MEMOIRS OF EXTRAORDINARY POPULAR DELUSIONS

VOLUME 1

CHARLES MACKAY

CAMBRIDGE

CAMBRIDGE LIBRARY COLLECTION

Books of enduring scholarly value

Spiritualism and Esoteric Knowledge

Magic, superstition, the occult sciences and esoteric knowledge appear regularly in the history of ideas alongside more established academic disciplines such as philosophy, natural history and theology. Particularly fascinating are periods of rapid scientific advances such as the Renaissance or the nineteenth century which also see a burgeoning of interest in the paranormal among the educated elite. This series provides primary texts and secondary sources for social historians and cultural anthropologists working in these areas, and all who wish for a wider understanding of the diverse intellectual and spiritual movements that formed a backdrop to the academic and political achievements of their day. It ranges from works on Babylonian and Jewish magic in the ancient world, through studies of sixteenth-century topics such as Cornelius Agrippa and the rapid spread of Rosicrucianism, to nineteenth-century publications by Sir Walter Scott and Sir Arthur Conan Doyle. Subjects include astrology, mesmerism, spiritualism, theosophy, clairvoyance, and ghost-seeing, as described both by their adherents and by sceptics.

Memoirs of Extraordinary Popular Delusions

This book is a joy to read and remains relevant in the current era of financial boom and bust. Mackay examines animal magnetism, money-mania, tulip-mania, the history of hair and facial hair, the crusades, haunted houses, and much more. Throughout history, the most extraordinary fashions and trends have been followed unthinkingly, and occasionally this crowd fever has overtaken not only a town but a whole country; in some cases much of western Europe was engulfed simultaneously. The ability of some manias to be so far-reaching, and for common sense and intelligence to abandon such large populations seems incredible, though the book is as thought-provoking now as it was when first published in 1852. Brought to life with exquisite engravings and witty commentary, the first volume focusses on the financial bubbles in Europe and the wide-ranging consequences of fashions in hair, prophecies and alchemy.

CAMBRIDGE UNIVERSITY PRESS

Cambridge, New York, Melbourne, Madrid, Cape Town, Singapore,
São Paolo, Delhi, Dubai, Tokyo, Mexico City

Published in the United States of America by Cambridge University Press, New York

www.cambridge.org
Information on this title: www.cambridge.org/9781108027618

© in this compilation Cambridge University Press 2010

This edition first published
This digitally printed version 2010

ISBN 978-1-108-02761-8 Paperback

THE MISSISSIPPI SCHEME: GARDENS OF THE HOTEL DE SOISSONS, 1720.

MEMOIRS

OF

EXTRAORDINARY POPULAR DELUSIONS.

VOLUME I.

THE BUBBLERS' ARMS—PROSPERITY.

LONDON:

OFFICE OF THE NATIONAL ILLUSTRATED LIBRARY,

227 STRAND.

1852.

MEMOIRS

OF

EXTRAORDINARY POPULAR DELUSIONS

AND THE

𝕸𝖆𝖉𝖓𝖊𝖘𝖘 𝖔𝖋 𝕮𝖗𝖔𝖜𝖉𝖘.

By CHARLES MACKAY, LL.D.

AUTHOR OF " EGERIA," " THE SALAMANDRINE," ETC.

ILLUSTRATED WITH NUMEROUS ENGRAVINGS.

N'en déplaise à ces fous nommés sages de Grèce,
En ce monde il n'est point de parfaite sagesse;
Tous les hommes sont fous, et malgré tous leurs soins
Ne different entre eux que du plus ou du moins.

BOILEAU.

VOL. I.

SECOND EDITION.

LONDON:

OFFICE OF THE NATIONAL ILLUSTRATED LIBRARY,

227 STRAND.

1852.

CONTENTS.

LIST OF ENGRAVINGS IN VOL. I.

LIST OF ENGRAVINGS.

Preface.

In reading the history of nations, we find that, like individuals, they have their whims and their peculiarities; their seasons of excitement and recklessness, when they care not what they do. We find that whole communities suddenly fix their minds upon one object, and go mad in its pursuit; that millions of people become simultaneously impressed with one delusion, and run after it, till their attention is caught by some new folly more captivating than the first. We see one nation suddenly seized, from its highest to its lowest members, with a fierce desire of military glory; another as suddenly becoming crazed upon a religious scruple; and neither of them recovering its senses until it has shed rivers of blood and sowed a harvest of groans and tears, to be reaped by its posterity. At an early age in the annals of Europe its population lost their wits about the sepulchre of Jesus, and crowded in frenzied multitudes to the Holy Land; another age went mad for fear of the devil, and offered up hundreds of thousands of victims to the delusion of witchcraft. At another time, the many became crazed on the subject of the philosopher's stone, and committed follies till then unheard of in the pursuit. It was once thought a venial offence, in very many countries of Europe, to destroy an enemy by slow poison. Persons who would have revolted at the idea of stabbing a man to the heart, drugged his pottage without scruple. Ladies of gentle birth and manners caught the contagion of murder, until poisoning, under their auspices, became quite fashionable. Some delusions, though notorious to all the world, have subsisted for ages, flourishing as widely among civilised and polished nations as among the early barbarians with whom they originated,—that of duelling, for instance, and the belief in omens and divination of the future, which seem to defy the progress of knowledge to eradicate them entirely from the popular mind.

Money, again, has often been a cause of the delusion of multitudes. Sober nations have all at once become desperate gamblers, and risked almost their existence upon the turn of a piece of paper. To trace the history of the most prominent of these delusions is the object of the present pages. Men, it has been well said, think in herds; it will be seen that they go mad in herds, while they only recover their senses slowly, and one by one.

Some of the subjects introduced may be familiar to the reader; but the Author hopes that sufficient novelty of detail will be found even in these, to render them acceptable, while they could not be wholly omitted in justice to the subject of which it was proposed to treat. The memoirs of the South-Sea madness and the Mississippi delusion are more complete and copious than are to be found elsewhere; and the same may be said of the history of the Witch Mania, which contains an account of its terrific progress in Germany, a part of the subject which has been left comparatively untouched by Sir Walter Scott in his *Letters on Demonology and Witchcraft*, the most important that have yet appeared on this fearful but most interesting subject.

Popular delusions began so early, spread so widely, and have lasted so long, that instead of two or three volumes, fifty would scarcely suffice to detail their history. The present may be considered more of a miscellany of delusions than a history—a chapter only in the great and awful book of human folly which yet remains to be written, and which Porson once jestingly said he would write in five hundred volumes! Interspersed are sketches of some lighter matters,—amusing instances of the imitativeness and wrongheadedness of the people, rather than examples of folly and delusion.

Religious matters have been purposely excluded as incompatible with the limits prescribed to the present work; a mere list of them would alone be sufficient to occupy a volume.

JOHN LAW.

MONEY MANIA.—THE MISSISSIPPI SCHEME.

Some in clandestine companies combine;
Erect new stocks to trade beyond the line;
With air and empty names beguile the town,
And raise new credits first, then cry 'em down;
Divide the empty nothing into shares,
And set the crowd together by the ears.—*Defoe.*

THE personal character and career of one man are so intimately connected with the great scheme of the years 1719 and 1720, that a history of the Mississippi madness can have no fitter introduction than a sketch of the life of its great author John Law. Historians are divided in opinion as to whether they should designate him a knave or a madman. Both epithets were unsparingly applied to him in his lifetime, and while the unhappy consequences of his projects were still deeply felt. Posterity, however, has found reason to doubt the justice of the accusation, and to confess that John Law was neither knave nor madman, but one more deceived than deceiving, more sinned against than sinning. He was thoroughly acquainted with the philosophy and true principles of credit. He understood the monetary question better than any man of his day; and if his system fell with a crash so tremendous, it was not so much his fault as that of the people amongst whom he had erected it. He did not calculate upon the avaricious frenzy of a whole nation; he did not see that confidence, like mistrust, could be increased almost *ad infinitum*, and that hope was as extravagant as fear. How was he to foretell that the French people, like the man in the fable, would kill, in their frantic eagerness, the fine goose he had brought to lay them so many golden eggs? His fate was like that which may be supposed to have overtaken the first adventurous boatman who rowed from Erie to Ontario. Broad and smooth was the river on which he embarked; rapid and pleasant was his progress; and who was to stay him in his career? Alas for him! the cataract was nigh. He saw, when it it was too late, that the tide which wafted him so joyously along was a tide of destruction; and when he endeavoured to retrace his way, he found that the current was too strong for his weak efforts to stem, and that he drew nearer every instant to the tremendous falls. Down he went over the sharp rocks, and the waters with him. *He* was dashed to pieces with his bark; but the waters, maddened and turned to foam by the rough descent, only boiled and bubbled for a time, and then flowed on again as smoothly as ever. Just so it was with Law and the French people. He was the boatman, and they were the waters.

John Law was born at Edinburgh in the year 1671. His father was the younger son of an ancient family in Fife, and carried on the business of a goldsmith and banker. He amassed considerable wealth in his trade, sufficient to enable him to gratify the wish, so common among his countrymen, of adding a territorial designation to his name. He purchased with this view the estates of Lauriston and Randleston, on the Frith of Forth, on the borders of West and Mid Lothian, and was thenceforth known as Law of Lauriston. The subject of our memoir, being the eldest son, was received into his father's counting-house at the age of fourteen, and for three years laboured hard to acquire an insight into the principles of banking as then carried on in Scotland. He had always manifested great love for the study of numbers, and his proficiency in the mathematics was considered extraordinary in one of his tender years. At the age of seventeen he was tall, strong, and well made; and his face, although deeply scarred with the small-pox, was agreeable in its expression, and full of intelligence. At this time he began to neglect his business, and becoming vain of his person, indulged in considerable extravagance of attire. He was a great favourite with the ladies, by whom he was called Beau Law; while the other sex, despising his foppery, nicknamed him Jessamy John. At the death of his father, which happened in 1688, he withdrew entirely from the desk, which had become so irksome, and being possessed of the revenues of the paternal estate of Lauriston, he proceeded to London, to see the world.

He was now very young, very vain, good-looking, tolerably rich, and quite uncontrolled. It is no wonder that, on his arrival in the capital, he should launch out into extravagance. He soon became a regular frequenter of the gaming-houses, and by pursuing a certain plan, based upon some abstruse calculation of chances, he contrived to gain considerable sums. All the gamblers envied him his luck, and many made it a point to watch his play, and stake their money on the same chances. In affairs of gallantry he was equally fortunate; ladies of the first rank smiled graciously upon the handsome Scotchman—the young, the rich, the witty, and the obliging. But all these successes only paved the way for reverses. After he had been for nine years exposed to the dangerous attractions of the gay life he was leading, he became an irrecoverable gambler. As his love of play increased in violence, it diminished in prudence. Great losses were only to be repaired by still greater ventures, and one unhappy day he lost more than he could repay without mortgaging his family estate. To that step he was driven at last. At the same time his gallantry brought him into trouble. A love affair, or slight flirtation, with a lady of the name of Villiers,* exposed him to the resentment of a Mr. Wilson, by whom he was challenged to fight a duel. Law accepted, and had the ill fortune to shoot his antagonist dead upon the spot. He was arrested the same day, and brought to trial for murder by the relatives of Mr. Wilson. He was afterwards found guilty, and sentenced to death. The sentence was commuted to a fine, upon the ground that the offence only amounted to manslaughter. An appeal being lodged by a brother of the deceased, Law was detained in the King's Bench, whence, by some means or other, which he never explained, he contrived to escape; and an action being instituted against the sheriffs, he was advertised in the Gazette, and a reward offered for his apprehension. He was described as

* Miss Elizabeth Villiers, afterwards Countess of Orkney.

"Captain John Law, a Scotchman, aged twenty-six; a very tall, black, lean man; well shaped, above six feet high, with large pock-holes in his face; big nosed, and speaking broad and loud." As this was rather a caricature than a description of him, it has been supposed that it was drawn up with a view to favour his escape. He succeeded in reaching the Continent, where he travelled for three years, and devoted much of his attention to the monetary and banking affairs of the countries through which he passed. He stayed a few months in Amsterdam, and speculated to some extent in the funds. His mornings were devoted to the study of finance and the principles of trade, and his evenings to the gaming-house. It is generally believed that he returned to Edinburgh in the year 1700. It is certain that he published in that city his *Proposals and Reasons for constituting a Council of Trade.* This pamphlet did not excite much attention.

In a short time afterwards he published a project for establishing what he called a Land-bank,* the notes issued by which were never to exceed the value of the entire lands of the state, upon ordinary interest, or were to be equal in value to the land, with the right to enter into possession at a certain time. The project excited a good deal of discussion in the Scottish Parliament, and a motion for the establishment of such a bank was brought forward by a neutral party, called the Squadrone, whom Law had interested in his favour. The Parliament ultimately passed a resolution to the effect, that, to establish any kind of paper credit, so as to force it to pass, was an improper expedient for the nation.

Upon the failure of this project, and of his efforts to procure a pardon for the murder of Mr. Wilson, Law withdrew to the Continent, and resumed his old habits of gaming. For fourteen years he continued to roam about, in Flanders, Holland, Germany, Hungary, Italy, and France. He soon became intimately acquainted with the extent of the trade and resources of each, and daily more confirmed in his opinion that no country could prosper without a paper currency. During the whole of this time he appears to have chiefly supported himself by successful play. At every gambling-house of note in the capitals of Europe he was known and appreciated as one better skilled in the intricacies of chance than any other man of the day. It is stated in the *Biographie Universelle* that he was expelled, first from Venice, and afterwards from Genoa, by the magistrates, who thought him a visitor too dangerous for the youth of those cities. During his residence in Paris he rendered himself obnoxious to D'Argenson, the lieutenant-general of the police, by whom he was ordered

* The wits of the day called it a *sand-bank*, which would wreck the vessel of the state.

to quit the capital. This did not take place, however, before he had made the acquaintance, in the saloons, of the Duke de Vendôme, the Prince de Conti, and of the gay Duke of Orleans, the latter of whom was destined afterwards to exercise so much influence over his fate. The Duke of Orleans was pleased with the vivacity and good sense of the Scottish adventurer, while the latter was no less pleased with the wit and amiability of a prince who promised to become his patron. They were often thrown into each other's society, and Law seized every opportunity to instil his financial doctrines into the mind of one whose proximity to the throne pointed him out as destined, at no very distant date, to play an important part in the government.

Shortly before the death of Louis XIV., or, as some say, in 1780, Law proposed a scheme of finance to Desmarets, the comptroller. Louis is reported to have inquired whether the projector were a Catholic, and on being answered in the negative, to have declined having any thing to do with him.[*]

It was after this repulse that he visited Italy. His mind being still occupied with schemes of finance, he proposed to Victor Amadeus, Duke of Savoy, to

THE REGENT OF FRANCE.

establish his land-bank in that country. The duke replied that his dominions were too circumscribed for the execution of so great a project, and that he was by far too poor a potentate to be ruined. He advised him, however, to try the king of France once more ; for he was sure, if he knew any thing of the French character, that the people would be delighted with a plan, not only so new, but so plausible.

Louis XIV. died in 1715, and the heir to the throne being an infant only seven years of age, the Duke of Orleans assumed the reigns of government, as regent, during his minority. Law now found himself in a more favourable position. The tide in his affairs had come, which, taken at the flood, was to waft him on to fortune.

* This anecdote, which is related in the correspondence of Madame de Bavière, Duchess of Orleans and mother of the Regent, is discredited by Lord John Russell in his *History of the principal States of Europe from the Peace of Utrecht;* for what reason he does not inform us. There is no doubt that Law proposed his scheme to Desmarets, and that Louis refused to hear of it. The reason given for the refusal is quite consistent with the character of that bigoted and tyrannical monarch.

The regent was his friend, already acquainted with his theory and pretensions, and inclined, moreover, to aid him in any efforts to restore the wounded credit of France, bowed down to the earth by the extravagance of the long reign of Louis XIV.

Hardly was that monarch laid in his grave ere the popular hatred, suppressed so long, burst forth against his memory. He who, during his life, had been flattered with an excess of adulation, to which history scarcely offers a parallel, was now cursed as a tyrant, a bigot, and a plunderer. His statues were pelted and disfigured ; his effigies torn down, amid the execrations of the populace, and his name rendered synonymous with selfishness and oppression. The glory of his arms was forgotten, and nothing was remembered but his reverses, his extravagance, and his cruelty.

The finances of the country were in a state of the utmost disorder. A profuse and corrupt monarch, whose profuseness and corruption were imitated by almost every functionary, from the highest to the lowest grade, had brought France to the verge of ruin. The national debt amounted to 3000 millions of livres, the revenue to 145 millions, and the expenses of government to 142 millions per annum ; leaving only three millions to pay the interest upon 3000 millions. The first care of the regent was to discover a remedy for an evil of such magnitude, and a council was early summoned to take the matter into consideration. The Duke de St. Simon was of opinion that nothing could save the country from revolution but a remedy at once bold and dangerous. He advised the regent to convoke the states-general, and declare a national bankruptcy. The Duke de Noailles, a man of accommodating principles, an accomplished courtier, and totally averse from giving himself any trouble or annoyance that ingenuity could escape from, opposed the project of St. Simon with all his influence. He represented the expedient as alike dishonest and ruinous. The regent was of the same opinion, and this desperate remedy fell to the ground.

The measures ultimately adopted, though they promised fair, only aggravated the evil. The first and most dishonest measure was of no advantage to the state. A recoinage was ordered, by which the currency was depreciated one-fifth ; those who took a thousand pieces of gold or silver to the mint received back an amount of coin of the same nominal value, but only four-fifths of the weight of metal. By this contrivance the treasury gained seventy-two millions of livres, and all the commercial operations of the country were disordered. A trifling diminution of the taxes silenced the clamours of the people, and for the slight present advantage the great prospective evil was forgotten.

A Chamber of Justice was next instituted to inquire into the mal-versations of the loan-contractors and the farmers of the revenues. Tax-collectors are never very popular in any country, but those of France at this period deserved all the odium with which they were loaded. As soon as these farmers-general, with all their hosts of subordinate agents, called *maltôtiers*,* were called to account for their misdeeds, the most extravagant joy took possession of the nation. The Chamber of Justice, instituted chiefly for this purpose, was endowed with very extensive powers. It was composed of the presidents and councils of the parliament, the judges of the Courts of Aid and of Requests, and the officers of the Chamber of Account, under the general presidence of the minister of finance. Informers were encouraged to give evidence against the offenders by the promise of one-fifth part of the fines and confiscations. A tenth of all concealed effects belonging to the guilty was promised to such as should furnish the means of discovering them.

The promulgation of the edict constituting this court caused a degree of consternation among those principally concerned, which can only be accounted for on the supposition that their peculation had been enormous. But they met with no sympathy. The proceedings against them justified their terror. The Bastille was soon unable to contain the prisoners that were sent to it, and the gaols all over the country teemed with guilty or suspected persons. An order was issued to all innkeepers and postmasters to refuse horses to such as endeavoured to seek safety in flight ; and all persons were forbidden, under heavy fines, to harbour them or favour their evasion. Some were condemned to the pillory, others to the galleys, and the least guilty to fine and imprisonment. One only, Samuel Bernard, a rich banker and farmer-general of a province remote from the capital, was sentenced to death. So great had been the illegal profits of this man,—looked upon as the tyrant and oppressor of his district,—that he offered six millions of livres, or 250,000*l.* sterling, to be allowed to escape.

His bribe was refused, and he suffered the penalty of death. Others, perhaps more guilty, were more fortunate. Confiscation, owing to the concealment of their treasures by the delinquents, often produced less money than a fine. The severity of the government relaxed, and fines, under the denomination of taxes, were indiscriminately levied upon all offenders ; but so corrupt was every department of the administration, that the country benefited but little by the sums which thus flowed into the treasury. Courtiers and courtiers' wives and mistresses came in for the chief share of the spoils. One

---

* From *maltôte*, an oppressive tax.

contractor had been taxed, in proportion to his wealth and guilt, at the sum of twelve millions of livres. The Count * * *, a man of some weight in the government, called upon him, and offered to procure a remission of the fine if he would give him a hundred thousand crowns. "Vous êtes trop tard, mon ami;" replied the financier; "I have already made a bargain with your wife for fifty thousand."*

About a hundred and eighty millions of livres were levied in this manner, of which eighty were applied in payment of the debts contracted by the government. The remainder found its way into the pockets of the courtiers. Madame de Maintenon, writing on this subject, says—"We hear every day of some new grant of the regent. The people murmur very much at this mode of employing the money taken from the peculators." The people, who, after the first burst of their resentment is over, generally express a sympathy for the weak, were indignant that so much severity should be used to so little purpose. They did not see the justice of robbing one set of rogues to fatten another. In a few months all the more guilty had been brought to punishment, and the Chamber of Justice looked for victims in humbler walks of life. Charges of fraud and extortion were brought against tradesmen of good character in consequence of the great inducements held out to common informers. They were compelled to lay open their affairs before this tribunal in order to establish their innocence. The voice of complaint resounded from every side; and at the expiration of a year the government found it advisable to discontinue further proceedings. The Chamber of Justice was suppressed, and a general amnesty granted to all against whom no charges had yet been preferred.

In the midst of this financial confusion Law appeared upon the scene. No man felt more deeply than the regent the deplorable state of the country, but no man could be more averse from putting his shoulders manfully to the wheel. He disliked business; he signed official documents without proper examination, and trusted to others what he should have undertaken himself. The cares inseparable from his high office were burdensome to him. He saw that something was necessary to be done; but he lacked the energy to do it, and had not virtue enough to sacrifice his ease and his pleasures in the attempt. No wonder that, with this character, he listened favourably

---

* This anecdote is related by M. de la Hode, in his *Life of Philippe of Orleans.* It would have looked more authentic if he had given the names of the dishonest contractor and the still more dishonest minister. But M. de la Hode's book is liable to the same objection as most of the French memoirs of that and of subsequent periods. It is sufficient with most of them that an anecdote be *ben trovato;* the *vero* is but matter of secondar consideration.

to the mighty projects, so easy of execution, of the clever adventurer whom he had formerly known, and whose talents he appreciated.

When Law presented himself at court he was most cordiallly received. He offered two memorials to the regent, in which he set forth the evils that had befallen France, owing to an insufficient currency, at different times depreciated. He asserted that a metallic currency, unaided by a paper money, was wholly inadequate to the wants of a commercial country, and particularly cited the examples of Great Britain and Holland to shew the advantages of paper. He used many sound arguments on the subject of credit, and proposed as a means of restoring that of France, then at so low an ebb among the nations, that he should be allowed to set up a bank, which should have the management of the royal revenues, and issue notes both on that and on landed security. He further proposed that this bank should be administered in the king's name, but subject to the control of commissioners to be named by the States-General.

While these memorials were under consideration, Law translated into French his essay on money and trade, and used every means to extend through the nation his renown as a financier. He soon became talked of. The confidants of the regent spread abroad his praise, and every one expected great things of Monsieur Lass.*

On the 5th of May, 1716, a royal edict was published, by which Law was authorised, in conjunction with his brother, to establish a bank under the name of Law and Company, the notes of which should be received in payment of the taxes. The capital was fixed at six millions of livres, in twelve thousand shares of five hundred livres each, purchasable one fourth in specie, and the remainder in *billets d'état*. It was not thought expedient to grant him the whole of the privileges prayed for in his memorials until experience should have shewn their safety and advantage.

Law was now on the high road to fortune. The study of thirty years was brought to guide him in the management of his bank. He made all his notes payable at sight, and in the coin current at the time they were issued. This last was a master-stroke of policy, and immediately rendered his notes more valuable than the precious metals. The latter were constantly liable to depreciation by the unwise tampering of the government. A thousand livres of silver might be worth their nominal value one day, and be reduced one-sixth the next, but a note of Law's bank retained its original value. He publicly declared at the same time, that a banker deserved death if he

---

* The French pronounced his name in this manner to avoid the ungallic sound, *aw*. After the failure of his scheme, the wags said the nation was *lasse de lui*, and proposed that he should in future be known by the name of Monsieur Helas!

made issues without having sufficient security to answer all demands. The consequence was, that his notes advanced rapidly in public estimation, and were received at one per cent more than specie. It was not long before the trade of the country felt the benefit. Languishing commerce began to lift up her head; the taxes were paid with greater regularity and less murmuring; and a degree of confidence was established that could not fail, if it continued, to become still more advantageous. In the course of a year, Law's notes rose to fifteen per cent premium, while the *billets d'état*, or notes issued by the government as security for the debts contracted by the extravagant Louis XIV., were at a discount of no less than seventy-eight and a half per cent. The comparison was too great in favour of Law not to attract the attention of the whole kingdom, and his credit extended itself day by day. Branches of his bank were almost simultaneously established at Lyons, Rochelle, Tours, Amiens, and Orleans.

The regent appears to have been utterly astonished at his success, and gradually to have conceived the idea that paper, which could so aid a metallic currency, could entirely supersede it. Upon this fundamental error he afterwards acted. In the mean time, Law commenced the famous project which has handed his name down to posterity. He proposed to the regent (who could refuse him nothing) to establish a company that should have the exclusive privilege of trading to the great river Mississippi and the province of Louisiana, on its western bank. The country was supposed to abound in the precious metals; and the company, supported by the profits of their exclusive commerce, were to be the sole farmers of the taxes and sole coiners of money. Letters patent were issued, incorporating the company, in August 1717. The capital was divided into two hundred thousand shares of five hundred livres each, the whole of which might be paid in *billets d'état*, at their nominal value, although worth no more than a hundred and sixty livres in the market.

It was now that the frenzy of speculating began to seize upon the nation. Law's bank had effected so much good, that any promises for the future which he thought proper to make were readily believed. The regent every day conferred new privileges upon the fortunate projector. The bank obtained the monopoly of the sale of tobacco, the sole right of refinage of gold and silver, and was finally erected into the Royal Bank of France. Amid the intoxication of success, both Law and the regent forgot the maxim so loudly proclaimed by the former, that a banker deserved death who made issues of paper without the necessary funds to provide for them. As soon as the bank, from a private, became a public institution, the regent caused a fabrication of notes to the amount of one thousand millions of livres. This was the first departure from sound principles, and one for which Law is not justly blameable. While the affairs of the bank were under his control, the issues had never exceeded sixty millions. Whether Law opposed the inordinate increase is not known; but as it took place as soon as the bank was made a royal establishment, it is but fair to lay the blame of the change of system upon the regent.

Law found that he lived under a despotic government; but he was not yet aware of the pernicious influence which such a government could exercise upon so delicate a framework as that of credit. He discovered it afterwards to his cost, but in the meantime suffered himself to be impelled by the regent into courses which his own reason must have disapproved. With a weakness most culpable, he lent his aid in inundating the country with paper money, which, based upon no solid foundation, was sure to fall, sooner or later. The extraordinary present fortune dazzled his eyes, and prevented him from seeing the evil day that would burst over his head, when once, from any cause or other, the alarm was sounded. The parliament were from the first jealous of his influence as a foreigner, and had, besides, their misgivings as to the safety of his projects. As his influence extended, their animosity increased. D'Aguesseau, the chancellor, was unceremoniously dismissed by the regent for his opposition to the vast increase of paper money, and the constant depreciation of the gold and silver coin of the realm. This only served to augment the enmity of the parliament, and when D'Argenson, a man devoted to the interests of the regent, was appointed to the vacant chancellorship, and made at the same time minister of finance, they became more violent than ever. The first measure of the new minister caused a further depreciation of the coin. In order to extinguish the *billets d'état*, it was ordered that persons bringing to the mint four thousand livres in specie and one thousand livres in *billets d'état*, should receive back coin to the amount of five thousand livres. D'Argenson plumed himself mightily upon thus creating five thousand new and smaller livres out of the four thousand old and larger ones, being too ignorant of the true principles of trade and credit to be aware of the immense injury he was inflicting upon both.

The parliament saw at once the impolicy and danger of such a system, and made repeated remonstrances to the regent. The latter refused to entertain their petitions, when the parliament, by a bold and very unusual stretch of authority, commanded that no money should be received in payment but that of the old standard. The regent summoned a *lit de justice*, and annulled the decree. The parliament resisted, and issued another. Again the regent exercised his privilege, and annulled it, till the parliament, stung to fiercer opposition, passed another decree, dated August 12th, 1718, by which they forbade the bank of Law to have any concern, either direct or indirect, in the administration of the revenue ; and prohibited all foreigners, under heavy penalties, from interfering, either in their own names or in that of others, in the management of the finances of the state. The parliament considered Law to be the author of all the evil, and some of the councillors, in the virulence of their enmity, proposed that he should be brought to trial, and, if found guilty, be hung at the gates of the Palais de Justice.

PALAIS ROYAL FROM THE GARDEN.

Law, in great alarm, fled to the Palais Royal, and threw himself on the protection of the regent, praying that measures might be taken to reduce the parliament to obedience. The regent had nothing so much at heart, both on that account and because of the disputes that had arisen relative to the legitimation of the Duke of Maine and the Count of Thoulouse, the sons of the late king. The parliament was ultimately overawed by the arrest of their president and two of the councillors, who were sent to distant prisons.

Thus the first cloud upon Law's prospects blew over : freed from apprehension of personal danger, he devoted his attention to his famous Mississippi project, the shares of which were rapidly rising, in spite of the parliament. At the commencement of the year 1719, an edict was published, granting to the Mississippi Company the exclusive privilege of trading to the East Indies, China, and the South Seas, and to all the possessions of the French East India Company, established by Colbert. The Company, in consequence of this great increase of their business, assumed, as more appropriate, the title of Company of the Indies, and created fifty thousand new shares. The prospects now held out by Law were most magnificent. He promised a yearly dividend of two hundred livres upon each share of five hundred, which, as the shares were paid for in *billets d'état*, at their nominal value, but worth only 100 livres, was at the rate of about 120 per cent profit.

LAW'S HOUSE; RUE DE QUINCAMPOIX.

The public enthusiasm, which had been so long rising, could not resist a vision so splendid. At least three hundred thousand applications were made for the fifty thousand new shares, and Law's house in the Rue de Quincampoix was beset from morning to night by the eager applicants. As it was impossible to satisfy them all, it was several weeks before a list of the fortunate new stockholders could be made out, during which time the public impatience rose to a pitch of frenzy. Dukes, marquises, counts, with their duchesses, marchionesses, and countesses, waited in the streets for hours every day before Mr. Law's door to know the result. At last, to avoid the jostling of the plebeian crowd, which, to the number of thousands, filled the whole thoroughfare, they took apartments in the adjoining houses, that they might be continually near the temple whence the new Plutus was diffusing wealth. Every day the value of the old shares increased, and the fresh applications, induced by the golden dreams of the whole nation, became so numerous that it was deemed advisable to create no less than three hundred thousand new shares, at five thousand livres each, in order that the regent might take advantage of the popular enthusiasm to pay off the national debt. For this purpose, the sum of fifteen hundred millions of livres was necessary. Such was the eagerness of the nation, that thrice the sum would have been subscribed if the government had authorised it.

Law was now at the zenith of his prosperity, and the people were rapidly approaching the zenith of their infatuation. The highest and the lowest classes were alike filled with a vision of boundless wealth. There was not a person of note among the aristocracy, with the exception of the Duke of St. Simon and Marshal Villars, who was not engaged in buying or selling stock. People of every age and sex and condition in life speculated in the rise and fall of the Mississippi bonds. The Rue de Quincampoix was the grand resort of the jobbers, and it being a narrow, inconvenient street, accidents continually occurred in it, from the tremendous pressure of the crowd. Houses in it, worth, in ordinary times, a thousand livres of yearly rent, yielded as much as twelve or sixteen thousand. A cobbler, who had a stall in it, gained about two hundred livres a day by letting it out, and furnishing writing materials to brokers and their clients. The story goes, that a hunchbacked man who stood in the street gained considerable sums by lending his hump as a writing-desk to the eager speculators! The great concourse of persons who assembled to do business brought a still greater concourse of spectators. These again drew all the thieves and immoral characters of Paris to the spot, and constant riots and disturbances took place. At nightfall, it was often found necessary to send a troop of soldiers to clear the street.

Law, finding the inconvenience of his residence, removed to the Place Vendôme, whither the crowd of *agioteurs* followed him. That spacious square soon became as thronged as the Rue de Quincampoix: from morning to night it presented the appearance of a fair. Booths and tents were erected for the transaction of business and the sale of refreshments, and gamblers with their roulette-tables stationed themselves in the very middle of the place, and reaped a golden, or rather a paper, harvest from the throng. The boulevards and public gardens were forsaken; parties of pleasure took their walks in preference in the Place Vendôme, which became the fashionable lounge of

THE HUNCHBACK.

the idle, as well as the general rendezvous of the busy. The noise was so great all day, that the chancellor, whose court was situated in the square, complained to the regent and the municipality that he could not hear the advocates. Law, when applied to, expressed his willingness to aid in the removal of the nuisance, and for this purpose entered into a treaty with the Prince de Carignan for the Hôtel de Soissons, which had a garden of several acres in the rear. A bargain was concluded, by which Law became the purchaser of the hotel at an enormous price, the prince reserving to himself the magnificent gardens as a new source of profit. They contained some fine statues and several fountains, and were altogether laid out with much taste. As soon as Law was installed in his new abode, an edict was published, forbidding all persons to buy or sell stock any where but in the gardens of the Hôtel de Soissons. In the midst, among the trees, about five hundred small tents and pavilions were erected, for the

HOTEL DE SOISSONS.

convenience of the stock-jobbers. Their various colours, the gay ribands and banners which floated from them, the busy crowds which passed continually in and out—the incessant hum of voices, the noise, the music, and the strange mixture of business and pleasure on the countenances of the throng, all combined to give the place an air of enchantment that quite enraptured the Parisians. The Prince de Carignan made enormous profits while the delusion lasted. Each tent was let at the rate of five hundred livres a month; and, as there were at least five hundred of them, his monthly revenue from this source alone must have amounted to 250,000 livres, or upwards of 10,000*l.* sterling.

The honest old soldier, Marshal Villars, was so vexed to see the folly which had smitten his countrymen, that he never could speak with temper on the subject. Passing one day through the Place Vendôme in his carriage, the choleric gentleman was so annoyed at the infatuation of the people, that he abruptly ordered his coachman to stop, and, putting his head out of the carriage-window, harangued them for full half an hour on their "disgusting avarice." This was nôt a very wise proceeding on his part. Hisses and shouts of laughter resounded from every side, and jokes without number were aimed at him. There being at last strong symptoms that something more tangible was flying through the air in the direction of his head, the marshal was glad to drive on. He never again repeated the experiment.

Two sober, quiet, and philosophic men of letters, M. de la Motte and the Abbé Terrason, congratulated each other, that they, at least, were free from this strange infatuation. A few days afterwards, as the worthy abbé was coming out of the Hôtel de Soissons, whither he had gone to buy shares in the Mississippi, whom should he see but his friend La Motte entering for the same purpose. " Ha !" said the abbé smiling, " is that *you ?*" " Yes," said La Motte, pushing past him as fast as he was able ; " and can that be *you ?*" The next time the two scholars met, they talked of philosophy, of science, and of religion, but neither had courage for a long time to breathe one syllable about the Mississippi. At last, when it was mentioned, they agreed that a man ought never to swear against his doing any one thing, and that there was no sort of extravagance of which even a wise man was not capable.

During this time, Law, the new Plutus, had become all at once the most important personage of the state. The ante-chambers of the regent were forsaken by the courtiers. Peers, judges, and bishops thronged to the Hôtel de Soissons; officers of the army and navy, ladies of title and fashion, and every one to whom hereditary rank or public employ gave a claim to precedence, were to be found waiting in his ante-chambers to beg for a portion of his India stock. Law was so pestered that he was unable to see one-tenth part of the applicants, and every manœuvre that ingenuity could suggest was employed to gain access to him. Peers, whose dignity would have been outraged if the regent had made them wait half an hour for an interview, were content to wait six hours for the chance of seeing Monsieur Law. Enormous fees were paid to his servants, if they would merely announce their names. Ladies of rank employed the blandishments of their smiles for the same object; but many of them came day after day for a fortnight before they could obtain an audience. When Law accepted an invitation, he was sometimes so surrounded by ladies, all asking to have their names put down in his lists as shareholders in the new stock, that, in spite of his well-known and habitual gallantry, he was obliged to tear himself away *par force*. The most ludicrous stratagems were employed to have an opportunity of speaking to him. One lady, who had striven in vain during several days, gave up in despair all attempts to see him at his own house, but ordered her coachman to keep a strict watch whenever she was out in her carriage, and if he saw Mr. Law coming, to drive against a post and upset her. The coachman promised obedience, and for three days the lady was driven incessantly through the town, praying inwardly for the opportunity to be overturned. At last she espied Mr. Law, and, pulling the string, called out to the coachman, " Upset us now ! for God's sake, upset us now !" The coachman drove against a post, the lady

screamed, the coach was overturned, and Law, who had seen the *accident*, hastened to the spot to render assistance. The cunning dame was led into the Hôtel de Soissons, where she soon thought it advisable to recover from her fright, and, after apologising to Mr. Law, confessed her stratagem. Law smiled, and entered the lady in his books as the purchaser of a quantity of India stock. Another story is told of a Madame de Boucha, who, knowing that Mr. Law was at dinner at a certain house, proceeded thither in her carriage, and gave the alarm of fire. The company started from table, and Law among the rest ; but, seeing one lady making all haste into the house towards him, while every body else was scampering away, he suspected the trick, and ran off in another direction.

Many other anecdotes are related, which even though they may be a little exaggerated, are nevertheless worth preserving, as shewing the spirit of that singular period.* The regent was one day mentioning, in the presence of D'Argenson, the Abbé Dubois, and some other persons, that he was desirous of deputing some lady, of the rank at least of a duchess, to attend upon his daughter at Modena; " but," added he, " I do not exactly know where to find one." " No !" replied one, in affected surprise ; " I can tell you where to find every duchess in France : you have only to go to Mr. Law's ; you will see them every one in his ante-chamber."

M. de Chirac, a celebrated physician, had bought stock at an unlucky period, and was very anxious to sell out. Stock, however, continued to fall for two or three days, much to his alarm. His mind was filled with the subject, when he was suddenly called upon to attend a lady who imagined herself unwell. He arrived, was shewn up stairs, and felt the lady's pulse. " It falls ! it falls ! good God ! it falls continually !" said he musingly, while the lady looked up in his face all anxiety for his opinion. " Oh, M. de Chirac," said she, starting to her feet and ringing the bell for assistance ; " I am dying ! I am dying ! it falls ! it falls ! it falls !" " What falls ?" inquired the doctor in amazement. " My pulse ! my pulse !" said the lady; " I must be dying." " Calm your apprehensions, my dear madam," said M. de Chirac ; " I was speaking of the stocks. The truth is, I have been a great loser, and my mind is so disturbed, I hardly know what I have been saying."

The price of shares sometimes rose ten or twenty per cent in the course of a few hours, and many persons in the humbler walks of life, who had risen poor in the morning, went to bed in affluence. An extensive holder of stock, being taken ill, sent his servant to sell two hundred and fifty shares, at eight thousand livres each, the price at which they were then quoted. The servant went, and, on his arrival in the Jardin de Soissons, found that in the interval the price had risen to ten thousand livres. The difference of two thousand livres on the two hundred and fifty shares, amounting to 500,000 livres, or 20,000*l.* sterling, he very coolly transferred to his own use, and giving the remainder to his master, set out the same evening for another country. Law's coachman in a very short time made money enough

* The curious reader may find an anecdote of the eagerness of the French ladies to retain Law in their company, which will make him blush or smile according as he happens to be very modest or the reverse. It is related in the *Letters of Madame Charlotte Elizabeth de Bavière, Duchess of Orleans*, vol. ii. p. 274.

to set up a carriage of his own, and requested permission to leave his service. Law, who esteemed the man, begged of him as a favour, that he would endeavour, before he went, to find a substitute as good as himself. The coachman consented, and in the evening brought two of his former comrades, telling Mr. Law to choose between them, and he would take the other. Cookmaids and footmen were now and then as lucky, and, in the full-blown pride of their easily-acquired wealth, made the most ridiculous mistakes. Preserving the language and manners of their old, with the finery of their new station, they afforded continual subjects for the pity of the sensible, the contempt of the sober, and the laughter of every body. But the folly and meanness of the higher ranks of society were still more disgusting. One instance alone, related by the Duke de St. Simon, will shew the unworthy avarice which infected the whole of society. A man of the name of André, without character or education, had, by a series of well-timed speculations in Mississippi bonds, gained enormous wealth in an incredibly short space of time. As St. Simon expresses it, " he had amassed mountains of gold." As he became rich, he grew ashamed of the lowness of his birth, and anxious above all things to be allied to nobility. He had a daughter, an infant only three years of age, and he opened a negotiation with the aristocratic and needy family of D'Oyse, that this child should, upon certain conditions, marry a member of that house. The Marquis D'Oyse, to his shame, consented, and promised to marry her himself on her attaining the age of twelve, if the father would pay him down the sum of a hundred thousand crowns, and twenty thousand livres every year until the celebration of the marriage. The marquis was himself in his thirty-third year. This scandalous bargain was duly signed and sealed, the stockjobber furthermore agreeing to settle upon his daughter, on the marriage-day, a fortune of several millions. The Duke of Brancas, the head of the family, was present throughout the negotiation, and shared in all the profits. St. Simon, who treats the matter with the levity becoming what he thought so good a joke, adds, "that people did not spare their animadversions on this beautiful marriage," and further informs us " that the project fell to the ground some months afterwards by the overthrow of Law, and the ruin of the ambitious Monsieur André." It would appear, however, that the noble family never had the honesty to return the hundred thousand crowns.

Amid events like these, which, humiliating though they be, partake largely of the ludicrous, others occurred of a more serious nature. Robberies in the streets were of daily occurrence, in consequence of the immense sums, in paper, which people carried about with them.

Assassinations were also frequent. One case in particular fixed the attention of the whole of France, not only on account of the enormity of the offence, but of the rank and high connexions of the criminal.

The Count d'Horn, a younger brother of the Prince d'Horn, and related to the noble families of D'Aremberg, De Ligne, and De Montmorency, was a young man of dissipated character, extravagant to a degree, and unprincipled as he was extravagant. In connexion with

two other young men as reckless as himself, named Mille, a Piedmontese captain, and one Destampes, or Lestang, a Fleming, he formed a design to rob a very rich broker, who was known, unfortunately for himself, to carry great sums about his person. The count pretended a desire to purchase of him a number of shares in the Company of the Indies, and for that purpose appointed to meet him in a *cabaret*, or low public-house, in the neighbourhood of the Place Vendôme. The unsuspecting broker was punctual to his appointment; so were the Count d'Horn and his two associates, whom he introduced as his particular friends. After a few moments' conversation, the Count d'Horn suddenly sprang upon his victim, and stabbed him three time in the breast with a poniard. The man fell heavily to the ground, and, while the count was employed in rifling his portfolio of bonds in the Mississippi and Indian schemes to the amount of one hundred thousand crowns, Mille, the Piedmontese, stabbed the unfortunate broker again and again, to make sure of his death. But the broker did not fall without a struggle, and his cries brought the people of the *cabaret* to his assistance. Lestang, the other assassin, who had been set to keep watch at a staircase, sprang from a window and escaped; but Mille and the Count d'Horn were seized in the very act.

This crime, committed in open day, and in so public a place as a *cabaret*, filled Paris with consternation. The trial of the assassins commenced on the following day; and the evidence being so clear, they were both found guilty, and condemned to be broken alive on the wheel. The noble relatives of the Count d'Horn absolutely blocked up the ante-chambers of the regent, praying for mercy on the misguided youth, and alleging that he was insane. The regent avoided them as long as possible, being determined that, in a case so atrocious, justice should take its course. But the importunity of these influential suitors was not to be overcome so silently; and they at last forced themselves into the presence of the regent, and prayed him to save their house the shame of a public execution. They hinted that the Princes d'Horn were allied to the illustrious family of Orleans; and added, that the regent himself would be disgraced if a kinsman of his should die by the hands of a common executioner. The regent, to his credit, was proof against all their solicitations, and replied to their last argument in the words of Corneille:

" Le crime fait la honte, et non pas l'échafaud:"

adding, that whatever shame there might be in the punishment he would very willingly share with the other relatives. Day after day they renewed their entreaties, but always with the same result. At last they thought, that if they could interest the Duke de St. Simon in their favour—a man for whom the regent felt sincere esteem—they might succeed in their object. The duke, a thorough aristocrat, was as shocked as they were that a noble assassin should die by the same death as a plebeian felon, and represented to the regent the impolicy of making enemies of so numerous, wealthy, and powerful a family.

He urged, too, that in Germany, where the family of D'Aremberg had large possessions, it was the law, that no relative of a person broken on the wheel could succeed to any public office or employ until a whole generation had passed away. For this reason, he thought the punishment of the guilty count might be transmuted into beheading, which was considered all over Europe as much less infamous. The regent was moved by this argument, and was about to consent, when Law, who felt peculiarly interested in the fate of the murdered man, confirmed him in his former resolution to let the law take its course.

The relatives of D'Horn were now reduced to the last extremity. The Prince de Robec Montmorency, despairing of other methods, found means to penetrate into the dungeon of the criminal, and offering him a cup of poison, implored him to save them from disgrace. The Count d'Horn turned away his head, and refused to take it. Montmorency pressed him once more ; and losing all patience at his continued refusal, turned on his heel, and exclaiming, " Die, then, as thou wilt, mean-spirited wretch ! thou art fit only to perish by the hands of the hangman !" left him to his fate.

D'Horn himself petitioned the regent that he might be beheaded ; but Law, who exercised more influence over his mind than any other person, with the exception of the notorious Abbé Dubois, his tutor, insisted that he could not in justice succumb to the self-interested views of the D'Horns. The regent had from the first been of the same opinion ; and within six days after the commission of their crime, D'Horn and Mille were broken on the wheel in the Place de Grève. The other assassin, Lestang, was never apprehended.

This prompt and severe justice was highly pleasing to the populace of Paris. Even M. de Quincampoix, as they called Law, came in for a share of their approbation for having induced the regent to shew no favour to a patrician. But the number of robberies and assassinations did not diminish ; no sympathy was shewn for rich jobbers when they were plundered. The general laxity of public morals, conspicuous enough before, was rendered still more so by its rapid pervasion of the middle classes, who had hitherto remained comparatively pure between the open vices of the class above and the hidden crimes of the class below them. The pernicious love of gambling diffused itself through society, and bore all public and nearly all private virtue before it.

For a time, while confidence lasted, an impetus was given to trade which could not fail to be beneficial. In Paris especially the good results were felt. Strangers flocked into the capital from every part, bent not only upon making money, but on spending it. The Duchess of Orleans, mother of the regent, computes the increase of the population during this time, from the great influx of strangers from all parts of the world, at 305,000 souls. The housekeepers were obliged to make up beds in garrets, kitchens, and even stables, for the accommodation of lodgers ; and the town was so full of carriages and vehicles of every description, that they were obliged, in the principal streets, to drive at a foot-pace for fear of accidents. The looms of the country worked with unusual activity to supply rich laces, silks, broad-cloth, and velvets, which being paid for in abundant paper, increased in price fourfold. Provisions shared the general advance. Bread, meat, and vegetables were sold at prices greater than had ever before been known ; while the wages of labour rose in exactly the same proportion. The artisan who formerly gained fifteen sous per diem now gained sixty. New houses were built in every direction ; an illusory prosperity shone over the land, and so dazzled the eyes of the whole nation, that none could see the dark cloud on the horizon announcing the storm that was too rapidly approaching.

Law himself, the magician whose wand had wrought so surprising a change, shared, of course, in the general prosperity. His wife and daughter were courted by the highest nobility, and their alliance sought by the heirs of ducal and princely houses. He bought two splendid estates in different parts of France, and entered into a negotiation with the family of the Duke de Sully for the purchase of the marquisate of Rosny. His religion being an obstacle to his advancement, the regent promised, if he would publicly conform to the Catholic faith, to make him comptroller-general of the finances. Law, who had no more real religion than any other professed gambler, readily agreed, and was confirmed by the Abbé de Tencin in the cathedral of Melun, in presence of a great crowd of spectators.* On the following day he was elected honorary churchwarden of the parish of St. Roch, upon which occasion he made it a present of the sum of five hundred thousand livres. His charities, always magnificent, were not always so ostentatious. He gave away great sums privately, and no tale of real distress ever reached his ears in vain.

---

* The following squib was circulated on the occasion :
> " Foin de ton zèle séraphique,
> Malheureux Abbé de Tencin,
> Depuis que Law est Catholique,
> Tout le royaume est Capucin!"

Thus somewhat weakly and paraphrastically rendered by Justandsond, in his translation of the *Memoirs of Louis XV.;*
> " Tencin, a curse on thy seraphic zeal,
> Which by persuasion hath contrived the means
> To make the Scotchman at our altars kneel,
> Since which we all are poor as Capucines!"

At this time he was by far the most influential person of the state. The Duke of Orleans had so much confidence in his sagacity and the success of his plans, that he always consulted him upon every matter of moment. He was by no means unduly elevated by his prosperity, but remained the same simple, affable, sensible man that he had shewn himself in adversity. His gallantry, which was always delightful to the fair objects of it, was of a nature so kind, so gentlemanly, and so respectful, that not even a lover could have taken offence at it. If upon any occasion he shewed any symptoms of haughtiness, it was to the cringing nobles who lavished their adulation upon him

LAW AS ATLAS.*

till it became fulsome. He often took pleasure in seeing how long he could make them dance attendance upon him for a single favour. To such of his own countrymen as by chance visited Paris, and sought an interview with him, he was, on the contrary, all politeness and attention. When Archibald Campbell, Earl of Islay, and afterwards Duke of Argyle, called upon him in the Place Vendôme, he had to pass through an ante-chamber crowded with persons of the first distinction, all anxious to see the great financier, and have their names put down as first on the list of some new subscription. Law himself was quietly sitting in his library, writing a letter to the gardener at his paternal estate of Lauriston about the planting of some cabbages! The earl stayed for a considerable time, played a game of piquet with his countryman, and left him charmed with his ease, good sense, and good breeding.

* From a print in a Dutch collection of satirical prints relating to the Mississippi Mania, entitled "Het groote Tafereel der Dwaasheid;" or, The great picture of Folly. The print of Atlas is styled, "L'Atlas actieux de Papier." Law is calling in Hercules to aid him in supporting the globe. Quoted in Wright's *England under the House of Hanover*.

Among the nobles who, by means of the public credulity at this time, gained sums sufficient to repair their ruined fortunes, may be mentioned the names of the Dukes de Bourbon, de Guiche, de la Force,* de Chaulnes, and d'Antin ; the Marechal d'Estrées ; the Princes de Rohan, de Poix, and de Léon. The Duke de Bourbon, son of Louis XIV. by Madame de Montespan, was peculiarly fortunate in his speculations in Mississippi paper. He rebuilt the royal residence of Chantilly in a style of unwonted magnificence ; and being passionately fond of horses, he erected a range of stables, which were long renowned throughout Europe, and imported a hundred and fifty of the finest racers from England to improve the breed in France. He bought a large extent of country in Picardy, and became possessed of nearly all the valuable lands lying between the Oise and the Somme.

When fortunes such as these were gained, it is no wonder that Law should have been almost worshipped by the mercurial population. Never was monarch more flattered than he was. All the small poets and *littérateurs* of the day poured floods of adulation upon him. According to them, he was the saviour of the country, the tutelary divinity of France ; wit was in all his words, goodness in all his looks, and wisdom in all his actions. So great a crowd followed his carriage whenever he went abroad, that the regent sent him a troop of horse as his permanent escort to clear the streets before him.

It was remarked at this time that Paris had never before been so full of objects of elegance and luxury. Statues, pictures, and tapestries were imported in great quantities from foreign countries, and found a ready market. All those pretty trifles in the way of furniture and ornament which the French excel in manufacturing were no longer the exclusive playthings of the aristocracy, but were to be found in abundance in the houses of traders and the middle classes in general. Jewellery of the most costly description was brought to Paris as the most favourable mart ; among the rest, the famous diamond bought by the regent, and called by his name, and which long adorned the crown of France. It was purchased for the sum of two millions of livres, under circumstances which shew that the regent was not so great a gainer as some of his subjects by the impetus which trade had received. When the diamond was first offered to him, he refused to buy it, although he desired above all things to possess it,

---

* The Duke de la Force gained considerable sums, not only by jobbing in the stocks, but in dealing in porcelain, spices, &c. It was debated for a length of time in the parliament of Paris whether he had not, in his quality of spice-merchant, forfeited his rank in the peerage. It was decided in the negative. A caricature of him was made, dressed as a street-porter, carrying a large bale of spices on his back, with the inscription, " Admirez LA FORCE."

alleging as his reason, that his duty to the country he governed would not allow him to spend so large a sum of the public money for a mere jewel. This valid and honourable excuse threw all the ladies of the court into alarm, and nothing was heard for some days but expressions of regret that so rare a gem should be allowed to go out of France, no private individual being rich enough to buy it. The regent was continually importuned about it, but all in vain, until the Duke de St. Simon, who with all his ability was something of a twaddler, undertook the weighty business. His entreaties being seconded by Law, the good-natured regent gave his consent, leaving to Law's ingenuity to find the means to pay for it. The owner took security for the payment of the sum of two millions of livres within a stated period, receiving in the mean time the interest of five per cent upon that amount, and being allowed, besides, all the valuable clippings of the gem. St. Simon, in his *Memoirs*, relates with no little complacency his share in this transaction. After describing the diamond to be as large as a greengage, of a form nearly round, perfectly white, and without flaw, and weighing more than five hundred grains, he concludes with a chuckle, by telling the world "that he takes great credit to himself for having induced the regent to make so illustrious a purchase." In other words, he was proud that he had induced him to sacrifice his duty, and buy a bauble for himself at an extravagant price out of the public money.

Thus the system continued to flourish till the commencement of the year 1720. The warnings of the parliament, that too great a creation of paper money would, sooner or later, bring the country to bankruptcy, were disregarded. The regent, who knew nothing whatever of the philosophy of finance, thought that a system which had produced such good effects could never be carried to excess. If five hundred millions of paper had been of such advantage, five hundred millions additional would be of still greater advantage. This was the grand error of the regent, and which Law did not attempt to dispel. The extraordinary avidity of the people kept up the delusion; and the higher the price of Indian and Mississippi stock, the more *billets de banque* were issued to keep pace with it. The edifice thus reared might not unaptly be compared to the gorgeous palace erected by Potemkin, that princely barbarian of Russia, to surprise and please his imperial mistress: huge blocks of ice were piled one upon another; ionic pillars of chastest workmanship, in ice, formed a noble portico; and a dome, of the same material, shone in the sun, which had just strength enough to gild, but not to melt it. It glittered afar, like a palace of crystals and diamonds; but there came one warm breeze from the south, and the stately building dissolved away, till none

were able even to gather up the fragments. So with Law and his
paper system. No sooner did the breath of popular mistrust blow
steadily upon it, than it fell to ruins, and none could raise it up again.
The first slight alarm that was occasioned was early in 1720. The
Prince de Conti, offended that Law should have denied him fresh
shares in India stock, at his own price, sent to his bank to demand
payment in specie of so enormous a quantity of notes, that three
wagons were required for its transport. Law complained to the
regent, and urged on his attention the mischief that would be done,
if such an example found many imitators. The regent was but too
well aware of it, and, sending for the Prince de Conti, ordered him,
under penalty of his high displeasure, to refund to the bank two-thirds
of the specie which he had withdrawn from it. The prince was forced
to obey the despotic mandate. Happily for Law's credit, De Conti
was an unpopular man : every body condemned his meanness and
cupidity, and agreed that Law had been hardly treated. It is strange,
however, that so narrow an escape should not have made both Law
and the regent more anxious to restrict their issues. Others were
soon found who imitated, from motives of distrust, the example which
had been set by De Conti in revenge. The more acute stockjobbers
imagined justly that prices could not continue to rise for ever. Bour-
don and La Richardière, renowned for their extensive operations in
the funds, quietly and in small quantities at a time, converted their
notes into specie, and sent it away to foreign countries. They also
bought as much as they could conveniently carry of plate and expensive jewellery, and sent it secretly away to England or to Holland.
Vermalet, a jobber, who sniffed the coming storm, procured gold and
silver coin to the amount of nearly a million of livres, which he packed
in a farmer's cart, and covered over with hay and cow-dung. He
then disguised himself in the dirty smock-frock, or *blouse*, of a peasant,
and drove his precious load in safety into Belgium. From thence he
soon found means to transport it to Amsterdam.

Hitherto no difficulty had been experienced by any class in procuring specie for their wants. But this system could not long be carried on without causing a scarcity. The voice of complaint was heard
on every side, and inquiries being instituted, the cause was soon discovered. The council debated long on the remedies to be taken, and
Law, being called on for his advice, was of opinion, that an edict
should be published, depreciating the value of coin five per cent
below that of paper. The edict was published accordingly ; but failing
of its intended effect, was followed by another, in which the depreciation was increased to ten per cent. The payments of the bank
were at the same time restricted to one hundred livres in gold, and

ten in silver. All these measures were nugatory to restore confidence in the paper, though the restriction of cash payments within limits so extremely narrow kept up the credit of the bank.

LUCIFER'S NEW ROW-BARGE.*

Notwithstanding every effort to the contrary, the precious metals continued to be conveyed to England and Holland. The little coin that was left in the country was carefully treasured, or hidden until the scarcity became so great, that the operations of trade could no longer be carried on. In this emergency, Law hazarded the bold experiment of forbidding the use of specie altogether. In February

* "Lucifer's New Row-Barge" exhibits Law in a barge, with a host of emblematic figures representing the Mississippi follies.—*From a Print in Mr. Hawkins' Collection.*

1720 an edict was published, which, instead of restoring the credit of
the paper, as was intended, destroyed it irrecoverably, and drove the
country to the very brink of revolution. By this famous edict it was
forbidden to any person whatever to have more than five hundred
livres (20*l.*) of coin in his possession, under pain of a heavy fine, and
confiscation of the sums found. It was also forbidden to buy up
jewellery, plate, and precious stones, and informers were encouraged
to make search for offenders, by the promise of one-half the amount
they might discover. The whole country sent up a cry of distress at
this unheard-of tyranny. The most odious persecution daily took
place. The privacy of families was violated by the intrusion of informers and their agents. The most virtuous and honest were denounced for the crime of having been seen with a *louis d'or* in their
possession. Servants betrayed their masters, one citizen became a
spy upon his neighbour, and arrests and confiscations so multiplied,
that the courts found a difficulty in getting through the immense increase of business thus occasioned. It was sufficient for an informer
to say that he suspected any person of concealing money in his house,
and immediately a search-warrant was granted. Lord Stair, the English ambassador, said, that it was now impossible to doubt of the sincerity of Law's conversion to the Catholic religion; he had established
the *inquisition*, after having given abundant evidence of his faith in
transubstantiation, by turning so much gold into paper.

Every epithet that popular hatred could suggest was showered
upon the regent and the unhappy Law. Coin, to any amount above
five hundred livres, was an illegal tender, and nobody would take
paper if he could help it. No one knew to-day what his notes would
be worth to-morrow. "Never," says Duclos, in his *Secret Memoirs
of the Regency*, "was seen a more capricious government—never was
a more frantic tyranny exercised by hands less firm. It is inconceivable to those who were witnesses of the horrors of those times, and
who look back upon them now as on a dream, that a sudden revolution did not break out—that Law and the regent did not perish by a
tragical death. They were both held in horror, but the people confined themselves to complaints; a sombre and timid despair, a stupid
consternation, had seized upon all, and men's minds were too vile
even to be capable of a courageous crime." It would appear that, at
one time, a movement of the people was organised. Seditious writings were posted up against the walls, and were sent, in hand-bills,
to the houses of the most conspicuous people. One of them, given
in the *Mémoires de la Régence*, was to the following effect :—" Sir
and madam,—This is to give you notice that a St. Bartholomew's
Day will be enacted again on Saturday and Sunday, if affairs do not

alter. You are desired not to stir out, nor you, nor your servants. God preserve you from the flames! Give notice to your neighbours. Dated, Saturday, May 25th, 1720." The immense number of spies with which the city was infested rendered the people mistrustful of one another, and beyond some trifling disturbances made in the evening by an insignificant group, which was soon dispersed, the peace of the capital was not compromised.

The value of shares in the Louisiana, or Mississippi stock, had fallen very rapidly, and few indeed were found to believe the tales that had once been told of the immense wealth of that region. A last effort was therefore tried to restore the public confidence in the Mississippi project. For this purpose, a general conscription of all the poor wretches in Paris was made by order of government. Upwards of six thousand of the very refuse of the population were im-

pressed, as if in time of war, and were provided with clothes and tools to be embarked for New Orleans, to work in the gold mines alleged to abound there. They were paraded day after day through the streets with their pikes and shovels, and then sent off in small detachments to the out-ports to be shipped for America. Two-thirds of them never reached their destination, but dispersed themselves over the country, sold their tools for what they could get, and returned to their old course of life. In less than three weeks afterwards, one-half of them were to be found again in Paris. The manœuvre, however, caused a

trifling advance in Mississippi stock. Many persons of superabundant
gullibility believed that operations had begun in earnest in the new
Golconda, and that gold and silver ingots would again be found in
France.

In a constitutional monarchy some surer means would have been
found for the restoration of public credit. In England, at a subsequent period, when a similar delusion had brought on similar distress,
how different were the measures taken to repair the evil; but in
France, unfortunately, the remedy was left to the authors of the mischief. The arbitrary will of the regent, which endeavoured to extricate the country, only plunged it deeper into the mire. All payments
were ordered to be made in paper, and between the 1st of February
and the end of May, notes were fabricated to the amount of upwards
of 1500 millions of livres, or 60,000,000l. sterling. But the alarm
once sounded, no art could make the people feel the slightest confidence in paper which was not exchangeable into metal. M. Lambert,
the president of the parliament of Paris, told the regent to his face
that he would rather have a hundred thousand livres in gold or silver
than five millions in the notes of his bank. When such was the general
feeling, the superabundant issues of paper but increased the evil, by
rendering still more enormous the disparity between the amount of
specie and notes in circulation. Coin, which it was the object of the
regent to depreciate, rose in value on every fresh attempt to diminish
it. In February, it was judged advisable that the Royal Bank should
be incorporated with the Company of the Indies. An edict to that
effect was published and registered by the parliament. The state
remained the guarantee for the notes of the bank, and no more were
to be issued without an order in council. All the profits of the bank,
since the time it had been taken out of Law's hands and made a national institution, were given over by the regent to the Company of
the Indies. This measure had the effect of raising for a short time
the value of the Louisiana and other shares of the company, but it
failed in placing public credit on any permanent basis.

A council of state was held in the beginning of May, at which
Law, D'Argenson (his colleague in the administration of the finances),
and all the ministers were present. It was then computed that the
total amount of notes in circulation was 2600 millions of livres, while
the coin in the country was not quite equal to half that amount. It
was evident to the majority of the council that some plan must be
adopted to equalise the currency. Some proposed that the notes
should be reduced to the value of the specie, while others proposed
that the nominal value of the specie should be raised till it was on an
equality with the paper. Law is said to have opposed both these pro-

jects, but failing in suggesting any other, it was agreed that the notes should be depreciated one half. On the 21st of May, an edict was accordingly issued, by which it was decreed that the shares of the Company of the Indies, and the notes of the bank, should gradually diminish in value, till at the end of a year they should only pass current for one-half of their nominal worth. The parliament refused to register the edict—the greatest outcry was excited, and the state of the country became so alarming, that, as the only means of preserving tranquillity, the council of the regency was obliged to stultify its own proceedings, by publishing within seven days another edict, restoring the notes to their original value.

On the same day (the 27th of May) the bank stopped payment in specie. Law and D'Argenson were both dismissed from the ministry. The weak, vacillating, and cowardly regent threw the blame of all the mischief upon Law, who, upon presenting himself at the Palais Royal, was refused admittance. At nightfall, however, he was sent for, and admitted into the palace by a secret door,* when the regent endeavoured to console him, and made all manner of excuses for the severity with which in public he had been compelled to treat him. So capricious was his conduct, that, two days afterwards, he took him publicly to the opera, where he sat in the royal box alongside of the regent, who treated him with marked consideration in face of all the people. But such was the hatred against Law that the experiment had well nigh proved fatal to him. The mob assailed his carriage with stones just as he was entering his own door ; and if the coachman had not made a sudden jerk into the court-yard, and the domestics closed the gate immediately, he would, in all probability, have been dragged out and torn to pieces. On the following day, his wife and daughter were also assailed by the mob as they were returning in their carriage from the races. When the regent was informed of these occurrences he sent Law a strong detachment of Swiss guards, who were stationed night and day in the court of his residence. The public indignation at last increased so much, that Law, finding his own house, even with this guard, insecure, took refuge in the Palais Royal, in the apartments of the regent.

The Chancellor, D'Aguesseau, who had been dismissed in 1718 for his opposition to the projects of Law, was now recalled to aid in the restoration of credit. The regent acknowledged too late, that he had treated with unjustifiable harshness and mistrust one of the ablest, and perhaps the sole honest public man of that corrupt period. He had retired ever since his disgrace to his country house at Fresnes, where, in the midst of severe but delightful philosophic studies, he

* Duclos, *Mémoires Secrets de la Régence.*

had forgotten the intrigues of an unworthy court. Law himself, and the Chevalier de Conflans, a gentleman of the regent's household, were despatched in a post-chaise with orders to bring the ex-chancellor to Paris along with them. D'Aguesseau consented to render what assistance he could, contrary to the advice of his friends, who did not approve that he should accept any recal to office of which Law was the bearer. On his arrival in Paris, five councillors of the parliament were admitted to confer with the Commissary of Finance ; and on the 1st of June an order was published abolishing the law which made

D'AGUESSEAU.

it criminal to amass coin to the amount of more than five hundred livres. Every one was permitted to have as much specie as he pleased. In order that the bank-notes might be withdrawn, twenty-five millions of new notes were created, on the security of the revenues of the city of Paris, at two and a half per cent. The bank-notes withdrawn were publicly burned in front of the Hôtel de Ville. The new notes were principally of the value of ten livres each ; and on the 10th of June the bank was re-opened, with a sufficiency of silver coin to give in change for them.

These measures were productive of considerable advantage. All the population of Paris hastened to the bank to get coin for their small notes ; and silver becoming scarce, they were paid in copper. Very few complained that this was too heavy, although poor fellows might be continually seen toiling and sweating along the streets, laden with more than they could comfortably carry, in the shape of change for fifty livres. The crowds around the bank were so great that hardly a day passed that some one was not pressed to death. On the 9th of July, the multitude was so dense and clamorous that the guards stationed at the entrance of the Mazarin Gardens closed the gate and refused to admit any more. The crowd became incensed, and flung stones through the railings upon the soldiers. The latter, incensed in their turn, threatened to fire upon the people. At that instant one of them was hit by a stone, and, taking up his piece, he fired into the crowd. One man fell dead immediately, and another was severely wounded. It was every instant expected that a general attack would have been commenced upon the bank ; but the gates of the Mazarin Gardens being opened to the crowd, who saw a whole troop of soldiers, with their bayonets fixed ready to receive them, they contented themselves by giving vent to their indignation in groans and hisses.

Eight days afterwards the concourse of people was so tremendous that fifteen persons were squeezed to death at the doors of the bank. The people were so indignant that they took three of the bodies on stretchers before them, and proceeded, to the number of seven or eight thousand, to the gardens of the Palais Royal, that they might shew the regent the misfortunes that he and Law had brought upon the country. Law's coachman, who was sitting on the box of his master's carriage, in the court-yard of the palace, happened to have more zeal than discretion, and, not liking that the mob should abuse his master, he said, loud enough to be overheard by several persons, that they were all blackguards, and deserved to be hanged. The mob immediately set upon him, and thinking that Law was in the carriage, broke it to pieces. The imprudent coachman narrowly escaped with his life. No further mischief was done ; a body of troops making their appearance, the crowd quietly dispersed, after an assurance had been given by the regent that the three bodies they had brought to shew him should be decently buried at his own expense. The parliament was sitting at the time of this uproar, and the president took upon himself to go out and see what was the matter. On his return he informed the councillors that Law's carriage had been broken by the mob. All the members rose simultaneously, and expressed their joy by a loud shout, while one man, more zealous in his hatred than the rest, exclaimed, " *And Law himself, is he torn to pieces ?*"*

Much, undoubtedly, depended on the credit of the Company of the Indies, which was answerable for so great a sum to the nation. It was therefore suggested in the council of the ministry, that any privileges which could be granted to enable it to fulfil its engagements, would be productive of the best results. With this end in view, it was proposed that the exclusive privilege of all maritime commerce should be secured to it, and an edict to that effect was published. But it was unfortunately forgotten that by such a measure all the merchants of the country would be ruined. The idea of such an immense privilege was generally scouted by the nation, and petition on petition was presented to the parliament that they would

---

* The Duchess of Orleans gives a different version of this story; but whichever be the true one, the manifestation of such feeling in a legislative assembly was not very creditable. She says that the president was so transported with joy, that he was seized with a rhyming fit, and returning into the hall, exclaimed to the members :

" *Messieurs ! Messieurs ! bonne nouvelle !*
Le carrosse de Lass est reduit en cannelle !"

refuse to register the decree. They refused accordingly, and the regent, remarking that they did nothing but fan the flame of sedition, exiled them to Blois. At the intercession of D'Aguesseau, the place of banishment was changed to Pontoise, and thither accordingly the councillors repaired, determined to set the regent at defiance. They made every arrangement for rendering their temporary exile as agreeable as possible. The president gave the most elegant suppers, to which he invited all the gayest and wittiest company of Paris. Every night there was a concert and ball for the ladies. The usually grave and solemn judges and councillors joined in cards and other diversions, leading for several weeks a life of the most extravagant pleasure, for no other purpose than to shew the regent of how little consequence they deemed their banishment, and that, when they willed it, they could make Pontoise a pleasanter residence than Paris.

Of all the nations in the world the French are the most renowned for singing over their grievances. Of that country it has been remarked with some truth, that its whole history may be traced in its songs. When Law, by the utter failure of his best-laid plans, rendered himself obnoxious, satire of course seized hold upon him ; and while caricatures of his person appeared in all the shops, the streets resounded with songs, in which neither he nor the regent was spared. Many of these songs were far from decent ; and one of them in particular counselled the application of all his notes to the most ignoble use to which paper can be applied. But the following, preserved in the letters of the Duchess of Orleans, was the best and the most popular, and was to be heard for months in all the *carrefours* in Paris. The application of the chorus is happy enough :

> Aussitôt que Lass arriva
> Dans notre bonne ville,
> Monsieur le Régent publia
> Que Lass serait utile
> Pour rétablir la nation.
> *La faridondaine! la faridondon!*
> Mais il nous a tous enrichi,
> *Biribi!*
> *A la façon de Barbari,*
> *Mon ami!*
>
> Ce parpaillot, pour attirer
> Tout l'argent de la France,
> Songea d'abord à s'assurer
> De notre confiance.
> Il fit son abjuration,
> *La faridondaine! la faridondon!*

> Mais le fourbe s'est converti,
> *Biribi !*
> A la façon de Barbari,
> *Mon ami !*

> Lass, le fils aîné de Satan
> Nous met tous à l'aumône,
> Il nous a pris tout notre argent
> Et n'en rend à personne.
> Mais le Régent, humain et bon,
> La faridondaine ! la faridondon !
> Nous rendra ce qu'on nous a pris,
> *Biribi !*
> A la facon de Barbari,
> *Mon ami !*

The following epigram is of the same date :

> *Lundi,* j'achetai des actions ;
> *Mardi,* je gagnai des millions ;
> *Mercredi,* j'arrangeai mon ménage,
> *Jeudi,* je pris un équipage,
> *Vendredi,* je m'en fus au bal,
> *Et Samedi,* à l'hôpital.

Among the caricatures that were abundantly published, and that shewed as plainly as graver matters that the nation had awakened to a sense of its folly, was one, a fac-simile of which is preserved in the *Mémoires de la Régence*. It was thus described by its author : " The ' Goddess of Shares,' in her triumphal car, driven by the Goddess of Folly. Those who are drawing the car are impersonations of the Mississippi, with his wooden leg, the South Sea, the Bank of England, the Company of the West of Senegal, and of various assurances. Lest the car should not roll fast enough, the agents of these companies, known by their long fox-tails and their cunning looks, turn round the spokes of the wheels, upon which are marked the names of the several stocks and their value, sometimes high and sometimes low, according to the turns of the wheel. Upon the ground are the merchandise, day-books and ledgers of legitimate commerce, crushed under the chariot of Folly. Behind is an immense crowd of persons, of all ages, sexes, and conditions, clamouring after Fortune, and fighting with each other to get a portion of the shares which she distributes so bountifully among them. In the clouds sits a demon, blowing bubbles of soap, which are also the objects of the admiration and cupidity of the crowd, who jump upon one another's backs to reach them ere they burst. Right in the pathway of the car, and blocking up the passage, stands a large building,

with three doors, through one of which it must pass, if it proceeds
farther, and all the crowd along with it. Over the first door are
the words, ' *Hôpital des Foux*,' over the second, ' *Hôpital des Ma-
lades*,' and over the third, ' *Hôpital des Gueux*.' " Another caricature represented Law sitting in a large cauldron, boiling over the
flames of popular madness, surrounded by an impetuous multitude,
who were pouring all their gold and silver into it, and receiving
gladly in exchange the bits of paper which he distributed among
them by handfuls.

While this excitement lasted, Law took good care not to expose
himself unguarded in the streets. Shut up in the apartments of the
regent, he was secure from all attack ; and whenever he ventured
abroad, it was either *incognito*, or in one of the royal carriages,
with a powerful escort. An amusing anecdote is recorded of the detestation in which he was held by the people, and the ill-treatment
he would have met had he fallen into their hands. A gentleman
of the name of Boursel was passing in his carriage down the Rue St.
Antoine, when his farther progress was stayed by a hackney-coach
that had blocked up the road. M. Boursel's servant called impatiently to the hackney-coachman to get out of the way, and, on his
refusal, struck him a blow on the face. A crowd was soon drawn
together by the disturbance, and M. Boursel got out of the carriage
to restore order. The hackney-coachman, imagining that he had
now another assailant, bethought him of an expedient to rid himself of both, and called out as loudly as he was able, " Help ! help !
murder ! murder ! Here are Law and his servant going to kill me !
Help ! help !" At this cry the people came out of their shops, armed
with sticks and other weapons, while the mob gathered stones to inflict summary vengeance upon the supposed financier. Happily for
M. Boursel and his servant, the door of the church of the Jesuits
stood wide open, and, seeing the fearful odds against them, they
rushed towards it with all speed. They reached the altar, pursued
by the people, and would have been ill-treated even there, if, finding the door open leading to the sacristy, they had not sprang
through, and closed it after them. The mob were then persuaded
to leave the church by the alarmed and indignant priests, and finding M. Boursel's carriage still in the streets, they vented their ill-
will against it, and did it considerable damage.

The twenty-five millions secured on the municipal revenues of
the city of Paris, bearing so low an interest as two and a half per
cent, were not very popular among the large holders of Mississippi
stock. The conversion of the securities was, therefore, a work of
considerable difficulty ; for many preferred to retain the falling paper

of Law's company, in the hope that a favourable turn might take place. On the 15th of August, with a view to hasten the conversion, an edict was passed, declaring that all notes for sums between one thousand and ten thousand livres should not pass current, except for the purchase of annuities and bank accounts, or for the payment of instalments still due on the shares of the company.

In October following another edict was passed, depriving these notes of all value whatever after the month of November next ensuing. The management of the mint, the farming of the revenue, and all the other advantages and privileges of the India, or Mississippi Company, were taken from them, and they were reduced to a mere private company. This was the death-blow to the whole system, which had now got into the hands of its enemies. Law had lost all influence in the Council of Finance, and the company, being despoiled of its immunities, could no longer hold out the shadow of a prospect of being able to fulfil its engagements. All those suspected of illegal profits at the time the public delusion was at its height, were sought out and amerced in heavy fines. It was previously ordered that a list of the original proprietors should be made out, and that such persons as still retained their shares should place them in deposit with the company, and that those who had neglected to complete the shares for which they had put down their names should now purchase them of the company, at the rate of 13,500 livres for each share of 500 livres. Rather than submit to pay this enormous sum for stock which was actually at a discount, the shareholders packed up all their portable effects, and endeavoured to find a refuge in foreign countries. Orders were immediately issued to the authorities at the ports and frontiers, to apprehend all travellers who sought to leave the kingdom, and keep them in custody, until it was ascertained whether they had any plate or jewellery with them, or were concerned in the late stock-jobbing. Against such few as escaped, the punishment of death was recorded, while the most arbitrary proceedings were instituted against those who remained.

Law himself, in a moment of despair, determined to leave a country where his life was no longer secure. He at first only demanded permission to retire from Paris to one of his country-seats—a permission which the regent cheerfully granted. The latter was much affected at the unhappy turn affairs had taken, but his faith continued unmoved in the truth and efficacy of Law's financial system. His eyes were opened to his own errors; and during the few remaining years of his life he constantly longed for an opportunity of again establishing the system upon a securer basis. At Law's last interview with the prince, he is reported to have said,— " I confess that I have committed many faults. I committed them because I am a man, and all men are liable to error; but I declare to you most solemnly that none of them proceeded from wicked or dishonest motives, and that nothing of the kind will be found in the whole course of my conduct."

LAW IN A CAR DRAWN BY COCKS.*

Two or three days after his departure the regent sent him a very kind letter, permitting him to leave the kingdom whenever he pleased, and stating that he had ordered his passports to be made ready. He at the same time offered him any sum of money he might require. Law respectfully declined the money, and set out for Brussels in a post-chaise belonging to Madame de Prie, the mistress of the Duke of Bourbon, escorted by six horse-guards. From thence he proceeded to Venice, where he remained for some months, the object of the greatest curiosity to the people, who believed him to be the possessor

* Law in a car drawn by cocks; from *Het groote Tafereel der Dwaasheid.*

of enormous wealth. No opinion, however, could be more erroneous. With more generosity than could have been expected from a man who during the greatest part of his life had been a professed gambler, he had refused to enrich himself at the expense of a ruined nation. During the height of the popular frenzy for Mississippi stock, he had never doubted of the final success of his projects in making France the richest and most powerful nation of Europe. He invested all his gains in the purchase of landed property in France—a sure proof of his own belief in the stability of his schemes. He had hoarded no plate or jewellery, and sent no money, like the dishonest jobbers, to foreign countries. His all, with the exception of one diamond, worth about five or six thousand pounds sterling, was invested in the French soil ; and when he left that country, he left it almost a beggar. This fact alone ought to rescue his memory from the charge of knavery, so often and so unjustly brought against him.

As soon as his departure was known, all his estates and his valuable library were confiscated. Among the rest, an annuity of 200,000 livres (8000*l.* sterling) on the lives of his wife and children, which had been purchased for five millions of livres, was forfeited, notwithstanding that a special edict, drawn up for the purpose in the days of his prosperity, had expressly declared that it should never be confiscated for any cause whatever. Great discontent existed among the people that Law had been suffered to escape. The mob and the parliament would have been pleased to have seen him hanged. The few who had not suffered by the commercial revolution rejoiced that the *quack* had left the country ; but all those (and they were by far the most numerous class) whose fortunes were implicated regretted that his intimate knowledge of the distress of the country, and of the causes that had led to it, had not been rendered more available in discovering a remedy.

At a meeting of the Council of Finance and the General Council of the Regency, documents were laid upon the table, from which it appeared that the amount of notes in circulation was 2700 millions. The regent was called upon to explain how it happened that there was a discrepancy between the dates at which these issues were made and those of the edicts by which they were authorised. He might have safely taken the whole blame upon himself, but he preferred that an absent man should bear a share of it ; and he therefore stated that Law, upon his own authority, had issued 1200 millions of notes at different times, and that he (the regent), seeing that the thing had been irrevocably done, had screened Law by antedating the decrees of the council which authorised the augmentation. It would have been more to his credit if he had told the whole truth while he was about it, and acknowledged that it was mainly through his extravagance and impatience that Law had been induced to overstep the bounds of safe speculation. It was also ascertained that the national debt, on the 1st of January, 1721, amounted to upwards of 3100 millions of livres, or more than 124,000,000*l.* sterling, the interest upon which was 3,196,000*l.* A commission, or *visa*, was forthwith appointed to examine into all the securities of the state creditors, who were to be divided into five classes; the first four comprising those who had purchased their securities with real effects, and the latter comprising those who could give no proofs that the transactions they had entered into were real and *bonâ fide*. The securities of the latter were ordered to be destroyed, while those of the first four classes were subjected to a most rigid and jealous scrutiny. The result of the labours of the *visa* was a report, in which they counselled the reduction of the interest upon these securities to fifty-six millions of livres.

D'ARGENSON.

They justified this advice by a statement of the various acts of peculation and extortion which they had discovered ; and an edict to that effect was accordingly published and duly registered by the parliaments of the kingdom.

Another tribunal was afterwards established under the title of the *Chambre de l'Arsenal*, which took cognisance of all the malversations committed in the financial departments of the government during the late unhappy period. A Master of Requests, named Falhonet, together with the Abbé Clement, and two clerks in their employ, had been concerned in divers acts of peculation to the amount of upwards of a million of livres. The first two were sentenced to be beheaded, and the latter to be hanged ; but their punishment was afterwards commuted into imprisonment for life in the Bastille. Numerous other acts of dishonesty were discovered, and punished by fine and imprisonment.

D'Argenson shared with Law and the regent the unpopularity which had alighted upon all those concerned in the Mississippi madness. He was dismissed from his post of Chancellor to make room for D'Aguesseau ; but he retained the title of Keeper of the Seals, and was allowed to attend the councils whenever he pleased. He thought it better, however, to withdraw from Paris, and live for a time a life of seclusion at his country seat. But he was not formed for retirement; and becoming moody and discontented, he aggravated a disease under which he had long laboured, and died in less than a twelvemonth. The populace of Paris so detested him, that they carried their hatred even to his grave. As his funeral procession passed to the church of St. Nicholas du Chardonneret, the burying-place of his family, it was beset by a riotous mob; and his two sons, who were following as chief mourners, were obliged to drive as fast as they were able down a by-street to escape personal violence.

As regards Law, he for some time entertained a hope that he should be recalled to France to aid in establishing its credit upon a firmer basis. The death of the regent in 1723, who expired suddenly as he was sitting by the fireside conversing with his mistress, the Duchess de Phalaris, deprived him of that hope, and he was reduced to lead his former life of gambling. He was more than once obliged to pawn his diamond, the sole remnant of his vast wealth, but successful play generally enabled him to redeem it. Being persecuted by his creditors at Rome, he proceeded to Copenhagen, where he received permission from the English ministry to reside in his native country, his pardon for the murder of Mr. Wilson having been sent over to him in 1719. He was brought over in the admiral's ship—a circumstance which gave occasion for a short debate in the House of Lords. Earl Coningsby complained that a man who had renounced both his country and his religion should have been treated with such honour, and expressed his belief that his presence in England, at a time when the people were so bewildered by the nefarious practices of the South-Sea directors, would be attended with no little danger. He gave notice of a motion on the subject; but it was allowed to drop, no other member of the House having the slightest participation in his lordship's fears. Law remained for about four years in England, and then proceeded to Venice, where he died in 1729, in very embarrassed circumstances. The following epitaph was written at the time :

> " Ci gît cet Ecossais célébre,
> Ce calculateur sans égal,
> Qui, par les régles de l'algébre,
> A mis la France à l'hôpital."

His brother, William Law, who had been concerned with him in the administration both of the bank and the Louisiana Company, was imprisoned in the Bastille for alleged malversation, but no guilt was ever proved against him. He was liberated after fifteen months, and became the founder of a family, which is still known in France under the title of Marquises of Lauriston.

NECK OR NOTHING.*

In the next chapter will be found an account of the madness which infected the people of England at the same time, and under very similar circumstances, but which, thanks to the energies and good sense of a constitutional government, was attended with results far less disastrous than those which were seen in France.

* Neck or nothing, or downfall of the Mississippi Company.—*From a Print in Mr. Hawkins' Collection.*

SOUTH-SEA HOUSE.

THE SOUTH-SEA BUBBLE.

At length corruption, like a general flood,
Did deluge all; and avarice creeping on,
Spread, like a low-born mist, and hid the sun.
Statesmen and patriots plied alike the stocks,
Peeress and butler shared alike the box;
And judges jobbed, and bishops bit the town,
And mighty dukes packed cards for half-a-crown:
Britain was sunk in lucre's sordid charms.—*Pope.*

THE South-Sea Company was originated by the celebrated Harley Earl of Oxford, in the year 1711, with the view of restoring public credit, which had suffered by the dismissal of the Whig ministry, and of providing for the discharge of the army and navy debentures, and other parts of the floating debt, amounting to nearly ten millions sterling. A company of merchants, at that time without a name, took this debt upon themselves, and the government agreed to secure them for a certain period the interest of six per cent. To provide for this interest, amounting to 600,000*l.* per annum, the duties upon wines, vinegar, India goods, wrought silks, tobacco, whale-fins, and some other articles, were rendered permanent. The monopoly of the trade to the South Seas was granted, and the company, being incorporated by act of parliament, assumed the title by which it has ever since been known. The minister took great credit to himself for his share in this transaction, and the scheme was always called by his flatterers "the Earl of Oxford's masterpiece."

Even at this early period of its history the most visionary ideas were formed by the company and the public of the immense riches of the eastern coast of South America. Every body had heard of the gold and silver mines of Peru and Mexico; every one believed them to be inexhaustible, and that it was only necessary to send the manufactures of England to the coast to be repaid a hundredfold in gold and silver ingots by the natives. A report, industriously spread, that Spain was willing to concede four ports on the coasts of Chili and Peru for the purposes of traffic, increased the general confidence, and for many years the South-Sea Company's stock was in high favour.

HARLEY EARL OF OXFORD

Philip V. of Spain, however, never had any intention of admitting the English to a free trade in the ports of Spanish America. Negotiations were set on foot, but their only result was the *assiento* contract, or the privilege of supplying the colonies with negroes for thirty years, and of sending once a year a vessel, limited both as to tonnage and value of cargo, to trade with Mexico, Peru, or Chili. The latter permission was only granted upon the hard condition, that the King of Spain should enjoy one-fourth of the profits, and a tax of five per cent on the remainder. This was a great disappointment to the Earl of Oxford and his party, who were reminded much oftener than they found agreeable of the

" Parturiunt montes, nascitur ridiculus mus."

But the public confidence in the South-Sea Company was not shaken. The Earl of Oxford declared that Spain would permit two ships, in addition to the annual ship, to carry out merchandise during the first year; and a list was published, in which all the ports and harbours of these coasts were pompously set forth as open to the trade of Great Britain. The first voyage of the annual ship was not made till the year 1717, and in the following year the trade was suppressed by the rupture with Spain.

The king's speech, at the opening of the session of 1717, made pointed allusion to the state of public credit, and recommended that proper measures should be taken to reduce the national debt. The two great monetary corporations, the South-Sea Company and the Bank of England, made proposals to parliament on the 20th of May ensuing. The South-Sea Company prayed that their capital stock of ten millions might be increased to twelve, by subscription or otherwise, and offered to accept five per cent instead of six upon the whole amount. The bank made proposals equally advantageous. The house debated for some time, and finally three acts were passed, called the South-Sea Act, the Bank Act, and the General Fund Act. By the first, the proposals of the South-Sea Company were accepted, and that body held itself ready to advance the sum of two millions towards discharging the principal and interest of the debt due by the state for the four lottery funds of the ninth and tenth years of Queen Anne. By the second act, the bank received a lower rate of interest for the sum of 1,775,027*l*. 15*s*. due to it by the state, and agreed to deliver up to be cancelled as many exchequer bills as amounted to two millions sterling, and to accept of an annuity of one hundred thousand pounds, being after the rate of five per cent, the whole redeemable at one year's notice. They were further required to be ready to advance, in case of need, a sum not exceeding 2,500,000*l*. upon the same terms of five per cent interest, redeemable by parliament. The General Fund Act recited the various deficiencies, which were to be made good by the aids derived from the foregoing sources.

The name of the South-Sea Company was thus continually before the public. Though their trade with the South American States produced little or no augmentation of their revenues, they continued to flourish as a monetary corporation. Their stock was in high request, and the directors, buoyed up with success, began to think of new means for extending their influence. The Mississippi scheme of John Law, which so dazzled and captivated the French people, inspired them with an idea that they could carry on the same game in England. The anticipated failure of his plans did not divert them from their intention. Wise in their own conceit, they imagined they could avoid his faults, carry on their schemes for ever, and stretch the cord of credit to its extremest tension, without causing it to snap asunder.

It was while Law's plan was at its greatest height of popularity, while people were crowding in thousands to the Rue Quincampoix, and ruining themselves with frantic eagerness, that the South-Sea directors laid before parliament their famous plan for paying off the national debt. Visions of boundless wealth floated before the fascinated eyes of the people in the two most celebrated countries of

Europe. The English commenced their career of extravagance somewhat later than the French ; but as soon as the delirium seized them, they were determined not to be outdone. Upon the 22d of January, 1720, the House of Commons resolved itself into a committee of the whole house, to take into consideration that part of the king's speech at the opening of the session which related to the public debts, and the proposal of the South-Sea Company towards the redemption and sinking of the same. The proposal set forth at great length, and under several heads, the debts of the state, amounting to 30,981,712*l*., which the company were anxious to take upon themselves, upon consideration of five per cent per annum, secured to them until Midsummer 1727 ; after which time, the whole was to become redeemable at the pleasure of the legislature, and the interest to be reduced to four per cent. The proposal was received with great favour ; but the Bank of England had many friends in the House of Commons, who were desirous that that body should share in the advantages that were likely to accrue. On behalf of this corporation it was represented, that they had performed great and eminent services to the state in the most difficult times, and deserved, at least, that if any advantage was to be made by public bargains of this nature, they should be preferred before a company that had never done any thing for the nation. The further consideration of the matter was accordingly postponed for five days. In the mean time, a plan was drawn up by the governors of the bank. The South-Sea Company, afraid that the bank might offer still more advantageous terms to the government than themselves, reconsidered their former proposal, and made some alterations in it, which they hoped would render it more acceptable. The principal change was a stipulation that the government might redeem these debts at the expiration of four years, instead of seven, as at first suggested. The bank resolved not to be outbidden in this singular auction, and the governors also reconsidered their first proposal, and sent in a new one.

Thus, each corporation having made two proposals, the house began to deliberate. Mr. Robert Walpole was the chief speaker in favour of the bank, and Mr. Aislabie, the Chancellor of the Exchequer, the principal advocate on behalf of the South-Sea Company. It was resolved, on the 2d of February, that the proposals of the latter were most advantageous to the country. They were accordingly received, and leave was given to bring in a bill to that effect.

Exchange Alley was in a fever of excitement. The company's stock, which had been at a hundred and thirty the previous day, gradually rose to three hundred, and continued to rise with the most astonishing rapidity during the whole time that the bill in its several

stages was under discussion. Mr. Walpole was almost the only statesman in the House who spoke out boldly against it. He warned them,
in eloquent and solemn language, of the evils that would ensue. It
countenanced, he said, "the dangerous practice of stock-jobbing, and
would divert the genius of the nation from trade and industry. It
would hold out a dangerous lure to decoy the unwary to their ruin,
by making them part with the earnings of their labour for a prospect
of imaginary wealth. The great principle of the project was an evil
of first-rate magnitude; it was to raise artificially the value of the
stock, by exciting and keeping up a general infatuation, and by promising dividends out of funds which could never be adequate to the
purpose." In a prophetic spirit he
added, that if the plan succeeded,
the directors would become masters
of the government, form a new and
absolute aristocracy in the kingdom, and control the resolutions of
the legislature. If it failed, which
he was convinced it would, the result would bring general discontent
and ruin upon the country. Such
would be the delusion, that when
the evil day came, as come it would,
the people would start up, as from
a dream, and ask themselves if these
things could have been true. All his
eloquence was in vain. He was looked

SIR ROBERT WALPOLE.

upon as a false prophet, or compared to the hoarse raven, croaking
omens of evil. His friends, however, compared him to Cassandra,
predicting evils which would only be believed when they come home
to men's hearths, and stared them in the face at their own boards.
Although, in former times, the House had listened with the utmost
attention to every word that fell from his lips, the benches became
deserted when it was known that he would speak on the South-Sea
question.

The bill was two months in its progress through the House of
Commons. During this time every exertion was made by the directors
and their friends, and more especially by the chairman, the noted Sir
John Blunt, to raise the price of the stock. The most extravagant
rumours were in circulation. Treaties between England and Spain
were spoken of, whereby the latter was to grant a free trade to all her
colonies; and the rich produce of the mines of Potosi-la-Paz was to
be brought to England until silver should become almost as plentiful

as iron. For cotton and woollen goods, with which we could supply them in abundance, the dwellers in Mexico were to empty their golden mines. The company of merchants trading to the South Seas would be the richest the world ever saw, and every hundred pounds invested in it would produce hundreds per annum to the stockholder. At last the stock was raised by these means to near four hundred ; but, after fluctuating a good deal, settled at three hundred and thirty, at which price it remained when the bill passed the Commons by a majority of 172 against 55.

In the House of Lords the bill was hurried through all its stages with unexampled rapidity. On the 4th of April it was read a first time ; on the 5th, it was read a second time ; on the 6th, it was committed ; and on the 7th, was read a third time and passed.

Several peers spoke warmly against the scheme ; but their warnings fell upon dull, cold ears. A speculating frenzy had seized them as well as the plebeians. Lord North and Grey said the bill was unjust in its nature, and might prove fatal in its consequences, being calculated to enrich the few and impoverish the many. The Duke of Wharton followed ; but, as he only retailed at second-hand the arguments so eloquently stated by Walpole in the Lower House, he was not listened to with even the same attention that had been bestowed upon Lord North and Grey. Earl Cowper followed on the same side, and compared the bill to the famous horse of the siege of Troy. Like that, it was ushered in and received with great pomp and acclamations of joy, but bore within it treachery and destruction. The Earl of Sunderland endeavoured to answer all objections ; and on the question being put, there appeared only seventeen peers against, and eighty-three in favour of the project. The very same day on which it passed the Lords, it received the royal assent, and became the law of the land.

It seemed at that time as if the whole nation had turned stock-jobbers. Exchange Alley was every day blocked up by crowds, and Cornhill was impassable for the number of carriages. Every body came to purchase stock. "Every fool aspired to be a knave." In the words of a ballad published at the time, and sung about the streets,*

> " Then stars and garters did appear
> Among the meaner rabble ;
> To buy and sell, to see and hear
> The Jews and Gentiles squabble.

---

* *A South-Sea Ballad ; or, Merry Remarks upon Exchange-Alley Bubbles. To a new Tune called " The Grand Elixir ; or, the Philosopher's Stone discovered."*

The greatest ladies thither came,
And plied in chariots daily,
Or pawned their jewels for a sum
To venture in the Alley."

The inordinate thirst of gain that had afflicted all ranks of society was not to be slaked even in the South Sea. Other schemes, of the most extravagant kind, were started. The share-lists were speedily

CORNHILL, 1720.

filled up, and an enormous traffic carried on in shares, while, of course, every means were resorted to to raise them to an artificial value in the market.

Contrary to all expectation, South-Sea stock fell when the bill received the royal assent. On the 7th of April the shares were quoted at three hundred and ten, and on the following day at two hundred and ninety. Already the directors had tasted the profits of their scheme, and it was not likely that they should quietly allow the stock to find its natural level without an effort to raise it. Immediately their busy emissaries were set to work. Every person interested in the success of the project endeavoured to draw a knot of listeners around him, to whom he expatiated on the treasures of the South American seas. Exchange Alley was crowded with attentive groups. One rumour alone, asserted with the utmost confidence, had an im-

mediate effect upon the stock.   It was said that Earl Stanhope had
received overtures in France from the Spanish government to exchange
Gibraltar and Port Mahon for some places on the coast of Peru, for
the security and enlargement of the trade in the South Seas.   Instead
of one annual ship trading to those ports, and allowing the king of
Spain twenty-five per cent out of the profits, the company might
build and charter as many ships as they pleased, and pay no per cent-
age whatever to any foreign potentate.

"Visions of ingots danced before their eyes,"

and stock rose rapidly.   On the 12th of April, five days after the bill
had become law, the directors opened their books for a subscription
of a million, at the rate of 300*l.* for every 100*l.* capital.   Such was
the concourse of persons of all ranks, that this first subscription was
found to amount to above two millions of original stock.   It was to
be paid at five payments, of 60*l.* each for every 100*l.*   In a few days
the stock advanced to three hundred and forty, and the subscriptions
were sold for double the price of the first payment.   To raise the stock
still higher, it was declared, in a general court of directors, on the
21st of April, that the midsummer dividend should be ten per cent,
and that all subscriptions should be entitled to the same.   These resolutions answering the end designed, the directors, to improve the
infatuation of the monied men, opened their books for a second subscription of a million, at four hundred per cent.   Such was the frantic
eagerness of people of every class to speculate in these funds, that in
the course of a few hours no less than a million and a half was subscribed at that rate.

In the mean time, innumerable joint-stock companies started up
every where.   They soon received the name of Bubbles, the most
appropriate that imagination could devise.   The populace are often
most happy in the nicknames they employ.   None could be more apt
than that of Bubbles.   Some of them lasted for a week or a fortnight,
and were no more heard of, while others could not even live out that
short span of existence.   Every evening produced new schemes, and
every morning new projects.   The highest of the aristocracy were as
eager in this hot pursuit of gain as the most plodding jobber in Cornhill.   The Prince of Wales became governor of one company, and
is said to have cleared 40,000*l.* by his speculations.*   The Duke of
Bridgewater started a scheme for the improvement of London and
Westminster, and the Duke of Chandos another.   There were nearly
a hundred different projects, each more extravagant and deceptive
than the other.   To use the words of the *Political State*, they were

* Coxe's *Walpole*, Correspondence between Mr. Secretary Craggs and Earl Stanhope.

"set on foot and promoted by crafty knaves, then pursued by multi-tudes of covetous fools, and at last appeared to be, in effect, what their vulgar appellation denoted them to be — bubbles and mere cheats." It was computed that near one million and a half sterling was won and lost by these unwarrantable practices, to the impoverish-ment of many a fool, and the enriching of many a rogue.

Some of these schemes were plausible enough, and, had they been undertaken at a time when the public mind was unexcited, might have been pursued with advantage to all concerned. But they were established merely with the view of raising the shares in the market. The projectors took the first opportunity of a rise to sell out, and next morning the scheme was at an end. Maitland, in his *History of London*, gravely informs us, that one of the projects which received great encouragement, was for the establishment of a company "to make deal boards out of saw-dust." This is no doubt intended as a joke; but there is abundance of evidence to shew that dozens of schemes, hardly a whit more reasonable, lived their little day, ruining hundreds ere they fell. One of them was for a wheel for perpetual motion—capital one million ; another was "for encouraging the breed of horses in England, and improving of glebe and church lands, and repairing and rebuilding parsonage and vicarage houses." Why the clergy, who were so mainly interested in the latter clause, should have taken so much interest in the first, is only to be explained on the supposition that the scheme was projected by a knot of the fox-hunting parsons, once so common in England. The shares of this company were rapidly subscribed for. But the most absurd and pre-posterous of all, and which shewed, more completely than any other, the utter madness of the people, was one started by an unknown ad-venturer, entitled "*A company for carrying on an undertaking of great advantage, but nobody to know what it is.*" Were not the fact stated by scores of credible witnesses, it would be impossible to be-lieve that any person could have been duped by such a project. The man of genius who essayed this bold and successful inroad upon public credulity, merely stated in his prospectus that the required capital was half a million, in five thousand shares of 100*l.* each, deposit 2*l.* per share. Each subscriber, paying his deposit, would be entitled to 100*l.* per annum per share. How this immense profit was to be ob-tained, he did not condescend to inform them at that time, but pro-mised that in a month full particulars should be duly announced, and a call made for the remaining 98*l.* of the subscription. Next morning, at nine o'clock, this great man opened an office in Cornhill. Crowds of people beset his door, and when he shut up at three o'clock, he found that no less than one thousand shares had been subscribed for,

and the deposits paid. He was thus, in five hours, the winner of
2000*l*. He was philosopher enough to be contented with his venture,
and set off the same evening for the Continent. He was never heard
of again.

Well might Swift exclaim, comparing Change Alley to a gulf in
the South Sea :

> " Subscribers here by thousands float,
>   And jostle one another down,
> Each paddling in his leaky boat,
>   And here they fish for gold and drown.
>
> Now buried in the depths below,
>   Now mounted up to heaven again,
> They reel and stagger to and fro,
>   At their wits' end, like drunken men.
>
> Meantime, secure on Garraway cliffs,
>   A savage race, by shipwrecks fed,
> Lie waiting for the foundered skiffs,
>   And strip the bodies of the dead."

Another fraud that was very successful was that of the " Globe
Permits," as they were called. They were nothing more than square
pieces of playing-cards, on which was the impression of a seal, in wax,
bearing the sign of the Globe Tavern, in the neighbourhood of Exchange Alley, with the inscription of " Sail-Cloth Permits." The
possessors enjoyed no other advantage than permission to subscribe
to subscribe at some future time to a new sail-cloth manufactory, projected by one who was then known to be a man of fortune, but who
was afterwards involved in the peculation and punishment of the
South-Sea directors. These permits sold for as much as sixty guineas
in the Alley.

Persons of distinction, of both sexes, were deeply engaged in all
these bubbles ; those of the male sex going to taverns and coffee-
houses to meet their brokers, and the ladies resorting for the same
purpose to the shops of milliners and haberdashers. But it did not
follow that all these people believed in the feasibility of the schemes
to which they subscribed ; it was enough for their purpose that their
shares would, by stock-jobbing arts, be soon raised to a premium, when
they got rid of them with all expedition to the really credulous. So
great was the confusion of the crowd in the alley, that shares in the
same bubble were known to have been sold at the same instant ten
per cent higher at one end of the alley than at the other. Sensible
men beheld the extraordinary infatuation of the people with sorrow
and alarm. There were some both in and out of parliament who fore-

saw clearly the ruin that was impending. Mr. Walpole did not cease his gloomy forebodings. His fears were shared by all the thinking few, and impressed most forcibly upon the government. On the 11th of June, the day the parliament rose, the king published a proclamation, declaring that all these unlawful projects should be deemed public nuisances, and prosecuted accordingly, and forbidding any broker, under a penalty of five hundred pounds, from buying or selling any shares in them. Notwithstanding this proclamation, roguish speculators still carried them on, and the deluded people still encouraged them. On the 12th of July, an order of the Lords Justices assembled in privy council was published, dismissing all the petitions that had been presented for patents and charters, and dissolving all the bubble companies. The following copy of their lordships' order, containing a list of all these nefarious projects, will not be deemed uninteresting at the present time, when, at periodic intervals, there is but too much tendency in the public mind to indulge in similar practices:

"At the Council Chamber, Whitehall, the 12th day of July, 1720. Present, their Excellencies the Lords Justices in Council.

"Their Excellencies the Lords Justices, in council, taking into consideration the many inconveniences arising to the public from several projects set on foot for raising of joint-stock for various purposes, and that a great many of his majesty's subjects have been drawn in to part with their money on pretence of assurances that their petitions for patents and charters to enable them to carry on the same would be granted: to prevent such impositions, their excellencies this day ordered the said several petitions, together with such reports from the Board of Trade, and from his majesty's attorney and solicitor-general, as had been obtained thereon, to be laid before them; and after mature consideration thereof, were pleased, by advice of his majesty's privy council, to order that the said petitions be dismissed, which are as follow:

"1. Petition of several persons, praying letters patent for carrying on a fishing trade by the name of the Grand Fishery of Great Britain.

"2. Petition of the Company of the Royal Fishery of England, praying letters patent for such further powers as will effectually contribute to carry on the said fishery.

"Petition of George James, on behalf of himself and divers persons of distinction concerned in a national fishery, praying letters patent of incorporation, to enable them to carry on the same.

"4. Petition of several merchants, traders, and others, whose names are thereunto subscribed, praying to be incorporated for reviving and carrying on a whale fishery to Greenland and elsewhere.

" 5. Petition of Sir John Lambert and others thereto subscribing, on behalf of themselves and a great number of merchants, praying to be incorporated for carrying on a Greenland trade, and particularly a whale fishery in Davis's Straits.

" 6. Another petition for a Greenland trade.

" 7. Petition of several merchants, gentlemen, and citizens, praying to be incorporated for buying and building of ships to let or freight.

" 8. Petition of Samuel Antrim and others, praying for letters patent for sowing hemp and flax.

" 9. Petition of several merchants, masters of ships, sail-makers, and manufacturers of sail-cloth, praying a charter of incorporation, to enable them to carry on and promote the said manufactory by a joint-stock.

" 10. Petition of Thomas Boyd and several hundred merchants, owners and masters of ships, sail-makers, weavers, and other traders, praying a charter of incorporation, empowering them to borrow money for purchasing lands, in order to the manufacturing sail-cloth and fine holland.

" 11. Petition on behalf of several persons interested in a patent granted by the late King William and Queen Mary for the making of linen and sail-cloth, praying that no charter may be granted to any persons whatsoever for making sail-cloth, but that the privilege now enjoyed by them may be confirmed, and likewise an additional power to carry on the cotton and cotton-silk manufactures.

" 12. Petition of several citizens, merchants, and traders in London, and others, subscribers to a British stock for a general insurance from fire in any part of England, praying to be incorporated for carrying on the said undertaking.

" 13. Petition of several of his majesty's loyal subjects of the city of London and other parts of Great Britain, praying to be incorporated for carrying on a general insurance from losses by fire within the kingdom of England.

" 14. Petition of Thomas Burges and others his majesty's subjects thereto subscribing, in behalf of themselves and others, subscribers to a fund of 1,200,000l. for carrying on a trade to his majesty's German dominions, praying to be incorporated by the name of the Harburg Company.

" 15. Petition of Edward Jones, a dealer in timber, on behalf of himself and others, praying to be incorporated for the importation of timber from Germany.

"16. Petition of several merchants of London, praying a charter of incorporation for carrying on a salt-work.

"17. Petition of Captain Macphedris of London, merchant, on behalf of himself and several merchants, clothiers, hatters, dyers, and other traders, praying a charter of incorporation empowering them to raise a sufficient sum of money to purchase lands for planting and rearing a wood called madder, for the use of dyers.

"18. Petition of Joseph Galendo of London, snuff-maker, praying a patent for his invention to prepare and cure Virginia tobacco for snuff in Virginia, and making it into the same in all his majesty's dominions."

LIST OF BUBBLES.

The following Bubble-Companies were by the same order declared to be illegal, and abolished accordingly :

1. For the importation of Swedish iron.

2. For supplying London with sea-coal. Capital, three millions.

3. For building and rebuilding houses throughout all England. Capital, three millions.

4. For making of muslin.

5. For carrying on and improving the British alum-works.

6. For effectually settling the island of Blanco and Sal Tartagus.

7. For supplying the town of Deal with fresh water.

8. For the importation of Flanders lace.

9. For improvement of lands in Great Britain. Capital, four millions.

10. For encouraging the breed of horses in England, and improving of glebe and church lands, and for repairing and rebuilding parsonage and vicarage houses.

11. For making of iron and steel in Great Britain.

12. For improving the land in the county of Flint. Capital, one million.

13. For purchasing lands to build on. Capital, two millions.

14. For trading in hair.

15. For erecting salt-works in Holy Island. Capital, two millions.

16. For buying and selling estates, and lending money on mortgage.

17. For carrying on an undertaking of great advantage; but nobody to know what it is.

18. For paving the streets of London. Capital, two millions.

19. For furnishing funerals to any part of Great Britain.

20. For buying and selling lands and lending money at interest. Capital, five millions.

21. For carrying on the royal fishery of Great Britain. Capital, ten millions.

22. For assuring of seamen's wages.

23. For erecting loan-offices for the assistance and encouragement of the industrious. Capital, two millions.

24. For purchasing and improving leaseable lands. Capital, four millions.

25. For importing pitch and tar, and other naval stores, from North Britain and America.

26. For the clothing, felt, and pantile trade.

27. For purchasing and improving a manor and royalty in Essex.

28. For insuring of horses. Capital, two millions.

29. For exporting the woollen manufacture, and importing copper, brass, and iron. Capital, four millions.

30. For a grand dispensary. Capital, three millions.

31. For erecting mills and purchasing lead-mines. Capital, two millions.

32. For improving the art of making soap.

33. For a settlement on the island of Santa Cruz.

34. For sinking pits and smelting lead ore in Derbyshire.

35. For making glass bottles and other glass.

36. For a wheel for perpetual motion. Capital, one million.

37. For improving of gardens.

38. For insuring and increasing children's fortunes.

39. For entering and loading goods at the Custom-house, and for negotiating business for merchants.

40. For carrying on a woollen manufacture in the north of England.

41. For importing walnut-trees from Virginia. Capital, two millions.

42. For making Manchester stuffs of thread and cotton.

43. For making Joppa and Castile soap.

44. For improving the wrought-iron and steel manufactures of this kingdom. Capital, four millions.

45. For dealing in lace, hollands, cambrics, lawns, &c. Capital, two millions.

46. For trading in and improving certain commodities of the produce of this kingdom, &c. Capital, three millions.

47. For supplying the London markets with cattle.

48. For making looking-glasses, coach-glasses, &c. Capital, two millions.

49. For working the tin and lead mines in Cornwall and Derbyshire.

50. For making rape-oil.

51. For importing beaver fur. Capital, two millions.

52. For making pasteboard and packing-paper.

53. For importing of oils and other materials used in the woollen manufacture.

54. For improving and increasing the silk manufactures.

55. For lending money on stock, annuities, tallies, &c.

56. For paying pensions to widows and others, at a small discount. Capital, two millions.

57. For improving malt liquors. Capital, four millions.

58. For a grand American fishery.

59. For purchasing and improving the fenny lands in Lincolnshire. Capital, two millions.

60. For improving the paper manufacture of Great Britain.

61. The Bottomry Company.

62. For drying malt by hot air.

63. For carrying on a trade in the river Oronooko.

64. For the more effectual making of baize, in Colchester and other parts of Great Britain.

65. For buying of naval stores, supplying the victualling, and paying the wages of the workmen.

66. For employing poor artificers, and furnishing merchants and others with watches.

67. For improvement of tillage and the breed of cattle.

68. Another for the improvement of our breed in horses.

69. Another for a horse-insurance.

70. For carrying on the corn trade of Great Britain.

71. For insuring to all masters and mistresses the losses they may sustain by servants. Capital, three millions.

72. For erecting houses or hospitals for taking in and maintaining illegitimate children. Capital, two millions.

73. For bleaching coarse sugars, without the use of fire or loss of substance.

74. For building turnpikes and wharfs in Great Britain.

75. For insuring from thefts and robberies.

76. For extracting silver from lead.

77. For making china and delft ware. Capital, one million.

78. For importing tobacco, and exporting it again to Sweden and the north of Europe. Capital, four millions.

79. For making iron with pit coal.

80. For furnishing the cities of London and Westminster with hay and straw. Capital, three millions.

81. For a sail and packing-cloth manufactory in Ireland.

82. For taking up ballast.

83. For buying and fitting out ships to suppress pirates.

84. For the importation of timber from Wales.   Capital, two millions.

85. For rock-salt.

86. For the transmutation of quicksilver into a malleable fine metal.

Besides these bubbles, many others sprang up daily, in spite of the condemnation of the government and the ridicule of the still

CHANGE-ALLEY.*

sane portion of the public. The print-shops teemed with caricatures, and the newspapers with epigrams and satires, upon the prevalent

---

* Stock-jobbing Card, or the humours of Change Alley. Copied from a print called the *Bubblers' Medley*, published by Carrington Bowles.

folly. An ingenious cardmaker published a pack of South-Sea playing-cards, which are now extremely rare, each card containing, besides the usual figures of a very small size, in one corner, a caricature of a bubble company, with appropriate verses underneath. One

TREE CARICATURE.*

of the most famous bubbles was "Puckle's Machine Company," for discharging round and square cannon-balls and bullets, and making a total revolution in the art of war. Its pretensions to public favour were thus summed up on the eight of spades :

> " A rare invention to destroy the crowd
> Of fools at home instead of fools abroad.
> Fear not, my friends, this terrible machine,
> They're only wounded who have shares therein."

* Tree, surrounded by water; people climbing up the tree. One of a series of bubble cards, copied from the *Bubblers' Medley*, published by Carrington Powles.

The nine of hearts was a caricature of the English Copper and Brass Company, with the following epigram :

> " The headlong fool that wants to be a swopper
> Of gold and silver coin for English copper,
> May, in Change Alley, prove himself an ass,
> And give rich metal for adultrate brass."

The eight of diamonds celebrated the company for the colonisation of Acadia, with this doggrel :

> " He that is rich and wants to fool away
> A good round sum in North America,
> Let him subscribe himself a headlong sharer,
> And asses' ears shall honour him or bearer."

And in a similar style every card of the pack exposed some knavish scheme, and ridiculed the persons who were its dupes.   It was computed that the total amount of the sums proposed for carrying on these projects was upwards of three hundred millions sterling.

MERCHANT'S GATEWAY.

It is time, however, to return to the great South-Sea gulf, that swallowed the fortunes of so many thousands of the avaricious and the credulous. On the 29th of May, the stock had risen as high as five hundred, and about two-thirds of the government annuitants had exchanged the securities of the state for those of the South-Sea company. During the whole of the month of May the stock continued to rise, and on the 28th it was quoted at five hundred and fifty. In four days after this it took a prodigious leap, rising suddenly from five hundred and fifty to eight hundred and ninety. It was now the general opinion that the stock could rise no higher, and many persons took that opportunity of selling out, with a view of realising their profits.   Many noblemen and persons in the train of the king, and about to accompany him to Hanover, were also anxious to sell out. So many sellers, and so few buyers, appeared in the Alley on the 3d of June, that the stock fell at once from eight hundred and ninety to six hundred and forty. The directors were alarmed, and gave their agents orders to buy. Their efforts succeeded. Towards evening, confidence was restored, and the stock advanced to seven hundred and fifty. It continued at this price, with some slight fluctuation, until the company closed their books on the 22d of June.

It would be needless and uninteresting to detail the various arts employed by the directors to keep up the price of stock. It will be sufficient to state that it finally rose to one thousand per cent. It was quoted at this price in the commencement of August. The bubble was then full-blown, and began to quiver and shake preparatory to its bursting.

Many of the government annuitants expressed dissatisfaction against the directors. They accused them of partiality in making out the lists for shares in each subscription. Further uneasiness was occasioned by its being generally known that Sir John Blunt the chairman, and some others, had sold out. During the whole of the month of August the stock fell, and on the 2d of September it was quoted at seven hundred only.

The state of things now became alarming. To prevent, if possible, the utter extinction of public confidence in their proceedings, the directors summoned a general court of the whole corporation, to meet in Merchant Tailors' Hall on the 8th of September. By nine o'clock in the morning, the room was filled to suffocation; Cheapside was blocked up by a crowd unable to gain admittance, and the greatest excitement prevailed. The directors and their friends mustered in great numbers. Sir John Fellowes, the sub-governor, was called to the chair. He acquainted the assembly with the cause of their meeting; read to them the several resolutions of the court of directors, and gave them an account of their proceedings; of the taking in the redeemable and unredeemable funds, and of the subscriptions in money. Mr. Secretary Craggs then made a short speech, wherein he commended the conduct of the directors, and urged that nothing could more effectually contribute to the bringing this scheme to perfection than union among themselves. He concluded with a motion for thanking the court of directors for their prudent and skilful management, and for desiring them to proceed in such manner as they should think most proper for the interest and advantage of the corporation. Mr. Hungerford, who had rendered himself very conspicuous in the House of Commons for his zeal in behalf of the South-

Sea company, and who was shrewdly suspected to have been a considerable gainer by knowing the right time to sell out, was very magniloquent on this occasion. He said that he had seen the rise and fall, the decay and resurrection of many communities of this nature, but that, in his opinion, none had ever performed such wonderful things in so short a time as the South-Sea company. They had done

more than the crown, the pulpit, or the bench could do. They had reconciled all parties in one common interest ; they had laid asleep, if not wholly extinguished, all the domestic jars and animosities of the nation. By the rise of their stock, monied men had vastly increased their fortunes; country gentlemen had seen the value of their lands doubled and trebled in their hands. They had at the same time done good to the Church, not a few of the reverend clergy having got great

MR. SECRETARY CRAGGS.

sums by the project. In short, they had enriched the whole nation, and he hoped they had not forgotten themselves. There was some hissing at the latter part of this speech, which for the extravagance of its eulogy was not far removed from satire ; but the directors and their friends, and all the winners in the room, applauded vehemently. The Duke of Portland spoke in a similar strain, and expressed his great wonder why any body should be dissatisfied ; of course, he was a winner by his speculations, and in a condition similar to that of the fat alderman in *Joe Miller's Jests*, who, whenever he had eaten a good dinner, folded his hands upon his paunch, and expressed his doubts whether there could be a hungry man in the world.

Several resolutions were passed at this meeting, but they had no effect upon the public. Upon the very same evening the stock fell to six hundred and forty, and on the morrow to five hundred and forty. Day after day it continued to fall, until it was as low as four hundred. In a letter dated September 13th, from Mr. Broderick, M.P., to Lord Chancellor Middleton, and published in Coxe's *Walpole*, the former says : " Various are the conjectures why the South-Sea directors have suffered the cloud to break so early. I made no doubt but they would do so when they found it to their advantage. They have stretched credit so far beyond what it would bear, that specie proves insufficient to support it. Their most considerable men have drawn out, securing themselves by the losses of the deluded, thoughtless

numbers, whose understandings have been overruled by avarice and
the hope of making mountains out of mole-hills. Thousands of families will be reduced to beggary. The consternation is inexpressible—
the rage beyond description, and the case altogether so desperate, that
I do not see any plan or scheme so much as thought of for averting
the blow; so that I cannot pretend to guess what is next to be done."
Ten days afterwards, the stock still falling, he writes: "The company
have yet come to no determination, for they are in such a wood that
they know not which way to turn. By several gentlemen lately come
to town, I perceive the very name of a South-Sea-man grows abominable in every country. A great many goldsmiths are already run off,
and more will daily. I question whether one-third, nay, one-fourth
of them can stand it. From the very beginning, I founded my judgment of the whole affair upon the unquestionable maxim, that ten
millions (which is more than our running cash) could not circulate
two hundred millions, beyond which our paper credit extended. That,
therefore, whenever that should become doubtful, be the cause what
it would, our noble state machine must inevitably fall to the ground.'

On the 12th of September, at the earnest solicitation of Mr. Secretary Craggs, several conferences were held between the directors of
the South Sea and the directors of the Bank. A report which was
circulated, that the latter had agreed to circulate six millions of the
South-Sea company's bonds, caused the stock to rise to six hundred and
seventy; but in the afternoon, as soon as the report was known to be
groundless, the stock fell again to five hundred and eighty; the next
day to five hundred and seventy, and so gradually to four hundred.*

The ministry were seriously alarmed at the aspect of affairs. The
directors could not appear in the streets without being insulted;
dangerous riots were every moment apprehended. Despatches were
sent off to the king at Hanover, praying his immediate return. Mr.
Walpole, who was staying at his country seat, was sent for, that he
might employ his known influence with the directors of the Bank of
England to induce them to accept the proposal made by the South-Sea
company for circulating a number of their bonds.

The Bank was very unwilling to mix itself up with the affairs of
the company; it dreaded being involved in calamities which it could

---

* Gay (the poet), in that disastrous year, had a present from young Craggs of some
South-Sea stock, and once supposed himself to be master of twenty thousand pounds.
His friends persuaded him to sell his share, but he dreamed of dignity and splendour,
and could not bear to obstruct his own fortune. He was then importuned to sell as much
as would purchase a hundred a year for life, " which," says Fenton, "will make you sure
of a clean shirt and a shoulder of mutton every day." This counsel was rejected; the
profit and principal were lost, and Gay sunk un ler the calamity so low that his life be_
came in danger.—*Johnson's Lives of the Poets.*

not relieve, and received all overtures with visible reluctance. But the universal voice of the nation called upon it to come to the rescue. Every person of note in commercial politics was called in to advise in the emergency. A rough draft of a contract drawn up by Mr. Walpole was ultimately adopted as the basis of further negociations, and the public alarm abated a little.

On the following day, the 20th of September, a general court of the South-Sea company was held at Merchant Tailors' Hall, in which resolutions were carried, empowering the directors to agree with the Bank of England, or any other persons, to circulate the company's bonds, or make any other agreement with the Bank which they should think proper. One of the speakers, a Mr. Pulteney, said it was most surprising to see the extraordinary panic which had seized upon the people. Men were running to and fro in alarm and terror, their imaginations filled with some great calamity, the form and dimensions of which nobody knew :

> " Black it stood as night—
> Fierce as ten furies—terrible as hell."

At a general court of the Bank of England, held two days afterwards, the governor informed them of the several meetings that had been held on the affairs of the South-Sea company, adding that the directors had not yet thought fit to come to any decision upon the matter. A resolution was then proposed, and carried without a dissentient voice, empowering the directors to agree with those of the South-Sea to circulate their bonds, to what sum, and upon what terms, and for what time, they might think proper.

Thus both parties were at liberty to act as they might judge best for the public interest. Books were opened at the Bank for a subscription of three millions for the support of public credit, on the usual terms of 15l. per cent deposit, 3l. per cent premium, and 5l. per cent interest. So great was the concourse of people in the early part of the morning, all eagerly bringing their money, that it was thought the subscription would be filled that day ; but before noon the tide turned. In spite of all that could be done to prevent it, the South-Sea company's stock fell rapidly. Their bonds were in such discredit, that a run commenced upon the most eminent goldsmiths and bankers, some of whom, having lent out great sums upon South-Sea stock, were obliged to shut up their shops and abscond. The Sword-blade company, who had hitherto been the chief cashiers of the South-Sea company, stopped payment. This being looked upon as but the beginning of evil, occasioned a great run upon the Bank, who were now obliged to pay out money much faster than they had received it upon the subscription in the morning. The day succeeding was a holiday (the 29th of September), and the Bank had a little breathing time. They bore up against the storm ; but their former rivals, the South-Sea company, were wrecked upon it. Their stock fell to one hundred and fifty, and gradually, after various fluctuations, to one hundred and thirty-five.

The Bank finding they were not able to restore public confidence, and stem the tide of ruin, without running the risk of being swept away with those they intended to save, declined to carry out the agreement into which they had partially entered. They were under no obligation whatever to continue ; for the so-called Bank contract was nothing more than the rough draft of an agreement, in which blanks had been left for several important particulars, and which contained no penalty for their secession. " And thus," to use the words of the Parliamentary History, "were seen, in the space of eight months, the rise, progress, and fall of that mighty fabric, which, being wound up by mysterious springs to a wonderful height, had fixed the eyes and expectations of all Europe, but whose foundation, being fraud, illusion, credulity, and infatuation, fell to the ground as soon as the artful management of its directors was discovered."

In the hey-day of its blood, during the progress of this dangerous delusion, the manners of the nation became sensibly corrupted. The parliamentary inquiry, set on foot to discover the delinquents, disclosed scenes of infamy, disgraceful alike to the morals of the offenders and the intellects of the people among whom they had arisen. It is a deeply interesting study to investigate all the evils that were the result. Nations, like individuals, cannot become desperate gamblers with impunity. Punishment is sure to overtake them sooner or later. A celebrated writer* is quite wrong when he says, " that such an era as this is the most unfavourable for a historian ; that no reader of sentiment and imagination can be entertained or interested by a detail of transactions such as these, which admit of no warmth, no colouring, no embellishment ; a detail of which only serves to exhibit an inanimate picture of tasteless vice and mean degeneracy." On the contrary,—and Smollett might have discovered it, if he had been in the humour,—the subject is capable of inspiring as much interest as even a novellist can desire. Is there no warmth in the despair of a plundered people?—no life and animation in the picture which might be drawn of the woes of hundreds of impoverished and ruined families ? of the wealthy of yesterday become the beggars of to-day ? of the powerful and influential changed into exiles and outcasts, and the voice of self-reproach and imprecation resounding from every corner of the land ? Is it a dull or uninstructive picture to see a whole people shaking suddenly off the trammels of reason, and running

* Smollett.

wild after a golden vision, refusing obstinately to believe that it is not real, till, like a deluded hind running after an *ignis fatuus*, they are plunged into a quagmire ? But in this false spirit has history too

CARICATURE.*

often been written. The intrigues of unworthy courtiers to gain the favour of still more unworthy kings, or the records of murderous battles and sieges, have been dilated on, and told over and over again, with all the eloquence of style and all the charms of fancy ; while the circumstances which have most deeply affected the morals and welfare of the people have been passed over with but slight notice, as dry and dull, and capable of neither warmth nor colouring.

During the progress of this famous bubble, England presented a singular spectacle. The public mind was in a state of unwholesome fermentation. Men were no longer satisfied with the slow but sure profits of cautious industry. The hope of boundless wealth for the

* Caricature, copied from the *Bubblers' Medley*, published by Carrington Bowles.

morrow made them heedless and extravagant for to-day. A luxury, till then unheard-of, was introduced, bringing in its train a corresponding laxity of morals. The over-bearing insolence of ignorant men, who had arisen to sudden wealth by successful gambling, made men of true gentility of mind and manners blush that gold should have power to raise the unworthy in the scale of society. The haughtiness of some of these " cyphering cits," as they were termed by Sir Richard Steele, was remembered against them in the day of their adversity. In the parliamentary inquiry, many of the directors suffered more for their insolence than for their peculation. One of them, who, in the full-blown pride of an ignorant rich man, had said that he would feed his horse upon gold, was reduced almost to bread and water for himself ; every haughty look, every overbearing speech, was set down, and repaid them a hundredfold in poverty and humiliation.

The state of matters all over the country was so alarming, that George I. shortened his intended stay in Hanover, and returned in all haste to England. He arrived on the 11th of November, and parliament was summoned to meet on the 8th of December. In the mean time, public meetings were held in every considerable town of the empire, at which petitions were adopted, praying the vengeance of the legislature upon the South-Sea directors, who, by their fraudulent practices, had brought the nation to the brink of ruin. Nobody seemed to imagine that the nation itself was as culpable as the South-Sea company. Nobody blamed the credulity and avarice of the people, —the degrading lust of gain, which had swallowed up every nobler quality in the national character, or the infatuation which had made the multitude run their heads with such frantic eagerness into the net held out for them by scheming projectors. These things were never mentioned. The people were a simple, honest, hard-working people, ruined by a gang of robbers, who were to be hanged, drawn, and quartered without mercy.

This was the almost unanimous feeling of the country. The two Houses of Parliament were not more reasonable. Before the guilt of the South-Sea directors was known, punishment was the only cry. The king, in his speech from the throne, expressed his hope that they would remember that all their prudence, temper, and resolution were necessary to find out and apply the proper remedy for their misfortunes. In the debate on the answer to the address, several speakers indulged in the most violent invectives against the directors of the South-Sea project. The Lord Molesworth was particularly vehement.

" It had been said by some, that there was no law to punish the directors of the South-Sea company, who were justly looked upon as the authors of the present misfortunes of the state. In his opinion,

they ought upon this occasion to follow the example of the ancient
Romans, who, having no law against parricide, because their legis-
lators supposed no son could be so unnaturally wicked as to embrue
his hands in his father's blood, made a law to punish this heinous
crime as soon as it was committed. They adjudged the guilty wretch
to be sown in a sack, and thrown alive into the Tiber. He looked

BRITANNIA STRIPT BY A SOUTH-SEA DIRECTOR.*

upon the contrivers and exe-
cutors of the villanous South-
Sea scheme as the parricides
of their country, and should
be satisfied to see them tied
in like manner in sacks, and
thrown into the Thames."
Other members spoke with
as much want of temper and
discretion. Mr. Walpole was
more moderate. He recom-
mended that their first care
should be to restore public
credit. " If the city of London were on fire, all wise
men would aid in extinguish-
ing the flames, and preventing the spread of the conflagration, before they inquired
after the incendiaries. Public
credit had received a dangerous wound, and lay bleeding,
and they ought to apply a
speedy remedy to it. It was
time enough to punish the
assassin afterwards." On the
9th of December an address, in answer to his majesty's speech, was
agreed upon, after an amendment, which was carried without a division, that words should be added expressive of the determination of
the House not only to seek a remedy for the national distresses, but
to punish the authors of them.

The inquiry proceeded rapidly. The directors were ordered to lay
before the House a full account of all their proceedings. Resolutions
were passed to the effect that the calamity was mainly owing to the
vile arts of stock-jobbers, and that nothing could tend more to the re-
establishment of public credit than a law to prevent this infamous

* Britannia stript by a South-Sea Director.   From *Het groote Tafereel der Dwaasheid.*

practice. Mr. Walpole then rose, and said, that "as he had previously hinted, he had spent some time upon a scheme for restoring public credit, but that the execution of it depending upon a position which had been laid down as fundamental, he thought it proper, before he opened out his scheme, to be informed whether he might rely upon that foundation. It was, whether the subscription of public debts and encumbrances, money subscriptions, and other contracts, made with the South-Sea company, should remain in the present state?" This question occasioned an animated debate. It was finally agreed, by a majority of 259 against 117, that all these contracts should remain in their present state, unless altered for the relief of the proprietors by a general court of the South-Sea company, or set aside by due course of law. On the following day, Mr. Walpole laid before a committee of the whole House his scheme for the restoration of public credit, which was, in substance, to engraft nine millions of South-Sea stock into the Bank of England, and the same sum into the East India company upon certain conditions. The plan was favourably received by the House. After some few objections, it was ordered that proposals should be received from the two great corporations. They were both unwilling to lend their aid, and the plan met with a warm but fruitless opposition at the general courts summoned for the purpose of deliberating upon it. They, however, ultimately agreed upon the terms on which they would consent to circulate the South-Sea bonds, and their report being presented to the committee, a bill was brought in under the superintendence of Mr. Walpole, and safely carried through both Houses of Parliament.

A bill was at the same time brought in for restraining the South-Sea directors, governor, sub-governor, treasurer, cashier, and clerks from leaving the kingdom for a twelvemonth, and for discovering their estates and effects, and preventing them from transporting or alienating the same. All the most influential members of the House supported the bill. Mr. Shippen, seeing Mr. Secretary Craggs in his place, and believing the injurious rumours that were afloat of that minister's conduct in the South-Sea business, determined to touch him to the quick. He said he was glad to see a British House of Commons resuming its pristine vigour and spirit, and acting with so much unanimity for the public good. It was necessary to secure the persons and estates of the South-Sea directors and their officers ; "but," he added, looking fixedly at Mr. Craggs as he spoke, "there were other men in high station, whom, in time, he would not be afraid to name, who were no less guilty than the directors." Mr. Craggs arose in great wrath, and said, that if the innuendo were directed against him, he was ready to give satisfaction to any man who questioned him, either in the House or out of it.   Loud cries of order immediately arose on every side.   In the midst of the uproar, Lord Molesworth got up, and expressed his wonder at the boldness of Mr. Craggs in challenging the whole House of Commons.   He, Lord Molesworth, though somewhat old, past sixty, would answer Mr. Craggs whatever he had to say in the House, and he trusted there were plenty of young men beside him, who would not be afraid to look Mr. Craggs in the face out of the House.   The cries of order again resounded from every side ; the members arose simultaneously ; every body seemed to be vociferating at once.   The Speaker in vain called order.   The confusion lasted several minutes, during which Lord Molesworth and Mr. Craggs were almost the only members who kept their seats.   At last, the call for Mr. Craggs became so violent, that he thought proper to submit to the universal feeling of the House, and explain his unparliamentary expression.   He said, that by giving satisfaction to the impugners of his conduct in that House, he did not mean that he would fight, but that he would explain his conduct. Here the matter ended, and the House proceeded to debate in what manner they should conduct their inquiry into the affairs of the South-Sea company, whether in a grand or a select committee.   Ultimately, a secret committee of thirteen was appointed, with power to send for persons, papers, and records.

The Lords were as zealous and as hasty as the Commons.   The Bishop of Rochester said the scheme had been like a pestilence.   The Duke of Wharton said the House ought to shew no respect of persons ; that, for his part, he would give up the dearest friend he had, if he had been engaged in the project.   The nation had been plundered in a most shameful and flagrant manner, and he would go as far as any body in the punishment of the offenders.   Lord Stanhope said, that every farthing possessed by the criminals, whether directors or not directors, ought to be confiscated, to make good the public losses.

During all this time the public excitement was extreme.   We learn from Coxe's *Walpole*, that the very name of a South-Sea director was thought to be synonymous with every species of fraud and villany.   Petitions from counties, cities, and boroughs, in all parts of the kingdom, were presented, crying for the justice due to an injured nation and the punishment of the villanous peculators.   Those moderate men, who would not go to extreme lengths, even in the punishment of the guilty, were accused of being accomplices, were exposed to repeated insults and virulent invectives, and devoted, both in anonymous letters and public writings, to the speedy vengeance of an injured people.   The accusations against Mr. Aislabie Chancellor of the Exchequer, and Mr. Craggs, another member of the ministry, were so loud, that the House of Lords resolved to proceed at once into the investigation concerning them. It was ordered, on the 21st of January, that all brokers concerned in the South-Sea scheme should lay before the House an account of the stock or subscriptions bought or sold by them for any of the officers of the Treasury or Exchequer, or in trust for any of them, since Michaelmas 1719. When this account was delivered, it appeared that large quantities of stock had been transferred to the use of Mr. Aislabie. Five of the South-Sea directors, including Mr. Edward Gibbon, the grandfather of the celebrated historian, were ordered into the custody of the black rod. Upon a motion made by Earl Stanhope, it was unanimously resolved, that the taking in or giving credit for stock without a valuable consideration actually paid or sufficiently secured ; or the purchasing stock by any director or agent of the South-Sea company, for the use or benefit of any member of the administration, or any member of either House of Parliament, during such time as the South-Sea bill was yet pending in Parliament, was a notorious and dangerous corruption. Another resolution was passed a few days afterwards, to the effect that several of the directors and officers of the company having, in a clandestine manner, sold their own stock to the company, had been guilty of a notorious fraud and breach of trust, and had thereby mainly caused the unhappy turn of affairs that had so much affected public credit. Mr. Aislabie resigned his office as Chancellor of the Exchequer, and absented himself from parliament, until the formal inquiry into his individual guilt was brought under the consideration of the legislature.

In the mean time, Knight, the treasurer of the company, and who was entrusted with all the dangerous secrets of the dishonest directors, packed up his books and documents, and made his escape from the country. He embarked in disguise, in a small boat on the river, and proceeding to a vessel hired for the purpose, was safely conveyed to Calais. The Committee of Secrecy informed the House of the circumstance, when it was resolved unanimously that two addresses should be presented to the king ; the first praying that he would issue a proclamation offering a reward for the apprehension of Knight ; and the second, that he would give immediate orders to stop the ports, and to take effectual care of the coasts, to prevent the said Knight, or any other officers of the South-Sea company, from escaping out of the kingdom. The ink was hardly dry upon these addresses before they were carried to the king by Mr. Methuen, deputed by the House for that purpose. The same evening a royal proclamation was issued, offering a reward of two thousand pounds for the apprehension of Knight. The Commons ordered the doors of

the House to be locked, and the keys to be placed on the table. General Ross, one of the members of the Committee of Secrecy, acquainted
them that they had already discovered a train of the deepest villany
and fraud that hell had ever contrived to ruin a nation, which in due
time they would lay before the House. In the mean time, in order
to a further discovery, the Committee thought it highly necessary to
secure the persons of some of the directors and principal South-Sea
officers, and to seize their papers. A motion to this effect having
been made, was carried unanimously. Sir Robert Chaplin, Sir Theodore Janssen, Mr. Sawbridge, and Mr. F. Eyles, members of the
House, and directors of the South-Sea company, were summoned to
appear in their places, and answer for their corrupt practices. Sir
Theodore Janssen and Mr. Sawbridge answered to their names, and
endeavoured to exculpate themselves. The House heard them patiently, and then ordered them to withdraw. A motion was then
made, and carried *nemine contradicente*, that they had been guilty of
a notorious breach of trust—had occasioned much loss to great numbers of his majesty's subjects, and had highly prejudiced the public
credit. It was then ordered that, for their offence, they should be
expelled the House, and taken into the custody of the sergeant-at-
arms. Sir Robert Chaplin and Mr. Eyles, attending in their places
four days afterwards, were also expelled the House. It was resolved
at the same time to address the king to give directions to his ministers at foreign courts to make application for Knight, that he might
be delivered up to the English authorities, in case he took refuge in
any of their dominions. The king at once agreed, and messengers
were despatched to all parts of the continent the same night.

Among the directors taken into custody was Sir John Blunt, the
man whom popular opinion has generally accused of having been the
original author and father of the scheme. This man, we are informed by Pope, in his epistle to Allen Lord Bathurst, was a Dis-
senter, of a most religious deportment, and professed to be a great
believer.* He constantly declaimed against the luxury and corrup-

---

* "'God cannot love,' says Blunt, with tearless eyes,
'The wretch he starves, and piously denies.' . . .
Much-injur'd Blunt! why bears he Britain's hate?
A wizard told him in these words our fate:
At length corruption, like a gen'ral flood,
So long by watchful ministers withstood,
Shall deluge all; and av'rice, creeping on,
Spread like a low-born mist, and blot the sun;
Statesman and patriot ply alike the stocks,
Peeress and butler share alike the box,
And judges job, and bishops bite the Town,
And mighty dukes pack cards for half-a-crown:

tion of the age, the partiality of parliaments, and the misery of party-spirit. He was particularly eloquent against avarice in great and noble persons. He was originally a scrivener, and afterwards became not only a director, but the most active manager of the South-Sea company. Whether it was during his career in this capacity that he first began to declaim against the avarice of the great, we are not informed. He certainly must have seen enough of it to justify his severest anathema ; but if the preacher had himself been free from the vice he condemned, his declamations would have had a better effect. He was brought up in custody to the bar of the House of Lords, and underwent a long examination. He refused to answer several important questions. He said he had been examined already by a committee of the House of Commons, and as he did not remember his answers, and might contradict himself, he refused to answer before another tribunal. This declaration, in itself an indirect proof of guilt, occasioned some commotion in the House. He was again asked peremptorily whether he had ever sold any portion of the stock to any member of the administration, or any member of either House of Parliament, to facilitate the passing of the bill. He again declined to answer. He was anxious, he said, to treat the House with all possible respect, but he thought it hard to be compelled to accuse himself. After several ineffectual attempts to refresh his memory, he was directed to withdraw. A violent discussion ensued between the friends and opponents of the ministry. It was asserted that the administration were no strangers to the convenient taciturnity of Sir John Blunt. The Duke of Wharton made a reflection upon the Earl Stanhope, which the latter warmly resented. He spoke under great excitement, and with such vehemence as to cause a sudden determination of blood to the head. He felt himself so ill that he was obliged to leave the House and retire to his chamber. He was cupped immediately, and also let blood on the following morning, but with slight relief. The fatal result was not anticipated. Towards evening he became drowsy, and turning himself on his face, expired. The sudden death of this statesman caused great grief to the nation. George I. was exceedingly affected, and shut himself up for some hours in his closet, inconsolable for his loss.

See Britain sunk in Lucre's forbid charms,
And France reveng'd of Ann's and Edward's arms ! '
'Twas no court-badge, great Scriv'ner ! fir'd thy brain,
Nor lordly luxury, nor city gain :
No, 'twas thy righteous end, asham'd to see
Senates degen'rate, patriots disagree,
And nobly wishing party-rage to cease,
To buy both sides, and give thy country peace."
Pope's Epistle to Allen Lord Bathurst.

Knight, the treasurer of the company, was apprehended at Tirlemont, near Liege, by one of the secretaries of Mr. Leathes, the British resident at Brussels, and lodged in the citadel of Antwerp. Repeated applications were made to the court of Austria to deliver him up, but in vain. Knight threw himself upon the protection of the states of Brabant, and demanded to be tried in that country. It was a privilege granted to the states of Brabant by one of the articles of the *Joyeuse Entrée*, that every criminal apprehended in that coun-

BRABANT SCREEN.*

try should be tried in that country. The states insisted on their privilege, and refused to deliver Knight to the British authorities. The latter did not cease their solicitations; but in the mean time, Knight escaped from the citadel.

On the 16th of February the Committee of Secrecy made their first report to the House. They stated that their inquiry had been attended with numerous difficulties and embarrassments; every one they had examined had endeavoured, as far as in him lay, to defeat the ends of justice. In some of the books produced before them, false and fictitious entries had been made; in others, there were entries of money with blanks for the name of the stockholders. There were frequent erasures and alterations, and in some of the books leaves were torn out. They also found that some books of great importance had been destroyed altogether, and that some had

* The Brabant Screen. This caricature represents the Duchess of Kendal behind the "Brabant Screen," supplying Mr. Knight with money to facilitate his escape; and is copied from a rare print of the time, in the collection of E. Hawkins, Esq. F.S.A.

been taken away or secreted. At the very entrance into their inquiry, they had observed that the matters referred to them were of great variety and extent. Many persons had been entrusted with various parts in the execution of the law, and under colour thereof had acted in an unwarrantable manner, in disposing of the properties of many thousands of persons amounting to many millions of money. They discovered that, before the South-Sea Act was passed, there was an entry in the company's books of the sum of 1,259,325*l*., upon account of stock stated to have been sold to the amount of 574,500*l.* This stock was all fictitious, and had been disposed of with a view to promote the passing of the bill. It was noted as sold on various days, and at various prices, from 150 to 325 per cent. Being surprised to see so large an account disposed of at a time when the company were not empowered to increase their capital, the Committee determined to investigate most carefully the whole transaction. The governor, sub-governor, and several directors were brought before them, and examined rigidly. They found that, at the time these entries were made, the company was not in possession of such a quantity of stock, having in their own right only a small quantity, not exceeding thirty thousand pounds at the utmost. Pursuing the inquiry, they found that this amount of stock was to be esteemed as taken in or holden by the company for the benefit of the pretended purchasers, although no mutual agreement was made for its delivery or acceptance at any certain time. No money was paid down, nor any deposit or security whatever given to the company by the supposed purchasers; so that if the stock had fallen, as might have been expected had the act not passed, they would have sustained no loss. If, on the contrary, the price of stock advanced (as it actually did by the success of the scheme), the difference by the advanced price was to be made good to them. Accordingly, after the passing of the act, the account of stock was made up and adjusted with Mr. Knight, and the pretended purchasers were paid the difference out of the company's cash. This fictitious stock, which had been chiefly at the disposal of Sir John Blunt, Mr. Gibbon, and Mr. Knight, was distributed among several members of the government and their connexions, by way of bribe, to facilitate the passing of the bill. To the Earl of Sunderland was assigned 50,000*l.* of this stock; to the Duchess of Kendal, 10,000*l.*; to the Countess of Platen, 10,000*l.*; to her two nieces, 10,000*l.*; to Mr. Secretary Craggs, 30,000*l.*; to Mr. Charles Stanhope (one of the secretaries of the Treasury), 10,000*l.*; to the Sword-blade company, 50,000*l.* It also appeared that Mr Stanhope had received the enormous sum of 250,000*l.* as the difference in the price of some stock, through the hands of Turner, Caswall, and Co., but that his name had been partly erased from their books, and altered to Stangape. Aislabie, the Chancellor of the Exchequer, had made profits still more abominable. He had an account with the same firm, who were also South-Sea directors, to the amount of 794,451l. He had, besides, advised the company to make their second subscription one million and a half, instead of a million, by their own authority, and without any warrant. The third subscription had been conducted in a manner as disgraceful. Mr. Aislabie's name was down for 70,000l.; Mr. Craggs, senior, for 659,000l.; the Earl of Sunderland's for 160,000l.; and Mr. Stanhope for 47,000l. This report was succeeded by six others, less important. At the end of the last, the committee declared, that the absence of Knight, who had been principally entrusted, prevented them from carrying on their inquiries.

The first report was ordered to be printed, and taken into consideration on the next day but one succeeding. After a very angry and animated debate, a series of resolutions were agreed to, condemnatory of the conduct of the directors, of the members of the parliament and of the administration concerned with them ; and declaring that they ought, each and all, to make satisfaction out of their own estates for the injury they had done the public. Their practices were declared to be corrupt, infamous, and dangerous ; and a bill was ordered to be brought in for the relief of the unhappy sufferers.

Mr. Charles Stanhope was the first person brought to account for his share in these transactions. He urged in his defence that, for some years past, he had lodged all the money he was possessed of in Mr. Knight's hands, and whatever stock Mr. Knight had taken in for him, he had paid a valuable consideration for it. As for the stock that had been bought for him by Turner, Caswall, and Co., he knew nothing about it. Whatever had been done in that matter was done without his authority, and he could not be responsible for it. Turner and Co. took the latter charge upon themselves ; but it was notorious to every unbiassed and unprejudiced person that Mr. Stanhope was a gainer of the 250,000l. which lay in the hands of that firm to his credit. He was, however, acquitted by a majority of three only. The greatest exertions were made to screen him. Lord Stanhope, the son of the Earl of Chesterfield, went round to the wavering members, using all the eloquence he was possessed of to induce them either to vote for the acquittal, or to absent themselves from the House. Many weakheaded country gentlemen were led astray by his persuasions, and the result was as already stated. The acquittal caused the greatest discontent throughout the country. Mobs of a menacing character assembled in different parts of London ; fears of riots were generally entertained, especially as the examination of a still greater delinquent was expected by many to have a similar termination. Mr. Aislabie, whose high office and deep responsibilities should have kept him honest, even had native principle been insufficient, was very justly regarded as perhaps the greatest criminal of all. His case was entered into on the day succeeding the acquittal of Mr. Stanhope. Great excitement prevailed, and the lobbies and avenues of the House were beset by crowds impatient to know the result. The debate lasted the whole day. Mr. Aislabie found few friends : his guilt was so apparent and so heinous that nobody had courage to stand up in his favour. It

BONFIRES ON TOWER HILL.

was finally resolved, without a dissentient voice, that Mr. Aislabie had encouraged and promoted the destructive execution of the South-Sea scheme with a view to his own exorbitant profit, and had combined with the directors in their pernicious practices, to the ruin of the public trade and credit of the kingdom : that he should for his offences be ignominiously expelled from the House of Commons, and committed a close prisoner to the Tower of London ; that he should be restrained from going out of the kingdom for a whole year, or till the end of the next session of parliament ; and that he should make out a correct account of all his estate, in order that it might be applied to the relief of those who had suffered by his mal-practices.

This verdict caused the greatest joy. Though it was delivered at half-past twelve at night, it soon spread over the city. Several persons illuminated their houses in token of their joy. On the following day, when Mr. Aislabie was conveyed to the Tower, the mob assembled on Tower-hill with the intention of hooting and pelting him. Not succeeding in this, they kindled a large bonfire, and danced around it in the exuberance of their delight. Several bonfires were made in other places; London presented the appearance of a holiday, and people congratulated one another as if they had just escaped from some great calamity. The rage upon the acquittal of Mr. Stanhope had grown to such a height, that none could tell where it would have ended, had Mr. Aislabie met with the like indulgence.

To increase the public satisfaction, Sir George Caswall, of the firm of Turner, Caswall, and Co., was expelled from the House on the following day, committed to the Tower, and ordered to refund the sum of 250,000*l*.

That part of the report of the Committee of Secrecy which related to the Earl of Sunderland was next taken into consideration. Every effort was made to clear his lordship from the imputation.

As the case against him rested chiefly on the evidence extorted from Sir John Blunt, great pains were taken to make it appear that Sir John's word was not to be believed, especially in a matter affecting the honour of a peer and privy councillor. All the friends of the ministry rallied around the earl, it being generally reported that a verdict of guilty against him would bring a Tory ministry into power. He was eventually acquitted by a majority of 233 against 172; but the country was convinced of his guilt. The greatest indignation was

EARL OF SUNDERLAND.

every where expressed, and menacing mobs again assembled in London. Happily no disturbance took place.

This was the day on which Mr. Craggs the elder expired. The morrow had been appointed for the consideration of his case. It was very generally believed that he had poisoned himself. It appeared, however, that grief for the loss of his son, one of the secretaries of the Treasury, who had died five weeks previously of the small-pox, preyed much on his mind. For this son, dearly beloved, he had been amassing vast heaps of riches : he had been getting money, but not honestly ; and he for whose sake he had bartered his honour and sullied his fame was now no more. The dread of further exposure increased his trouble of mind, and ultimately brought on an apoplectic fit, in which he expired. He left a fortune of a million and a half, which was afterwards confiscated for the benefit of the sufferers by the unhappy delusion he had been so mainly instrumental in raising.

One by one the case of every director of the company was taken into consideration. A sum amounting to two millions and fourteen thousand pounds was confiscated from their estates towards repairing the mischief they had done, each man being allowed a certain residue in proportion to his conduct and circumstances, with which he might begin the world anew. Sir John Blunt was only allowed 5000*l.* out of his fortune of upwards of 183,000*l.*; Sir John Fellows was allowed 10,000*l.* out of 243,000*l.* ; Sir Theodore Janssen, 50,000*l.* out of 243,000*l.*; Mr. Edward Gibbon, 10,000*l.* out of 106,000*l.*; Sir John Lambert, 5000*l.* out of 72,000*l.* Others, less deeply involved, were treated with greater liberality. Gibbon, the historian, whose grandfather was the Mr. Edward Gibbon so severely mulcted, has given, in the *Memoirs of his Life and Writings,* an interesting account of the proceedings in parliament at this time. He owns that he is not an unprejudiced witness ; but, as all the writers from which it is possible to extract any notice of the proceedings of these disastrous years were prejudiced on the other side, the statements of the great historian become of additional value. If only on the principle of *audi alteram partem,* his opinion is entitled to consideration. " In the year 1716," he says, " my grandfather was elected one of the directors of the South-Sea company, and his books exhibited the proof that before his acceptance of that fatal office, he had acquired an independent fortune of 60,000*l.* But his fortune was overwhelmed in the shipwreck of the year 1720, and the labours of thirty years were blasted in a single day. Of the use or abuse of the South-Sea scheme, of the guilt or innocence of my grandfather and his brother directors, I am neither a competent nor a disinterested judge. Yet the equity of modern times must condemn the violent and arbitrary proceedings, which would have disgraced the cause of justice, and rendered injustice still more odious. No sooner had the nation awakened from its golden dream, than a popular and even a parliamentary clamour demanded its victims ; but it was acknowledged on all sides, that the directors, however guilty, could not be touched by any known laws of the land. The intemperate notions of Lord Molesworth were not literally acted on; but a bill of pains and penalties was introduced—a retroactive statute, to punish the offences which did not exist at the time they were committed. The legislature restrained the persons of the directors, imposed an exorbitant security for their appearance, and marked their character with a previous note of ignominy. They were compelled to deliver, upon oath, the strict value of their estates, and were disabled from making any transfer or alienation of any part of their property. Against a bill of pains and penalties, it is the common right of every subject to be heard by his counsel at the bar. They prayed to be heard. Their prayer was refused, and their oppressors, who required no evidence, would listen to no defence. It had been at first proposed, that one-eighth of

THE SOUTH-SEA BUBBLE.—CARICATURE BY HOGARTH.*

their respective estates should be allowed for the future support of the directors; but it was especially urged that, in the various shades of opulence and guilt, such a proportion would be too light for many, and for some might possibly be too heavy. The character and conduct of each man were separately weighed; but, instead of the calm solemnity of a judicial inquiry, the fortune and honour of thirty-three Englishmen were made the topics of hasty conversation, the sport of a lawless majority; and the basest member of the com-

* Emblematic print of the South-Sea Scheme. By W. Hogarth.

mittee, by a malicious word or a silent vote, might indulge his general spleen or personal animosity. Injury was aggravated by insult, and insult was embittered by pleasantry. Allowances of 20*l.* or 1*s.* were facetiously moved. A vague report that a director had formerly been concerned in another project, by which some unknown persons had lost their money, was admitted as a proof of his actual guilt. One man was ruined because he had dropped a foolish speech, that his horses should feed upon gold ; another, because he was grown so proud, that one day, at the Treasury, he had refused a civil answer to persons much above him. All were condemned, absent and unheard, in arbitrary fines and forfeitures, which swept away the greatest part of their substance. Such bold oppression can scarcely be shielded by the omnipotence of parliament. My grandfather could not expect to be treated with more lenity than his companions. His Tory principles and connexions rendered him obnoxious to the ruling powers. His name was reported in a suspicious secret. His well-known abilities could not plead the excuse of ignorance or error. In the first proceedings against the South-Sea directors, Mr. Gibbon was one of the first taken into custody, and in the final sentence the measure of his fine proclaimed him eminently guilty. The total estimate, which he delivered on oath to the House of Commons, amounted to 106,543*l.* 5*s.* 6*d.*, exclusive of antecedent settlements. Two different allowances of 15,000*l.* and of 10,000*l.* were moved for Mr. Gibbon ; but on the question being put, it was carried without a division for the smaller sum. On these ruins, with the skill and credit of which parliament had not been able to despoil him, my grandfather, at a mature age, erected the edifice of a new fortune. The labours of sixteen years were amply rewarded ; and I have reason to believe that the second structure was not much inferior to the first."

The next consideration of the legislature, after the punishment of the directors, was to restore public credit. The scheme of Walpole had been found insufficient, and had fallen into disrepute. A computation was made of the whole capital stock of the South-Sea company at the end of the year 1720. It was found to amount to thirty-seven millions eight hundred thousand pounds, of which the stock allotted to all the proprietors only amounted to twenty-four millions five hundred thousand pounds. The remainder of thirteen millions three hundred thousand pounds belonged to the company in their corporate capacity, and was the profit they had made by the national delusion. Upwards of eight millions of this were taken from the company, and divided among the proprietors and subscribers generally, making a dividend of about 33*l.* 6*s.* 8*d.* per cent. This was a great relief. It was further ordered, that such persons as had borrowed money from the South-Sea company upon stock actually transferred and pledged at the time of borrowing to or for the use of the company, should be free from all demands, upon payment of ten per cent of the sums so borrowed. They had lent about eleven millions in this manner, at a time when prices were unnaturally raised ; and they now received back one million one hundred thousand, when prices had sunk to their ordinary level.

But it was a long time before public credit was thoroughly restored. Enterprise, like Icarus, had soared too high, and melted the wax of her wings ; like Icarus, she had fallen into a sea, and learned, while floundering in its waves, that her proper element was the solid ground. She has never since attempted so high a flight.

In times of great commercial prosperity there has been a tendency to over-speculation on several occasions since then. The success of one project generally produces others of a similar kind. Popular imitativeness will always, in a trading nation, seize hold of such successes, and drag a community too anxious for profits into an abyss from which extrication is difficult. Bubble companies, of a kind similar to those engendered by the South-Sea project, lived their little day in the famous year of the panic, 1825. On that occasion, as in 1720, knavery gathered a rich harvest from cupidity, but both suffered when the day of reckoning came. The schemes of the year 1836 threatened, at one time, results as disastrous ; but they were happily averted before it was too late.*

BUBBLERS' ARMS—DESPAIR—FROM A PRINT IN THE COLLECTION OF E. HAWKINS, ESQ.

* The South-Sea project remained until 1845 the greatest example in British history of the infatuation of the people for commercial gambling. The first edition of these volumes was published some time before the outbreak of the Great Railway Mania of that and the following year.

THE TULIPOMANIA.

Quis furor, ô cives!—Lucan.

THE tulip,—so named, it is said, from a Turkish word, signifying a turban,—was introduced into western Europe about the middle of the sixteenth century. Conrad Gesner, who claims the merit of having brought it into repute,—little dreaming of the commotion it was shortly afterwards to make in the world,—says that he first saw it in the year 1559, in a garden at Augsburg, belonging to the learned Counsellor Herwart, a man very famous in his day for his collection of rare exotics. The bulbs were sent to this gentleman by a friend at Constantinople, where the flower had long been a favourite. In the course of ten or eleven years after this period, tulips were much sought after by the wealthy, especially in Holland and Germany. Rich people at Amsterdam sent for the bulbs direct to Constantinople, and paid the most extravagant prices for them. The first roots planted in England were brought from Vienna in 1600. Until the year 1634 the tulip annually increased in reputation, until it was deemed a proof of bad taste in any man of fortune to be without a collection of them. Many learned men, including Pompeius de Angelis, and the celebrated Lipsius of Leyden, the author of the treatise " De Constantia," were passionately fond of tulips. The rage for possessing them soon caught the middle classes of society, and merchants and shopkeepers, even of moderate means, began to vie with each other in the rarity of these flowers and the preposterous prices they paid for them. A trader at Harlaem was known to pay one-half of his fortune for a single root, not with the design of selling it again at a profit, but to keep in his own conservatory for the admiration of his acquaintance.

One would suppose that there must have been some great virtue in this flower to have made it so valuable in the eyes of so prudent a people as the Dutch ; but it has neither the beauty nor the perfume of the rose—hardly the beauty of the " sweet, sweet-pea ;" neither is it as enduring as either. Cowley, it is true, is loud in its praise. He says—

> " The tulip next appeared, all over gay,
> But wanton, full of pride, and full of play ;
> The world can't shew a dye but here has place ;
> Nay, by new mixtures, she can change her face ;
> Purple and gold are both beneath her care,
> The richest needlework she loves to wear ;
> Her only study is to please the eye,
> And to outshine the rest in finery."

This, though not very poetical, is the description of a poet. Beck-mann, in his *History of Inventions*, paints it with more fidelity, and in prose more pleasing than Cowley's poetry. He says, " There are few plants which acquire, through accident, weakness, or disease, so many variegations as the tulip. When uncultivated, and in its natural state, it is almost of one colour, has large leaves, and an extraordinarily long stem. When it has been weakened by cultivation, it becomes more agreeable in the eyes of the florist. The petals are then paler, smaller, and more diversified in hue ; and the leaves acquire a softer green colour. Thus this masterpiece of culture, the more beautiful it turns, grows so much the weaker, so that, with the greatest skill and most careful attention, it can scarcely be trans-planted, or even kept alive."

Many persons grow insensibly attached to that which gives them a great deal of trouble, as a mother often loves her sick and ever-ailing child better than her more healthy offspring. Upon the same principle we must account for the unmerited encomia lavished upon these fragile blossoms. In 1634, the rage among the Dutch to possess them was so great that the ordinary industry of the country was neglected, and the population, even to its lowest dregs, embarked in the tulip trade. As the mania increased, prices augmented, until, in the year 1635, many persons were known to invest a fortune of 100,000 florins in the purchase of forty roots. It then became necessary to sell them by their weight in *perits*, a small weight less than a grain. A tulip of the species called *Admiral Liefken*, weighing 400 *perits*, was worth 4400 florins; an *Admiral Van der Eyck*, weighing 446 *perits*, was worth 1260 florins; a *Childer* of 106 *perits* was worth 1615 florins; a *Viceroy* of 400 *perits*, 3000 florins; and, most precious of all, a *Semper Augustus*, weighing 200 *perits*, was thought to be very cheap at 5500 florins. The latter was much sought after, and even an inferior bulb might command a price of 2000 florins. It is related that, at one time, early in 1636, there were only two roots of this description to be had in all Holland, and those not of the best. One was in the possession of a dealer in Amsterdam, and the other in Harlaem. So anxious were the speculators to obtain them, that one person offered the fee-simple of twelve acres of building-ground for the Harlaem tulip That of Amsterdam was bought for 4600 florins, a new carriage, two grey horses, and a complete suit of harness. Munting, an industrious author of that day, who wrote a folio volume of one thousand pages upon the tulipomania, has preserved the following list of the various articles, and their value, which were delivered for one single root of the rare species called the *Viceroy*:

	florins.
Two lasts of wheat	448
Four lasts of rye	558
Four fat oxen	480
Eight fat swine	240
Twelve fat sheep	120
Two hogsheads of wine	70
Four tuns of beer	32
Two tuns of butter	192
One thousand lbs. of cheese	120
A complete bed	100
A suit of clothes	80
A silver drinking-cup	60
	2500

People who had been absent from Holland, and whose chance it was to return when this folly was at its maximum, were sometimes led into awkward dilemmas by their ignorance. There is an amusing instance of the kind related in Blainville's *Travels*. A wealthy merchant, who prided himself not a little on his rare tulips, received upon one occasion a very valuable consignment of merchandise from the Levant. Intelligence of its arrival was brought him by a sailor, who presented himself for that purpose at the counting-house, among bales of goods of every description. The merchant, to reward him for his news, munificently made him a present of a fine red herring for his breakfast. The sailor had, it appears, a great partiality for onions, and seeing a bulb very like an onion lying upon the counter of this liberal trader, and thinking it, no doubt, very much out of its place among silks and velvets, he slily seized an opportunity and slipped it into his pocket, as a relish for his herring. He got clear off with his prize, and proceeded to the quay to eat his breakfast. Hardly was his back turned when the merchant missed his valuable *Semper Augustus*, worth three thousand florins, or about 280*l*. sterling. The whole establishment was instantly in an uproar; search was every where made for the precious root, but it was not to be found. Great was the merchant's distress of mind. The search was renewed, but again without success. At last some one thought of the sailor.

The unhappy merchant sprang into the street at the bare suggestion. His alarmed household followed him. The sailor, simple soul! had not thought of concealment. He was found quietly sitting on a coil of ropes, masticating the last morsel of his "*onion*." Little did he dream that he had been eating a breakfast whose cost might have regaled a whole ship's crew for a twelvemonth; or, as the plundered merchant himself expressed it, "might have sumptuously feasted the Prince of Orange and the whole court of the Stadtholder." Anthony caused pearls to be dissolved in wine to drink the health of Cleopatra; Sir Richard Whittington was as foolishly magnificent in an entertainment to King Henry V.; and Sir Thomas Gresham drank a diamond dissolved in wine to the health of Queen Elizabeth, when she opened the Royal Exchange; but the breakfast of this roguish Dutchman was as splendid as either. He had an advantage, too, over his wasteful predecessors: *their* gems did not improve the taste or the wholesomeness of *their* wine, while *his* tulip was quite delicious with his red herring. The most unfortunate part of the business for him was, that he remained in prison for some months on a charge of felony preferred against him by the merchant.

Another story is told of an English traveller, which is scarcely less ludicrous. This gentleman, an amateur botanist, happened to see a tulip-root lying in the conservatory of a wealthy Dutchman. Being ignorant of its quality, he took out his penknife, and peeled off its coats, with the view of making experiments upon it. When it was by this means reduced to half its size, he cut it into two equal sections, making all the time many learned remarks on the singular appearances of the unknown bulb. Suddenly the owner pounced upon him, and, with fury in his eyes, asked him if he knew what he had been doing? "Peeling a most extraordinary onion," replied the philosopher. "*Hundert tausend duyvel!*" said the Dutchman; "it's an *Admiral Van der Eyck*." "Thank you," replied the traveller, taking out his note-book to make a memorandum of the same; "are these admirals common in your country?" "Death and the devil!" said the Dutchman, seizing the astonished man of science by the collar; "come before the syndic, and you shall see." In spite of his remonstrances, the traveller was led through the streets followed by a mob of persons. When brought into the presence of the magistrate, he learned, to his consternation, that the root upon which he had been experimentalising was worth four thousand florins; and, notwithstanding all he could urge in extenuation, he was lodged in prison until he found securities for the payment of this sum.

The demand for tulips of a rare species increased so much in the year 1636, that regular marts for their sale were established on the Stock Exchange of Amsterdam, in Rotterdam, Harlaem, Leyden, Alkmar, Hoorn, and other towns. Symptoms of gambling now became, for the first time, apparent. The stock-jobbers, ever on the alert for a new speculation, dealt largely in tulips, making use of all the means they so well knew how to employ, to cause fluctuations in prices. At first, as in all these gambling mania, confidence was at its height, and every body gained. The tulip-jobbers speculated in the rise and fall of the tulip stocks, and made large profits by buying when prices fell, and selling out when they rose. Many individuals grew suddenly rich. A golden bait hung temptingly out before the people, and one after the other, they rushed to the tulip-marts, like flies around a honey-pot. Every one imagined that the passion for tulips would last for ever, and that the wealthy from every part of the world would send to Holland, and pay whatever prices were asked for them. The riches of Europe would be concentrated on the shores of the Zuyder Zee, and poverty banished from the favoured clime of Holland. Nobles, citizens, farmers, mechanics, seamen, footmen, maid-servants, even chimney-sweeps and old clothes-women, dabbled in tulips. People of all grades converted their property into cash, and invested it in flowers. Houses and lands were offered for sale at ruinously low prices, or assigned in payment of bargains made at the tulip-mart. Foreigners became smitten with the same frenzy, and money poured into Holland from all directions. The prices of the necessaries of life rose again by degrees: houses and lands, horses and carriages, and luxuries of every sort, rose in value with them, and for some months Holland seemed the very antechamber of Plutus. The operations of the trade became so extensive and so intricate, that it was found necessary to draw up a code of laws for the guidance of the dealers. Notaries and clerks were also appointed, who devoted themselves exclusively to the interests of the trade. The designation of public notary was hardly known in some towns, that of tulip-notary usurping its place. In the smaller towns, where there was no exchange, the principal tavern was usually selected as the "show-place," where high and low traded in tulips, and confirmed their bargains over sumptuous entertainments. These dinners were sometimes attended by two or three hundred persons, and large vases of tulips, in full bloom, were placed at regular intervals upon the tables and sideboards for their gratification during the repast.

At last, however, the more prudent began to see that this folly could not last for ever. Rich people no longer bought the flowers to keep them in their gardens, but to sell them again at cent per cent profit. It was seen that somebody must lose fearfully in the end. As this conviction spread, prices fell, and never rose again. Confidence was destroyed, and a universal panic seized upon the dealers. *A* had agreed to purchase ten *Semper Augustines* from *B*, at four thousand florins each, at six weeks after the signing of the contract. *B* was ready with the flowers at the appointed time; but the price had fallen to three or four hundred florins, and *A* refused either to pay the difference or receive the tulips. Defaulters were announced day after day in all the towns of Holland. Hundreds who, a few months previously, had begun to doubt that there was such a thing as poverty in the land, suddenly found themselves the possessors of a few bulbs, which nobody would buy, even though they offered them at one quarter of the sums they had paid for them. The cry of distress resounded every where, and each man accused his neighbour. The few who had contrived to enrich themselves hid their wealth from the knowledge of their fellow-citizens, and invested it in the English or other funds. Many who, for a brief season, had emerged from the humbler walks of life, were cast back into their original obscurity. Substantial merchants were reduced almost to beggary, and many a representative of a noble line saw the fortunes of his house ruined beyond redemption.

When the first alarm subsided, the tulip-holders in the several towns held public meetings to devise what measures were best to be taken to restore public credit. It was generally agreed that deputies should be sent from all parts to Amsterdam, to consult with the government upon some remedy for the evil. The government at first refused to interfere, but advised the tulip-holders to agree to some plan among themselves. Several meetings were held for this purpose; but no measure could be devised likely to give satisfaction to the deluded people, or repair even a slight portion of the mischief that had been done. The language of complaint and reproach was in every body's mouth, and all the meetings were of the most stormy character. At last, however, after much bickering and ill-will, it was agreed, at Amsterdam, by the assembled deputies, that all contracts made in the height of the mania, or prior to the month of November 1636, should be declared null and void, and that, in those made after that date, purchasers should be freed from their engagements, on paying ten per cent to the vendor. This decision gave no satisfaction. The vendors who had their tulips on hand were, of course, discontented, and those who had pledged themselves to purchase, thought themselves hardly treated. Tulips which had, at one time, been worth six thousand florins, were now to be procured for five hundred; so that the composition of ten per cent was one hundred florins more than the actual value. Actions for breach of contract were threatened in all the courts of the country; but the latter refused to take cognisance of gambling transactions.

The matter was finally referred to the Provincial Council at the Hague, and it was confidently expected that the wisdom of this body would invent some measure by which credit should be restored. Expectation was on the stretch for its decision, but it never came. The members continued to deliberate week after week, and at last, after thinking about it for three months, declared that they could offer no final decision until they had more information. They advised, however, that, in the mean time, every vendor should, in the presence of witnesses, offer the tulips *in natura* to the purchaser for the sums agreed upon. If the latter refused to take them, they might be put up for sale by public auction, and the original contractor held responsible for the difference between the actual and the stipulated price. This was exactly the plan recommended by the deputies, and which was already shewn to be of no avail. There was no court in Holland which would enforce payment. The question was raised in Amsterdam, but the judges unanimously refused to interfere, on the ground that debts contracted in gambling were no debts in law.

Thus the matter rested. To find a remedy was beyond the power of the government. Those who were unlucky enough to have had stores of tulips on hand at the time of the sudden reaction were left to bear their ruin as philosophically as they could; those who had made profits were allowed to keep them; but the commerce of the country suffered a severe shock, from which it was many years ere it recovered.

The example of the Dutch was imitated to some extent in England. In the year 1636 tulips were publicly sold in the Exchange of London, and the jobbers exerted themselves to the utmost to raise

them to the fictitious value they had acquired in Amsterdam. In
Paris also the jobbers strove to create a tulipomania. In both cities
they only partially succeeded. However, the force of example brought
the flowers into great favour, and amongst a certain class of people
tulips have ever since been prized more highly than any other flowers
of the field. The Dutch are still notorious for their partiality to them,
and continue to pay higher prices for them than any other people.
As the rich Englishman boasts of his fine race-horses or his old pictures, so does the wealthy Dutchman vaunt him of his tulips.

In England, in our day, strange as it may appear, a tulip will produce more money than an oak. If one could be found, *rara in terris*,
and black as the black swan of Juvenal, its price would equal that
of a dozen acres of standing corn. In Scotland, towards the close of
the seventeenth century, the highest price for tulips, according to the
authority of a writer in the supplement to the third edition of the
Encyclopedia Britannica, was ten guineas. Their value appears to
have diminished from that time till the year 1769, when the two most
valuable species in England were the *Don Quevedo* and the *Valenti-
nier*, the former of which was worth two guineas and the latter two
guineas and a half. These prices appear to have been the minimum.
In the year 1800, a common price was fifteen guineas for a single bulb.
In 1835, a bulb of the species called the Miss Fanny Kemble was sold
by public auction in London for seventy-five pounds. Still more remarkable was the price of a tulip in the possession of a gardener in
the King's Road, Chelsea ; — in his catalogues it was labelled at two
hundred guineas.

THE ALCHYMISTS;

OR

Searchers for the Philosopher's Stone and the Water of Life.

Mercury (loquitur) The mischief a secret any of them know, above the consuming of coals and drawing of usquebaugh! howsoever they may pretend, under the specious names of Geber, Arnold, Lulli, or bombast of Hohenheim, to commit miracles in art, and treason against nature! As if the title of philosopher. that creature of glory were to be fetched out of a furnace! I am their crude and their sublimate, their precipitate and their unctions; their male and their female, sometimes their hermaphrodite—what they list to style me! They will calcine you a grave matron, as it might be a mother of the maids, and spring up a young virgin out of her ashes, as fresh as a phœnix; lay you an old courtier on the coals, like a sausage or a bloat-herring, and, after they have broiled him enough, blow a soul into him with a pair of bellows! See, they begin to muster again, and draw their forces out against me! The genius of the place defend me!—BEN JONSON'S *Masque: Mercury vindicated from the Alchymists.*

DISSATISFACTION with his lot seems to be the characteristic of man in all ages and climates. So far, however, from being an evil, as at first might be supposed, it has been the great civiliser of our race; and has tended, more than any thing else, to raise us above the condition of the brutes. But the same discontent which has been the source of all improvement, has been the parent of no small progeny of follies and absurdities; to trace these latter is our present object.

Vast as the subject appears, it is easily reducible within such limits as will make it comprehensive without being wearisome, and render its study both instructive and amusing.

Three causes especially have excited the discontent of mankind; and, by impelling us to seek for remedies for the irremediable, have bewildered us in a maze of madness and error. These are death, toil, and ignorance of the future—the doom of man upon this sphere, and for which he shews his antipathy by his love of life, his longing for abundance, and his craving curiosity to pierce the secrets of the days to come. The first has led many to imagine that they might find means to avoid death, or failing in this, that they might, nevertheless, so prolong existence as to reckon it by centuries instead of units. From this sprang the search, so long continued and still pursued, for the *elixir vitæ*, or *water of life*, which has led thousands to pretend to it and millions to believe in it. From the second sprang the search for the philosopher's stone, which was to create plenty by changing all metals into gold; and from the third, the false sciences of astrology, divination, and their divisions of necromancy, chiromancy, augury, with all their train of signs, portents, and omens.

In tracing the career of the erring philosophers, or the wilful cheats, who have encouraged or preyed upon the credulity of mankind, it will simplify and elucidate the subject, if we divide it into three classes: the first comprising alchymists, or those in general who have devoted themselves to the discovering of the philosopher's stone and the water of life; the second comprising astrologers, necromancers, sorcerers, geomancers, and all those who pretended to discover futurity; and the third consisting of the dealers in charms, amulets, philters, universal-panacea mongers, touchers for the evil, seventh sons of a seventh son, sympathetic powder compounders, homœopathists, animal magnetisers, and all the motley tribe of quacks, empirics, and charlatans.

But in narrating the career of such men, it will be found that many of them united several or all of the functions just mentioned; that the alchymist was a fortune-teller, or a necromancer—that he pretended to cure all maladies by touch or charm, and to work miracles of every kind. In the dark and early ages of European history that is most especially the case. Even as we advance to more recent periods, we shall find great difficulty in separating the characters. The alchymist seldom confined himself strictly to his pretended science—the sorcerer and necromancers to theirs, or the medical charlatan to his. Beginning with alchymy, some confusion of these classes is unavoidable; but the ground will clear for us as we advance.

Let us not, in the pride of our superior knowledge, turn with contempt from the follies of our predecessors. The study of the errors into which great minds have fallen in the pursuit of truth can never be uninstructive. As the man looks back to the days of his childhood and his youth, and recalls to his mind the strange notions and false opinions that swayed his actions at that time, that he may wonder at them ; so should society, for its edification, look back to the opinions which governed the ages fled. He is but a superficial thinker who would despise and refuse to hear of them merely because they are absurd. No man is so wise but that he may learn some wisdom from his past errors, either of thought or action ; and no society has made such advances as to be capable of no improvement from the retrospect of its past folly and credulity. And not only is such a study instructive : he who reads for amusement only will find no chapter in the annals of the human mind more amusing than this. It opens out the whole realm of fiction—the wild, the fantastic, and the wonderful, and all the immense variety of things " that are not, and cannot be ; but that have been imagined and believed."

For more than a thousand years the art of alchymy captivated many noble spirits, and was believed in by millions. Its origin is involved in obscurity. Some of its devotees have claimed for it an antiquity coeval with the creation of man himself; others, again, would trace it no further back than the time of Noah. Vincent de Beauvais argues, indeed, that all the antediluvians must have possessed a knowledge of alchymy ; and particularly cites Noah as having been acquainted with the *elixir vitæ*, or he could not have lived to so prodigious an age, and have begotten children when upwards of five hundred. Lenglet du Fresnoy, in his *History of the Hermetic Philosophy*, says, " Most of them pretended that Shem, or Chem, the son of Noah, was an adept in the art, and thought it highly probable that the words *chem*istry and al*chym*y are both derived from his name." Others say, the art was derived from the Egyptians, amongst whom it was first founded by Hermes Trismegistus. Moses, who is looked upon as a first-rate alchymist, gained his knowledge in Egypt; but he kept it all to himself, and would not instruct the children of Israel in its mysteries. All the writers upon alchymy triumphantly cite the story of the golden calf, in the 32d chapter of Exodus, to prove that this great lawgiver was an adept, and could make or unmake gold at his pleasure. It is recorded, that Moses was so wrath with the Israelites for their idolatry, " that he took the calf which they had made, and burned it in the fire, and ground it to powder, and strewed it upon the water, and made the children of Israel drink of it." This, say the alchymists, he never could have done had he not been in possession of the philosopher's stone ; by no other means could he have made the powder of gold float upon the water. But we must leave this knotty point for the consideration of the adepts in the art, if any such there be, and come to more modern periods of its history. The Jesuit, Father Martini, in his *Historia Sinica*, says, it was practised by the Chinese two thousand five hundred years before the birth of Christ ; but his assertion, being unsupported, is worth nothing. It would appear, however, that pretenders to the art of making gold and silver existed in Rome in the first centuries after the Christian era, and that, when discovered, they were liable to punishment as knaves and impostors. At Constantinople, in the fourth century, the transmutation of metals was very generally believed in, and many of the Greek ecclesiastics wrote treatises upon the subject. Their names are preserved, and some notice of their works given, in the third volume of Lenglet du Fresnoy's *History of the Hermetic Philosophy.* Their notion appears to have been, that all metals were composed of two substances ; the one, metallic earth ; and the other, a red inflammable matter, which they called sulphur. The pure union of these substances formed gold ; but other metals were mixed with and contaminated by various foreign ingredients. The object of the philosopher's stone was to dissolve or neutralise all these ingredients, by which iron, lead, copper, and all metals would be transmuted into the original gold. Many learned and clever men wasted their time, their health, and their energies, in this vain pursuit ; but for several centuries it took no great hold upon the imagination of the people. The history of the delusion appears, in a manner, lost from this time till the eighth century, when it appeared amongst the Arabians. From this period it becomes easier to trace its progress. A master then appeared, who was long looked upon as the father of the science, and whose name is indissolubly connected with it.

GEBER.

Of this philosopher, who devoted his life to the study of alchymy, but few particulars are known. He is thought to have lived in the year 730. His true name was Abou Moussah Djafar, to which was added Al Sofi, or "The Wise," and he was born at Houran, in Mesopotamia.[*] Some have thought he was a Greek, others a Spaniard, and others a prince of Hindostan ; but of all the mistakes which have been made respecting him, the most ludicrous was that made by the French translator of Sprenger's *History of Medicine,* who thought,

[*] *Biographie Universelle.*

from the sound of his name, that he was a German, and rendered it as the "Donnateur," or Giver. No details of his life are known; but it is asserted, that he wrote more than five hundred works upon the philosopher's stone and the water of life. He was a great enthusiast in his art, and compared the incredulous to little children shut up in a narrow room, without windows or aperture, who, because they saw nothing beyond, denied the existence of the great globe itself. He thought that a preparation of gold would cure all maladies, not only in man, but in the inferior animals and plants. He also imagined that all the metals laboured under disease, with the exception of gold, which was the only one in perfect health. He affirmed, that the secret of the philosopher's stone had been more than once discovered; but that the ancient and wise men who had hit upon it would never, by word or writing, communicate it to men, because of their unworthiness and incredulity.* But the life of Geber, though spent in the pursuit of this vain chimera, was not altogether useless. He stumbled upon discoveries which he did not seek; and science is indebted to him for the first mention of corrosive sublimate, the red oxide of mercury, nitric acid, and the nitrate of silver.†

For more than two hundred years after the death of Geber, the Arabian philosophers devoted themselves to the study of alchymy, joining with it that of astrology. Of these the most celebrated was

ALFARABI.

Alfarabi flourished at the commencement of the tenth century, and enjoyed the reputation of being one of the most learned men of his age. He spent his life in travelling from country to country, that he might gather the opinions of philosophers upon the great secrets of nature. No danger dismayed him; no toil wearied him of the pursuit. Many sovereigns endeavoured to retain him at their courts; but he refused to rest until he had discovered the great object of his life—the art of preserving it for centuries, and of making gold as much as he needed. This wandering mode of life at last proved fatal to him. He had been on a visit to Mecca, not so much for religious as for philosophical purposes, when, returning through Syria, he stopped at the court of the Sultan Seifeddoulet, who was re-

---

* His sum "of perfection," or instructions to students to aid them in the laborious search for the stone and elixir, has been translated into most of the languages of Europe. An English translation, by a great enthusiast in alchymy, one Richard Russell, was published in London in 1686. The preface is dated eight years previously from the house of the alchymist, "at the Star, in Newmarket, in Wapping, near the Dock." His design in undertaking the translation was, as he informs us, to expose the false pretences of the many ignorant pretenders to the science who abounded in his day.

† Article, Geber, *Biographie Universelle*.

nowned as the patron of learning. He presented himself in his travelling attire in the presence of that monarch and his courtiers ; and,
without invitation, coolly sat himself down on the sofa beside the
prince. The courtiers and wise men were indignant; and the sultan, who did not know the intruder, was at first inclined to follow
their example. He turned to one of his officers, and ordered him to
eject the presumptuous stranger from the room ; but Alfarabi, without moving, dared them to lay hands upon him ; and, turning himself calmly to the prince, remarked, that he did not know who was
his guest, or he would treat him with honour, not with violence.
The sultan, instead of being still further incensed, as many potentates would have been, admired his coolness ; and, requesting him
to sit still closer to him on the sofa, entered into a long conversation
with him upon science and divine philosophy. All the court were
charmed with the stranger. Questions for discussion were pro-
pounded, on all of which he shewed superior knowledge. He convinced every one who ventured to dispute with him ; and spoke so
eloquently upon the science of alchymy, that he was at once recognised as only second to the great Geber himself. One of the doctors
present inquired whether a man who knew so many sciences was acquainted with music ? Alfarabi made no reply, but merely requested
that a lute should be brought him. The lute was brought ; and he
played such ravishing and tender melodies, that all the court were
melted into tears. He then changed his theme, and played airs so
sprightly, that he set the grave philosophers, sultan and all, dancing
as fast as their legs could carry them. He then sobered them again
by a mournful strain, and made them sob and sigh as if broken-
hearted. The sultan, highly delighted with his powers, entreated
him to stay, offering him every inducement that wealth, power, and
dignity could supply ; but the alchymist resolutely refused, it being
decreed, he said, that he should never repose till he had discovered
the philosopher's stone. He set out accordingly the same evening,
and was murdered by some thieves in the deserts of Syria. His biographers give no further particulars of his life beyond mentioning
that he wrote several valuable treatises on his art, all of which,
however, have been lost. His death happened in the year 954.

AVICENNA.

Avicenna, whose real name was Ebn Cinna, another great alchymist,
was born at Bokhara in 980. His reputation as a physician and
a man skilled in all sciences was so great, that the Sultan Magdal
Douleth resolved to try his powers in the great science of government.
He was accordingly made Grand Vizier of that prince, and ruled the

state with some advantage; but in a science still more difficult, he failed completely. He could not rule his own passions, but gave himself up to wine and women, and led a life of shameless debauchery. Amid the multifarious pursuits of business and pleasure, he nevertheless found time to write seven treatises upon the philosopher's stone, which were for many ages looked upon as of great value by pretenders to the art. It is rare that an eminent physician, as Avicenna appears to have been, abandons himself to sensual gratification; but so completely did he become enthralled in the course of a few years, that he was dismissed from his high office, and died shortly afterwards of premature old age and a complication of maladies, brought on by debauchery. His death took place in the year 1036. After his time few philosophers of any note in Arabia are heard of as devoting themselves to the study of alchymy; but it began shortly afterwards to attract greater attention in Europe. Learned men in France, England, Spain, and Italy, expressed their belief in the science, and many devoted their whole energies to it. In the twelfth and thirteenth centuries especially, it was extensively pursued, and some of the brightest names of that age are connected with it. Among the most eminent of them are

ALBERTUS MAGNUS AND THOMAS AQUINAS.

The first of these philosophers was born in the year 1193, of a noble family at Lawingen, in the Duchy of Neuburg, on the Danube. For the first thirty years of his life he appeared remarkably dull and stupid, and it was feared by every one that no good could come of him. He entered a Dominican monastery at an early age; but made so little progress in his studies, that he was more than once upon the point of abandoning them in despair, but he was endowed with extraordinary perseverance. As he advanced to middle age, his mind expanded, and he learned whatever he applied himself to with extreme facility. So remarkable a change was not in that age to be accounted for but by a miracle. It was asserted and believed that the Holy Virgin, touched with his great desire to become learned and famous, took pity upon his incapacity, and appeared to him in the cloister where he sat almost despairing, and asked him whether he wished to excel in philosophy or divinity. He chose philosophy, to the chagrin of the Virgin, who reproached him in mild and sorrowful accents that he had not made a better choice. She, however, granted his request, that he should become the most excellent philosopher of the age; but set this drawback to his pleasure, that he should relapse, when at the height of his fame, into his former incapacity and stupidity. Albertus never took the trouble to contradict the story, but prosecuted his studies with such unremitting zeal, that his reputation speedily spread over all Europe. In the year 1244, the celebrated Thomas Aquinas placed himself under his tuition. Many extraordinary stories are told of the master and his pupil. While

ALBERTUS MAGNUS.

they paid all due attention to other branches of science, they never neglected the pursuit of the philosopher's stone and the *elixir vitæ*. Although they discovered neither, it was believed that Albert had seized some portion of the secret of life, and found means to animate a brazen statue, upon the formation of which, under proper conjunctions of the planets, he had been occupied many years of his life. He and Thomas Aquinas completed it together, endowed it with the faculty of speech, and made it perform the functions of a domestic servant. In this capacity it was exceedingly useful; but, through some defect in the machinery, it chattered much more than was agreeable to either philosopher. Various remedies were tried to cure it of its garrulity, but in vain ; and one day, Thomas Aquinas was so enraged at the noise it made when he was in the midst of a mathematical problem, that he seized a ponderous hammer and smashed it to pieces.* He was sorry afterwards for what he had done, and was reproved by his master for giving way to his anger, so unbecoming in a philosopher. They made no attempt to reanimate the statue.

Such stories as these shew the spirit of the age. Every great man who attempted to study the secrets of nature was thought a magician ; and it is not to be wondered at that, when philosophers themselves pretended to discover an elixir for conferring immortality, or a red stone which was to create boundless wealth, that popular opinion should have enhanced upon their pretensions, and have endowed them with powers still more miraculous. It was believed of Albertus Magnus that he could even change the course of the seasons, a feat which the many thought less difficult than the discovery of the grand elixir. Albertus was desirous of obtaining a piece of ground on which to build a monastery in the neighbourhood of Cologne. The ground belonged to William Count of Holland and King of the Romans, who for some reason or other did not wish to part with it. Albertus is reported to have gained it by the following extraordinary method :

* Naudé, *Apologie des Grands Hommes accusés de Magie*, chap. xviii.

He invited the prince as he was passing through Cologne to a magnificent entertainment prepared for him and all his court. The prince accepted it, and repaired with a lordly retinue to the residence of the sage. It was in the midst of winter, the Rhine was frozen over, and the cold was so bitter, that the knights could not sit on horseback without running the risk of losing their toes by the frost. Great, therefore, was their surprise, on arriving at Albert's house, to find that the repast was spread in his garden, in which the snow had drifted to the depth of several feet. The earl in high dudgeon remounted his steed, but Albert at last prevailed upon him to take his seat at the table. He had no sooner done so, than the dark clouds rolled away from the sky—a warm sun shone forth—the cold north wind veered suddenly round and blew a mild breeze from the south —the snows melted away—the ice was unbound upon the streams, and the trees put forth their green leaves and their fruit—flowers sprang up beneath their feet, while larks, nightingales, blackbirds, cuckoos, thrushes, and every sweet song-bird sang hymns from every tree. The earl and his attendants wondered greatly ; but they ate their dinner, and in recompense for it, Albert got his piece of ground to build a convent on. He had not, however, shewn them all his power. Immediately that the repast was over, he gave the word, and dark clouds obscured the sun—the snow fell in large flakes—the singing-birds fell dead—the leaves dropped from the trees, and the winds blew so cold and howled so mournfully, that the guests wrapped themselves up in their thick cloaks, and retreated into the house to warm themselves at the blazing fire in Albert's kitchen.*

Thomas Aquinas also could work wonders as well as his master. It is related of him that he lodged in a street at Cologne, where he was much annoyed by the incessant clatter made by the horses' hoofs, as they were led through it daily to exercise by their grooms. He had entreated the latter to select some other spot, where they might not disturb a philosopher ; but the grooms turned a deaf ear to all his solicitations. In this emergency he had recourse to the aid of magic. He constructed a small horse of bronze, upon which he inscribed certain cabalistic characters, and buried it at midnight in the midst of the highway. The next morning a troop of grooms came riding along as usual ; but the horses, as they arrived at the spot where the magic horse was buried, reared and plunged violently—their nostrils distended with terror—their manes grew erect, and the perspiration ran down their sides in streams. In vain the riders applied the spur— in vain they coaxed or threatened, the animals would not pass the

* Lenglet, *Histoire de la Philosophie Hermétique.* See also Godwin's *Lives of the Necromancers.*

spot. On the following day their success was no better. They were at length compelled to seek another spot for their exercise, and Thomas Aquinas was left in peace.*

Albertus Magnus was made Bishop of Ratisbon in 1259; but he occupied the see only four years, when he resigned, on the ground that its duties occupied too much of the time which he was anxious to devote to philosophy. He died in Cologne in 1280, at the advanced age of eighty-seven. The Dominican writers deny that he ever sought the philosopher's stone, but his treatise upon minerals sufficiently proves that he did.

ARTEPHIUS.

Artephius, a name noted in the annals of alchymy, was born in the early part of the twelfth century. He wrote two famous treatises; the one upon the philosopher's stone, and the other on the art of prolonging human life. In the latter he vaunts his great qualifications for instructing mankind on such a matter, as he was at that time in the thousand and twenty-fifth year of his age! He had many disciples who believed in his extreme age, and who attempted to prove that he was Apollonius of Tyana, who lived soon after the advent of Jesus Christ, and the particulars of whose life and pretended miracles have been so fully described by Philostratus. He took good care never to contradict a story which so much increased the power he was desirous of wielding over his fellow-mortals. On all convenient occasions he boasted of it; and having an excellent memory, a fertile imagination, and a thorough knowledge of all existing history, he was never at a loss for an answer when questioned as to the personal appearance, the manners, or the character of the great men of antiquity. He also pretended to have found the philosopher's stone; and said that, in search of it, he had descended to hell, and seen the devil sitting on a throne of gold, with a legion of imps and fiends around him. His works on alchymy have been translated into French, and were published in Paris in 1609 or 1610.

ALAIN DE LISLE.

Contemporary with Albertus Magnus was Alain de Lisle of Flanders, who was named, from his great learning, the "universal doctor." He was thought to possess a knowledge of all the sciences, and, like Artephius, to have discovered the *elixir vitæ*. He became one of the friars of the abbey of Citeaux, and died in 1298, aged about one hundred and ten years. It was said of him that he was at the point of death when in his fiftieth year, but that the fortunate discovery of

* Naudé, *Apologie des Grands Hommes accusés de Magie,* chap. xvii.

the elixir enabled him to add sixty years to his existence. He wrote a commentary on the prophecies of Merlin.

ARNOLD DE VILLENEUVE.

This philosopher has left a much greater reputation. He was born in the year 1245, and studied medicine with great success in the university of Paris. He afterwards travelled for twenty years in Italy and Germany, where he made acquaintance with Pietro d'Apone, a man of a character akin to his own, and addicted to the same pursuits. As a physician, he was thought, in his own lifetime, to be the most able the world had ever seen. Like all the learned men of that day, he dabbled in astrology and alchymy, and was thought to have made immense quantities of gold from lead and copper. When Pietro d'Apone was arrested in Italy, and brought to trial as a sorcerer, a similar accusation was made against Arnold; but he managed to leave the country in time, and escape the fate of his unfortu-
nate friend. He lost some credit by predicting the end of the world, but afterwards regained it. The time of his death is not exactly known; but it must have been prior to the year 1311, when Pope Clement V. wrote a circular letter to all the clergy of Europe who lived under his obedience, praying them to use their utmost efforts to discover the famous treatise of Arnold on *The Practice of*

ARNOLD DE VILLENEUVE.

Medicine. The author had promised, during his lifetime, to make a present of the work to the Holy See, but died without fulfilling it.

In a very curious work by Monsieur Longeville Harcouet, entitled *The History of the Persons who have lived several centuries and then grown young again,* there is a receipt, said to have been given by Arnold de Villeneuve, by means of which any one might prolong his life for a few hundred years or so. In the first place, say Arnold and Monsieur Harcouet, "the person intending so to prolong his life must rub himself well, two or three times a week, with the juice or marrow of cassia (*moëlle de la casse*). Every night, upon going to bed, he must put upon his heart a plaster, composed of a certain quantity of oriental saffron, red rose-leaves, sandal-wood, aloes, and amber, liquified in oil of roses and the best white wax.   In the morning, he must take it off, and enclose it carefully in a leaden box till the next night, when it must be again applied.   If he be of a sanguine temperament, he shall take sixteen chickens; if phlegmatic, twenty-five; and if melancholy, thirty, which he shall put into a yard where the air and the water are pure.   Upon these he is to feed, eating one a day; but previously the chickens are to be fattened by a peculiar method, which will impregnate their flesh with the qualities that are to produce longevity in the eater.   Being deprived of all other nourishment till they are almost dying of hunger, they are to be fed upon broth made of serpents and vinegar, which broth is to be thickened with wheat and bran." Various ceremonies are to be performed in the cooking of this mess, which those may see in the book of M. Harcouet who are at all interested in the matter; and the chickens are to be fed upon it for two months.   They are then fit for table, and are to be washed down with moderate quantities of good white wine or claret. This regimen is to be followed regularly every seven years, and any one may live to be as old as Methuselah !   It is right to state that M. Harcouet has but little authority for attributing this precious composition to Arnold of Villeneuve.   It is not found in the collected works of that philosopher; but was first brought to light by a M. Poirier, at the commencement of the sixteenth century, who asserted that he had discovered it in Ms. in the undoubted writing of Arnold.

PIETRO D'APONE.

This unlucky sage was born at Apone, near Padua, in the year 1250.   Like his friend Arnold de Villeneuve, he was an eminent physician, and a pretender to the arts of astrology and alchymy.   He practised for many years in Paris, and made great wealth by killing and curing, and telling fortunes.   In an evil day for him, he returned to his own country, with the reputation of being a magician of the first order.   It was universally believed that he had drawn seven evil spirits from the infernal regions, whom he kept enclosed in seven crystal vases until he required their services, when he sent them forth to the ends of the earth to execute his pleasure.   One spirit excelled in philosophy; a second, in alchymy; a third, in astrology; a fourth, in physic; a fifth, in poetry; a sixth, in music; and the seventh, in painting; and whenever Pietro wished for information or instruction in any of these arts, he had only to go to his crystal vase and liberate the presiding spirit.   Immediately all the secrets of the art were revealed to him; and he might, if it pleased him, excel Homer in poetry, Apelles in painting, or Pythagoras himself in philosophy.   Although he could make gold out of brass, it was said of him that he was very sparing of his powers in that respect, and kept himself constantly supplied with money by other and less creditable means. Whenever he disbursed gold, he muttered a certain charm, known only to himself, and next morning the gold was safe again in his own possession. The trader to whom he gave it might lock it in his strong box and have it guarded by a troop of soldiers, but the charmed metal flew back to its old master. Even if it were buried in the earth, or thrown into the sea, the dawn of the next morning would behold it in the pockets of Pietro. Few people, in consequence, liked to have dealings with such a personage, especially for gold. Some, bolder than the rest, thought that his power did not extend over silver; but, when they made the experiment, they found themselves mistaken. Bolts and bars could not restrain it, and it sometimes became invisible in their very hands, and was whisked through the air to the purse of the magician. He necessarily acquired a very bad character; and having given utterance to some sentiments regarding religion which were the very reverse of orthodox, he was summoned before the tribunals of the Inquisition to answer for his crimes as a heretic and a sorcerer. He loudly protested his innocence, even upon the rack, where he suffered more torture than nature could support. He died in prison ere his trial was concluded, but was afterwards found guilty. His bones were ordered to be dug up and publicly burned. He was also burned in effigy in the streets of Padua.

RAYMOND LULLI.

While Arnold de Villeneuve and Pietro d'Apone flourished in France and Italy, a more celebrated adept than either appeared in Spain. This was Raymond Lulli, a name which stands in the first rank among the alchymists. Unlike many of his predecessors, he made no pretensions to astrology or necromancy; but, taking Geber for his model, studied intently the nature and composition of metals, without reference to charms, incantations, or any foolish ceremonies. It was not, however, till late in life that he commenced his study of the art. His early and middle age were spent in a different manner, and his whole history is romantic in the extreme. He was born of an illustrious family, in Majorca, in the year 1235. When that island was taken from the Saracens by James I. king of Aragon, in 1230, the father of Raymond, who was originally of Catalonia, settled there, and received a considerable appointment from the crown. Raymond married at an early age; and, being fond of pleasure, he left the solitudes of his native isle, and passed over with his bride into Spain. He was made Grand Seneschal at the court of King James, and led a gay life for several years. Faithless to his wife, he was always in the pursuit of some new beauty, till his heart was fixed at last by the lovely but unkind Ambrosia de Castello. This lady, like her admirer, was married; but, unlike him, was faithful to her vows, and treated all his solicitations with disdain. Raymond was so enamoured, that repulse only increased his flame; he lingered all night under her windows, wrote passionate verses in her praise, neglected his affairs, and made himself the butt of all the courtiers. One day, while watching under her lattice, he by chance caught sight of her bosom, as her neckerchief was blown aside by the wind. The fit of inspiration came over him, and he sat down and composed some tender stanzas upon

RAYMOND LULLI.

the subject, and sent them to the lady. The fair Ambrosia had never before condescended to answer his letters; but she replied to this. She told him that she could never listen to his suit; that it was unbecoming in a wise man to fix his thoughts, as he had done, on any other than his God; and entreated him to devote himself to a religious life, and conquer the unworthy passion which he had suffered to consume him. She, however, offered, if he wished it, to shew him the *fair* bosom which had so captivated him. Raymond was delighted. He thought the latter part of this epistle but ill corresponded with the former, and that Ambrosia, in spite of the good advice she gave him, had at last relented, and would make him as happy as he desired. He followed her about from place to place, entreating her to fulfil her promise: but still Ambrosia was cold, and implored him with tears to importune her no longer; for that she never could be his, and never would, if she were free to-morrow. "What means your letter, then?" said the despairing lover. "I will shew you!" replied Ambrosia, who immediately uncovered her bosom, and exposed to the eyes of her horror-stricken admirer a large cancer which had extended to both breasts. She saw that he was shocked; and extending her hand to him, she prayed him once more to lead a religious life, and set his heart upon the Creator, and not upon the creature. He went home an altered man. He threw up, on the morrow, his valuable

appointment at the court, separated from his wife, and took a farewell of his children, after dividing one-half of his ample fortune
among them. The other half he shared among the poor. He then
threw himself at the foot of a crucifix, and devoted himself to the
service of God, vowing, as the most acceptable atonement for his
errors, that he would employ the remainder of his days in the task of
converting the Mussulmans to the Christian religion. In his dreams
he saw Jesus Christ, who said to him, " Raymond! Raymond! follòw
me !" The vision was three times repeated, and Raymond was convinced that it was an intimation direct from heaven. Having put his
affairs in order, he set out on a pilgrimage to the shrine of St. James
of Compostello, and afterwards lived for ten years in solitude amid
the mountains of Aranda. Here he learned the Arabic, to qualify
himself for his mission of converting the Mahometans. He also
studied various sciences, as taught in the works of the learned men
of the East, and first made acquaintance with the writings of Geber,
which were destined to exercise so much influence over his future
life.

At the end of this probation, and when he had entered his fortieth
year, he emerged from his solitude into more active life. With some
remains of his fortune, which had accumulated during his retirement,
he founded a college for the study of Arabic, which was approved of
by the pope, with many commendations upon his zeal and piety. At
this time he narrowly escaped assassination from an Arabian youth
whom he had taken into his service. Raymond had prayed to God,
in some of his accesses of fanaticism, that he might suffer martyrdom
in his holy cause. His servant had overheard him ; and being as
great a fanatic as his master, he resolved to gratify his wish, and
punish him at the same time for the curses which he incessantly
launched against Mahomet and all who believed in him, by stabbing
him to the heart. He therefore aimed a blow at his master as
he sat one day at table; but the instinct of self-preservation being
stronger than the desire of martyrdom, Raymond grappled with his
antagonist, and overthrew him. He scorned to take his life himself ;
but handed him over to the authorities of the town, by whom he was
afterwards found dead in his prison.

After this adventure Raymond travelled to Paris, where he resided
for some time, and made the acquaintance of Arnold de Villeneuve.
From him he probably received some encouragement to search for
the philosopher's stone, as he began from that time forth to devote
less of his attention to religious matters, and more to the study of
alchymy. Still he never lost sight of the great object for which he
lived—the conversion of the Mahometans—and proceeded to Rome,

to communicate personally with Pope John XXI. on the best measures to be adopted for that end. The Pope gave him encouragement in words, but failed to associate any other persons with him in the enterprise which he meditated. Raymond, therefore, set out for Tunis alone, and was kindly received by many Arabian philosophers, who had heard of his fame as a professor of alchymy. If he had stuck to alchymy while in their country, it would have been well for him ; but he began cursing Mahomet, and got himself into trouble. While preaching the doctrines of Christianity in the great bazaar of Tunis, he was arrested and thrown into prison. He was shortly afterwards brought to trial, and sentenced to death. Some of his philosophic friends interceded hard for him, and he was pardoned upon condition that he left Africa immediately, and never again set foot in it. If he was found there again, no matter what his object might be, or whatever length of time might intervene, his original sentence would be carried into execution. Raymond was not at all solicitous of martyrdom when it came to the point, whatever he might have been when there was no danger, and he gladly accepted his life upon these conditions, and left Tunis with the intention of proceeding to Rome. He afterwards changed his plan, and established himself at Milan, where, for a length of time, he practised alchymy, and some say astrology, with great success.

Most writers who believed in the secrets of alchymy, and who have noticed the life of Raymond Lulli, assert, that while in Milan, he received letters from Edward King of England, inviting him to settle in his states. They add that Lulli gladly accepted the invitation, and had apartments assigned for his use in the Tower of London, where he refined much gold ; superintended the coinage of " rose-nobles," and made gold out of iron, quicksilver, lead, and pewter, to the amount of six millions. The writers in the *Biographie Universelle*, an excellent authority in general, deny that Raymond was ever in England, and say, that in all these stories of his wondrous powers as an alchymist, he has been mistaken for another Raymond, a Jew of Tarragona. Naudé, in his *Apologie*, says simply, " that six millions were given by Raymond Lulli to King Edward, to make war against the Turks and other infidels :" not that he transmuted so much metal into gold ; but, as he afterwards adds, that he advised Edward to lay a tax upon wool, which produced that amount. To shew that Raymond went to England, his admirers quote a work attributed to him, *De Transmutatione Animæ Metallorum*, in which he expressly says that he was in England at the intercession of the king.* The her-

* Vidimus omnia ista *dum ad Angliam transiimus, propter intercessionem domini Regis Edoardi illustrissimi.*

metic writers are not agreed whether it was Edward I. or Edward II. who invited him over ; but, by fixing the date of his journey in 1312, they make it appear that it was Edward II. Edmond Dickenson, in his work on the *Quintessences of the Philosophers*, says, that Raymond worked in Westminster Abbey, where, a long time after his departure, there was found in the cell which he had occupied a great quantity of golden dust, of which the architects made a great profit. In the biographical sketch of John Cremer, Abbot of Westminster, given by Lenglet, it is said that it was chiefly through his instrumentality that Raymond came to England. Cremer had been himself for thirty years occupied in the vain search for the philosopher's stone, when he accidentally met Raymond in Italy, and endeavoured to induce him to communicate his grand secret. Raymond told him that he must find it for himself, as all great alchymists had done before him. Cremer, on his return to England, spoke to King Edward in high terms of the wonderful attainments of the philosopher, and a letter of invitation was forthwith sent him. Robert Constantinus, in the *Nomenclator Scriptorum Medicorum*, published in 1515, says, that after a great deal of research, he found that Raymond Lulli resided for some time in London, and that he actually made gold, by means of the philosopher's stone, in the Tower ; that he had seen the golden pieces of his coinage, which were still named in England the nobles of Raymond, or rose-nobles. Lulli himself appears to have boasted that he made gold ; for, in his well-known *Testamentum*, he states that he converted no less than fifty thousand pounds weight of quicksilver, lead, and pewter into that metal.* It seems highly probable that the English king, believing in the extraordinary powers of the alchymist, invited him to England to make test of them, and that he was employed in refining gold and in coining. Camden, who is not credulous in matters like these, affords his countenance to the story of his coinage of nobles ; and there is nothing at all wonderful in the fact of a man famous for his knowledge of metals being employed in such a capacity. Raymond was at this time an old man, in his seventy-seventh year, and somewhat in his dotage. He was willing enough to have it believed that he had discovered the grand secret, and supported the rumour rather than contradicted it. He did not long remain in England, but returned to Rome to carry out the projects which were nearer to his heart than the profession of alchymy. He had proposed them to several successive popes with little or no success. The first was a plan for the introduction of the oriental languages into all the monasteries of Europe ; the second, for the

---

* Converti una vice in aurum ad L millia pondo argenti vivi, plumbi, et stauni.— *Lullii Testamentum.*

reduction into one of all the military orders, that, being united, they might move more efficaciously against the Saracens ; and the third, that the sovereign pontiff should forbid the works of Averroes to be read in the schools, as being more favourable to Mahometanism than to Christianity. The pope did not receive the old man with much cordiality ; and, after remaining for about two years in Rome, he proceeded once more to Africa, alone and unprotected, to preach the Gospel of Jesus. He landed at Bona in 1314, and so irritated the Mahometans by cursing their prophet, that they stoned him, and left him for dead on the sea-shore. He was found some hours afterwards by a party of Genoese merchants, who conveyed him on board their vessel, and sailed towards Majorca. The unfortunate man still breathed, but could not articulate. He lingered in this state for some days, and expired just as the vessel arrived within sight of his native shores. His body was conveyed with great pomp to the church of St. Eulalia, at Palma, where a public funeral was instituted in his honour. Miracles were afterwards said to have been worked at his tomb.

Thus ended the career of Raymond Lulli, one of the most extraordinary men of his age ; and, with the exception of his last boast about the six millions of gold, the least inclined to quackery of any of the professors of alchymy. His writings were very numerous, and include nearly five hundred volumes, upon grammar, rhetoric, morals, theology, politics, civil and canon law, physics, metaphysics, astronomy, medicine, and chemistry.

Roger Bacon.

The powerful delusion of alchymy seized upon a mind still greater than that of Raymond Lulli. Roger Bacon firmly believed in the philosopher's stone, and spent much of his time in search of it. His example helped to render all the learned men of the time more convinced of its practicability, and more eager in the pursuit. He was born at Ilchester, in the county of Somerset, in the year 1214. He studied for some time in the University of Oxford, and afterwards in that of Paris, in which he received the degree of doctor of divinity. Returning to England in 1240, he became a monk of the order of St. Francis. He was by far the most learned man of his age ; and his acquirements were so much above the comprehension of his contemporaries, that they could only account for them by supposing that he was indebted for them to the devil. Voltaire has not inaptly designated him " De l'or encroute de toutes les ordures de son siècle ;" but the crust of superstition that enveloped his powerful mind, though it may have dimmed, could not obscure the brightness of his genius. To him, and apparently to him only, among all the inquiring spirits of the time, were known the properties of the concave and convex lens. He also invented the magic-lantern ; that pretty plaything of modern days, which acquired for him a reputation that embittered his life. In a history of alchymy, the name of this great man cannot be omitted, although, unlike many others of whom we shall have occasion to speak, he only made it secondary to other pursuits. The love of universal knowledge that filled his mind, would not allow him to neglect one branch of science, of which neither he nor the world could yet see the absurdity. He made ample amends for his time lost in this pursuit by his knowledge in physics and his acquaintance with astronomy. The telescope, burning-glasses, and gunpowder, are discoveries which may well carry his fame to the remotest time, and make the world blind to the one spot of folly—the diagnosis of the age in which he lived, and the circumstances by which he was surrounded. His treatise on the *Admirable Power of Art and Nature in the Production of the Philosopher's Stone* was translated into French by Girard de Tormes, and published at Lyons in 1557. His *Mirror of Alchymy* was also published in French in the same year, and in Paris in 1612, with some additions from the works of Raymond Lulli. A complete list of all the published treatises upon the subject may be seen in Lenglet du Fresnoy.

POPE JOHN XXII.

This prelate is said to have been the friend and pupil of Arnold de Villeneuve, by whom he was instructed in all the secrets of alchymy. Tradition asserts of him, that he made great quantities of gold, and died as rich as Crœsus. He was born at Cahors, in the province of Guienne, in the year 1244. He was a very eloquent preacher, and soon reached high dignity in the Church. He wrote a work on the transmutation of metals, and had a famous laboratory at Avignon. He issued two bulls against the numerous pretenders to the art, who had sprung up in every part of Christendom ; from which it might be inferred that he was himself free from the delusion. The alchymists claim him, however, as one of the most distinguished and successful professors of their art, and say that his bulls were not directed against the real adepts, but the false pretenders. They lay particular stress upon these words in his bull, " Spondent, quas non exhibent, divitias, *pauperes* alchymistæ." These, it is clear, they say, relate only to *poor* alchymists, and therefore false ones. He died in the year 1344, leaving in his coffers a sum of eighteen millions of florins. Popular belief alleged that he had made, and not amassed, this treasure; and alchymists complacently cite this as a proof that the philosopher's stone was not such a chimera as the incredulous pretended. They take it for granted that John really left this money, and ask by what possible means he could have accumulated it. Replying to their own question, they say triumphantly, " His book shews it was by alchymy, the secrets of which he learned from Arnold de Villeneuve and Raymond Lulli. But he was as prudent as all other hermetic philosophers. Whoever would read his book to find out his secret, would employ all his labour in vain ; the pope took good care not to divulge it." Unluckily for their own credit, all these gold-makers are in the same predicament ; their great secret loses its worth most wonderfully in the telling, and therefore they keep it snugly to themselves. Perhaps they thought that, if every body could transmute metals, gold would be so plentiful that it would be no longer valuable, and that some new art would be requisite to transmute it back again into steel and iron. If so, society is much indebted to them for their forbearance.

JEAN DE MEUNG.

All classes of men dabbled in the art at this time ; the last mentioned was a pope, the one of whom we now speak was a poet. Jean de Meung, the celebrated author of the *Roman de la Rose*, was born in the year 1279 or 1280, and was a great personage at the courts of Louis X., Philip the Long, Charles IV., and Philip de Valois. His famous poem of the *Roman de la Rose*, which treats of every subject in vogue at that day, necessarily makes great mention of alchymy. Jean was a firm believer in the art, and wrote, besides his Roman, two shorter poems, the one entitled, *The Remonstrance of Nature to the wandering Alchymist* and *The Reply of the Alchymist to Nature*. Poetry and alchymy were his delight, and priests and women were his abomination. A pleasant story is related of him and the ladies of the court of Charles IV. He had written the following libellous couplet upon the fair sex :

> " Toutes êtes, serez, ou fûtes,
> De fait ou de volonté, putains ;
> Et qui très bien vous chercherait,
> Toutes putains vous trouverait."*

This naturally gave great offence ; and being perceived one day in the king's antechamber, by some ladies who were waiting for an audience, they resolved to punish him. To the number of ten or twelve, they armed themselves with canes and rods, and surrounding the unlucky poet, called upon the gentlemen present to strip him naked, that they might wreak just vengeance upon him, and lash him through the

* These verses are but a coarser expression of the slanderous line of Pope, that " every woman is at heart a rake."

streets of the town. Some of the lords present were in no wise loath, and promised themselves great sport from his punishment. But Jean de Meung was unmoved by their threats, and stood up calmly in the midst of them, begging them to hear him first, and then, if not satisfied, they might do as they liked with him. Silence being restored, he stood upon a chair, and entered on his defence. He acknowledged that he was the author of the obnoxious verses, but denied that they bore reference to all womankind. He only meant to speak of the vicious and abandoned, whereas those whom he saw around him were patterns of virtue, loveliness, and modesty. If, however, any lady present thought herself aggrieved, he would consent to be stripped, and she might lash him till her arms were wearied. It is added, that by this means Jean escaped his flogging, and that the wrath of the fair ones immediately subsided. The gentlemen present were, however, of opinion, that if every lady in the room whose character corresponded with the verses had taken him at his word, the poet would in all probability have been beaten to death. All his life long he evinced a great animosity towards the priesthood, and his famous poem abounds with passages reflecting upon their avarice, cruelty, and immorality. At his death he left a large box, filled with some weighty material, which he bequeathed to the Cordeliers, as a peace-offering for the abuse he had lavished upon them. As his practice of alchymy was well known, it was thought the box was filled with gold and silver, and the Cordeliers congratulated each other on their rich acquisition. When it came to be opened, they found to their horror that it was filled only with *slates*, scratched with hieroglyphic and cabalistic characters. Indignant at the insult, they determined to refuse him Christian burial, on pretence that he was a sorcerer. He was, however, honourably buried in Paris, the whole court attending his funeral.

NICHOLAS FLAMEL.

The story of this alchymist, as handed down by tradition, and enshrined in the pages of Lenglet du Fresnoy, is not a little marvellous. He was born at Pontoise, of a poor but respectable family, at the end of the thirteenth, or beginning of the fourteenth century. Having no patrimony, he set out for Paris at an early age, to try his fortune as a public scribe. He had received a good education, was well skilled in the learned languages, and was an excellent penman. He soon procured occupation as a letter-writer and copyist, and used to sit at the corner of the Rue de Marivaux, and practise his calling; but he hardly made profit enough to keep body and soul together. To mend his fortunes he tried poetry; but this was a more wretched occupation still. As a transcriber he had at least gained bread and cheese; but his rhymes were not worth a crust. He then tried painting with as little success; and as a last resource, began to search for the philosopher's stone and tell fortunes. This was a happier idea; he soon increased in substance, and had wherewithal to live comfortably. He therefore took unto himself his wife Petronella, and began to save money; but continued to all outward appearance as poor and miserable as before. In the course of a few years, he became desperately addicted to the study of alchymy, and thought of nothing but the philosopher's stone, the elixir of life, and the universal alkahest. In the year 1257, he bought by chance an old book for two florins, which soon became his sole study. It was written with a steel instrument upon the bark of trees, and contained twenty-one, or as he himself always expressed it, three times seven, leaves. The writing was very elegant and in the Latin language. Each seventh leaf contained a picture and no writing. On the first of these was a serpent swallowing rods; on the second, a cross with a serpent crucified; and on the third, the representation of a desert, in the midst of which was a fountain, with serpents crawling from side to side. It purported to be written by no less a personage than "Abraham, patriarch, Jew, prince, philosopher, priest, Levite, and astrologer;" and invoked curses upon any one who should cast eyes upon it, without being "a sacrificer or a scribe." Nicholas Flamel never thought it extraordinary that Abraham should have known Latin, and was convinced that the characters on his book had been traced by the hands of that great patriarch himself. He was at first afraid to read it, after he became aware of the curse it contained; but he got over that difficulty by recollecting that, although he was not a sacrificer, he had practised as a scribe. As he read he was filled with admiration, and found that it was a perfect treatise upon the transmutation of metals. All the processes were clearly explained; the vessels, the retorts, the mixtures, and the proper times and seasons for experiment. But as ill-luck would have it, the possession of the philosopher's stone, or prime agent in the work, was presupposed. This was a difficulty which was not to be got over. It was like telling a starving man how to cook a beefsteak, instead of giving him the money to buy one. But Nicholas did not despair, and set about studying the hieroglyphics and allegorical representations with which the book abounded. He soon convinced himself that it had been one of the sacred books of the Jews, and that it was taken from the temple of Jerusalem on its destruction by Titus. The process of reasoning by which he arrived at this conclusion is not stated.

From some expression in the treatise, he learned that the allegorical drawings on the fourth and fifth leaves enshrined the secret of the philosopher's stone, without which all the fine Latin of the directions was utterly unavailing. He invited all the alchymists and learned men of Paris to come and examine them, but they all departed as wise as they came. Nobody could make any thing either of Nicholas or his pictures; and some even went so far as to say that his invaluable book was not worth a farthing. This was not to be borne; and Nicholas resolved to discover the great secret by himself, without troubling the philosophers. He found on the first page of the fourth leaf the picture of Mercury attacked by an old man resembling Saturn or Time. The latter had an hour-glass on his head, and in his hand a scythe, with which he aimed a blow at Mercury's feet. The reverse of the leaf represented a flower growing on a mountain-top, shaken rudely by the wind, with a blue stalk, red and white blossoms, and leaves of pure gold. Around it were a great number of dragons and griffins. On the first page of the fifth leaf was a fine garden, in the midst of which was a rose-tree in full bloom, supported against the trunk of a gigantic oak. At the foot of this there bubbled up a fountain of milk-white water, which, forming a small stream, flowed through the garden, and was afterwards lost in the sands. On the second page was a king, with a sword in his hand, superintending a number of soldiers, who, in execution of his orders, were killing a great multitude of young children, spurning the prayers and tears of their mothers, who tried to save them from destruction. The blood of the children was carefully collected by another party of soldiers, and put into a large vessel, in which two allegorical figures of the sun and moon were bathing themselves.

For twenty-one years poor Nicholas wearied himself with the study of these pictures, but still he could make nothing of them. His wife Petronella at last persuaded him to find out some learned rabbi; but there was no rabbi in Paris learned enough to be of any service to him. The Jews met but small encouragement to fix their abode in France, and all the chiefs of that people were located in Spain. To Spain accordingly Nicholas Flamel repaired. He left his book in Paris, for fear, perhaps, that he might be robbed of it on the road; and telling his neighbours that he was going on a pilgrimage to the shrine of St. James of Compostello, he trudged on foot towards Madrid in search of a rabbi. He was absent two years in that country, and made himself known to a great number of Jews, descendants of those who had been expelled from France in the reign of Philip Augustus. The believers in the philosopher's stone give the following account of his adventures: They say that at Leon he made the acquaintance of a converted Jew, named Cauches, a very learned physician, to whom he explained the title and nature of his little book. The doctor was transported with joy as soon as he heard it named, and immediately resolved to accompany Nicholas to Paris, that he might have a sight of it. The two set out together; the doctor on the way entertaining his companion with the history of his book, which, if the genuine book he thought it to be, from the description he had heard of it, was in the handwriting of Abraham himself, and had been in the possession of personages no less distinguished than Moses, Joshua, Solomon, and Esdras. It contained all the secrets of alchymy and of many other sciences, and was the most valuable book that had ever existed in this world. The doctor was himself no mean adept, and Nicholas profited greatly by his discourse, as in the garb of poor pilgrims they wended their way to Paris, convinced of their power to turn every old shovel in that capital into pure gold. But, unfortunately, when they reached Orleans, the doctor was taken dangerously ill. Nicholas watched by his bedside, and acted the double part of a physician and nurse to him; but he died after a few days, lamenting with his last breath that he had not lived long enough to see the precious volume. Nicholas rendered the last honours to his body; 'and with a sorrowful heart, and not one *sou* in his pocket, proceeded home to his wife Petronella. He immediately recommenced the study of his pictures; but for two whole years he was as far from understanding them as ever. At last, in the third year, a glimmer of light stole over his understanding. He recalled some expression of his friend the doctor, which had hitherto escaped his memory, and he found that all his previous experiments had been conducted on a wrong basis. He recommenced them now with renewed energy, and at the end of the year had the satisfaction to see all his toils rewarded. On the 13th January 1382, says Lenglet, he made a projection on mercury, and had some very excellent silver. On the 25th April following, he converted a large quantity of mercury into gold, and the great secret was his.

Nicholas was now about eighty years of age, and still a hale and stout old man. His friends say that by a simultaneous discovery of the elixir of life, he found means to keep death at a distance for another quarter of a century; and that he died in 1415, at the age of 116. In this interval he made immense quantities of gold, though to all outward appearance he was as poor as a mouse. At an early period of his changed fortune, he had, like a worthy man, taken counsel with his old wife Petronella, as to the best use he could make of his wealth. Petronella replied, that as unfortunately they had no children,-the best thing he could do, was to build hospitals and endow churches. Nicholas thought so too, especially when he began to find that his elixir could not keep off death, and that the grim foe was making rapid advances upon him. He richly endowed the church of St. Jacques de la Boucherie, near the Rue de Marivaux, where he had all his life resided, besides seven others in different parts of the kingdom. He also endowed fourteen hospitals, and built three chapels.

The fame of his great wealth and his munificent benefactions soon spread over all the country, and he was visited, among others, by the celebrated doctors of that day, Jean Gerson, Jean de Courtecuisse, and Pierre d'Ailli. They found him in his humble apartment, meanly clad, and eating porridge out of an earthen vessel ; and with regard to his secret, as impenetrable as all his predecessors in alchymy. His fame reached the ears of the king, Charles VI., who sent M. de Cramoisi, the Master of Requests, to find out whether Nicholas had indeed discovered the philosopher's stone. But M. de Cramoisi took nothing by his visit; all his attempts to sound the alchymist were unavailing, and he returned to his royal master no wiser than he came. It was in this year, 1414, that he lost his faithful Petronella. He did not long survive her, but died in the following year, and was buried with great pomp by the grateful priests of St. Jacques de la Boucherie.

The great wealth of Nicholas Flamel is undoubted, as the records of several churches and hospitals in France can testify. That he practised alchymy is equally certain, as he left behind several works upon the subject. Those who knew him well, and who were incredulous about the philosopher's stone, give a satisfactory solution of the secret of his wealth. They say that he was always a miser and a usurer ; that his journey to Spain was undertaken with very different motives from those pretended by the alchymists ; that, in fact, he went to collect debts due from Jews in that country to their brethren in Paris, and that he charged a commission of fully cent per cent in consideration of the difficulty of collecting and the dangers of the road ; that when he possessed thousands, he lived upon almost nothing ; and was the general money-lender, at enormous profits, to all the dissipated young men at the French court.

Among the works written by Nicholas Flamel on the subject of alchymy is *The Philosophic Summary,* a poem, reprinted in 1735, as an appendix to the third volume of the *Roman de la Rose.* He also wrote three treatises upon natural philosophy, and an alchymic allegory, entitled *Le Désir désiré.* Specimens of his writing, and a fac-simile of the drawings in his book of Abraham, may be seen in Salmon's *Bibliothèque des Philosophes Chimiques.* The writer of the article *Flamel* in the *Biographie Universelle* says, that for a hundred years after the death of Flamel, many of the adepts believed that he was still alive, and that he would live for upwards of six hundred years. The house he formerly occupied, at the corner of the Rue de Marivaux, has been often taken by credulous speculators, and ransacked from top to bottom, in the hopes that gold might be found. A report was current in Paris, not long previous to the year 1816, that some lodgers had found in the cellars several jars filled with a dark-coloured ponderous matter. Upon the strength of the rumour, a believer in all the wondrous tales told of Nicholas Flamel bought the house, and nearly pulled it to pieces in ransacking the walls and wainscoting for hidden gold. He got nothing for his pains, however, and had a heavy bill to pay to restore his dilapidations.

GEORGE RIPLEY.

While alchymy was thus cultivated on the continent of Europe, it was not neglected in the isles of Britain. Since the time of Roger Bacon, it had fascinated the imagination of many ardent men in England. In the year 1404 an act of parliament was passed declaring the making of gold and silver to be felony. Great alarm was felt at that time lest any alchymist should succeed in his projects, and perhaps bring ruin upon the state by furnishing boundless wealth to some designing tyrant, who would make use of it to enslave his country. This alarm appears to have soon subsided ; for, in the year 1455, King Henry VI., by advice of his council and parliament, granted four successive patents and commissions to several knights, citizens of London, chemists, monks, mass priests, and others, to find out the philosopher's stone and elixir, "to the great benefit," said the patent, " of the realm, and the enabling of the king to pay all the debts of the crown in real gold and silver." Prinn, in his *Aurum Reginæ*, observes, as a note to this passage, that the king's reason for granting this patent to ecclesiastics was, that "they were such good artists in transubstantiating bread and wine in the eucharist, and therefore the more likely to be able to effect the transmutation of baser metals into better." No gold, of course, was ever made ; and next year the king, doubting very much of the practicability of the thing, took further advice, and appointed a commission of ten learned men and persons of eminence to judge and certify to him whether the transmutation of metals were a thing practicable or no. It does not appear whether the commission ever made any report upon the subject.

In the succeeding reign an alchymist appeared who pretended to have discovered the secret. This was George Ripley, the canon of Bridlington, in Yorkshire. He studied for twenty years in the universities of Italy, and was a great favourite with Pope Innocent VIII., who made him one of his domestic chaplains, and master of the ceremonies in his household. Returning to England in 1477, he dedicated to King Edward IV. his famous work, *The Compound of Alchymy; or, the Twelve Gates leading to the Discovery of the Philosopher's Stone.* These gates he described to be calcination, solution, separation, conjunction, putrefaction, congelation, cibation, sublimation, fermentation, exaltation, multiplication, and projection ; to which he might have added botheration, the most important process of all. He was very rich, and allowed it to be believed that he could make gold out of iron. Fuller, in his *Worthies of England*, says that an English gentleman of good credit reported, that in his travels abroad he saw a record in the island of Malta which declared that Ripley gave yearly to the knights of that island, and of Rhodes, the enormous sum of one hundred thousand pounds sterling to enable them to carry on the war against the Turks. In his old age he became an anchorite near Boston, and wrote twenty-five volumes upon the subject of alchymy, the most important of which is the *Duodecim Partarum* already mentioned. Before he died, he seems to have acknowledged that he had mis-spent his life in this vain study, and requested that all men, when they met with any of his books, would burn them, or afford them no credit, as they had been written merely from his opinion and not from proof ; and that subsequent trial had made manifest to him that they were false and vain.*

Basil Valentine.

Germany also produced many famous alchymists in the fifteenth century, the chief of whom are Basil Valentine, Bernard of Trèves, and the Abbot Trithemius. Basil Valentine was born at Mayence, and was made prior of St. Peter's, at Erfurt, about the year 1414. It was known during his life, that he diligently sought the philosopher's stone, and that he had written some works upon the process of transmutation. They were thought for many years to be lost, but were, after his death, discovered enclosed in the stonework of one of the pillars in the abbey. They were twenty-one in number, and are fully set forth in the third volume of Lenglet's *History of the Hermetic Philosophy.* The alchymists asserted that heaven itself conspired to bring to light these extraordinary works ; and that the pillar in which they were enclosed was miraculously shattered by a thunderbolt ; and that as soon as the manuscripts were liberated, the pillar closed up again of its own accord !

Bernard of Treves.

The life of this philosopher is a remarkable instance of talent and perseverance misapplied. In the search of his chimera nothing could

* Fuller's *Worthies of England*

daunt him. Repeated disappointment never diminished his hopes; and from the age of fourteen to that of eighty-five he was incessantly employed among the drugs and furnaces of his laboratory, wasting his life with the view of prolonging it, and reducing himself to beggary in the hopes of growing rich.

He was born at either Trèves or Padua in the year 1406. His father is said by some to have been a physician in the latter city, and by others to have been Count of the Marches of Trèves, and one of the most wealthy nobles of his country. At all events, whether noble or physician, he was a rich man, and left his son a magnificent estate. At the age of fourteen he first became enamoured of the science of alchymy, and read the Arabian authors in their own language. He himself has left a most interesting record of his labours and wanderings, from which the following particulars are chiefly extracted. The first book which fell into his hands was that of the Arabian phisosopher Rhazes, from the reading of which he imagined that he had discovered the means of augmenting gold a hundredfold. For four years he worked in his laboratory, with the book of Rhazes continually before him. At the end of that time, he found that he had spent no less than eight hundred crowns upon his experiment, and had got nothing but fire and smoke for his pains. He now began to lose confidence in Rhazes, and turned to the works of Geber. He studied him assiduously for two years; and being young, rich, and credulous, was beset by all the alchymists of the town, who kindly assisted him in spending his money. He did not lose his faith in Geber, or patience with his hungry assistants, until he had lost two thousand crowns— a very considerable sum in those days.

Among all the crowd of pretended men of science who surrounded him, there was but one as enthusiastic and as disinterested as himself. With this man, who was a monk of the order of St. Francis, he contracted an intimate friendship, and spent nearly all his time. Some obscure treatises of Rupecissa and Sacrobosco having fallen into their hands, they were persuaded, from reading them, that highly rectified spirits of wine was the universal alkahest, or dissolvent, which would aid them greatly in the process of transmutation. They rectified the alcohol thirty times, till they made it so strong as to burst the vessels which contained it. After they had worked three years, and spent three hundred crowns in the liquor, they discovered that they were on the wrong track. They next tried alum and copperas; but the great secret still escaped them. They afterwards imagined that there was a marvellous virtue in all excrement, especially the human, and actually employed more than two years in experimentalising upon it with mercury, salt, and molten lead! Again the adepts flocked around him from far and near to aid him with their counsels. He received them all hospitably, and divided his wealth among them so generously and unhesitatingly, that they gave him the name of the "Good Trevisan," by which he is still often mentioned in works that treat on alchymy. For twelve years he led this life, making experiments every day upon some new substance, and praying to God night and morning that he might dicover the secret of transmutation.

In this interval he lost his friend the monk, and was joined by a magistrate of the city of Trèves, as ardent as himself in the search. His new acquaintance imagined that the ocean was the mother of gold, and that sea-salt would change lead or iron into the precious metals. Bernard resolved to try; and, transporting his laboratory to a house on the shores of the Baltic, he worked upon salt for more than a year, melting it, sublimating it, crystallising it, and occasionally drinking it, for the sake of other experiments. Still the strange enthusiast was not wholly discouraged, and his failure in one trial only made him the more anxious to attempt another.

He was now approaching the age of fifty, and had as yet seen nothing of the world. He therefore determined to travel through Germany, Italy, France, and Spain. Wherever he stopped he made inquiries whether there were any alchymists in the neighbourhood. He invariably sought them out; and if they were poor, relieved, and if affluent, encouraged them. At Citeaux he became acquainted with one Geoffrey Leuvier, a monk of that place, who persuaded him that the essence of egg-shells was a valuable ingredient. He tried, therefore, what could be done; and was only prevented from wasting a year or two on the experiment by the opinions of an attorney, at Berghem, in Flanders, who said that the great secret resided in vinegar and copperas. He was not convinced of the absurdity of this idea until he had nearly poisoned himself. He resided in France for about five years, when, hearing accidentally that one Master Henry, confessor to the Emperor Frederick III., had discovered the philosopher's stone, he set out for Germany to pay him a visit. He had, as usual, surrounded himself with a set of hungry dependants, several of whom determined to accompany him. He had not heart to refuse them, and he arrived at Vienna with five of them. Bernard sent a polite invitation to the confessor, and gave him a sumptuous entertainment, at which were present nearly all the alchymists of Vienna. Master Henry frankly confessed that he had not discovered the philosopher's stone, but that he had all his life been employed in searching for it, and would so continue till he found it, or died. This was a man after Bernard's own heart, and they vowed with each other an eternal friendship. It was resolved, at supper, that each alchymist present should contribute a certain sum towards raising forty-two marks of gold, which, in five days, it was confidently asserted by Master Henry, would increase, in his furnace, fivefold. Bernard, being the richest man, contributed the lion's share, ten marks of gold, Master Henry five, and the others one or two a-piece, except the dependants of Bernard, who were obliged to borrow their quota from their patron. The grand experiment was duly made; the golden marks were put into a crucible, with a quantity of salt, copperas, aquafortis, egg-shells, mercury, lead, and dung. The alchymists watched this precious mess with intense interest, expecting that it would agglomerate into one lump of pure gold. At the end of three weeks they gave up the trial, upon some excuse that the crucible was not strong enough, or that some necessary ingredient was wanting. Whether any thief had put his hands into the crucible is not known, but it is alleged that the gold found therein at the close of the experiment was worth only sixteen marks, instead of the forty-two which were put there at the beginning.

Bernard, though he made no gold at Vienna, made away with a very considerable quantity. He felt the loss so acutely that he vowed to think no more of the philosopher's stone. This wise resolution he kept for two months; but he was miserable. He was in the condition of the gambler, who cannot resist the fascination of the game while he has a coin remaining, but plays on with the hope of retrieving former losses, till hope forsakes him, and he can live no longer. He returned once more to his beloved crucibles, and resolved to prosecute his journey in search of a philosopher who had discovered the secret, and would communicate it to so zealous and persevering an adept as himself. From Vienna he travelled to Rome, and from Rome to Madrid. Taking ship at Gibraltar, he proceeded to Messina; from Messina to Cyprus; from Cyprus to Greece; from Greece to Constantinople; and thence into Egypt, Palestine, and Persia. These wanderings occupied him about eight years. From Persia he made his way back to Messina, and from thence into France. He afterwards passed over into England, still in search of his great chimera; and this occupied four years more of his life. He was now growing both old and poor; for he was sixty-two years of age, and had been obliged to sell a great portion of his patrimony to provide for his expenses. His journey to Persia had cost upwards of thirteen thousand crowns, about one-half of which had been fairly melted in his all-devouring furnaces; the other half was lavished upon the sycophants that he made it his business to search out in every town he stopped at.

On his return to Trèves he found, to his sorrow, that, if not an actual beggar, he was not much better. His relatives looked upon him as a madman, and refused even to see him. Too proud to ask for favours from any one, and still confident that, some day or other, he would be the possessor of unbounded wealth, he made up his mind to retire to the island of Rhodes, where he might, in the mean time, hide his poverty from the eyes of the world. Here he might have lived unknown and happy; but, as ill luck would have it, he fell in with a monk as mad as himself upon the subject of transmutation. They were, however, both so poor that they could not afford to buy the proper materials to work with. They kept up each other's spirits by learned discourses on the hermetic philosophy, and in the reading of all the great authors who had written upon the subject. Thus did they nurse their folly, as the good wife of Tam O'Shanter did her wrath, "to keep it warm." After Bernard had resided about a year in Rhodes, a merchant, who knew his family, advanced him the sum of eight thousand florins, upon the security of the last-remaining acres of his formerly large estate. Once more provided with funds, he recommenced his labours with all the zeal and enthusiasm of a young man. For three years he hardly stepped out of his laboratory: he ate there, and slept there, and did not even give himself time to wash his hands and clean his beard, so intense was his application. It is melancholy to think that such wonderful perseverance should have been wasted in so vain a pursuit, and that energies so unconquerable should have had no worthier field to strive in. Even when he had fumed away his last coin, and had nothing left in prospective to keep his old age from starvation, hope never forsook him. He still dreamed of ultimate success, and sat down a grey-headed man of eighty, to read over all the authors on the hermetic mysteries, from Geber to his own day, lest he should have misunderstood some process, which it was not yet too late to recommence. The alchymists say, that he succeeded at last, and discovered the secret of transmutation in his eighty-second year. They add that he lived three years afterwards to enjoy his wealth. He lived, it is true, to this great age, and made a valuable discovery—more valuable than gold or gems. He learned, as he himself informs us, just before he had attained his eighty-third year, that the great secret of philosophy was contentment with our lot. Happy would it have been for him if he had discovered it sooner, and before he became decrepit, a beggar, and an exile!

He died at Rhodes, in the year 1490, and all the alchymists of Europe sang elegies over him, and sounded his praise as the "good Trevisan." He wrote several treatises upon his chimera, the chief of which are, the *Book of Chemistry*, the *Verbum dimissum*, and an essay *De Natura Ovi*.

TRITHEMIUS.

The name of this eminent man has become famous in the annals of alchymy, although he did but little to gain so questionable an honour. He was born in the year 1462, at the village of Trittheim, in the electorate of Trèves. His father was John Heidenberg, a vine-grower, in easy circumstances, who, dying when his son was but seven years old, left him to the care of his mother. The latter married again very shortly afterwards, and neglected the poor boy, the offspring of her first marriage. At the age of fifteen he did not even know his letters, and was, besides, half-starved, and otherwise ill-treated by his step-father; but the love of knowledge germinated in the breast of the unfortunate youth, and he learned to read at the house of a neighbour. His father-in-law set him to work in the vineyards, and thus occupied all his days; but the nights were his own. He often stole out unheeded, when all the household were fast asleep, poring over his studies in the fields, by the light of the moon; and thus taught himself Latin and the rudiments of Greek. He was subjected to so much ill-usage at home, in consequence of this love of study, that he determined to leave it. Demanding the patrimony which his father had left him, he proceeded to Trèves; and assuming the name of Trithemius, from that of his native village of Trittheim, lived there for some months under the tuition of eminent masters, by whom he was prepared for the university. At the age of twenty, he took it into his head that he should like to see his mother once more; and he set out on foot from the distant university for that purpose. On his arrival near Spannheim, late in the evening of a gloomy winter's day, it came on to snow so thickly, that he could not proceed onwards to the town. He therefore took refuge for the night in a neighbouring monastery; but the storm continued several days, the roads became impassable, and the hospitable monks would not hear of his departure. He was so pleased with them and their manner of life, that he suddenly resolved to fix his abode among them, and renounce the world. They were no less pleased with him, and gladly received him as a brother. In the course of two years, although still so young, he was unanimously elected their abbot. The financial affairs of the establishment had been greatly neglected, the walls of the building were falling into ruin, and every thing was in disorder. Trithemius, by his good management and regularity, introduced a reform in every branch of expenditure. The monastery was repaired, and a yearly surplus, instead of a deficiency, rewarded him for his pains. He did not like to see the monks idle, or occupied solely between prayers for their business, and chess for their relaxation. He, therefore, set them to work to copy the writings of eminent authors. They laboured so assiduously, that, in the course of a few years, their library, which had contained only about forty volumes, was enriched with several hundred valuable manuscripts, comprising many of the classical Latin authors, besides the works of the early fathers, and the principal historians and philosophers of more modern date. He retained the dignity of Abbot of Spannheim for twenty-one years, when the monks, tired of the severe discipline he maintained, revolted against him, and chose another abbot in his place. He was afterwards made Abbot of St. James, in Wurzburg, where he died in 1516.

During his learned leisure at Spannheim, he wrote several works upon the occult sciences, the chief of which are an essay on geomancy, or divination by means of lines and circles on the ground; another upon sorcery; a third upon alchymy; and a fourth upon the government of the world by its presiding angels, which was translated into English, and published by the famous William Lilly in 1647.

It has been alleged by the believers in the possibility of transmutation, that the prosperity of the abbey of Spannheim, while under his superintendence, was owing more to the philosopher's stone than to wise economy. Trithemius, in common with many other learned men, has been accused of magic; and a marvellous story is told of his having raised from the grave the form of Mary of Burgundy, at the intercession of her widowed husband, the Emperor Maximilian. His work on steganographia, or cabalistic writing, was denounced to the Count Palatine, Frederic II., as magical and devilish; and it was by him taken from the shelves of his library and thrown into the fire. Trithemius is said to be the first writer who makes mention of the wonderful story of the devil and Dr. Faustus, the truth of which he firmly believed. He also recounts the freaks of a spirit named *Hudekin*, by whom he was at times tormented.*

THE MARECHAL DE RAYS.

One of the greatest encouragers of alchymy in the fifteenth century was Gilles de Laval, Lord of Rays and a Marshal of France. His name and deeds are little known; but in the annals of crime and folly they might claim the highest and worst pre-eminence. Fiction has never invented any thing wilder or more horrible than his career; and were not the details but too well authenticated by legal and other documents which admit no doubt, the lover of romance might easily imagine they were drawn to please him from the stores of the prolific brain, and not from the page of history.

* *Biographie Universelle.*

He was born about the year 1420, of one of the noblest families of Brittany. His father dying when Gilles had attained his twentieth year, he came into uncontrolled possession, at that early age, of a fortune which the monarchs of France might have envied him. He was a near kinsman of the Montmorencys, the Roncys, and the Craons; possessed fifteen princely domains, and had an annual revenue of about three hundred thousand livres. Besides this, he was handsome, learned, and brave. He distinguished himself greatly in the wars of Charles VII., and was rewarded by that monarch with the dignity of a marshal of France. But he was extravagant and magnificent in his style of living, and accustomed from his earliest years to the gratification of every wish and passion; and this, at last, led him from vice to vice and from crime to crime, till a blacker name than his is not to be found in any record of human iniquity.

In his castle of Champtocé he lived with all the splendour of an eastern caliph. He kept up a troop of two hundred horsemen to accompany him wherever he went; and his excursions for the purposes of hawking and hunting were the wonder of all the country around, so magnificent were the caparisons of his steeds and the dresses of his retainers. Day and night his castle was open all the year round to comers of every degree. He made it a rule to regale even the poorest beggar with wine and hippocrass. Every day an ox was roasted whole in his spacious kitchens, besides sheep, pigs, and poultry sufficient to feed five hundred persons. He was equally magnificent in his devotions. His private chapel at Champtocé was the most beautiful in France, and far surpassed any of those in the richly-endowed cathedrals of Notre Dame in Paris, of Amiens, of Beauvais, or of Rouen. It was hung with cloth-of-gold and rich velvet. All the chandeliers were of pure gold curiously inlaid with silver. The great crucifix over the altar was of solid silver, and the chalices and incense-burners were of pure gold. He had besides a fine organ, which he caused to be carried from one castle to another on the shoulders of six men, whenever he changed his residence. He kept up a choir of twenty-five young children of both sexes, who were instructed in singing by the first musicians of the day. The master of his chapel he called a bishop, who had under him his deans, arch-deacons, and vicars, each receiving great salaries; the bishop four hundred crowns a year, and the rest in proportion.

He also maintained a whole troop of players, including ten dancing girls and as many ballad-singers, besides morris-dancers, jugglers, and mountebanks of every description. The theatre on which they performed was fitted up without any regard to expense, and they played mysteries or danced the morris-dance every evening for the amusement of himself and household, and such strangers as were sharing his prodigal hospitality.

At the age of twenty-three he married Catherine, the wealthy heiress of the house of Touars, for whom he refurnished his castle at an expense of a hundred thousand crowns. His marriage was the signal for new extravagance, and he launched out more madly than ever he had done before; sending for fine singers or celebrated dancers from foreign countries to amuse him and his spouse; and instituting tilts and tournaments in his great court-yard almost every week for all the knights and nobles of the province of Brittany. The Duke of Brittany's court was not half so splendid as that of the Maréchal de Rays. His utter disregard for wealth was so well known, that he was made to pay three times its value for every thing he purchased. His castle was filled with needy parasites and panderers to his pleasures, amongst whom he lavished rewards with an unsparing hand. But the ordinary round of sensual gratification ceased at last to afford him delight; he was observed to be more abstemious in the pleasures of the table, and to neglect the beauteous dancing girls who used formerly to occupy so much of his attention. He was sometimes gloomy and reserved, and there was an unnatural wildness in his eye which gave indications of incipient madness. Still his discourse was as reasonable as ever, his urbanity to the guests that flocked from far and near to Champtocé suffered no diminution; and learned priests, when they conversed with him, thought to themselves that few of the nobles of France were so well informed as Gilles de Laval. But dark rumours spread gradually over the country; murder, and, if possible, still more atrocious deeds were hinted at; and it was remarked that many young children of both sexes suddenly disappeared, and were never afterwards heard of. One or two had been traced to the castle of Champtocé, and had never been seen to leave it; but no one dared to accuse openly so powerful a man as the Maréchal de Rays. Whenever the subject of the lost children was mentioned in his presence, he manifested the greatest astonishment at the mystery which involved their fate, and indignation against those who might be guilty of l idnapping them. Still the world was not wholly deceived; his name became as formidable to young children as that of the devouring ogre in fairy tales, and they were taught to go miles round, rather than pass under the turrets of Champtocé.

In the course of a few years, the reckless extravagance of the marshal drained him of all his funds, and he was obliged to put up some of his estates for sale. The Duke of Brittany entered into a treaty with him for the valuable seignory of Ingrande; but the heirs of Gilles implored the interference of Charles VII. to stay the sale.

Charles immediately issued an edict, which was confirmed by the provincial parliament of Brittany, forbidding him to alienate his paternal estates. Gilles had no alternative but to submit. He had nothing to support his extravagance but his allowance as a marshal of France, which did not cover the one-tenth of his expenses. A man of his habits and character could not retrench his wasteful expenditure, and live reasonably; he could not dismiss without a pang his horsemen, his jesters, his morris-dancers, his choristers, and his parasites, or confine his hospitality to those who really needed it. Notwithstanding his diminished resources, he resolved to live as he had lived before, and turn alchymist, that he might make gold out of iron, and be still the wealthiest and most magnificent among the nobles of Brittany.

In pursuance of this determination, he sent to Paris, Italy, Germany, and Spain, inviting all the adepts in the science to visit him at Champtocé. The messengers he despatched on this mission were two of his most needy and unprincipled dependants, Gilles de Sillé and Roger de Bricqueville. The latter, the obsequious panderer to his most secret and abominable pleasures, he had entrusted with the education of his motherless daughter, a child but five years of age, with permission that he might marry her at the proper time to any person he chose, or to himself if he liked it better. This man entered into the new plans of his master with great zeal, and introduced to him one Prelati, an alchymist of Padua, and a physician of Poitou, who was adicted to the same pursuits.

The marshal caused a splendid laboratory to be fitted up for them, and the three commenced the search for the philosopher's stone. They were soon afterwards joined by another pretended philosopher, named Anthony Palermo, who aided in their operations for upwards of a year. They all fared sumptuously at the marshal's expense, draining him of the ready money he possessed, and leading him on from day to day with the hope that they would succeed in the object of their search. From time to time new aspirants from the remotest parts of Europe arrived at his castle, and for months he had upwards of twenty alchymists at work, trying to transmute copper into gold, and wasting the gold which was still his own in drugs and elixirs.

But the Lord of Rays was not a man to abide patiently their lingering processes. Pleased with their comfortable quarters, they jogged on from day to day, and would have done so for years, had they been permitted. But he suddenly dismissed them all, with the exception of the Italian Prelati, and the physician of Poitou. These he retained to aid him to discover the secret of the philosopher's stone by a bolder method. The Poitousan had persuaded him that the devil was the great depository of that and all other secrets, and that he would raise him before Gilles, who might enter into any contract he pleased with him. Gilles expressed his readiness, and promised to give the devil any thing but his soul, or do any deed that the arch-enemy might impose upon him. Attended solely by the physician, he proceeded at midnight to a wild-looking place in a neighbouring forest; the physician drew a magic circle around them on the sward, and muttered for half an hour an invocation to the evil spirit to arise at his bidding, and disclose the secrets of alchymy. Gilles looked on with intense interest, and expected every moment to see the earth open, and deliver to his gaze the great enemy of mankind. At last the eyes of the physician became fixed, his hair stood on end, and he spoke, as if addressing the fiend. But Gilles saw nothing except his companion. At last the physician fell down on the sward as if insensible. Gilles looked calmly on to see the end. After a few minutes the physician arose, and asked him if he had not seen how angry the devil looked? Gilles replied that he had seen nothing; upon which his companion informed him that Beelzebub had appeared in the form of a wild leopard, growled at him savagely, and said nothing; and that the reason why the marshal had neither seen nor heard him was, that he hesitated in his own mind as to devoting himself entirely to the service. De Rays owned that he had indeed misgivings, and inquired what was to be done to make the devil speak out, and unfold his secret? The physician replied, that some person must go to Spain and Africa to collect certain herbs which only grew in those countries, and offered to go himself, if De Rays would provide the necessary funds. De Rays at once consented; and the physician set out on the following day with all the gold that his dupe could spare him. The marshal never saw his face again.

But the eager Lord of Champtocé could not rest. Gold was necessary for his pleasures; and unless by supernatural aid, he had no means of procuring any further supplies. The physician was hardly twenty leagues on his journey, before Gilles resolved to make another effort to force the devil to divulge the art of gold-making. He went out alone for that purpose; but all his conjurations were of no effect. Beelzebub was obstinate, and would not appear. Determined to conquer him if he could, he unbosomed himself to the Italian alchymist, Prelati. The latter offered to undertake the business, upon condition that De Rays did not interfere in the conjurations, and consented besides to furnish him with all the charms and talismans that might be required. He was further to open a vein in his arm, and sign with his blood a contract that "he would work the devil's will in all things," and offer up to him a sacrifice of the heart, lungs, hands, eyes, and blood of a young child. The grasping monomaniac made no hesitation, but agreed at once to the disgusting terms proposed to him. On the following night, Prelati went out alone, and after having been absent for three or four hours, returned to Gilles, who sat anxiously awaiting him. Prelati then informed him that he had seen the devil in the shape of a handsome youth of twenty. He further said, that the devil desired to be called *Barron* in all future invocations; and had shewn him a great number of ingots of pure gold, buried under a large oak in the neighbouring forest, all of which, and as many more as he desired, should become the property of the Maréchal de Rays if he remained firm, and broke no condition of the contract. Prelati further shewed him a small casket of black dust, which would turn iron into gold; but as the process was very troublesome, he advised that they should be contented with the ingots they found under the oak-tree, and which would more than supply all the wants that the most extravagant imagination could desire. They were not, however, to attempt to look for the gold till a period of seven times seven weeks, or they would find nothing but slates and stones for their pains. Gilles expressed the utmost chagrin and disappointment, and at once said that he could not wait for so long a period; if the devil were not more prompt, Prelati might tell him that the Maréchal de Rays was not to be trifled with, and would decline all further communication with him. Prelati at last persuaded him to wait seven times seven days. They then went at midnight with picks and shovels to dig up the ground under the oak, where they found nothing to reward them but a great quantity of slates, marked with hieroglyphics. It was now Prelati's turn to be angry; and he loudly swore that the devil was nothing but a liar and a cheat. The marshal joinèd cordially in the opinion, but was easily persuaded by the cunning Italian to make one more trial. He promised at the same time that he would endeavour on the following night to discover the reason why the devil had broken his word. He went out alone accordingly, and on his return informed his patron that he had seen Barron, who was exceedingly angry that they had not waited the proper time ere they looked for the ingots. Barron had also said, that the Maréchal de Rays could hardly expect any favours from him, at a time when he must know that he had been meditating a pilgrimage to the Holy Land to make atonement for his sins. The Italian had doubtless surmised this from some incautious expression of his patron, for De Rays frankly confessed that there were times when, sick of the world and all its pomps and vanities, he thought of devoting himself to the service of God.

In this manner the Italian lured on from month to month his credulous and guilty patron, extracting from him all the valuables he possessed, and only waiting a favourable opportunity to decamp with his plunder. But the day of retribution was at hand for both. Young girls and boys continued to disappear in the most mysterious manner; and the rumours against the owner of Champtocé grew so loud and distinct, that the Church was compelled to interfere. Representations were made by the Bishop of Nantes to the Duke of Brittany, that it would be a public scandal if the accusations against the Maréchal de Rays were not inquired into. He was arrested accordingly in his own castle, along with his accomplice Prelati, and thrown into a dungeon at Nantes to await his trial.

The judges appointed to try him were the Bishop of Nantes Chancellor of Brittany, the Vicar of the Inquisition in France, and the celebrated Pierre l'Hôpital, the President of the provincial Parliament. The offences laid to his charge were, sorcery, sodomy, and murder. Gilles, on the first day of his trial, conducted himself with the utmost insolence. He braved the judges on the judgment-seat, calling them simoniacs and persons of impure life, and said he would rather be hanged by the neck like a dog without trial, than plead either guilty or not guilty before such contemptible miscreants. But his confidence forsook him as the trial proceeded, and he was found guilty on the clearest evidence of all the crimes laid to his charge. It was proved that he took insane pleasure in stabbing the victims of his lust and in observing the quivering of their flesh, and the fading lustre of their eyes as they expired. The confession of Prelati first made the judges acquainted with this horrid madness, and Gilles himself confirmed it before his death. Nearly a hundred children of the villagers around his two castles of Champtocé and Machecoue, had been missed within three years, the greater part, if not all, of whom were immolated to the lust or the cupidity of this monster. He imagined that he thus made the devil his friend, and that his recompense would be the secret of the philosopher's stone.

Gilles and Prelati were both condemned to be burned alive. At the place of execution they assumed the air of penitence and religion. Gilles tenderly embraced Prelati, saying, " *Farewell, friend Francis ! In this world we shall never meet again ; but let us place our hopes in God ; we shall see each other in Paradise.*" Out of consideration for his high rank and connexions, the punishment of the marshal was so far mitigated, that he was not burned alive like Prelati. He was first strangled, and then thrown into the flames : his body, when half consumed, was given over to his relatives for interment, while that of the Italian was burned to ashes, and then scattered to the winds.*

JACQUES CŒUR.

This remarkable pretender to the secret of the philosopher's stone was contemporary with the last mentioned. He was a great personage at the court of Charles VII., and in the events of his reign played a prominent part. From a very humble origin he rose to the highest honours of the state, and amassed enormous wealth by peculation and plunder of the country which he should have served. It was to hide his delinquencies in this respect, and to divert attention from the real source of his riches, that he boasted of having discovered the art of transmuting the inferior metals into gold and silver.

His father was a goldsmith in the city of Bourges ; but so reduced in circumstances towards the latter years of his life, that he was unable to pay the necessary fees to procure his son's admission into the guild. Young Jacques became, however, a workman in the Royal Mint of Bourges, in 1428, and behaved himself so well, and shewed so much knowledge of metallurgy, that he attained rapid promotion in that establishment. He had also the good fortune to make the acquaintance of the fair Agnes Sorel, by whom he was patronised and much esteemed. Jacques had now three things in his favour—ability, perseverance, and the countenance of the king's mistress. Many a man succeeds with but one of these to help him forward ; and it would have been strange indeed if Jacques Cœur, who had them all, should have languished in obscurity. While still a young man, he was made master of the mint, in which he had been a journeyman, and installed at the same time into the vacant office of grand treasurer of the royal household.

He possessed an extensive knowledge of finance, and turned it wonderfully to his own advantage, as soon as he became entrusted with extensive funds. He speculated in articles of the first necessity, and made himself popular by buying up grain, honey, wines, and other produce, till there was a scarcity, when he sold it again at enormous profit. Strong in the royal favour, he did not hesitate to oppress the poor by continual acts of forestalling and monopoly. As there is no enemy so bitter as the estranged friend, so, of all the tyrants and tramplers upon the poor, there is none so fierce and reckless as the upstart that sprang from their ranks. The offensive pride of Jacques Cœur to his inferiors was the theme of indignant reproach

---

For full details of this extraordinary trial, see Lobineau's *Nouvelle Histoire de Bretagne*, and D'Argentré's work on the same subject. The character and life of Gilles de Rays are believed to have suggested the famous Blue Beard of the nursery tale.

in his own city, and his cringing humility to those above him was as much an object of contempt to the aristocrats into whose society he thrust himself. But Jacques did not care for the former, and to the latter he was blind. He continued his career till he became the richest man in France, and so useful to the king that no important enterprise was set on foot until he had been consulted. He was sent, in 1446, on an embassy to Genoa, and in the following year to Pope Nicholas V. In both these missions he acquitted himself to the satisfaction of his sovereign, and was rewarded with a lucrative appointment, in addition to those which he already held.

In the year 1449, the English in Normandy, deprived of their great general, the Duke of Bedford, broke the truce with the French king, and took possession of a small town belonging to the Duke of Brittany. This was the signal for the recommencement of a war, in which the French regained possession of nearly the whole province. The money for this war was advanced, for the most part, by Jacques Cœur. When Rouen yielded to the French, and Charles made his triumphal entry into that city, accompanied by Dunois and his most famous generals, Jacques was among the most brilliant of his *cortége*. His chariot and horses vied with those of the king in the magnificence of their trappings ; and his enemies said of him that he publicly boasted that he alone had driven out the English, and that the valour of the troops would have been nothing without his gold.

Dunois appears, also, to have been partly of the same opinion Without disparaging the courage of the army, he acknowledged the utility of the able financier, by whose means they had been fed and paid, and constantly afforded him his powerful protection.

When peace returned, Jacques again devoted himself to commerce, and fitted up several galleys to trade with the Genoese. He also bought large estates in various parts of France ; the chief of which were the baronies of St. Fargeau, Meneton, Salone, Maubranche, Meaune, St. Gerant de Vaux, and St. Aon de Boissy ; the earldoms or counties of La Palisse, Champignelle, Beaumont, and Villeneuve la Genêt, and the marquisate of Toucy. He also procured for his son, Jean Cœur, who had chosen the Church for his profession, a post no less distinguished than that of Archbishop of Bourges.

Every body said that so much wealth could not have been honestly acquired ; and both rich and poor longed for the day that should humble the pride of the man, whom the one class regarded as an upstart and the other as an oppressor. Jacques was somewhat alarmed at the rumours that were afloat respecting him, and of dark hints that he had debased the coin of the realm and forged the king's seal to an important document, by which he had defrauded the state of very considerable sums. To silence these rumours, he invited many alchymists from foreign countries to reside with him, and circulated a counter rumour, that he had discovered the secret of the philosopher's stone. He also built a magnificent house in his native city, over the entrance of which he caused to be sculptured the emblems of that science. Some time afterwards he built another, no less splendid, at Montpellier, which he inscribed in a similar manner. He also wrote a treatise upon the hermetic philosophy, in which he pretended that he knew the secret of transmuting metals.

But all these attempts to disguise his numerous acts of peculation proved unavailing ; and he was arrested in 1452, and brought to trial on several charges. Upon one only, which the malice of his enemies

HOUSE OF JACQUES CŒUR, BOURGES.

invented to ruin him, was he acquitted; which was, that he had been accessory to the death, by poison, of his kind patroness, Agnes Sorel. Upon the others he was found guilty, and sentenced to be banished the kingdom, and to pay the enormous fine of four hundred thousand crowns. It was proved that he had forged the king's seal ; that in his capacity of master of the mint of Bourges, he had debased, to a very great extent, the gold and silver coin of the realm ; and that he had not hesitated to supply the Turks with arms and money to enable them to carry on war against their Christian neighbours, for which service he had received the most munificent recompenses. Charles VII. was deeply grieved at his condemnation, and believed to the last that he was innocent. By his means the fine was reduced within a sum which Jacques Cœur could pay. After remaining for some time in prison, he was liberated, and left France with a large sum of money, part of which, it was alleged, was secretly paid him by Charles out of the produce of his confiscated estates. He retired to Cyprus, where he died about 1460, the richest and most conspicuous personage of the island.

The writers upon alchymy all claim Jacques Cœur as a member of their fraternity, and treat as false and libellous the more rational explanation of his wealth which the records of his trial afford. Pierre Borel, in his *Antiquités Gauloises*, maintains the opinion that Jacques was an honest man, and that he made his gold out of lead and copper by means of the philosopher's stone. The alchymic adepts in general were of the same opinion ; but they found it difficult to persuade even his contemporaries of the fact. Posterity is still less likely to believe it.

INFERIOR ADEPTS OF THE FOURTEENTH AND FIFTEENTH CENTURIES.

Many other pretenders to the secrets of the philosopher's stone appeared in every country in Europe, during the fourteenth and fifteenth centuries. The possibility of transmutation was so generally admitted, that every chemist was more or less an alchymist. Germany, Holland, Italy, Spain, Poland, France, and England produced thousands of obscure adepts, who supported themselves, in the pursuit of their chimera, by the more profitable resources of astrology and divination. The monarchs of Europe were no less persuaded than their subjects of the possibility of discovering the philosopher's stone. Henry VI. and Edward IV of England encouraged alchymy. In Germany, the Emperors Maximilian, Rodolph, and Frederick II. devoted much of their attention to it ; and every inferior potentate within their dominions imitated their example. It was a common practice in Germany, among the nobles and petty sovereigns, to invite an alchymist to take up his residence among them, that they might confine him in a dungeon till he made gold enough to pay millions for his ransom. Many poor wretches suffered perpetual imprisonment in consequence. A similar fate appears to have been intended by Edward II. for Raymond Lulli, who, upon the pretence that he was thereby honoured, was accommodated with apartments in the Tower of London. He found out in time the trick that was about to be played him, and managed to make his escape ; some of his biographers say, by jumping into the Thames, and swimming to a vessel that lay waiting to receive him. In the sixteenth century, the same system was pursued, as will be shewn more fully in the life of Seton the Cosmopolite. The following is a catalogue of the chief authors upon alchymy who flourished during this epoch, and whose lives and adventures are either unknown or are unworthy of more detailed notice. John Dowston, an Englishman, lived in 1315, and wrote two treatises on the philosopher's stone. Richard, or, as some call him Robert, also an Englishman, lived in 1330, and wrote a work entitled *Correctorium Alchymiæ*, which was much esteemed till the time of Paracelsus. In the same year lived Peter of Lombardy, who wrote what he called a *Complete Treatise upon the Hermetic Science*, an abridgment of which was afterwards published by Lacini, a monk of Calabria. In 1330 the most famous alchymist of Paris was one Odomare, whose work, *De Practica Magistri*, was for a long time a hand-book among the brethren of the science. John de Rupecissa, a French monk of the order of St. Francis, flourished in 1357, and pretended to be a prophet as well as an alchymist. Some of his prophecies were so disagreeable to Pope Innocent VI., that the pontiff determined to put a stop to them, by locking up the prophet in the dungeons of the Vatican. It is generally believed that he died there, though there is no evidence of the fact. His chief works are, the *Book of Light*, the *Five Essences*, the *Heaven of Philosophers*, and his grand work, *De Confectione Lapidis*. He was not thought a shining light among the adepts. Ortholani was another pretender, of whom nothing is known, but that he exercised the arts of alchymy and astrology at Paris, shortly before the time of Nicholas Flamel. His work on the practice of alchymy was written in that city in 1358. Isaac of Holland wrote, it is supposed, about this time ; and his son also devoted himself to the science. Nothing worth repeating is known of their lives. Boerhaave speaks with commendation of many passages in their works, and Paracelsus esteemed them highly : the chief are, *De Triplici Ordine Elixiris et Lapidis Theoria*, printed at Berne, in 1608; and *Mineralia Opera, seu de Lapide Philosophico*, printed at Middleburg in 1600. They also wrote eight other works upon the same subject. Koffstky, a Pole, wrote an alchymical treatise, entitled *The Tincture of Minerals*, about the year 1488. In this list of authors a royal name must not be forgotten. Charles VI. of France, one of the most credulous princes of the day, whose court absolutely swarmed with alchymists, conjurers, astrologers, and quacks of every description, made several attempts to discover the philosopher's stone, and thought he knew so much about it, that he determined to enlighten the world with a treatise ; it is called the *Royal Work of Charles VI. of France, and the Treasure of Philosophy*.

It is said to be the original from which Nicholas Flamel took the idea of his *Désir désiré*. Lenglet du Fresnoy says it is very allegorical, and utterly incomprehensible. For a more complete list of the hermetic philosophers of the fourteenth and fifteenth centuries, the reader is referred to the third volume of Lenglet's History, already quoted.

PROGRESS OF THE INFATUATION DURING THE SIXTEENTH AND SEVEN-
TEENTH CENTURIES.—PRESENT STATE OF THE SCIENCE.

During the sixteenth and seventeenth centuries, the search for the philosopher's stone was continued by thousands of the enthusiastic and the credulous ; but a great change was introduced during this period. The eminent men who devoted themselves to the study totally changed its aspect, and referred to the possession of their wondrous stone and elixir, not only the conversion of the base into the precious metals, but the solution of all the difficulties of other sciences. They pretended that by its means man would be brought into closer communion with his Maker ; that disease and sorrow would be banished from the world ; and that "the millions of spiritual beings who walk the earth unseen" would be rendered visible, and become the friends, companions, and instructors of mankind. In the seventeenth century more especially, these poetical and fantastic doctrines excited the notice of Europe ; and from Germany, where they had been first disseminated by Rosencreutz, spread into France and England, and ran away with the sound judgment of many clever but too enthusiastic searchers for the truth. Paracelsus, Dee, and many others of less note, were captivated by the grace and beauty of the new mythology, which was arising to adorn the literature of Europe. Most of the alchymists of the sixteenth century, although ignorant of the Rosicrucians as a sect, were, in some degree, tinctured with their fanciful tenets : but before we speak more fully of those poetical visionaries, it will be necessary to resume the history of the hermetic folly, and trace the gradual change that stole over the dreams of the adepts. It will be seen that the infatuation increased rather than diminished as the world grew older.

AUGURELLO.

Among the alchymists who were born in the fifteenth, and distinguished themselves in the sixteenth century, the first in point of date is John Aurelio Augurello. He was born at Rimini in 1441, and became professor of the *belles lettres* at Venice and Trevisa. He was early convinced of the truth of the hermetic science, and used to pray to God that he might be happy enough to discover the philosopher's stone. He was continually surrounded by the paraphernalia of chemistry, and expended all his wealth in the purchase of drugs and metals. He was also a poet, but of less merit than pretensions. His *Chrysopeia*, in which he pretended to teach the art of making gold, he dedicated to Pope Leo X., in the hope that the pontiff would reward him handsomely for the compliment; but the pope was too good a judge of poetry to be pleased with the worse than mediocrity of his poem, and too good a philosopher to approve of the strange doctrines which it inculcated; he was, therefore, far from gratified at the dedication. It is said, that when Augurello applied to him for a reward, the pope, with great ceremony and much apparent kindness and cordiality, drew an empty purse from his pocket, and presented it to the alchymist, saying, that since he was able to make gold, the most appropriate present that could be made him, was a purse to put it in. This scurvy reward was all that the poor alchymist ever got either for his poetry or his alchymy. He died in a state of extreme poverty, in the eighty-third year of his age.

CORNELIUS AGRIPPA.

This alchymist has left a distinguished reputation. The most

CORNELIUS AGRIPPA.

extraordinary tales were told and believed of his powers. He could turn iron into gold by his mere word. All the spirits of the air and demons of the earth were under his command, and bound to obey him in every thing. He could raise from the dead the forms of the great men of other days, and make them appear, "in their habit as they lived," to the gaze of the curious who had courage enough to abide their presence.

He was born at Cologne in 1486, and began at an early age the study of chemistry and philosophy. By some means or other, which have never been very clearly explained, he managed to impress his contemporaries with a great idea of his wonderful attainments. At the early age of twenty, so great was his reputation as an alchymist, that the principal adepts of Paris wrote to Cologne, inviting him to settle in France, and aid them with his experience in discovering the philosopher's stone. Honours poured upon him in thick succession ; and he was highly esteemed by all the learned men of his time. Melancthon speaks of him with respect and commendation. Erasmus also bears testimony in his favour ; and the general voice of his age proclaimed him a light of literature and an ornament to philosophy. Some men, by dint of excessive egotism, manage to persuade their contemporaries that they are very great men indeed : they publish their acquirements so loudly in people's ears, and keep up their own praises so incessantly, that the world's applause is actually taken by storm. Such seems to have been the case with Agrippa. He called himself a sublime theologian, an excellent jurisconsult, an able physician, a great philosopher, and a successful alchymist. The world at last took him at his word ; and thought that a man who talked so big must have some merit to recommend him,—that it was, indeed, a great trumpet which sounded so obstreperous a blast. He was made secretary to the Emperor Maximilian, who conferred upon him the title of chevalier, and gave him the honorary command of a regiment. He afterwards became professor of Hebrew and the *belles lettres* at the University of Dôle, in France ; but quarrelling with the Franciscan monks upon some knotty points of divinity, he was obliged to quit the town. He took refuge in London, where he taught Hebrew and cast nativities, for about a year. From London he proceeded to Pavia, and gave lectures upon the writings, real or supposed, of Hermes Trismegistus ; and might have lived there in peace and honour, had he not again quarrelled with the clergy. By their means his position became so disagreeable that he was glad to accept an offer made him by the magistracy of Metz, to become their syndic and advocate-general. Here, again, his love of disputation made him enemies : the theological wiseacres of that city asserted that St. Ann had three husbands, in which opinion they were confirmed by the popular belief of the day. Agrippa needlessly ran foul of this opinion, or prejudice as he called it, and thereby lost much of his influence. Another dispute, more creditable to his character, occurred soon after, and sank him for ever in the estimation of the Metzians. Humanely taking the part of a young girl who was accused of witchcraft, his enemies asserted that he was himself a sorcerer, and raised such a storm over his head, that he was forced to fly the city. After this he became physician to Louisa de Savoy, mother of King Francis I. This lady was curious to know the future, and required her physician to cast her nativity. Agrippa replied that he would not encourage such idle curiosity. The result was, he lost her confidence, and was forthwith dismissed. If it had been through his belief in the worthlessness of astrology that he had made his answer, we might admire his honest and fearless independence; but when it is known that, at the very same time, he was in the constant habit of divination and fortune-telling, and that he was predicting splendid success, in all his undertakings, to the Constable of Bourbon, we can only wonder at his thus estranging a powerful friend through mere petulance and perversity.

He was about this time invited, both by Henry VIII. of England, and Margaret of Austria, governess of the Low Countries, to fix his residence in their dominions. He chose the service of the latter, by whose influence he was made historiographer to the Emperor Charles V. Unfortunately for Agrippa, he never had stability enough to remain long in one position, and offended his patrons by his restlessness and presumption. After the death of Margaret he was imprisoned at Brussels, on a charge of sorcery. He was released after a year; and quitting the country, experienced many vicissitudes. He died in great poverty in 1534, aged forty-eight years.

While in the service of Margaret of Austria, he resided principally at Louvain, in which city he wrote his famous work on the *Vanity and Nothingness of Human Knowledge*. He also wrote, to please his royal mistress, a treatise upon the *Superiority of the Female Sex*, which he dedicated to her in token of his gratitude for the favours she had heaped upon him. The reputation he left behind him in these provinces was any thing but favourable. A great number of the marvellous tales that are told of him relate to this period of his life. It was said, that the gold which he paid to the traders with whom he dealt, always looked remarkably bright, but invariably turned into pieces of slate and stone in the course of four and-twenty hours. Of this spurious gold he was believed to have made large quantities by the aid of the devil, who, it would appear from this, had but a very superficial knowledge of alchymy, and much less than the Maréchal de Rays gave him credit for. The Jesuit Delrio, in his book on magic and sorcery, relates a still more extraordinary story of him. One day, Agrippa left his house at Louvain, and intending to be absent for some time, gave the key of his study to his wife, with strict orders that no one should enter it during his absence. The lady herself, strange as it may appear, had no curiosity to pry into her husband's secrets, and never once thought of entering the forbidden room; but a young student, who had been accommodated with an attic in the philosopher's house, burned with a fierce desire to examine the study; hoping, perchance, that he might purloin some book or implement which would instruct him in the art of transmuting metals. The youth, being handsome, eloquent, and, above all, highly complimentary to the charms of the lady, she was persuaded without much difficulty to lend him the key, but gave him strict orders not to remove any thing. The student promised implicit obedience, and entered Agrippa's study. The first object that caught his attention was a large *grimoire*, or book of spells, which lay open on the philosopher's desk. He sat himself down immediately and began to read. At the first word he uttered, he fancied he heard a knock at the door. He listened, but all was silent. Thinking that his imagination had deceived him, he read on, when immediately a louder knock was heard, which so terrified him, that he started to his feet. He tried to say " come in," but his tongue refused its office, and he could not articulate a sound. He fixed his eyes upon the door, which, slowly opening, disclosed a stranger of majestic form, but scowling features, who demanded sternly why he was summoned? "I did not summon you," said the trembling student. "You did!" said the stranger, advancing angrily ; " and the demons are not to be invoked in vain." The student could make no reply ; and the demon, enraged that one of the uninitiated should have summoned him out of mere presumption, seized him by the throat and strangled him. When Agrippa returned, a few days afterwards, he found his house beset with devils. Some of them were sitting on the chimney-pots, kicking up their legs in the air; while others were playing at leapfrog on the very edge of the parapet. His study was so filled with them, that he found it difficult to make his way to his desk. When, at last, he had elbowed his way through them, he found his book open, and the student lying dead upon the floor. He saw immediately how the mischief had been done ; and dismissing all the inferior imps, asked the principal demon how he could have been so rash as to kill the young man. The demon replied, that he had been needlessly invoked by an insulting youth, and could do no less than kill him for his presumption. Agrippa reprimanded him severely, and ordered him immediately to reanimate the dead body, and walk about with it in the market-place for the whole of the afternoon. The demon did so ; the student revived, and putting his arm through that of his unearthly murderer, walked very lovingly with him in sight of all the people. At sunset, the body fell down again cold and lifeless as before, and was carried by the crowd to the hospital, it being the general opinion that he had expired in a fit of apoplexy. His conductor immediately disappeared. When the body was examined, marks of strangulation were found on the neck, and prints of the long claws of the demon on various parts of it. These appearances, together with a story, which soon obtained currency, that the companion of the young man had vanished in a cloud of flame and smoke, opened people's eyes to the truth. The magistrates of Louvain instituted inquiries, and the result was, that Agrippa was obliged to quit the town.

Other authors besides Delrio relate similar stories of this philosopher. The world in those days was always willing enough to believe in tales of magic and sorcery; and when, as in Agrippa's case, the alleged magician gave himself out for such, and claimed credit for the wonders he worked, it is not surprising that the age should have allowed his pretensions. It was dangerous boasting, which sometimes led to the stake or the gallows, and therefore was thought to be not without foundation. Paulus Jovius, in his *Eulogia Doctorum Virorum*, says, that the devil, in the shape of a large black dog, attended Agrippa wherever he went. Thomas Nash, in his *Adventures of Jack Wilton*, relates, that, at the request of Lord Surrey, Erasmus, and some other learned men, Agrippa called up from the grave many of the great philosophers of antiquity; among others, Tully, whom he caused to re-deliver his celebrated oration for Roscius. He also shewed Lord Surrey, when in Germany, an exact resemblance in a glass of his mistress, the fair Geraldine. She was represented on a couch weeping for the absence of her lover. Lord Surrey made a note of the exact time at which he saw this vision, and ascertained afterwards that his mistress was actually so employed at the very minute. To Thomas Lord Cromwell, Agrippa represented King Henry VIII. hunting in Windsor Park, with the principal lords of his court; and to please the Emperor Charles V. he summoned King David and King Solomon from the tomb.

Naudé, in his *Apology for the great Men who have been falsely suspected of Magic*, takes a great deal of pains to clear Agrippa from the imputations cast upon him by Delrio, Paulus Jovius, and other such ignorant and prejudiced scribblers. Such stories demanded refutation in the days of Naudé, but they may now be safely left to decay in their own absurdity. That they should have attached, however, to the memory of a man who claimed the power of making iron obey him when he told it to become gold, and who wrote such a work as that upon magic which goes by his name, is not at all surprising.

PARACELSUS.

This philosopher, called by Naudé "the zenith and rising sun of all the alchymists," was born at Einsiedeln, near Zurich, in the year 1493. His true name was Hohenheim; to which, as he himself informs us, were prefixed the baptismal names of Aureolus Theophrastus Bombastes Paracelsus. The last of these he chose for his common designation while he was yet a boy ; and rendered it, before he died, one of the most famous in the annals of his time. His father, who was a physician, educated his son for the same pursuit. The latter was an apt scholar, and made great progress. By chance the work of Isaac Hollandus fell into his hands, and from that time he became smitten with the mania of the philosopher's stone. All his thoughts henceforth were devoted to metallurgy ; and he travelled into Sweden that he might visit the mines of that country, and examine the ores while they yet lay in the bowels of the earth. He also visited Trithemius at the monastery of Spannheim, and obtained instructions from him in the science of alchymy. Continuing his travels, he proceeded through Prussia and Austria into Turkey, Egypt, and Tartary, and thence returning to Constantinople, learned, as he boasted, the art of transmutation, and became possessed of the *elixir vitæ*. He then established himself as a physician in his native

PARACELSUS.

Switzerland at Zurich, and commenced writing works upon alchymy and medicine, which immediately fixed the attention of Europe. Their great obscurity was no impediment to their fame ; for the less the author was understood, the more the demonologists, fanatics, and philosopher's-stone hunters seemed to appreciate him. His fame as a physician kept pace with that which he enjoyed as an alchymist, owing to his having effected some happy cures by means of mercury and opium,—drugs unceremoniously condemned by his professional brethren. In the year 1526, he was chosen professor of physics and natural philosophy in the University of Basle, where his lectures attracted vast numbers of students. He denounced the writings of all former physicians, as tending to mislead ; and publicly burned the works of Galen and Avicenna, as quacks and impostors. He exclaimed, in presence of the admiring and half-bewildered crowd who assembled to witness the ceremony, that there was more knowledge in his shoe-strings than in the writings of these physicians. Continuing in the same strain, he said, all the Universities in the world were full of ignorant quacks ; but that he, Paracelsus, overflowed with wisdom " You will all follow my new system," said he, with furious gesticulations, " Avicenna, Galen, Rhazis, Montagnana, Memé,—you will all follow me, ye professors of Paris, Montpellier, Germany, Cologne, and Vienna ! and all ye that dwell on the Rhine and the Danube,—ye that inhabit the isles of the sea ; and ye also, Italians, Dalmatians, Athenians, Arabians, Jews,—ye will all follow my doctrines, for I am the monarch of medicine!"

But he did not long enjoy the esteem of the good people of Basle. It is said that he indulged in wine so freely, as not unfrequently to be seen in the streets in a state of intoxication. This was ruinous for a physician, and his good fame decreased rapidly. His ill fame increased in still greater proportion, especially when he assumed the airs of a sorcerer. He boasted of the legions of spirits at his command ; and of one especially, which he kept imprisoned in the hilt of his sword. Wetterus, who lived twenty-seven months in his service, relates that he often threatened to invoke a whole army of demons, and shew him the great authority which he could exercise over them. He let it be believed that the spirit in his sword had custody of the elixir of life, by means of which he could make any one live to be as old as the antediluvians. He also boasted that he had a spirit at his command, called "Azoth," whom he kept imprisoned in a jewel; and in many of the old portraits he is represented with a jewel, inscribed with the word " Azoth," in his hand.

If a sober prophet has little honour in his own country, a drunken one has still less. Paracelsus found it at last convenient to quit Basle, and establish himself at Strasbourg. The immediate cause of this change of residence was as follows. A citizen lay at the point of death, and was given over by all the physicians of the town. As a last resource Paracelsus was called in, to whom the sick man promised a magnificent recompense, if, by his means, he were cured. Paracelsus gave him two small pills, which the man took, and rapidly recovered. When he was quite well, Paracelsus sent for his fee ; but the citizen had no great opinion of the value of a cure which had been so speedily effected. He had no notion of paying a handful of gold for two pills, although they had saved his life, and he refused to pay more than the usual fee for a single visit. Paracelsus brought an action against him and lost it. This result so exasperated him, that he left Basle in high dudgeon. He resumed his wandering life and travelled in Germany and Hungary, supporting himself as he went on the credulity and infatuation of all classes of society. He cast nativities— told fortunes —aided those who had money to throw away upon the experiment, to find the philosopher's stone—prescribed remedies for cows and pigs, and aided in the recovery of stolen goods. After residing successively at Nuremburg, Augsburg, Vienna, and Mindelheim, he retired in the year 1541 to Saltzbourg, and died in a state of abject poverty in the hospital of that town.

If this strange charlatan found hundreds of admirers during his life, he found thousands after his death. A sect of Paracelsists sprang up in France and Germany, to perpetuate the extravagant doctrines of their founder upon all the sciences, and upon alchymy in particular. The chief leaders were Bodenstein and Dorneus. The following is a summary of his doctrine, founded upon the supposed existence of the philosopher's stone ; it is worth preserving from its very absurdity, and is altogether unparalleled in the history of philosophy. First of all, he maintained that the contemplation of the perfection of the Deity sufficed to procure all wisdom and knowledge ; that the Bible was the key to the theory of all diseases, and that it was necessary to search into the Apocalypse to know the signification of magic medicine. The man who blindly obeyed the will of God, and who succeeded in identifying himself with the celestial intelligences, possessed the philosopher's stone—he could cure all diseases, and prolong life to as many centuries as he pleased ; it being by the very same means that Adam and the antediluvian patriarchs prolonged theirs. Life was an emanation from the stars—the sun governed the heart, and the moon the brain. Jupiter governed the liver, Saturn the gall, Mercury the lungs, Mars the bile, and Venus the loins. In the stomach of every human being there dwelt a demon, or intelligence, that was a sort of alchymist in his way, and mixed, in their due proportions, in his crucible, the various aliments that were sent into that grand laboratory, the belly.* He was proud of the title of magician, and boasted that he kept up a regular correspondence with Galen from hell ; and that he often summoned Avicenna from the same regions to dispute with him on the false notions he had promulgated respecting alchymy, and especially regarding potable gold and the elixir of life. He imagined that gold could cure ossification of the heart, and, in fact, all diseases, if it were gold which had been transmuted from an inferior metal by means of the philosopher's stone, and if it were applied under certain conjunctions of the planets. The mere list of the works in which he advances these frantic imaginings, which he called a doctrine, would occupy several pages.

George Agricola.

This alchymist was born in the province of Misnia, in 1494. His real name was *Bauer*, meaning a husbandman, which, in accordance with the common fashion of his age, he latinised into Agricola. From his early youth, he delighted in the visions of the hermetic science. Ere he was sixteen, he longed for the great elixir which was to make him live for seven hundred years, and for the stone which

* See the article "Paracelsus," by the learned Renaudin, in the *Biographie Universelle*.

was to procure him wealth to cheer him in his multiplicity of days. He published a small treatise upon the subject at Cologne, in 1531, which obtained him the patronage of the celebrated Maurice duke of Saxony. After practising for some years as a physician at Joachimsthal, in Bohemia, he was employed by Maurice as superintendent of the silver mines of Chemnitz, he led a happy life among the miners, making various experiments in alchymy while deep in the bowels of the earth. He acquired a great knowledge of metals, and gradually got rid of his extravagant notions about the philosopher's stone. The miners had no faith in alchymy ; and they converted him to their way of thinking, not only in that but in other respects. From their legends, he became firmly convinced that the bowels of the earth were inhabited by good and evil spirits, and that firedamp and other explosions sprang from no other causes than the mischievous propensities of the latter. He died in the year 1555, leaving behind him the reputation of a very able and intelligent man.

DENIS ZACHAIRE.

Autobiography, written by a wise man who was once a fool, is not only the most instructive, but the most delightful of reading. Denis Zachaire, an alchymist of the sixteenth century, has performed this task, and left a record of his folly and infatuation in pursuit of the philosopher's stone, which well repays perusal. He was born in the year 1510, of an ancient family in Guienne, and was early sent to the university of Bordeaux, under the care of a tutor to direct his studies. Unfortunately his tutor was a searcher for the grand elixir, and soon rendered his pupil as mad as himself upon the subject. With this introduction, we will allow Denis Zachaire to speak for himself, and continue his narrative in his own words : " I received from home," says he, "the sum of two hundred crowns for the expenses of myself and master ; but before the end of the year, all our money went away in the smoke of our furnaces. My master, at the same time, died of a fever, brought on by the parching heat of our laboratory, from which he seldom or never stirred, and which was scarcely less hot than the arsenal of Venice. His death was the more unfortunate for me, as my parents took the opportunity of reducing my allowance, and sending me only sufficient for my board and lodging, instead of the sum I required to continue my operations in alchymy.

" To meet this difficulty and get out of leading-strings, I returned home at the age of twenty-five, and mortgaged part of my property for four hundred crowns. This sum was necessary to perform an operation of the science, which had been communicated to me by an

Italian at Toulouse, and who, as he said, had proved its efficacy. I retained this man in my service, that we might see the end of the experiment. I then, by means of strong distillations, tried to calcinate gold and silver; but all my labour was in vain. The weight of the gold I drew out of my furnace was diminished by one-half since I put it in, and my four hundred crowns were very soon reduced to two hundred and thirty. I gave twenty of these to my Italian, in order that he might travel to Milan, where the author of the receipt resided, and ask him the explanation of some passages which we thought obscure. I remained at Toulouse all the winter, in the hope of his return; but I might have remained there till this day if I had waited for him, for I never saw his face again.

"In the succeeding summer there was a great plague, which forced me to quit the town. I did not, however, lose sight of my work. I went to Cahors, where I remained six months, and made the acquaintance of an old man, who was commonly known to the people as 'the Philosopher;' a name which, in country places, is often bestowed upon people whose only merit is, that they are less ignorant than their neighbours. I shewed him my collection of alchymical receipts, and asked his opinion upon them. He picked out ten or twelve of them, merely saying that they were better than the others. When the plague ceased, I returned to Toulouse, and recommenced my experiments in search of the stone. I worked to such effect that my four hundred crowns were reduced to one hundred and seventy.

"That I might continue my work on a safer method, I made acquaintance, in 1537, with a certain abbé who resided in the neighbourhood. He was smitten with the same mania as myself, and told me that one of his friends, who had followed to Rome in the retinue of the Cardinal d'Armagnac, had sent him from that city a new receipt which could not fail to transmute iron and copper, but which would cost two hundred crowns. I provided half this money, and the abbé the rest; and we began to operate at our joint expense. As we required spirits of wine for our experiment, I bought a tun of excellent *vin de Gaillac.* I extracted the spirit, and rectified it several times. We took a quantity of this, into which we put four marks of silver and one of gold that had been undergoing the process of calcination for a month. We put this mixture cleverly into a sort of horn-shaped vessel, with another to serve as a retort; and placed the whole apparatus upon our furnace to produce congelation. This experiment lasted a year; but, not to remain idle, we amused ourselves with many other less important operations. We drew quite as much profit from these as from our great work.

"The whole of the year 1537 passed over without producing any change whatever; in fact we might have waited till doomsday for the congelation of our spirits of wine. However, we made a projection with it upon some heated quicksilver; but all was in vain. Judge of our chagrin, especially of that of the abbé, who had already boasted to all the monks of his monastery, that they had only to bring the large pump which stood in a corner of the cloister, and he would convert it into gold : but this ill luck did not prevent us from persevering. I once more mortgaged my paternal lands for four hundred crowns, the whole of which I determined to devote to a renewal of my search for the great secret. The abbé contributed the same sum; and with these eight hundred crowns I proceeded to Paris, a city more abounding with alchymists than any other in the world, resolved never to leave it until I had either found the philosopher's stone or spent all my money. This journey gave the greatest offence to all my relations and friends, who, imagining that I was fitted to be a great lawyer, were anxious that I should establish myself in that profession. For the sake of quietness, I pretended, at last, that such was my object.

"After travelling for fifteen days, I arrived in Paris on the 9th of January 1539. I remained for a month almost unknown; but I had no sooner begun to frequent the amateurs of the science, and visited the shops of the furnace-makers, than I had the acquaintance of more than a hundred operative alchymists, each of whom had a different theory and a different mode of working. Some of them preferred cementation; others sought the universal alkahest or dissolvent; and some of them boasted the great efficacy of the essence of emery. Some of them endeavoured to extract mercury from other metals, to fix it afterwards; and, in order that each of us should be thoroughly acquainted with the proceedings of the others, we agreed to meet somewhere every night and report progress. We met sometimes at the house of one, and sometimes in the garret of another; not only on week-days, but on Sundays and the great festivals of the Church. 'Ah!' one used to say, 'if I had the means of recommencing this experiment, I should do something.' 'Yes,' said another, 'if my crucible had not cracked, I should have succeeded before now;' while a third exclaimed, with a sigh, 'If I had but had a round copper vessel of sufficient strength, I would have fixed mercury with silver.' There was not one among them who had not some excuse for his failure; but I was deaf to all their speeches. I did not want to part with my money to any of them, remembering how often I had been the dupe of such promises.

"A Greek at last presented himself; and with him I worked a long time uselessly upon nails made of cinnabar or vermilion. I was also acquainted with a foreign gentleman newly arrived in Paris, and often accompanied him to the shops of the goldsmiths to sell pieces of gold and silver, the produce, as he said, of his experiments. I stuck closely to him for a long time, in the hope that he would impart his secret. He refused for a long time, but acceded at last on my earnest entreaty, and I found that it was nothing more than an ingenious trick. I did not fail to inform my friend the abbé, whom I had left at Toulouse, of all my adventures; and sent him, among other matters, a relation of the trick by which this gentleman pretended to turn lead into gold. The abbé still imagined that I should succeed at last, and advised me to remain another year in Paris, where I had made so good a beginning. I remained there three years; but, notwithstanding all my efforts, I had no more success than I had had elsewhere.

"I had just got to the end of my money, when I received a letter from the abbé, telling me to leave every thing, and join him immediately at Toulouse. I went accordingly, and found that he had received letters from the king of Navarre (grandfather of Henry IV.). This prince was a great lover of philosophy, full of curiosity, and had written to the abbé that I should visit him at Pau; and that he would give me three or four thousand crowns if I would communicate the secret I had learned from the foreign gentleman. The abbé's ears were so tickled with the four thousand crowns, that he let me have no peace night or day until he had fairly seen me on the road to Pau. I arrived at that place in the month of May 1542. I worked away, and succeeded, according to the receipt I had obtained. When I had finished to the satisfaction of the king, he gave me the reward that I expected. Although he was willing enough to do me further service, he was dissuaded from it by the lords of his court; even by many of those who had been most anxious that I should come. He sent me then about my business, with many thanks; saying, that if there was any thing in his kingdom which he could give me—such as the produce of confiscations or the like—he should be most happy. I thought I might stay long enough for these prospective confiscations, and never get them at last; and I therefore determined to go back to my friend the abbé.

"I learned that, on the road between Pau and Toulouse, there resided a monk who was very skilful in all matters of natural philosophy. On my return, I paid him a visit. He pitied me very much, and advised me, with much warmth and kindness of expression, not to amuse myself any longer with such experiments as these, which were all false and sophistical; but that I should read the good books of the old philosophers, where I might not only find the true matter of the science of alchymy, but learn also the exact order of operations which ought to be followed. I very much approved of this wise advice; but before I acted upon it, I went back to my abbé of Toulouse, to give him an account of the eight hundred crowns which we had had in common, and, at the same time, share with him such reward as I had received from the king of Navarre. If he was little satisfied with the relation of my adventures since our first separation, he appeared still less satisfied when I told him I had formed a resolution to renounce the search for the philosopher's stone. The reason was that he thought me a good artist. Of our eight hundred crowns, there remained but one hundred and seventy-six. When I quitted the abbé, I went to my own house with the intention of remaining there till I had read all the old philosophers, and of then proceeding to Paris.

" I arrived in Paris on the day after All Saints, of the year 1546, and devoted another year to the assiduous study of great authors. Among others, the *Turba Philosophorum* of the Good Trevisan, the *Remonstrance of Nature to the Wandering Alchymist*, by Jean de Meung, and several others of the best books; but, as I had no right principles, I did not well know what course to follow.

" At last I left my solitude, not to see my former acquaintances, the adepts and operators, but to frequent the society of true philosophers. Among them I fell into still greater uncertainties; being, in fact, completely bewildered by the variety of operations which they shewed me. Spurred on, nevertheless, by a sort of frenzy or inspiration, I threw myself into the works of Raymond Lulli and of Arnold de Villeneuve. The reading of these, and the reflections I made upon them, occupied me for another year, when I finally determined on the course I should adopt. I was obliged to wait, however, until I had mortgaged another very considerable portion of my patrimony. This business was not settled until the beginning of Lent 1549, when I commenced my operations. I laid in a stock of all that was necessary, and began to work the day after Easter. It was not, however, without some disquietude and opposition from my friends who came about me; one asking me what I was going to do, and whether I had not already spent money enough upon such follies? Another assured me that, if I bought so much charcoal, I should strengthen the suspicion already existing, that I was a coiner of base money. Another advised me to purchase some place in the magistracy, as I was already a Doctor of Laws. My relations spoke in terms still more annoying to me, and even threatened that, if I continued to make such a fool of myself, they would send a posse of police-officers into my house, and break all my furnaces and crucibles into atoms. I was wearied almost to death by this continued persecution; but I found comfort in my work and in the progress of my experiment, to which I was very attentive, and which went on bravely from day to day. About this time, there was a dreadful plague in Paris, which interrupted all intercourse between man and man, and left me as much to myself as I could desire. I soon had the satisfaction to remark the progress and succession of the three colours which, according to the philosophers, always prognosticate the approaching perfection of the work. I observed them distinctly, one after the other; and next day, being Easter Sunday, 1550, I made the great trial. Some common quicksilver, which I put into a small crucible on the fire, was, in less than an hour, converted into very good gold. You may judge how great was my joy, but I took care not to boast of it. I returned thanks to God for the favour he had shewn me, and prayed that I might only be permitted to make such use of it as would redound to his glory.

"On the following day, I went towards Toulouse to find the abbé, in accordance with a mutual promise, that we should communicate our discoveries to each other. On my way, I called in to see the sage monk who had assisted me with his counsels; but I had the sorrow to learn that they were both dead. After this, I would not return to my own home, but retired to another place, to await one of my relations whom I had left in charge of my estate. I gave him orders to sell all that belonged to me, as well movable as immovable — to pay my debts with the proceeds, and divide all the rest among those in any way related to me who might stand in need of it, in order that they might enjoy some share of the good fortune which had befallen me. There was a great deal of talk in the neighbourhood about my precipitate retreat; the wisest of my acquaintance imagining that, broken down and ruined by my mad expenses, I sold my little remaining property, that I might go and hide my shame in distant countries.

"My relative already spoken of rejoined me on the 1st of July, after having performed all the business I had entrusted him with. We took our departure together, to seek a land of liberty. We first retired to Lausanne, in Switzerland, when, after remaining there for some time, we resolved to pass the remainder of our days in some of the most celebrated cities of Germany, living quietly and without splendour."

Thus ends the story of Denis Zachaire, as written by himself. He has not been so candid at its conclusion as at its commencement, and has left the world in doubt as to his real motives for pretending that he had discovered the philosopher's stone. It seems probable that the sentence he puts into the mouths of his wisest acquaintances was the true reason of his retreat; that he was, in fact, reduced to poverty, and hid his shame in foreign countries. Nothing further is known of his life, and his real name has never yet been discovered. He wrote a work on alchymy, entitled *The true Natural Philosophy of Metals.*

DR. DEE AND EDWARD KELLY.

John Dee and Edward Kelly claim to be mentioned together, having been so long associated in the same pursuits, and undergone so many strange vicissitudes in each other's society. Dee was altogether a wonderful man, and had he lived in an age when folly and superstition were less rife, he would, with the same powers which he enjoyed, have left behind him a bright and enduring reputation. He

DR. DEE.

was born in London in the year 1527, and very early manifested a love for study. At the age of fifteen he was sent to Cambridge, and delighted so much in his books, that he passed regularly eighteen hours every day among them. Of the other six, he devoted four to sleep and two for refreshment. Such intense application did not injure his health, and could not fail to make him one of the first scholars of his time. Unfortunately, however, he quitted the mathematics and the pursuits of true philosophy, to indulge in the unprofitable reveries of the occult sciences. He studied alchymy, astrology, and magic, and thereby rendered himself obnoxious to the authorities at Cambridge. To avoid persecution, he was at last obliged to retire to the university of Louvain; the rumours of sorcery that were current respecting him rendering his longer stay in England not altogether without danger. He found at Louvain many kindred spirits who had known Cornelius Agrippa while he resided among them, and by whom he was constantly entertained with the wondrous deeds of that great master of the hermetic mysteries. From their conversation he received much encouragement to continue the search for the philosopher's stone, which soon began to occupy nearly all his thoughts.

He did not long remain on the Continent, but returned to England in 1551, being at that time in the twenty-fourth year of his age. By the influence of his friend Sir John Cheek, he was kindly received at the court of King Edward VI., and rewarded (it is difficult to say for what) with a pension of one hundred crowns. He continued for several years to practise in London as an astrologer; casting nativities, telling fortunes, and pointing out lucky and unlucky days.

During the reign of Queen Mary he got into trouble, being suspected of heresy, and charged with attempting Mary's life by means of enchantments. He was tried for the latter offence, and acquitted; but was retained in prison on the former charge, and left to the tender mercies of Bishop Bonner. He had a very narrow escape from being burned in Smithfield, but he somehow or other contrived to persuade that fierce bigot that his orthodoxy was unimpeachable, and was set at liberty in 1555.

On the accession of Elizabeth, a brighter day dawned upon him. During her retirement at Woodstock, her servants appear to have consulted him as to the time of Mary's death, which circumstance no doubt first gave rise to the serious charge for which he was brought to trial. They now came to consult him more openly as to the fortunes of their mistress; and Robert Dudley, the celebrated Earl of Leicester, was sent by command of the Queen herself to know the most auspicious day for her coronation. So great was the favour he enjoyed, that, some years afterwards, Elizabeth condescended to pay him a visit at his house in Mortlake, to view his museum of curiosities, and when he was ill, sent her own physician to attend upon him.

Astrology was the means whereby he lived, and he continued to practise it with great assiduity; but his heart was in alchymy. The philosopher's stone and the elixir of life haunted his daily thoughts and his nightly dreams. The Talmudic mysteries, which he had also deeply studied, impressed him with the belief, that he might hold converse with spirits and angels, and learn from them all the mysteries of the universe. Holding the same idea as the then obscure sect of the Rosicrucians, some of whom he had perhaps encountered in his travels in Germany, he imagined that, by means of the philosopher's stone, he could summon these kindly spirits at his will. By dint of continually brooding upon the subject, his imagination became so diseased, that he at last persuaded himself that an angel appeared to him, and promised to be his friend and companion as long as he lived. He relates that, one day, in November 1582, while he was engaged in fervent prayer, the window of his museum looking towards the west suddenly glowed with a dazzling light, in the midst of which, in all his glory, stood the great angel Uriel. Awe and wonder rendered him speechless; but the angel smiling graciously upon him, gave him a crystal, of a convex form, and told him that whenever he wished to hold converse with the beings of another sphere, he had only to gaze intently upon it, and they would appear in the crystal, and unveil to him all the secrets of futurity.* Thus saying, the angel disap-

* The "crystal" alluded to appears to have been a black stone, or piece of polished coal. The following account of it is given in the supplement to Granger's *Biographical*

peared. Dee found from experience of the crystal that it was necessary that all the faculties of the soul should be concentrated upon it,
otherwise the spirits did not appear. He also found that he could
never recollect the conversations he had with the angels. He therefore determined to communicate the secret to another person, who
might converse with the spirit while he (Dee) sat in another part of
the room, and took down in writing the revelations which they
made.

SHEW-STONE OF DR. DEE, IN THE BRITISH MUSEUM.

He had at this time in his service, as his assistant, one Edward
Kelly, who, like himself, was crazy upon the subject of the philosopher's stone. There was this difference, however, between them,
that, while Dee was more of an enthusiast than an impostor, Kelly
was more of an impostor than an enthusiast. In early life he was a
notary, and had the misfortune to lose both his ears for forgery. This
mutilation, degrading enough in any man, was destructive to a philosopher ; Kelly, therefore, lest his wisdom should suffer in the world's
opinion, wore a black skull-cap, which, fitting close to his head, and
descending over both his cheeks, not only concealed his loss, but gave
him a very solemn and oracular appearance. So well did he keep his
secret, that even Dee, with whom he lived so many years, appears
never to have discovered it. Kelly, with this character, was just the
man to carry on any piece of roguery for his own advantage, or to
nurture the delusions of his master for the same purpose. No sooner
did Dee inform him of the visit he had received from the glorious
Uriel, than Kelly expressed such a fervour of belief, that Dee's heart
glowed with delight. He set about consulting his crystal forthwith,

History. " The black stone into which Dee used to call his spirits was in the collection
of the Earls of Peterborough, from whence it came to Lady Elizabeth Germaine. It was
next the property of the late Duke of Argyle, and is now Mr. Walpole's. It appears
upon examination to be nothing more than a polished piece of cannel coal ; but this is
what Butler means when he says,

> ' Kelly did all his feats upon
> The devil's looking-glass—a stone.' "

and on the 2d of December, 1581, the spirits appeared, and held a very extraordinary discourse with Kelly, which Dee took down in writing. The curious reader may see this farrago of nonsense among the Harleian Mss. in the British Museum. The later consultations were published in a folio volume, in 1659, by Dr. Meric Casaubon, under the title of *A true and faithful Relation of what passed between Dr. John Dee and some Spirits; tending, had it succeeded, to a general Alteration of most States and Kingdoms in the World.*[*]

The fame of these wondrous colloquies soon spread over the country, and even reached the Continent. Dee at the same time pretended to be in possession of the *elixir vitæ*, which he stated he had found among the ruins of Glastonbury Abbey, in Somersetshire. People flocked from far and near to his house at Mortlake to have their nativities cast, in preference to visiting astrologers of less renown. They also longed to see a man who, according to his own account, would never die. Altogether, he carried on a very profitable trade, but spent so much in drugs and metals to work out some peculiar process of transmutation, that he never became rich.

About this time there came into England a wealthy Polish nobleman, named Albert Laski, Count Palatine of Siradz. His object was principally, he said, to visit the court of Queen Elizabeth, the fame of whose glory and magnificence had reached him in distant Poland. Elizabeth received this flattering stranger with the most splendid hospitality, and appointed her favourite Leicester to shew him all that was worth seeing in England. He visited all the curiosities of London and Westminster, and from thence proceeded to Oxford and Cambridge, that he might converse with some of the great scholars whose writings shed lustre upon the land of their birth. He was very much disappointed at not finding Dr. Dee among them, and told the Earl of Leicester that he would not have gone to Oxford if he had known that Dee was not there. The earl promised to introduce him to the great alchymist on their return to London, and the Pole was satisfied. A few days afterwards, the earl and Laski being in the antechamber of the Queen, awaiting an audience of her majesty, Dr. Dee arrived on the same errand, and was introduced to the Pole.[†] An interest-

---

[*] Lilly the astrologer, in his *Life*, written by himself, frequently tells of prophecies delivered by the angels in a manner similar to the angels of Dr. Dee. He says, "The prophecies were not given vocally by the angels, but by inspection of the crystal in types and figures, or by apparition the circular way; where, at some distance, the angels appear, representing by forms, shapes, and creatures, what is demanded. It is very rare, yea even in our days," quoth that wiseacre, "for any operator or master to hear the angels speak articulately : when they do speak, *it is like the Irish, much in the throat!*"

[†] Albert Laski, son of Jaroslav, was Palatine of Siradz, and afterwards of Sendomir, and chiefly contributed to the election of Henry of Valois, the Third of France, to the throne of Poland, and was one of the delegates who went to France in order to announce

ing conversation ensued, which ended by the stranger inviting himself to dine with the astrologer at his house at Mortlake. Dee returned home in some tribulation, for he found he had not money enough, without pawning his plate, to entertain Count Laski and his retinue in a manner becoming their dignity. In this emergency he sent off an express to the Earl of Leicester, stating frankly the embarrassment he laboured under, and praying his good offices in representing the matter to her majesty. Elizabeth immediately sent him a present of twenty pounds.

On the appointed day Count Laski came, attended by a numerous retinue, and expressed such open and warm admiration of the wonderful attainments of his host, that Dee turned over in his own mind how he could bind irretrievably to his interests a man who seemed so well inclined to become his friend. Long acquaintance with Kelly had imbued him with all the roguery of that personage, and he resolved to make the Pole pay dearly for his dinner. He found out before many days that he possessed great estates in his own country, as well as great influence, but that an extravagant disposition had reduced him to temporary embarrassment. He also discovered that he was a firm believer in the philosopher's stone and the water of life. He was therefore just the man upon whom an adventurer might fasten himself. Kelly thought so too; and both of them set to work to weave a web, in the meshes of which they might firmly entangle the rich and credulous stranger. They went very cautiously about it; first throwing out obscure hints of the stone and the elixir, and finally of the spirits, by means of whom they could turn over the pages of the book of futurity, and read the awful secrets inscribed therein. Laski eagerly implored that he might be admitted to one of their mysterious interviews with Uriel and the angels; but they knew human nature too well to accede at once to the request. To the count's entreaties they only replied by hints of the difficulty or impropriety of summoning the spirits in the presence of a stranger, or of one who might perchance have no other motive than the gratification of a vain curiosity; but they only meant to whet the edge of his appetite by this delay, and would have been sorry indeed if the count had been discouraged. To shew how exclusively the thoughts both of Dee and

---

to the new monarch his elevation to the sovereignty of Poland. After the deposition of Henry, Albert Laski voted for Maximilian of Austria. In 1583 he visited England, when Queen Elizabeth received him with great distinction. The honours which were shewn him during his visit to Oxford, by the especial command of the Queen, were equal to those rendered to sovereign princes. His extraordinary prodigality rendered his enormous wealth insufficient to defray his expenses, and he therefore became a zealous adept in alchymy, and took from England to Poland with him two known alchymists.—Count Valerian Krasinski's *Historical Sketch of the Reformation in Poland.*

Kelly were fixed upon their dupe at this time, it is only necessary to read the introduction to their first interview with the spirits, related in the volume of Dr. Casaubon. The entry made by Dee, under the date of the 25th of May, 1583, says, that when the spirit appeared to them, "I [John Dee] and E. K. [Edward Kelly] sat together, conversing of that noble Polonian Albertus Laski, his great honour here with us obtained, and of his great liking among all sorts of the people." No doubt they were discussing how they might make the most of the "noble Polonian," and concocting the fine story with which they afterwards excited his curiosity, and drew him firmly within their toils. "Suddenly," says Dee, as they were thus employed, "there seemed to come out of the oratory a spiritual creature, like a pretty girl of seven or nine years of age, attired on her head, with her hair rolled up before and hanging down behind, with a gown of silk, of changeable red and green, and with a train. She seemed to play up and down, and seemed to go in and out behind the books; and as she seemed to go between them, the books displaced themselves, and made way for her."

With such tales as these they lured on the Pole from day to day, and at last persuaded him to be a witness of their mysteries. Whether they played off any optical delusions upon him, or whether, by the force of a strong imagination, he deluded himself, does not appear, but certain it is that he became a complete tool in their hands, and consented to do whatever they wished him. Kelly, at these interviews, placed himself at a certain distance from the wondrous crystal, and gazed intently upon it, while Dee took his place in a corner, ready to set down the prophecies as they were uttered by the spirits. In this manner they prophesied to the Pole that he should become the fortunate possessor of the philosopher's stone; that he should live for centuries, and be chosen King of Poland, in which capacity he should gain many great victories over the Saracens, and make his name illustrious over all the earth. For this purpose it was necessary, however, that Laski should leave England, and take them with him, together with their wives and families; that he should treat them all sumptuously, and allow them to want for nothing. Laski at once consented; and very shortly afterwards they were all on the road to Poland.

It took them upwards of four months to reach the count's estates in the neighbourhood of Cracow. In the mean time, they lead a pleasant life, and spent money with an unsparing hand. When once established in the count's palace, they commenced the great hermetic operation of transmuting iron into gold. Laski provided them with all necessary materials, and aided them himself with his knowledge of alchymy; but, somehow or other, the experiment always failed at the very moment it ought to have succeeded, and they were obliged to recommence operations on a grander scale. But the hopes of Laski were not easily extinguished. Already, in idea, the possessor of countless millions, he was not to be cast down for fear of present expenses. He thus continued from day to day, and from month to month, till he was at last obliged to sell a portion of his deeply-mortgaged estates to find aliment for the hungry crucibles of Dee and Kelly, and the no less hungry stomachs of their wives and families. It was not till ruin stared him in the face that he awoke from his dream of infatuation, too happy, even then, to find that he had escaped utter beggary. Thus restored to his senses, his first thought was how to rid himself of his expensive visitors. Not wishing to quarrel with them, he proposed that they should proceed to Prague, well furnished with letters of recommendation to the Emperor Rudolph. Our alchymists too plainly saw that nothing more was to be made of the almost destitute Count Laski. Without hesitation, therefore, they accepted the proposal, and set out forthwith to the imperial residence. They had no difficulty, on their arrival at Prague, in obtaining an audience of the emperor. They found him willing enough to believe that such a thing as the philosopher's stone existed, and flattered themselves that they had made a favourable impression upon him ; but, from some cause or other—perhaps the look of low cunning and quackery upon the face of Kelly—the emperor conceived no very high opinion of their abilities. He allowed them, however, to remain for some months at Prague, feeding themselves upon the hope that he would employ them ; but the more he saw of them, the less he liked them ; and when the pope's nuncio represented to him that he ought not to countenance such heretic magicians, he gave orders that they should quit his dominions within four-and-twenty hours. It was fortunate for them that so little time was given them ; for, had they remained six hours longer, the nuncio had received orders to procure a perpetual dungeon or the stake for them.

Not knowing well whither to direct their steps, they resolved to return to Cracow, where they had still a few friends ; but by this time the funds they had drawn from Laski were almost exhausted, and they were many days obliged to go dinnerless and supperless. They had great difficulty to keep their poverty a secret from the world; but they managed to bear privation without murmuring, from a conviction that if the fact were known, it would militate very much against their pretensions. Nobody would believe that they were possessors of the philosopher's stone, if it were once suspected that they did not know how to procure bread for their subsistence. They still gained a little by casting nativities, and kept starvation at arm's length, till a new dupe, rich enough for their purposes, dropped into their toils, in the shape of a royal personage. Having procured an introduction to Stephen king of Poland, they predicted to him that the Emperor Rudolph would shortly be assassinated, and that the Germans would look to Poland for his successor. As this prediction was not precise enough to satisfy the king, they tried their crystal again, and a spirit appeared who told them that the new sovereign of Germany would be Stephen of Poland. Stephen was credulous enough to believe them, and was once present when Kelly held his mystic conversations with the shadows of his crystal. He also appears to have furnished them with money to carry on their experiments in alchymy; but he grew tired, at last, of their broken promises and their constant drains upon his pocket, and was on the point of discarding them with disgrace, when they met with another dupe, to whom they eagerly transferred their services. This was Count Rosenberg, a nobleman of large estates at Trebona in Bohemia. So comfortable did they find themselves in the palace of this munificent patron, that they remained nearly four years with him, faring sumptuously, and having an almost unlimited command of his money. The count was more ambitious than avaricious : he had wealth enough, and did not care for the philosopher's stone on account of the gold, but of the length of days it would bring him. They had their predictions, accordingly, all ready framed to suit his character. They prophesied that he should be chosen king of Poland ; and promised, moreover, that he should live for five hundred years to enjoy his dignity, provided always that he found them sufficient money to carry on their experiments.

But now, while fortune smiled upon them, while they revelled in the rewards of successful villany, retributive justice came upon them in a shape they had not anticipated. Jealousy and mistrust sprang up between the two confederates, and led to such violent and frequent quarrels, that Dee was in constant fear of exposure. Kelly imagined himself a much greater personage than Dee ; measuring, most likely, by the standard of impudent roguery ; and was displeased that on all occasions, and from all persons, Dee received the greater share of honour and consideration. He often threatened to leave Dee to shift for himself ; and the latter, who had degenerated into the mere tool of his more daring associate, was distressed beyond measure at the prospect of his desertion. His mind was so deeply imbued with superstition, that he believed the rhapsodies of Kelly to be, in a great measure, derived from his intercourse with angels ; and he knew not where, in the whole world, to look for a man of depth and wisdom enough to succeed him. As their quarrels every day became more and more frequent, Dee wrote letters to Queen Elizabeth to secure a favourable reception on his return to England, whither he intended to proceed if Kelly forsook him. He also sent her a round piece of silver, which he pretended he had made of a portion of brass cut out of a warming-pan. He afterwards sent her the warming-pan also, that she might convince herself that the piece of silver corresponded exactly with the hole which was cut into the brass. While thus preparing for the worst, his chief desire was to remain in Bohemia with Count Rosenberg, who treated him well, and reposed much confidence in him. Neither had Kelly any great objection to remain ; but a new passion had taken possession of his breast, and he was laying deep schemes to gratify it. His own wife was ill-favoured and ill-natured ; Dee's was comely and agreeable ; and he longed to make an exchange of partners without exciting the jealousy or shocking the morality of Dee. This was a difficult matter ; but to a man like Kelly, who was as deficient in rectitude and right feeling as he was full of impudence and ingenuity, the difficulty was not insurmountable. He had also deeply studied the character and the foibles of Dee ; and he took his measures accordingly. The next time they consulted the spirits, Kelly pretended to be shocked at their language, and refused to tell Dee what they had said. Dee insisted, and was informed that they were henceforth to have their wives in common. Dee, a little startled, inquired whether the spirits might not mean that they were to live in common harmony and good-will ? Kelly tried again, with apparent reluctance, and said the spirits insisted upon the literal interpretation. The poor fanatic Dee resigned himself to their will ; but it suited Kelly's purpose to appear coy a little longer. He declared that the spirits must be spirits not of good, but of evil ; and refused to consult them any more. He thereupon took his departure, saying that he would never return.

Dee, thus left to himself, was in sore trouble and distress of mind. He knew not on whom to fix as the successor to Kelly for consulting the spirits ; but at last chose his son Arthur, a boy of eight years of age. He consecrated him to this service with great ceremony, and impressed upon the child's mind the dignified and awful nature of the duties he was called upon to perform ; but the poor boy had neither the imagination, the faith, nor the artifice of Kelly. He looked intently upon the crystal as he was told ; but could see nothing and hear nothing. At last, when his eyes ached, he said he could see a vague indistinct shadow, but nothing more. Dee was in despair. The deception had been carried on so long, that he was never so happy as when he fancied he was holding converse with superior beings ; and he cursed the day that had put estrangement between him and his dear friend Kelly. This was exactly what Kelly had foreseen; and, when he thought the doctor had grieved sufficiently for his absence, he returned unexpectedly, and entered the room where the little Arthur was in vain endeavouring to distinguish something in the crystal. Dee, in entering this circumstance in his journal, ascribes this sudden return to a "miraculous fortune" and a "divine fate;" and goes on to record that Kelly immediately saw the spirits which had remained invisible to little Arthur. One of these spirits reiterated the previous command, that they should have their wives in common. Kelly bowed his head and submitted; and Dee, in all humility, consented to the arrangement.

This was the extreme depth of the wretched man's degradation. In this manner they continued to live for three or four months, when, new quarrels breaking out, they separated once more. This time their separation was final. Kelly, taking the *elixir* which he had found in Glastonbury Abbey, proceeded to Prague, forgetful of the abrupt mode in which he had previously been expelled from that city. Almost immediately after his arrival, he was seized by order of the Emperor Rudolph, and thrown into prison. He was released after some months' confinement, and continued for five years to lead a vagabond life in Germany, telling fortunes at one place, and pretending to make gold at another. He was a second time thrown into prison, on a charge of heresy and sorcery; and he then resolved, if ever he obtained his liberty, to return to England. He soon discovered that there was no prospect of this, and that his imprisonment was likely to be for life. He twisted his bed-clothes into a rope, one stormy night in February 1595, and let himself down from the window of his dungeon, situated at the top of a very high tower. Being a corpulent man, the rope gave way, and he was precipitated to the ground. He broke two of his ribs and both his legs; and was otherwise so much injured, that he expired a few days afterwards.

Dee, for a while, had more prosperous fortune. The warming-pan he had sent to Queen Elizabeth was not without effect. He was rewarded soon after Kelly had left him with an invitation to return to England. His pride, which had been sorely humbled, sprang up again to its pristine dimensions, and he set out from Bohemia with a train of attendants becoming an ambassador. How he procured the money does not appear, unless from the liberality of the rich Bohemian Rosenberg, or perhaps from his plunder. He travelled with three coaches for himself and family, and three wagons to carry his baggage. Each coach had four horses, and the whole train was protected by a guard of four and twenty soldiers. This statement may be doubted; but it is on the authority of Dee himself, who made it on oath before the commissioners appointed by Elizabeth to inquire into his circumstances. On his arrival in England he had an audience of the queen, who received him kindly, as far as words went, and gave orders that he should not be molested in his pursuits of chemistry and philosophy. A man who boasted of the power to turn baser metals into gold, could not, thought Elizabeth, be in want of money; and she therefore gave him no more substantial marks of her approbation than her countenance and protection.

Thrown thus unexpectedly upon his own resources, Dee began in earnest the search for the philosopher's stone. He worked incessantly among his furnaces, retorts, and crucibles, and almost poisoned himself with deleterious fumes. He also consulted his miraculous crystal; but the spirits appeared not to him. He tried one Bartholomew to supply the place of the invaluable Kelly; but he being a man of some little probity, and of no imagination at all, the spirits would not hold any communication with him. Dee then tried another pretender to philosophy, of the name of Hickman, but had no better fortune. The crystal had lost its power since the departure of its great high priest. From this quarter, then, Dee could get no information on the stone or elixir of the alchymists, and all his efforts to discover them by other means were not only fruitless but expensive. He was soon reduced to great distress, and wrote piteous letters to the queen, praying relief. He represented that, after he left England with Count Laski, the mob had pillaged his house at Mortlake, accusing him of being a necromancer and a wizard; and had broken all his furniture, burned his library, consisting of four thousand rare volumes, and destroyed all the philosophical instruments and curiosities in his museum. For this damage he claimed compensation; and furthermore stated, that, as he had come to England by the queen's command, she ought to pay the expenses of his journey. Elizabeth sent him small sums of money at various times; but Dee still continuing his complaints, a commission was appointed to inquire into his circumstances. He finally obtained a small appointment as Chancellor of St. Paul's cathedral, which he exchanged, in 1595, for the wardenship of the college at Manchester. He remained in this capacity till 1602 or 1603, when, his strength and intellect beginning to fail him, he was compelled to resign. He retired to his old dwelling at Mortlake, in a state not far removed from actual want, supporting himself as a common fortune-teller; and being often obliged to sell or pawn his books to procure a dinner. James I. was often applied to on his behalf, but he refused to do any thing for him. It may be said, to the discredit of this king, that the only reward he would grant the indefatigable Stowe, in his days of old age and want, was the royal permission to beg ; but no one will blame him for neglecting such a quack as John Dee. He died in 1608, in the eighty-first year of his age, and was buried at Mortlake.

THE COSMOPOLITE.

Many disputes have arisen as to the real name of the alchymist who wrote several works under the above designation. The general opinion is that he was a Scotsman named Seton, and that by a fate very common to alchymists who boasted too loudly of their powers of transmutation, he ended his days miserably in a dungeon, into which he was thrown by a German potentate until he made a million of gold to pay his ransom. By some he has been confounded with Michael Sendivog, or Sendivogius, a Pole, a professor of the same art, who made a great noise in Europe at the commencement of the seventeenth century. Lenglet du Fresnoy, who is in general well informed with respect to the alchymists, inclines to the belief that these personages were distinct ; and gives the following particulars of the Cosmopolite, extracted from George Morhoff, in his *Epistola ad Langelottum,* and other writers.

About the year 1600, one Jacob Haussen, a Dutch pilot, was shipwrecked on the coast of Scotland. A gentleman, named Alexander Seton, put off in a boat, and saved him from drowning, and afterwards entertained him hospitably for many weeks at his house on the shore. Haussen saw that he was addicted to the pursuits of chemistry, but no conversation on the subject passed between them at the time. About a year and a half afterwards, Haussen being then at home at Enkhuysen, in Holland, received a visit from his former host. He endeavoured to repay the kindness that had been shewn him ; and so great a friendship arose between them that Seton, on his departure, offered to make him acquainted with the great secret of the philosopher's stone. In his presence the Scotsman transmuted a great quantity of base metal into pure gold, and gave it him as a mark of his esteem. Seton then took leave of his friend, and travelled into Germany. At Dresden he made no secret of his wonderful powers, having, it is said, performed transmutations successfully before a great assemblage of the learned men of that city. The circumstance coming to the ears of the Duke or Elector of Saxony, he gave orders for the arrest of the alchymist. He caused him to be imprisoned in a high tower, and set a guard of forty men to watch that he did not escape, and that no strangers were admitted to his presence. The unfortunate Seton received several visits from the elector, who used every art of persuasion to make him divulge his secret. Seton obstinately refused either to communicate his secret, or to make any gold for the tyrant; on which he was stretched upon the rack, to see if the argument of torture would render him more tractable. The result was still the same; neither hope of reward nor fear of anguish could shake him. For several months he remained in prison, subjected alternately to a sedative and a violent regimen, till his health broke, and he wasted away almost to a skeleton.

There happened at that time to be at Dresden a learned Pole, named Michael Sendivogius, who had wasted a good deal of his time and substance in the unprofitable pursuits of alchymy. He was touched with pity for the hard fate, and admiration for the intrepidity of Seton; and determined, if possible, to aid him in escaping from the clutch of his oppressor. He requested the elector's permission to see the alchymist, and obtained it with some difficulty. He found him in a state of great wretchedness, shut up from the light of day in a noisome dungeon, and with no better couch or fare than those allotted to the worst of criminals. Seton listened eagerly to the proposal of escape, and promised the generous Pole that he would make him richer than an eastern monarch if by his means he were liberated. Sendivogius immediately commenced operations; he sold some property which he possessed near Cracow, and with the proceeds led a merry life at Dresden. He gave the most elegant suppers, to which he regularly invited the officers of the guard, and especially those who did duty at the prison of the alchymist. He insinuated himself at last into their confidence, and obtained free ingress to his friend as often as he pleased; pretending that he was using his utmost endeavours to conquer his obstinacy and worm his secret out of him. When their project was ripe, a day was fixed upon for the grand attempt; and Sendivogius was ready with a post-chariot to convey him with all speed into Poland. By drugging some wine which he presented to the guards of the prison, he rendered them so drowsy that he easily found means to scale a wall unobserved, with Seton, and effect his escape. Seton's wife was in the chariot awaiting him, having safely in her possession a small packet of a black powder, which was, in fact, the philosopher's stone, or ingredient for the transmutation of iron and copper into gold. They all arrived in safety at Cracow; but the frame of Seton was so wasted by torture of body and starvation, to say nothing of the anguish of mind he had endured, that he did not long survive. He died in Cracow, in 1603 or 1604, and was buried under the cathedral church of that city. Such is the story related of the author of the various works which bear the name of the Cosmopolite. A list of them may be found in the third volume of the *History of the Hermetic Philosophy*.

SENDIVOGIUS.

On the death of Seton, Sendivogius married his widow, hoping to learn from her some of the secrets of her deceased lord in the art of transmutation. The ounce of black powder stood him, however, in better service ; for the alchymists say, that by its means he converted great quantities of quicksilver into the purest gold. It is also said that he performed this experiment successfully before the Emperor Rudolph II., at Prague ; and that the emperor, to commemorate the circumstance, caused a marble tablet to be affixed to the wall of the room in which it was performed, bearing this inscription, "Faciat hoc quispiam alius, quod fecit Sendivogius Polonus." M. Desnoyers, secretary to the Princess Mary of Gonzaga, Queen of Poland, writing from Warsaw in 1651, says that he saw this tablet, which existed at that time, and was often visited by the curious.

The after-life of Sendivogius is related in a Latin memoir of him by one Brodowski, his steward ; and is inserted by Pierre Borel in his *Treasure of Gaulish Antiquities*. The Emperor Rudolph, according to this authority, was so well pleased with his success, that he made him one of his councillors of state, and invited him to fill a station in the royal household and inhabit the palace. But Sendivogius loved his liberty, and refused to become a courtier. He preferred to reside on his own patrimonial estate of Gravarna, where, for many years he exercised a princely hospitality. His philosophic powder, which, his steward says, was red, and not black, he kept in a little box of gold ; and with one grain of it he could make five hundred ducats, or a thousand rix-dollars. He generally made his projection upon quicksilver. When he travelled, he gave this box to his steward, who hung it round his neck by a gold chain next his skin. But the greatest part of the powder he used to hide in a secret place cut into the step of his chariot. He thought that, if attacked at any time by robbers, they would not search such a place as that. When he anticipated any danger, he would dress himself in his valet's clothes, and, mounting the coach-box, put the valet inside. He was induced to take these precautions, because it was no secret that he possessed the philosopher's stone ; and many unprincipled adventurers were on the watch for an opportunity to plunder him. A German prince, whose name Brodowski has not thought fit to chronicle, served him a scurvy trick, which ever afterwards put him on his guard. This prince went on his knees to Sendivogius, and entreated him in the most pressing terms to satisfy his curiosity, by converting some quicksilver into gold before him. Sendivogius, wearied by his importunity, consented, upon a promise of inviolable secrecy. After his departure, the prince called a German alchymist, named Muhlenfels, who resided in his house, and told him all that had been done. Muhlenfels entreated that he might have a dozen mounted horsemen at his command, that he might instantly ride after the philosopher, and either rob him of all his powder, or force from him the secret of making it. The prince desired nothing better; Muhlenfels, being provided with twelve men well mounted and armed, pursued Sendivogius in hot haste. He came up with him at a lonely inn by the road-side, just as he was sitting down to dinner. He at first endeavoured to persuade him to divulge the secret; but finding this of no avail, he caused his accomplices to strip the unfortunate Sendivogius and tie him naked to one of the pillars of the house. He then took from him his golden box, containing a small quantity of the powder; a manuscript book on the philosopher's stone; a golden medal, with its chain, presented to him by the Emperor Rudolph; and a rich cap, ornamented with diamonds, of the value of one hundred thousand rix-dollars. With this booty he decamped, leaving Sendivogius still naked and firmly bound to the pillar. His servant had been treated in a similar manner; but the people of the inn released them all as soon as the robbers were out of sight.

Sendivogius proceeded to Prague, and made his complaint to the emperor. An express was instantly sent off to the prince, with orders that he should deliver up Muhlenfels and all his plunder. The prince, fearful of the emperor's wrath, caused three large gallows to be erected in his court-yard; on the highest of which he hanged Muhlenfels, with another thief on each side of him. He thus propitiated the emperor, and got rid of an ugly witness against himself. He sent back at the same time, the bejewelled hat, the medal and chain, and the treatise upon the philosopher's stone, which had been stolen from Sendivogius. As regarded the powder, he said he had not seen it, and knew nothing about it.

This adventure made Sendivogius more prudent; he would no longer perform the process of transmutation before any strangers, however highly recommended. He pretended also to be very poor; and sometimes lay in bed for weeks together, that people might believe he was suffering from some dangerous malady, and could not therefore, by any possibility, be the owner of the philosopher's stone. He would occasionally coin false money, and pass it off as gold; preferring to be esteemed a cheat rather than a successful alchymist.

Many other extraordinary tales are told of this personage by his steward Brodowski, but they are not worth repeating. He died in 1636, aged upwards of eighty, and was buried in his own chapel at

Gravarna. Several works upon alchymy have been published under his name.

THE ROSICRUCIANS.

It was during the time of the last-mentioned author that the sect of the Rosicrucians first began to create a sensation in Europe. The influence which they exercised upon opinion during their brief career, and the permanent impression which they have left upon European literature, claim for them especial notice. Before their time, alchymy was but a grovelling delusion ; and theirs is the merit of having spiritualised and refined it. They also enlarged its sphere, and supposed the possession of the philosopher's stone to be, not only the means of wealth, but of health and happiness, and the instrument by which man could command the services of superior beings, control the elements to his will, defy the obstructions of time and space, and acquire the most intimate knowledge of all the secrets of the universe. Wild and visionary as they were, they were not without their uses ; if it were only for having purged the superstitions of Europe of the dark and disgusting forms with which the monks had peopled it, and substituted, in their stead, a race of mild, graceful, and beneficent beings.

They are said to have derived their name from Christian Rosencreutz, or " Rose-cross," a German philosopher, who travelled in the Holy Land towards the close of the fourteenth century. While dangerously ill at a place called Damcar, he was visited by some learned Arabs, who claimed him as their brother in science, and unfolded to him, by inspiration, all the secrets of his past life, both of thought and of action. They restored him to health by means of the philosopher's stone, and afterwards instructed him in all their mysteries. He returned to Europe in 1401, being then only twenty-three years of age ; and drew a chosen number of his friends around him, whom he initiated into the new science, and bound by solemn oaths to keep it secret for a century. He is said to have lived eighty-three years after this period, and to have died in 1484.

Many have denied the existence of such a personage as Rosencreutz, and have fixed the origin of this sect at a much later epoch. The first dawning of it, they say, is to be found in the theories of Paracelsus and the dreams of Dr. Dee, who, without intending it, became the actual, though never the recognised founders of the Rosicrucian philosophy. It is now difficult, and indeed impossible, to determine whether Dee and Paracelsus obtained their ideas from the then obscure and unknown Rosicrucians, or whether the Rosicrucians did but follow and improve upon them. Certain it is, that their existence was never suspected till the year 1605, when they began to excite attention in Germany. No sooner were their doctrines promulgated, than all the visionaries, Paracelsists, and alchymists, flocked around their standard, and vaunted Rosencreutz as the new regenerator of the human race. Michael Mayer, a celebrated physician of that day, and who had impaired his health and wasted his fortune in searching for the philosopher's stone, drew up a report of the tenets and ordinances of the new fraternity, which was published at Cologne, in the year 1615. They asserted, in the first place, "that the meditations of their founders surpassed every thing that had ever been imagined since the creation of the world, without even excepting the revelations of the Deity; that they were destined to accomplish the general peace and regeneration of man before the end of the world arrived; that they possessed all wisdom and piety in a supreme degree; that they possessed all the graces of nature, and could distribute them among the rest of mankind according to their pleasure; that they were subject to neither hunger, nor thirst, nor disease, nor old age, nor to any other inconvenience of nature; that they knew by inspiration, and at the first glance, every one who was worthy to be admitted into their society; that they had the same knowledge then which they would have possessed if they had lived from the beginning of the world, and had been always acquiring it; that they had a volume in which they could read all that ever was or ever would be written in other books till the end of time; that they could force to, and retain in their service the most powerful spirits and demons; that, by the virtue of their songs, they could attract pearls and precious stones from the depths of the sea or the bowels of the earth; that God had covered them with a thick cloud, by means of which they could shelter themselves from the malignity of their enemies, and that they could thus render themselves invisible from all eyes; that the first eight brethren of the ' Rose-cross' had power to cure all maladies; that, by means of the fraternity, the triple diadem of the pope would be reduced into dust; that they only admitted two sacraments, with the ceremonies of the primitive Church, renewed by them; that they recognised the Fourth Monarchy and the Emperor of the Romans as their chief and the chief of all Christians; that they would provide him with more gold, their treasures being inexhaustible, than the King of Spain had ever drawn from the golden regions of Eastern and Western Ind." This was their confession of faith. Their rules of conduct were six in number, and as follow :

First. That, in their travels, they should gratuitously cure all diseases.

Secondly. That they should always dress in conformity to the fashion of the country in which they resided.

Thirdly. That they should, once every year, meet together in the place appointed by the fraternity, or send in writing an available excuse.

Fourthly. That every brother, whenever he felt inclined to die, should choose a person worthy to succeed him.

Fifthly. That the words "Rose-cross" should be the marks by which they should recognise each other.

Sixthly. That their fraternity should be kept secret for six times twenty years.

They asserted that these laws had been found inscribed in a golden book in the tomb of Rosencreutz, and that the six times twenty years from his death expired in 1604. They were consequently called upon from that time forth to promulgate their doctrine for the welfare of mankind.*

For eight years these enthusiasts made converts in Germany, but they excited little or no attention in other parts of Europe. At last they made their appearance in Paris, and threw all the learned, all the credulous, and all the lovers of the marvellous into commotion. In the beginning of March 1623, the good folks of that city, when they arose one morning, were surprised to find all their walls placarded with the following singular manifesto:

"*We, the deputies of the principal College of the brethren of the Rose-cross have taken up our abode, visible and invisible, in this city, by the grace of the Most High, towards whom are turned the hearts of the just. We shew and teach without books or signs, and speak all sorts of languages in the countries where we dwell, to draw mankind, our fellows, from error and from death.*"

For a long time this strange placard was the sole topic of conver-

---

* The following legend of the tomb of Rosencreutz, written by Eustace Budgell, appears in No. 379 of the *Spectator:*—"A certain person, having occasion to dig somewhat deep in the ground where this philosopher lay interred, met with a small door, having a wall on each side of it. His curiosity, and the hope of finding some hidden treasure, soon prompted him to force open the door. He was immediately surprised by a sudden blaze of light, and discovered a very fair vault. At the upper end of it was a statue of a man in armour, sitting by a table, and leaning on his left arm. He held a truncheon in his right hand, and had a lamp burning before him. The man had no sooner set one foot within the vault, than the statue, erecting itself from its leaning posture, stood bolt upright; and, upon the fellow's advancing another step, lifted up the truncheon in his right hand. The man still ventured a third step; when the statue, with a furious blow, broke the lamp into a thousand pieces, and left his guest in sudden darkness. Upon the report of this adventure, the country people came with lights to the sepulchre, and discovered that the statue, which was made of brass, was nothing more than a piece of clock-work; that the floor of the vault was all loose, and underlaid with several springs, which, upon any man's entering, naturally produced that which had happened.

"Rosicreucius, say his disciples, made use of this method to shew the world that he had re-invented the ever-burning lamps of the ancients, though he was resolved no one should reap any advantage from the discovery."

sation in all public places. Some few wondered, but the greater number only laughed at it. In the course of a few weeks two books were published, which raised the first alarm respecting this mysterious society, whose dwelling-place no one knew, and no members of which had ever been seen. The first was called a history of *The frightful Compacts entered into between the Devil and the pretended 'Invisibles;' with their damnable Instructions, the deplorable Ruin of their Disciples, and their miserable end.* The other was called an *Examination of the new and unknown Cabala of the Brethren of the Rose-cross, who have lately inhabited the City of Paris; with the History of their Manners, the Wonders worked by them, and many other particulars.*

These books sold rapidly. Every one was anxious to know something of this dreadful and secret brotherhood. The *badauds* of Paris were so alarmed that they daily expected to see the arch-enemy walking *in propria persona* among them. It was said in these volumes that the Rosicrucian society consisted of six-and-thirty persons in all, who had renounced their baptism and hope of resurrection. That it was not by means of good angels, as they pretended, that they worked their prodigies ; but that it was the devil who gave them power to transport themselves from one end of the world to the other with the rapidity of thought ; to speak all languages ; to have their purses always full of money, however much they might spend ; to be invisible, and penetrate into the most secret places, in spite of fastenings of bolts and bars ; and to be able to tell the past and future. These thirty-six brethren were divided into bands or companies : six of them only had been sent on the mission to Paris, six to Italy, six to Spain, six to Germany, four to Sweden, and two into Switzerland, two into Flanders, two into Lorraine, and two into Franche Comté. It was generally believed that the missionaries to France resided somewhere in the Marais du Temple. That quarter of Paris soon acquired a bad name, and people were afraid to take houses in it, lest they should be turned out by the six invisibles of the Rose-cross. It was believed by the populace, and by many others whose education should have taught them better, that persons of a mysterious aspect used to visit the inns and hotels of Paris, and eat of the best meats and drink of the best wines, and then suddenly melt away into thin air when the landlord came with the reckoning. That gentle maidens, who went to bed alone, often awoke in the night and found men in bed with them, of shape more beautiful than the Grecian Apollo, who immediately became invisible when an alarm was raised. It was also said that many persons found large heaps of gold in their houses without knowing from whence they came. All Paris was in alarm. No man thought himself secure of his goods, no maiden of her virginity, or wife of her chastity, while these Rosicrucians were abroad. In the midst of the commotion, a second placard was issued to the following effect :

"*If any one desires to see the brethren of the Rose-cross from curiosity only, he will never communicate with us. But if his will really induces him to inscribe his name in the register of our brotherhood, we, who can judge of the thoughts of all men, will convince him of the truth of our promises. For this reason we do not publish to the world the place of our abode. Thought alone, in unison with the sincere will of those who desire to know us, is sufficient to make us known to them, and them to us.*"

Though the existence of such a society as that of the Rose-cross was problematical, it was quite evident that somebody or other was concerned in the promulgation of these placards, which were stuck up on every wall in Paris. The police endeavoured in vain to find out the offenders, and their want of success only served to increase the perplexity of the public. The Church very soon took up the question ; and the Abbé Gaultier, a Jesuit, wrote a book to prove that, by their enmity to the pope, they could be no other than disciples of Luther sent to promulgate his heresy. Their very name, he added, proved that they were heretics ; a *cross* surmounted by a *rose* being the heraldic device of the arch-heretic Luther. One Garasse said they were a confraternity of drunken impostors ; and that their name was derived from the garland of roses, in the form of a cross, hung over the tables of taverns in Germany as the emblem of secrecy, and from whence was derived the common saying, when one man communicated a secret to another, that it was said " under the rose." Others interpreted the letters F. R. C. to mean, not Brethren of the Rose-Cross, but *Fratres Roris Cocti,* or Brothers of Boiled Dew ; and explained this appellation by alleging that they collected large quantities of morning dew, and boiled it, in order to extract a very valuable ingredient in the composition of the philosopher's stone and the water of life.

The fraternity thus attacked defended themselves as well as they were able. They denied that they used magic of any kind, or that they consulted the devil. They said they were all happy ; that they had lived more than a century, and expected to live many centuries more ; and that the intimate knowledge which they possessed of all nature was communicated to them by God himself as a reward for their piety and utter devotion to his service. Those were in error who derived their name from a cross of roses, or called them drunkards. To set the world right on the first point, they reiterated that they derived their name from Christian Rosencreutz, their founder ; and to answer the latter charge, they repeated that they knew not what thirst was, and had higher pleasures than those of the palate. They did not desire to meddle with the politics or religion of any man or set of men, although they could not help denying the supremacy of the pope, and looking upon him as a tyrant. Many slanders, they said, had been repeated respecting them, the most unjust of which was, that they indulged in carnal appetites, and, under the cloak of their invisibility, crept into the chambers of beautiful maidens. They asserted, on the contrary, that the first vow they took on entering the society was a vow of chastity, and that any one among them who transgressed in that particular would immediately lose all the advantages he enjoyed, and be exposed once more to hunger, woe, disease, and death, like other men. So strongly did they feel on the subject of chastity, that they attributed the fall of Adam solely to his want of this virtue. Besides defending themselves in this manner, they entered into a further confession of their faith. They discarded for ever all the old tales of sorcery and witchcraft, and communion with the devil. They said there were no such horrid, unnatural, and disgusting beings as the incubi and succubi, and the innumerable grotesque imps that men had believed in for so many ages. Man was not surrounded with enemies like these, but with myriads of beautiful and beneficent beings, all anxious to do him service. The air was peopled with sylphs, the water with undines or naiads, the bowels of the earth with gnomes, and the fire with salamanders. All these beings were the friends of man, and desired nothing so much as that men should purge themselves of all uncleanness, and thus be enabled to see and converse with them. They possessed great power, and were unrestrained by the barriers of space or the obstructions of matter. But man was in one particular their superior. He had an immortal soul, and they had not. They might, however, become sharers in man's immortality if they could inspire one of that race with the passion of love towards them. Hence it was the constant endeavour of the female spirits to captivate the admiration of men, and of the male gnomes, sylphs, salamanders, and undines to be beloved by a woman. The object of this passion, in returning their love, imparted a portion of that celestial fire, the soul; and from that time forth the beloved became equal to the lover, and both, when their allotted course was run, entered together into the mansions of felicity. These spirits, they said, watched constantly over mankind by night and day. Dreams, omens, and presentiments were all their works, and the means by which they gave warning of the approach of danger. But though so well inclined to befriend man for their own sakes, the want of a soul rendered them at times capricious and revengeful; they took offence on slight causes, and heaped injuries instead of benefits on the heads of those who extinguished the light of reason that was in them by gluttony, debauchery, and other appetites of the body.

The excitement produced in Paris by the placards of the brotherhood and the attacks of the clergy wore itself away after a few months. The stories circulated about them became at last too absurd even for that age of absurdity, and men began to laugh once more at those invisible gentlemen and their fantastic doctrines. Gabriel Naudé at that conjuncture brought out his *Avis à la France sur les Frères de la Rose-croix*, in which he very successfully exposed the folly of the new sect. This work, though not well written, was well timed. It quite extinguished the Rosicrucians of France; and after that year little more was heard of them. Swindlers in different parts of the country assumed the name at times to cloak their depredations; and now and then one of them was caught and hanged for his too great ingenuity in enticing pearls and precious stones from the pockets of other people into his own, or for passing off lumps of gilded brass for pure gold, made by the agency of the philosopher's stone. With these exceptions, oblivion shrouded them.

The doctrine was not confined to a sphere so narrow as France alone; it still flourished in Germany, and drew many converts in England. The latter countries produced two great masters in the persons of Jacob Böhmen and Robert Fludd—pretended philosophers, of whom it is difficult to say which was the more absurd and extravagant. It would appear that the sect was divided into two classes—the brothers *Rosæ Crucis*, who devoted themselves to the wonders of this sublunary sphere, and the brothers *Auræ Crucis*, who were wholly occupied in the contemplation of things divine. Fludd belonged to the first class, and Böhmen to the second. Fludd may be called the father of the English Rosicrucians, and as such merits a conspicuous niche in the temple of Folly.

He was born in the year 1574 at Milgate, in Kent, and was the son of Sir Thomas Fludd, Treasurer of War to Queen Elizabeth. He was originally intended for the army; but he was too fond of study, and of a disposition too quiet and retiring, to shine in that sphere. His father would not therefore press him to adopt a course of life for which he was unsuited, and encouraged him in the study of medicine, for which he early manifested a partiality. At the age of twenty-five he proceeded to the continent; and being fond of the abstruse, the marvellous, and the incomprehensible, he became an ardent disciple of the school of Paracelsus, whom he looked upon as the regenerator not only of medicine, but of philosophy. He remained six years in Italy, France, and Germany, storing his mind with fantastic notions, and seeking the society of enthusiasts and visionaries. On his return to England in 1605, he received the degree of Doctor of Medicine from the University of Oxford, and began to practise as a physician in London.

He soon made himself conspicuous. He latinised his name from Robert Fludd into Robertus à Fluctibus, and began the promulgation of many strange doctrines. He avowed his belief in the philosopher's stone, the water of life, and the universal alkahest ; and maintained that there were but two principles of all things—which were, condensation, the boreal or northern virtue ; and rarefaction, the southern or austral virtue. A number of demons, he said, ruled over the human frame, whom he arranged in their places in a rhomboid. Every disease had its peculiar demon who produced it, which demon could only be combated by the aid of the demon whose place was directly opposite to his in the rhomboidal figure. Of his medical notions we shall have further occasion to speak in another part of this book, when we consider him in his character as one of the first founders of the magnetic delusion, and its offshoot, animal magnetism, which has created so much sensation in our own day.

As if the doctrines already mentioned were not wild enough, he joined the Rosicrucians as soon as they began to make a sensation in Europe, and succeeded in raising himself to high consideration among them. The fraternity having been violently attacked by several German authors, and among others by Libavius, Fludd volunteered a reply, and published, in 1616, his defence of the Rosicrucian philosophy, under the title of the *Apologia compendiaria Fraternitatem de Rosea-cruce suspicionis et infamiæ maculis aspersam abluens.* This work immediately procured him great renown upon the Continent, and he was henceforth looked upon as one of the high-priests of the sect. Of so much importance was he considered, that Keppler and Gassendi thought it necessary to refute him ; and the latter wrote a complete examination of his doctrine. Mersenne also, the friend of Descartes, and who had defended that philosopher when accused of having joined the Rosicrucians, attacked Dr. à Fluctibus, as he preferred to be called, and shewed the absurdity of the brothers of the Rose-cross in general, and of Dr. à Fluctibus in particular. Fluctibus wrote a long reply, in which he called Mersenne an ignorant calumniator, and reiterated that alchymy was a profitable science, and the Rosicrucians worthy to be the regenerators of the world. This book was published at Frankfort, and was entitled *Summum Bonum, quod est Magiæ, Cabalæ, Alchimiæ, Fratrum Roseæ-Crucis verorum, et adversus Mersenium Calumniatorem.* Besides this, he wrote several other works upon alchymy, a second answer to Libavius upon the Rosicrucians, and many medical works He died in London in 1637.

After his time there was some diminution of the sect in England. They excited but little attention, and made no effort to bring themselves into notice. Occasionally some obscure and almost incomprehensible work made its appearance, to shew the world that the folly was not extinguished. Eugenius Philalethes, a noted Alchymist, who has veiled his real name under this assumed one, translated *The Fame and Confession of the Brethren of the Rosie Cross,* which was published in London in 1652. A few years afterwards, another enthusiast, named John Heydon, wrote two works on the subject : the one entitled *The Wise Man's Crown, or the Glory of the Rosie Cross;* and the other, *The Holy Guide, leading the way to unite Art and Nature with the Rosie Crosse uncovered.* Neither of these attracted much notice. A third book was somewhat more successful ; it was called *A new Method of Rosicrucian Physic; by John Heydon, the servant of God and the Secretary of Nature.* A few extracts will shew the ideas of the English Rosicrucians about this period. Its author was an attorney, "practising (to use his own words) at Westminster Hall all term times as long as he lived, and in the vacations devoting himself to alchymical and Rosicrucian meditation." In his preface, called by him an Apologue for an Epilogue, he enlightens the public upon the true history and tenets of his sect. Moses, Elias, and Ezekiel were, he says, the most ancient masters of the Rosicrucian philosophy. Those few then existing in England and the rest of Europe, were as the eyes and ears of the great king of the universe, seeing and hearing all things; seraphically illuminated; companions of the holy company of unbodied souls and immortal angels ; turning themselves, Proteus-like, into any shape, and having the power of working miracles. The most pious and abstracted brethren could slack the plague in cities, silence the violent winds and tempests, calm the rage of the sea and rivers, walk in the air, frustrate the malicious aspect of witches, cure all diseases, and turn all metals into gold. He had known in his time two famous brethren of the Rosie Cross, named Walfourd and Williams, who had worked miracles in his sight, and taught him many excellent predictions of astrology and earthquakes. "I desired one of these to tell me," says he, "whether my complexion were capable of the society of my good genius. 'When I see you again,' said he (which was when he pleased to come to me, for I knew not where to go to him), 'I will tell you.' When I saw him afterwards, he said, 'You should pray to God ; for a good and holy man can offer no greater or more acceptable service to God than the oblation of himself—his soul.' He said also, that the good genii were the benign eyes of God, running to and fro in the world, and with love and pity beholding the innocent endeavours of harmless and single-hearted men, ever ready to do them good and to help them."

Heydon held devoutly true that dogma of the Rosicrucians which said that neither eating nor drinking was necessary to men. He maintained that any one might exist in the same manner as that singular people dwelling near the source of the Ganges, of whom mention was made in the travels of his namesake, Sir Christopher Heydon, who had no mouths, and therefore could not eat, but lived by the breath of their nostrils; except when they took a far journey, and then they mended their diet with the smell of flowers. He said that in really pure air "there was a fine foreign fatness," with which it was sprinkled by the sunbeams, and which was quite sufficient for the nourishment of the generality of mankind. Those who had enormous appetites, he had no objection to see take animal food, since they could not do without it; but he obstinately insisted that there was no necessity why they should *eat* it. If they put a plaster of nicely-cooked meat upon their epigastrium, it would be sufficient for the wants of the most robust and voracious! They would by that means let in no diseases, as they did at the broad and common gate, the mouth, as any one might see by example of drink; for all the while a man sat in water he was never athirst. He had known, he said, many Rosicrucians who, by applying wine in this manner, had fasted for years together. In fact, quoth Heydon, we may easily fast all our life, though it be three hundred years, without any kind of meat, and so cut off all danger of disease.

This "sage philosopher" further informed his wondering contemporaries that the chiefs of the doctrine always carried about with them to their place of meeting their symbol, called the R. C. which was an ebony cross, flourished and decked with roses of gold; the cross typifying Christ's sufferings upon the cross for our sins, and the roses of gold the glory and beauty of his Resurrection. This symbol was carried alternately to Mecca, Mount Calvary, Mount Sinai, Haran, and to three other places, which must have been in mid-air, called *Cascle, Apamia,* and *Chaulateau Virissa Caunuch,* where the Rosicrucian brethren met when they pleased, and made resolution of all their actions. They always took their pleasures in one of these places, where they resolved all questions of whatsoever had been done, was done, or should be done in the world, from the beginning to the end thereof. "And these," he concludes, "are the men called Rosicrucians!"

Towards the end of the seventeenth century, more rational ideas took possession of the sect, which still continued to boast of a few members. They appear to have considered that contentment was the true philosopher's stone, and to have abandoned the insane search for a mere phantom of the imagination. Addison, in *The Spectator*,* gives an account of his conversation with a Rosicrucian ; from which it may be inferred that the sect had grown wiser in their deeds, though in their talk they were as foolish as ever. "I was once," says he, "engaged in discourse with a Rosicrucian about the great secret. He talked of the secret as of a spirit which lived within an emerald, and converted every thing that was near it to the highest perfection that it was capable of. 'It gives a lustre,' says he, 'to the sun, and water to the diamond. It irradiates every metal, and enriches lead with all the properties of gold. It heightens smoke into flame, flame into light, and light into glory.' He further added, 'that a single ray of it dissipates pain and care and melancholy from the person on whom it falls. In short,' says he, 'its presence naturally changes every place into a kind of heaven.' After he had gone on for some time in this unintelligible cant, I found that he jumbled natural and moral ideas together into the same discourse, and that his great secret was nothing else but content."

JACOB BÖHMEN.

It is now time to speak of Jacob Böhmen, who thought he could discover the secret of the transmutation of metals in the Bible, and who invented a strange heterogeneous doctrine of mingled alchymy and religion, and founded upon it the sect of the Aurea-crucians. He was born at Görlitz, in Upper Lusatia, in 1575, and followed till his thirtieth year the occupation of a shoemaker. In this obscurity he remained, with the character of a visionary and a man of unsettled mind, until the promulgation of the Rosicrucian philosophy in his part of Germany, toward the year 1607 or 1608. From that time he began to neglect his leather, and buried his brain under the rubbish of metaphysics. The works of Paracelsus fell into his hands ; and these, with the reveries of the Rosicrucians, so completely engrossed his attention, that he abandoned his trade altogether, sinking, at the same time, from a state of comparative independence into poverty and destitution. But he was nothing daunted by the miseries and privations of the flesh ; his mind was fixed upon the beings of another sphere, and in thought he was already the new apostle of the human race. In the year 1612, after a meditation of four years, he published his first work, entitled *Aurora, or the Rising of the Sun;* embodying the ridiculous notions of Paracelsus, and worse confounding the confusion of that writer. The philosopher's stone might, he contended, be discovered by a diligent search of the Old

* No. 574. Friday, July 30th, 1714.

and New Testaments, and more especially of the Apocalypse, which alone contained all the secrets of alchymy. He contended that the divine grace operated by the same rules, and followed the same methods, that the divine providence observed in the natural world; and that the minds of men were purged from their vices and corruptions in the very same manner that metals were purified from their dross, namely, by fire.

Besides the sylphs, gnomes, undines, and salamanders, he acknowledged various ranks and orders of demons. He pretended to invisibility and absolute chastity. He also said that, if it pleased him, he could abstain for years from meat and drink, and all the necessities of the body. It is needless, however, to pursue his follies any further. He was reprimanded for writing this work by the magistrates of Görlitz, and commanded to leave the pen alone and stick to his wax, that his family might not become chargeable to the parish. He neglected this good advice, and continued his studies; burning minerals and purifying metals one day, and mystifying the Word of God on the next. He afterwards wrote three other works, as sublimely ridiculous as the first. The one was entitled *Metallurgia*, and has the slight merit of being the least obscure of his compositions. Another was called *The Temporal Mirror of Eternity;* and the last his *Theosophy revealed*, full of allegories and metaphors,

> " All strange and geason,
> Devoid of sense and ordinary reason."

Böhmen died in 1624, leaving behind him a considerable number of admiring disciples. Many of them became, during the seventeenth century, as distinguished for absurdity as their master; amongst whom may be mentioned Gifftheil, Wendenhagen, John Jacob Zimmermann, and Abraham Frankenberg. Their heresy rendered them obnoxious to the Church of Rome; and many of them suffered long imprisonment and torture for their faith. One, named Kuhlmann, was burned alive at Moscow, in 1684, on a charge of sorcery. Böhmen's works were translated into English, and published, many years afterwards, by an enthusiast named William Law.

MORMIUS.

Peter Mormius, a notorious alchymist and contemporary of Böhmen, endeavoured, in 1630, to introduce the Rosicrucian philosophy into Holland. He applied to the States-General to grant him a public audience, that he might explain the tenets of the sect, and disclose a plan for rendering Holland the happiest and richest country on the earth, by means of the philosopher's stone and the service of the elementary spirits. The States-General wisely resolved to have nothing to do with him. He thereupon determined to shame them by printing his book, which he did at Leyden the same year. It was entitled *The Book of the most Hidden Secrets of Nature*, and was divided into three parts; the first treating of "perpetual motion;" the second of the "transmutation of metals;" and the third of the "universal medicine." He also published some German works upon the Rosicrucian philosophy, at Frankfort, in 1617.

Poetry and romance are deeply indebted to the Rosicrucians for many a graceful creation. The literature of England, France, and Germany contains hundreds of sweet fictions, whose machinery has been borrowed from their day-dreams. The "delicate Ariel" of Shakspeare stands pre-eminent among the number. From the same source Pope drew the airy tenants of Belinda's dressing-room, in his charming *Rape of the Lock;* and La Motte Fouqué, the beautiful and capricious water-nymph Undine, around whom he has thrown more grace and loveliness, and for whose imaginary woes he has excited more sympathy, than ever were bestowed on a supernatural being. Sir Walter Scott also endowed the White Lady of Avenel with many of the attributes of the undines or water-sprites. German romance and lyrical poetry teem with allusions to sylphs, gnomes, undines, and salamanders; and the French have not been behind in substituting them, in works of fiction, for the more cumbrous mythology of Greece and Rome. The sylphs, more especially, have been the favourites of the bards, and have become so familiar to the popular mind as to be, in a manner, confounded with that other race of ideal beings, the fairies, who can boast of an antiquity much more venerable in the annals of superstition. Having these obligations to the Rosicrucians, no lover of poetry can wish, however absurd they were, that such a sect of philosophers had never existed.

BORRI.

Just at the time that Michael Mayer was making known to the world the existence of such a body as the Rosicrucians, there was born in Italy a man who was afterwards destined to become the most conspicuous member of the fraternity. The alchymic mania never called forth the ingenuity of a more consummate or more successful impostor than Joseph Francis Borri. He was born in 1616, according to some authorities, and in 1627 according to others, at Milan ; where his father, the Signor Branda Borri, practised as a physician. At the age of sixteen Joseph was sent to finish his education at the Jesuits' college in Rome, where he distinguished himself by his extraordinary memory. He learned every thing to which he applied

himself with the utmost ease.   In the most voluminous works no
fact was too minute for his retention, and no study was so abstruse
but that he could master it; but any advantages he might have
derived from this facility were neutralised by his ungovernable passions and his love of turmoil and debauchery.   He was involved in
continual difficulty, as well with the heads of the college as with
the police of Rome, and acquired so bad a character that years could
not remove it.   By the aid of his friends he established himself as a
physician in Rome, and also obtained some situation in the pope's
household.   In one of his fits of studiousness he grew enamoured of
alchymy, and determined to devote his energies to the discovery of
the philosopher's stone.   Of unfortunate propensities he had quite
sufficient, besides this, to bring him to poverty.   His pleasures were
as expensive as his studies, and both were of a nature to destroy his
health and ruin his fair fame.   At the age of thirty-seven he found
that he could not live by the practice of medicine, and began to look
about for some other employment.   He became, in 1653, private
secretary to the Marquis di Mirogli, the minister of the Archduke of
Innsprück at the court of Rome.   He continued in this capacity for
two years; leading, however, the same abandoned life as heretofore,
frequenting the society of gamesters, debauchees, and loose women,
involving himself in disgraceful street quarrels, and alienating the
patrons who were desirous to befriend him.

All at once a sudden change was observed in his conduct.   The
abandoned rake put on the outward sedateness of a philosopher; the
scoffing sinner proclaimed that he had forsaken his evil ways, and
would live thenceforth a model of virtue.   To his friends this
reformation was as pleasing as it was unexpected; and Borri gave
obscure hints that it had been brought about by some miraculous
manifestation of a superior power.   He pretended that he held converse with beneficent spirits; that the secrets of God and nature
were revealed to him; and that he had obtained possession of the
philosopher's stone.   Like his predecessor, Jacob Böhmen, he mixed
up religious questions with his philosophical jargon, and took measures for declaring himself the founder of a new sect.   This, at Rome
itself, and in the very palace of the pope, was a hazardous proceeding; and Borri just awoke to a sense of it in time to save himself
from the dungeons of the Castle of St. Angelo.   He fled to Innsprück,
where he remained about a year, and then returned to his native city
of Milan.

The reputation of his great sanctity had gone before him; and he
found many persons ready to attach themselves to his fortunes.   All
who were desirous of entering into the new communion took an oath

of poverty, and relinquished their possessions for the general good of the fraternity. Borri told them that he had received from the arch-angel Michael a heavenly sword, upon the hilt of which were engraven the names of the seven celestial intelligences. "Whoever shall refuse," said he, "to enter into my new sheepfold shall be destroyed by the papal armies, of whom God has predestined me to be the chief. To those who follow me all joy shall be granted. I shall soon

INNSPRUCK.

bring my chemical studies to a happy conclusion by the discovery of the philosopher's stone, and by this means we shall all have as much gold as we desire. I am assured of the aid of the angelic hosts, and more especially of the archangel Michael's. When I began to walk in the way of the spirit, I had a vision of the night, and was assured by an angelic voice that I should become a prophet. In sign of it, I saw a palm-tree surrounded with all the glory of paradise. The angels come to me whenever I call, and reveal to me all the secrets of the universe. The sylphs and elementary spirits obey me, and fly to the uttermost ends of the world to serve me, and those whom I delight to honour." By force of continually repeating such stories as these, Borri soon found himself at the head of a very considerable number of adherents. As he figures in these pages as an alchymist, and not as a religious sectarian, it will be unnecessary to repeat the doctrines which he taught with regard to some of the dogmas of the Church of Rome, and which exposed him to the fierce resentment of the papal authority. They were to the full as ridiculous as his philosophical pretensions. As the number of his followers increased, he appears to have cherished the idea of becoming one day a new Mahomet, and of founding, in his native city of Milan, a monarchy and religion of which he should be the king and the prophet. He had taken measures, in the year 1658, for seizing the guards at all the gates of that city, and formally declaring himself the monarch of the Milanese. Just as he thought the plan ripe for execution, it was discovered. Twenty of his followers were arrested, and he himself managed, with the utmost difficulty, to escape to the neutral territory of Switzerland, where the papal displeasure could not reach him.

The trial of his followers commenced forthwith, and the whole of them were sentenced to various terms of imprisonment. Borri's trial proceeded in his absence, and lasted for upwards of two years. He was condemned to death as a heretic and sorcerer in 1661, and was burned in effigy in Rome by the common hangman.

Borri, in the mean time, lived quietly in Switzerland, indulging himself in railing at the Inquisition and its proceedings. He afterwards went to Strasbourg, intending to fix his residence in that town. He was received with great cordiality, as a man persecuted for his religious opinions, and withal a great alchymist. He found that sphere too narrow for his aspiring genius, and retired in the same year to the more wealthy city of Amsterdam. He there hired a magnificent house, established an equipage which eclipsed in brilliancy those of the richest merchants, and assumed the title of Excellency. Where he got the money to live in this expensive style was long a secret : the adepts in alchymy easily explained it, after their fashion. Sensible people were of opinion that he had come by it in a less wonderful manner ; for it was remembered that among his unfortunate disciples in Milan, there were many rich men, who, in conformity with one of the fundamental rules of the sect, had given up all their earthly wealth into the hands of their founder. In whatever manner the money was obtained, Borri spent it in Holland with an unsparing hand, and was looked up to by the people with no little respect and veneration. He performed several able cures, and increased his reputation so much that he was vaunted as a prodigy. He continued diligently the operations of alchymy, and was in daily expectation that he should succeed in turning the inferior metals into gold. This hope never abandoned him, even in the worst extremity of his fortunes ; and in his prosperity it led him into the most foolish expenses : but he could not long continue to live so magnificently upon the funds he had brought from Italy ; and the philosopher's stone, though it promised all for the wants of the morrow, never brought any thing for the necessities of to-day. He was obliged in a few months to retrench, by giving up his large house, his gilded coach and valuable blood-horses, his liveried domestics, and his luxurious entertainments. With this diminution of splendour came a diminution of renown. His cures did not appear so miraculous when he went out on foot to perform them, as they had seemed when "his Excellency" had driven to a poor man's door in his carriage with six horses. He sank from a prodigy into an ordinary man. His great friends shewed him the cold shoulder, and his humble flatterers carried their incense to some other shrine. Borri now thought it high time to change his quarters. With this view he borrowed money wherever he could get it, and succeeded in obtaining two hundred thousand florins from a merchant named De Meer, to aid, as he said, in discovering the water of life. He also obtained six diamonds of great value, on pretence that he could remove the flaws from them without diminishing their weight. With this booty he stole away secretly by night, and proceeded to Hamburgh.

On his arrival in that city, he found the celebrated Christina, the ex-queen of Sweden. He procured an introduction to her, and requested her patronage in his endeavour to discover the philosopher's stone. She gave him some encouragement ; but Borri, fearing that the merchants of Amsterdam, who had connexions in Hamburgh, might expose his delinquencies if he remained in the latter city, passed over to Copenhagen, and sought the protection of Frederick III., the king of Denmark.

This prince was a firm believer in the transmutation of metals. Being in want of money, he readily listened to the plans of an adventurer who had both eloquence and ability to recommend him. He provided Borri with the means to make experiments, and took a great interest in the progress of his operations. He expected every month to possess riches that would buy Peru ; and, when he was disappointed, accepted patiently the excuses of Borri, who, upon every failure, was always ready with some plausible explanation. He became in time much attached to him ; and defended him from the jealous attacks of his courtiers, and the indignation of those who were grieved to see their monarch the easy dupe of a charlatan. Borri endeavoured, by every means in his power, to find aliment for this good opinion. His knowledge of medicine was useful to him in this respect, and often stood between him and disgrace. He lived six years in this manner at the court of Frederick ; but that monarch dying in 1670, he was léft without a protector.

As he had made more enemies than friends in Copenhagen, and had nothing to hope from the succeeding sovereign, he sought an asylum in another country. He went first to Saxony ; but met so little encouragement and encountered so much danger from the emissaries of the Inquisition, that he did not remain there many months. Anticipating nothing but persecution in every country that acknowledged the spiritual authority of the pope, he appears to have taken the resolution to dwell in Turkey, and turn Mussulman. On his arrival at the Hungarian frontier, on his way to Constantinople, he was arrested on suspicion of being concerned in the conspiracy of the Counts Nadasdi and Frangipani, which had just been discovered. In vain he protested his innocence, and divulged his real name and profession. He was detained in prison, and a letter despatched to the Emperor Leopold, to know what should be done with him. The star of his fortunes was on the decline. The letter reached Leopold at an unlucky moment. The pope's nuncio was closeted with his majesty ; and he no sooner heard the name of Joseph Francis Borri, than he demanded him as a prisoner of the Holy See. The request was complied with ; and Borri, closely manacled, was sent under an escort of soldiers to the prison of the Inquisition at Rome. He was too much of an impostor to be deeply tinged with fanaticism, and was not unwilling to make a public recantation of his heresies, if he could thereby save his life. When the proposition was made to him, he accepted it with eagerness. His punishment was to be commuted into the hardly less severe one of perpetual imprisonment ; but he was too happy to escape the clutch of the executioner at any price, and he made the *amende honorable* in face of the assembled multitudes of Rome on the 27th of October 1672. He was then transferred to the prisons of the Castle of St. Angelo, where he remained till his death, twenty-three years·afterwards. It is said that, towards the close of his life, considerable indulgence was granted him ; that he was allowed to have a laboratory, and to cheer the solitude of his dungeon by searching for the philosopher's stone. Queen Christina, during her residence at Rome, frequently visited the old man, to converse with him upon chemistry and the doctrines of the Rosicrucians. She even obtained permission that he should leave his prison occasionally for a day or two, and reside in her palace, she being responsible for his return to captivity. She encouraged him to search for the great secret of the alchymists, and provided him with money for the purpose. It may well be supposed that Borri benefited most by this acquaintance, and that Christina got nothing but experience. It is not sure that she gained even that; for until her dying day she was convinced of the possibility of finding the philosopher's stone, and ready to assist any adventurer either zealous or impudent enough to pretend to it.

After Borri had been about eleven years in confinement, a small volume was published at Cologne, entitled *The Key of the Cabinet of the Chevalier Joseph Francis Borri, in which are contained many curious Letters upon Chemistry and other Sciences, written by him, together with a Memoir of his Life.* This book contained a complete exposition of the Rosicrucian philosophy, and afforded materials to the Abbé de Villars for his interesting *Count de Gabalis*, which excited so much attention at the close of the seventeenth century.

Borri lingered in the prison of St. Angelo till 1695, when he died, in his eightieth year. Besides *The Key of the Cabinet*, written originally in Copenhagen, in 1666, for the edification of King Frederick III., he published a work upon alchymy and the secret sciences, under the title of *The Mission of Romulus to the Romans.*

INFERIOR ALCHYMISTS OF THE SEVENTEENTH CENTURY.

Besides the pretenders to the philosopher's stone whose lives have been already narrated, this and the preceding century produced a great number of writers, who inundated literature with their books upon the subject. In fact, most of the learned men of that age had some faith in it. Van Helmont, Borrichius, Kircher, Boerhaave, and a score of others, though not professed alchymists, were fond of the science and countenanced its professors. Helvetius, the grandfather of the celebrated philosopher of the same name, asserts that he saw an inferior metal turned into gold by a stranger at the Hague, in 1666. He says, that, sitting one day in his study, a man, who was dressed as a respectable burgher of North Holland, and very modest and simple in his appearance, called upon him, with the intention of dispelling his doubts relative to the philosopher's stone. He asked Helvetius if he thought he should know that rare gem if he saw it. To which Helvetius replied, that he certainly should not. The burgher immediately drew from his pocket a small ivory box, containing three pieces of metal, of the colour of brimstone, and extremely heavy; and assured Helvetius, that of them he could make as much as twenty tons of gold. Helvetius informs us, that he examined them very attentively ; and seeing that they were very brittle, he took the opportunity to scrape off a small portion with his thumb-nail. He then returned them to the stranger, with an entreaty that he would perform the process of transmutation before him. The stranger replied, that he was not allowed to do so, and went away. After his departure, Helvetius procured a crucible and a portion of lead, into which, when in a state of fusion, he threw the stolen grain from the philosopher's stone. He was disappointed to find that the grain evaporated altogether, leaving the lead in its original state.

Some weeks afterwards, when he had almost forgotten the subject, he received another visit from the stranger. He again entreated him to explain the processes by which he pretended to transmute lead. The stranger at last consented, and informed him, that one grain was sufficient ; but that it was necessary to envelope it in a ball of wax before throwing it on the molten metal ; otherwise its extreme volatility would cause it to go off in vapour. They tried the experiment, and succeeded to their heart's content. Helvetius repeated the experiment alone, and converted six ounces of lead into very pure gold.

The fame of this event spread all over the Hague, and all the notable persons of the town flocked to the study of Helvetius to convince themselves of the fact. Helvetius performed the experiment again, in the presence of the Prince of Orange, and several times afterwards, until he exhausted the whole of the powder he had received from the stranger, from whom, it is necessary to state, he never received another visit, nor did he ever discover his name or condition. In the following year, Helvetius published his *Golden Calf*,* in which he detailed the above circumstances.

About the same time, the celebrated Father Kircher published his *Subterranean World*, in which he called the alchymists a congregation of knaves and impostors, and their science a delusion. He admitted that he had himself been a diligent labourer in the field, and had only come to this conclusion after mature consideration and repeated fruitless experiments. All the alchymists were in arms immediately, to refute this formidable antagonist. One Solomon de Blauenstein was the first to grapple with him, and attempted to convict him of wilful misrepresentation, by recalling to his memory the transmutations by Sendivogius before the Emperor Frederick III. and the Elector of Mayence, all performed within a recent period. Zwelfer

---

* " Vitulus Aureus quem Mundus adorat et orat, in quo tractatur de naturæ miraculo transmutandi metalla." *Hagæ*, 1667.

and Glauber also entered into the dispute, and attributed the enmity of Father Kircher to spite and jealousy against adepts who had been more successful than himself.

It was also pretended that Gustavus Adolphus transmuted a quantity of quicksilver into pure gold. The learned Borrichius relates, that he saw coins which had been struck of this gold; and Lenglet du Fresnoy deposes to the same circumstance. In the *Travels of Monconis* the story is told in the following manner: " A merchant of Lubeck, who carried on but little trade, but who knew how to change lead into very good gold, gave the King of Sweden a lingot which he had made, weighing at least one hundred pounds. The king immediately caused it to be coined into ducats; and because he knew positively that its origin was such as had been stated to him, he had his own arms graven upon the one side, and emblematical figures of Mercury and Venus on the other. I (continued Monconis) have one of these ducats in my possession ; and was credibly informed that, after the death of the Lubeck merchant, who had never appeared very rich, a sum of no less than one million seven hundred thousand crowns was found in his coffers."*

Such stories as these, confidently related by men high in station, tended to keep up the infatuation of the alchymists in every country of Europe. It is astonishing to see the number of works which were written upon the subject during the seventeenth century alone, and the number of clever men who sacrificed themselves to the delusion. Gabriel de Castaigne, a monk of the order of St. Francis, attracted so much notice in the reign of Louis XIII., that that monarch secured him in his household, and made him his Grand Almoner. He pretended to find the elixir of life, and Louis expected by his means to have enjoyed the crown for a century. Van Helmont also pretended to have once performed with success the process of transmuting quicksilver, and was in consequence invited by the Emperor Rudolph II. to fix his residence at the court of Vienna. Glauber, the inventor of the salts which still bear his name, and who practised as a physician at Amsterdam about the middle of the seventeenth century, established a public school in that city for the study of alchymy, and gave lectures himself upon the science. John Joachim Becher of Spire acquired great reputation at the same period, and was convinced that much gold might be made out of flint-stones by a peculiar process, and the aid of that grand and incomprehensible substance the philosopher's stone. He made a proposition to the Emperor Leopold of Austria to aid him in these experiments ; but the hope of success was too remote, and the present expense too great, to tempt that mon-

* *Voyages de Monconis*, tome ii. p. 379.

arch, and he therefore gave Becher much of his praise, but none of his money. Becher afterwards tried the States-General of Holland with no better success.

With regard to the innumerable tricks by which impostors persuaded the world that they had succeeded in making gold, and of which so many stories were current about this period, a very satisfactory report was read by M. Geoffroy the elder, at the sitting of the Royal Academy of Sciences at Paris, on the 15th of April 1722. As it relates principally to the alchymic cheats of the sixteenth and seventeenth centuries, the following abridgment of it may not be out of place in this portion of our history. The instances of successful transmutation were so numerous, and apparently so well authenticated, that nothing short of so able an exposure as that of M. Geoffroy could disabuse the public mind. The trick to which they oftenest had recourse was to use a double-bottomed crucible, the under surface being of iron or copper, and the upper one of wax, painted to resemble the same metal. Between the two they placed as much gold or silver dust as was necessary for their purpose. They then put in their lead, quicksilver, or other ingredients, and placed their pot upon the fire. Of course, when the experiment was concluded, they never failed to find a lump of gold at the bottom. The same result was produced in many other ways. Some of them used a hollow wand, filled with gold or silver dust, and stopped at the ends with wax or butter. With this they stirred the boiling metal in their crucibles, taking care to accompany the operation with many ceremonies, to divert attention from the real purpose of the manœuvre. They also drilled holes in lumps of lead, into which they poured molten gold, and carefully closed the aperture with the original metal. Sometimes they washed a piece of gold with quicksilver. When in this state, they found no difficulty in palming it off upon the uninitiated as an inferior metal, and very easily transmuted it into fine sonorous gold again with the aid of a little aquafortis.

Others imposed by means of nails, half iron and half gold or silver. They pretended that they really transmuted the precious half from iron, by dipping it in a strong alcohol. M. Geoffroy produced several of these nails to the Academy of Sciences, and shewed how nicely the two parts were soldered together. The golden or silver half was painted black to resemble iron, and the colour immediately disappeared when the nail was dipped into aquafortis. A nail of this description was for a long time in the cabinet of the Grand Duke of Tuscany. Such also, said M. Geoffroy, was the knife presented by a monk to Queen Elizabeth of England; the blade of which was half gold and half steel. Nothing at one time was more common than to see coins, half gold and half silver, which had been operated upon by alchymists, for the same purposes of trickery. In fact, says M. Geoffroy, in concluding his long report, there is every reason to believe that all the famous histories which have been handed down to us about the transmutation of metals into gold or silver, by means of the powder of projection or philosophical elixirs, are founded upon some successful deception of the kind above narrated. These pretended philosophers invariably disappeared after the first or second experiment, or their powders or elixirs have failed to produce their effect, either because attention being excited they have found no opportunity to renew the trick without being discovered, or because they have not had sufficient gold dust for more than one trial.

The disinterestedness of these would-be philosophers looked, at first sight, extremely imposing. Instances were not rare in which they generously abandoned all the profits of their transmutations—even the honour of the discovery. But this apparent disinterestedness was one of the most cunning of their manœuvres. It served to keep up the popular expectation ; it seemed to shew the possibility of discovering the philosopher's stone, and provided the means of future advantages, which they were never slow to lay hold of—such as entrances into royal households, maintenance at the public expense, and gifts from ambitious potentates, too greedy after the gold they so easily promised.

It now only remains to trace the progress of the delusion from the commencement of the eighteenth century until the present day. It will be seen that, until a very recent period, there were but slight signs of a return to reason.

JEAN DELISLE.

In the year 1705, there was much talk in France of a blacksmith, named Delisle, who had discovered the philosopher's stone, and who went about the country turning lead into gold. He was a native of Provence, from which place his fame soon spread to the capital. His early life is involved in obscurity ; but Lenglet du Fresnoy has industriously collected some particulars of his later career, which possess considerable interest. He was a man without any education, and had been servant in his youth to an alchymist, from whom he learned many of the tricks of the fraternity. The name of his master has never been discovered ; but it is pretended that he rendered himself in some manner obnoxious to the government of Louis XIV., and was obliged, in consequence, to take refuge in Switzerland. Delisle accompanied him as far as Savoy, and there, it is said, set upon him in a solitary mountain-pass and murdered and robbed him. He then disguised himself as a pilgrim, and returned to France. At a lonely inn, by the road-side, where he stopped for the night, he became acquainted with a woman, named Aluys ; and so sudden a passion was enkindled betwixt them, that she consented to leave all, follow him, and share his good or evil fortune wherever he went. They lived together for five or six years in Provence, without exciting any attention, apparently possessed of a decent independence. At last, in 1706, it was given out that he was the possessor of the philosopher's stone ; and people from far and near came flocking to his residence, at the Château de la Palu, at Sylanez, near Barjaumont, to witness the wealth he could make out of pumps and fire-shovels. The following account of his operations is given in a letter addressed by M. de Cerisy, the Prior of Châteauneuf, in the Diocese of Riez, in Provence, to the Vicar of St. Jacques du Hautpas, at Paris, and dated the 18th of November, 1706 :

"I have something to relate to you, my dear cousin, which will be interesting to you and your friends. The philosopher's stone, which so many persons have looked upon as a chimera, is at last found. It is a man named Delisle, of the parish of Sylanez, and residing within a quarter of a league of me, that has discovered this great secret. He turns lead into gold, and iron into silver, by merely heating these metals red-hot, and pouring upon them in that state some oil and powder he is possessed of ; so that it would not be impossible for any man to make a million a day, if he had sufficient of this wondrous mixture. Some of the pale gold which he had made in this manner he sent to the jewellers of Lyons, to have their opinion on its quality. He also sold twenty pounds weight of it to a merchant of Digne, named Taxis. All the jewellers say they never saw such fine gold in their lives. He makes nails, part gold, part iron, and part silver. He promised to give me one of them, in a long conversation which I had with him the other day, by order of the Bishop of Senés, who saw his operations with his own eyes, and detailed all the circumstances to me.

"The Baron and Baroness de Rheinwald shewed me a lingot of gold made out of pewter before their eyes by M. Delisle. My brother-in-law Sauveur, who has wasted fifty years of his life in this great study, brought me the other day a nail which he had seen changed into gold by Delisle, and fully convinced me that all his previous experiments were founded on an erroneous principle. This excellent workman received, a short time ago, a very kind letter from the superintendent of the royal household, which I read. He offered to use all his influence with the ministers to prevent any attempts upon his liberty, which has twice been attacked by the agents of government. It is believed that the oil he makes use of is gold or silver reduced to that state. He leaves it for a long time exposed to the rays of the sun. He told me that it generally took him six months to make all his preparations. I told him that, apparently, the king wanted to see him. He replied that he could not exercise his art in every place, as a certain climate and temperature were absolutely necessary to his success. The truth is, that this man appears to have no ambition. He only keeps two horses and two men-servants. Besides, he loves his liberty, has no politeness, and speaks very bad French ; but his judgment seems to be solid. He was formerly no more than a blacksmith, but excelled in that trade without having been taught it. All the great lords and seigneurs from far and near come to visit him, and pay such court to him, that it seems more like idolatry than any thing else. Happy would France be if this man would discover his secret to the king, to whom the superintendent has already sent some lingots! But the happiness is too great to be hoped for; for I fear that the workman and his secret will expire together. There is no doubt that this discovery will make a great noise in the kingdom, unless the character of the man, which I have just depicted to you, prevent it. At all events, posterity will hear of him."

In another letter to the same person, dated the 27th of January 1707, M. de Cerisy says, "My dear cousin, I spoke to you in my last letter of the famous alchymist of Provence, M. Delisle. A good deal of that was only hearsay, but now I am enabled to speak from my own experience. I have in my possession a nail, half iron and half silver, which I made myself. That great and admirable workman also bestowed a still greater privilege upon me—he allowed me to turn a piece of lead which I had brought with me into pure gold, by means of his wonderful oil and powder. All the country have their eyes upon this gentleman ; some deny loudly, others are incredulous; but those who have seen acknowledge the truth. I have read the passport that has been sent to him from court, with orders that he should present himself at Paris early in the spring. He told me that he would go willingly, and that it was himself who fixed the spring for his departure ; as he wanted to collect his materials, in order that, immediately on his introduction to the king, he might make an experiment worthy of his majesty, by converting a large quantity of lead into the finest gold. I sincerely hope that he will not allow his secret to die with him, but that he will communicate it to the king. As I had the honour to dine with him on Thursday last, the 20th of this month, being seated at his side, I told him in a whisper that he could, if he liked, humble all the enemies of France. He did not deny it, but began to smile. In fact, this man is the miracle of art. Sometimes he employs the oil and powder mixed, sometimes the powder only; but in so small a quantity that, when the lingot which I made was rubbed all over with it, it did not shew at all."

This soft-headed priest was by no means the only person in the neighbourhood who lost his wits in hopes of the boundless wealth held out by this clever impostor. Another priest named De Lions, a chanter in the cathedral of Grenoble, writing on the 30th January 1707, says: "M. Mesnard, the curate of Montier, has written to me, stating that there is a man, about thirty-five years of age, named Delisle, who turns lead and iron into gold and silver; and that this transmutation is so veritable and so true, that the goldsmiths affirm that his gold and silver are the purest and finest they ever saw. For five years this man was looked upon as a madman or a cheat; but the public mind is now disabused with respect to him. He now resides with M. de la Palu, at the château of the same name. M. de la Palu is not very easy in his circumstances, and wants money to portion his daughters, who have remained single till middle age, no man being willing to take them without a dowry. M. Delisle has promised to make them the richest girls in the province before he goes to court, having been sent for by the king. He has asked for a little time before his departure, in order that he may collect powder enough to make several quintals of gold before the eyes of his majesty, to whom he intends to present them. The principal matter of his wonderful powder is composed of simples, principally the herbs *Lunaria major* and *minor*. There is a good deal of the first planted by him in the gardens of La Palu; and he gets the other from the mountains that stretch about two leagues from Montier. What I tell you now is not a mere story invented for your diversion : M. Mesnard can bring forward many witnesses to its truth ; among others the Bishop of Senés, who saw these surprising operations performed ; and M. de Cerisy, whom you know well. Delisle transmutes his metals in public. He rubs the lead or iron with his powder, and puts it over burning charcoal. In a short time it changes colour ; the lead becomes yellow, and is found to be converted into excellent gold ; the iron becomes white, and is found to be pure silver. Delisle is altogether an illiterate person. M. de St. Auban endeavoured to teach him to read and write, but he profited very little by his lessons. He is unpolite, fantastic, and a dreamer, and acts by fits and starts."

Delisle, it would appear, was afraid of venturing to Paris. He knew that his sleight of hand would be too narrowly watched in the royal presence ; and upon some pretence or other he delayed the journey for more than two years. Desmarets, the Minister of Finance to Louis XIV., thinking the "philosopher" dreaded foul play, twice sent him a safe-conduct under the king's seal ; but Delisle still refused. Upon this, Desmarets wrote to the Bishop of Senés for his real opinion as to these famous transmutations. The following was the answer of that prelate :

" Copy of a report addressed to M. Desmarets, Comptroller-General of the Finances to His Majesty Louis XIV., by the Bishop of Senés, dated March 1709.

" SIR,—A twelvemonth ago, or a little more, I expressed to you my joy at hearing of your elevation to the ministry ; I have now the honour to write you my opinion of the Sieur Delisle, who has been working at the transmutation of metals in my diocese. I have, during the last two years, spoken of him several times to the Count de Pontchartrain, because he asked me ; but I have not written to you, sir, or to M. de Chamillart, because you neither of you requested my opinion upon the subject. Now, however, that you have given me to understand that you wish to know my sentiments on the matter, I will unfold myself to you in all sincerity, for the interests of the king and the glory of your ministry.

" There are two things about the Sieur Delisle which, in my opinion, should be examined without prejudice : the one relates to his secret ; the other, to his person ; that is to say, whether his transmutations are real, and whether his conduct has been regular. As regards the secret of the philosopher's stone, I deemed it impossible, for a long time ; and for more than three years I was more mistrustful of the pretensions of this Sieur Delisle than of any other person. During this period I afforded him no countenance ; I even aided a person, who was highly recommended to me by an influential family of this province, to prosecute Delisle for some offence or other which it was alleged he had committed. But this person, in his anger against him, having told me that he had himself been several times the bearer of gold and silver to the goldsmiths of Nice, Aix, and Avignon, which had been transmuted by Delisle from lead and iron, I began to waver a little in my opinions respecting him. I afterwards met Delisle at the house of one of my friends. To please me, the family asked Delisle to operate before me, to which he immediately consented. I offered him some iron nails, which he changed into silver in the chimney-place before six or seven credible witnesses. I took the nails thus transmuted, and sent them by my almoner to Imbert, the jeweller of Aix, who, having subjected them to the necessary trial, returned them to me, saying they were very good silver. Still, however, I was not quite satisfied. M. de Pontchartrain having hinted to me, two years previously, that I should do a thing agreeable to his majesty if I examined into this business of Delisle, I resolved to do so now. I therefore summoned the alchymist to come to me at Castellane. He came; and I had him escorted by eight or ten vigilant men, to whom I had given notice to watch his hands strictly. Before all of us he changed two pieces of lead into gold and silver. I sent them both to M. de Pontchartrain; and he afterwards informed me by a letter, now lying before me, that he had shewn them to the most experienced goldsmiths of Paris, who unanimously pronounced them to be gold and silver of the very purest quality, and without alloy. My former bad opinion of Delisle was now indeed shaken. It was much more so when he performed transmutation five or six times before me at Senés, and made me perform it myself before him without his putting his hand to any thing. You have seen, sir, the letter of my nephew, the Père Berard, of the Oratoire at Paris, on the experiment that he performed at Castellane, and the truth of which I hereby attest. Another nephew of mine, the Sieur Bourget, who was here three weeks ago, performed the same experiment in my presence, and will detail all the circumstances to you personally at Paris. A hundred persons in my diocese have been witnesses of these things. I confess to you, sir, that, after the testimony of so many spectators and so many goldsmiths, and after the repeatedly successful experiments that I saw performed, all my prejudices vanished. My reason was convinced by my eyes; and the phantoms of impossibility which I had conjured up were dissipated by the work of my own hands.

"It now only remains for me to speak to you on the subject of his person and conduct. Three suspicions have been excited against him : the first, that he was implicated in some criminal proceeding at Cisteron, and that he falsified the coin of the realm ; the second, that the king sent him two safe-conducts without effect ; and the third, that he still delays going to court to operate before the king. You may see, sir, that I do not hide or avoid any thing. As regards the business at Cisteron, the Sieur Delisle has repeatedly assured me that there was nothing against him which could reasonably draw him within the pale of justice, and that he had never carried on any calling injurious to the king's service. It was true that, six or seven years ago, he had been to Cisteron to gather herbs necessary for his powder, and that he had lodged at the house of one Pelouse, whom he thought an honest man. Pelouse was accused of clipping Louisd'ors ; and as he had lodged with him, he was suspected of being his accomplice. This mere suspicion, without any proof whatever, had caused him to be condemned for contumacy ; a common case enough with judges, who always proceed with much rigour against those who are absent. During my own sojourn at Aix, it was well known that a man, named André Aluys, had spread about reports injurious to the character of Delisle, because he hoped thereby to avoid paying him a sum of forty *Louis* that he owed him. But permit me, sir, to go further, and to add that, even if there were well-founded suspicions against Delisle, we should look with some little indulgence on the faults of a man who possesses a secret so useful to the state. As regards the two safe-conducts sent him by the king, I think I can answer certainly that it was through no fault of his that he paid so little attention to them. His year, strictly speaking, consists only of the four summer months; and when by any means he is prevented from making the proper use of them, he loses a whole year. Thus the first safe-conduct became useless by the irruption of the Duke of Savoy in 1707; and the second had hardly been obtained, at the end of June 1708, when the said Delisle was insulted by a party of armed men, pretending to act under the authority of the Count de Grignan, to whom he wrote several letters of complaint, without receiving any answer, or promise that his safety would be attended to. What I have now told you, sir, removes the third objection, and is the reason why, at the present time, he cannot go to Paris to the king, in fulfilment of his promises made two years ago. Two, or even three, summers have been lost to him, owing to the continual inquietude he has laboured under. He has, in consequence, been unable to work, and has not collected a sufficient quantity of his oil and powder, or brought what he has got to the necessary degree of perfection. For this reason also he could not give the Sieur de Bourget the portion he promised him for your inspection. If the other day he changed some lead into gold with a few grains of his powder, they were assuredly all he had; for he told me that such was the fact long before he knew my nephew was coming. Even if he had preserved this small quantity to operate before the king, I am sure that, on second thoughts, he would never have adventured with so little; because the slightest obstacles in the metals (their being too hard or too soft, which is only discovered in operating,) would have caused him to be looked upon as an impostor, if, in case his first powder had proved ineffectual, he had not been possessed of more to renew the experiment and surmount the difficulty.

"Permit me, sir, in conclusion, to repeat, that such an artist as this should not be driven to the last extremity, nor forced to seek an asylum offered to him in other countries, but which he has despised, as much from his own inclinations as from the advice I have given him. You risk nothing in giving him a little time, and in hurrying him you may lose a great deal. The genuineness of his gold can no longer be doubted, after the testimony of so many jewellers of Aix, Lyons, and Paris in its favour. As it is not his fault that the previous safe-conducts sent to him have been of no service, it will be necessary to send him another ; for the success of which I will be answerable, if you will confide the matter to me, and trust to my zeal for the service of his majesty, to whom I pray you to communicate this letter, that I may be spared the just reproaches he might one day heap upon me if he remained ignorant of the facts I have now written to you. Assure him, if you please, that, if you send me such a safe-conduct, I will oblige the Sieur Delisle to depose with me such precious pledges of his fidelity as shall enable me to be responsible myself to the king. These are my sentiments, and I submit them to your superior knowledge ; and have the honour to remain, with much respect, &c.   " ✠ John Bishop of Senes.

" To M. Desmarets, Minister of State, and
Comptroller-General of the Finances, at Paris."

That Delisle was no ordinary impostor, but a man of consummate cunning and address, is very evident from this letter. The bishop was fairly taken in by his clever legerdemain, and when once his first distrust was conquered, appeared as anxious to deceive himself as even Delisle could have wished. His faith was so abundant that he made the case of his *protégé* his own, and would not suffer the breath of suspicion to be directed against him. Both Louis and his minister appear to have been dazzled by the brilliant hopes he had excited, and a third pass, or safe-conduct, was immediately sent to the alchymist, with a command from the king that he should forthwith present himself at Versailles, and make public trial of his oil and powder. But this did not suit the plans of Delisle. In the provinces he was regarded as a man of no small importance ; the servile flattery that awaited him wherever he went was so grateful to his mind that he could not willingly relinquish it, and run upon certain detection at the court of the monarch. Upon one pretext or another he delayed his journey, notwithstanding the earnest solicitations of his good friend the bishop. The latter had given his word to the minister, and pledged his honour that he would induce Delisle to go, and he began to be alarmed when he found he could not subdue the obstinacy of that individual. For more than two years he continued to remonstrate with him, and was always met by some excuse, that there was not sufficient powder, or that it had not been long enough exposed to the rays of the sun. At last his patience was exhausted ; and fearful that he might suffer in the royal estimation by longer delay, he wrote to the king for a *lettre de cachet*, in virtue of which the alchymist was seized at the castle of La Palu, in the month of June 1711, and carried off to be imprisoned in the Bastille.

The gendarmes were aware that their prisoner was supposed to be the lucky possessor of the philosopher's stone, and on the road they conspired to rob and murder him. One of them pretended to be touched with pity for the misfortunes of the philosopher, and offered to give him an opportunity of escape whenever he could divert the attention of his companions. Delisle was profuse in his thanks, little dreaming of the snare that was laid for him. His treacherous friend gave notice of the success of the stratagem so far ; and it was agreed that Delisle should be allowed to struggle with and overthrow one of them while the rest were at some distance. They were then to pursue him and shoot him through the heart ; and after robbing the corpse of the philosopher's stone, convey it to Paris on a cart, and tell M. Desmarets that the prisoner had attempted to escape, and would have succeeded if they had not fired after him and shot him through the body. At a convenient place the scheme was executed. On a given signal from the friendly gendarme, Delisle fled, while another gendarme took aim and shot him through the thigh. Some peasants arriving at the instant, they were prevented from killing him as they intended, and he was transported to Paris, maimed and bleeding. He was thrown into a dungeon in the Bastille, and obstinately tore away the bandages which the surgeons applied to his wound. He never afterwards rose from his bed.

The Bishop of Senés visited him in prison, and promised him his liberty if he would transmute a certain quantity of lead into gold before the king. The unhappy man had no longer the means of carrying on the deception ; he had no gold, and no double-bottomed crucible or hollow wand to conceal it in, even if he had. He would not, however, confess that he was an impostor; but merely said he did not know how to make the powder of projection, but had received a quantity from an Italian philosopher, and had used it all in his various transmutations in Provence. He lingered for seven or eight months in the Bastille, and died from the effects of his wound, in the forty-first year of his age.

Albert Aluys.

This pretender to the philosopher's stone was the son, by a former husband, of the woman Aluys, with whom Delisle became acquainted at the commencement of his career, in the cabaret by the road-side, and whom he afterwards married. Delisle performed the part of a father towards him, and thought he could shew no stronger proof of his regard, than by giving him the necessary instructions to carry on the deception which had raised himself to such a pitch of greatness. The young Aluys was an apt scholar, and soon mastered all the jargon of the alchymists. He discoursed learnedly upon projections, cimentations, sublimations, the elixir of life, and the universal alkahest; and on the death of Delisle gave out that the secret of that great adept had been communicated to him, and to him only. His mother aided in the fraud, with the hope they might both fasten themselves, in the true alchymical fashion, upon some rich dupe, who would entertain them magnificently while the operation was in progress. The fate of Delisle was no inducement for them to stop in France. The Provencals, it is true, entertained as high an opinion as ever of his skill, and were well inclined to believe the tales of the young adept on whom his mantle had fallen; but the dungeons of the Bastille were yawning for their prey, and Aluys and his mother decamped with all convenient expedition. They travelled about the Continent for several years, sponging upon credulous rich men, and now and then performing successful transmutations by the aid of double-bottomed crucibles and the like. In the year 1726, Aluys, without his mother, who appears to have died in the interval, was at Vienna, where he introduced himself to the Duke de Richelieu, at that time ambassador from the court of France. He completely deceived this nobleman; he turned lead into gold (apparently) on several occasions, and even made the ambassador himself turn an iron nail into a silver one. The duke afterwards boasted to Lenglet du Fresnoy of his achievements as an alchymist, and regretted that he had not been able to discover the secret of the precious powder by which he performed them.

Aluys soon found that, although he might make a dupe of the Duke de Richelieu, he could not get any money from him. On the contrary, the duke expected all his pokers and fire-shovels to be made silver, and all his pewter utensils gold; and thought the honour of his acquaintance was reward sufficient for a *roturier*, who could not want wealth since he possessed so invaluable a secret. Aluys, seeing that so much was expected of him, bade adieu to his excellency, and proceeded to Bohemia accompanied by a pupil, and by a young girl who had fallen in love with him in Vienna. Some noblemen in Bohemia received him kindly, and entertained him at their houses for months at a time. It was his usual practice to pretend that he possessed only a few grains of his powder, with which he would operate in any house where he intended to fix his quarters for the season. He would make the proprietor the present of a piece of gold thus transmuted, and promise him millions, if he could only be provided with leisure to gather his *lunaria major* and *minor* on their mountain-tops, and board, lodging, and loose cash for himself, his wife, and his pupil, in the interval.

He exhausted in this manner the patience of some dozen of people, when, thinking that there was less danger for him in France under the young king Louis XV. than under his old and morose predecessor, he returned to Provence. On his arrival at Aix, he presented himself before M. le Bret, the president of the province, a gentleman who was much attached to the pursuits of alchymy, and had great hopes of being himself able to find the philosopher's stone. M. le Bret, contrary to his expectations, received him very coolly in consequence of some rumours that were spread abroad respecting him ; and told him to call upon him on the morrow. Aluys did not like the tone of the voice, or the expression of the eye of the learned president, as that functionary looked down upon him. Suspecting that all was not right, he left Aix secretly the same evening, and proceeded to Marseilles. But the police were on the watch for him ; and he had not been there four-and-twenty hours, before he was arrested on a charge of coining, and thrown into prison.

As the proofs against him were too convincing to leave him much hope of an acquittal, he planned an escape from durance. It so happened that the gaoler had a pretty daughter, and Aluys soon discovered that she was tender-hearted. He endeavoured to gain her in his favour, and succeeded. The damsel, unaware that he was a married man, conceived and encouraged a passion for him, and generously provided him with the means of escape. After he had been nearly a year in prison he succeeded in getting free, leaving the poor girl behind to learn that he was already married, and to lament in solitude that she had given her heart to an ungrateful vagabond.

When he left Marseilles, he had not a shoe to his foot or a decent garment to his back, but was provided with some money and clothes by his wife in a neighbouring town. They then found their way to Brussels, and by dint of excessive impudence, brought themselves into notice. He took a house, fitted up a splendid laboratory, and gave out that he knew the secret of transmutation. In vain did M. Percel, the brother-in-law of Lenglet du Fresnoy, who resided in that city, expose his pretensions, and hold him up to contempt as an ignorant impostor : the world believed him not. They took the alchymist at his word, and besieged his doors to see and wonder at the clever legerdemain by which he turned iron nails into gold and silver. A rich *greffier* paid him a large sum of money that he might be instructed in the art, and Aluys gave him several lessons on the most common principles of chemistry. The greffier studied hard for a twelvemonth, and then discovered that his master was a quack. He demanded his money back again ; but Aluys was not inclined to give it him, and the affair was brought before the civil tribunal of the province. In the mean time, however, the greffier died suddenly ; poisoned, according to the popular rumour, by his debtor, to avoid repayment. So great an outcry arose in the city, that Aluys, who may have been innocent of the crime, was nevertheless afraid to remain and brave it. He withdrew secretly in the night, and retired to Paris. Here all trace of him is lost. He was never heard of again ; but Lenglet du Fresnoy conjectures that he ended his days in some obscure dungeon, into which he was cast for coining or other malpractices.

The Count de St. Germain.

This adventurer was of a higher grade than the last, and played a distinguished part at the court of Louis XV. He pretended to have discovered the elixir of life, by means of which he could make any one live for centuries ; and allowed it to be believed that his own age was upwards of two thousand years. He entertained many of the opinions of the Rosicrucians ; boasted of his intercourse with sylphs and salamanders ; and of his power of drawing diamonds from the earth, and pearls from the sea, by the force of his incantations. He did not lay claim to the merit of having discovered the philosopher's stone ; but devoted so much of his time to the operations of alchymy, that it was very generally believed, that if such a thing as the philosopher's stone had ever existed, or could be called into existence, he was the man to succeed in finding it.

It has never yet been discovered what was his real name, or in what country he was born. Some believed, from the Jewish cast of his handsome countenance, that he was the "wandering Jew ;" others asserted that he was the issue of an Arabian princess, and that his rather was a salamander ; while others, more reasonable, affirmed him to be the son of a Portuguese Jew established at Bourdeaux. He first carried on his imposture in Germany, where he made considerable sums by selling an elixir to arrest the progress of old age. The Maréchal de Belle-Isle purchased a dose of it ; and was so captivated with the wit, learning, and good manners of the charlatan, and so convinced of the justice of his most preposterous pretensions, that he induced him to fix his residence in Paris. Under the marshal's patronage, he first appeared in the gay circles of that capital. Every one was delighted with the mysterious stranger ; who, at this period of his life, appears to have been about seventy years of age, but did not look more than forty-five. His easy assurance imposed upon most people. His reading was extensive, and his memory extraordinarily tenacious of the slightest circumstances. His pretension to have lived for so many centuries naturally exposed him to some puzzling questions, as to the appearance, life, and conversation of the great men of former days; but he was never at a loss for an answer. Many who questioned him for the purpose of scoffing at him, refrained in perplexity, quite bewildered by his presence of mind, his ready replies, and his astonishing accuracy on every point mentioned in history. To increase the mystery by which he was surrounded, he permitted no person to know how he lived. He dressed in a style of the greatest magnificence; sported valuable diamonds in his hat, on his fingers, and in his shoe-buckles; and sometimes made the most costly presents to the ladies of the court. It was suspected by many that he was a spy, in the pay of the English ministry; but there never was a tittle of evidence to support the charge. The king looked upon him with marked favour, was often closeted with him for hours together, and would not suffer any body to speak disparagingly of him. Voltaire constantly turned him into ridicule; and, in one of his letters to the King of Prussia, mentions him as "un comte pour rire ;" and states that he pretended to have dined with the holy fathers at the Council of Trent!

In the *Memoirs of Madame du Hausset,* chamber-woman to Madame du Pompadour, there are some amusing anecdotes of this personage. Very soon after his arrival in Paris, he had the *entrée* of her dressing-room; a favour only granted to the most powerful lords at the court of her royal lover. Madame was fond of conversing with him; and, in her presence, he thought fit to lower his pretensions very considerably; but he often allowed her to believe that he had lived two or three hundred years at least. "One day," says Madame du Hausset, "madame said to him, in my presence, 'What was the personal appearance of Francis I. ? He was a king I should have liked.' 'He was, indeed, very captivating,' replied St. Germain; and he proceeded to describe his face and person, as that of a man whom he had accurately observed. 'It is a pity he was too ardent. I could have given him some good advice, which would have saved him from all his misfortunes: but he would not have followed it ; for it seems as if a fatality attended princes, forcing them to shut their ears to the wisest counsel.' 'Was his court very brilliant?' inquired Madame du Pompadour. 'Very,' replied the count; 'but those of his grandsons surpassed it. In the time of Mary Stuart and Margaret of Valois, it was a land of enchantment—a temple sacred to pleasures of every kind.' Madame said, laughing, 'You seem to have seen all this.' 'I have an excellent memory,' said he, 'and have read the history of France with great care. I sometimes amuse myself, not by making, but by letting, it be believed that I lived in old times.'

" 'But you do not tell us your age,' said Madame du Pompadour to him on another occasion; 'and yet you pretend you are very old. The Countess de Gergy, who was, I believe, ambassadress at Vienna some fifty years ago, says she saw you there, exactly the same as you now appear.'

" 'It is true, madame,' replied St. Germain; 'I knew Madame de Gergy many years ago.'

" 'But, according to her account, you must be more than a hundred years old?'

" 'That is not impossible,' said he, laughing; 'but it is much more possible that the good lady is in her dotage.'

" 'You gave her an elixir, surprising for the effects it produced; for she says, that during a length of time she only appeared to be eighty-four, the age at which she took it. Why don't you give it to the king?'

" 'Oh, madame,' he exclaimed, 'the physicians would have me broken on the wheel, were I to think of drugging his majesty.' "

When the world begins to believe extraordinary things of an individual, there is no telling where its extravagance will stop. People, when once they have taken the start, vie with each other who shall believe most. At this period all Paris resounded with the wonderful adventures of the Count de St. Germain; and a company of waggish young men tried the following experiment upon its credulity: A clever mimic, who, on account of the amusement he afforded, was admitted into good society, was taken by them, dressed as the Count de St. Germain, into several houses in the Rue du Marais. He imitated the count's peculiarities admirably, and found his auditors open-mouthed to believe any absurdity he chose to utter. No fiction was too monstrous for their all-devouring credulity. He spoke of the Saviour of the world in terms of the greatest familiarity; said he had supped with him at the marriage in Cana of Galilee, where the water was miraculously turned into wine. In fact, he said he was an intimate friend of his, and had often warned him to be less romantic and imprudent, or he would finish his career miserably. This infamous blasphemy, strange to say, found believers; and ere three days had elapsed, it was currently reported that St. Germain was born soon after the deluge, and that he would never die!

St. Germain himself was too much a man of the world to assert any thing so monstrous; but he took no pains to contradict the story. In all his conversations with persons of rank and education, he advanced his claims modestly, and as if by mere inadvertency, and seldom pretended to a longevity beyond three hundred years, except when he found he was in company with persons who would believe any thing. He often spoke of Henry VIII. as if he had known him intimately, and of the Emperor Charles V. as if that monarch had delighted in his society. He would describe conversations which took place with such an apparent truthfulness, and be so exceedingly minute and particular as to the dress and appearance of the individuals, and even the weather at the time and the furniture of the room, that three persons out of four were generally inclined to credit him. He had constant applications from rich old women for an elixir to make them young again, and it would appear gained large sums in this manner. To those whom he was pleased to call his friends he said his mode of living and plan of diet were far superior to any elixir, and that any body might attain a patriarchal age by refraining from drinking at meals, and very sparingly at any other time. The Baron de Gleichen followed this system, and took great quantities of senna-leaves, expecting to live for two hundred years. He died, however, at seventy-three. The Duchess de Choiseul was desirous of following the same system, but the duke her husband in much wrath forbade her to follow any system prescribed by a man who had so equivocal a reputation as M. de St. Germain.

Madame du Hausset says she saw St. Germain and conversed with him several times. He appeared to her to be about fifty years of age, was of the middle size, and had fine expressive features. His dress was always simple, but displayed much taste. He usually wore diamond rings of great value, and his watch and snuff-box were ornamented with a profusion of precious stones. One day, at Madame du Pompadour's apartments, where the principal courtiers were assembled, St. Germain made his appearance in diamond knee and shoe buckles of so fine a water, that madame said she did not think the king had any equal to them. He was entreated to pass into the antechamber and undo them, which he did, and brought them to madame for closer inspection. M. de Gontant, who was present, said their value could not be less than two hundred thousand livres, or upwards of eight thousand pounds sterling. The Baron de Gleichen, in his *Memoirs*, relates that the count one day shewed him so many diamonds, that he thought he saw before him all the treasures of Aladdin's lamp ; and adds, that he had had great experience in precious stones, and was convinced that all those possessed by the count were genuine. On another occasion St. Germain shewed Madame du Pompadour a small box, containing topazes, emeralds, and diamonds worth half a million of livres. He affected to despise all this wealth, to make the world more easily believe that he could, like the Rosicru-

cians, draw precious stones out of the earth by the magic of his song
He gave away a great number of these jewels to the ladies of the
court ; and Madame du Pompadour was so charmed with his generosity, that she gave him a richly enamelled snuff-box as a token of her
regard, on the lid of which was beautifully painted a portrait of So-
crates, or some other Greek sage, to whom she compared him. He
was not only lavish to the mistresses, but to the maids. Madame du
Hausset says : " The count came to see Madame du Pompadour, who
was very ill, and lay on the sofa. He shewed her diamonds enough
to furnish a king's treasury. Madame sent for me to see all those
beautiful things. I looked at them with an air of the utmost astonishment ; but I made signs to her that I thought them all false. The
count felt for something in a pocket-book about twice as large as a
spectacle-case, and at length drew out two or three little paper packets,
which he unfolded, and exhibited a superb ruby. He threw on the
table, with a contemptuous air, a little cross of green and white
stones. I looked at it, and said it was not to be despised. I then
put it on, and admired it greatly. The count begged me to accept
it ; I refused. He urged me to take it. At length he pressed so
warmly, that madame, seeing it could not be worth more than a thousand livres, made me a sign to accept it. I took the cross, much
pleased with the count's politeness."

How the adventurer obtained his wealth remains a secret. He
could not have made it all by the sale of his *elixir vitæ* in Germany,
though no doubt some portion of it was derived from that source.
Voltaire positively says he was in the pay of foreign governments ;
and in his letter to the King of Prussia, dated the 5th of April 1758,
says that he was initiated in all the secrets of Choiseul, Kaunitz, and
Pitt. Of what use he could be to any of those ministers, and to Choiseul especially, is a mystery of mysteries.

There appears no doubt that he possessed the secret of removing
spots from diamonds ; and in all probability he gained considerable
sums by buying at inferior prices such as had flaws in them, and afterwards disposing of them at a profit of cent per cent. Madame du
Hausset relates the following anecdote on this particular : " The
king," says she, " ordered a middling-sized diamond, which had a flaw
in it, to be brought to him. After having it weighed, his majesty
said to the count, 'The value of this diamond as it is, and with the
flaw in it, is six thousand livres ; without the flaw, it would be worth
at least ten thousand. Will you undertake to make me a gainer of
four thousand livres ?' St. Germain examined it very attentively, and
said, 'It is possible ; it may be done. I will bring it you again in a
month.' At the time appointed the count brought back the diamond

without a spot, and gave it to the king. It was wrapped in a cloth of amianthos, which he took off. The king had it weighed immediately, and found it very little diminished. His majesty then sent it to his jeweller by M. de Gontant, without telling him of any thing that had passed. The jeweller gave nine thousand six hundred livres for it. The king, however, sent for the diamond back again, and said he would keep it as a curiosity. He could not overcome his surprise, and said M. de St. Germain must be worth millions, especially if he possessed the secret of making large diamonds out of small ones. The count neither said that he could or could not, but positively asserted that he knew how to make pearls grow, and give them the finest water. The king paid him great attention, and so did Madame du Pompadour. M. du Quesnoy once said that St. Germain was a quack, but the king reprimanded him. In fact, his majesty appears infatuated by him, and sometimes talks of him as if his descent were illustrious."

St. Germain had a most amusing vagabond for a servant, to whom he would often appeal for corroboration, when relating some wonderful event that happened centuries before. The fellow, who was not without ability, generally corroborated him in a most satisfactory manner. Upon one occasion, his master was telling a party of ladies and gentlemen, at dinner, some conversation he had had in Palestine with King Richard I. of England, whom he described as a very particular friend of his. Signs of astonishment and incredulity were visible on the faces of the company; upon which St. Germain very coolly turned to his servant, who stood behind his chair, and asked him if he had not spoken truth? "I really cannot say," replied the man, without moving a muscle; "you forget, sir, I have only been five hundred years in your service!" "Ah! true," said his master; "I remember now; it was a little before your time!"

Occasionally, when with men whom he could not so easily dupe, he gave utterance to the contempt with which he could scarcely avoid regarding such gaping credulity. "These fools of Parisians," said he to the Baron de Gleichen, "believe me to be more than five hundred years old; and, since they will have it so, I confirm them in their idea. Not but that I really am much older than I appear."

Many other stories are related of this strange impostor; but enough have been quoted to shew his character and pretensions. It appears that he endeavoured to find the philosopher's stone; but never boasted of possessing it. The Prince of Hesse Cassel, whom he had known years before, in Germany, wrote urgent letters to him, entreating him to quit Paris, and reside with him. St. Germain at last consented. Nothing further is known of his career. There were no gossiping memoir-writers at the court of Hesse Cassel to chronicle his sayings and doings. He died at Sleswig, under the roof of his friend the prince, in the year 1784.

CAGLIOSTRO.

This famous charlatan, the friend and successor of St. Germain, ran a career still more extraordinary. He was the arch-quack of his age, the last of the great pretenders to the philosopher's stone and the water of life, and during his brief season of prosperity, one of the most conspicuous characters of Europe.

His real name was Joseph Balsamo. He was born at Palermo, about the year 1743, of humble parentage. He had the misfortune to lose his father during his infancy, and his education was left in consequence to some relatives of his mother, the latter being too poor to afford him any instruction beyond mere reading and writing. He was sent in his fifteenth year to a monastery, to be taught the elements of chemistry and physic ; but his temper was so impetuous, his indolence so invincible, and his vicious habits so deeply rooted, that he made no progress. After remaining some years, he left it with the character of an uninformed and dissipated young man, with good natural talents but a bad disposition. When he became of age, he abandoned himself to a life of riot and debauchery, and entered himself, in fact, into that celebrated fraternity, known in France and Italy as the "Knights of Industry," and in England as the "Swell Mob." He was far from being an idle or unwilling member of the corps. The first way in which he distinguished himself was by forging orders of admission to the theatres. He afterwards robbed his uncle, and counterfeited a will. For acts like these, he paid frequent compulsory visits to the prisons of Palermo. Somehow or other he acquired the character of a sorcerer—of a man who had failed in discovering the secrets of alchymy, and had sold his soul to the devil for the gold which he was not able to make by means of transmutation. He took no pains to disabuse the popular mind on this particular, but rather encouraged the belief than otherwise. He at last made use of it to cheat a silversmith named Marano, of about sixty ounces of gold, and was in consequence obliged to leave Palermo. He persuaded this man that he could shew him a treasure hidden in a cave, for which service he was to receive the sixty ounces of gold, while the silversmith was to have all the treasure for the mere trouble of digging it up. They went together at midnight to an excavation in the vicinity of Palermo, where Balsamo drew a magic circle, and invoked the devil to shew his treasures. Suddenly there appeared half a dozen fellows, the accomplices of the swindler, dressed to represent devils, with horns on their heads, claws to their fingers, and vomiting apparently red and blue flame. They were armed with pitchforks, with which they belaboured poor Marano till he was almost dead, and robbed him of his sixty ounces of gold and all the valuables he carried about his person. They then made off, accompanied by Balsamo, leaving the unlucky silversmith to recover or die at his leisure. Nature chose the former course; and soon after daylight he was restored to his senses, smarting in body from his blows, and in spirit for the deception of which he had been the victim. His first impulse was to denounce Balsamo to the magistrates of the town; but on further reflection he was afraid of the ridicule that a full exposure of all the circumstances would draw upon him; he therefore took the truly Italian resolution of being revenged on Balsamo, by murdering him at the first convenient opportunity. Having given utterance to this threat in the hearing of a friend of Balsamo, it was reported to the latter, who immediately packed up his valuables and quitted Europe.

He chose Medina, in Arabia, for his future dwelling-place, and there became acquainted with a Greek named Altotas, a man exceedingly well versed in all the languages of the East, and an indefatigable student of alchymy. He possessed an invaluable collection of Arabian manuscripts on his favourite science, and studied them with such unremitting industry, that he found he had not sufficient time to attend to his crucibles and furnaces without neglecting his books. He was looking about for an assistant, when Balsamo opportunely presented himself, and made so favourable an impression that he was at once engaged in that capacity. But the relation of master and servant did not long subsist between them; Balsamo was too ambitious and too clever to play a secondary part, and within fifteen days of their first acquaintance they were bound together as friends and partners. Altotas, in the course of a long life devoted to alchymy, had stumbled upon some valuable discoveries in chemistry, one of which was an ingredient for improving the manufacture of flax, and imparting to goods of that material a gloss and softness almost equal to silk. Balsamo gave him the good advice to leave the philosopher's stone for the present undiscovered, and make gold out of their flax. The advice was taken, and they proceeded together to Alexandria to trade, with a large stock of that article. They stayed forty days in Alexandria, and gained a considerable sum by their venture. They afterwards visited other cities in Egypt, and were equally successful. They also visited Turkey, where they sold drugs and amulets. On their return to Europe, they were driven by stress of weather into Malta, and were hospitably received by Pinto, the Grand Master of the

Knights, and a famous alchymist. They worked in his laboratory for some months, and tried hard to change a pewter platter into a silver one. Balsamo, having less faith than his companions, was sooner wearied; and obtaining from his host many letters of introduction to Rome and Naples, he left him and Altotas to find the philosopher's stone and transmute the pewter platter without him.

He had long since dropped the name of Balsamo on account of the many ugly associations that clung to it; and during his travels had assumed at least half a score others, with titles annexed to them. He called himself sometimes the Chevalier de Fischio, the Marquis de Melissa, the Baron de Belmonte, de Pelligrini, d'Anna, de Fenix, de Harat, but most commonly the Count de Cagliostro. Under the latter title he entered Rome, and never afterwards changed it. In this city he gave himself out as the restorer of the Rosicrucian philosophy; said he could transmute all metals into gold; that he could render himself invisible, cure all diseases, and administer an elixir against old age and decay. His letters from the Grand Master Pinto procured him an introduction into the best families. He made money rapidly by the sale of his *elixir vitæ;* and, like other quacks, performed many remarkable cures by inspiring his patients with the most complete faith and reliance upon his powers; an advantage which the most impudent charlatans often possess over the regular practitioner.

While thus in a fair way of making his fortune he became acquainted with the beautiful Lorenza Feliciana, a young lady of noble birth, but without fortune. Cagliostro soon discovered that she possessed accomplishments that were invaluable. Besides her ravishing beauty, she had the readiest wit, the most engaging manners, the most fertile imagination, and the least principle of any of the maidens of Rome. She was just the wife for Cagliostro, who proposed himself to her, and was accepted. After their marriage, he instructed his fair Lorenza in all the secrets of his calling—taught her pretty lips to invoke angels, and genii, sylphs, salamanders, and undines, and, when need required, devils and evil spirits. Lorenza was an apt scholar; she soon learned all the jargon of the alchymists and all the spells of the enchanters; and thus accomplished, the hopeful pair set out on their travels, to levy contributions on the superstitious and the credulous.

They first went to Sleswig on a visit to the Count de St. Germain, their great predecessor in the art of making dupes, and were received by him in the most magnificent manner. They no doubt fortified their minds for the career they had chosen by the sage discourse of that worshipful gentleman; for immediately after they left him, they began their operations. They travelled for three or four years in Russia, Poland, and Germany, transmuting metals, telling fortunes, raising spirits, and selling the *elixir vitæ* wherever they went; but there is no record of their doings from whence to draw a more particular detail. It was not until they made their appearance in England in 1776, that the names of the Count and Countess di Cagliostro began to acquire a European reputation. They arrived in London in the July of that year, possessed of property, in plate, jewels, and specie, to the amount of about three thousand pounds. They hired apartments in Whitcombe Street, and lived for some months quietly. In the same house there lodged a Portuguese woman, named Blavary, who, being in necessitous circumstances, was engaged by the count as interpreter. She was constantly admitted into his laboratory, where he spent much of his time in search of the philosopher's stone. She spread abroad the fame of her entertainer in return for his hospitality, and laboured hard to impress every body with as full a belief in his extraordinary powers as she felt herself; but as a female interpreter of the rank and appearance of Madame Blavary did not exactly correspond with the count's notions either of dignity or decorum, he hired a person named Vitellini, a teacher of languages, to act in that capacity. Vitellini was a desperate gambler, a man who had tried almost every resource to repair his ruined fortunes, including among the rest the search for the philosopher's stone. Immediately that he saw the count's operations, he was convinced that the great secret was his, and that the golden gates of the palace of fortune were open to let him in. With still more enthusiasm than Madame Blavary, he held forth to his acquaintance, and in all public places, that the count was an extraordinary man, a true adept, whose fortune was immense, and who could transmute into pure and solid gold as much lead, iron, and copper as he pleased. The consequence was, that the house of Cagliostro was besieged by crowds of the idle, the credulous, and the avaricious, all eager to obtain a sight of the "philosopher," or to share in the boundless wealth which he could call into existence.

Unfortunately for Cagliostro, he had fallen into evil hands. Instead of duping the people of England, as he might have done, he became himself the victim of a gang of swindlers, who, with the fullest reliance on his occult powers, only sought to make money of him. Vitellini introduced to him a ruined gambler like himself, named Scot, whom he represented as a Scottish nobleman, attracted to London solely by his desire to see and converse with the extraordinary man whose fame had spread to the distant mountains of the north. Cagliostro received him with great kindness and cordiality; and "Lord" Scot thereupon introduced a woman named Fry as Lady Scot, who was to act as chaperone to the Countess di Cagliostro, and make her acquainted with all the noble families of Britain. Thus things went swimmingly. " His lordship," whose effects had not arrived from Scotland, and who had no banker in London, borrowed two hundred pounds of the count. They were lent without scruple, so flattered was Cagliostro by the attentions they paid him, the respect, nay veneration they pretended to feel for him, and the complete deference with which they listened to every word that fell from his lips.

Superstitious like all desperate gamesters, Scot had often tried magical and cabalistic numbers, in the hope of discovering lucky numbers in the lottery or at the roulette-tables. He had in his possession a cabalistic manuscript, containing various arithmetical combinations of the kind, which he submitted to Cagliostro, with an urgent request that he would select a number. Cagliostro took the manuscript and studied it, but, as he himself informs us, with no confidence in its truth. He, however, predicted twenty as the successful number for the 6th of November following. Scot ventured a small sum upon this number out of the two hundred pounds he had borrowed, and won. Cagliostro, incited by this success, prognosticated number twenty-five for the next drawing. Scot tried again, and won a hundred guineas. The numbers fifty-five and fifty-seven were announced with equal success for the 18th of the same month, to the no small astonishment and delight of Cagliostro, who thereupon resolved to try fortune for himself, and not for others. To all the entreaties of Scot and his lady that he would predict more numbers for them, he turned a deaf ear, even while he still thought him a lord and a man of honour; but when he discovered that he was a mere swindler, and the pretended Lady Scot an artful woman of the town, he closed his door upon them and on all their gang.

Having complete faith in the supernatural powers of the count, they were in the deepest distress at having lost his countenance. They tried by every means their ingenuity could suggest to propitiate him again. They implored, they threatened, and endeavoured to bribe him; but all was vain. Cagliostro would neither see nor correspond with them. In the mean time they lived extravagantly, and in the hope of future, exhausted all their present gains. They were reduced to the last extremity, when Miss Fry obtained access to the countess, and received a guinea from her on the representation that she was starving. Miss Fry, not contented with this, begged her to intercede with her husband, that for the last time he would point out a lucky number in the lottery. The countess promised to exert her influence; and Cagliostro, thus entreated, named the number eight, at the same time reiterating his determination to have no more to do with any of them. By an extraordinary hazard, which filled Cagliostro with surprise and pleasure, number eight was the greatest prize in the lottery. Miss Fry and her associates cleared fifteen hundred guineas by the adventure, and became more than ever convinced of the occult powers of Cagliostro, and strengthened in their determination never to quit him until they had made their fortunes. Out of the proceeds Miss Fry bought a handsome necklace at a pawnbroker's for ninety guineas. She then ordered a richly chased gold box, having two compartments, to be made at a jeweller's, and putting the necklace in the one, filled the other with a fine aromatic snuff. She then sought another interview with Madame di Cagliostro, and urged her to accept the box as a small token of her esteem and gratitude, without mentioning the valuable necklace that was concealed in it. Madame di Cagliostro accepted the present, and was from that hour exposed to the most incessant persecution from all the confederates—Blavary, Vitellini, and the pretended Lord and Lady Scot. They flattered themselves they had regained their lost footing in the house, and came day after day to know lucky numbers in the lottery, sometimes forcing themselves up the stairs, and into the count's laboratory, in spite of the efforts of the servants to prevent them. Cagliostro, exasperated at their pertinacity, threatened to call in the assistance of the magistrates, and taking Miss Fry by the shoulders, pushed her into the street.

From that time may be dated the misfortunes of Cagliostro. Miss Fry, at the instigation of her paramour, determined on vengeance. Her first act was to swear a debt of two hundred pounds against Cagliostro, and to cause him to be arrested for that sum. While he was in custody in a sponging-house, Scot, accompanied by a low attorney, broke into his laboratory, and carried off a small box, containing, as they believed, the powder of transmutation, and a number of cabalistic manuscripts and treatises upon alchymy. They also brought an action against him for the recovery of the necklace; and Miss Fry accused both him and his countess of sorcery and witchcraft, and of foretelling numbers in the lottery by the aid of the Devil. This latter charge was actually heard before Mr. Justice Miller. The action of trover for the necklace was tried before the Lord Chief Justice of the Common Pleas, who recommended the parties to submit to arbitration. In the mean time Cagliostro remained in prison for several weeks, till having procured bail, he was liberated. He was soon after waited upon by an attorney named Reynolds, also deep in the plot, who offered to compromise all the actions upon certain conditions. Scot, who had accompanied him, concealed himself behind the door, and suddenly rushing out, presented a pistol at the heart of Cagliostro, swearing he would shoot him instantly, if he would not tell him truly the art of predicting lucky numbers and of transmuting metals. Reynolds pretending to be very angry, disarmed his accomplice, and entreated the count to satisfy them by fair means, and disclose his secrets, promising that if he would do so, they would discharge all the actions, and offer him no further molestation. Cagliostro replied, that threats and entreaties were alike useless; that he knew no secrets; and that the powder of transmutation of which they had robbed him, was of no value to any body but himself. He offered, however, if they would discharge the actions, and return the powder and the manuscripts, to forgive them all the money they had swindled him out of. These conditions were refused; and Scot and Reynolds departed, swearing vengeance against him.

Cagliostro appears to have been quite ignorant of the forms of law in England, and to have been without a friend to advise him as to the best course he should pursue. While he was conversing with his countess on the difficulties that beset them, one of his bail called, and invited him to ride in a hackney coach to the house of a person who would see him righted. Cagliostro consented, and was driven to the King's Bench prison, where his friend left him. He did not discover for several hours that he was a prisoner, or, in fact, understand the process of being surrendered by one's bail.

He regained his liberty in a few weeks; and the arbitrators between him and Miss Fry made their award against him. He was ordered to pay the two hundred pounds she had sworn against him, and to restore the necklace and gold box which had been presented to the countess. Cagliostro was so disgusted, that he determined to quit England. His pretensions, besides, had been unmercifully exposed by a Frenchman, named Morande, the editor of the *Courrier de l'Europe*, published in London. To add to his distress, he was recognised in Westminster Hall as Joseph Balsamo, the swindler of Palermo. Such a complication of disgrace was not to be borne. He and his countess packed up their small effects, and left England with no more than fifty pounds, out of the three thousand they had brought with them.

They first proceeded to Brussels, where fortune was more auspicious. They sold considerable quantities of the elixir of life, performed many cures, and recruited their finances. They then took their course through Germany to Russia, and always with the same success. Gold flowed into their coffers faster than they could count it. They quite forgot all the woes they had endured in England, and learned to be more circumspect in the choice of their acquaintance.

In the year 1780, they made their appearance in Strasbourg.

Their fame had reached that city before them. They took a magnificent hotel, and invited all the principal persons of the place to their table. Their wealth appeared to be boundless, and their hospitality equal to it. Both the count and countess acted as physicians, and gave money, advice, and medicine to all the necessitous and suffering of the town. Many of the cures they performed astonished those regular practitioners who did not make sufficient allowance for the wonderful influence of imagination in certain cases. The countess, who at this time was not more than five-and-twenty, and all radiant with grace, beauty, and cheerfulness, spoke openly of her eldest son as a fine young man of eight-and-twenty, who had been for some years a captain in the Dutch service. The trick succeeded to admiration. All the ugly old women in Strasbourg, and for miles around, thronged the saloon of the countess to purchase the liquid which was to make them as blooming as their daughters; the young women came in equal abundance, that they might preserve their charms, and when twice as old as Ninon de l'Enclos, be more captivating than she; while men were not wanting who were fools enough to imagine that they might keep off the inevitable stroke of the grim foe by a few drops of the same incomparable elixir. The countess, sooth to say, looked like an incarnation of immortal loveliness, a very goddess of youth and beauty; and it is possible that the crowds of young men and old, who at all convenient seasons haunted the perfumed chambers of this enchantress, were attracted less by their belief in her occult powers than from admiration of her languishing bright eyes and sparkling conversation. But amid all the incense that was offered at her shrine, Madame di Cagliostro was ever faithful to her spouse. She encouraged hopes, it is true, but she never realised them; she excited admiration, yet kept it within bounds; and made men her slaves, without ever granting a favour of which the vainest might boast.

In this city they made the acquaintance of many eminent persons, and, among others, of the Cardinal Prince de Rohan, who was destined afterwards to exercise so untoward an influence over their fate. The cardinal, who seems to have had great faith in him as a philosopher, persuaded him to visit Paris in his company, which he did, but remained only thirteen days. He preferred the society of Strasbourg, and returned thither with the intention of fixing his residence far from the capital. But he soon found that the first excitement of his arrival had passed away. People began to reason with themselves, and to be ashamed of their own admiration. The populace, among whom he had lavished his charity with a bountiful hand, accused him of being the Antichrist, the Wandering Jew, the man of fourteen hundred years of age, a demon in human shape, sent to lure the ignorant to their destruction ; while the more opulent and better informed called him a spy in the pay of foreign governments, an agent of the police, a swindler, and a man of evil life. The outcry grew at last so strong, that he deemed it prudent to try his fortune elsewhere.

He went first to Naples, but that city was too near Palermo ; he dreaded recognition from some of his early friends, and, after a short stay, returned to France. He chose Bourdeaux as his next dwelling-place, and created as great a sensation there as he had done in Strasbourg. He announced himself as the founder of a new school of medicine and philosophy, boasted of his ability to cure all diseases, and invited the poor and suffering to visit him, and he would relieve the distress of the one class, and cure the ailings of the other. All day long the street opposite his magnificent hotel was crowded by the populace ; the halt and the blind, women with sick babes in their arms, and persons suffering under every species of human infirmity, flocked to this wonderful doctor. The relief he afforded in money more than counterbalanced the failure of his nostrums ; and the affluence of people from all the surrounding country became so great, that the *jurats* of the city granted him a military guard, to be stationed day and night before his door, to keep order. The anticipations of Cagliostro were realised. The rich were struck with admiration of his charity and benevolence, and impressed with a full conviction of his marvellous powers. The sale of the elixir went on admirably. His saloons were thronged with wealthy dupes who came to purchase immortality. Beauty, that would endure for centuries, was the attraction for the fair sex ; health and strength for the same period were the baits held out to the other. His charming countess, in the meantime, brought grist to the mill by telling fortunes and casting nativities, or granting attendant sylphs to any ladies who would pay sufficiently for their services. What was still better, as tending to keep up the credit of her husband, she gave the most magnificent parties in Bourdeaux.

But as at Strasbourg, the popular delusion lasted for a few months only, and burned itself out ; Cagliostro forgot, in the intoxication of success, that there was a limit to quackery which once passed inspired distrust. When he pretended to call spirits from the tomb, people became incredulous. He was accused of being an enemy to religion, of denying Christ, and of being the Wandering Jew. He despised these rumours as long as they were confined to a few ; but when they spread over the town, when he received no more fees, when his parties were abandoned, and his acquaintance turned away when they met him in the street, he thought it high time to shift his quarters.

He was by this time wearied of the provinces, and turned his thoughts to the capital. On his arrival he announced himself as the restorer of Egyptian Freemasonry, and the founder of a new philosophy. He immediately made his way into the best society by means of his friend the Cardinal de Rohan. His success as a magician was quite extraordinary: the most considerable persons of the time visited him. He boasted of being able, like the Rosicrucians, to converse

HOUSE OF CAGLIOSTRO, PARIS.

with the elementary spirits; to invoke the mighty dead from the grave, to transmute metals, and to discover occult things by means of the special protection of God towards him. Like Dr. Dee, he summoned the angels to reveal the future; and they appeared and conversed with him in crystals and under glass bells.* "There was hardly," says the *Biographie des Contemporains*, "a fine lady in Paris who would not sup with the shade of Lucretius in the apartments of Cagliostro; a military officer who would not discuss the art of war with Cæsar, Hannibal, or Alexander; or an advocate or counsellor who would not argue legal points with the ghost of Cicero." These interviews with the departed were very expensive; for, as Cagliostro

* See the Abbe Fiard, and *Anecdotes of the Reign of Louis XVI.* p. 400.

said, the dead would not rise for nothing. The countess, as usual,
exercised all her ingenuity to support her husband's credit. She was
a great favourite with her own sex, to many a delighted and wondering auditory of whom she detailed the marvellous powers of Cagliostro. She said he could render himself invisible, traverse the
world with the rapidity of thought, and be in several places at the
same time.*

He had not been long at Paris before he became involved in the
celebrated affair of the queen's necklace. His friend the Cardinal de
Rohan, enamoured of the charms of Marie Antoinette, was in sore
distress at her coldness, and the displeasure she had so often manifested against him. There was at that time a lady named La Motte
in the service of the queen, of whom the cardinal was foolish enough
to make a confidant. Madame de la Motte, in return, endeavoured
to make a tool of the cardinal, and succeeded but too well in her projects. In her capacity of chamber-woman, or lady of honour to the
queen, she was present at an interview between her majesty and
M. Boehmer, a wealthy jeweller of Paris, when the latter offered for
sale a magnificent diamond necklace, valued at 1,600,000 francs, or
about 64,000*l.* sterling. The queen admired it greatly, but dismissed
the jeweller, with the expression of her regret that she was too poor
to purchase it. Madame de la Motte formed a plan to get this costly
ornament into her own possession, and determined to make the Cardinal de Rohan the instrument by which to effect it. She therefore
sought an interview with him, and pretending to sympathise in his
grief for the queen's displeasure, told him she knew a way by which
he might be restored to favour. She then mentioned the necklace,
and the sorrow of the queen that she could not afford to buy it. The
cardinal, who was as wealthy as he was foolish, immediately offered
to purchase the necklace, and make a present of it to the queen.
Madame de la Motte told him by no means to do so, as he would
thereby offend her majesty. His plan would be to induce the jeweller to give her majesty credit, and accept her promissory note for the
amount at a certain date, to be hereafter agreed upon. The cardinal
readily agreed to the proposal, and instructed the jeweller to draw
up an agreement, and he would procure the queen's signature. He
placed this in the hands of Madame de la Motte, who returned it
shortly afterwards, with the words, " Bon, bon—approuvé—Marie
Antoinette," written in the margin. She told him at the same time
that the queen was highly pleased with his conduct in the matter,
and would appoint a meeting with him in the gardens of Versailles,

when she would present him with a flower, as a token of her regard. The cardinal shewed the forged document to the jeweller, obtained the necklace, and delivered it into the hands of Madame de la Motte. So far all was well. Her next object was to satisfy the cardinal, who awaited impatiently the promised interview with his royal mistress. There was at that time in Paris a young woman named D'Oliva, noted for her resemblance to the queen; and Madame de la Motte, on the promise of a handsome reward, found no difficulty in persuading her to personate Marie Antoinette, and meet the Cardinal de Rohan at the evening twilight in the gardens of Versailles. The meeting took place accordingly. The cardinal was deceived by the uncertain light, the great resemblance of the counterfeit, and his own hopes; and having received the flower from Mademoiselle D'Oliva, went home with a lighter heart than had beat in his bosom for many a day.*

In the course of time the forgery of the queen's signature was discovered. Boehmer the jeweller immediately named the Cardinal de Rohan and Madame de la Motte as the persons with whom he had negotiated, and they were both arrested and thrown into the Bastille. La Motte was subjected to a rigorous examination, and the disclosures she made implicating Cagliostro, he was seized, along with his wife, and also sent to the Bastille. A story involving so much scandal necessarily excited great curiosity. Nothing was to be heard of in Paris but the queen's necklace, with surmises of the guilt or innocence of the several parties implicated. The husband of Madame de la Motte escaped to England, and in the opinion of many took the necklace with him, and there disposed of it to different jewellers in small quantities at a time. But Madame de la Motte insisted that she had entrusted it to Cagliostro, who had seized and taken it to pieces, to "swell the treasures of his immense unequalled fortune." She spoke of him as "an empiric, a mean alchymist, a dreamer on the philosopher's stone, a false prophet, a profaner of the true worship, the self-dubbed Count Cagliostro!" She further said that he originally conceived the project of ruining the Cardinal de Rohan; that he persuaded her, by the exercise of some magic influence over her mind, to aid and abet the scheme; and that he was a robber, a swindler, and a sorcerer!

After all the accused parties had remained for upwards of six months in the Bastille, the trial commenced. The depositions of the

---

* The enemies of the unfortunate Queen of France, when the progress of the Revolution embittered their animosity against her, maintained that she was really a party in this transaction; that she, and not Mademoiselle D'Oliva, met the cardinal and rewarded him with the flower; and that the story above related was merely concocted between her, La Motte, and others to cheat the jeweller of his 1,600,000 francs.

witnesses having been heard, Cagliostro, as the principal culprit, was first called upon for his defence. He was listened to with the most breathless attention. He put himself into a theatrical attitude, and thus began :—" I am oppressed!—I am accused!—I am calumniated! Have I deserved this fate? I descend into my conscience, and I there find the peace that men refuse me! I have travelled a great deal— I am known over all Europe, and a great part of Asia and Africa. I have every where shewn myself the friend of my fellow-creatures. My knowledge, my time, my fortune have ever been employed in the relief of distress. I have studied and practised medicine; but I have never degraded that most noble and most consoling of arts by mercenary speculations of any kind. Though always giving, and never receiving, I have preserved my independence. I have even carried my delicacy so far as to refuse the favours of kings. I have given gratuitously my remedies and my advice to the rich; the poor have received from me both remedies and money. I have never contracted any debts, and my manners are pure and uncorrupted." After much more self-laudation of the same kind, he went on to complain of the great hardships he had endured in being separated for so many months from his innocent and loving wife, who, as he was given to understand, had been detained in the Bastille, and perhaps chained in an unwholesome dungeon. He denied unequivocally that he had the necklace, or that he had ever seen it; and to silence the rumours and accusations against him, which his own secrecy with regard to the events of his life had perhaps originated, he expressed himself ready to satisfy the curiosity of the public, and to give a plain and full account of his career. He then told a romantic and incredible tale, which imposed upon no one. He said he neither knew the place of his birth nor the name of his parents, but that he spent his infancy in Medina, in Arabia, and was brought up under the name of Acharat. He lived in the palace of the Great Muphti in that city, and always had three servants to wait upon him, besides his preceptor, named Althotas. This Althotas was very fond of him, and told him that his father and mother, who were Christians and nobles, died when he was three months old, and left him in the care of the Muphti. He could never, he said, ascertain their names, for whenever' he asked Althotas the question, he was told that it would be dangerous for him to know. Some incautious expressions dropped by his preceptor gave him reason to think they were from Malta. At the age of twelve he began his travels, and learned the various languages of the East. He remained three years in Mecca, where the cherif, or governor, shewed him so much kindness, and spoke to him so tenderly and affectionately, that he sometimes thought that personage was his father. He quitted this good man with tears in his eyes, and never saw him afterwards ; but he was convinced that he was, even at that moment, indebted to his care for all the advantages he enjoyed. Whenever he arrived in any city, either of Europe or Asia, he found an account opened for him at the principal bankers' or merchants'. He could draw upon them to the amount of thousands and hundreds of thousands ; and no questions were ever asked beyond his name. He had only to mention the word 'Acharat,' and all his wants were supplied. He firmly believed that the Cherif of Mecca was the friend to whom all was owing. This was the secret of his wealth, and he had no occasion to resort to swindling for a livelihood. It was not worth his while to steal a diamond necklace when he had wealth enough to purchase as many as he pleased, and more magnificent ones than had ever been worn by a queen of France. As to the other charges brought against him by Madame de la Motte, he had but a short answer to give. She had called him an empiric. He was not unfamiliar with the word. If it meant a man who, without being a physician, had some knowledge of medicine, and took no fees—who cured both rich and poor, and took no money from either, he confessed that he was such a man, that he was an empiric. She had also called him a mean alchymist. Whether he were an alchymist or not, the epithet *mean* could only be applied to those who begged and cringed, and he had never done either. As regarded his being a dreamer about the philosopher's stone, whatever his opinions upon that subject might be, he had been silent, and had never troubled the public with his dreams. Then, as to his being a false prophet, he had not always been so ; for he had prophesied to the Cardinal de Rohan, that Madame de la Motte would prove a dangerous woman, and the result had verified the prediction. He denied that he was a profaner of the true worship, or that he had ever striven to bring religion into contempt ; on the contrary, he respected every man's religion, and never meddled with it. He also denied that he was a Rosicrucian, or that he had ever pretended to be three hundred years of age, or to have had one man in his service for a hundred and fifty years. In conclusion, he said every statement that Madame de la Motte had made regarding him was false, and that she was *mentiris impudentissime*, which two words he begged her counsel to translate for her, as it was not polite to tell her so in French.

Such was the substance of his extraordinary answer to the charges against him ; an answer which convinced those who were before doubtful that he was one of the most impudent impostors that had ever run the career of deception. Counsel was then heard on behalf o the Cardinal de Rohan and Madame de la Motte. It appearing clearly that the cardinal was himself the dupe of a vile conspiracy, and there being no evidence against Cagliostro, they were both acquitted. Madame de la Motte was found guilty, and sentenced to be publicly whipped, and branded with a hot iron on the back.

Cagliostro and his wife were then discharged from custody. On applying to the officers of the Bastille for the papers and effects which had been seized at his lodgings, he found that many of them had been abstracted. He thereupon brought an action against them for the recovery of his Mss. and a small portion of the powder of transmutation. Before the affair could be decided, he received orders to quit Paris within four-and-twenty hours. Fearing that if he were once more enclosed in the dungeons of the Bastille he should never see daylight again, he took his departure immediately and proceeded to England. On his arrival in London he made the acquaintance of the notorious Lord George Gordon, who espoused his cause warmly, and inserted a letter in the public papers, animadverting upon the conduct of the Queen of France in the affair of the necklace, and asserting that she was really the guilty party. For this letter Lord George was exposed to a prosecution at the instance of the French ambassador, found guilty of libel, and sentenced to fine and a long imprisonment.

Cagliostro and the countess afterwards travelled in Italy, where they were arrested by the Papal government in 1789, and condemned to death. The charges against him were, that he was a freemason, a heretic, and a sorcerer. This unjustifiable sentence was afterwards commuted into one of perpetual imprisonment in the Castle of St. Angelo. His wife was allowed to escape severer punishment by immuring herself in a nunnery. Cagliostro did not long survive. The loss of liberty preyed upon his mind—accumulated misfortunes had injured his health and broken his spirit, and he died early in 1790. His fate may have been no better than he deserved, but it is impossible not to feel that his sentence for the crimes assigned was utterly disgraceful to the government that pronounced it.

PRESENT STATE OF ALCHYMY.

We have now finished the list of the persons who have most distinguished themselves in this unprofitable pursuit. Among them are men of all ranks, characters, and conditions : the truth-seeking but erring philosopher; the ambitious prince and the needy noble, who have believed in it; as well as the designing charlatan, who has not believed in it, but has merely made the pretension to it the means of cheating his fellows, and living upon their credulity. One or more of all these classes will be found in the foregoing pages. It will be seen, from the record of their lives, that the delusion was not altogether without its uses. Men, in striving to gain too much, do not always overreach themselves; if they cannot arrive at the inaccessible mountain-top, they may perhaps get half-way towards it, and pick up some scraps of wisdom and knowledge on the road. The useful science of chemistry is not a little indebted to its spurious brother of alchymy. Many valuable discoveries have been made in that search for the impossible, which might otherwise have been hidden for centuries yet to come. Roger Bacon, in searching for the philosopher's stone, discovered gunpowder, a still more extraordinary substance. Van Helmont, in the same pursuit, discovered the properties of gas; Geber made discoveries in chemistry which were equally important; and Paracelsus, amidst his perpetual visions of the transmutation of metals, found that mercury was a remedy for one of the most odious and excruciating of all the diseases that afflict humanity.

In our day little mention is made in Europe of any new devotees of the science, though it is affirmed that one or two of our most illustrious men of science do not admit the pursuit to be so absurd and vain as it has been commonly considered in recent times. The belief in witchcraft, which is scarcely more absurd, still lingers in the popular mind; but few are so credulous as to believe that any elixir could make man live for centuries, or turn all our iron and pewter into gold. Alchymy, in Europe, may be said to be almost wholly exploded; but in the East it still flourishes in as great repute as ever. Recent travellers make constant mention of it, especially in China, Hindostan, Persia, Tartary, Egypt, and Arabia.

MODERN PROPHECIES.

A N epidemic terror of the end of the world has several times spread over the nations. The most remarkable was that which seized Christendom about the middle of the tenth century. Numbers of fanatics appeared in France, Germany, and Italy at that time, preaching that the thousand years prophesied in the Apocalypse as the term of the world's duration were about to expire, and that the Son of Man would appear in the clouds to judge the godly and the ungodly. The delusion appears to have been discouraged by the Church, but it nevertheless spread rapidly among the people.[*]

The scene of the last judgment was expected to be at Jerusalem. In the year 999, the number of pilgrims proceeding eastward, to await the coming of the Lord in that city, was so great that they were compared to a desolating army. Most of them sold their goods and possessions before they quitted Europe, and lived upon the proceeds in the Holy Land. Buildings of every sort were suffered to fall into ruins. It was thought useless to repair them, when the end of the world was so near. Many noble edifices were deliberately pulled down. Even churches, usually so well maintained, shared the general neglect. Knights, citizens, and serfs, travelled eastwards in company, taking with them their wives and children, singing psalms as they went, and looking with fearful eyes upon the sky, which they expected each minute to open, to let the Son of God descend in his glory.

During the thousandth year the number of pilgrims increased. Most of them were smitten with terror as with a plague. Every phenomenon of nature filled them with alarm. A thunder-storm sent them all upon their knees in mid-march. It was the opinion that

[*] See Gibbon and Voltaire for further notice of this subject

thunder was the voice of God, announcing the day of judgment. Numbers expected the earth to open, and give up its dead at the sound. Every meteor in the sky seen at Jerusalem brought the whole Christian population into the streets to weep and pray. The pilgrims on the road were in the same alarm:

> "Lorsque, pendant la nuit, un globe de lumière
> S'échappa quelquefois de la voûte de cieux,
> Et traca dans sa chûte un long sillon de feux,
> La troupe suspendit sa marche solitaire."[*]

Fanatic preachers kept up the flame of terror. Every shooting star furnished occasion for a sermon, in which the sublimity' of the approaching judgment was the principal topic.

The appearance of comets has been often thought to foretell the speedy dissolution of this world. Part of this belief still exists ; but the comet is no longer looked upon as the sign, but the agent of destruction. So lately as in the year 1832 the greatest alarm spread over the continent of Europe, especially in Germany, lest the comet, whose appearance was then foretold by astronomers, should destroy the earth. The danger of our globe was gravely discussed. Many persons refrained from undertaking or concluding any business during that year, in consequence solely of their apprehension that this terrible comet would dash us and our world to atoms.

During seasons of great pestilence, men have often believed the prophecies of crazed fanatics, that the end of the world was come. Credulity is always greatest in times of calamity. During the great plague, which ravaged all Europe between the years 1345 and 1350, it was generally considered that the end of the world was at hand. Pretended prophets were to be found in all the principal cities of Germany, France, and Italy, predicting that within ten years the trump of the archangel would sound, and the Saviour appear in the clouds to call the earth to judgment.

No little consternation was created in London in 1736 by the prophecy of the famous Whiston, that the world would be destroyed in that year, on the 13th of October. Crowds of people went out on the appointed day to Islington, Hampstead, and the fields intervening, to see the destruction of London, which was to be the "beginning of the end." A satirical account of this folly is given in Swift's *Miscellanies*, vol. iii., entitled *A true and faithful Narrative of what passed in London on a Rumour of the Day of Judgment*. An authentic narrative of this delusion would be interesting ; but this solemn witticism of Pope and Gay is not to be depended upon.

Charlemagne: Poëme épique, par Lucien Buonaparte.

In the year 1761 the citizens of London were alarmed by two shocks of an earthquake, and the prophecy of a third, which was to destroy them altogether. The first shock was felt on the 8th of February, and threw down several chimneys in the neighbourhood of Limehouse and Poplar; the second happened on the 8th of March, and was chiefly felt in the north of London, and towards Hampstead and Highgate. It soon became the subject of general remark, that there was exactly an interval of a month between the shocks; and a crack-brained fellow, named Bell, a soldier in the Life Guards, was so impressed with the idea that there would be a third in another month, that he lost his senses altogether, and ran about the streets predicting the destruction of London on the 5th of April. Most people thought that the *first* would have been a more appropriate day; but there were not wanting thousands who confidently believed the prediction, and took measures to transport themselves and families from the scene of the impending calamity. As the awful day approached, the excitement became intense, and great numbers of credulous people resorted to all the villages within a circuit of twenty miles, awaiting the doom of London. Islington, Highgate, Hampstead, Harrow, and Blackheath, were crowded with panic-stricken fugitives, who paid exorbitant prices for accommodation to the housekeepers of these secure retreats. Such as could not afford to pay for lodgings at any of those places, remained in London until two or three days before the time, and then encamped in the surrounding fields, awaiting the tremendous shock which was to lay their high city all level with the dust. As happened during a similar panic in the time of Henry VIII., the fear became contagious, and hundreds who had laughed at the prediction a week before, packed up their goods, when they saw others doing so, and hastened away. The river was thought to be a place of great security, and all the merchant-vessels in the port were filled with people, who passed the night between the 4th and 5th on board, expecting every instant to see St. Paul's totter, and the towers of Westminster Abbey rock in the wind and fall amid a cloud of dust. The greater part of the fugitives returned on the following day, convinced that the prophet was a false one; but many judged it more prudent to allow a week to elapse before they trusted their dear limbs in London. Bell lost all credit in a short time, and was looked upon even by the most credulous as a mere madman. He tried some other prophecies, but nobody was deceived by them; and, in a few months afterwards, he was confined in a lunatic asylum.

A panic terror of the end of the world seized the good people of Leeds and its neighbourhood in the year 1806. It arose from the following circumstances. A hen, in a village close by, laid eggs, on which were inscribed the words, " *Christ is coming.*" Great numbers visited the spot, and examined these wondrous eggs, convinced that the day of judgment was near at hand. Like sailors in a storm, expecting every instant to go to the bottom, the believers suddenly became religious, prayed violently, and flattered themselves that they repented them of their evil courses. But a plain tale soon put them down, and quenched their religion entirely. Some gentlemen, hearing of the matter, went one fine morning, and caught the poor hen in the act of laying one of her miraculous eggs. They soon ascertained beyond doubt that the egg had been inscribed with some corrosive ink, and cruelly forced up again into the bird's body. At this explanation, those who had prayed, now laughed, and the world wagged as merrily as of yore.

At the time of the plague in Milan, in 1630, of which so affecting a description has been left us by Ripamonte, in his interesting work, *De Peste Mediolani*, the people, in their distress, listened with avidity to the predictions of astrologers and other impostors. It is singular enough that the plague was foretold a year before it broke out. A large comet appearing in 1628, the opinions of astrologers were divided with regard to it. Some insisted that it was a forerunner of a bloody war; others maintained that it predicted a great famine; but the greater number, founding their judgment upon its pale colour, thought it portended a pestilence. The fulfilment of their prediction brought them into great repute while the plague was raging.

Other prophecies were current, which were asserted to have been delivered hundreds of years previously. They had a most pernicious effect upon the mind of the vulgar, as they induced a belief in fatalism. By taking away the hope of recovery—that greatest balm in every malady—they increased threefold the ravages of the disease. One singular prediction almost drove the unhappy people mad. An ancient couplet, preserved for ages by tradition, foretold, that in the year 1630 the devil would poison all Milan. Early one morning in April, and before the pestilence had reached its height, the passengers were surprised to see that all the doors in the principal streets of the city were marked with a curious daub, or spot, as if a sponge, filled with the purulent matter of the plague-sores, had been pressed against them. The whole population were speedily in movement to remark the strange appearance, and the greatest alarm spread rapidly. Every means was taken to discover the perpetrators, but in vain. At last the ancient prophecy was remembered, and prayers were offered up in all the churches, that the machinations of the Evil One might be defeated. Many persons were of opinion that the emissaries of foreign powers were employed to spread infectious poison over the city; but by far the greater number were convinced that the powers of hell had conspired against them, and that the infection was spread by supernatural agencies. In the mean time the plague increased fearfully. Distrust and alarm took possession of every mind. Every thing was believed to have been poisoned by the Devil; the waters of the wells, the standing corn in the fields, and the fruit upon the trees. It was believed that all objects of touch were poisoned; the walls of the houses, the pavements of the streets, and the very handles of the doors. The populace were raised to a pitch of ungovernable fury. A strict watch was kept for the Devil's emissaries, and any man who wanted to be rid of an enemy, had only to say that he had seen him besmearing a door with ointment; his fate was certain death at the hands of the mob. An old man, upwards of eighty years of age, a daily frequenter of the church of St. Antonio, was seen, on rising from his knees, to wipe with the skirt of his cloak the stool on which he was about to sit down. A cry was raised immediately that he was besmearing the seat with poison. A mob of women, by whom the church was crowded, seized hold of the feeble old man, and dragged him out by the hair of his head, with horrid oaths and imprecations. He was trailed in this manner through the mire to the house of the municipal judge, that he might be put to the rack, and forced to discover his accomplices; but he expired on the way. Many other victims were sacrificed to the popular fury. One Mora, who appears to have been half a chemist and half a barber, was accused of being in league with the Devil to poison Milan. His house was surrounded, and a number of chemical preparations were found. The poor man asserted, that they were intended as preservatives against infection; but some physicians, to whom they were submitted, declared they were poison. Mora was put to the rack, where he for a long time asserted his innocence. He confessed at last, when his courage was worn down by torture, that he was in league with the Devil and foreign powers to poison the whole city; that he had anointed the doors, and infected the fountains of water. He named several persons as his accomplices, who were apprehended and put to a similar torture. They were all found guilty, and executed. Mora's house was rased to the ground, and a column erected on the spot, with an inscription to commemorate his guilt.

While the public mind was filled with these marvellous occurrences, the plague continued to increase. The crowds that were brought together to witness the executions spread the infection among one another. But the fury of their passions, and the extent of their credulity, kept pace with the violence of the plague; every wonderful and preposterous story was believed. One, in particular, occupied them to the exclusion, for a long time, of every other. The Devil himself had been seen. He had taken a house in Milan, in which he prepared his poisonous unguents, and furnished them to his emissaries for distribution. One man had brooded over such tales till he became firmly convinced that the wild flights of his own fancy were realities. He stationed himself in the market-place of Milan, and related the following story to the crowds that gathered round him. He was standing, he said, at the door of the cathedral, late in the evening; and when there was nobody nigh, he saw a dark-coloured chariot, drawn by six milk-white horses, stop close beside him. The chariot was followed by a numerous train of domestics in dark liveries, mounted on dark-coloured steeds. In the chariot there sat a tall stranger of a majestic aspect; his long black hair floated in the wind —fire flashed from his large black eyes, and a curl of ineffable scorn dwelt upon his lips. The look of the stranger was so sublime that he was awed, and trembled with fear when he gazed upon him. His complexion was much darker than that of any man he had ever seen, and the atmosphere around him was hot and suffocating. He perceived immediately that he was a being of another world. The stranger, seeing his trepidation, asked him blandly, yet majestically, to mount beside him. He had no power to refuse, and before he was well aware that he had moved, he found himself in the chariot. Onwards they went, with the rapidity of the wind, the stranger speaking no word, until they stopped before a door in the high-street of Milan. There was a crowd of people in the street, but, to his great surprise, no one seemed to notice the extraordinary equipage and its numerous train. From this he concluded that they were invisible. The house at which they stopped appeared to be a shop, but the interior was like a vast half-ruined palace. He went with his mysterious guide through several large and dimly-lighted rooms. In one of them, surrounded by huge pillars of marble, a senate of ghosts was assembled, debating on the progress of the plague. Other parts of the building were enveloped in the thickest darkness, illumined at intervals by flashes of lightning, which allowed him to distinguish a number of gibing and chattering skeletons, running about and pursuing each other, or playing at leap-frog over one another's backs. At the rear of the mansion was a wild, uncultivated plot of ground, in the midst of which arose a black rock. Down its sides rushed with fearful noise a torrent of poisonous water, which, insinuating itself through the soil, penetrated to all the springs of the city, and rendered them unfit for use. After he had been shewn all this, the stranger led him into another large chamber, filled with gold and

precious stones, all of which he offered him if he would kneel down
and worship him, and consent to smear the doors and houses of Milan
with a pestiferous salve which he held out to him. He now knew
him to be the Devil, and in that moment of temptation prayed to
God to give him strength to resist. His prayer was heard—he refused the bribe. The stranger scowled horribly upon him—a loud
clap of thunder burst over his head—the vivid lightning flashed in
his eyes, and the next moment he found himself standing alone at
the porch of the cathedral. He repeated this strange tale day after
day, without any variation, and all the populace were firm believers
in its truth. Repeated search was made to discover the mysterious
house, but all in vain. The man pointed out several as resembling it,
which were searched by the police; but the Demon of the Pestilence
was not to be found, nor the hall of ghosts, nor the poisonous fountain. But the minds of the people were so impressed with the idea,
that scores of witnesses, half crazed by disease, came forward to swear
that they also had seen the diabolical stranger, and had heard his
chariot, drawn by the milk-white steeds, rumbling over the streets
at midnight with a sound louder than thunder.

The number of persons who confessed that they were employed
by the Devil to distribute poison is almost incredible. An epidemic
frenzy was abroad, which seemed to be as contagious as the plague.
Imagination was as disordered as the body, and day after day persons
came voluntarily forward to accuse themselves. They generally had
the marks of disease upon them, and some died in the act of confession.

During the great plague of London, in 1665, the people listened
with similar avidity to the predictions of quacks and fanatics. Defoe
says, that at that time the people were more addicted to prophecies
and astronomical conjurations, dreams, and old wives' tales than ever
they were before or since. Almanacs, and their predictions, frightened
them terribly. Even the year before the plague broke out, they were
greatly alarmed by the comet which then appeared, and anticipated
that famine, pestilence, or fire would follow. Enthusiasts, while yet
the disease had made but little progress, ran about the streets, predicting that in a few days London would be destroyed.

A still more singular instance of the faith in predictions occurred
in London in the year 1524. The city swarmed at that time with
fortune-tellers and astrologers, who were consulted daily by people of
every class in society on the secrets of futurity. As early as the month
of June 1523, several of them concurred in predicting that, on the
1st day of February 1524, the waters of the Thames would swell to
such a height as to overflow the whole city of London, and wash away
ten thousand houses. The prophecy met implicit belief. It was

reiterated with the utmost confidence month after month, until so much alarm was excited that many families packed up their goods, and removed into Kent and Essex. As the time drew nigh, the number of these emigrants increased. In January, droves of workmen might be seen, followed by their wives and children, trudging on foot to the villages within fifteen or twenty miles, to await the catastrophe. People of a higher class were also to be seen in wagons and other vehicles bound on a similar errand. By the middle of January, at least twenty thousand persons had quitted the doomed city, leaving nothing but the bare walls of their homes to be swept away by the impending floods. Many of the richer sort took up their abode on the heights of Highgate, Hampstead, and Blackheath; and some erected tents as far away as Waltham Abbey on the north, and Croydon on the south of the Thames. Bolton, the prior of St. Bartholomew's, was so alarmed, that he erected, at a very great expense, a sort of fortress at Harrow-on-the-Hill, which he stocked with provisions for two months. On the 24th of January, a week before the awful day which was to see the destruction of London, he removed thither, with the brethren and officers of the priory and all his household. A number of boats were conveyed in wagons to his fortress, furnished abundantly with expert rowers, in case the flood, reaching so high as Harrow, should force them to go farther for a resting-place. Many wealthy citizens prayed to share his retreat; but the prior, with a prudent forethought, admitted only his personal friends, and those who brought stores of eatables for the blockade.

At last the morn, big with the fate of London, appeared in the east. The wondering crowds were astir at an early hour to watch the rising of the waters. The inundation, it was predicted, would be gradual, not sudden; so that they expected to have plenty of time to escape as soon as they saw the bosom of old Thames heave beyond the usual mark. But the majority were too much alarmed to trust to this, and thought themselves safer ten or twenty miles off. The Thames, unmindful of the foolish crowds upon its banks, flowed on quietly as of yore. The tide ebbed at its usual hour, flowed to its usual height, and then ebbed again, just as if twenty astrologers had not pledged their words to the contrary. Blank were their faces as evening approached, and as blank grew the faces of the citizens to think that they had made such fools of themselves. At last night set in, and the obstinate river would not lift its waters to sweep away even one house out of the ten thousand. Still, however, the people were afraid to go to sleep. Many hundreds remained up till dawn of the next day, lest the deluge should come upon them like a thief in the night.

On the morrow, it was seriously discussed whether it would not
be advisable to duck the false prophets in the river. Luckily for
them, they thought of an expedient which allayed the popular fury.
They asserted that, by an error (a very slight one,) of a little figure,
they had fixed the date of this awful inundation a whole century too
early. The stars were right after all, and they, erring mortals, were
wrong. The present generation of cockneys was safe, and London
would be washed away, not in 1524, but in 1624. At this announcement, Bolton the prior dismantled his fortress, and the weary emigrants came back.

An eye-witness of the great fire of London, in an account preserved among the Harleian Mss. in the British Museum, and published in the transactions of the Royal Society of Antiquaries, relates
another instance of the credulity of the Londoners. The writer, who
accompanied the Duke of York day by day through the district in-
cluded between the Fleet-bridge and the Thames, states that, in their
efforts to check the progress of the flames, they were much impeded
by the superstition of the people. Mother Shipton, in one of her prophecies, had said that London would be reduced to ashes, and they
refused to make any efforts to prevent it.* A son of the noted Sir
Kenelm Digby, who was also a pretender to the gifts of prophecy,
persuaded them that no power on earth could prevent the fulfilment
of the prediction; for it was written in the great book of fate that
London was to be destroyed. Hundreds of persons, who might have
rendered valuable assistance, and saved whole parishes from devastation, folded their arms and looked on. As many more gave themselves up, with the less compunction, to plunder a city which they
could not save.†

This prophecy seems to have been that set forth at length in the popular *Life of
Mother Shipton:*   " When fate to England shall restore
                         A king to reign as heretofore,
                         Great death in London shall be though,
                         And many houses be laid low."

† The *London Saturday Journal* of March 12th, 1842, contains the following :—" An
absurd report is gaining ground among the weak-minded, that London will be destroyed
by an earthquake on the 17th of March, or St. Patrick's day. This rumour is founded on
the following ancient prophecies : one professing to be pronounced in the year 1203 ; the
other, by Dr. Dee the astrologer, in 1598 :

                         " In eighteen hundred and forty-two
                         Four things the sun shall view :
                         London's rich and famous town
                         Hungry earth shall swallow down.
                         Storm and rain in France shall be,
                         Till every river runs a sea.
                         Spain shall be rent in twain,
                         And famine waste the land again.

The prophecies of Mother Shipton are still believed in many of the rural districts of England. In cottages and servants' halls her reputation is great; and she rules, the most popular of British prophets, among all the uneducated, or half-educated, portions of the community. She is generally supposed to have been born at Knaresborough, in the reign of Henry VII., and to have sold her soul to the Devil for the power of foretelling future events. Though during her lifetime she was looked upon as a witch, she yet escaped the witch's fate, and died peaceably in her bed at an extreme old age, near Clifton in Yorkshire. A stone is said to have been erected to her memory in the churchyard of that place, with the following epitaph :

> "Here lies she who never lied,
> Whose skill often has been tried :
> Her prophecies shall still survive,
> And ever keep her name alive."

"Never a day passed," says her traditionary biography, "wherein she did not relate something remarkable, and that required the most serious consideration. People flocked to her from far and near, her fame was so great. They went to her of all sorts, both old and young, rich and poor, especially young maidens, to be resolved of their doubts relating to things to come; and all returned wonderfully satisfied in the explanations she gave to their questions." Among the rest, went the Abbot of Beverley, to whom she foretold the suppression of the monasteries by Henry VIII., his marriage with Anne Boleyn, the fires for heretics in Smithfield, and the execution of Mary Queen of Scots. She also foretold the accession of James I., adding that, with him,

> "From the cold North
> Every evil should come forth."

> So say I, the Monk of Dree,
> In the twelve hundredth year and three."
>
> *Harleian Collection (British Museum), 800 b, fol. 319*

> " The Lord have mercy on you all—
> Prepare yourselves for dreadful fall
> Of house and land and human soul—
> The measure of your sins is full.
> In the year one, eight, and forty-two,
> Of the year that is so new ;
> In the third month of that sixteen,
> It may be a day or two between—
> Perhaps you'll soon be stiff and cold.
> Dear Christian, be not stout and bold—
> The mighty, kingly-proud will see
> This comes to pass as my name's Dee."
>
> *1598. Ms. in the British Museum.*

The alarm of the population of London did not on this occasion extend beyond the wide circle of the uneducated classes, but among them it equalled that recorded in the text. It was soon afterwards stated that no such prophecy is to be found in the Harleian Ms.

On a subsequent visit she uttered another prophecy, which, in the opinion of her believers, still remains unfulfilled, but may be expected to be realised during the present century :

> " The time shall come when seas of blood
> Shall mingle with a greater flood.
> Great noise there shall be heard—great shouts and cries,
> And seas shall thunder louder than the skies ;
> Then shall three lions fight with three and bring
> Joy to a people, honour to a king.
> That fiery year as soon as o'er,
> Peace shall then be as before ;
> Plenty shall every where be found,
> And men with swords shall plough the ground."

But the most famous of all her prophecies is one relating to London. Thousands of persons still shudder to think of the woes that are to burst over this unhappy realm, when London and Highgate are joined by one continuous line of houses. This junction, which, if the rage for building lasts much longer, in the same proportion as heretofore, bids fair to be soon accomplished, was predicted by her shortly before her death. Revolutions—the fall of mighty monarchs, and the shedding of much blood are to signalise that event. The very angels, afflicted by our woes, are to turn aside their heads, and weep for hapless Britain.

But great as is the fame of Mother Shipton, she ranks but second in the list of British prophets. Merlin, the mighty Merlin, stands alone in his high pre-eminence—the first and greatest. As old Drayton sings, in his *Poly-olbion :*

> " Of Merlin and his skill what region doth not hear ?
> The world shall still be full of Merlin every year.
> A thousand lingering years his prophecies have run,
> And scarcely shall have end till time itself be done."

Spenser, in his divine poem, has given us a powerful description of this renowned seer—

> " who had in magic more insight
> Than ever him before, or after, living wight.
> For he by words could call out of the sky
> Both sun and moon, and make them him obey ;
> The land to sea, and sea to mainland dry,
> And darksome night he eke could turn to day—
> Huge hosts of men he could, alone, dismay.
> And hosts of men and meanest things could frame,
> Whenso him list his enemies to fray,
> That to this day, for terror of his name,
> The fiends do quake, when any him to them does name.

> And soothe men say that he was not the sonne
> Of mortal sire or other living wighte,
> But wondrously begotten and begoune
> By false illusion of a guileful sprite
> On a faire ladye nun."

In these verses the poet has preserved the popular belief with regard to Merlin, who is generally supposed to have been a contemporary of Vortigern. Opinion is divided as to whether he were a real personage, or a mere impersonation, formed by the poetic fancy of a credulous people. It seems most probable that such a man did exist, and that, possessing knowledge as much above the comprehension of his age, as that possessed by Friar Bacon was beyond the reach of his, he was endowed by the wondering crowd with the supernatural attributes that Spenser has enumerated.

Geoffrey of Monmouth translated Merlin's poetical odes, or prophecies, into Latin prose; and he was much reverenced not only by Geoffrey, but by most of the old annalists. In a *Life of Merlin, with his Prophecies and Predictions interpreted and made good by our English Annals*, by Thomas Heywood, published in the reign of Charles I., we find several of these pretended prophecies. They seem, however, to have been all written by Heywood himself. They are in terms too plain and positive to allow any one to doubt for a moment of their having been composed *ex post facto*. Speaking of Richard I., he says:

> " The Lion's heart will 'gainst the Saracen rise,
> And purchase from him many a glorious prize;
> The rose and lily shall at first unite,
> But, parting of the prey prove opposite.　*　*　*
> But while abroad these great acts shall be done,
> All things at home shall to disorder run.
> Cooped up and caged then shall the Lion be,
> But, after sufferance, ransomed and set free."

The simple-minded Thomas Heywood gravely goes on to inform us, that all these things actually came to pass. Upon Richard III. he is equally luminous. He says:

> " A hunch-backed monster, who with teeth is born,
> The mockery of art and nature's scorn;
> Who from the womb preposterously is hurled,
> And with feet forward thrust into the world,
> Shall, from the lower earth on which he stood,
> Wade, every step he mounts, knee-deep in blood.
> He shall to th' height of all his hopes aspire,
> And, clothed in state, his ugly shape admire;
> But, when he thinks himself most safe to stand,
> From foreign parts a native whelp shall land."

Another of these prophecies after the event tells us that Henry VIII. should take the power from Rome, " and bring it home unto his British bower ;" that he should " root out from the land all the razored skulls ;" and that he should neither spare " man in his rage nor woman in his lust ;" and that, in the time of his next successor but one, "there should come in the fagot and the stake." Master Heywood closes Merlin's prophecies at his own day, and does not give even a glimpse of what was to befall England after his decease. Many other prophecies, besides those quoted by him, were, he says, dispersed abroad, in his day, under the name of Merlin ; but he gives his readers a taste of one only, and that is the following :

> " When hempe is ripe and ready to pull,
> Then, Englishman, beware thy skull."

This prophecy, which, one would think, ought to have put him in mind of the gallows, at that time the not unusual fate of false prophets, he explains thus : " In this word HEMPE be five letters. Now, by reckoning the five successive princes from Henry VIII., this prophecy is easily explained : H signifieth King Henry before-named; E, Edward, his son, the sixth of that name ; M, Mary, who succeeded him; P, Philip of Spain, who, by marrying Queen Mary, participated with her in the English diadem ; and, lastly, E signifieth Queen Elizabeth, after whose death there was a great feare that some troubles might have arisen about the crown." As this did not happen, Heywood, who was a sly rogue in a small way, gets out of the scrape by saying, " Yet proved this augury true, though not according to the former expectation ; for, after the peaceful inauguration of King James, there was great mortality, not in London only, but through the whole kingdom, and from which the nation was not quite clean in seven years after."

This is not unlike the subterfuge of Peter of Pontefract, who had prophesied the death and deposition of King John, and who was hanged by that monarch for his pains. A very graphic and amusing account of this pretended prophet is given by Grafton, in his *Chronicles of England.** " In the meanwhile," says he, " the priestes within England had provided them a false and counterfeated prophet, called Peter Wakefielde, a Yorkshire man, who was an hermite, an idle gadder about, and a pratlyng marchant. Now, to bring this Peter in credite, and the kyng out of all credite with his people, diverse vaine persons bruted dayly among the commons of the realme, that Christe had twice appered unto him in the shape of a childe, between the prieste's handes, once at Yorke, another tyme at Pom-

---

* *Chronicles of England,* by Richard Grafton; London, 1568, p. 106.

fret; and that he had breathed upon him thrice, saying, '*Peace, peace, peace,*' and teachyng many things, which he anon declared to the bishops, and bid the people amend their naughtie living. Being rapt also in spirite, they sayde he behelde the joyes of heaven and sorrowes of hell; for scant were there three in the realme, sayde he, that lived christianly.

"This counterfeated soothsayer prophesied of King John, that he should reigne no longer than the Ascension-day next followyng, which was in the yere of our Lord 1211, and was the thirteenth yere from his coronation; and this, he said, he had by revelation. Then it was of him demanded, whether he should be slaine or be deposed, or should voluntarily give over the crowne? He aunswered, that he could not tell; but of this he was sure (he sayd), that neither he nor any of his stock or lineage should reigne after that day.

"The king, hering of this, laughed much at it, and made but a scoff thereat. 'Tush!' saith he, 'it is but an ideot knave, and such an one as lacketh his right wittes.' But when this foolish prophet had so escaped the daunger of the kinge's displeasure, and that he made no more of it, he gate him abroad, and prated thereof at large, as he was a very idle vagabond, and used to trattle and talke more than ynough; so that they which loved the king caused him anon after to be apprehended as a malefactor, and to be throwen in prison, the king not yet knowing thereof.

"Anone after the fame of this phantasticall prophet went all the realme over, and his name was knowen every where, as foolishnesse is much regarded of the people, where wisdome is not in place; specially because he was then imprisoned for the matter, the rumour was the larger, their wonderynges were the wantoner, their practises the foolisher, their busye talkes and other idle doinges the greater. Continually from thence, as the rude manner of people is, old gossyps tales went abroad, new tales were invented, fables were added to fables, and lyes grew upon lyes. So that every daye newe slanders were laide upon the king, and not one of them true. Rumors arose, blasphemyes were sprede, the enemyes rejoyced, and treasons by the priestes were mainteyned; and what lykewise was surmised, or other subtiltye practised, all was then fathered upon this foolish prophet, as 'thus saith Peter Wakefield;' 'thus hath he prophesied;' 'and thus it shall come to pass;' yea, many times, when he thought nothing lesse. And when the Ascension-day was come, which was prophecyed of before, King John commanded his royal tent to be spread in the open fielde, passing that day with his noble counseyle and men of honour in the greatest solemnitie that ever he did before; solacing himself with musickale instrumentes and songs, most in sight among his trustie friendes. When that day was paste in all prosperitie and myrth, his enemyes being confused, turned all into an allegorical understanding to make the prophecie good, and sayde, ' He is no longer king, for the pope reigneth, and not he.' [King John was labouring under a sentence of excommunication at the time.]

" Then was the king by his council perswaded that this false prophet had troubled the realme, perverted the heartes of the people, and raysed the Commons against him ; for his wordes went over the sea, by the help of his prelates, and came to the French king's eare, and gave to him a great encouragement to invade the lande. He had not else done it so sodeinely. But he was most fowly deceived, as all they are and shall be that put their trust in such dark drowsye dreames of hipocrites. The king therefore commended that he should be hanged up, and his sonne also with him, lest any more false prophets should arise of that race."

Heywood, who was a great stickler for the truth of all sorts of prophecies, gives a much more favourable account of this Peter of Pomfret, or Pontefract, whose fate he would, in all probability, have shared, if he had had the misfortune to have flourished in the same age. He says, that Peter, who was not only a prophet, but a bard, predicted divers of King John's disasters, which fell out accordingly. On being taxed for a lying prophet in having predicted that the king would be deposed before he entered into the fifteenth year of his reign, he answered him boldly, that all he had said was justifiable and true ; for that, having given up the crown to the pope, and paying him an annual tribute, the pope reigned, and not he. Heywood thought this explanation to be perfectly satisfactory, and the prophet's faith for ever established.

But to return to Merlin. Of him even to this day it may be said, in the words which Burns has applied to another notorious personage :

" Great was his power and great his fame;
Far kenned and noted is his name."

His reputation is by no means confined to the land of his birth, but extends through most of the nations of Europe. A very curious volume of his *Life, Prophecies, and Miracles*, written, it is supposed, by Robert de Bosron, was printed at Paris in 1498, which states, that the devil himself was his father, and that he spoke the instant he was born, and assured his mother, a very virtuous young woman, that she should not die in childbed with him, as her ill-natured neighbours had predicted. The judge of the district, hearing of so marvellous an occurrence, summoned both mother and child to appear before him ; and they went accordingly the same day. To put the wisdom of the young prophet most effectively to the test, the judge asked him if he knew his own father ? To which the infant Merlin replied, in a clear sonorous voice, ' Yes, my father is the Devil ; and I have his power, and know all things, past, present, and to come." His worship clapped his hands in astonishment, and took the prudent resolution of not molesting so awful a child or its mother either.

Early tradition attributes the building of Stonehenge to the power of Merlin. It was believed that those mighty stones were whirled through the air, at his command, from Ireland to Salisbury Plain ; and that he arranged them in the form in which they now stand, to commemorate for ever the unhappy fate of three hundred British chiefs, who were massacred on that spot by the Saxons.

At Abergwylly, near Carmarthen, is still shewn the cave of the prophet and the scene of his incantations. How beautiful is the description of it given by Spenser in his *Faerie Queene !* The lines need no apology for their repetition here, and any sketch of the great prophet of Britain would be incomplete without them :

> " There the wise Merlin, whilom wont (they say,)
>   To make his wonne low underneath the ground,
>   In a deep delve far from the view of day,
>   That of no living wight he mote be found,
> Whenso he counselled with his sprites encompassed round.

> And if thou ever happen that same way
>   To travel, go to see that dreadful place ;
>   It is a hideous, hollow cave, they say,
>   Under a rock that lies a little space
>   From the swift Barry, tumbling down apace
>   Amongst the woody hills of Dynevoure ;
>   But dare thou not, I charge, in any case,
>   To enter into that same baleful bower,
> For fear the cruel fiendes should thee unwares devour !

> But, standing high aloft, low lay thine eare,
>   And there such ghastly noise of iron chaines
> And brazen caudrons thou shalt rombling heare,
>   Which thousand sprites with long-enduring paines
>   Doe tosse, that it will stun thy feeble braines ;
>   And often times great groans and grievous stownds,
>   When too huge toile and labour them constraines ;
>   And often times loud strokes and ringing sounds
> From under that deep rock most horribly rebounds.

> The cause, they say, is this. A little while
>   Before that Merlin died, he did intend
>   A brazen wall in compass, to compile
>   About Cayr Merdin, and did it commend
>   Unto these sprites to bring to perfect end ;

> During which work the Lady of the Lake,
>   Whom long he loved, for him in haste did send,
> Who thereby forced his workmen to forsake,
>   Them bound till his return their labour not to slake.
>
> In the mean time, through that false ladie's traine,
>   He was surprised, and buried under biere,
> Ne ever to his work returned again;
>   Natheless these fiendes may not their work forbeare,
> So greatly his commandement they fear,
> But there doe toile and travaile day and night,
>   Until that brazen wall they up doe reare."*

Amongst other English prophets, a belief in whose power has not been entirely effaced by the light of advancing knowledge, is Robert Nixon, the Cheshire idiot, a contemporary of Mother Shipton. The popular accounts of this man say, that he was born of poor parents, not far from Vale Royal, on the edge of the forest of Delamere. He was brought up to the plough, but was so ignorant and stupid, that nothing could be made of him. Every body thought him irretrievably insane, and paid no attention to the strange, unconnected discourses which he held. Many of his prophecies are believed to have been lost in this manner. But they were not always destined to be wasted upon dull and inattentive ears. An incident occurred which brought him into notice, and established his fame as a prophet of the first calibre. He was ploughing in a field, when he suddenly stopped from his labour, and with a wild look and strange gesture, exclaimed, "*Now, Dick! now, Harry! O, ill done, Dick! O, well done, Harry! Harry has gained the day!*" His fellow-labourers in the field did not know what to make of this rhapsody; but the next day cleared up the mystery. News was brought by a messenger, in hot haste, that at the very instant when Nixon had thus ejaculated, Richard III. had been slain at the battle of Bosworth, and Henry VII. proclaimed king of England.

It was not long before the fame of the new prophet reached the ears of the king, who expressed a wish to see and converse with him. A messenger was accordingly despatched to bring him to court; but long before he reached Cheshire, Nixon knew and dreaded the honours that awaited him. Indeed it was said, that at the very instant the king expressed the wish, Nixon was, by supernatural means, made acquainted with it, and that he ran about the town of Over in great distress of mind, calling out, like a madman, that Henry had sent for him, and that he must go to court, and be *clammed*, that is, starved to death. These expressions excited no little won-

* *Faerie Queene*, b. 3, c. 3, s. 6-13.

der ; but, on the third day, the messenger arrived, and carried him to court, leaving on the minds of the good people of Cheshire an impression that their prophet was one of the greatest ever born. On his arrival King Henry appeared to be troubled exceedingly at the loss of a valuable diamond, and asked Nixon if he could inform him where it was to be found Henry had hidden the diamond himself, with a view to test the prophet's skill. Great, therefore, was his surprise when Nixon answered him in the words of the old proverb, " Those who hide can find." From that time forth the king implicitly believed that he had the gift of prophecy, and ordered all his words to be taken down.

During all the time of his residence at court he was in constant fear of being starved to death, and repeatedly told the king that such would be his fate, if he were not allowed to depart, and return into his own country. Henry would not suffer it, but gave strict orders to all his officers and cooks to give him as much to eat as he wanted. He lived so well, that for some time he seemed to be thriving like a nobleman's steward, and growing as fat as an alderman. One day the king went out hunting, when Nixon ran to the palace gate, and entreated on his knees that he might not be left behind to be starved. The king laughed, and calling an officer, told him to take especial care of the prophet during his absence, and rode away to the forest. After his departure, the servants of the palace began to jeer at and insult Nixon, whom they imagined to be much better treated than he deserved. Nixon complained to the officer, who, to prevent him from being further molested, locked him up in the king's own closet, and brought him regularly his four meals a day. But it so happened that a messenger arrived from the king to this officer, requiring his immediate presence at Winchester, on a matter of life and death. So great was his haste to obey the king's command, that he mounted on the horse behind the messenger, and rode off, without bestowing a thought upon poor Nixon. He did not return till three days afterwards, when, remembering the prophet for the first time, he went to the king's closet, and found him lying upon the floor, starved to death, as he had predicted.

Among the prophecies of his which are believed to have been fulfilled are the following, which relate to the times of the Pretender :

> " A great man shall come into England,
> But the son of a king
> Shall take from him the victory."

> " Crows shall drink the blood of many nobles,
> And the North shall rise against the South."

> " *The cock of the North shall be made to flee,*
> *And his feather be plucked for his pride,*
> *That he shall almost curse the day that he was born.*"

All these, say his admirers, are as clear as the sun at noon-day. The first denotes the defeat of Prince Charles Edward, at the battle of Culloden, by the Duke of Cumberland; the second, the execution of Lords Derwentwater, Balmerino, and Lovat; and the third, the retreat of the Pretender from the shores of Britain. Among the prophecies that still remain to be accomplished are the following:

> " *Between seven, eight, and nine,*
> *In England wonders shall be seen;*
> *Between nine and thirteen*
> *All sorrow shall be done.*"

> " *Through our own money and our men,*
> *Shall a dreadful war begin.*
> *Between the sickle and the suck*
> *All England shall have a pluck.*"

> " *Foreign nations shall invade England with snow on their helmets, and shall bring plague, famine, and murder in the skirts of their garments.*"

> " *The town of Nantwich shall be swept away by a flood.*"

Of the two first of these no explanation has yet been attempted; but some event or other will doubtless be twisted into such a shape as will fit them. The third, relative to the invasion of England by a nation with snow on their helmets, is supposed by the old women to foretell most clearly a coming war with Russia. As to the last, there are not a few in the town mentioned who devoutly believe that' such will be its fate. Happily for their peace of mind, the prophet said nothing of the year that was to witness the awful calamity; so that they think it as likely to be two centuries hence as now.

The popular biographers of Nixon conclude their account of him by saying, that "his prophecies are by some persons thought fables; yet by what has come to pass, it is now thought, and very plainly appears, that most of them have proved, or will prove, true; for which we, on all occasions, ought not only to exert our utmost might to repel by force our enemies, but to refrain from our abandoned and wicked course of life, and to make our continual prayer to God for protection and safety." To this, though a *non sequitur*, every one will cry, Amen!

Besides the prophets, there have been the almanac-makers Lilly, Poor Robin, Partridge, and Francis Moore, physician, in England; and Matthew Laensbergh, in France and Belgium. But great as were their pretensions, they were modesty itself in comparison with

Merlin, Shipton, and Nixon, who fixed their minds upon higher things than the weather, and were not so restrained as to prophesy for only one year at a time. After such prophets the almanac-makers hardly deserve to be mentioned ; not even the renowned Partridge, whose prognostications set all England agog in 1708, and whose death while still alive was so pleasantly and satisfactorily proved by Isaac Bickerstaff. The anti-climax would be too palpable, and they and their doings must be left uncommemorated.

MOTHER SHIPTON'S HOUSE.*

* Although other places claim the honour (!) of Mother Shipton's birth, her residence is asserted, by oral tradition, to have been for many years a cottage at Winslow-cum-Shipton, in Buckinghamshire, of which the above is a representation. We give the contents of one of the popular books containing her prophecies :

The Strange and Wonderful History and Prophecies of Mother Shipton, plainly setting forth her Birth, Life, Death, and Burial. 12mo. Newcastle. Chap. 1.—Of her birth and parentage. 2. How Mother Shipton's mother proved with child ; how she fitted the justice, and what happened at her delivery. 3. By what name Mother Shipton was christened, and how her mother went into a monastery. 4. Several other pranks play'd by Mother Shipton in revenge of such as abused her. 5. How Ursula married a young man named Tobias Shipton, and how strangely she discovered a thief. 6. Her prophecy against Cardinal Wolsey. 7. Some other prophecies of Mother Shipton relating to those times. 8. Her prophecies in verse to the Abbot of Beverly. 9. Mother Shipton's life, death, and burial

FORTUNE-TELLING.

———◆———

And men still grope t' anticipate
The cabinet designs of Fate;
Apply to wizards to foresee
What shall and what shall never be.
Hudibras, part iii. canto 3.

IN accordance with the plan laid down, we proceed to the consideration of the follies into which men have been led by their eager desire to pierce the thick darkness of futurity. God himself, for his own wise purposes, has more than once undrawn the impenetrable veil which shrouds those awful secrets; and, for purposes just as wise, he has decreed that, except in these instances, ignorance shall be our lot for ever. It is happy for man that he does not know what the morrow is to bring forth; but, unaware of this great blessing, he has, in all ages of the world, presumptuously endeavoured to trace the events of unborn centuries, and anticipate the march of time. He has reduced this presumption into a study. He has divided it into sciences and systems without number, employing his whole life in the vain pursuit. Upon no subject has it been so easy to deceive the world as upon this. In every breast the curiosity exists in a greater or less degree, and can only be conquered by a long course of self-examination, and a firm reliance that the future would not be hidden from our sight, if it were right that we should be acquainted with it.

An undue opinion of our own importance in the scale of creation is at the bottom of all our unwarrantable notions in this respect. How flattering to the pride of man to think that the stars in their courses watch over him, and typify, by their movements and aspects, the joys or the sorrows that await him! He, less in proportion to the universe than the all-but invisible insects that feed in myriads on a summer's leaf are to this great globe itself, fondly imagines that eternal worlds were chiefly created to prognosticate his fate. How we should pity the arrogance of the worm that crawls at our feet, if we knew that it also desired to know the secrets of futurity, and imagined that meteors shot athwart the sky to warn it that a tom-tit was hovering near to gobble it up; that storms and earthquakes, the revolutions of empires, or the fall of mighty monarchs, only happened to predict its birth, its progress, and its decay! Not a whit less presuming has man shewn himself; not a whit less arrogant are the sciences, so called, of astrology, augury, necromancy, geomancy, palmistry, and divination of every kind.

Leaving out of view the oracles of pagan antiquity and religious predictions in general, and confining ourselves solely to the persons who, in modern times, have made themselves most conspicuous in foretelling the future, we shall find that the sixteenth and seventeenth centuries were the golden age of these impostors. Many of them have been already mentioned in their character of alchymists. The union of the two pretensions is not at all surprising. It was to be expected that those who assumed a power so preposterous as that of prolonging the life of man for several centuries, should pretend, at the same time, to foretell the events which were to mark that preternatural span of existence. The world would as readily believe that they had discovered all secrets, as that they had only discovered one. The most celebrated astrologers of Europe, three centuries ago, were alchymists. Agrippa, Paracelsus, Dr. Dee, and the Rosicrucians, all laid as much stress upon their knowledge of the days to come, as upon their pretended possession of the philosopher's stone and the elixir of life. In their time, ideas of the wonderful, the diabolical, and the supernatural, were rifer than ever they were before. The devil or the stars were universally believed to meddle constantly in the affairs of men; and both were to be consulted with proper ceremonies. Those who were of a melancholy and gloomy temperament betook themselves to necromancy and sorcery; those more cheerful and aspiring devoted themselves to astrology. The latter science was encouraged by all the monarchs and governments of that age. In England, from the time of Elizabeth to that of William and Mary, judicial astrology was in high repute. During that period flourished Drs. Dee, Lamb, and Forman; with Lilly, Booker, Gadbury, Evans, and scores of nameless impostors in every considerable town and village in the country, who made it their business to cast nativities, aid in the recovery of stolen goods, prognosticate happy or unhappy marriages, predict whether journeys would be prosperous, and note lucky moments for the commencement of any enterprise, from the setting up of a cobbler's shop to the marching of an army. Men who, to use the words of Butler, did

> "Deal in Destiny's dark counsel,
> And sage opinion of the moon sell;
> To whom all people far and near
> On deep importance did repair,

> When brass and pewter pots did stray,
> And linen slunk out of the way."

In Lilly's *Memoirs of his Life and Times*, there are many notices of the inferior quacks who then abounded, and upon whom he pretended to look down with supreme contempt; not because they were astrologers, but because they debased that noble art by taking fees for the recovery of stolen property. From Butler's *Hudibras*, and its curious notes, we may learn what immense numbers of these fellows lived upon the credulity of mankind in that age of witchcraft and diablerie. Even in our day, how great is the reputation enjoyed by the almanac-makers, who assume the name of Francis Moore! But in the time of Charles I. and the Commonwealth the most learned, the most noble, and the most conspicuous characters did not hesitate to consult astrologers in the most open manner. Lilly, whom Butler has immortalised under the name of Sydrophel, relates, that he proposed to write a work called *An Introduction to Astrology*, in which he would satisfy the whole kingdom of the lawfulness of that art Many

HENRY ANDREWS, THE ORIGINAL "FRANCIS MOORE."

of the soldiers were for it, he says, and many of the Independent party, and abundance of worthy men in the House of Commons, his assured friends, and able to take his part against the Presbyterians, who would have silenced his predictions if they could. He afterwards carried his plan into execution, and when his book was published, went with another astrologer named Booker to the head-quarters of the parliamentary army at Windsor, where they were welcomed and feasted in the garden where General Fairfax lodged. They were afterwards introduced to the general, who received them very kindly, and made allusion to some of their predictions. He hoped their art was lawful and agreeable to God's word; but he did not understand it himself. He did not doubt, however, that the two astrologers feared God, and therefore he had a good opinion of them. Lilly assured him that the art of astrology was quite consonant to the Scriptures; and confidently predicted from his knowledge of the stars, that the parliamentary army would overthrow all its enemies. In Oliver's Protectorate, this quack informs us that he wrote freely enough. He became an Independent, and all the soldiery were his friends. When he went to Scotland, he saw a soldier standing in front of the army with a book of prophecies in his hand, exclaiming to the several companies as they passed by him, "Lo! hear what Lilly saith: you are in this month promised victory! Fight it out, brave boys! and then read that month's prediction!"

After the great fire of London, which Lilly said he had foretold, he was sent for by the committee of the House of Commons appointed to inquire into the causes of the calamity. In his *Monarchy or no Monarchy*, published in 1651, he had inserted an hieroglyphical plate representing on one side persons in winding-sheets digging graves; and on the other a large city in flames. After the great fire, some sapient member of the legislature bethought him of Lilly's book, and having mentioned it in the house, it was agreed that the astrologer should be summoned. Lilly attended accordingly, when Sir Robert Brook told him the reason of his summons, and called upon him to declare what he knew. This was a rare opportunity for the vainglorious Lilly to vaunt his abilities; and he began a long speech in praise of himself and his pretended science. He said that, after the execution of Charles I., he was extremely desirous to know what might from that time forth happen to the parliament and to the nation in general. He therefore consulted the stars, and satisfied himself. The result of his judgment he put into emblems and hieroglyphics, without any commentary, so that the true meaning might be concealed from the vulgar, and made manifest only to the wise; imitating in this the example of many wise philosophers who had done the like.

"Did you foresee the year of the fire?" said a member. "No," quoth Lilly, "nor was I desirous. Of that I made no scrutiny." After some further parley, the house found they could make nothing of the astrologer, and dismissed him with great civility.

One specimen of the explanation of a prophecy given by Lilly, and related by him with much complacency, will be sufficient to shew the sort of trash by which he imposed upon the million. "In the year 1588," says he, "there was a prophecy printed in Greek characters, exactly deciphering the long troubles of the English nation from 1641 to 1660." And it ended thus: "And after him shall come a dreadful dead man, and with him a royal G, of the best blood in the world; and he shall have the crown, and shall set England on the right way, and put out all heresies." The following is the explanation of this oracular absurdity:

"*Monkery being extinguished above eighty or ninety years, and the Lord General's name being Monk, is the dead man. The royal G or C [it is gamma in the Greek, intending C in the Latin, being the third letter in the alphabet] is Charles II., who for his extraction may be said to be of the best blood of the world.*"

In France and Germany astrologers met even more encouragement than they received in England. In very early ages Charlemagne and his successors fulminated their wrath against them in common with sorcerers. Louis XI., that most superstitious of men, entertained great numbers of them at his court; and Catherine di Medicis, that most superstitious of women, hardly ever undertook any affair of importance without consulting them. She chiefly favoured her own countrymen; and during the time she governed France, the land was overrun by Italian conjurors, necromancers, and fortune-tellers of every kind.

NOSTRADAMUS — FROM THE FRONTISPIECE TO A COLLECTION OF HIS PROPHECIES, PUBLISHED AT AMSTERDAM, A.D. 1666.

But the chief astrologer of that day, beyond all doubt, was the celebrated Nostradamus, physician to her husband, King Henry II. He was born in 1503 at the town of St. Remi, in Provence, where his father was a notary. He did not acquire much fame till he was past his fiftieth year, when his famous *Centuries*, a collection of verses, written in obscure and almost unintelligible language, began to excite attention. They were so much spoken of in 1556, that Henry II. resolved to attach so skilful a man to his service, and appointed him his physician. In a biographical notice of him, prefixed to the edition of his *Vraies Centuries*, published at Amsterdam in 1668, we are informed that he often discoursed with his royal master on the secrets of futurity, and received many great presents as his reward, besides his usual allowance for medical attendance. After the death of Henry he retired to his native place, where Charles IX. paid him a visit in 1564; and was so impressed with veneration for his wondrous knowledge of the things that were to be, not in France only, but in the whole world for hundreds of years to come, that he made him a counsellor of state and his own physician, besides treating him in other matters with a royal liberality. " In fine," continues his biographer, " I should be too prolix were I to tell all the honours conferred upon him, and all the great nobles and learned men that arrived at his house from the very ends of the earth, to see and converse with him as if he had been an oracle. Many strangers, in fact, came to France for no other purpose than to consult him."

The prophecies of Nostradamus consist of upwards of a thousand stanzas, each of four lines, and are to the full as obscure as the oracles of old. They take so great a latitude, both as to time and space, that they are almost sure to be fulfilled somewhere or other in the course of a few centuries. A little ingenuity, like that evinced by Lilly in his explanation about General Monk and the dreadful dead man, might easily make events to fit some of them.*

He is to this day extremely popular in France and the Walloon country of Belgium, where old farmer-wives consult him with great confidence and assiduity.

Catherine di Medicis was not the only member of her illustrious house who entertained astrologers. At the beginning of the fifteenth century there was a man, named Basil, residing in Florence, who was noted over all Italy for his skill in piercing the darkness of futurity. It is said that he foretold to Cosmo di Medicis, then a private citizen, that he would attain high dignity, inasmuch as the ascendant of his nativity was adorned with the same propitious aspects as those of Augustus Cæsar and the Emperor Charles V.† Another astrologer foretold the death of Prince Alexander di Medicis ; and so very minute and particular was he in all the circumstances, that he was suspected of being chiefly instrumental in fulfilling his own prophecy—

---

* Let us try. In his second century, prediction 66, he says:

"From great dangers the captive is escaped.
A little time, great fortune changed.
In the palace the people are caught.
By good augury the city is besieged."

" What is this," a believer might exclaim, "but the escape of Napoleon from Elba—his changed fortune, and the occupation of Paris by the allied armies?"

Let us try again. In his third century, prediction 98, he says:

"Two royal brothers will make fierce war on each other;
So mortal shall be the strife between them,
That each one shall occupy a fort against the other;
For their reign and life shall be the quarrel."

Some Lillius Redivivus would find no difficulty in this prediction. To use a vulgar phrase, it is as clear as a pikestaff. Had not the astrologer in view Don Miguel and Don Pedro when he penned this stanza, so much less obscure and oracular than the rest?

† *Hermippus Redivivus,* p. 142.

a very common resource with these fellows to keep up their credit. He foretold confidently that the prince should die by the hand of his own familiar friend, a person of a slender habit of body, a small face, a swarthy complexion, and of most remarkable taciturnity. So it afterwards happened, Alexander having been murdered in his chamber by his cousin Lorenzo, who corresponded exactly with the above description.* The author of *Hermippus Redivivus*, in relating this story, inclines to the belief that the astrologer was guiltless of any participation in the crime, but was employed by some friend of Prince Alexander to warn him of his danger.

A much more remarkable story is told of an astrologer who lived in Romagna in the fifteenth century, and whose name was Antiochus Tibertus.† At that time nearly all the petty sovereigns of Italy retained such men in their service ; and Tibertus, having studied the mathematics with great success at Paris, and delivered many predictions, some of which, for guesses, were not deficient in shrewdness, was taken into the household of Pandolfo di Malatesta, the sovereign of Rimini. His reputation was so great, that his study was continually thronged either with visitors who were persons of distinction, or with clients who came to him for advice ; and in a short time he acquired a considerable fortune. Notwithstanding all these advantages, he passed his life miserably, and ended it on the scaffold. The following story afterwards got into circulation, and has been often triumphantly cited by succeeding astrologers as an irrefragable proof of the truth of their science. It was said that, long before he died, he uttered three remarkable prophecies—one relating to himself, another to his friend, and the third to his patron, Pandolfo di Malatesta. The first delivered was that relating to his friend Guido di Bogni, one of the greatest captains of the time. Guido was exceedingly desirous to know his fortune, and so importuned Tibertus, that the latter consulted the stars and the lines on his palm to satisfy him. He afterwards told him with a sorrowful face, that, according to all the rules of astrology and palmistry, he should be falsely suspected by his best friend, and should lose his life in consequence. Guido then asked the astrologer if he could foretell his own fate ; upon which Tibertus again consulted the stars, and found that it was decreed from all eternity that he should end his days on the scaffold. Malatesta, when he heard these predictions, so unlikely, to all present appearance, to prove true, desired his astrologer to predict his fate also, and to hide nothing from him, however unfavourable it might be. Tibertus complied, and told his patron, at that time one of the most flour-

---

* *Jovii Elog.* p. 320.
† *Les Anecdotes de Florence, ou l'Histoire secrète de la Maison di Medicis,* p. 318.

ishing and powerful princes of Italy, that he should suffer great want, and die at last like a beggar in the common hospital of Bologna. And so it happened in all three cases. Guido di Bogni was accused by his own father-in-law, the Count di Bentivoglio, of a treasonable design to deliver up the city of Rimini to the papal forces, and was assassinated afterwards, by order of the tyrant Malatesta, as he sat at the supper-table, to which he had been invited in all apparent friendship. The astrologer was at the same time thrown into prison, as being concerned in the treason of his friend. He attempted to escape, and had succeeded in letting himself down from his dungeon-window into a moat, when he was discovered by the sentinels. This being reported to Malatesta, he gave orders for his execution on the following morning.

Malatesta had, at this time, no remembrance of the prophecy, and his own fate gave him no uneasiness ; but events were silently working its fulfilment. A conspiracy had been formed, though Guido di Bogni was innocent of it, to deliver up Rimini to the pope ; and all the necessary measures having been taken, the city was seized by the Count de Valentinois. In the confusion, Malatesta had barely time to escape from his palace in disguise. He was pursued from place to place by his enemies, abandoned by all his former friends, and, finally, by his own children. He at last fell ill of a languishing disease, at Bologna ; and, nobody caring to afford him shelter, he was carried to the hospital, where he died. The only thing that detracts from the interest of this remarkable story is the fact, that the prophecy was made after the event.

For some weeks before the birth of Louis XIV., an astrologer from Germany, who had been sent for by the Marshal de Bassompierre and other noblemen of the court, had taken up his residence in the palace, to be ready, at a moment's notice, to draw the horoscope of the future sovereign of France. When the queen was taken in labour, he was ushered into a contiguous apartment, that he might receive notice of the very instant the child was born. The result of his observations were the three words, *diu, durè, feliciter ;* meaning, that the new-born prince should live and reign long, with much labour, and with great glory. No prediction less favourable could have been expected from an astrologer, who had his bread to get, and who was at the same time a courtier. A medal was afterwards struck in commemoration of the event ; upon one side of which was figured the nativity of the prince, representing him as driving the chariot of Apollo, with the inscription " Ortus solis Gallici,"—the rising of the Gallic sun.

The best excuse ever made for astrology was that offered by the great astronomer, Kepler, himself an unwilling practiser of the art.

He had many applications from his friends to cast nativities for them, and generally gave a positive refusal to such as he was not afraid of offending by his frankness. In other cases he accommodated himself to the prevailing delusion. In sending a copy of his *Ephemerides* to Professor Gerlach, he wrote, that *they were nothing but worthless conjectures;* but he was obliged to devote himself to them, or he would have starved. " Ye overwise philosophers," he exclaimed, in his *Tertius Interveniens;* "ye censure this daughter of astronomy beyond her deserts ! *Know ye not that she must support her mother by her charms ?* The scanty reward of an astronomer would not provide him with bread, if men did not entertain hopes of reading the future in the heavens."

NECROMANCY was, next to astrology, the pretended science most resorted to, by those who wished to pry into the future. The earliest instance upon record is that of the witch of Endor and the spirit of Samuel. Nearly all the nations of antiquity believed in the possibility of summoning departed ghosts to disclose the awful secrets that God made clear to the disembodied. Many passages in allusion to this subject will at once suggest themselves to the classical reader ; but this art was never carried on openly in any country. All governments looked upon it as a crime of the deepest dye. While astrology was encouraged, and its professors courted and rewarded, necromancers were universally condemned to the stake or the gallows. Roger Bacon, Albertus Magnus, Arnold of Villeneuve, and many others, were accused by the public opinion of many centuries, of meddling in these unhallowed matters. So deep-rooted has always been the popular delusion with respect to accusations of this kind, that no crime was ever disproved with such toil and difficulty. That it met great encouragement, nevertheless, is evident from the vast numbers of pretenders to it ; who, in spite of the danger, have existed in all ages and countries.

GEOMANCY, or the art of foretelling the future by means of lines and circles, and other mathematical figures drawn on the earth, is still extensively practised in Asiatic countries, but is almost unknown in Europe.

AUGURY, from the flight or entrails of birds, so favourite a study among the Romans, is, in like manner, exploded in Europe. Its most assiduous professors, at the present day, are the abominable Thugs of India.

DIVINATION, of which there are many kinds, boasts a more enduring reputation. It has held an empire over the minds of men from the earliest periods of recorded history, and is, in all probability, coeval with time itself. It was practised alike by the Jews, the Egyptians, the Chaldeans, the Persians, the Greeks, and the Romans; is equally known to all modern nations, in every part of the world ; and is not unfamiliar to the untutored tribes that roam in the wilds of Africa and America. Divination, as practised in civilised Europe at the present day, is chiefly from cards, the tea-cup, and the lines on the palm of the hand. Gipsies alone make a profession of it; but there are thousands and tens of thousands of humble families in which the good-wife, and even the good-man, resort to the grounds at the bottom of their tea-cups, to know whether the next harvest will be abundant, or their sow bring forth a numerous litter ; and in which the young maidens look to the same place to know when they are to be married, and whether the man of their choice is to be dark or fair, rich or poor, kind or cruel. Divination by cards, so great a favourite among the moderns, is, of course, a modern science ; as cards do not yet boast an antiquity of much more than four hundred years. Divination by the palm, so confidently believed in by half the village lasses in Europe, is of older date, and seems to have been known to the Egyptians in the time of the patriarchs ; as well as divination by the cup, which, as we are informed in Genesis, was practised by Joseph. Divination by the rod was also practised by the Egyptians. In comparatively recent times, it was pretended that by this means hidden treasures could be discovered. It now appears to be altogether exploded in Europe. Onomancy, or the foretelling a man's fate by the letters of his name, and the various transpositions of which they are capable, is a more modern sort of divination ; but it reckons comparatively few believers.

The following list of the various species of divination formerly in use, is given by Gaule in his *Magastromancer*, and quoted in Hone's *Year-Book*, p. 1517.

Stereomancy, or divining by the elements.

Aeromancy, or divining by the air.

Pyromancy, by fire.

Hydromancy, by water.

Geomancy, by earth.

Theomancy, pretending to divine by the revelation of the Spirit, and by the Scriptures, or word of God.

Demonomancy, by the aid of devils and evil spirits.

Idolomancy, by idols, images, and figures.

Psychomancy, by the soul, affections, or dispositions of men.

Anthropomancy, by the entrails of human beings.
Theriomancy, by beasts.
Ornithomancy, by birds.
Ichthyomancy, by fishes.
Botanomancy, by herbs.
Lithomancy, by stones.
Kleromancy, by lots.
Oneiromancy, by dreams.
Onomancy, by names.
Arithmancy, by numbers.
Logarithmancy, by logarithms.
Sternomancy, by the marks from the breast to the belly.
Gastromancy, by the sound of, or marks upon the belly.
Omphalomancy, by the naval.
Chiromancy, by the hands.
Podomancy, by the feet.
Onchyomancy, by the nails.
Cephaleonomancy, by asses' heads.
Tephromancy, by ashes.
Kapnomancy, by smoke.
Knissomancy, by the burning of incense.
Ceromancy, by the melting of wax.
Lecanomancy, by basins of water.
Katoptromancy, by looking-glasses.
Chartomancy, by writing in papers, and by Valentines.
Macharomancy, by knives and swords.
Crystallomancy, by crystals.
Dactylomancy, by rings.
Koskinomancy, by sieves.
Axinomancy, by saws.
Chalcomancy, by vessels of brass, or other metal.
Spatilomancy, by skins, bones, &c.
Astromancy, by stars.
Sciomancy, by shadows.
Astragalomancy, by dice.
Oinomancy, by the lees of wine.
Sycomancy, by figs.
Tyromancy, by cheese.
Alphitomancy, by meal, flour, or bran.
Krithomancy, by corn or grain.
Alectromancy, by cocks.
Gyromancy, by circles.
Lampadomancy, by candles and lamps.

ONEIRO-CRITICISM, or the art of interpreting dreams, is a relic of the most remote ages, which has subsisted through all the changes that moral or physical revolutions have operated in the world. The records of five thousand years bear abundant testimony to the universal diffusion of the belief, that the skilful could read the future in dreams. The rules of the art, if any existed in ancient times, are not known; but in our day, one simple rule opens the whole secret. Dreams, say all the wiseacres in Christendom, are to be interpreted by contraries. Thus, if you dream of filth, you will acquire something valuable; if you dream of the dead, you will hear news of the living; if you dream of gold and silver, you run a risk of being without either; and if you dream you have many friends, you will be persecuted by many enemies. The rule, however, does not hold good in all cases. It is fortunate to dream of little pigs, but unfortunate to dream of big bullocks. If you dream you have lost a tooth, you may be sure that you will shortly lose a friend; and if you dream that your house is on fire, you will receive news from a far country. If you dream of vermin, it is a sign that there will be sickness in your family; and if you dream of serpents, you will have friends who, in the course of time, will prove your bitterest enemies; but, of all dreams, it is most fortunate if you dream that you are wallowing up to your neck in mud and mire. Clear water is a sign of grief; and great troubles, distress, and perplexity are predicted, if you dream that you stand naked in the public streets, and know not where to find a garment to shield you from the gaze of the multitude.

In many parts of Great Britain, and the continents of Europe and America, there are to be found elderly women in the villages and country-places whose interpretations of dreams are looked upon with as much reverence as if they were oracles. In districts remote from towns it is not uncommon to find the members of a family regularly every morning narrating their dreams at the breakfast-table, and becoming happy or miserable for the day according to their interpretation. There is not a flower that blossoms, or fruit that ripens, that, dreamed of, is not ominous of either good or evil to such people. Every tree of the field or the forest is endowed with a similar influence over the fate of mortals, if seen in the night-visions. To dream of the ash, is the sign of a long journey; and of an oak, prognosticates long life and prosperity. To dream you stript the bark off any tree, is a sign to a maiden of an approaching loss of a character; to a married woman, of a family bereavement; and to a man, of an accession of fortune. To dream of a leafless tree, is a sign of great sorrow; and of a branchless trunk, a sign of despair and suicide. The elder-tree is more auspicious to the sleeper ; while the fir-tree, better still, betokens all manner of comfort and prosperity. The lime-tree predicts a voyage across the ocean ; while the yew and the alder are ominous of sickness to the young and of death to the old.* Among the flowers and fruits charged with messages for the future, the following is a list of the most important, arranged from approved sources, in alphabetical order :

Asparagus, gathered and tied up in bundles, is an omen of tears. If you see it growing in your dreams, it is a sign of good fortune.

Aloes, without a flower, betokens long life ; in flower, betokens a legacy.

Artichokes. This vegetable is a sign that you will receive, in a short time, a favour from the hands of those from whom you would least expect it.

Agrimony. This herb denotes that there will be sickness in your house.

Anemone predicts love.

Auriculas, in beds, denote luck ; in pots, marriage ; while to gather them, foretells widowhood.

Bilberries predict a pleasant excursion.

Broom-flowers an increase of family.

Cauliflowers predict that all your friends will slight you, or that you will fall into poverty and find no one to pity you.

Dock-leaves, a present from the country.

Daffodils. Any maiden who dreams of daffodils is warned by her good angel to avoid going into a wood with her lover, or into any dark or retired place where she might not be able to make people hear her if she cried out. Alas for her if she pay no attention to the warning !

> " Never again shall she put garland on ;
> Instead of it she'll wear sad cypress now,
> And bitter elder broken from the bough."

---

* It is quite astonishing to see the great demand there is, both in England and France, for dream-books, and other trash of the same kind. Two books in England enjoy an extraordinary popularity, and have run through upwards of fifty editions in as many years in London alone, besides being reprinted in Manchester, Edinburgh, Glasgow, and Dublin. One is *Mother Bridget's Dream-book and Oracle of Fate;* the other is the *Norwood Gipsy*. It is stated, on the authority of one who is curious in these matters, that there is a demand for these works, which are sold at sums varying from a penny to sixpence, chiefly to servant-girls and imperfectly-educated people, all over the country, of upwards of eleven thousand annually; and that at no period during the last thirty years has the average number sold been less than this. The total number during this period would thus amount to 330,000.

Figs, if green, betoken embarrassment; if dried, money to the poor, and mirth to the rich.

Heart's-ease betokens heart's pain.

Lilies predict joy; *water-lilies*, danger from the sea.

Lemons betoken a separation.

Pomegranates predict happy wedlock to those who are single, and reconciliation to those who are married and have disagreed.

Quinces prognosticate pleasant company.

Roses denote happy love, not unmixed with sorrow from other sources.

Sorrel. To dream of this herb is a sign that you will shortly have occasion to exert all your prudence to overcome some great calamity.

Sunflowers shew that your pride will be deeply wounded.

Violets predict evil to the single, and joy to the married.

Yellow-flowers of any kind predict jealousy.

Yew-berries predict loss of character to both sexes.

It should be observed that the rules for the interpretation of dreams are far from being universal. The cheeks of the peasant girl of England glow with pleasure in the morning after she has dreamed of a rose, while the *paysanne* of Normandy dreads disappointment and vexation for the very same reason. The Switzer who dreams of an oak-tree does not share in the Englishman's joy; for he imagines that the vision was a warning to him that, from some trifling cause, an overwhelming calamity will burst over him. Thus do the ignorant and the credulous torment themselves; thus do they spread their nets to catch vexation, and pass their lives between hopes which are of no value and fears which are a positive evil.

OMENS. Among the other means of self-annoyance upon which men have stumbled, in their vain hope of discovering the future, signs and omens hold a conspicuous place. There is scarcely an occurrence in nature which, happening at a certain time, is not looked upon by some persons as a prognosticator either of good or evil. The latter are in the greatest number, so much more ingenious are we in tormenting ourselves than in discovering reasons for enjoyment in the things that surround us. We go out of our course to make ourselves uncomfortable; the cup of life is not bitter enough to our palate, and we distil superfluous poison to put into it, or conjure up hideous things to frighten ourselves at, which would never exist if we did not make them. " We suffer," says Addison,* " as much from

* *Spectator*, No. 7, March 8, 1710-11.

trifling accidents as from real evils. I have known the shooting of
a star spoil a night's rest, and have seen a man in love grow pale and
lose his appetite upon the plucking of a merrythought. A screech-
owl at midnight has alarmed a family more than a band of robbers;
nay, the voice of a cricket has struck more terror than the roaring
of a lion. There is nothing so inconsiderable which may not appear
dreadful to an imagination that is filled with omens and prognostics.
A rusty nail or a crooked pin shoot up into prodigies."

The century and a quarter that has passed away since Addison
wrote has seen the fall of many errors. Many fallacies and delusions
have been crushed under the foot of Time since then; but this has
been left unscathed, to frighten the weak-minded and embitter their
existence. A belief in omens is not confined to the humble and uninformed. A general who led an army with credit has been known
to feel alarmed at a winding-sheet in the candle; and learned men,
who had honourably and fairly earned the highest honours of literature, have been seen to gather their little ones around them, and fear
that one would be snatched away, because,

> " When stole upon the time the dead of night,
> And heavy sleep had closed up mortal eyes,"

a dog in the street was howling at the moon. Persons who would
acknowledge freely that the belief in omens was unworthy of a man
of sense, have yet confessed at the same time that, in spite of their
reason, they have been unable to conquer their fears of death when
they heard the harmless insect called the death-watch ticking in the
wall, or saw an oblong hollow coal fly out of the fire.

Many other evil omens besides those mentioned above alarm the
vulgar and the weak. If a sudden shivering comes over such people,
they believe that, at that instant, an enemy is treading over the spot
that will one day be their grave. If they meet a sow when they first
walk abroad in the morning, it is an omen of evil for that day. To
meet an ass, is in like manner unlucky. It is also very unfortunate
to walk under a ladder; to forget to eat goose on the festival of St.
Michael; to tread upon a beetle, or to eat the twin nuts that are
sometimes found in one shell. Woe, in like manner, is predicted
to that wight who inadvertently upsets the salt; each grain that is
overthrown will bring to him a day of sorrow. If thirteen persons
sit at table, one of them will die within the year; and all of them
will be unhappy. Of all evil omens this is the worst. The facetious
Dr. Kitchener used to observe that there was one case in which he
believed that it was really unlucky for thirteen persons to sit down
to dinner, and that was when there was only dinner enough for twelve.

Unfortunately for their peace of mind, the great majority of people do not take this wise view of the matter. In almost every country of Europe the same superstition prevails, and some carry it so far as to look upon the number thirteen as in every way ominous of evil ; and if they find thirteen coins in their purse, cast away the odd one like a polluted thing. The philosophic Beranger, in his exquisite song, *Thirteen at Table*, has taken a poetical view of this humiliating superstition, and mingled, as is his wont, a lesson of genuine wisdom in his lay. Being at dinner, he overthrows the salt, and, looking round the room, discovers that he is the thirteenth guest. While he is mourning his unhappy fate, and conjuring up visions of disease and suffering and the grave, he is suddenly startled by the apparition of Death herself, not in the shape of a grim foe, with skeleton-ribs and menacing dart, but of an angel of light, who shews the folly of tormenting ourselves with the dread of her approach, when she is the friend, rather than the enemy, of man, and frees us from the fetters which bind us to the dust.

If men could bring themselves to look upon death in this manner, living well and wisely till her inevitable approach, how vast a store of grief and vexation would they spare themselves !

Among good omens, one of the most conspicuous is to meet a piebald horse. To meet two of these animals is still more fortunate ; and if on such an occasion you spit thrice, and form any reasonable wish, it will be gratified within three days. It is also a sign of good fortune if you inadvertently put on your stocking wrong side out. If you wilfully wear your stocking in this fashion, no good will come of it. It is very lucky to sneeze twice; but if you sneeze a third time, the omen loses its power, and your good fortune will be nipped in the bud. If a strange dog follow you, and fawn on you, and wish to attach itself to you, it is a sign of very great prosperity. Just as fortunate is it if a strange male cat comes to your house and manifests friendly intentions towards your family. If a she cat, it is an omen, on the contrary, of very great misfortune. If a swarm of bees alight in your garden, some very high honour and great joys await you.

Besides these glimpses of the future, you may know something of your fate by a diligent attention to every itching that you may feel in your body. Thus, if the eye or the nose itches, it is a sign you will be shortly vexed; if the foot itches, you will tread upon strange ground ; and if the elbow itches, you will change your bedfellow. Itching of the right hand prognosticates that you will soon have a sum of money ; and, of the left, that you will be called upon to disburse it.

These are but a few of the omens which are generally credited in modern Europe. A complete list of them would fatigue from its length, and sicken from its absurdity. It would be still more unprofitable to attempt to specify the various delusions of the same kind which are believed among oriental nations. Every reader will remember the comprehensive formula of cursing preserved in *Tristram Shandy*—curse a man after any fashion you remember or can invent, you will be sure to find it there. The oriental creed of omens is not less comprehensive. Every movement of the body, every emotion of the mind, is at certain times an omen. Every form and object in nature, even the shape of the clouds and the changes of the weather ; every colour, every sound, whether of men or animals, or birds or insects, or inanimate things, is an omen. Nothing is too trifling or inconsiderable to inspire a hope which is not worth cherishing, or a fear which is sufficient to embitter existence.

From the belief in omens springs the superstition that has, from very early ages, set apart certain days, as more favourable than others, for prying into the secrets of futurity. The following, copied verbatim from the popular *Dream and Omen Book* of Mother Bridget, will shew the belief of the people of England at the present day. Those who are curious as to the ancient history of these observances, will find abundant aliment in the *Every-day Book*.

" *The 1st of January.*—If a young maiden drink, on going to bed, a pint of cold spring water, in which is beat up an amulet, composed of the yolk of a pullet's egg, the legs of a spider, and the skin of an eel pounded, her future destiny will be revealed to her in a dream. This charm fails of its effect if tried any other day of the year.

" *Valentine Day.*—Let a single woman go out of her own door very early in the morning, and if the first person she meets be a woman, she will not be married that year ; if she meet a man she will be married within three months.

" *Lady Day.*—The following charm may be tried this day with certain success : String thirty-one nuts on a string, composed of red worsted mixed with blue silk, and tie it round your neck on going to bed, repeating these lines :

> " Oh, I wish ! oh, I wish to see
> Who my true love is to be !

Shortly after midnight, you will see your lover in a dream, and be informed at the same time of all the principal events of your future life.

" *St. Swithin's Eve.*—Select three things you most wish to know ; write them down with a new pen and red ink on a sheet of fine wove paper, from which you must previously cut off all the corners and burn them. Fold the paper into a true lover's knot, and wrap round it three hairs from your head. Place the paper under your pillow for three successive nights, and your curiosity to know the future will be satisfied.

"*St. Mark's Eve.*—Repair to the nearest churchyard as the clock strikes twelve, and take from a grave on the south side of the church three tufts of grass (the longer and ranker the better), and on going to bed place them under your pillow, repeating earnestly three several times,

> 'The Eve of St. Mark by prediction is blest,
> Set therefore my hopes and my fears all to rest:
> Let me know my fate, whether weal or woe;
> Whether my rank's to be high or low;
> Whether to live single, or be a bride,
> And the destiny my star doth provide.'

Should you have no dream that night, you will be single and miserable all your life. If you dream of thunder and lightning, your life will be one of great difficulty and sorrow.

"*Candlemas Eve.*—On this night (which is the purification of the Virgin Mary), let three, five, seven, or nine young maidens assemble together in a square chamber. Hang in each corner a bundle of sweet herbs, mixed with rue and rosemary. Then mix a cake of flour, olive-oil, and white sugar; every maiden having an equal share in the making and the expense of it. Afterwards it must be cut into equal pieces, each one marking the piece as she cuts it with the initials of her name. It is then to be baked one hour before the fire, not a word being spoken the whole time, and the maidens sitting with their arms and knees across. Each piece of cake is then to be wrapped up in a sheet of paper, on which each maiden shall write the love part of Solomon's Songs. If she put this under her pillow she will dream true. She will see her future husband and every one of her children, and will know besides whether her family will be poor or prosperous, a comfort to her or the contrary.

"*Midsummer.*—Take three roses, smoke them with sulphur, and exactly at three in the day bury one of the roses under a yew-tree; the second in a newly made grave, and put the third under your pillow for three nights, and at the end of that period burn it in a fire of charcoal. Your dreams during that time will be prophetic of your future destiny, and, what is still more curious and valuable, says Mother Bridget, the man whom you are to wed will enjoy no peace till he comes and visits you. Besides this, you will perpetually haunt his dreams.

" *St. John's Eve.*—Make a new pincushion of the very best black velvet (no inferior quality will answer the purpose), and on one side stick your name at full length with the very smallest pins that can be bought (none other will do). On the other side make a cross with some very large pins, and surround it with a circle. Put this into your stocking when you take it off at night, and hang it up at the foot of the bed. All your future life will pass before you in a dream.

" *First New Moon of the year.*—On the first new moon in the year take a pint of clear spring water, and infuse into it the *white* of an egg laid by a *white* hen, a glass of *white* wine, three almonds peeled *white*, and a tablespoonful of *white* rose-water. Drink this on going to bed, not making more nor less than three draughts of it; repeating the following verses three several times in a clear distinct voice, but not so loud as to be overheard by any body :

> ' If I dream of water pure
>   Before the coming morn,
>   'Tis a sign I shall be poor,
>   And unto wealth not born.
>   If I dream of tasting beer,
>   Middling then will be my cheer—
>   Chequer'd with the good and bad,
>   Sometimes joyful, sometimes sad ;
>   But should I dream of drinking wine,
>   Wealth and pleasure will be mine.
>   The stronger the drink, the better the cheer—
>   Dreams of my destiny, appear, appear !'

" *Twenty-ninth of February.*—This day, as it only occurs in four years, is peculiarly auspicious to those who desire to have a glance at futurity, especially to young maidens burning with anxiety to know the appearance and complexion of their future lords. The charm to be adopted is the following : Stick twenty-seven of the smallest pins that are made, three by three, into a tallow candle. Light it up at the wrong end, and then place it in a candlestick made out of clay, which must be drawn from a virgin's grave. Place this on the chimney-place, in the left-hand corner, exactly as the clock strikes twelve, and go to bed immediately. When the candle is burnt out, take the pins and put them into your left shoe ; and before nine nights have elapsed your fate will be revealed to you."

We have now taken a hasty review of the various modes of seeking to discover the future, especially as practised in modern times. The main features of the folly appear essentially the same in all countries. National character and peculiarities operate some difference of interpretation. The mountaineer makes the natural phenomena which he most frequently witnesses prognosticative of the future. The dweller in the plains, in a similar manner, seeks to know his fate among the signs of the things that surround him, and tints his superstition with the hues of his own clime. The same spirit animates them all—the same desire to know that which Infinite Mercy has concealed. There is but little probability that the curiosity of mankind in this respect will ever be wholly eradicated. Death and ill fortune are continual bugbears to the weak-minded, the irreligious, and the ignorant; and while such exist in the world, divines will preach upon its impiety and philosophers discourse upon its absurdity in vain. Still it is evident that these follies have greatly diminished. Soothsayers and prophets have lost the credit they formerly enjoyed, and skulk in secret now where they once shewed their faces in the blaze of day. So far there is manifest improvement.

THE MAGNETISERS.

HE wonderful influence of imagination in
the cure of diseases is well known. A
motion of the hand, or a glance of the
eye, will throw a weak and credulous patient into a fit ; and a pill made of bread,
if taken with sufficient faith, will operate a
cure better than all the drugs in the pharma-
copœia. The Prince of Orange, at the siege
of Breda, in 1625, cured all his soldiers, who
were dying of the scurvy, by a philanthropic
piece of quackery, which he played upon them
with the knowledge of the physicians, when
all other means had failed.* Many hundreds
of instances, of a similar kind, might be related, especially from the history of witchcraft.
The mummeries, strange gesticulations, and barbarous jargon of witches and sorcerers, which frightened
credulous and nervous women, brought on all those
symptoms of hysteria and other similar diseases, so
well understood now, but which were then supposed
to be the work of the Devil, not only by the victims
and the public in general, but by the operators
themselves.

In the age when alchymy began to fall into some
disrepute, and learning to lift up its voice against

* See Van der Mye's account of the siege of Breda. The garrison, being afflicted with
scurvy, the Prince of Orange sent the physicians two or three small phials, containing a
decoction of camomile, wormwood, and camphor, telling them to pretend that it was a
medicine of the greatest value and extremest rarity, which had been procured with very
much danger and difficulty from the East; and so strong, that two or three drops would
impart a healing virtue to a gallon of water. The soldiers had faith in their commander; they took the medicine with cheerful faces, and grew well rapidly. They
afterwards thronged about the prince in groups of twenty and thirty at a time, praising
his skill, and loading him with protestations of gratitude.

it, a new delusion, based upon this power of imagination, suddenly arose, and found apostles among all the alchymists. Numbers of them, forsaking their old pursuits, made themselves magnetisers. It appeared first in the shape of mineral, and afterwards of animal, magnetism, under which latter name it survives to this day, and numbers its dupes by thousands.

The mineral magnetisers claim the first notice, as the worthy predecessors of the quacks of the present day. The honour claimed for Paracelsus, of being the first of the Rosicrucians, has been disputed; but his claim to be considered the first of the magnetisers can scarcely be challenged. It has been already mentioned of him, in the part of this work which treats of alchymy, that, like nearly all the distinguished adepts, he was a physician; and pretended, not only to make gold and confer immortality, but to cure all diseases. He was the first who, with the latter view, attributed occult and miraculous powers to the magnet. Animated apparently by a sincere conviction that the magnet was the philosopher's stone, which, if it could not transmute metals, could soothe all human suffering and arrest the progress of decay, he travelled for many years in Persia and Arabia, in search of the mountain of adamant, so famed in oriental fables. When he practised as a physician at Basle, he called one of his nostrums by the name of azoth—a stone or crystal, which, he said, contained magnetic properties, and cured epilepsy, hysteria, and spasmodic affections. He soon found imitators. His fame spread far and near; and thus were sown the first seeds of that error which has since taken root and flourished so widely. In spite of the denial of modern practitioners, this must be considered the origin of magnetism; for we find that, beginning with Paracelsus, there was a regular succession of mineral magnetisers until Mesmer appeared, and gave a new feature to the delusion.

Paracelsus boasted of being able to *transplant* diseases from the human frame into the earth, by means of the magnet. He said there were six ways by which this might be effected. One of them will be quite sufficient as a specimen. "If a person suffer from disease, either local or general, let the following remedy be tried. Take a magnet, impregnated with mummy,* and mixed with rich earth. In

* Mummies were of several kinds, and were all of great use in magnetic medicines. Paracelsus enumerates six kinds of mummies; the first four only differing in the composition used by different people for preserving their dead, are the Egyptian, Arabian, Pisasphaltos, and Libyan. The fifth mummy of peculiar power was made from criminals that had been hanged; "for from such there is a gentle siccation, that expungeth the watery humour, without destroying the oil and spirituall, which is cherished by the heavenly luminaries, and strengthened continually by the affluence and impulses of the celestial spirits; whence it may be properly called by the name of constellated or celes

this earth sow some seeds that have a congruity or homogeneity with
the disease; then let this earth, well sifted and mixed with mummy,
be laid in an earthen vessel; and let the seeds committed to it be
watered daily with a lotion in which the diseased limb or body has
been washed. Thus will the disease be transplanted from the human
body to the seeds which are in the earth. Having done this, transplant the seeds from the earthen vessel to the ground, and wait till
they begin to sprout into herbs; as they increase, the disease will
diminish; and when they have arrived at their full growth, it will
disappear altogether."

Kircher the Jesuit, whose quarrel with the alchymists was the
means of exposing many of their impostures, was a firm believer in
the efficacy of the magnet. Having been applied to by a patient
afflicted with hernia, he directed the man to swallow a small magnet
reduced to powder, while he applied at the same time to the external
swelling, a poultice made of filings of iron. He expected that by this
means the magnet, when it got to the corresponding place inside,
would draw in the iron, and with it the tumour; which would thus,
he said, be safely and expeditiously reduced.

As this new doctrine of magnetism spread, it was found that
wounds inflicted with any metallic substance could be cured by the
magnet. In process of time, the delusion so increased, that it was
deemed sufficient to magnetise a sword, to cure any hurt which that
sword might have inflicted! This was the origin of the celebrated
" weapon-salve," which excited so much attention about the middle
of the seventeenth century. The following was the recipe given by
Paracelsus for the cure of any wounds inflicted by a sharp weapon,
except such as had penetrated the heart, the brain, or the arteries.
" Take of moss growing on the head of a thief who has been hanged
and left in the air; of real mummy; of human blood, still warm—of
each, one ounce; of human suet, two ounces; of linseed oil, turpen-
tine, and Armenian bole—of each, two drachms. Mix all well in a
mortar, and keep the salve in an oblong, narrow urn." With this
salve the weapon, after being dipped in the blood from the wound,
was to be carefully anointed, and then laid by in a cool place. In the
mean time, the wound was to be duly washed with fair clean water,
covered with a clean, soft, linen rag, and opened once a day to cleanse
off purulent or other matter. Of the success of this treatment, says

tial mummie." The sixth kind of mummy was made of corpuscles, or spiritual effluences,
radiated from the living body; though we cannot get very clear ideas on this head, or
respecting the manner in which they were caught.—*Medicina Diatastica; or, Sympa-
thetical Mummie, abstracted from the Works of Paracelsus, and translated out of the Latin*, by
Fernando Parkhurst, Gent. London, 1653, pp. 2, 7. Quoted by the *Foreign Quarterly
Review*, vol. xii. p. 415.

the writer of the able article on Animal Magnetism, in the twelfth volume of the *Foreign Quarterly Review*, there cannot be the least doubt ; "for surgeons at this moment follow exactly the same method, *except* anointing the weapon !"

The weapon-salve continued to be much spoken of on the Continent, and many eager claimants appeared for the honour of the invention. Dr. Fludd, or A Fluctibus, the Rosicrucian, who has been already mentioned in a previous part of this volume, was very zealous in introducing it into England. He tried it with great success in several cases, and no wonder, for while he kept up the spirits of his patients by boasting of the great efficacy of the salve, he never neglected those common, but much more important remedies, of washing, bandaging, &c. which the experience of all ages had declared sufficient for the purpose. Fludd moreover declared, that the magnet was a remedy for all diseases, if properly applied ; but that man having, like the earth, a north and a south pole, magnetism could only take place when his body was in a boreal position ! In the midst of his popularity, an attack was made upon him and his favourite remedy, the salve ; which, however, did little or nothing to diminish the belief in its efficacy. One "Parson Foster" wrote a pamphlet, entitled *Hyplocrisma Spongus ; or, a Spünge to wipe away the Weapon-Salve ;* in which he declared, that it was as bad as witchcraft to use or recommend such an unguent ; that it was invented by the Devil, who, at the last day, would seize upon every person who had given it the slightest encouragement. "In fact," said Parson Foster, "the Devil himself gave it to Paracelsus ; Paracelsus to the emperor ; the emperor to the courtier ; the courtier to Baptista Porta ; and Baptista Porta to Dr. Fludd, a doctor of physic, yet living and practising in the famous city of London, who now stands tooth and nail for it." Dr. Fludd, thus assailed, took up the pen in defence of his unguent, in a reply called *The Squeezing of Parson Foster's Spunge ; wherein the Spunge-bearer's immodest carriage and behaviour towards his brethren is detected ; the bitter flames of his slanderous reports are, by the sharp vinegar of truth, corrected and quite extinguished ; and lastly, the virtuous validity of his spünge in wiping away the weapon-salve, is crushed out aňd clean abolished.*

Shortly after this dispute a more distinguished believer in the weapon-salve made his appearance in the person of Sir Kenelm Digby, the son of Sir Everard Digby, who was executed for his participation in the Gunpowder Plot. This gentleman, who, in other respects, was an accomplished scholar and an able man, was imbued with all the extravagant notions of the alchymists. He believed in the philosopher's stone, and wished to engage Descartes to devote his energies

to the discovery of the elixir of life, or some other means by which
the existence of man might be prolonged to an indefinite period. He
gave his wife, the beautiful Venetia Anastasia Stanley, a dish of
capons fed upon vipers, according to the plan supposed to have been
laid down by Arnold of Villeneuve, in the hope that she might thereby preserve her loveliness for a century. If such a man once took up
the idea of the weapon-salve, it was to be expected that he would
make the most of it. In his hands, however, it was changed from
an unguent into a powder, and was called the *powder of sympathy*.
He pretended that he had acquired the knowledge of it from a Car-
melite friar, who had learned it in Persia or Armenia, from an oriental
philosopher of great renown. King James, the Prince of Wales, the
Duke of Buchingham, and many other noble personages, believed in
its efficacy. The following remarkable instance of his mode of cure
was read by Sir Kenelm to a society of learned men at Montpellier.
Mr. James Howell, the well-known author of the *Dendrologia*, and
of various letters, coming by chance as two of his best friends were
fighting a duel, rushed between them and endeavoured to part them.
He seized the sword of one of the combatants by the hilt, while, at
the same time, he grasped the other by the blade. Being transported
with fury one against the other, they struggled to rid themselves of
the hindrance caused by their friend ; and in so doing, the one whose
sword was held by the blade by Mr. Howell, drew it away roughly,
and nearly cut his hand off, severing the nerves and muscles, and
penetrating to the bone. The other, almost at the same instant,
disengaged his sword, and aimed a blow at the head of his antagonist,
which Mr. Howell observing, raised his wounded hand with the
rapidity of thought to prevent the blow. The sword fell on the back
of his already wounded hand, and cut it severely. " It seemed,"
said Sir Kenelm Digby, " as if some unlucky star raged over them,
that they should have both shed the blood of that dear friend for
whose life they would have given their own, if they had been in their
proper mind at the time." Seeing Mr. Howell's face all besmeared
with blood from his wounded hand, they both threw down their
swords and embraced him, and bound up his hand with a garter, to
close the veins which were cut and bled profusely. They then conveyed him home, and sent for a surgeon. King James, who was
much attached to Mr. Howell, afterwards sent his own surgeon to
attend him. We must continue the narrative in the words of Sir
Kenelm Digby : " It was my chance," says he, " to be lodged hard
by him ; and four or five days after, as I was making myself ready,
he came to my house, and prayed me to view his wounds. ' For I
understand,' said he, ' that you have extraordinary remedies on such

occasions; and my surgeons apprehend some fear that it may grow to a gangrene, and so the hand must be cut off.' In effect, his countenance discovered that he was in much pain, which, he said, was insupportable in regard of the extreme inflammation. I told him I would willingly serve him; but if, haply, he knew the manner how I could cure him, without touching or seeing him, it might be that he would not expose himself to my manner of curing; because he would think it, peradventure, either ineffectual or superstitious. He replied, ' The many wonderful things which people have related unto me of your way of medicinement makes me nothing doubt at all of its efficacy; and all that I have to say unto you is comprehended in the Spanish proverb, *Hagase el milagro y hagalo Mahoma*—Let the miracle be done, though Mahomet do it.'

" I asked him then for any thing that had the blood upon it: so he presently sent for his garter, wherewith his hand was first bound; and as I called for a basin of water, as if I would wash my hands, I took a handful of powder of vitriol, which I had in my study, and presently dissolved it. As soon as the bloody garter was brought me, I put it in the basin, observing, in the interim, what Mr. Howell did, who stood talking with a gentleman in a corner of my chamber, not regarding at all what I was doing. He started suddenly, as if he had found some strange alteration in himself. I asked him what he ailed? ' I know not what ails me, but I find that I feel no more pain. Methinks that a pleasing kind of freshness, as it were a wet cold napkin, did spread over my hand, which hath taken away the inflammation that tormented me before.' I replied, ' Since, then, you feel already so much good of my medicament, I advise you to cast away all your plasters; only keep the wound clean, and in a moderate temper betwixt heat and cold.' This was presently reported to the Duke of Buckingham, and, a little after, to the king, who were both very curious to know the circumstances of the business; which was, that after dinner I took the garter out of the water, and put it to dry before a great fire. It was scarce dry before Mr. Howell's servant came running, and saying that his master felt as much burning as ever he had done, if not more; for the heat was such as if his hand were betwixt coals of fire. I answered that, although that had happened at present, yet he should find ease in a short time; for I knew the reason of this new accident, and would provide accordingly; for his master should be free from that inflammation, it might be before he could possibly return to him. But, in case he found no ease, I wished him to come presently back again; if not, he might forbear coming. Thereupon he went, and, at the instant I did put the garter again into the water; thereupon he found his master without any pain at all. To be brief, there was no cense of pain afterwards; but within five or six days the wounds were cicatrised and entirely healed."

Such is the marvellous story of Sir Kenelm Digby. Other practitioners of that age were not behind him in their pretensions. It was not always thought necessary to use either the powder of sympathy, or the weapon-salve, to effect a cure. It was sufficient to magnetise the sword with the hand (the first faint dawn of the *animal* theory), to relieve any pain the same weapon had caused. They asserted, that if they stroked the sword *upwards* with their fingers, the wounded person would feel immediate relief; but if they stroked it *downwards*, he would feel intolerable pain.*

Another very singular notion of the power and capabilities of magnetism was entertained at the same time. It was believed that a *sympathetic alphabet* could be made on the flesh, by means of which persons could correspond with each other, and communicate all their ideas with the rapidity of volition, although thousands of miles apart. From the arms of two persons a piece of flesh was cut, and mutually transplanted, while still warm and bleeding. The piece so severed grew to the new arm on which it was placed; but still retained so close a sympathy with its native limb, that its old possessor was always sensible of any injury done to it. Upon these transplanted pieces were tatooed the letters of the alphabet; so that, when a communication was to be made, either of the persons, though the wide Atlantic rolled between them, had only to prick his arm with a magnetic needle, and straightway his friend received intimation that the telegraph was at work. Whatever letter he pricked on his own arm pained the same letter on the arm of his correspondent.

Contemporary with Sir Kenelm Digby was the no less famous Mr. Valentine Greatraks, who, without mentioning magnetism, or laying claim to any theory, practised upon himself and others a deception much more akin to the animal magnetism of the present day than the mineral magnetism it was then so much the fashion to study. He was the son of an Irish gentleman, of good education and property, in the county of Cork. He fell, at an early age, into a sort of melancholy derangement. After some time he had an impulse, or strange persuasion in his mind, which continued to present itself, whether he were sleeping or waking, that God had given him the power of curing the king's evil. He mentioned this persuasion to his

---

* Reginald Scott, quoted by Sir Walter Scott, in the notes to the *Lay of the last Minstrel*, c. iii. v. xxiii.

wife, who very candidly told him that he was a fool. He was not quite sure of this, notwithstanding the high authority from which it came, and determined to make trial of the power that was in him. A few days afterwards, he went to one William Maher, of Salters-bridge, in the parish of Lismore, who was grievously afflicted with the king's evil in his eyes, cheek, and throat. Upon this man, who was of abundant faith, he laid his hands, stroked him, and prayed fervently. He had the satisfaction to see him heal considerably in the course of a few days; and finally, with the aid of other remedies, to be quite cured. This success encouraged him in the belief that he had a divine mission. Day after day he had further impulses from on high that he was called upon to cure the ague also. In the course of time he extended his powers to the curing of epilepsy, ulcers, aches, and lameness. All the county of Cork was in a commotion to see this extraordinary physician, who certainly operated some very great benefit in cases where the disease was heightened by hypochondria and depression of spirits. According to his own account,* such great multitudes resorted to him from divers places, that he had no time to follow his own business, or enjoy the company of his family and friends. He was obliged to set aside three days in the week, from six in the morning till six at night, during which time only he laid hands upon all that came. Still the crowds which thronged around him were so great, that the neighbouring towns were not able to accommodate them. He thereupon left his house in the country, and went to Youghal, where the resort of sick people, not only from all parts of Ireland, but from England, continued so great, that the magistrates were afraid they would infect the place by their diseases. Several of these poor credulous people no sooner saw him than they fell into fits, and he restored them by waving his hand in their faces, and praying over them. Nay, he affirmed that the touch of his glove had driven pains away, and, on one occasion, cast out from a woman several devils, or evil spirits, who tormented her day and night. "Every one of these devils," says Greatraks, "was like to choke her when it came up into her throat." It is evident from this that the woman's complaint was nothing but hysteria.

The clergy of the diocese of Lismore, who seem to have had much clearer notions of Greatraks' pretensions than their parishioners, set their faces against the new prophet and worker of miracles. He was cited to appear in the Dean's Court, and prohibited from laying on his hands for the future : but he cared nothing for the Church. He imagined that he derived his powers direct from heaven, and con-

* Greatraks' Account of himself, in a letter to the Honourable Robert Boyle.

tinued to throw people into fits, and bring them to their senses again, as usual, almost exactly after the fashion of modern magnetisers. His reputation became, at last, so great, that Lord Conway sent to him from London, begging that he would come over immediately to cure a grievous headache which his lady had suffered for several years, and which the principal physicians of England had been unable to relieve.

Greatraks accepted the invitation, and tried his manipulations and prayers upon Lady Conway. He failed, however, in affording any relief. The poor lady's headache was excited by causes too serious to allow her any help, even from faith and a lively imagination. He lived for some months in Lord Conway's house, at Ragley, in Warwickshire, operating cures similar to those he had performed in Ireland. He afterwards removed to London, and took a house in Lincoln's-Inn Fields, which soon became the daily resort of all the nervous and credulous women of the metropolis. A very amusing account of Greatraks at this time (1665) is given in the second volume of the *Miscellanies of St. Evremond*, under the title of the Irish prophet. It is the most graphic sketch ever made of this early magnetiser. Whether his pretensions were more or less absurd than those of some of his successors, who have lately made their appearance among us, would be hard to say.

"When M. de Comminges," says St. Evremond, "was ambassador from his most Christian majesty to the king of Great Britain, there came to London an Irish prophet, who passed himself off as a great worker of miracles. Some persons of quality having begged M. de Comminges to invite him to his house, that they might be witnesses of some of his miracles, the ambassador promised to satisfy them, as much to gratify his own curiosity as from courtesy to his friends; and gave notice to Greatraks that he would be glad to see him.

"A rumour of the prophet's coming soon spread all over the town, and the hotel of M. de Comminges was crowded by sick persons, who came full of confidence in their speedy cure. The Irishman made them wait a considerable time for him, but came at last, in the midst of their impatience, with a grave and simple countenance, that shewed no signs of his being a cheat. Monsieur de Comminges prepared to question him strictly, hoping to discourse with him on the matters that he had read of in Van Helmont and Bodinus; but he was not able to do so, much to his regret, for the crowd became so great, and cripples and others pressed around so impatiently to be the first cured, that the servants were obliged to use threats, and even force, before they could establish order among them, or place them in proper ranks.

"The prophet affirmed that all diseases were caused by evil spirits. Every infirmity was with him a case of diabolical possession. The first that was presented to him was a man suffering from gout and rheumatism, and so severely that the physicians had been unable to cure him. 'Ah,' said the miracle-worker, 'I have seen a good deal of this sort of spirits when I was in Ireland. They are watery spirits, who bring on cold shivering, and excite an overflow of aqueous humours in our poor bodies.' Then addressing the man, he said, 'Evil spirit, who hast quitted thy dwelling in the waters to come and afflict this miserable body, I command thee to quit thy new abode, and to return to thine ancient habitation!' This said, the sick man was ordered to withdraw, and another was brought forward in his place. This new comer said he was tormented by the melancholy vapours. In fact, he looked like a hypochondriac; one of those persons, diseased in imagination, and who but too often become so in reality. 'Aerial spirit,' said the Irishman, 'return, I command thee, into the air;—exercise thy natural vocation of raising tempests, and do not excite any more wind in this sad unlucky body!' This man was immediately turned away to make room for a third patient, who, in the Irishman's opinion, was only tormented by a little bit of a sprite, who could not withstand his command for an instant. He pretended that he recognised this sprite by some marks which were invisible to the company, to whom he turned with a smile, and said, 'This sort of spirit does not often do much harm, and is always very diverting.' To hear him talk, one would have imagined that he knew all about spirits,—their names, their rank, their numbers, their employment, and all the functions they were destined to; and he boasted of being much better acquainted with the intrigues of demons than he was with the affairs of men. You can hardly imagine what a reputation he gained in a short time. Catholics and Protestants visited him from every part, all believing that power from heaven was in his hands."

After relating a rather equivocal adventure of a husband and wife, who implored Greatraks to cast out the devil of dissension which had crept in between them, St. Evremond thus sums up the effect he produced on the popular mind: "So great was the confidence in him, that the blind fancied they saw the light which they did not see—the deaf imagined that they heard—the lame that they walked straight, and the paralytic that they had recovered the use of their limbs. An idea of health made the sick forget for a while their maladies; and imagination, which was not less active in those merely drawn by curiosity than in the sick, gave a false view to the one class, from the desire of seeing, as it operated a false cure on the other from the strong desire of being healed. Such was the power of the Irishman over the mind, and such was the influence of the mind upon the body. Nothing was spoken of in London but his prodigies; and these prodigies were supported by such great authorities, that the bewildered multitude believed them almost without examination, while more enlightened people did not dare to reject them from their own knowledge. The public opinion, timid and enslaved, respected this imperious and, apparently, well-authenticated error. Those who saw through the delusion kept their opinion to themselves, knowing how useless it was to declare their disbelief to a people filled with prejudice and admiration."

About the same time that Valentine Greatraks was thus *magnetising* the people of London, an Italian enthusiast, named Francisco Bagnone, was performing the same tricks in Italy, and with as great success. He had only to touch weak women with his hands, or sometimes (for the sake of working more effectively upon their fanaticism) with a relic, to make them fall into fits, and manifest all the symptoms of magnetism.

Besides these, several learned men, in different parts of Europe, directed their attention to the study of the magnet, believing that it might be rendered efficacious in many diseases. Van Helmont, in particular, published a work on the effects of magnetism on the human frame; and Balthazar Gracian, a Spaniard, rendered himself famous for the boldness of his views on the subject. " The magnet," said the latter, " attracts iron ; iron is found every where ; every thing, therefore, is under the influence of magnetism. It is only a modification of the general principle, which establishes harmony or foments divisions among men. It is the same agent that gives rise to sympathy, antipathy, and the passions."*

Baptista Porta, who, in the whimsical genealogy of the weapon-salve, given by Parson Foster, in his attack upon Dr. à Fluctibus, is mentioned as one of its fathers, had also great faith in the efficacy of the magnet, and operated upon the imagination of his patients in a manner which was then considered so extraordinary that he was accused of being a magician, and prohibited from practising by the court of Rome. Among others who distinguished themselves by their faith in magnetism, Sebastian Wirdig and William Maxwell claim especial notice. Wirdig was professor of medicine at the university

* *Introduction to the Study of Animal Magnetism*, by Baron Dupotet de Sennevoy, p. 315.

of Rostock in Mecklenburg, and wrote a treatise called *The New Medicine of the Spirits*, which he presented to the Royal Society of London. An edition of this work was printed in 1673, in which the author maintained that a magnetic influence took place, not only between the celestial and terrestrial bodies, but between all living things. The whole world, he said, was under the influence of magnetism : life was preserved by magnetism ; death was the consequence of magnetism !

Maxwell, the other enthusiast, was an admiring disciple of Paracelsus, and boasted that he had irradiated the obscurity in which too many of the wonder-working recipes of that great philosopher were enveloped. His works were printed at Frankfort in 1679. It would seem, from the following passage, that he was aware of the great influence of imagination, as well in the production as in the cure of diseases. " If you wish to work prodigies," says he, " abstract from the materiality of beings—increase the sum of spirituality in bodies —rouse the spirit from its slumbers. Unless you do one or other of these things—unless you can bind the idea, you can never perform any thing good or great." Here, in fact, lies the whole secret of magnetism, and all delusions of a similar kind : increase the spirituality—rouse the spirit from its slumbers, or, in other words, work upon the imagination — induce belief and blind confidence, and you may do any thing. This passage, which is quoted with approbation by M. Dupotet* in a work, as strongly corroborative of the theory now advanced by the animal magnetists, is just the reverse. If they believe they can work all their wonders by the means so dimly shadowed forth by Maxwell, what becomes of the universal fluid pervading all nature, and which they pretend to pour into weak and diseased bodies from the tips of their fingers ?

Early in the eighteenth century the attention of Europe was directed to a very remarkable instance of fanaticism, which has been claimed by the animal magnetists as a proof of their science. The *Convulsionaries of St. Medard*, as they were called, assembled in great numbers round the tomb of their favourite saint, the Jansenist priest Paris, and taught one another how to fall into convulsions. They believed that St. Paris would cure all their infirmities ; and the number of hysterical women and weak-minded persons of all descriptions that flocked to the tomb from far and near was so great as daily to block up all the avenues leading to it. Working themselves up to a pitch of excitement, they went off one after the other into fits, while some of them, still in apparent possession of all their faculties, volun-

* *Introduction to the Study of Animal Magnetism*, p. 318.

tarily exposed themselves to sufferings which on ordinary occasions would have been sufficient to deprive them of life. The scenes that occurred were a scandal to civilisation and to religion—a strange mixture of obscenity, absurdity, and superstition. While some were praying on bended knees at the shrine of St. Paris, others were shrieking and making the most hideous noises. The women especially exerted themselves. On one side of the chapel there might be seen a score of them, all in convulsions; while at another as many more, excited to a sort of frenzy, yielded themselves up to gross indecencies. Some of them took an insane delight in being beaten and trampled upon. One in particular, according to Montégre, whose account we quote,* was so enraptured with this ill-usage, that nothing but the hardest blows would satisfy her. While a fellow of Herculean strength was beating her with all his might with a heavy bar of iron, she kept continually urging him to renewed exertion. The harder he struck the better she liked it, exclaiming all the while, " Well done, brother, well done ! Oh, how pleasant it is ! what good you are doing me ! Courage, my brother, courage ; strike harder, strike harder still!" Another of these fanatics had, if possible, a still greater love for a beating. Carré de Montgeron, who relates the circumstance, was unable to satisfy her with sixty blows of a large sledge-hammer. He afterwards used the same weapon with the same degree of strength, for the sake of experiment, and succeeded in battering a hole in a stone wall at the twenty-fifth stroke. Another woman, named Sonnet, laid herself down on a red-hot brazier without flinching, and acquired for herself the nickname of the *Salamander;* while others, desirous of a more illustrious martyrdom, attempted to crucify themselves. M. Deleuze, in his critical history of *Animal Magnetism,* attempts to prove that this fanatical frenzy was produced by magnetism, and that these mad enthusiasts magnetised each other without being aware of it. As well might he insist that the fanaticism which tempts the Hindoo bigot to keep his arms stretched in a horizontal position till the sinews wither, or his fingers closed upon his palms till the nails grow out of the backs of his hands, is also an effect of magnetism !

For a period of sixty or seventy years magnetism was almost wholly confined to Germany. Men of sense and learning devoted their attention to the properties of the loadstone ; and one Father Hell, a Jesuit, and professor of astronomy at the University of Vienna, rendered himself famous by his magnetic cures. About the year 1771 or 1772 he invented steel-plates of a peculiar form, which he applied to the naked

* *Dictionnaire des Sciences Médicales*—Article *Convulsionnaires,* par Montégre.

body as a cure for several diseases. In the year 1774 he communicated his system to Anthony Mesmer. The latter improved upon the ideas of Father Hell, constructed a new theory of his own, and became the founder of ANIMAL MAGNETISM.

It has been the fashion among the enemies of the new delusion to decry Mesmer as an unprincipled adventurer, while his disciples have extolled him to the skies as a regenerator of the human race. In nearly the same words as the Rosicrucians applied to their founders, he has been called the discoverer of the secret which brings man into more intimate connexion with his Creator, the deliverer of the soul from the debasing trammels of the flesh, the man who enables us to set time at defiance, and conquer the obstructions of space. A careful sifting of his pretensions, and examination of the evidence brought forward to sustain them, will soon shew which opinion is the more correct. That the writer of these pages considers him in the light of a man who, deluding himself, was the means of deluding others, may be inferred from his finding a place in these volumes, and figuring among the Flamels, the Agrippas, the Borris, the Böhmens, and the Cagliostros.

He was born in May 1734, at Mersburg, in Swabia, and studied medicine at the University of Vienna. He took his degrees in 1766, and chose the influence of the planets on the human body as the subject of his inaugural dissertation. Having treated the matter quite in the style of the old astrological physicians, he was exposed to some ridicule both then and afterwards. Even at this early period some faint ideas of his great theory were germinating in his mind. He maintained in his dissertàtion "that the sun, moon, and fixed stars mutually affect each other in their orbits; that they cause and direct in our earth a flux and reflux not only in the sea, but in the atmosphere, and affect in a similar manner all organised bodies through the medium of a subtile and mobile fluid, which pervades the universe, and associates all things together in mutual intercourse and harmony." This influence, he said, was particularly exercised on the nervous system, and produced two states, which he called *intension* and *remission*, which seemed to him to account for the different periodical revolutions observable in several maladies. When in after-life he met with Father Hell, he was confirmed by that person's observations in the truth of many of his own ideas. Having caused Hell to make him some magnetic plates, he determined to try experiments with them himself for his further satisfaction.

He tried accordingly, and was astonished at his success. The faith of their wearers operated wonders with the metallic plates. Mesmer made due reports to Father Hell of all he had done, and the latter published them as the results of his own happy invention, and speaking of Mesmer as a physician whom he had employed to work under him. Mesmer took offence at being thus treated, considering himself a far greater personage than Father Hell. He claimed the invention as his own, accused Hell of a breach of confidence, and stigmatised him as a mean person, anxious to turn the discoveries of others to his own account. Hell replied, and a very pretty quarrel was the result, which afforded small talk for months to the literati of Vienna. Hell ultimately gained the victory. Mesmer, nothing daunted, continued to promulgate his views till he stumbled at last upon the animal theory.

One of his patients was a young lady, named Œsterline, who suffered under a convulsive malady. Her attacks were periodical, and attended by a rush of blood to the head, followed by delirium and syncope. These symptoms he soon succeeded in reducing under his system of planetary influence, and imagined he could foretell the periods of accession and remission. Having thus accounted satisfactorily to himself for the origin of the disease, the idea struck him that he could operate a certain cure if he could ascertain beyond doubt, what he had long believed, that there existed between the bodies which compose our globe an action equally reciprocal and similar to that of the heavenly bodies, by means of which he could imitate artificially the periodical revolutions of the flux and reflux before mentioned. He soon convinced himself that this action did exist. When trying the metallic plates of Father Hell, he thought their efficacy depended on their form ; but he found afterwards that he could produce the same effects without using them at all, merely by passing his hands downwards towards the feet of the patient, even when at a considerable distance.

This completed the theory of Mesmer. He wrote an account of his discovery to all the learned societies of Europe, soliciting their investigation. The Academy of Sciences at Berlin was the only one that answered him, and their answer was any thing but favourable to his system or flattering to himself. Still he was not discouraged. He maintained to all who would listen to him that the magnetic matter, or fluid, pervaded all the universe — that every human body contained it, and could communicate the superabundance of it to another by an exertion of the will. Writing to a friend from Vienna, he said, " I have observed that the magnetic is almost the same thing as the electric fluid, and that it may be propagated in the same manner, by means of intermediate bodies. Steel is not the only substance adapted to this purpose. I have rendered paper, bread, wool, silk, stones, leather, glass, wood, men, and dogs—in short, every thing I touched, magnetic to such a degree, that these substances produced the same effects as the loadstone on diseased persons. I have charged jars with magnetic matter in the same way as is done with electricity."

Mesmer did not long find his residence at Vienna as agreeable as he wished. His pretensions were looked upon with contempt or indifference, and the case of Mademoiselle Œsterline brought him less fame than notoriety. He determined to change his sphere of action, and travelled into Swabia and Switzerland. In the latter country he met with the celebrated Father Gassner, who, like Valentine Greatraks, amused himself by casting out devils, and healing the sick by merely laying hands upon them. At his approach, delicate girls fell into convulsions, and hypochondriacs fancied themselves cured. His house was daily besieged by the lame, the blind, and the hysteric. Mesmer at once acknowledged the efficacy of his cures, and declared that they were the obvious result of his own newly-discovered power of magnetism. A few of the father's patients were forthwith subjected to the manipulations of Mesmer, and the same symptoms were induced. He then tried his hand upon some paupers in the hospitals of Berne and Zurich, and succeeded, according to his own account, but no other person's, in curing an opththalmia and a gutta serena. With memorials of these achievements he returned to Vienna, in the hope of silencing his enemies, or at least forcing them to respect his newly-acquired reputation, and to examine his system more attentively.

His second appearance in that capital was not more auspicious than the first. He undertook to cure a Mademoiselle Paradis, who was quite blind, and subject to convulsions. He magnetised her several times, and then declared that she was cured; at least, if she was not, it was her fault and not his. An eminent oculist of that day, named Barth, went to visit her, and declared that she was as blind as ever; while her family said she was as much subject to convulsions as before. Mesmer persisted that she was cured. Like the French philosopher, he would not allow facts to interfere with his theory.* He declared that there was a conspiracy against him ; and that Mademoiselle Paradis, at the instigation of her family, feigned blindness in order to injure his reputation !

The consequences of this pretended cure taught Mesmer that

* An enthusiastic philosopher, of whose name we are not informed, had constructed a very satisfactory theory on some subject or other, and was not a little proud of it. " But the facts, my dear fellow,' said his friend, " the facts do not agree with your theory."— " Don't they?" replied the philosopher, shrugging his shoulders, " then, *tant pis pour les faits ;*"—so much the worse for the facts !

Vienna was not the sphere for him. Paris, the idle, the debauched,
the pleasure-hunting, the novelty-loving, was the scene for a philosopher like him, and thither he repaired accordingly. He arrived at
Paris in 1778, and began modestly by making himself and his theory
known to the principal physicians. At first, his encouragement was
but slight; he found people more inclined to laugh at than to patronise him. But he was a man who had great confidence in himself,
and of a perseverance which no difficulties could overcome. He hired
a sumptuous apartment, which he opened to all comers who chose to
make trial of the new power of nature. M. D'Eslon, a physician of
great reputation, became a convert ; and from that time, animal
magnetism, or, as some called it, mesmerism, became the fashion in
Paris. The women were quite enthusiastic about it, and their
admiring tattle wafted its fame through every grade of society. Mesmer was the rage ; and high and low, rich and poor, credulous and
unbelieving, all hastened to convince themselves of the power of this
mighty magician, who made such magnificent promises. Mesmer,
who knew as well as any man living the influence of the imagination,
determined that, on that score, nothing should be wanting to heighten
the effect of the magnetic charm. In all Paris, there was not a house
so charmingly furnished as Monsieur Mesmer's. Richly-stained glass
shed a dim religious light on his spacious saloons, which were almost
covered with mirrors. Orange-blossoms scented all the air of his
corridors ; incense of the most expensive kinds burned in antique
vases on his chimney-pieces ; æolian harps sighed melodious music
from distant chambers ; while sometimes a sweet female voice, from
above or below, stole softly upon the mysterious silence that was kept
in the house, and insisted upon from all visitors. "*Was ever any
thing so delightful!*" cried all the Mrs. Wittitterleys of Paris, as they
thronged to his house in search of pleasant excitement ; "*So wonderful!*" said the pseudo-philosophers, who would believe any thing if
it were the fashion ; "*So amusing!*" said the worn-out debauchés,
who had drained the cup of sensuality to its dregs, and who longed to
see lovely women in convulsions, with the hope that they might gain
some new emotions from the sight.

The following was the mode of operation : In the centre of the
saloon was placed an oval vessel, about four feet in its longest diameter,
and one foot deep. In this were laid a number of wine-bottles, filled
with magnetised water, well corked-up, and disposed in radii, with
their necks outwards. Water was then poured into the vessel so as
just to cover the bottles, and filings of iron were thrown in occasionally
to heighten the magnetic effect. The vessel was then covered with an

iron cover, pierced through with many holes, and was called the *baquet*. From each hole issued a long movable rod of iron, which the patients were to apply to such parts of their bodies as were afflicted. Around this *baquet* the patients were directed to sit, holding each other by the hand, and pressing their knees together as closely as possible, to facilitate the passage of the magnetic fluid from one to the other.

Then came in the assistant magnetisers, generally strong, handsome young men, to pour into the patient from their finger-tips fresh streams of the wondrous fluid. They embraced the patient between the knees, rubbed them gently down the spine and the course of the nerves, using gentle pressure upon the breasts of the ladies, and staring them out of countenance to magnetise them by the eye! All this time the most rigorous silence was maintained, with the exception of a few wild notes on the harmonica or the piano-forte, or the melodious voice of a hidden opera-singer swelling softly at long intervals. Gradually the cheeks of the ladies began to glow, their imaginations to become inflamed; and off they went, one after the other, in convulsive fits. Some of them sobbed and tore their hair, others laughed till the tears ran from their eyes, while others shrieked and screamed and yelled till they became insensible altogether.

This was the crisis of the delirium. In the midst of it, the chief actor made his appearance, waving his wand, like Prospero, to work new wonders. Dressed in a long robe of lilac-coloured silk richly embroidered with gold flowers, bearing in his hand a white magnetic rod, and with a look of dignity which would have sat well on an eastern caliph, he marched with solemn strides into the room. He awed the still sensible by his eye, and the violence of their symptoms diminished. He stroked the insensible with his hands upon the eyebrows and down the spine; traced figures upon their breast and abdomen with his long white wand, and they were restored to consciousness. They became calm, acknowledged his power, and said they felt streams of cold or burning vapour passing through their frames, according as he waved his wand or his fingers before them.

"It is impossible," says M. Dupotet, "to conceive the sensation which Mesmer's experiments created in Paris. No theological controversy, in the earlier ages of the Catholic Church, was ever conducted with greater bitterness." His adversaries denied the discovery; some calling him a quack, others a fool, and others again, like the Abbé Fiard, a man who had sold himself to the Devil! His friends were as extravagant in their praise, as his foes were in their censure. Paris was inundated with pamphlets upon the subject, as many defending as attacking the doctrine. At court, the queen expressed herself in favour of it, and nothing else was to be heard of in society.

By the advice of M. D'Eslon, Mesmer challenged an examination of his doctrine by the Faculty of Medicine. He proposed to select twenty-four patients, twelve of whom he would treat magnetically, leaving the other twelve to be treated by the faculty according to the old and approved methods. He also stipulated that, to prevent disputes, the government should nominate certain persons who were not physicians, to be present at the experiments; and that the object of the inquiry should be, not how these effects were produced, but whether they were really efficacious in the cure of any disease. The faculty objected to limit the inquiry in this manner, and the proposition fell to the ground.

Mesmer now wrote to Marie Antoinette, with the view of securing her influence in obtaining for him the protection of government. He wished to have a château and its lands given to him, with a handsome yearly income, that he might be enabled to continue his experiments at leisure, untroubled by the persecution of his enemies. He hinted the duty of governments to support men of science, and expressed his fear, that if he met no more encouragement, he should be compelled to carry his great discovery to some other land more willing to appreciate him. "In the eyes of your majesty," said he, "four or five hundred thousand francs, applied to a good purpose, are of no account. The welfare and happiness of your people are every thing. My discovery ought to be received and rewarded with a munificence worthy of the monarch to whom I shall attach myself." The government at last offered him a pension of twenty thousand francs, and the cross of the order of St. Michael, if he had made any discovery in medicine, and would communicate it to physicians nominated by the king. The latter part of the proposition was not agreeable to Mesmer. He feared the unfavourable report of the king's physicians; and, breaking off the negotiation, spoke of his disregard of money, and his wish to have his discovery at once recognised by the government. He then retired to Spa, in a fit of disgust, upon pretence of drinking the waters for the benefit of his health.

After he had left Paris, the Faculty of Medicine called upon M. D'Eslon, for the third and last time, to renounce the doctrine of animal magnetism, or be expelled from their body. M. D'Eslon, so far from doing this, declared that he had discovered new secrets, and solicited further examination. A royal commission of the Faculty of Medicine was, in consequence, appointed on the 12th of March 1784, seconded by another commission of the Académie des Sciences, to investigate the phenomena and report upon them. The first commission was composed of the principal physicians of Paris; while, among the eminent men comprised in the latter, were Benjamin Franklin, Lavoisier, and Bailly the historian of astronomy. Mesmer was formally invited to appear before this body, but absented himself from day to day, upon one pretence or another. M. D'Eslon was more honest, because he thoroughly believed in the phenomena, which it is to be questioned if Mesmer ever did, and regularly attended the sittings and performed experiments.

Bailly has thus described the scenes of which he was a witness in the course of this investigation. "The sick persons, arranged in great numbers and in several rows around the *baquet*, receive the magnetism by all these means: by the iron rods which convey it to them from the *baquet*—by the cords wound round their bodies—by the connexion of the thumb, which conveys to them the magnetism of their neighbours—and by the sounds of a piano-forte, or of an agreeable voice, diffusing the magnetism in the air. The patients were also directly magnetised by means of the finger and wand of the magnetiser moved slowly before their faces, above or behind their heads, and on the diseased parts, always observing the direction of the holes. The magnetiser acts by fixing his eyes on them. But above all, they are magnetised by the application of his hands and the pressure of his fingers on the hypochondres and on the regions of the abdomen; an application often continued for a long time—sometimes for several hours.

"Meanwhile the patients in their different conditions present a very varied picture. Some are calm, tranquil, and experience no effect. Others cough, spit, feel slight pains, local or general heat, and have sweatings. Others again are agitated and tormented with convulsions. These convulsions are remarkable in regard to the number affected with them, to their duration and force. As soon as one begins to be convulsed, several others are affected. The commissioners have observed some of these convulsions last more than three hours. They are accompanied with expectorations of a muddy viscous water, brought away by violent efforts. Sometimes streaks of blood have been observed in this fluid. These convulsions are characterised by the precipitous, involuntary motion of all the limbs, and of the whole body; by the contraction of the throat—by the leaping motions of the hypochondria and the epigastrium—by the dimness and wandering of the eyes—by piercing shrieks, tears, sobbing, and immoderate laughter. They are preceded or followed by a state of languor or reverie, a kind of depression, and sometimes drowsiness. The smallest sudden noise occasions a shuddering; and it was remarked, that the change of measure in the airs played on the piano-forte had a great influence on the patients. A quicker motion, a livelier melody, agitated them more, and renewed the vivacity of their convulsions.

" Nothing is more astonishing than the spectacle of these convulsions. One who has not seen them can form no idea of them. The spectator is as much astonished at the profound repose of one portion of the patients as at the agitation of the rest—at the various accidents which are repeated, and at the sympathies which are exhibited. Some of the patients may be seen devoting their attention exclusively to one another, rushing towards each other with open arms, smiling, soothing, and manifesting every symptom of attachment and affection. All are under the power of the magnetiser; it matters not in what state of drowsiness they may be, the sound of his voice—a look, a motion of his hand—brings them out of it. Among the patients in convulsions there are always observed a great many women, and very few men."*

These experiments lasted for about five months. They had hardly commenced, before Mesmer, alarmed at the loss both of fame and profit, determined to return to Paris. Some patients of rank and fortune, enthusiastic believers in his doctrine, had followed him to Spa. One of them named Bergasse, proposed to open a subscription for him, of one hundred shares, at one hundred louis each, on condition that he would disclose his secret to the subscribers, who were to be permitted to make whatever use they pleased of it. Mesmer readily embraced the proposal; and such was the infatuation, that the subscription was not only filled in a few days, but exceeded by no less a sum than one hundred and forty thousand francs.

With this fortune he returned to Paris, and recommenced his experiments, while the royal commission continued theirs. His admiring pupils, who had paid him so handsomely for his instructions, spread his fame over the country, and established in all the principal towns of France, " Societies of Harmony," for trying experiments and curing all diseases by means of magnetism. Some of these societies were a scandal to morality, being joined by profligate men of depraved appetites, who took a disgusting delight in witnessing young girls in convulsions. Many of the pretended magnetisers were asserted at the time to be notorious libertines, who took that opportunity of gratifying their passions.

At last the commissioners published their report, which was drawn up by the illustrious and unfortunate Bailly. For clearness of reasoning and strict impartiality it has never been surpassed. After detail-

* *Rapport des Commissaires*, rédigé par M. Bailly. Paris. 1784.

ing the various experiments made, and their results, they came to the conclusion that the only proof advanced in support of animal magnetism was the effects it produced on the human body—that those effects could be produced without passes or other magnetic manipulations— that all these manipulations and passes and ceremonies never produce any effect at all if employed without the patient's knowledge ; and that therefore imagination did, and animal magnetism did not, account for the phenomena.

This report was the ruin of Mesmer's reputation in France. He quitted Paris shortly after, with the three hundred and forty thousand francs which had been subscribed by his admirers, and retired to his own country, where he died in 1815, at the advanced age of eighty-one. But the seeds he had sown fructified of themselves, nourished and brought to maturity by the kindly warmth of popular credulity. Imitators sprang up in France, Germany, and England, more extravagant than their master, and claiming powers for the new science which its founder had never dreamt of. Among others, Cagliostro made good use of the delusion in extending his claims to be considered a master of the occult sciences. But he made no discoveries worthy to be compared to those of the Marquis de Puysegur and the Chevalier Barbarin, honest men, who began by deceiving themselves before they deceived others.

The Marquis de Puysegur, the owner of a considerable estate at Busancy, was one of those who had entered into the subscription for Mesmer. After that individual had quitted France, he retired to Busancy, with his brother, to try animal magnetism upon his tenants, and cure the country people of all manner of diseases. He was a man of great simplicity and much benevolence, and not only magnetised but fed the sick that flocked around him. In all the neighbourhood, and indeed within a circumference of twenty miles, he was looked upon as endowed with a power almost divine. His great discovery, as he called it, was made by chance. One day he had magnetised his gardener ; and observing him to fall into a deep sleep, it occurred to him that he would address a question to him, as he would have done to a natural somnambulist. He did so, and the man replied with much clearness and precision. M. de Puysegur was agreeably surprised : he continued his experiments, and found that, in this state of magnetic somnambulism, *the soul of the sleeper was enlarged, and brought into more intimate communion with all nature, and more especially with him, M. de Puysegur.* He found that all further manipulations were unnecessary ; that, without speaking or making any sign, he could convey his will to the patient ; that he could, in fact, converse with him, soul to soul, without the employment of any physical operation whatever !

Simultaneously with this marvellous discovery he made another, which reflects equal credit upon his understanding. Like Valentine Greatraks, he found it hard work to magnetise all that came—that he had not even time to take the repose and relaxation which were necessary for his health. In this emergency he hit upon a clever expedient. He had heard Mesmer say that he could magnetise bits of wood : why should he not be able to magnetise a whole tree? It was no sooner thought than done. There was a large elm on the village green at Busancy, under which the peasant girls used to dance on festive occasions, and the old men to sit, drinking their *vin du pays*, on the fine summer evenings. M. de Puysegur proceeded to this tree and magnetised it, by first touching it with his hands, and then retiring a few steps from it ; all the while directing streams of the magnetic fluid from the branches toward the trunk, and from the trunk toward the root. This done, he caused circular seats to be erected round it, and cords suspended from it in all directions. When the patients had seated themselves, they twisted the cords round the diseased parts of their bodies, and held one another firmly by their thumbs to form a direct channel of communication for the passage of the fluid.

M. de Puysegur had now two "hobbies"—the man with the enlarged soul and the magnetic elm. The infatuation of himself and his patients cannot be better expressed than in his own words. Writing to his brother, on the 17th of May 1784, he says, " If you do not come, my dear friend, you will not see my extraordinary man, for his health is now almost quite restored. I continue to make use of the happy power for which I am indebted to M. Mesmer. Every day I bless his name ; for I am very useful, and produce many salutary effects on all the sick poor in the neighbourhood. They flock around my tree ; there were more than one hundred and thirty of them this morning. It is the best *baquet* possible ; *not a leaf of it but communicates health !* all feel, more or less, the good effects of it. You will be delighted to see the charming picture of humanity which this presents. I have only one regret—it is, that I cannot touch all who come. But my magnetised man—my intelligence—sets me at ease. He teaches me what conduct I should adopt. According to him, it is not at all necessary that I should touch every one ; a look, a gesture, even a wish, is sufficient. And it is one of the most ignorant peasants of the country that teaches me this ! When he is in a crisis, I know of nothing more profound, more prudent, more clearsighted (*clairvoyant*) than he is."

In another letter, describing his first experiment with the magnetic tree, he says, " Yesterday evening I brought my first patient to it. As soon as I had put the cord round him he gazed at the tree ; and, with an air of astonishment which I cannot describe, exclaimed, ' What is it that I see there?' His head then sunk down, and he fell into a perfect fit of somnambulism. At the end of an hour, I took him home to his house again, when I restored him to his senses. Several men and women came to tell him what he had been doing. He maintained it was not true ; that, weak as he was, and scarcely able to walk, it would have been scarcely possible for him to have gone down stairs and walked to the tree. To-day I have repeated the experiment on him, and with the same success. I own to you that my head turns round with pleasure to think of the good I do. Madame de Puysegur, the friends she has with her, my servants, and, in fact, all who are near me, feel an amazement, mingled with admiration, which cannot be described ; but they do not experience the half of my sensations. Without my tree, which gives me rest, and which will give me still more, I should be in a state of agitation, inconsistent, I believe, with my health. I exist too much, if I may be allowed to use the expression."

In another letter, he descants still more poetically upon his gardener with the enlarged soul. He says, " It is from this simple man, this tall and stout rustic, twenty-three years of age, enfeebled by disease, or rather by sorrow, and therefore the more predisposed to be affected by any great natural agent,—it is from this man, I repeat, that I derive instruction and knowledge. When in the magnetic state, he is no longer a peasant who can hardly utter a single sentence ; he is a being, to describe whom I cannot find a name. I need not speak ; *I have only to think before him, when he instantly understands and answers me.* Should any body come into the room, he sees him, if I desire it (but not else), and addresses him, and says what I wish to say ; not indeed exactly as I dictate to him, but as truth requires. When he wants to add more than I deem it prudent strangers should hear, I stop the flow of his ideas, and of his conversation in the middle of a word, and give it quite a different turn !"

Among other persons attracted to Busancy by the report of these extraordinary occurrences was M. Cloquet, the Receiver of Finance. His appetite for the marvellous being somewhat insatiable, he readily believed all that was told him by M. de Puysegur. He also has left a record of what he saw, and what he credited, which throws a still clearer light upon the progress of the delusion.* He says that the patients he saw in the magnetic state had an appearance of deep sleep,

* *Introduction to the Study of Animal Magnetism,* by Baron Dupotet, p. 73.

during which all the physical faculties were suspended, to the advantage of the intellectual faculties. The eyes of the patients were closed, the sense of hearing was abolished; and they awoke only at the voice of their magnetiser. "If any one touched a patient during a crisis, or even the chair on which he was seated," says M. Cloquet, "it would cause him much pain and suffering, and throw him into convulsions. During the crisis, they possess an extraordinary and supernatural power, by which, on touching a patient presented to them, they can feel what part of his body is diseased, even by merely passing their hand over the clothes." Another singularity was, that these sleepers who could thus discover diseases, see into the interior of other men's stomachs, and point out remedies, remembered absolutely nothing after the magnetiser thought proper to disenchant them. The time that elapsed between their entering the crisis and their coming out of it was obliterated. Not only had the magnetiser the power of making himself heard by the somnambulists, but he could make them follow him by merely pointing his finger at them from a distance, though they had their eyes the whole time completely closed.

Such was animal magnetism under the auspices of the Marquis de Puysegur. While he was exhibiting these phenomena around his elm-tree, a magnetiser of another class appeared in Lyons, in the person of the Chevalier de Barbarin. This gentleman thought the effort of the will, without any of the paraphernalia of wands or *baquets*, was sufficient to throw patients into the magnetic sleep. He tried it and succeeded. By sitting at the bedside of his patients, and praying that they might be magnetised, they went off into a state very similar to that of the persons who fell under the notice of M. de Puysegur. In the course of time a very considerable number of magnetisers, acknowledging Barbarin for their model, and called after him Barbarinists, appeared in different parts, and were believed to have effected some remarkable cures. In Sweden and Germany this sect of fanatics increased rapidly, and were called *spiritualists*, to distinguish them from the followers of M. de Puysegur, who were called *experimentalists*. They maintained that all the effects of animal magnetism, which Mesmer believed to be producible by a magnetic fluid dispersed through nature, were produced by the mere effort of one human soul acting upon another; that when a connexion had once been established between a magnetiser and his patient, the former could communicate his influence to the latter from any distance, even hundreds of miles, by the will. One of them thus described the blessed state of a magnetic patient: "In such a man animal instinct ascends to the highest degree admissible in this world. The *clairvoyant* is then a pure animal, without any admixture of matter. His observations are those of a spirit. He is similar to God: his eye penetrates all the secrets of nature. When his attention is fixed on any of the objects of this world—on his disease, his death, his well-beloved, his friends, his relations, his enemies—in spirit he sees them acting; he penetrates into the causes and the consequences of their actions; he becomes a physician, a prophet, a divine!"*

Let us now see what progress these mysteries made in England. In the year 1788 Dr. Mainauduc, who had been a pupil, first of Mesmer and afterwards of D'Eslon, arrived in Bristol, and gave public lectures upon magnetism. His success was quite extraordinary. People of rank and fortune hastened from London to Bristol to be magnetised, or to place themselves under his tuition. Dr. George Winter, in his *History of Animal Magnetism,* gives the following list of them: "They amounted to one hundred and twenty-seven, among whom there were one duke, one duchess, one marchioness, two countesses, one earl, one baron, three baronesses, one bishop, five right honourable gentlemen and ladies, two baronets, seven members of parliament, one clergyman, two physicians, seven surgeons, besides ninety-two gentlemen and ladies of respectability." He afterwards established himself in London, where he performed with equal success.

He began by publishing proposals to the ladies for the formation of a Hygeian Society. In this paper he vaunted highly the curative effects of animal magnetism, and took great credit to himself for being the first person to introduce it into England, and thus concluded: "As this method of cure is not confined to sex or college education, and the fair sex being in general the most sympathising part of the creation, and most immediately concerned in the health and care of its offspring, I think myself bound in gratitude to you, ladies, for the partiality you have shewn me in midwifery, to contribute, as far as lies in my power, to render you additionally useful and valuable to the community. With this view I propose forming my Hygeian Society, to be incorporated with that of Paris. As soon as twenty ladies have given in their names, the day shall be appointed for the first meeting at my house, when they are to pay fifteen guineas, which will include the whole expense."

Hannah More, in a letter addressed to Horace Walpole in September 1788, speaks of the "demoniacal mummeries" of Dr. Mainauduc, and says he was in a fair way of gaining a hundred thousand pounds by them, as Mesmer had done by his exhibitions in Paris.

So much curiosity was excited by the subject, that, about the same time, a man named Holloway gave a course of lectures on ani-

* See *Foreign Review and Continental Miscellany,* vol. v. p. 113.

mal magnetism in London, at the rate of five guineas for each pupil, and realised a considerable fortune. Loutherbourg the painter and his wife followed the same profitable trade; and such was the infatuation of the people to be witnesses of their strange manipulations, that at times upwards of three thousand persons crowded around their house at Hammersmith, unable to gain admission. The tickets sold at prices varying from one to three guineas. Loutherbourg performed his cures by the touch, after the manner of Valentine Greatraks, and finally pretended to a divine mission. An account of his miracles, as they were called, was published in 1789, entitled *A List of New Cures performed by Mr. and Mrs. de Loutherbourg, of Hammersmith Terrace, without Medicine; by a Lover of the Lamb of God. Dedicated to his Grace the Archbishop of Canterbury.*

This "Lover of the Lamb of God" was a half-crazy old woman, named Mary Pratt, who conceived for Mr. and Mrs. de Loutherbourg a veneration which almost prompted her to worship them. She chose for the motto of her pamphlet a verse in the thirteenth chapter of the Acts of the Apostles: "Behold, ye despisers, and wonder and perish! for I will work a work in your days which ye shall not believe, though a man declare it unto you." Attempting to give a religious character to the cures of the painter, she thought a *woman* was the proper person to make them known, since the apostle had declared that a *man* should not be able to conquer the incredulity of the people. She stated, that from Christmas 1788 to July 1789, De Loutherbourg and his wife had cured two thousand people, "having been made *proper recipients to receive divine manuductions;* which heavenly and divine influx, coming from the radix *God*, his Divine Majesty had most graciously bestowed upon them to diffuse healing to all, be they deaf, dumb, blind, lame, or halt."

In her dedication to the Archbishop of Canterbury she implored him to compose a new form of prayer, to be used in all churches and chapels, that nothing might impede this inestimable gift from having its due course. She further entreated all the magistrates and men of authority in the land to wait on Mr. and Mrs. de Loutherbourg, to consult with them on the immediate erection of a large hospital, with a pool of Bethesda attached to it. All the magnetisers were scandalised at the preposterous jabber of this old woman, and De Loutherbourg appears to have left London to avoid her,—continuing, however, in conjunction with his wife, the fantastic tricks which had turned the brain of this poor fanatic, and deluded many others who pretended to more sense than she had.

From this period until 1798 magnetism excited little or no attention in England. An attempt to revive the belief in it was made in that year, but it was in the shape of mineral rather than of animal magnetism. One Benjamin Douglas Perkins, an American, practising as a surgeon in Leicester Square, invented and took out a patent for the celebrated "Metallic Tractors." He pretended that these tractors, which were two small pieces of metal strongly magnetised, something resembling the steel plates which were first brought into notice by Father Hell, would cure gout, rheumatism, palsy, and, in fact, almost every disease the human frame was subject to, if applied externally to the afflicted part, and moved about gently, touching the surface only. The most wonderful stories soon obtained general circulation, and the press groaned with pamphlets, all vaunting the curative effects of the tractors, which were sold at five guineas the pair. Perkins gained money rapidly. Gouty subjects forgot their pains in the presence of this new remedy; the rheumatism fled at its approach; and toothache, which is often cured by the mere sight of a dentist, vanished before Perkins and his marvellous steel-plates. The benevolent Society of Friends, of whose body he was a member, warmly patronised the invention. Desirous that the poor, who could not afford to pay Mr. Perkins five guineas, or even five shillings for his tractors, should also share in the benefits of that sublime discovery, they subscribed a large sum, and built an hospital, called the "Perkinean Institution," in which all comers might be magnetised free of cost. In the course of a few months they were in very general use, and their lucky inventor in possession of five thousand pounds.

Dr. Haygarth, an eminent physician at Bath, recollecting the influence of imagination in the cure of disease, hit upon an expedient to try the real value of the tractors. Perkins's cures were too well established to be doubted; and Dr. Haygarth, without gainsaying them, quietly, but in the face of numerous witnesses, exposed the delusion under which people laboured with respect to the curative medium. He suggested to Dr. Falconer that they should make wooden tractors, paint them to resemble the steel ones, and see if the very same effects would not be produced. Five patients were chosen from the hospital in Bath, upon whom to operate. Four of them suffered severely from chronic rheumatism in the ankle, knee, wrist, and hip; and the fifth had been afflicted for several months with the gout. On the day appointed for the experiments Dr. Haygarth and his friends assembled at the hospital, and with much solemnity brought forth the fictitious tractors. Four out of the five patients said their pains were immediately relieved; and three of them said they were not only relieved but very much benefited. One felt his knee warmer, and said he could walk across the room. He tried and succeeded, although on the previous day he had not been able to stir. The gouty man felt his pains diminish rapidly, and was quite easy for nine hours, until he went to bed, when the twitching began again. On the following day the real tractors were applied to all the patients, when they described their symptoms in nearly the same terms.

To make still more sure, the experiment was tried in the Bristol infirmary, a few weeks afterwards, on a man who had a rheumatic affection in the shoulder, so severe as to incapacitate him from lifting his hand from his knee. The fictitious tractors were brought and applied to the afflicted part, one of the physicians, to add solemnity to the scene, drawing a stop-watch from his pocket to calculate the time exactly, while another, with a pen in his hand, sat down to write the change of symptoms from minute to minute as they occurred. In less than four minutes the man felt so much relieved, that he lifted his hand several inches without any pain in the shoulder!

An account of these matters was published by Dr. Haygarth, in a small volume entitled, *Of the Imagination, as a Cause and Cure of Disorders, exemplified by Fictitious Tractors.* The exposure was a *coup de grace* to the system of Mr. Perkins. His friends and patrons, still unwilling to confess that they had been deceived, tried the tractors upon sheep, cows, and horses, alleging that the animals received benefit from the metallic plates, but none at all from the wooden ones. But they found nobody to believe them; the Perkinean institution fell into neglect; and Perkins made his exit from England, carrying with him about ten thousand pounds, to soothe his declining years in the good city of Pennsylvania.

Thus was magnetism laughed out of England for a time. In France the revolution left men no leisure for studying it. The *Sociétés de l'Harmonie* of Strasbourg, and other great towns lingered for a while, till sterner matters occupying men's attention, they were one after the other abandoned, both by pupils and professors. The system, thus driven from the first two nations of Europe, took refuge among the dreamy philosophers of Germany. There the wonders of the magnetic sleep grew more and more wonderful every day; the patients acquired the gift of prophecy; their vision extended over all the surface of the globe; they could hear and see with their toes and fingers, and read unknown languages, and understand them too, by merely having the book placed on their stomachs. Ignorant peasants, when once entranced by the grand mesmeric fluid, could spout philosophy diviner than Plato ever wrote, descant upon the mysteries of the mind with more eloquence and truth than the profoundest metaphysicians the world ever saw, and solve knotty points of divinity with as much ease as waking men could undo their shoe-buckles!

During the first twelve years of the present century little was heard of animal magnetism in any country of Europe. Even the Germans forgot their airy fancies, recalled to the knowledge of this every-day world by the roar of Napoleon's cannon and the fall or the establishment of kingdoms. During this period a cloud of obscurity hung over the science, which was not dispersed until M. Deleuze published, in 1813, his *Histoire Critique du Magnétisme Animal*. This work gave a new impulse to the half-forgotten fancy. Newspapers, pamphlets, and books again waged war upon each other on the question of its truth or falsehood ; and many eminent men in the profession of medicine recommenced inquiry with an earnest design to discover the truth.

The assertions made in the celebrated treatise of Deleuze are thus summed up :* " There is a fluid continually escaping from the human body," and " forming an atmosphere around us," which, as " it has no determined current," produces no sensible effects on surrounding individuals. It is, however, " capable of being directed by the will;" and, when so directed, " is sent forth in currents," with a force corresponding to the energy we possess. Its motion is " similar to that of the rays from burning bodies ;" " it possesses different qualities in different individuals." It is capable of a high degree of concentration, " and exists also in trees." The will of the magnetiser, " guided by a motion of the hand, several times repeated in the same direction," can fill a tree with this fluid. Most persons, when this fluid is poured into them from the body and by the will of the magnetiser, " feel a sensation of heat or cold" when he passes his hand before them, without even touching them. Some persons, when sufficiently charged with this fluid, fall into a state of somnambulism, or magnetic ecstasy; and when in this state, " they see the fluid encircling the magnetiser like a halo of light, and issuing in luminous streams from his mouth and nostrils, his head and hands, possessing a very agreeable smell, and communicating a particular taste to food and water."

One would think that these " notions" were quite enough to be insisted upon by any physician who wished to be considered sane ; but they form only a small portion of the wondrous things related by M. Deleuze. He further said, " When magnetism produces somnambulism, the person who is in this state acquires a prodigious extension of all his faculties. Several of his external organs, especially those of sight and hearing, become inactive ; but the sensations which

---

* See the very clear and dispassionate article upon the subject in the fifth volume (1830) of *The Foreign Review*, p. 96 et seq.

depend upon them take place internally. Seeing and hearing are carried on by the magnetic fluid, which transmits the impressions immediately, and without the intervention of any nerves or organs directly to the brain. Thus the somnambulist, though his eyes and ears are closed, not only sees and hears, but sees and hears much better than he does when awake. In all things he feels the will of the magnetiser, although that will be not expressed. He sees into the interior of his own body, and the most secret organisation of the bodies of all those who may be put *en rapport*, or in magnetic connexion, with him. Most commonly, he only sees those parts which are diseased and disordered, and intuitively prescribes a remedy for them. He has prophetic visions and sensations, which are generally true, but sometimes erroneous. He expresses himself with astonishing eloquence and facility. He is not free from vanity. He becomes a more perfect being of his own accord for a certain time, if guided wisely by the magnetiser, but wanders if he is ill-directed."

According to M. Deleuze, any person could become a magnetiser and produce these effects, by conforming to the following conditions, and acting upon the following rules :

"Forget for a while all your knowledge of physics and metaphysics.

"Remove from your mind all objections that may occur.

"Imagine that it is in your power to take the malady in hand, and throw it on one side.

"*Never reason for six weeks after you have commenced the study.*

"Have an active desire to do good ; a firm belief in the power of magnetism, and an entire confidence in employing it. In short, repel all doubts ; desire success, and act with simplicity and attention."

That is to say, "be very credulous; be very persevering; reject all past experience, and do not listen to reason," and you are a magnetiser after M. Deleuze's own heart.

Having brought yourself into this edifying state, "remove from the patient all persons who might be troublesome to you ; keep with you only the necessary witnesses—a single person if need be ; desire them not to occupy themselves in any way with the processes you employ and the effects which result from them, but to join with you in the desire of doing good to your patient. Arrange yourself so as neither to be too hot nor too cold, and in such a manner that nothing may obstruct the freedom of your motions ; and take precautions to prevent interruption during the sitting. Make your patient then sit as commodiously as possible, and place yourself opposite to him, on a seat a little more elevated, in such a manner that his knees may be betwixt yours, and your feet at the side of his. First, request him to resign himself ; to think of nothing ; not to perplex himself by examining the effects which may be produced; to banish all fear; to surrender himself to hope, and not to be disturbed or discouraged if the action of magnetism should cause in him momentary pains. After having collected yourself, take his thumbs between your fingers in such a way that the internal part of your thumbs may be in contact with the internal part of his, *and then fix your eyes upon him !* You must remain from two to five minutes in this situation, or until you feel an equal heat between your thumbs and his. This done, you will withdraw your hands, removing them to the right and left; and at the same time turning them till their internal surface be outwards, and you will raise them to the height of the head. You will now place them upon the two shoulders, and let them remain there about a minute; afterwards drawing them gently along the arms to the extremities of the fingers, touching very slightly as you go. You will renew this pass five or six times, always turning your hands, and removing them a little from the body before you lift them. You will then place them above the head; and after holding them there for an instant, lower them, passing them before the face, at the distance of one or two inches, down to the pit of the stomach. There you will stop them two minutes also, putting your thumbs upon the pit of the stomach and the rest of your fingers below the ribs. You will then descend slowly along the body to the knees, or rather, if you can do so without deranging yourself, to the extremity of the feet. You will repeat the same processes several times during the remainder of the sitting. You will also occasionally approach your patient, so as to place your hands behind his shoulders, in order to descend slowly along the spine of the back and the thighs, down to the knees or the feet. After the first passes, you may dispense with putting your hands upon the head, and may make the subsequent passes upon the arms, beginning at the shoulders, and upon the body, beginning at the stomach."

Such was the process of magnetising recommended by Deleuze. That delicate, fanciful, and nervous women, when subjected to it, should have worked themselves into convulsions will be readily believed by the sturdiest opponent of animal magnetism. To sit in a constrained posture—be stared out of countenance by a fellow who enclosed her knees between his, while he made *passes* upon different parts of her body, was quite enough to throw any weak woman into a fit, especially if she were predisposed to hysteria, and believed in the efficacy of the treatment. It is just as evident that those of stronger minds and healthier bodies should be sent to sleep by the process. That these effects have been produced by these means, there are thousands of instances to shew. But are they testimony in favour of animal magnetism ?—do they prove the existence of the magnetic fluid ? It needs neither magnetism, nor ghost from the grave, to tell us that silence, monotony, and long recumbency in one position, must produce sleep; or that excitement, imitation, and a strong imagination acting upon a weak body, will bring on convulsions.

M. Deleuze's book produced quite a sensation in France; the study was resumed with redoubled vigour. In the following year, a journal was established devoted exclusively to the science, under the title of *Annales du Magnétisme Animal;* and shortly afterwards appeared the *Bibliothèque du Magnétisme Animal*, and many others. About the same time, the Abbé Faria, "the man of wonders," began to magnetise; and the belief being that he had more of the mesmeric fluid about him, and a stronger will, than most men, he was very successful in his treatment. His experiments afford a convincing proof that imagination can operate all, and the supposed fluid none, of the results so confidently claimed as evidence of the new science. He placed his patients in an arm-chair; told them to shut their eyes; and then, in a loud commanding voice, pronounced the single word, "Sleep!" He used no manipulations whatever—had no *baquet*, or conductor of the fluid ; but he nevertheless succeeded in causing sleep in hundreds of patients. He boasted of having in his time produced five thousand somnambulists by this method. It was often necessary to repeat the command three or four times; and if the patient still remained awake, the abbé got out of the difficulty by dismissing him from the chair, and declaring that he was incapable of being acted on. And it should be especially remarked that the magnetisers do not lay claim to universal efficacy for their fluid; the strong and the healthy cannot be magnetised; the incredulous cannot be magnetised; those who reason upon it cannot be magnetised; those who firmly believe in it can be magnetised; the weak in body can be magnetised, and the weak in mind can be magnetised. And lest, from some cause or other, individuals of the latter classes should resist the magnetic charm, the apostles of the science declare that there are times when even *they* cannot be acted upon ; the presence of one scorner or unbeliever may weaken the potency of the fluid and destroy its efficacy. In M. Deleuze's instructions to a magnetiser, he expressly says, " Never magnetise before inquisitive persons !"*

Here we conclude the subject, as it would serve no good purpose to extend to greater length the history of Animal Magnetism; especially at a time when many phenomena, the reality of which it is impossible to dispute, are daily occurring to startle and perplex the

* *Histoire Critique du Magnetisme Animal*, p. 60.

most learned, impartial, and truth-loving of mankind. Enough, however, has been stated to shew, that if there be some truth in magnetism, there has been much error, misconception, and exaggeration. Taking its history from the commencement, it can hardly be said to have been without its uses. To quote the words of Bailly, in 1784, " Magnetism has not been altogether unavailing to the philosophy which condemns it : it is an additional fact to record among the errors of the human mind, and a great experiment on the strength of the imagination." Over that vast inquiry of the influence of mind over matter,—an inquiry which the embodied intellect of mankind will never be able to fathom completely,—it will at least have thrown a feeble and imperfect light. It will have afforded an additional proof of the strength of the unconquerable will, and the weakness of matter as compared with it ; another illustration of the words of the inspired Psalmist, that " we are fearfully and wonderfully made."

INFLUENCE OF POLITICS AND RELIGION

ON THE

HAIR AND BEARD.

———◆———

Speak with respect and honour
Both of the beard and the beard's owner.
Hudibras.

THE famous declaration of St. Paul, "that long hair was a shame unto a man," has been made the pretext for many singular enactments, both of civil and ecclesiastical governments. The fashion of the hair and the cut of the beard were state questions in France and England, from the establishment of Christianity until the fifteenth century.

We find, too, that in much earlier times, men were not permitted to do as they liked with their own hair. Alexander the Great thought that the beards of the soldiery afforded convenient handles for the enemy to lay hold of, preparatory to cutting off their heads; and, with a view of depriving them of this advantage, he ordered the whole of his army to be closely shaven. His notions of courtesy towards an enemy were quite different from those entertained by the North American Indians, and amongst whom it is held a point of honour to allow one " chivalrous lock" to grow, that the foe, in taking the scalp, may have something to catch hold of.

At one time, long hair was the symbol of sovereignty in Europe. We learn from Gregory of Tours, that, among the successors of Clovis, it was the exclusive privilege of the royal family to have their hair long and curled. The nobles, equal to kings in power, would not shew any inferiority in this respect, and wore not only their hair, but their beards of an enormous length. This fashion lasted, with but slight changes, till the time of Louis the Debonnaire; but his successors, up to Hugh Capet, wore their hair short, by way of distinction. Even the serfs had set all regulation at defiance, and allowed their locks and beards to grow.

At the time of the invasion of England by William the Conqueror, the Normans wore their hair very short. Harold, in his progress towards Hastings, sent forward spies to view the strength and number of the enemy. They reported, amongst other things, on their return, that "the host did almost seem to be priests, because they had all their face and both their lips shaven." The fashion among the English at the time was to wear the hair long upon the head and the upper lip, but to shave the chin. When the haughty victors had divided the broad lands of the Saxon thanes and franklins among them, when tyranny of every kind was employed to make the English feel that they were indeed a subdued and broken nation, the latter encouraged the growth of their hair, that they might resemble as little as possible their cropped and shaven masters.

This fashion was exceedingly displeasing to the clergy, and prevailed to a considerable extent in France and Germany. Towards the end of the eleventh century, it was decreed by the pope, and zealously supported by the ecclesiastical authorities all over Europe, that such persons as wore long hair should be excommunicated while living, and not be prayed for when dead. William of Malmesbury relates, that the famous St. Wulstan, Bishop of Worcester, was peculiarly indignant whenever he saw a man with long hair. He declaimed against the practice as one highly immoral, criminal, and beastly. He continually carried a small knife in his pocket, and whenever any body offending in this respect knelt before him to receive his blessing, he would whip it out slily, and cut off a handful, and then, throwing it in his face, tell him to cut off all the rest, or he would go to hell.

But fashion, which at times it is possible to move with a wisp, stands firm against a lever; and men preferred to run the risk of

damnation to parting with the superfluity of their hair. In the time
of Henry I., Anselm, Archbishop of Canterbury, found it necessary
to republish the famous decree of excommunication and outlawry
against the offenders ; but, as the court itself had begun to patronise
curls, the fulminations of the Church were unavailing. Henry I. and
his nobles wore their hair in long ringlets down their backs and
shoulders, and became a *scandalum magnatum* in the eyes of the
godly. One Serlo, the king's chaplain, was so grieved in spirit at the
impiety of his master, that he preached a sermon from the well-known
text of St. Paul before the assembled court, in which he drew so
dreadful a picture of the torments that awaited them in the other
world, that several of them burst into tears, and wrung their hair, as
if they would have pulled it out by the roots. Henry himself was
observed to weep. The priest, seeing the impression he had made,
determined to strike while the iron was hot, and pulling a pair of
scissors from his pocket, cut the king's hair in presence of them all.
Several of the principal courtiers consented to do the like, and for a
short time long hair appeared to be going out of fashion. But the
courtiers thought, after the first glow of their penitence had been
cooled by reflection, that the clerical Delilah had shorn them of their
strength, and in less than six months they were as great sinners as
ever.

Anselm, the Archbishop of Canterbury, who had been a monk of
Bec, in Normandy, and who had signalised himself at Rouen by his
fierce opposition to long hair, was still anxious to work a reformation
in this matter. But his pertinacity was far from pleasing to the
king, who had finally made up his mind to wear ringlets. There
were other disputes, of a more serious nature, between them ; so that
when the archbishop died, the king was so glad to be rid of him, that
he allowed the see to remain vacant for five years. Still the cause
had other advocates, and every pulpit in the land resounded with
anathemas against that disobedient and long-haired generation. But
all was of no avail. Stowe, in writing of this period, asserts, on the
authority of some more ancient chronicler, "that men, forgetting
their birth, transformed themselves, by the length of their haires, into
the semblance of woman kind;" and that when their hair decayed
from age, or other causes, "they knit about their heads certain rolls
and braidings of false hair." At last accident turned the tide of
fashion. A knight of the court, who was exceedingly proud of his
beauteous locks, dreamed one night that, as he lay in bed, the devil
sprang upon him, and endeavoured to choke him with his own hair.
He started in affright, and actually found that he had a great quantity
of hair in his mouth. Sorely stricken in conscience, and looking

upon the dream as a warning from heaven, he set about the work of reformation, and cut off his luxuriant tresses the same night. The story was soon bruited abroad; of course it was made the most of by the clergy, and the knight, being a man of influence and consideration, and the acknowledged leader of the fashion, his example, aided by priestly exhortations, was very generally imitated. Men appeared almost as decent as St. Wulstan himself could have wished, the dream of a dandy having proved more efficacious than the entreaties of a saint. But, as Stowe informs us, "scarcely was one year past, when all that thought themselves courtiers fell into the former vice, and contended with women in their long haires." Henry, the king, appears to have been quite uninfluenced by the dreams of others, for even his own would not induce him a second time to undergo a cropping from priestly shears. It is said, that he was much troubled at this time by disagreeable visions. Having offended the Church in this and other respects, he could get no sound, refreshing sleep, and used to imagine that he saw all the bishops, abbots, and monks of every degree, standing around his bed-side, and threatening to belabour him with their pastoral staves; which sight, we are told, so frightened him, that he often started naked out of his bed, and attacked the phantoms sword in hand. Grimbalde, his physician, who, like most of his fraternity at that day, was an ecclesiastic, never hinted that his dreams were the result of a bad digestion, but told him to shave his head, be reconciled to the Church, and reform himself with alms and prayer. But he would not take this good advice, and it was not until he had been nearly drowned a year afterwards, in a violent storm at sea, that he repented of his evil ways, cut his hair short, and paid proper deference to the wishes of the clergy.

In France, the thunders of the Vatican with regard to long curly hair were hardly more respected than in England. Louis VII., however, was more obedient than his brother-king, and cropped himself as closely as a monk, to the great sorrow of all the gallants of his court. His queen, the gay, haughty, and pleasure-seeking Eleanor of Guienne, never admired him in this trim, and continually reproached him with imitating, not only the head-dress, but the asceticism of the monks. From this cause a coldness arose between them. The lady proving at last unfaithful to her shaven and indifferent lord, they were divorced, and the kings of France lost the rich provinces of Guienne and Poitou, which were her dowry. She soon after bestowed her hand and her possessions upon Henry Duke of Normandy, afterwards Henry II. of England, and thus gave the English sovereigns that strong footing in France which was for so many centuries the cause of such long and bloody wars between the nations.

When the Crusades had drawn all the smart young fellows into Palestine, the clergy did not find it so difficult to convince the staid burghers who remained in Europe, of the enormity of long hair. During the absence of Richard Cœur de Lion, his English subjects not only cut their hair close, but shaved their faces. William Fitz-osbert, or Long-beard, the great demagogue of that day, reintroduced among the people who claimed to be of Saxon origin the fashion of long hair. He did this with the view of making them as unlike as possible to the citizens and the Normans. He wore his own beard hanging down to his waist, from whence the name by which he is best known to posterity.

The Church never shewed itself so great an enemy to the beard as to long hair on the head. It generally allowed fashion to take its own course, both with regard to the chin and the upper lip. This fashion varied continually; for we find that, in little more than a century after the time of Richard I., when beards were short, that they had again become so long as to be mentioned in the famous epigram made by the Scots who visited London in 1327, when David, son of Robert Bruce, was married to Joan, the sister of King Edward. This epigram, which was stuck on the church-door of St. Peter Stangate, ran as follows :

> "Long beards heartlesse,
> Painted hoods witlesse,
> Gray coats gracelesse,
> Make England thriftlesse."

When the Emperor Charles V. ascended the throne of Spain he had no beard. It was not to be expected that the obsequious para-sites who always surround a monarch, could presume to look more virile than their master. Immediately all the courtiers appeared beardless, with the exception of such few grave old men as had out-grown the influence of fashion, and who had determined to die bearded as they had lived. Sober people in general saw this revolu-tion with sorrow and alarm, and thought that every manly virtue would be banished with the beard. It became at the time a common saying,—

> "Desde que no hay barba, no hay mas alma."
> We have no longer souls since we have lost our beards.

In France also the beard fell into disrepute after the death of Henry IV., from the mere reason that his successor was too young to have one. Some of the more immediate friends of the great Béarnais, and his minister Sully among the rest, refused to part with their beards, notwithstanding the jeers of the new generation.

Who does not remember the division of England into the two great parties of Roundheads and Cavaliers ? In those days every species of vice and iniquity was thought by the Puritans to lurk in the long curly tresses of the monarchists, while the latter imagined that their opponents were as destitute of wit, of wisdom, and of virtue, as they were of hair. A man's locks were the symbol of his creed, both in politics and religion. The more abundant the hair, the more scant the faith ; and the balder the head, the more sincere the piety.

But among all the instances of the interference of governments with men's hair, the most extraordinary, not only for its daring, but for its success, is that of Peter the Great, in 1705. By this time fashion had condemned the beard in every other country in Europe, and with a voice more potent than popes or emperors, had banished it from civilised society. But this only made the Russians cling more fondly to their ancient ornament, as a mark to distinguish them from foreigners, whom they hated. Peter, however, resolved that they should be shaven. If he had been a man deeply read in history, he might have hesitated before he attempted so despotic an attack upon

PETER THE GREAT.

the time-hallowed customs and prejudices of his countrymen ; but he was not. He did not know or consider the danger of the innovation ; he only listened to the promptings of his own indomitable will, and his fiat went forth, that not only the army, but all ranks of citizens, from the nobles to the serfs, should shave their beards. A certain time was given, that people might get over the first throes of their repugnance, after which every man who chose to retain his beard was to pay a tax of one hundred roubles. The priests and the serfs were put on a lower footing, and allowed to retain theirs upon payment of a copeck every time they passed the gate of a city. Great discontent existed in consequence, but the dreadful fate of the Strelitzes was too recent to be forgotten, and thousands who had the will had not the courage to revolt. As is well remarked by a writer in the *Encyclopædia Britannica*, they thought it wiser to cut off their beards than to run the risk of incensing a man who would make no scruple in cutting off their heads. Wiser, too, than the popes and bishops of a former age, he did not threaten them with eternal damnation, but made them pay in hard cash the penalty of their disobedience. For many years, a very considerable revenue was collected from this source. The collectors gave in receipt for its payment a small copper coin, struck expressly for the purpose, and called the "*borodováia*," or "the bearded." On one side it bore the figure of a nose, mouth, and moustaches, with a long bushy beard, surmounted by the words, "*Deuyee Vyeatee*," "money received;" the whole encircled by a wreath, and stamped with the black eagle of Russia. On the reverse, it bore the date of the year. Every man who chose to wear a beard was obliged to produce this receipt on his entry into a town. Those who were refractory, and refused to pay the tax, were thrown into prison.

Since that day, the rulers of modern Europe have endeavoured to persuade, rather than to force, in all matters pertaining to fashion. The Vatican troubles itself no more about beards or ringlets, and men may become hairy as bears, if such is their fancy, without fear of excommunication or deprivation of their political rights. Folly has taken a new start, and cultivates the moustache.

Even upon this point governments will not let men alone. Religion as yet has not meddled with it; but perhaps it will; and politics already influence it considerably. Before the revolution of 1830, neither the French nor Belgian citizens were remarkable for their moustaches; but after that event there was hardly a shopkeeper either in Paris or Brussels whose upper lip did not suddenly become hairy with real or mock moustaches. During a temporary triumph gained by the Dutch soldiers over the citizens of Louvain, in October 1830, it became a standing joke against the patriots, that they shaved their faces clean immediately; and the wits of the Dutch army asserted that they had gathered moustaches enough from the denuded lips of the Belgians to stuff mattresses for all the sick and wounded in their hospital.

The last folly of this kind is still more recent. In the German newspapers, of August 1838, appeared an ordonnance, signed by the king of Bavaria, forbidding civilians, on any pretence whatever, to wear moustaches, and commanding the police and other authorities to arrest, and cause to be shaved, the offending parties. "Strange to say," adds *Le Droit*, the journal from which this account is taken, "moustaches disappeared immediately, like leaves from the trees in autumn; everybody made haste to obey the royal order, and not one person was arrested."

The king of Bavaria, a rhymester of some celebrity, has taken a good many poetical licences in his time. His licence in this matter appears neither poetical nor reasonable. It is to be hoped that he will not take it into his royal head to make his subjects shave theirs ; nothing but that is wanting to complete their degradation.

BAYEAUX TAPESTRY.*

* The above engraving, shewing two soldiers of William the Conqueror's army, is taken from the celebrated Bayeux Tapestry.—See *ante*, p. 297

END OF VOL. I.

LEVEY, ROBSON, AND FRANKLYN, GREAT NEW STREET.

Breinigsville, PA USA
15 March 2011
257712BV00001B/30/P

CAMBRIDGE LIBRARY COLLECTION

Books of enduring scholarly value

Spiritualism and Esoteric Knowledge

Magic, superstition, the occult sciences and esoteric knowledge appear regularly in the history of ideas alongside more established academic disciplines such as philosophy, natural history and theology. Particularly fascinating are periods of rapid scientific advances such as the Renaissance or the nineteenth century which also see a burgeoning of interest in the paranormal among the educated elite. This series provides primary texts and secondary sources for social historians and cultural anthropologists working in these areas, and all who wish for a wider understanding of the diverse intellectual and spiritual movements that formed a backdrop to the academic and political achievements of their day. It ranges from works on Babylonian and Jewish magic in the ancient world, through studies of sixteenth-century topics such as Cornelius Agrippa and the rapid spread of Rosicrucianism, to nineteenth-century publications by Sir Walter Scott and Sir Arthur Conan Doyle. Subjects include astrology, mesmerism, spiritualism, theosophy, clairvoyance, and ghost-seeing, as described both by their adherents and by sceptics.

Memoirs of Extraordinary Popular Delusions

This book is a joy to read and remains relevant in the current era of financial boom and bust. Mackay examines animal magnetism, money-mania, tulip-mania, the history of hair and facial hair, haunted houses, and much more. Throughout history, the most extraordinary fashions and trends have been followed unthinkingly, and occasionally this crowd fever has overtaken not only a town but a whole country; in some cases much of western Europe was engulfed simultaneously. The ability of some manias to be so far-reaching, and for common sense and intelligence to abandon such large populations seems incredible, though the book is as thought-provoking now as it was when first published in 1852. Volume 2 examines the fervour of the crusades and of witch trials, both of which engulfed Europe at different times. Explored on a lighter note are haunted houses and a fashion for lady poisoners.

Memoirs of
Extraordinary
Popular Delusions

VOLUME 2

CHARLES MACKAY

CAMBRIDGE
UNIVERSITY PRESS

CAMBRIDGE UNIVERSITY PRESS

Cambridge, New York, Melbourne, Madrid, Cape Town, Singapore,
São Paolo, Delhi, Dubai, Tokyo, Mexico City

Published in the United States of America by Cambridge University Press, New York

www.cambridge.org
Information on this title: www.cambridge.org/9781108027656

© in this compilation Cambridge University Press 2010

This edition first published 1852
This digitally printed version 2010

ISBN 978-1-108-02765-6 Paperback

page 9.

POPE URBAN PREACHING THE CRUSADES.

MEMOIRS

OF

EXTRAORDINARY POPULAR DELUSIONS.

VOLUME II.

VIEW IN THE HARZ MOUNTAINS.

LONDON:

OFFICE OF THE NATIONAL ILLUSTRATED LIBRARY,

227 STRAND.

1852.

MEMOIRS

OF

EXTRAORDINARY POPULAR DELUSIONS

AND THE

𝕸𝖆𝖉𝖓𝖊𝖘𝖘 𝖔𝖋 𝕮𝖗𝖔𝖜𝖉𝖘.

~~✦~~

By CHARLES MACKAY, LL.D.

AUTHOR OF " EGERIA," "THE SALAMANDRINE," ETC.

ILLUSTRATED WITH NUMEROUS ENGRAVINGS.

> N'en déplaise à ces fous nommés sages de Grèce,
> En ce monde il n'est point de parfaite sagesse;
> Tous les hommes sont fous, et malgré tours leurs soins
> Ne diffèrent entre eux que du plus ou du moins.
> BOILEAU.

VOL. II.

SECOND EDITION.

LONDON:

OFFICE OF THE NATIONAL ILLUSTRATED LIBRARY,

227 STRAND.

1852.

LONDON:
PRINTED BY LEVEY, ROBSON, AND FRANKLYN,
Great New Street, Fetter Lane.

CONTENTS.

⁓⊶ↄ◝⊙⊙◜ↄ⊷⁓

LIST OF ENGRAVINGS IN VOL. II.

MEMOIRS

OF

EXTRAORDINARY POPULAR DELUSIONS.

THE CRUSADES.

> They heard, and up they sprung upon the wing
> Innumerable. As when the potent rod
> Of Amram's son, in Egypt's evil day,
> Waved round the coast, up call'd a pitchy cloud
> Of locusts, warping on the eastern wind
> That o'er the realm of impious Pharaoh hung
> Like night, and darken'd all the realm of Nile,
> So numberless were they.   *   *   *   *
> All in a moment through the gloom were seen
> Ten thousand banners rise into the air,
> With orient colours waving. With them rose
> A forest huge of spears ; and thronging helms
> Appear'd, and serried shields, in thick array,
> Of depth immeasurable.   *Paradise Lost.*

VERY age has its peculiar folly ; some scheme, project, or phantasy into which it plunges, spurred on either by the love of gain, the necessity of excitement, or the mere force of imitation. Failing in these, it has some madness, to which it is goaded by political or religious causes, or both combined. Every one of these causes influenced the Crusades, and conspired to render them the most extraordinary instance upon record of the extent to which popular enthusiasm can be carried. History in her solemn page informs us, that the Crusaders were but ignorant and savage men, that their motives were those of bigotry unmitigated, and that their pathway was one of blood and tears. Romance, on the other hand, dilates upon their piety and heroism, and portrays, in her most glowing and impassioned hues, their virtue and magnanimity, the imperishable honour they acquired for themselves, and the great services they rendered to Christianity. In the following pages we shall ransack the stores of both, to discover the true spirit that animated the motley multitude who took up arms in the service of the cross, leaving history to vouch for facts, but not disdaining the aid of contemporary poetry and romance, to throw light upon feelings, motives, and opinions.

In order to understand thoroughly the state of public feeling in Europe at the time when Peter the Hermit preached the holy war, it will be necessary to go back for many years anterior to that event. We must make acquaintance with the pilgrims of the eighth, ninth, and tenth centuries, and learn the tales they told of the dangers they had passed and the wonders they had seen. Pilgrimages to the Holy Land seem at first to have been undertaken by converted Jews, and by Christian devotees of lively imagination, pining with a natural curiosity to visit the scenes which of all others were most interesting in their eyes. The pious and the impious alike flocked to Jerusalem,— the one class to feast their sight on the scenes hallowed by the life and sufferings of their Lord, and the other, because it soon became a generally received opinion, that such a pilgrimage was sufficient to rub off the long score of sins, however atrocious. Another and very numerous class of pilgrims were the idle and roving, who visited Palestine then as the moderns visit Italy or Switzerland now, because it was the fashion, and because they might please their vanity by retailing, on their return, the adventures they had met with. But the really pious formed the great majority. Every year their numbers increased, until at last they became so numerous as to be called the " armies of the Lord." Full of enthusiasm, they set the dangers and difficulties of the way at defiance, and lingered with holy rapture on every scene described by the Evangelists. To them it was bliss indeed to drink the clear waters of the Jordan, or be baptised in the same stream where John had baptised the Saviour. They wandered with awe and pleasure in the purlieus of the Temple, on the solemn Mount of Olives, or the awful Calvary, where a God had bled for sinful men. To these pilgrims every object was precious. Relics were eagerly sought after ; flagons of water from Jordan, or panniers of mould from the hill of the Crucifixion, were brought home, and sold at extravagant prices to churches and monasteries. More apocryphal relics, such as the wood of the true cross, the tears of the Virgin Mary, the hems of her garments, the toe-nails and hair of the Apostles—even the tents that Paul had helped to manufacture—were exhibited for sale by the knavish in Palestine, and brought back to Europe "with wondrous cost and care." A grove of a hundred oaks would not have furnished all the wood sold in little morsels as remnants of the true cross; and the tears of Mary, if collected together, would have filled a cistern.

For upwards of two hundred years the pilgrims met with no impediment in Palestine. The enlightened Haroun Al Reschid, and his more immediate successors, encouraged the stream which brought so much wealth into Syria, and treated the wayfarers with the utmost courtesy. The race of Fatemite caliphs,—who, although in other respects as tolerant, were more distressed for money, or more unscrupulous in obtaining it, than their predecessors of the house of Abbas,—imposed a tax of a bezant for each pilgrim that entered Jerusalem. This was a serious hardship upon the poorer sort, who had begged their weary way across Europe, and arrived at the bourne of all their hopes without a coin. A great outcry was immediately raised, but still the tax was rigorously levied. The pilgrims unable to pay were compelled to remain at the gate of the holy city until some rich devotee arriving with his train, paid the tax and let them in. Robert of Normandy, father of William the Conqueror, who, in common with many other nobles of the highest rank, undertook the pilgrimage, found on his arrival scores of pilgrims at the gate, anxiously expecting his coming to pay the tax for them. Upon no occasion was such a boon refused.

The sums drawn from this source were a mine of wealth to the Moslem governors of Palestine, imposed as the tax had been at a time when pilgrimages had become more numerous than ever. A strange idea had taken possession of the popular mind at the close of the tenth and commencement of the eleventh century. It was universally believed that the end of the world was at hand; that the thousand years of the Apocalypse were near completion, and that Jesus Christ would descend upon Jerusalem to judge mankind. All Christendom was in commotion. A panic terror seized upon the weak, the credulous, and the guilty, who in those days formed more than nineteen-twentieths of the population. Forsaking their homes, kindred, and occupation, they crowded to Jerusalem to await the coming of the Lord, lightened, as they imagined, of a load of sin by their weary pilgrimage. To increase the panic, the stars were observed to fall from heaven, earthquakes to shake the land, and violent hurricanes to blow down the forests. All these, and more especially the meteoric phenomena, were looked upon as the forerunners of the approaching judgments. Not a meteor shot athwart the horizon that did not fill a district with alarm, and send away to Jerusalem a score of pilgrims, with staff in hand and wallet on their back, praying as they went for the remission of their sins. Men, women, and even children, trudged in droves to the holy city, in expectation of the day when the heavens would open, and the Son of God descend in his glory. This extraordinary delusion, while it augmented the numbers, increased also the hardships of the pilgrims. Beggars became so numerous on all the highways between the west of Europe and Constantinople, that the monks, the great almsgivers upon these occasions, would have brought starvation within sight of their own doors, if they had not economised their resources, and left the devotees to shift for themselves as they could. Hundreds of them were glad to subsist upon the berries that ripened by the road, who, before this great flux, might have shared the bread and flesh of the monasteries.

But this was not the greatest of their difficulties. On their arrival in Jerusalem they found that a sterner race had obtained possession of the Holy Land. The caliphs of Bagdad had been succeeded by the harsh Turks of the race of Seljook, who looked upon the pilgrims with contempt and aversion. The Turks of the eleventh century were more ferocious and less scrupulous than the Saracens of the tenth. They were annoyed at the immense number of pilgrims who overran the country, and still more so because they shewed no intention of quitting it. The hourly expectation of the last judgment kept them waiting ; and the Turks, apprehensive of being at last driven from the soil by the swarms that were still arriving, heaped up difficulties in their way. Persecution of every kind awaited them. They were plundered, and beaten with stripes, and kept in suspense for months at the gates of Jerusalem, unable to pay the golden bezant that was to procure them admission.

When the first epidemic terror of the day of judgment began to subside, a few pilgrims ventured to return to Europe, their hearts big with indignation at the insults they had suffered. Every where as they passed they related to a sympathising auditory the wrongs of Christendom. Strange to say, even these recitals increased the mania for pilgrimage. The greater the dangers of the way, the fairer chance that sins of deep dye would be atoned for. Difficulty and suffering only heightened the merit, and fresh hordes issued from every town and village, to win favour in the sight of heaven by a visit to the holy sepulchre. Thus did things continue during the whole of the eleventh century.

The train that was to explode so fearfully was now laid, and there wanted but the hand to apply the torch. At last the man appeared upon the scene. Like all who have ever achieved so great an end, Peter the Hermit was exactly suited to the age; neither behind it nor in advance of it; but acute enough to penetrate its mystery ere it was discovered by any other. Enthusiastic, chivalrous, bigoted, and, if not insane, not far removed from insanity, he was the very prototype of the time. True enthusiasm is always persevering and always eloquent, and these two qualities were united in no common degree in the person of this extraordinary preacher. He was a monk of Amiens, and ere he assumed the hood had served as a soldier. He is represented as having been ill-favoured and low in stature, but with an eye of surpassing brightness and intelligence. Having been seized with the mania of the age, he visited Jerusalem, and remained there till his blood boiled to see the cruel persecution heaped upon the devotees. On his return home he shook the world by the eloquent story of their wrongs.

Before entering into any further details of the marvellous results of his preaching, it will be advisable to cast a glance at the state of the mind of Europe, that we may understand all the better the causes of his success. First of all, there was the priesthood, which, exercising as it did the most conspicuous influence upon the fortunes of society, claims the largest share of attention. Religion was the ruling idea of that day, and the only civiliser capable of taming such wolves as then constituted the flock of the faithful. The clergy were all in all; and though they kept the popular mind in the most slavish subjection with regard to religious matters, they furnished it with the means of defence against all other oppression except their own. In the ecclesiastical ranks were concentrated all the true piety, all the learning, all the wisdom of the time; and, as a natural consequence, a great portion of power, which their very wisdom perpetually incited them to extend. The people knew nothing of kings and nobles, except in the way of injuries inflicted. The first ruled for, or more properly speaking against, the barons, and the barons only existed to brave the power of the kings, or to trample with their iron heels upon the neck of prostrate democracy. The latter had no friend but the clergy, and these, though they necessarily instilled the superstition from which they themselves were not exempt, yet taught the cheering doctrine that all men were equal in the sight of heaven. Thus, while Feudalism told them they had no rights in this world, Religion told them they had every right in the next. With this consolation they were for the time content, for political ideas had as yet taken no root. When the clergy, for other reasons, recommended the Crusade, the people joined in it with enthusiasm. The subject of Palestine filled all minds; the pilgrims' tales of two centuries warmed every imagination; and when their friends, their guides, and their instructors preached a war so much in accordance with their own prejudices and modes of thinking, the enthusiasm rose into a frenzy.

But while religion inspired the masses, another agent was at work upon the nobility. These were fierce and lawless; tainted with every vice, endowed with no virtue, and redeemed by one good quality alone, that of courage. The only religion they felt was the religion of fear. That and their overboiling turbulence alike combined to guide them to the Holy Land. Most of them had sins enough to answer for. They lived with their hand against every man, and with no law but their own passions. They set at defiance the secular power of the clergy; but their hearts quailed at the awful denunciations of the pulpit with regard to the life to come. War was the business and the delight of their existence; and when they were promised remission of all their sins upon the easy condition of following their favourite bent, it is not to be wondered at that they rushed with enthusiasm to the onslaught, and became as zealous in the service of the cross as the great majority of the people, who were swayed by more purely religious motives. Fanaticism and the love of battle alike impelled them to the war, while the kings and princes of Europe had still another motive for encouraging their zeal. Policy opened their eyes to the great advantages which would accrue to themselves by the absence of so many restless, intriguing, and bloodthirsty men, whose insolence it required more than the small power of royalty to restrain within due bounds. Thus every motive was favourable to the Crusades. Every class of society was alike incited to join or encourage the war: kings and the clergy by policy, the nobles by turbulence and the love of dominion, and the people by religious zeal and the concentrated enthusiasm of two centuries, skilfully directed by their only instructors.

It was in Palestine itself that Peter the Hermit first conceived the grand idea of rousing the powers of Christendom to rescue the Christians of the East from the thraldom of the Mussulmans, and the sepulchre of Jesus from the rude hands of the infidel. The subject engrossed his whole mind. Even in the visions of the night he was full of it. One dream made such an impression upon him, that he devoutly believed the Saviour of the world himself appeared before him, and promised him aid and protection in his holy undertaking. If his zeal had ever wavered before, this was sufficient to fix it for ever.

Peter, after he had performed all the penances and duties of his pilgrimage, demanded an interview with Simeon, the Patriarch of the Greek Church at Jerusalem. Though the latter was a heretic in Peter's eyes, yet he was still a Christian, and felt as acutely as himself for the persecutions heaped by the Turks upon the followers of Jesus. The good prelate entered fully into his views, and, at his suggestion, wrote letters to the pope, and to the most influential monarchs of Christendom, detailing the sorrows of the faithful, and urging them to take up arms in their defence. Peter was not a laggard in the work. Taking an affectionate farewell of the Patriarch, he returned in all haste to Italy. Pope Urban II. occupied the apostolic chair. It was at that time far from being an easy seat. His predecessor Gregory had bequeathed him a host of disputes with the Emperor Henry IV. of Germany, and he had converted Philip I. of France into an enemy by his strenuous opposition to an adulterous connexion formed by that monarch. So many dangers encompassed him, that the Vatican was no secure abode, and he had taken refuge in Apulia, under the protection of the renowned Robert Guiscard. Thither Peter appears to have followed him, though in what spot their meeting took place is not stated with any precision by ancient chroniclers or modern historians. Urban received him most kindly ; read, with tears in his eyes, the epistle from the Patriarch Simeon, and listened to the eloquent story of the Hermit with an attention which shewed how deeply he sympathised with the woes of the Christian Church. Enthusiasm is contagious ; and the pope appears to have caught it instantly from one whose zeal was so unbounded. Giving the Hermit full powers, he sent him abroad to preach the holy war to all the nations and potentates of Christendom. The Hermit preached, and countless thousands answered to his call. France, Germany, and Italy started at his voice, and prepared for the deliverance of Zion. One of the early historians of the Crusade, who was himself an eyewitness of the rapture of Europe,* describes the personal appearance of the Hermit at this time. He says, that there appeared to be something of divine in every thing which he said or did. The people so highly reverenced him, that they plucked hairs from the mane of his mule that they might keep them as relics. While preaching he wore in general a woollen tunic, with a dark-coloured mantle, which fell down to his heels. His arms and feet were bare ; and he ate neither flesh nor bread, supporting himself chiefly upon fish and wine. "He set out," says the chronicler, "from whence I know not; but we saw him passing through the towns and villages, preaching every where, and the people surrounding him in crowds, loading him with offerings, and celebrating his sanctity with such great praises, that I

Guibert de Nogent.

never remember to have seen such honours bestowed upon any one.
Thus he went on, untired, inflexible, and full of devotion, communicating his own madness to his hearers, until Europe was stirred from
its very depths.

While the Hermit was appealing with such signal success to the
people, the pope appealed with as much success to those who were to
become the chiefs and leaders of the expedition. His first step was to
call a council at Placentia, in the autumn of the year 1095. Here, in
the assembly of the clergy, the pope debated the grand scheme, and
gave audience to emissaries who had been sent from Constantinople
by the Emperor of the East, to detail the progress made by the Turks
in their design of establishing themselves in Europe. The clergy
were of course unanimous in support of the Crusade ; and the council
separated, each individual member of it being empowered to preach it
to his people.

But Italy could not be expected to furnish all the aid required;
and the pope crossed the Alps to inspire the fierce and powerful
nobility and chivalrous population of Gaul. His boldness in entering
the territory, and placing himself in the power of his foe King Philip
of France, is not the least surprising feature of his mission. Some
have imagined that cool policy alone actuated him ; while others
assert that it was mere zeal, as warm and as blind as that of Peter the
Hermit. The latter opinion seems to be the true one. Society did
not calculate the consequences of what it was doing. Every man
seemed to act from impulse only ; and the pope, in throwing himself
into the heart of France, acted as much from impulse as the thousands who responded to his call. A council was eventually summoned
to meet him at Clermont, in Auvergne, to consider the state of the
Church, reform abuses, and above all, make preparations for the
war. It was in the midst of an extremely cold winter, and the
ground was covered with snow. During seven days the council sat
with closed doors, while immense crowds from all parts of France
flocked into the town, in expectation that the pope himself would
address the people. All the towns and villages for miles around were
filled with the multitude ; even the fields were encumbered with
people, who, unable to procure lodging, pitched their tents under the
trees and by the way-side. All the neighbourhood presented the
appearance of a vast camp.

During the seven days' deliberation, a sentence of excommunication was passed upon King Philip for adultery with Bertrade de
Montfort, Countess of Anjou, and for disobedience to the supreme
authority of the apostolic see. This bold step impressed the people
with reverence for so stern a Church, which in the discharge of its

duty shewed itself no respecter of persons. Their love and their fear were alike increased, and they were prepared to listen with more intense devotion to the preaching of so righteous and inflexible a pastor. The great square before the cathedral church of Clermont

THE CATHEDRAL OF CLERMONT.

became every instant more densely crowded as the hour drew nigh when the pope was to address the populace. Issuing from the church in his full canonicals, surrounded by his cardinals and bishops in all the splendour of Romish ecclesiastical costume, the pope stood before the populace on a high scaffolding erected for the occasion, and covered with scarlet cloth. A brilliant array of bishops and cardinals surrounded him; and among them, humbler in rank, but more important in the world's eye, the Hermit Peter, dressed in his simple and austere habiliments. Historians differ as to whether or not Peter addressed the crowd, but as all agree that he was present, it seems reasonable to suppose that he spoke. But it was the oration of the pope that was most important. As he lifted up his hands to ensure attention, every voice immediately became still. He began by detailing the miseries endured by their brethren in the Holy Land; how the plains of Palestine were desolated by the outrageous heathen, who with the sword and the firebrand carried wailing into the dwellings and flames into the possessions of the faithful; how Christian wives and daughters were defiled by pagan lust; how the altars of the true God were desecrated, and the relics of the saints trodden under foot. "You," continued the eloquent pontiff (and Urban II. was one of the most eloquent men of the day), "you, who hear me, and who have received the true faith, and been endowed by God with power, and strength, and greatness of soul,—whose ancestors have been the prop of Christendom, and whose kings have put a barrier against the progress of the infidel,—I call upon you to wipe off these impurities from the face of the earth, and lift your oppressed fellow-Christians from the depths into which they have been trampled. The sepulchre of Christ is possessed by the heathen, the sacred places dishonoured by their vileness. Oh, brave knights and faithful people! offspring of invincible fathers! ye will not degenerate from your ancient renown. Ye will not be restrained from embarking in this great cause by the tender ties of wife or little ones, but will remember the words of the Saviour of the world himself, ' Whosoever loves father and mother more than me is not worthy of me. Whosoever shall abandon for my name's sake his house, or his brethren, or his sisters, or his father, or his mother, or his wife, or his children, or his lands, shall receive a hundredfold, and shall inherit eternal life.'"

The warmth of the pontiff communicated itself to the crowd, and the enthusiasm of the people broke out several times ere he concluded his address. He went on to portray, not only the spiritual but the temporal advantages that would accrue to those who took up arms in the service of the cross. Palestine was, he said, a land flowing with milk and honey, and precious in the sight of God, as the scene of the grand events which had saved mankind. That land, he promised, should be divided among them. Moreover, they should have full pardon for all their offences, either against God or man. "Go, then," he added, "in expiation of your sins; and go assured, that after this world shall have passed away, imperishable glory shall be yours in the world which is to come." The enthusiasm was no longer to be restrained, and loud shouts interrupted the speaker ; the people exclaiming as if with one voice, " *Dieu le veult ! Dieu le veult !*" With great presence of mind Urban took advantage of the outburst, and as soon as silence was obtained, continued : "Dear brethren, to-day is shewn forth in you that which the Lord has said by his Evangelist, ' When two or three are gathered together in my name, there will I be in the midst of them to bless them.' If the Lord God had not been in your souls, you would not all have pronounced the same words ; or rather God himself pronounced them by your lips, for it was he that put them in your hearts. Be they, then, your war-cry in the combat, for those words came forth from God. Let the army of the Lord, when it rushes upon his enemies, shout but that one cry, ' *Dieu le veult ! Dieu le veult !*' Let whoever is inclined to devote himself to this holy cause make it a solemn engagement, and bear the cross of the Lord either on his breast or his brow till he set out ; and let him who is ready to begin his march place the holy emblem on his shoulders, in memory of that precept of our Saviour, ' He who does not take up his cross and follow me is not worthy of me.'"

The news of this council spread to the remotest parts of Europe in an incredibly short space of time. Long before the fleetest horseman could have brought the intelligence, it was known by the people in distant provinces ; a fact which was considered as nothing less than supernatural. But the subject was in every body's mouth, and the minds of men were prepared for the result. The enthusiastic merely asserted what they wished, and the event tallied with their prediction. This was, however, quite enough in those days for a miracle, and as a miracle every one regarded it.

For several months after the Council of Clermont, France and Germany presented a singular spectacle. The pious, the fanatic, the needy, the dissolute, the young and the old, even women and children, and the halt and lame, enrolled themselves by hundreds. In every village the clergy were busied in keeping up the excitement, promising eternal rewards to those who assumed the red cross, and fulminating the most awful denunciations against all the worldly-minded who refused or even hesitated. Every debtor who joined the Crusade was freed by the papal edict from the claims of his creditors ; outlaws of every grade were made equal with the honest upon the same conditions. The property of those who went was placed under the protection of the Church, and St. Paul and St. Peter themselves were believed to descend from their high abode, to watch over the chattels of the absent pilgrims. Signs and portents were seen in the air, to increase the fervour of the multitude. An aurora-borealis of unusual brilliancy appeared, and thousands of the Crusaders came out to gaze upon it, prostrating themselves upon the earth in adoration. It was thought to be a sure prognostic of the interposition of the Most High, and a representation of his armies fighting with and overthrowing the infidels. Reports of wonders were every where rife. A monk had seen two gigantic warriors on horseback, the one representing a Christian and the other a Turk, fighting in the sky with flaming swords, the Christian of course overcoming the Paynim. Myriads of stars were said to have fallen from heaven, each representing the fall of a pagan foe. It was believed at the same time that the Emperor Charlemagne would rise from the grave, and lead on to victory the embattled armies of the Lord. A singular feature of the popular madness was the enthusiasm of the women. Every where they encouraged their lovers and husbands to forsake all things for the holy war. Many of them burned the sign of the cross upon their breasts and arms, and coloured the wound with a red dye, as a lasting memorial of their zeal. Others, still more zealous, impressed the mark by the same means upon the tender limbs of young children and infants at the breast.

Guibert de Nogent tells of a monk who made a large incision upon his forehead in the form of a cross, which he coloured with some powerful ingredient, telling the people that an angel had done it when he was asleep. This monk appears to have been more of a rogue than a fool, for he contrived to fare more sumptuously than any of his brother pilgrims, upon the strength of his sanctity. The Crusaders every where gave him presents of food and money, and he became quite fat ere he arrived at Jerusalem, notwithstanding the fatigues of the way. If he had acknowledged in the first place that he had made the wound himself, he would not have been thought more holy than his fellows; but the story of the angel was a clincher.

All those who had property of any description rushed to the mart to change it into hard cash. Lands and houses could be had for a quarter of their value, while arms and accoutrements of war rose in the same proportion. Corn, which had been excessively dear in anticipation of a year of scarcity, suddenly became plentiful; and such was the diminution in the value of provisions, that seven sheep were sold for five *deniers*.* The nobles mortgaged their estates for mere trifles to Jews and unbelievers, or conferred charters of immunity upon the towns and communes within their fiefs, for sums which, a few years previously, they would have rejected with disdain. The farmer endeavoured to sell his plough, and the artisan his tools, to purchase a sword for the deliverance of Jerusalem. Women disposed of their

* Guibert de Nogent.

trinkets for the same purpose. During the spring and summer of this year (1096) the roads teemed with Crusaders, all hastening to the towns and villages appointed as the rendezvous of the district. Some were on horseback, some in carts, and some came down the rivers in boats and rafts, bringing their wives and children, all eager to go to Jerusalem. Very few knew where Jerusalem was. Some thought it fifty thousand miles away, and others imagined that it was but a month's journey ; while at sight of every town or castle the children exclaimed, " Is that Jerusalem ? Is that the city ? "* Parties of knights and nobles might be seen travelling eastward, and amusing themselves as they went with the knightly diversion of hawking, to lighten the fatigues of the way.

Guibert de Nogent, who did not write from hearsay, but from actual observation, says the enthusiasm was so contagious, that when any one heard the orders of the pontiff, he went instantly to solicit his neighbours and friends to join with him in " the way of God," for so they called the proposed expedition. The counts palatine were full of the desire to undertake the journey, and all the inferior knights were animated with the same zeal. Even the poor caught the flame so ardently, that no one paused to think of the inadequacy of his means, or to consider whether he ought to yield up his farm, his vineyard, or his fields. Each one set about selling his property at as low a price as if he had been held in some horrible captivity, and sought to pay his ransom without loss of time. Those who had not determined upon the journey joked and laughed at those who were thus disposing of their goods at such ruinous prices, prophesying that the expedition would be miserable and their return worse. But they held this language only for a day ; the next they were suddenly seized with the same frenzy as the rest. Those who had been loudest in their jeers gave up all their property for a few crowns, and set out with those they had so laughed at a few hours before. In most cases the laugh was turned against them ; for when it became known that a man was hesitating, his more zealous neighbours sent him a present of a knitting-needle or a distaff, to shew their contempt of him. There was no resisting this ; so that the fear of ridicule contributed its fair contingent to the armies of the Lord.

Another effect of the Crusade was, the religious obedience with which it inspired the people and the nobility for that singular institution " The Truce of God." At the commencement of the eleventh century, the clergy of France, sympathising for the woes of the people, but unable to diminish them, by repressing the rapacity and insolence of the feudal chiefs, endeavoured to promote universal good-will by

* Guibert de Nogent.

the promulgation of the famous "Peace of God." All who conformed to it bound themselves by oath not to take revenge for any injury, not to enjoy the fruits of property usurped from others, nor to use deadly weapons ; in reward of which they would receive remission of all their sins. However benevolent the intention of this "Peace," it led to nothing but perjury, and violence reigned as uncontrolled as before. In the year 1041, another attempt was made to soften the angry passions of the semi-barbarous chiefs, and the "Truce of God" was solemnly proclaimed. The *truce* lasted from the Wednesday evening to the Monday morning of every week, in which interval it was strictly forbidden to recur to violence on any pretext, or to seek revenge for any injury. It was impossible to civilise men by these means. Few even promised to become peaceable for so unconscionable a period as five days a week ; or if they did, they made ample amends on the two days left open to them. The truce was afterwards shortened from the Saturday evening to the Monday morning ; but little or no diminution of violence and bloodshed was the consequence. At the Council of Clermont, Urban II. again solemnly proclaimed the truce. So strong was the religious feeling, that every one hastened to obey. All minor passions disappeared before the grand passion of crusading. The feudal chief ceased to oppress, the robber to plunder, the people to complain ; but one idea was in all hearts, and there seemed to be no room for any other.

The encampments of these heterogeneous multitudes offered a singular aspect. Those vassals who ranged themselves under the banners of their lord erected tents around his castle ; while those who undertook the war on their own account constructed booths and huts in the neighbourhood of the towns or villages, preparatory to their joining some popular leader of the expedition. The meadows of France were covered with tents. As the belligerents were to have remission of all their sins on their arrival in Palestine, hundreds of them gave themselves up to the most unbounded licentiousness. The courtesan, with the red cross upon her shoulders, plied her shameless trade with sensual pilgrims without scruple on either side ; the lover of good cheer gave loose reign to his appetite, and drunkenness and debauchery flourished. Their zeal in the service of the Lord was to wipe out all faults and follies, and they had the same surety of salvation as the rigid anchorite. This reasoning had charms for the ignorant, and the sounds of lewd revelry and the voice of prayer rose at the same instant from the camp.

It is now time to speak of the leaders of the expedition. Great multitudes ranged themselves under the command of Peter the Hermit, whom, as the originator, they considered the most appropriate leader of the war. Others joined the banner of a bold adventurer, whom history has dignified with no other name than that of Gautier sans Avoir, or Walter the Pennyless, but who is represented as having been of noble family, and well skilled in the art of war. A third multitude from Germany flocked around the standard of a monk named Gottschalk, of whom nothing is known except that he was a fanatic of the deepest dye. All these bands, which together are said to have amounted to three hundred thousand men, women, and children, were composed of the vilest rascality of Europe. Without discipline, principle, or true courage, they rushed through the nations like a pestilence, spreading terror and death wherever they went. The first multitude that set forth was led by Walter the Pennyless early in the spring of 1096, within a very few months after the Council of Clermont. Each man of that irregular host aspired to be his own master. Like their nominal leader, each was poor to penury, and trusted for subsistence on his journey to the chances of the road. Rolling through Germany like a tide, they entered Hungary, where, at first, they were received with some degree of kindness by the people. The latter had not yet caught sufficient of the fire of enthusiasm to join the Crusade themselves, but were willing enough to forward the cause by aiding those embarked in it. Unfortunately this good understanding did not last long. The swarm were not contented with food for their necessities, but craved for luxuries also. They attacked and plundered the dwellings of the country people, and thought nothing of murder where resistance was offered. On their arrival before Semlin, the outraged Hungarians collected in large numbers, and, attacking the rear of the crusading host, slew a great many of the stragglers, and, taking away their arms and crosses, affixed them as trophies to the walls of the city. Walter appears to have been in no mood or condition to make reprisals; for his army, destructive as a plague of locusts when plunder urged them on, were useless against any regular attack from a determined enemy. Their rear continued to be thus harassed by the wrathful Hungarians until they were fairly out of their territory. On his entrance into Bulgaria, Walter met with no better fate. The cities and towns refused to let him pass; the villages denied him provisions; and the citizens and country people uniting, slaughtered his followers by hundreds. The progress of the army was more like a retreat than an advance; but as it was impossible to stand still, Walter continued his course till he arrived at Constantinople with a force which famine and the sword had diminished to one-third of its original number.

The greater multitude, led by the enthusiastic Hermit, followed close upon his heels, with a bulky train of baggage, and women and children sufficient to form a host of themselves. If it were possible to find a rabble more vile than the army of Walter the Pennyless, it was that led by Peter the Hermit. Being better provided with means, they were not reduced to the necessity of pillage in their progress through Hungary; and had they taken any other route than that which led through Semlin, might perhaps have traversed the country without molestation. On their arrival before that city, their fury was raised at seeing the arms and red crosses of their predecessors hanging as trophies over the gates. Their pent-up ferocity exploded at the sight. The city was tumultuously attacked, and the besiegers entering, not by dint of bravery, but of superior numbers, it was given up to all the horrors which follow when victory, brutality, and licentiousness are linked together. Every evil passion was allowed to revel with impunity, and revenge, lust, and avarice,—each had its hundreds of victims in unhappy Semlin. Any maniac can kindle a conflagration, but it may require many wise men to put it out. Peter the Hermit had blown the popular fury into a flame, but to cool it again was beyond his power. His followers rioted unrestrained, until the fear of retaliation warned them to desist. When the king of Hungary was informed of the disasters of Semlin, he marched with a sufficient force to chastise the Hermit, who, at the news, broke up his camp and retreated towards the Morava, a broad and rapid stream that joins the Danube a few miles to the eastward of Belgrade. Here a party of indignant Bulgarians awaited him, and so harassed him, as to make the passage of the river a task both of difficulty and danger. Great numbers of his infatuated followers perished in the waters, and many fell under the swords of the Bulgarians. The ancient chronicles do not mention the amount of the Hermit's loss at this passage, but represent it in general terms as very great.

At Nissa, the Duke of Bulgaria fortified himself, in fear of an assault; but Peter, having learned a little wisdom from experience, thought it best to avoid hostilities. He passed three nights in quietness under the walls, and the duke, not wishing to exasperate unnecessarily so fierce and rapacious a host, allowed the townspeople to supply them with provisions. Peter took his departure peaceably on the following morning; but some German vagabonds, falling behind the main body of the army, set fire to the mills and house of a Bulgarian, with whom, it appears, they had had some dispute on the previous evening. The citizens of Nissa, who had throughout mistrusted the Crusaders, and were prepared for the worst, sallied out immediately, and took signal vengeance. The spoilers were cut to pieces, and the townspeople pursuing the Hermit, captured all the women and children who had lagged in the rear, and a great quantity of baggage. Peter hereupon turned round and marched back to Nissa, to demand explanation of the Duke of Bulgaria. The latter fairly stated the provocation given, and the Hermit could urge nothing in palliation of so gross an outrage. A negotiation was entered into, which promised to be successful, and the Bulgarians were about to deliver up the women and children, when a party of undisciplined Crusaders, acting solely upon their own suggestion, endeavoured to scale the walls and seize upon the town. Peter in vain exerted his authority; the confusion became general, and after a short but desperate battle, the Crusaders threw down their arms, and fled in all directions. Their vast host was completely routed, the slaughter being so great among them, as to be counted, not by hundreds, but by thousands.

It is said that the Hermit fled from this fatal field to a forest a few miles from Nissa, abandoned by every human creature. It would be curious to know whether, after so dire a reverse,

> "His enpierced breast
> Sharp sorrow did in thousand pieces rive,"

or whether his fiery zeal still rose superior to calamity, and pictured the eventual triumph of his cause. He, so lately the leader of a hundred thousand men, was now a solitary skulker in the forests, liable at every instant to be discovered by some pursuing Bulgarian, and cut off in mid career. Chance at last brought him within sight of an eminence, where two or three of his bravest knights had collected five hundred of the stragglers. These gladly received the Hermit, and a consultation having taken place, it was resolved to gather together the scattered remnants of the army. Fires were lighted on the hill, and scouts sent out in all directions for the fugitives. Horns were sounded at intervals, to make known that friends were near; and before nightfall the Hermit saw himself at the head of seven thousand men. During the succeeding day, he was joined by twenty thousand more, and with this miserable remnant of his force, he pursued his route towards Constantinople. The bones of the rest mouldered in the forests of Bulgaria.

On his arrival at Constantinople, where he found Walter the Pennyless awaiting him, he was hospitably received by the Emperor Alexius. It might have been expected that the sad reverses they had undergone would have taught his followers common prudence; but, unhappily for them, their turbulence and love of plunder was not to be restrained. Although they were surrounded by friends, by whom all their wants were liberally supplied, they could not refrain from rapine. In vain the Hermit exhorted them to tranquillity; he possessed no more power over them, in subduing their passions, than

the obscurest soldier of the host.   They set fire to several public
buildings in Constantinople out of pure mischief, and stripped the
lead from the roofs of the churches, which they afterwards sold for
old metal in the purlieus of the city.   From this time may be dated
the aversion which the Emperor Alexius entertained for the Crusaders,
and which was afterwards manifested in all his actions, even when he
had to deal with the chivalrous and more honourable armies which
arrived after the Hermit.   He seems to have imagined that the Turks
themselves were enemies less formidable to his power than these out-
pourings of the refuse of Europe : he soon found a pretext to hurry
them into Asia Minor.   Peter crossed the Bosphorus with Walter;
but the excesses of his followers were such, that, despairing of accom-
plishing any good end by remaining at their head, he left them to
themselves, and returned to Constantinople, on the pretext of making
arrangements with the government of Alexius for a proper supply of
provisions.   The Crusaders, forgetting that they were in the enemy's
country, and that union, above all things, was desirable, gave themselves up to dissensions.   Violent disputes arose between the Lom-
bards and Normans commanded by Walter the Pennyless, and the
Franks and Germans led out by Peter.   The latter separated themselves from the former, and choosing for their leader one Reinaldo,
or Reinhold, marched forward, and took possession of the fortress of
Exorogorgon.   The Sultan Solimaun was on the alert, with a superior
force.   A party of Crusaders, which had been detached from the fort,
and stationed at a little distance as an ambuscade, were surprised
and cut to pieces, and Exorogorgon invested on all sides.   The siege
was protracted for eight days, during which the Christians suffered
the most acute agony from the want of water.   It is hard to say how
long the hope of succour or the energy of despair would have enabled
them to hold out : their treacherous leader cut the matter short by
renouncing the Christian faith, and delivering up the fort into the
hands of the sultan.   He was followed by two or three of his officers ;
all the rest, refusing to become Mahometans, were ruthlessly put to
the sword.   Thus perished the last wretched remnant of the vast
multitude which had traversed Europe with Peter the Hermit.

　　Walter the Pennyless and his multitude met as miserable a fate.
On the news of the disasters of Exorogorgon, they demanded to be
led instantly against the Turks.   Walter, who only wanted good soldiers to have made a good general, was cooler of head, and saw all
the dangers of such a step.   His force was wholly insufficient to make
any decisive movement in a country where the enemy was so much
superior, and where, in case of defeat, he had no secure position to
fall back upon ; and he therefore expressed his opinion against ad-

vancing until the arrival of reinforcements. This prudent counsel found no favour: the army loudly expressed their dissatisfaction at their chief, and prepared to march forward without him. Upon this, the brave Walter put himself at their head, and rushed to destruction. Proceeding towards Nice, the modern Isnik, he was inter-

ISNIK.

cepted by the army of the sultan: a fierce battle ensued, in which the Turks made fearful havoc; out of twenty-five thousand Christians, twenty-two thousand were slain, and among them Gautier himself, who fell pierced by seven mortal wounds. The remaining three thousand retreated upon Civitot, where they entrenched themselves.

Disgusted as was Peter the Hermit at the excesses of the multitude, who, at his call, had forsaken Europe, his heart was moved with grief and pity at their misfortunes. All his former zeal revived: casting himself at the feet of the Emperor Alexius, he implored him, with tears in his eyes, to send relief to the few survivors at Civitot. The emperor consented, and a force was sent, which arrived just in time to save them from destruction. The Turks had beleaguered the place, and the Crusaders were reduced to the last extremity. Negotiations were entered into, and the last three thousand were conducted in safety to Constantinople. Alexius had suffered too much by their former excesses to be very desirous of retaining them in his capital; he therefore caused them all to be disarmed, and, furnishing each with a sum of money, he sent them back to their own country.

While these events were taking place, fresh hordes were issuing from the woods and wilds of Germany, all bent for the Holy Land. They were commanded by a fanatical priest, named Gottschalk, who, like Gautier and Peter the Hermit, took his way through Hungary. History is extremely meagre in her details of the conduct and fate of this host, which amounted to at least one hundred thousand men. Robbery and murder seem to have journeyed with them, and the poor Hungarians were rendered almost desperate by their numbers and rapacity. Karloman, the king of the country, made a bold effort to get rid of them; for the resentment of his people had arrived at such a height, that nothing short of the total extermination of the Crusaders would satisfy them. Gottschalk had to pay the penalty, not only for the ravages of his own bands, but for those of the swarms that had come before him. He and his army were induced, by some means or other, to lay down their arms: the savage Hungarians, seeing them thus defenceless, set upon them, and slaughtered them in great numbers. How many escaped their arrows we are not informed; but not one of them reached Palestine.

Other swarms, under nameless leaders, issued from Germany and France, more brutal and more frantic than any that had preceded them. Their fanaticism surpassed by far the wildest freaks of the followers of the Hermit. In bands, varying in numbers from one to five thousand, they traversed the country in all directions, bent upon plunder and massacre. They wore the symbol of the Crusade upon their shoulders, but inveighed against the folly of proceeding to the Holy Land to destroy the Turks, while they left behind them so many Jews, the still more inveterate enemies of Christ. They swore fierce vengeance against this unhappy race, and murdered all the Hebrews they could lay their hands on, first subjecting them to the most horrible mutilation. According to the testimony of Albert Aquensis, they lived among each other in the most shameless profligacy, and their vice was only exceeded by their superstition. Whenever they were in search of Jews, they were preceded by a goose and goat, which they believed to be holy, and animated with divine power to discover the retreats of the unbelievers. In Germany alone they slaughtered more than a thousand Jews, notwithstanding all the efforts of the clergy to save them. So dreadful was the cruelty of their tormentors, that great numbers of Jews committed self-destruction to avoid falling into their hands.

Again it fell to the lot of the Hungarians to deliver Europe from these pests. When there were no more Jews to murder, the bands collected in one body, and took the old route to the Holy Land, a route stained with the blood of three hundred thousand who had gone before, and destined also to receive theirs. The number of these swarms has never been stated; but so many of them perished in Hungary, that contemporary writers, despairing of giving any adequate idea of their multitudes, state that the fields were actually heaped with their corpses, and that for miles in its course the waters of the Danube were dyed with their blood. It was at Mersburg, on the Danube, that the greatest slaughter took place,—a slaughter so great as to amount almost to extermination. The Hungarians for a while disputed the passage of the river, but the Crusaders forced their way across, and attacking the city with the blind courage of madness, succeeded in making a breach in the walls. At this moment of victory an unaccountable fear came over them. Throwing down their arms, they fled panic-stricken, no one knew why, and no one knew whither. The Hungarians followed, sword in hand, and cut them down without remorse, and in such numbers, that the stream of the Danube is said to have been choked up by their unburied bodies.

This was the worst paroxysm of the madness of Europe; and this passed, her chivalry stepped upon the scene. Men of cool heads, mature plans, and invincible courage stood forward to lead and direct the grand movement of Europe upon Asia. It is upon these men that romance has lavished her most admiring epithets, leaving to the condemnation of history the vileness and brutality of those who went before. Of these leaders the most distinguished were Godfrey of Bouillon duke of Lorraine, and Raymond count of Toulouse. Four other chiefs of the royal blood of Europe also assumed the cross, and led each his army to the Holy Land; Hugh count of Vermandois, brother of the king of France; Robert duke of Normandy, the elder brother of William Rufus; Robert count of Flanders, and Bohemund prince of Tarentum, eldest son of the celebrated Robert Guiscard. These men were all tinged with the fanaticism of the age, but none of them acted entirely from religious motives. They were neither utterly reckless like Gautier sans Avoir, crazy like Peter the Hermit, nor brutal like Gottschalk the Monk, but possessed each of these qualities in a milder form; their valour being tempered by caution, their religious zeal by worldly views, and their ferocity by the spirit of chivalry. They saw whither led the torrent of the public will; and it being neither their wish nor their interest to stem it, they allowed themselves to be carried with it, in the hope that it would lead them at last to a haven of aggrandisement. Around them congregated many minor chiefs, the flower of the nobility of France and Italy, with some few from Germany, England, and Spain. It was wisely conjectured that armies so numerous would find a difficulty in procuring provisions if they all journeyed by the same road. They therefore resolved to separate; Godfrey de Bouillon proceeding through Hungary and Bulgaria,

GODFREY DE BOUILLON.

the Count of Toulouse through Lombardy and Dalmatia, and the other leaders through Apulia to Constantinople, where the several divisions were to reunite. The forces under these leaders have been variously estimated. The Princess Anna Comnena talks of them as having been as numerous as the sands on the sea-shore, or the stars in the firmament. Fulcher of Chartres is more satisfactory, and exaggerates less magnificently, when he states, that all the divisions, when they had sat down before Nice in Bithynia, amounted to one hundred thousand horsemen, and six hundred thousand men on foot, exclusive of the priests, women, and children. Gibbon is of opinion that this amount is exaggerated ; but thinks the actual numbers did not fall very far short of the calculation. The Princess Anna afterwards gives the number of those under Godfrey of Bouillon as eighty thousand foot and horse; and supposing that each of the other chiefs led an army as numerous, the total would be near half a million. This must be over rather than under the mark, as the army of Godfrey of Bouillon was confessedly the largest when it set out, and suffered less by the way than any other.

The Count of Vermandois was the first who set foot on the Grecian territory. On his arrival at Durazzo he was received with every mark of respect and courtesy by the agents of the emperor, and his followers were abundantly supplied with provisions. Suddenly, however, and without cause assigned, the count was arrested by order of the Emperor Alexius, and conveyed a close prisoner to Constantinople. Various motives have been assigned by different authors as having induced the emperor to this treacherous and imprudent proceeding. By every writer he has been condemned for so flagrant a breach of hospitality and justice. The most probable reason for his conduct appears to be that suggested by Guibert of Nogent, who states that Alexius, fearful of the designs of the Crusaders upon his throne, resorted to this extremity in order afterwards to force the count to take the oath of allegiance to him, as the price of his liberation. The example of a prince so eminent as the brother of the king of France, would, he thought, be readily followed by the other chiefs of the Crusade. In the result he was wofully disappointed, as every man deserves to be who commits positive evil that doubtful good may ensue. But this line of policy accorded well enough with the narrowmindedness of the emperor, who, in the enervating atmosphere of his highly civilised and luxurious court, dreaded the influx of the hardy and ambitious warriors of the West, and strove to nibble away by unworthy means the power which he had not energy enough to confront. If danger to himself had existed from the residence of the chiefs in his dominions, he might easily have averted it, by the simple means of placing himself at the head of the European movement, and directing its energies to their avowed object, the conquest of the Holy Land. But the emperor, instead of being, as he might have been, the lord and leader of the Crusades, which he had himself aided in no inconsiderable degree to suscitate by his embassies to the Pope, became the slave of men who hated and despised him. No doubt the barbarous excesses of the followers of Gautier and Peter the Hermit made him look upon the whole body of them with disgust, but it was the disgust of a little mind, which is glad of any excuse to palliate or justify its own irresolution and love of ease.

Godfrey of Bouillon traversed Hungary in the most quiet and orderly manner. On his arrival at Mersburg he found the country strewed with the mangled corpses of the Jew-killers, and demanded of the king of Hungary for what reason his people had set upon them. The latter detailed the atrocities they had committed, and made it so evident to Godfrey that the Hungarians had only acted in self-defence, that the high-minded leader declared himself satisfied, and passed on without giving or receiving molestation. On his arrival at Philippopoli he was informed for the first time of the imprisonment of the count of Vermandois. He immediately sent messengers to the emperor, demanding the count's release, and threatening, in case of refusal, to lay waste the country with fire and sword. After waiting a day at Philippopoli, he marched on to Adrianople, where he was met by his messengers returning with the emperor's refusal. Godfrey, the bravest and most determined of the leaders of the Crusade, was not a man to swerve from his word, and the country was given up to pillage. Alexius here committed another blunder. No sooner did he learn from dire experience that the Crusader was not an utterer of idle threats, than he consented to the release of the prisoner. As he had been unjust in the first instance, he became cowardly in the second, and taught his enemies (for so the Crusaders were forced to consider themselves) a lesson which they took care to remember to his cost, that they could hope nothing from his sense of justice, but every thing from his fears. Godfrey remained encamped for several weeks in the neighbourhood of Constantinople, to the great annoyance of Alexius, who sought by every means to extort from him the homage he had extorted from Vermandois. Sometimes he acted as if at open and declared war with the Crusaders, and sent his troops against them. Sometimes he refused to supply them with food, and ordered the markets to be shut against them, while at other times he was all for peace and good-will, and sent costly presents to Godfrey. The honest, straightforward Crusader was at last so wearied by his false kindness, and so pestered by his attacks, that, allowing his indignation to get the better of his judgment, he gave up the country around Constantinople to be plundered by his soldiers. For six days the flames of the farm-houses around struck terror into the heart of Alexius; but, as Godfrey anticipated, they convinced him of his error. Fearing that Constantinople itself would be the next object of attack, he sent messengers to demand an interview with Godfrey, offering at the same time to leave his son as a hostage for his good faith. Godfrey agreed to meet him; and, whether to put an end to these use-less dissensions, or for some other unexplained reason, he rendered homage to Alexius as his liege lord. He was thereupon loaded with honours, and, according to a singular custom of that age, underwent the ceremony of the "adoption of honour" as son to the emperor. Godfrey and his brother Baudouin de Bouillon conducted themselves with proper courtesy on this occasion, but were not able to restrain the insolence of their followers, who did not conceive themselves bound to keep any terms with a man so insincere as he had shewn himself. One barbarous chieftain, Count Robert of Paris, carried his insolence so far as to seat himself upon the throne; an insult which Alexius merely resented with a sneer, but which did not induce him to look with less mistrust upon the hordes that were still advancing.

It is impossible, notwithstanding his treachery, to avoid feeling some compassion for the emperor, whose life at this time was rendered one long scene of misery by the presumption of the Crusaders, and his not altogether groundless fears of the evil they might inflict upon him, should any untoward circumstance force the current of their ambition to the conquest of his empire. His daughter Anna Comnena feelingly deplores his state of life at this time, and a learned German,* in a recent work, describes it, on the authority of the princess, in the following manner:

"To avoid all occasion of offence to the Crusaders, Alexius complied with all their whims and their (on many occasions) unreasonable demands, even at the expense of great bodily exertion, at a time when he was suffering severely under the gout, which eventually brought him to his grave. No Crusader who desired an interview with him was refused access; he listened with the utmost patience to the long-winded harangues which their loquacity or zeal continually wearied him with; he endured, without expressing any impatience, the unbecoming and haughty language which they permitted themselves to employ towards him, and severely reprimanded his officers when they undertook to defend the dignity of the imperial station from these rude assaults, for he trembled with apprehension at the slightest disputes, lest they might become the occasion of greater evil. Though the counts often appeared before him with trains altogether unsuitable to their dignity and to his—sometimes with an entire troop, which completely filled the royal apartment—the emperor held his peace. He listened to them at all hours; he often seated himself on his throne at day-break to attend to their wishes and requests, and the evening twilight saw him still in the same place. Very frequently he could not snatch time to refresh himself with meat and drink.

* M. Wilken's *Geschichte der Kreuzzüge.*

During many nights he could not obtain any repose, and was obliged to indulge in an unrefreshing sleep upon his throne, with his head resting on his hands. Even this slumber was continually disturbed by the appearance and harangues of some newly-arrived rude knights. When all the courtiers, wearied out by the efforts of the day and by night-watching, could no longer keep themselves on their feet, and sank down exhausted—some upon benches and others on the floor— Alexius still rallied his strength to listen with seeming attention to the wearisome chatter of the Latins, that they might have no occasion or pretext for discontent. In such a state of fear and anxiety, how could Alexius comport himself with dignity and like an emperor?"

Alexius, however, had himself to blame, in a great measure, for the indignities he suffered: owing to his insincerity, the Crusaders mistrusted him so much, that it became at last a common saying, that the Turks and Saracens were not such inveterate foes to the Western or Latin Christians as the Emperor Alexius and the Greeks.[*] It would be needless in this sketch, which does not profess to be so much a history of the Crusades, as of the madness of Europe, from which they sprang, to detail the various acts of bribery and intimidation, cajolery and hostility, by which Alexius contrived to make each of the leaders in succession, as they arrived, take the oath of allegiance to him as their suzerain. One way or another he exacted from each the barren homage on which he had set his heart, and they were then allowed to proceed into Asia Minor. One only, Raymond de St. Gilles count of Toulouse, obstinately refused the homage.

Their residence in Constantinople was productive of no good to the armies of the cross. Bickerings and contentions on the one hand, and the influence of a depraved and luxurious court on the other, destroyed the elasticity of their spirits, and cooled the first ardour of their enthusiasm. At one time the army of the Count of Toulouse was on the point of disbanding itself; and, had not their leader energetically removed them across the Bosphorus, this would have been the result. Once in Asia, their spirits in some degree revived, and the presence of danger and difficulty nerved them to the work they had undertaken. The first operation of the war was the siege of Nice, to gain possession of which all their efforts were directed.

Godfrey of Bouillon and the Count of Vermandois were joined under its walls by each host in succession as it left Constantinople. Among the celebrated Crusaders who fought at this siege we find, besides the leaders already mentioned, the brave and generous Tancred, whose name and fame have been immortalised in the

* Wilken.

Gerusalemme Liberata, the valorous Bishop of Puy, Baldwin, afterwards king of Jerusalem, and Peter the Hermit, now an almost solitary soldier, shorn of all the power and influence he had formerly possessed. Kilij Aslaun the sultan of Roum and chief of the Seljukian Turks, whose deeds, surrounded by the false halo of romance, are familiar to the readers of Tasso, under the name of Soliman, marched to defend this city, but was defeated after several obstinate engagements, in which the Christians shewed a degree of heroism that quite astonished him. The Turkish chief had expected to find a wild undisciplined multitude, like that under Peter the Hermit, without leaders capable of enforcing obedience ; instead of which, he found the most experienced leaders of the age at the head of armies that had just fanaticism enough to be ferocious, but not enough to render them ungovernable. In these engagements, many hundreds fell on both sides ; and on both sides the most revolting barbarity was practised : the Crusaders cut off the heads of the fallen Mussulmans, and sent them in panniers to Constantinople, as trophies of their victory. After the temporary defeat of Kilij Aslaun, the siege of Nice was carried on with redoubled vigour. The Turks defended themselves with the greatest obstinacy, and discharged showers of poisoned arrows upon the Crusaders. When any unfortunate wretch was killed under the walls, they let down iron hooks from above, and drew the body up, which, after stripping and mutilating, they threw back again at the besiegers. The latter were well supplied with provisions, and for six-and-thirty days the siege continued without any relaxation of the efforts on either side. Many tales are told of the almost superhuman heroism of the Christian leaders—how one man put a thousand to flight; and how the arrows of the faithful never missed their mark. One anecdote of Godfrey of Bouillon, related by Albert of Aix, is worth recording, not only as shewing the high opinion entertained of his valour, but as shewing the contagious credulity of the armies—a credulity which has often led them to the very verge of defeat, as it incited them to victory. One Turk, of gigantic stature, took his station day by day on the battlements of Nice, and, bearing an enormous bow, committed great havoc among the Christian host. Not a shaft he sped but bore death upon its point ; and although the Crusaders aimed repeatedly at his breast, and he stood in the most exposed position, their arrows fell harmless at his feet. He seemed to be invulnerable to attack ; and a report was soon spread abroad, that he was no other than the Arch Fiend himself, and that mortal hand could not prevail against him. Godfrey of Bouillon, who had no faith in the supernatural character of the Mussulman, determined, if possible, to put an end to the dismay which was rapidly paralysing the exertions of his best soldiers. Taking a huge cross-bow, he stood forward in front of the army, to try the steadiness of his hand against the much-dreaded archer: the shaft was aimed directly at his heart, and took fatal effect. The Moslem fell amid the groans of the besieged and the shouts of *Deus adjuva! Deus adjuva!* the war-cry of the besiegers.

At last the Crusaders imagined that they had overcome all obstacles, and were preparing to take possession of the city, when, to their great astonishment, they saw the flag of the Emperor Alexius flying from the battlements. An emissary of the emperor, named Faticius or Tatin, had contrived to gain admission, with a body of Greek troops, at a point which the Crusaders had left unprotected, and had persuaded the Turks to surrender to him rather than to the crusading forces. The greatest indignation prevailed in the army when this stratagem was discovered, and the soldiers were, with the utmost difficulty, prevented from renewing the attack and besieging the Greek emissary.

The army, however, continued its march, and, by some means or other, was broken into two divisions; some historians say accidentally,* while others affirm by mutual consent, and for the convenience of obtaining provisions on the way.† The one division was composed of the forces under Bohemund, Tancred, and the Duke of Normandy; while the other, which took a route at some distance on the right, was commanded by Godfrey of Bouillon and the other chiefs. The Sultan of Roum, who, after his losses at Nice, had been silently making great efforts to crush the Crusaders at one blow, collected in a very short time all the multitudinous tribes that owed him allegiance, and with an army which, according to a moderate calculation, amounted to two hundred thousand men, chiefly cavalry, he fell upon the first division of the Christian host in the valley of Dorylæum. It was early in the morning of the 1st of July 1097, when the Crusaders saw the first companies of the Turkish horsemen pouring down upon them from the hills. Bohemund had hardly time to set himself in order, and transport his sick and helpless to the rear, when the overwhelming force of the Orientals was upon him. The Christian army, composed principally of men on foot, gave way on all sides, and the hoofs of the Turkish steeds, and the poisoned arrows of their bowmen, mowed them down by hundreds. After having lost the flower of their chivalry, the Christians retreated upon their baggage, when a dreadful slaughter took place. Neither

* Fulcher of Chartres; Guibert de Nogent; Vital.
† William of Tyre; Mills; Wilken, &c.

women nor children, nor the sick, were spared. Just as they were reduced to the last extremity, Godfrey of Bouillon and the Count of Toulouse made their appearance on the field, and turned the tide of battle. After an obstinate engagement the Turks fled, and their rich camp fell into the hands of the enemy. The loss of the Crusaders amounted to about four thousand men, with several chiefs of renown, among whom were Count Robert of Paris and William the brother of Tancred. The loss of the Turks, which did not exceed this number, taught them to pursue a different mode of warfare. The sultan was far from being defeated. With his still gigantic army, he laid waste all the country on either side of the Crusaders. The latter, who were unaware of the tactics of the enemy, found plenty of provisions in the Turkish camp; but so far from economising these resources, they gave themselves up for several days to the most unbounded extravagance. They soon paid dearly for their heedlessness. In the ravaged country of Phrygia, through which they advanced towards Antiochetta, they suffered dreadfully for want of food for themselves and pasture for their cattle. Above them was a scorching sun, almost sufficient of itself to dry up the freshness of the land, a task which the firebrands of the sultan had but too surely effected, and water was not to be had after the first day of their march. The pilgrims died at the rate of five hundred a day. The horses of the knights perished on the road, and the baggage which they had aided to transport was either placed upon dogs, sheep, and swine, or abandoned altogether. In some of the calamities that afterwards befel them, the Christians gave themselves up to the most reckless profligacy; but upon this occasion, the dissensions which prosperity had engendered were all forgotten. Religion, often disregarded, arose in the stern presence of misfortune, and cheered them as they died by the promises of eternal felicity.

At length they reached Antiochetta, where they found water in abundance, and pastures for their expiring cattle. Plenty once more surrounded them, and here they pitched their tents. Untaught by the bitter experience of famine, they again gave themselves up to luxury and waste.

On the 18th of October they sat down before the strong city of Antioch, the siege of which, and the events to which it gave rise, are among the most extraordinary incidents of the Crusade. The city, which is situated on an eminence, and washed by the river Orontes, is naturally a very strong position, and the Turkish garrison were well supplied with provisions to endure a long siege. In this respect the Christians were also fortunate, but unluckily for themselves, unwise. Their force amounted to three hundred thousand fighting men; and we are informed by Raymond d'Argilles, that they had so much provision, that they threw away the greater part of every animal they killed, being so dainty, that they would only eat particular parts of the beast. So insane was their extravagance, that in less than ten days famine began to stare them in the face. After making a fruitless attempt to gain possession of the city by a *coup de main*, they, starving themselves, sat down to starve out the enemy. But with want came a cooling of enthusiasm. The chiefs began to grow weary of the expedition. Baldwin had previously detached himself from the main body of the army, and, proceeding to Edessa, had intrigued himself into the supreme power in that little principality. The other leaders were animated with less zeal than heretofore. Stephen of Chartres and Hugh of Vermandois began to waver, unable to endure the privations which their own folly and profusion had brought upon them. Even Peter the Hermit became sick at heart ere all was over. When the famine had become so urgent that they were reduced to eat human flesh in the extremity of their hunger, Bohemund and Robert of Flanders set forth on an expedition to procure a supply. They were in a slight degree successful; but the relief they brought was not economised, and in two days they were as destitute as before. Faticius, the Greek commander and representative of Alexius, deserted with his division under pretence of seeking for food, and his example was followed by various bodies of Crusaders.

Misery was rife among those who remained, and they strove to alleviate it by a diligent attention to signs and omens. These, with extraordinary visions seen by the enthusiastic, alternately cheered and depressed them according as they foretold the triumph or pictured the reverses of the cross. At one time a violent hurricane arose, levelling great trees with the ground, and blowing down the tents of the Christian leaders. At another time an earthquake shook the camp, and was thought to prognosticate some great impending evil to the cause of Christendom. But a comet which appeared shortly afterwards raised them from the despondency into which they had fallen; their lively imaginations making it assume the form of a flaming cross leading them on to victory. Famine was not the least of the evils they endured. Unwholesome food, and the impure air from the neighbouring marshes, engendered pestilential diseases, which carried them off more rapidly than the arrows of the enemy. A thousand of them died in a day, and it became at last a matter of extreme difficulty to afford them burial. To add to their misery, each man grew suspicious of his neighbour; for the camp was infested by Turkish spies, who conveyed daily to the besieged intelligence of the movements and distresses of the enemy. With a ferocity, engendered by despair, Bohemund caused two spies, whom he had detected, to be roasted alive in presence of the army, and within sight of the battlements of Antioch. But even this example failed to reduce their numbers, and the Turks continued to be as well informed as the Christians themselves of all that was passing in the camp.

The news of the arrival of a reinforcement of soldiers from Europe, with an abundant stock of provisions, came to cheer them when reduced to the last extremity. The welcome succour landed at St. Simeon, the port of Antioch, and about six miles from that city. Thitherwards the famishing Crusaders proceeded in tumultuous bands, followed by Bohemund and the Count of Toulouse, with strong detachments of their retainers and vassals, to escort the supplies in safety to the camp. The garrison of Antioch, forewarned of this arrival, was on the alert, and a corps of Turkish archers was despatched to lie in ambuscade among the mountains and intercept their return. Bohemund, laden with provisions, was encountered in the rocky passes by the Turkish host. Great numbers of his followers were slain, and he himself had just time to escape to the camp with the news of his defeat. Godfrey of Bouillon, the Duke of Normandy, and the other leaders had heard the rumour of this battle, and were at that instant preparing for the rescue. The army was immediately in motion, animated both by zeal and by hunger, and marched so rapidly as to intercept the victorious Turks before they had time to reach Antioch with their spoil. A fierce battle ensued, which lasted from noon till the going down of the sun. The Christians gained and maintained the advantage, each man fighting as if upon himself alone had depended the fortune of the day. Hundreds of Turks perished in the Orontes, and more than two thousand were left dead upon the field of battle. All the provision was recaptured and brought in safety to the camp, whither the Crusaders returned singing *Alleluia!* or shouting *Deus adjuva! Deus adjuva!*

This relief lasted for some days, and, had it been duly economised, would have lasted much longer; but the chiefs had no authority, and were unable to exercise any control over its distribution. Famine again approached with rapid strides, and Stephen count of Blois, not liking the prospect, withdrew from the camp with four thousand of his retainers, and established himself at Alexandretta. The moral influence of this desertion was highly prejudicial upon those who remained; and Bohemund, the most impatient and ambitious of the chiefs, foresaw that, unless speedily checked, it would lead to the utter failure of the expedition. It was necessary to act decisively; the army murmured at the length of the siege, and the sultan was collecting his forces to crush them. Against the efforts of the Crusaders

Antioch might have held out for months; but treason within effected that which courage without might have striven for in vain.

Baghasihan, the Turkish prince or emir of Antioch, had under his command an Armenian of the name of Phirouz, whom he had entrusted with the defence of a tower on that part of the city wall which overlooked the passes of the mountains. Bohemund, by means of a spy who had embraced the Christian religion, and to whom he had given his own name at baptism, kept up a daily communication with this captain, and made him the most magnificent promises of reward, if he would deliver up his post to the Crusaders. Whether the proposal was first made by Bohemund or by the Armenian is uncertain, but that a good understanding soon existed between them is undoubted ; and a night was fixed for the execution of the project. Bohemund communicated the scheme to Godfrey and the Count of Toulouse, with the stipulation that, if the city were won, he, as the soul of the enterprise, should enjoy the dignity of Prince of Antioch. The other leaders hesitated : ambition and jealousy prompted them to refuse their aid in furthering the views of the intriguer. More mature consideration decided them to acquiesce, and seven hundred of the bravest knights were chosen for the expedition, the real object of which, for fear of spies, was kept a profound secret from the rest of the army. When all was ready, a report was promulgated that the seven hundred were intended to form an ambuscade for a division of the sultan's army, which was stated to be approaching.

Every thing favoured the treacherous project of the Armenian captain, who, on his solitary watch-tower, received due intimation of the approach of the Crusaders. The night was dark and stormy; not a star was visible above, and the wind howled so furiously as to overpower all other sounds : the rain fell in torrents, and the watchers on the towers adjoining to that of Phirouz could not hear the tramp of the armed knights for the wind, nor see them for the obscurity of the night and the dismalness of the weather. When within shot of the walls, Bohemund sent forward an interpreter to confer with the Armenian. The latter urged them to make haste, and seize the favourable interval, as armed men, with lighted torches, patrolled the battlements every half hour, and at that instant they had just passed. The chiefs were instantly at the foot of the wall : Phirouz let down a rope ; Bohemund attached it to the end of a ladder of hides, which was then raised by the Armenian, and held while the knights mounted. A momentary fear came over the spirits of the adventurers, and every one hesitated. At last Bohemund,* encouraged by

* Vide William of Tyre.

Phirouz from above, ascended a few steps on the ladder, and was followed by Godfrey, Count Robert of Flanders, and a number of other knights. As they advanced, others pressed forward, until their

SIEGE OF ANTIOCH.

weight became too great for the ladder, which, breaking, precipitated about a dozen of them to the ground, where they fell one upon the other, making a great clatter with their heavy coats of mail. For a moment they thought that all was lost; but the wind made so loud a howling as it swept in fierce gusts through the mountain gorges, and the Orontes, swollen by the rain, rushed so noisily along, that the guards heard nothing. The ladder was easily repaired, and the knights ascended two at a time, and reached the platform in safety. When sixty of them had thus ascended, the torch of the coming patrol was seen to gleam at the angle of the wall. Hiding themselves behind a buttress, they awaited his coming in breathless silence. As soon as he arrived at arm's length, he was suddenly seized, and, before he could open his lips to raise an alarm, the silence of death closed them up for ever. They next descended rapidly the spiral staircase of the tower, and opening the portal, admitted the whole of their companions. Raymond of Toulouse, who, cognisant of the whole plan, had been left behind with the main body of the army, heard at this instant the signal horn, which announced that an entry had been effected, and, leading on his legions, the town was attacked from within and without.

Imagination cannot conceive a scene more dreadful than that presented by the devoted city of Antioch on that night of horror. The Crusaders fought with a blind fury, which fanaticism and suffering alike incited. Men, women, and children were indiscriminately slaughtered, till the streets ran with blood. Darkness increased the destruction, for when morning dawned the Crusaders found themselves with their swords at the breasts of their fellow-soldiers, whom they had mistaken for foes. The Turkish commander fled, first to the citadel, and that becoming insecure, to the mountains, whither he was pursued and slain, and his grey head brought back to Antioch as a trophy. At daylight the massacre ceased, and the Crusaders gave themselves up to plunder. They found gold, and jewels, and silks, and velvets in abundance, but of provisions, which were of more importance to them, they found but little of any kind. Corn was excessively scarce, and they discovered to their sorrow that in this respect the besieged had been but little better off than the besiegers.

Before they had time to instal themselves in their new position, and take the necessary measures for procuring a supply, the city was invested by the Turks. The sultan of Persia had raised an immense army, which he entrusted to the command of Kerbogha, the emir of Mosul, with instructions to sweep the Christian locusts from the face of the land. The emir effected a junction with Kilij Aslaun, and the two armies surrounded the city. Discouragement took complete possession of the Christian host, and numbers of them contrived to elude the vigilance of the besiegers, and escape to Count Stephen of Blois at Alexandretta, to whom they related the most exaggerated tales of the misery they had endured, and the utter hopelessness of continuing the war. Stephen forthwith broke up his camp and retreated towards Constantinople. On his way he was met by the Emperor Alexius, at the head of a considerable force. hastening to take possession of the conquests made by the Christians in Asia. As soon as he heard of their woful plight, he turned back, and proceeded with the Count of Blois to Constantinople, leaving the remnant of the Crusaders to shift for themselves.

The news of this defection increased the discouragement at Antioch. All the useless horses of the army had been slain and eaten, and dogs, cats, and rats were sold at enormous prices. Even vermin were becoming scarce. With increasing famine came a pestilence, so that in a short time but sixty thousand remained of the three hundred thousand that had originally invested Antioch. But this bitter extremity, while it annihilated the energy of the host, only served to knit the leaders more firmly together ; and Bohemund, Godfrey, and Tancred swore never to desert the cause as long as life lasted. The former strove in vain to reanimate the courage of his followers. They were weary and sick at heart, and his menaces and promises were alike thrown away. Some of them had shut themselves up in the houses, and refused to come forth. Bohemund, to drive them to their duty, set fire to the whole quarter, and many of them perished in the flames, while the rest of the army looked on with the utmost indifference. Bohemund, animated himself by a worldly spirit, did not know the true character of the Crusaders, nor understand the religious madness which had brought them in such shoals from Europe. A priest, more clear-sighted, devised a scheme which restored all their confidence, and inspired them with a courage so wonderful as to make the poor sixty thousand emaciated, sick, and starving zealots put to flight the well-fed and six times as numerous legions of the Sultan of Persia.

This priest, a native of Provence, was named Peter Barthelemy, and whether he were a knave or an enthusiast, or both ; a principal, or a tool in the hands of others, will ever remain a matter of doubt. Certain it is, however, that he was the means of raising the siege of Antioch, and causing the eventual triumph of the armies of the cross. When the strength of the Crusaders was completely broken by their sufferings, and hope had fled from every bosom, Peter came to Count Raymond of Toulouse, and demanded an interview on matters of serious moment. He was immediately admitted. He said that, some weeks previously, at the time the Christians were besieging Antioch, he was reposing alone in his tent, when he was startled by the shock of the earthquake which had so alarmed the whole host. Through violent terror of the shock he could only ejaculate, God help me! when turning round he saw two men standing before him, whom he at once recognised by the halo of glory around them as beings of another world. One of them appeared to be an aged man, with reddish hair sprinkled with grey, black eyes, and a long flowing grey beard. The other was younger, larger, and handsomer, and had something more divine in his aspect. The elderly man alone spoke, and informed him that he was the holy apostle St. Andrew, and desired him to seek out the Count Raymond, the Bishop of Puy, and Raymond of Altapulto, and ask them why the bishop did not exhort the people, and sign them with the cross which he bore. The apostle then took him, naked in his shirt as he was, and transported him through the air into the heart of the city of Antioch, where he led him into the church of St. Peter, at that time a Saracen mosque. The apostle made him stop by the pillar close to the steps by which they ascend on the south side to the altar, where hung two lamps, which gave out a light brighter than that of the noonday sun ; the younger man, whom he did not at that time know, standing afar off, near the steps of the altar. The apostle then descended into the ground and brought up a lance, which he gave into his hand, telling him that it was the very lance that had opened the side whence had flowed the salvation of the world. With tears of joy he held the holy lance, and implored the apostle to allow him to take it away and deliver it into the hands of Count Raymond. The apostle refused, and buried the lance again in the ground, commanding him, when the city was won from the infidels, to go with twelve chosen men, and dig it up again in the same place. The apostle then transported him back to his tent, and the two vanished from his sight. He had neglected, he said, to deliver this message, afraid that his wonderful tale would not obtain credence from men of such high rank. After some days he again saw the holy vision, as he was going out of the camp to look for food. This time the divine eyes of the younger looked reproachfully upon him. He implored the apostle to choose some one else more fitted for the mission, but the apostle refused, and smote him with a disorder of the eyes, as a punishment for his disobedience. With an obstinacy unaccountable even to himself, he had still delayed. A third time the apostle and his companion had appeared to him, as he was in a tent with his master William at St. Simeon. On that occasion St. Andrew told him to bear his command to the Count of Toulouse not to bathe in the waters of the Jordan when he came to it, but to cross over in a boat, clad in a shirt and breeches of linen, which he should sprinkle with the sacred waters of the river. These clothes he was afterwards to preserve along with the holy lance. His master William, although he could not see the saint, distinctly heard the voice giving orders to that effect. Again he neglected to execute the commission, and again the saints appeared to him, when he was at the port of Mamistra, about to sail for Cyprus, and St. Andrew threatened him with eternal perdition if he refused longer. Upon this he made up his mind to divulge all that had been revealed to him.

The Count of Toulouse, who, in all probability, concocted this tale with the priest, appeared struck with the recital, and sent immediately for the Bishop of Puy and Raymond of Altapulto. The bishop at once expressed his disbelief of the whole story, and refused to have any thing to do in the matter. The Count of Toulouse, on the contrary, saw abundant motives, if not for believing, for pretending to believe; and, in the end, he so impressed upon the mind of the bishop the advantage that might be derived from it, in working up the popular mind to its former excitement, that the latter reluctantly agreed to make search in due form for the holy weapon. The day after the morrow was fixed upon for the ceremony; and, in the mean time, Peter was consigned to the care of Raymond, the count's chaplain, in order that no profane curiosity might have an opportunity of cross-examining him, and putting him to a nonplus.

Twelve devout men were forthwith chosen for the undertaking, among whom were the Count of Toulouse and his chaplain. They began digging at sunrise, and continued unwearied till near sunset, without finding the lance; they might have dug till this day with no better success, had not Peter himself sprung into the pit, praying to God to bring the lance to light, for the strengthening and victory of his people. Those who hide know where to find; and so it was with Peter, for both he and the lance found their way into the hole at the same time. On a sudden he and Raymond the chaplain beheld its point in the earth, and Raymond, drawing it forth, kissed it with tears of joy, in sight of the multitude which had assembled in the church. It was immediately enveloped in a rich purple cloth, already prepared to receive it, and exhibited in this state to the faithful, who made the building resound with their shouts of gladness.

THE HOLY LANCE

Peter had another vision the same night, and became from that day forth " dreamer of dreams" in general to the army. He stated on the following day, that the Apostle Andrew and "the youth with the divine aspect" appeared to him again, and directed that the Count of Toulouse, as a reward for his persevering piety, should carry the Holy Lance at the head of the army, and that the day on which it was found should be observed as a solemn festival throughout Christendom. St. Andrew shewed him at the same time the holes in the feet and hands of his benign companion ; and he became convinced that he stood in the awful presence of THE REDEEMER.

Peter gained so much credit by his visions that dreaming became contagious. Other monks beside himself were visited by the saints, who promised victory to the host if it would valiantly hold out to the last, and crowns of eternal glory to those who fell in the fight. Two deserters, wearied of the fatigues and privations of the war, who had stealthily left the camp, suddenly returned, and seeking Bohemund, told him that they had been met by two apparitions, who, with great anger, had commanded them to return. The one of them said, that he recognised his brother, who had been killed in battle some months before, and that he had a halo of glory around his head. The other, still more hardy, asserted that the apparition which had spoken to him was the Saviour himself, who had promised eternal happiness as his reward if he returned to his duty, but the pains of eternal fire if he rejected the cross. No one thought of disbelieving these men. The courage of the army immediately revived ; despondency gave way to hope ; every arm grew strong again, and the pangs of hunger were for a time disregarded. The enthusiasm which had led them from Europe burned forth once more as brightly as ever, and they demanded, with loud cries, to be led against the enemy. The leaders were not unwilling. In a battle lay their only chance of salvation ; and although Godfrey, Bohemund, and Tancred received the story of the lance with much suspicion, they were too wise to throw discredit upon an imposture which bade fair to open the gates of victory.

Peter the Hermit was previously sent to the camp of Kerbogha to propose that the quarrel between the two religions should be decided by a chosen number of the bravest soldiers of each army. Kerbogha turned from him with a look of contempt, and said he could agree to no proposals from a set of such miserable beggars and robbers. With this uncourteous answer Peter returned to Antioch. Preparations were immediately commenced for an attack upon the enemy : the latter continued to be perfectly well informed of all the proceedings of the Christian camp. The citadel of Antioch, which remained in their possession, overlooked the town, and the commander of the fortress could distinctly see all that was passing within. On the morning of the 28th of June, 1098, a black flag, hoisted from its highest tower, announced to the besieging army that the Christians were about to sally forth.

The Moslem leaders knew the sad inroads that famine and disease had made upon the numbers of the foe ; they knew that not above two hundred of the knights had horses to ride upon, and that the foot soldiers were sick and emaciated ; but they did not know the almost incredible valour which superstition had infused into their hearts. The story of the lance they treated with the most supreme contempt, and, secure of an easy victory, they gave themselves no trouble in preparing for the onslaught. It is related that Kerbogha was playing a game at chess, when the black flag on the citadel gave warning of the enemy's approach, and that, with true oriental coolness, he insisted upon finishing the game ere he bestowed any of his attention upon a foe so unworthy. The defeat of his advanced post of two thousand men aroused him from his apathy.

The Crusaders, after this first victory, advanced joyfully towards the mountains, hoping to draw the Turks to a place where their cavalry would be unable to manœuvre. Their spirits were light and their courage high, as, led on by the Duke of Normandy, Count Robert of Flanders, and Hugh of Vermandois, they came within sight of the splendid camp of the enemy. Godfrey of Bouillon and Adhemar Bishop of Puy followed immediately after these leaders, the latter clad in complete armour, and bearing the Holy Lance within sight of the whole army : Bohemund and Tancred brought up the rear.

Kerbogha, aware at last that his enemy was not so despicable, took vigorous measures to remedy his mistake, and, preparing himself to meet the Christians in front, he despatched the Sultan Soliman of Roum to attack them in the rear. To conceal this movement, he set fire to the dried weeds and grass with which the ground was covered, and Soliman, taking a wide circuit with his cavalry, succeeded, under cover of the smoke, in making good his position in the rear. The battle raged furiously in front ; the arrows of the Turks fell thick as hail, and their well-trained squadrons trod the Crusaders under their hoofs like stubble. Still the affray was doubtful ; for the Christians had the advantage of the ground, and were rapidly gaining upon the enemy, when the overwhelming forces of Soliman arrived in the rear. Godfrey and Tancred flew to the rescue of Bohemund, spreading dismay in the Turkish ranks by their fierce impetuosity. The Bishop of Puy was left almost alone with the Provencals to oppose the legions commanded by Kerbogha in person ; but the presence of the Holy Lance made a hero of the meanest soldier in his train. Still, however, the numbers of the enemy seemed inter-

minable. The Christians, attacked on every side, began at last to
give way, and the Turks made sure of victory.

At this moment a cry was raised in the Christian host that the
saints were fighting on their side. The battle-field was clear of the
smoke from the burning weeds, which had curled away, and hung in
white clouds of fantastic shape on the brow of the distant mountains.
Some imaginative zealot, seeing this dimly through the dust of the
battle, called out to his fellows, to look at the army of saints, clothed
in white, and riding upon white horses, that were pouring over the
hills to the rescue. All eyes were immediately turned to the distant
smoke; faith was in every heart; and the old battle-cry, *God wills it!*
God wills it! resounded through the field, as every soldier, believing
that God was visibly sending his armies to his aid, fought with an
energy unfelt before. A panic seized the Persian and Turkish hosts,
and they gave way in all directions. In vain Kerbogha tried to rally
them. Fear is more contagious than enthusiasm, and they fled over
the mountains like deer pursued by the hounds. The two leaders,
seeing the uselessness of further efforts, fled with the rest; and that
immense army was scattered over Palestine, leaving nearly seventy
thousand of its dead upon the field of battle.

Their magnificent camp fell into the hands of the enemy, with its
rich stores of corn, and its droves of sheep and oxen. Jewels, gold, and
rich velvets in abundance, were distributed among the army. Tancred
followed the fugitives over the hills, and reaped as much plunder as
those who had remained in the camp. The way, as they fled, was
covered with valuables, and horses of the finest breed of Arabia became so plentiful that every knight of the Christians was provided
with a steed. The Crusaders, in this battle, acknowledge to have lost
nearly ten thousand men.

Their return to Antioch was one of joy indeed : the citadel was
surrendered at once, and many of the Turkish garrison embraced the
Christian faith, and the rest were suffered to depart. A solemn thanks-
giving was offered up by the Bishop of Puy, in which the whole army
joined, and the Holy Lance was visited by every soldier.

The enthusiasm lasted for some days, and the army loudly demanded to be led forward to Jerusalem, the grand goal of all their
wishes : but none of their leaders was anxious to move ;—the more
prudent among them, such as Godfrey and Tancred, for reasons of
expediency ; and the more ambitious, such as the Count of Toulouse
and Bohemund, for reasons of self-interest. Violent dissensions sprang
up again between all the chiefs. Raymond of Toulouse, who was left
at Antioch to guard the town, had summoned the citadel to surrender,
as soon as he saw that there was no fear of any attack upon the part of

the Persians; and the other chiefs found, upon their return, his banner waving on its walls. This had given great offence to Bohemund, who had stipulated the principality of Antioch as his reward for winning the town in the first instance. Godfrey and Tancred supported his claim, and, after a great deal of bickering, the flag of Raymond was lowered from the tower, and that of Bohemund hoisted in its stead, who assumed from that time the title of Prince of Antioch. Raymond, however, persisted in retaining possession of one of the city gates and its adjacent towers, which he held for several months, to the great annoyance of Bohemund and the scandal of the army The count became in consequence extremely unpopular, although his ambition was not a whit more unreasonable than that of Bohemund himself, nor of Baldwin, who had taken up his quarters at Edessa, where he exercised the functions of a petty sovereign.

The fate of Peter Barthelemy deserves to be recorded. Honours and consideration had come thick upon him after the affair of the lance, and he consequently felt bound in conscience to continue the dreams which had made him a personage of so much importance. The mischief of it was, that, like many other liars, he had a very bad memory, and he contrived to make his dreams contradict each other in the most palpable manner. St. John one night appeared to him, and told one tale ; while, a week after, St. Paul told a totally different story, and held out hopes quite incompatible with those of his apostolic brother. The credulity of that age had a wide maw, and Peter's visions must have been absurd and outrageous indeed, when the very men who had believed in the lance refused to swallow any more of his wonders. Bohemund at last, for the purpose of annoying the Count of Toulouse, challenged poor Peter to prove the truth of his story of the lance by the fiery ordeal. Peter could not refuse a trial so common in that age, and being besides encouraged by the count and his chaplain Raymond, an early day was appointed for the ceremony. The previous night was spent in prayer and fasting, according to custom, and Peter came forth in the morning bearing the lance in his hand, and walked boldly up to the fire. The whole army gathered round, impatient for the result, many thousands still believing that the lance was genuine, and Peter a holy man. Prayers having been said by Raymond d'Agilles, Peter walked into the flames, and had got nearly through, when pain caused him to lose his presence of mind : the heat, too, affected his eyes, and, in his anguish, he turned round unwittingly, and passed through the fire again, instead of stepping out of it, as he should have done. The result was, that he was burned so severely that he never recovered, and, after lingering for some days, he expired in great agony.

Most of the soldiers were suffering either from wounds, disease, or weariness ; and it was resolved by Godfrey,—the tacitly acknowledged chief of the enterprise,—that the army should have time to refresh itself ere they advanced upon Jerusalem. It was now July, and he proposed that they should pass the hot months of August and September within the walls of Antioch, and march forward in October with renewed vigour, and numbers increased by fresh arrivals from Europe. This advice was finally adopted, although the enthusiasts of the army continued to murmur at the delay. In the mean time the Count of Vermandois was sent upon an embassy to the Emperor Alexius at Constantinople, to reproach him for his base desertion of the cause, and urge him to send the reinforcements he had promised. The count faithfully executed his mission (of which, by the way, Alexius took no notice whatever), and remained for some time at Constantinople, till his zeal, never very violent, totally evaporated. He then returned to France, sick of the Crusade, and determined to intermeddle with it no more.

The chiefs, though they had determined to stay at Antioch for two months, could not remain quiet for so long a time. They would, in all probability, have fallen upon each other, had there been no Turks in Palestine upon whom they might vent their impetuosity. Godfrey proceeded to Edessa, to aid his brother Baldwin in expelling the Saracens from his principality, and the other leaders carried on separate hostilities against them as caprice or ambition dictated. At length the impatience of the army to be led against Jerusalem became so great that the chiefs could no longer delay, and Raymond, Tancred, and Robert of Normandy marched forward with their divisions, and laid siege to the small but strong town of Marah. With their usual improvidence, they had not food enough to last a beleaguering army for a week. They suffered great privations in consequence, till Bohemund came to their aid and took the town by storm. In connexion with this siege, the chronicler, Raymond d'Agilles (the same Raymond the chaplain who figured in the affair of the holy lance), relates a legend, in the truth of which he devoutly believed, and upon which Tasso has founded one of the most beautiful passages of his poem. It is worth preserving, as shewing the spirit of the age and the source of the extraordinary courage manifested by the Crusaders on occasions of extreme difficulty. "One day," says Raymond, "Anselme de Ribeaumont beheld young Engelram, the son of the Count de St. Paul, who had been killed at Marah, enter his tent. ' How is it,' said Anselme to him, ' that you, whom I saw lying dead on the field of battle, are full of life?'—'You must know,' replied Engelram, ' that those who fight for Jesus Christ never die.' ' But whence,' re-

sumed Anselme, ' comes that strange brightness that surrounds you ?'
Upon this Engelram pointed to the sky, where Anselme saw a palace
of diamond and crystal. ' It is thence,' said he, ' that I derive the
beauty which surprises you. My dwelling is there; a still finer one is
prepared for you, and you shall soon come to inhabit it. Farewell!
we shall meet again to-morrow.' With these words Engelram returned
to heaven. Anselme, struck by the vision, sent the next morning
for the priests, received the sacrament, and although full of health,
took a last farewell of all his friends, telling them that he was about
to leave this world. A few hours afterwards, the enemy having made
a sortie, Anselme went out against them sword in hand, and was
struck on the forehead by a stone from a Turkish sling, which sent
him to heaven, to the beautiful palace that was prepared for him."

New disputes arose between the Prince of Antioch and the Count
of Toulouse with regard to the capture of this town, which were with
the utmost difficulty appeased by the other chiefs. Delays also took

SHRINE OF THE NATIVITY.

place in the progress of the army, especially before Archas, and the
soldiery were so exasperated that they were on the point of choosing
new leaders to conduct them to Jerusalem. Godfrey, upon this, set

fire to his camp at Archas, and marched forward. He was immediately joined by hundreds of the Provençals of the Count of Toulouse. The latter, seeing the turn affairs were taking, hastened after them, and the whole host proceeded towards the holy city, so long desired amid sorrow, and suffering, and danger. At Emmaus they were met by a deputation from the Christians of Bethlehem, praying for immediate aid against the oppression of the infidels. The very name of Bethlehem, the birthplace of their Saviour, was music to their ears, and many of them wept with joy to think they were approaching a spot so hallowed. Albert of Aix informs us that their hearts were so touched that sleep was banished from the camp, and that, instead of waiting till the morning's dawn to recommence their march, they set out shortly after midnight, full of hope and enthusiasm. For upwards of four hours the mail-clad legions tramped stedfastly forward in the dark, and when the sun arose in unclouded splendour, the towers and pinnacles of Jerusalem gleamed upon their sight. All the

THE PILGRIMS AT THE FIRST SIGHT OF JERUSALEM.

tender feelings of their nature were touched; no longer brutal fanatics, but meek and humble pilgrims, they knelt down upon the sod, and with tears in their eyes, exclaimed to one another, "*Jerusalem! Jerusalem!*" Some of them kissed the holy ground, others stretched themselves at full length upon it, in order that their bodies might come in contact with the greatest possible extent of it, and others prayed aloud. The women and children who had followed the camp from Europe, and shared in all its dangers, fatigues, and privations, were more boisterous in their joy; the former from long-nourished enthusiasm, and the latter from mere imitation,* and prayed, and wept, and laughed till they almost put the more sober to the blush.

The first ebullition of their gladness having subsided, the army marched forward and invested the city on all sides. The assault was almost immediately begun; but after the Christians had lost some of their bravest knights, that mode of attack was abandoned, and the army commenced its preparations for a regular siege. Mangonels, movable towers, and battering-rams, together with a machine called a sow, made of wood, and covered with raw hides, inside of which miners worked to undermine the walls, were forthwith constructed; and to restore the courage and discipline of the army, which had suffered from the unworthy dissensions of the chiefs, the latter held out the hand of friendship to each other, and Tancred and the Count of Toulouse embraced in sight of the whole camp. The clergy aided the cause with their powerful voice, and preached union and goodwill to the highest and the lowest. A solemn procession was also ordered round the city, in which the entire army joined, prayers being offered up at every spot which gospel records had taught them to consider as peculiarly sacred.

The Saracens upon the ramparts beheld all these manifestations without alarm. To incense the Christians, whom they despised, they constructed rude crosses, and fixed them upon the walls, and spat upon and pelted them with dirt and stones. This insult to the symbol of their faith raised the wrath of the Crusaders to that height that bravery became ferocity, and enthusiasm madness. When all the engines of war were completed, the attack was recommenced, and every soldier of the Christian army fought with a vigour which the sense of private wrong invariably inspires. Every man had been personally outraged, and the knights worked at the battering-rams with as much readiness as the meanest soldiers. The Saracen arrows and balls of fire fell thick and fast among them, but the tremendous

---

* Guibert de Nogent relates a curious instance of the imitativeness of these juvenile Crusaders. He says that, during the siege of Antioch, the Christian and Saracen boys used to issue forth every evening from the town and camp in great numbers, under the command of captains chosen from among themselves. Armed with sticks instead of swords, and stones instead of arrows, they ranged themselves in battle order, and, shouting each the war-cry of their country, fought with the utmost desperation. Some of them lost their eyes, and many became cripples for life from the injuries they received on these occasions.

rams still heaved against the walls, while the best marksmen of the host were busily employed in the several floors of the movable towers in dealing death among the Turks upon the battlements. Godfrey, Raymond, Tancred, and Robert of Normandy, each upon his tower, fought for hours with unwearied energy, often repulsed, but ever ready to renew the struggle. The Turks, no longer despising the enemy, defended themselves with the utmost skill and bravery till darkness brought a cessation of hostilities. Short was the sleep that night in the Christian camp. The priests offered up solemn prayers in the midst of the attentive soldiery for the triumph of the cross in this last great struggle; and as soon as morning dawned, every one was in readiness for the affray. The women and children lent their aid, the latter running unconcerned to and fro while the arrows fell fast around them, bearing water to the thirsty combatants. The saints were believed to be aiding their efforts, and the army, impressed with this idea, surmounted difficulties under which a force thrice as numerous, but without their faith, would have quailed and been defeated. Raymond of Toulouse at last forced his way into the city by escalade, while at the very same moment Tancred and Robert of Normandy succeeded in bursting open one of the gates. The Turks flew to repair the mischief, and Godfrey of Bouillon, seeing the battlements comparatively deserted, let down the drawbridge of his movable tower, and sprang forward, followed by all the knights of his train. In an instant after, the banner of the cross floated upon the walls of Jerusalem. The Crusaders, raising once more their redoubtable war-cry, rushed on from every side, and the city was taken. The battle raged in the streets for several hours, and the Christians, remembering their insulted faith, gave no quarter to young or old, male or female, sick or strong. Not one of the leaders thought himself at liberty to issue orders for staying the carnage, and if he had, he would not have been obeyed. The Saracens fled in great numbers to the mosque of Soliman, but they had not time to fortify themselves within it ere the Christians were upon them. Ten thousand persons are said to have perished in that building alone.

Peter the Hermit, who had remained so long under the veil of neglect, was repaid that day for all his zeal and all his sufferings. As soon as the battle was over, the Christians of Jerusalem issued forth from their hiding-places to welcome their deliverers. They instantly recognised the Hermit as the pilgrim who, years before, had spoken to them so eloquently of the wrongs and insults they had endured, and promised to stir up the princes and people of Europe in their behalf. They clung to the skirts of his garments in the fervour of their gratitude, and vowed to remember him for ever in their prayers. Many of them shed tears about his neck, and attributed the deliverance of Jerusalem solely to his courage and perseverance. Peter afterwards held some ecclesiastical office in the holy city, but

SIEGE OF JERUSALEM.

what it was, or what was his ultimate fate, history has forgotten to inform us. Some say that he returned to France and founded a monastery, but the story does not rest upon sufficient authority.

The grand object for which the popular swarms of Europe had forsaken their homes was now accomplished. The Moslem mosques of Jerusalem were converted into churches for a purer faith, and the Mount of Calvary and the sepulchre of Christ were profaned no longer by the presence or the power of the infidel. Popular frenzy had fulfilled its mission, and, as a natural consequence, it began to subside from that time forth. The news of the capture of Jerusalem brought numbers of pilgrims from Europe, and, among others, Stephen count of Chartres and Hugh of Vermandois, to atone for their desertion; but nothing like the former enthusiasm existed among the nations.

Thus, then, ends the history of the first Crusade. For the better understanding of the second, it will be necessary to describe the interval between them, and to enter into a slight sketch of the history of Jerusalem under its Latin kings, the long and fruitless wars they continued to wage with the unvanquished Saracens, and the poor and miserable results which sprang from so vast an expenditure of zeal and so deplorable a waste of human life.

The necessity of having some recognised chief was soon felt by the Crusaders, and Godfrey de Bouillon, less ambitious than Bohemund or Raymond of Toulouse, gave his cold consent to wield a sceptre which the latter chiefs would have clutched with eagerness. He was hardly invested with the royal mantle before the Saracens menaced his capital. With much vigour and judgment he exerted himself to follow up the advantages he had gained, and marching out to meet the enemy before they had time to besiege him in Jerusalem, he gave them battle at Ascalon, and defeated them with great loss. He did not, however, live long to enjoy his new dignity, being seized with a fatal illness when he had only reigned nine months. To him succeeded his brother, Baldwin of Edessa. The latter monarch did much to improve the condition of Jerusalem and to extend its territory, but was not able to make a firm footing for his successors. For fifty years, in which the history of Jerusalem is full of interest to the historical student, the Crusaders were exposed to fierce and constant hostilities, often gaining battles and territory, and as often losing them, but becoming every day weaker and more divided, while the Saracens became stronger and more united to harass and root them out. The battles of this period were of the most chivalrous character, and deeds of heroism were done by the handful of brave knights that remained in Syria which have hardly their parallel in the annals of war. In the course of time, however, the Christians could not avoid feeling some respect for the courage, and admiration for the polished manners and advanced civilisation of the Saracens, so much superior to the rudeness and semi-barbarism of Europe at that day. Difference of faith

JERUSALEM.

did not prevent them from forming alliances with the dark-eyed maidens of the East.   One of the first to set the example of taking

BIBLE OF BALDWIN'S QUEEN.

a Paynim spouse was King Baldwin himself, and these connexions in time became not only frequent, but almost universal, among such of the knights as had resolved to spend their lives in Palestine. These Eastern ladies were obliged, however, to submit to the ceremony of baptism before they could be received to the arms of a Christian lord. These, and their offspring, naturally looked upon the Saracens with less hatred than did the zealots who conquered Jerusalem, and who thought it a sin deserving the wrath of God to spare an unbeliever. We find, in consequence, that the most obstinate battles waged during the reigns of the later kings of Jerusalem were fought by the new and raw levies who from time to time arrived from Europe, lured by the hope of glory or spurred by fanaticism.   The latter broke without scruple the truces established between the original settlers and the Saracens, and drew down severe retaliation upon many thousands of their brethren in the faith, whose prudence was stronger than their zeal, and whose chief desire was to live in peace.

Things remained in this unsatisfactory state till the close of the year 1145, when Edessa, the strong frontier town of the Christian kingdom, fell into the hands of the Saracens.   The latter were commanded by Zenghi, a powerful and enterprising monarch, and, after his death, by his son Nourheddin, as powerful and enterprising as his father.   An unsuccessful attempt was made by the Count of Edessa to regain the fortress, but Nourheddin with a large army came to the rescue, and after defeating the count with great slaughter, marched into Edessa and caused its fortifications to be razed to the ground, that the town might never more be a bulwark of defence for the kingdom of Jerusalem. The road to the capital was now open, and consternation seized the hearts of the Christians. Nourheddin, it was known, was only waiting for a favourable opportunity to advance upon Jerusalem, and the armies of the cross, weakened and divided, were not in a condition to make any available resistance. The clergy were filled with grief and alarm, and wrote repeated letters to the Pope and the sovereigns of Europe, urging the expediency of a new Crusade for the relief of Jerusalem. By far the greater number of the priests of Palestine were natives of France, and these naturally looked first to their own country. The solicitations they sent to Louis VII. were urgent and oft repeated, and the chivalry of France began to talk once more of arming in defence of the birthplace of Jesus. The kings of Europe, whose interest it had not been to take any part in the first Crusade, began to bestir themselves in this; and a man appeared, eloquent as Peter the Hermit, to arouse the people as that preacher had done.

We find, however, that the enthusiasm of the second did not equal that of the first Crusade; in fact, the mania had reached its climax in the time of Peter the Hermit, and decreased regularly from that period. The third Crusade was less general than the second, and the fourth than the third, and so on, until the public enthusiasm was quite extinct, and Jerusalem returned at last to the dominion of its old masters without a convulsion in Christendom. Various reasons have been assigned for this; and one very generally put forward is, that Europe was wearied with continued struggles, and had become sick of "precipitating itself upon Asia." M. Guizot, in his admirable lectures upon European civilisation, successfully combats this opinion, and offers one of his own, which is far more satisfactory. He says, in his eighth lecture, "It has been often repeated that Europe was tired of continually invading Asia. This expression appears to me exceedingly incorrect. It is not possible that human beings can be wearied with what they have not done—that the labours of their forefathers can fatigue them. Weariness is a personal, not an inherited feeling. The men of the thirteenth century were not fatigued by the Crusades of the twelfth. They were influenced by another cause. A great change had taken place in ideas, sentiments, and social conditions. The same desires and the same wants were no longer felt. The same things were no longer believed. The people refused to believe what their ancestors were persuaded of."

This is, in fact, the secret of the change; and its truth becomes more apparent as we advance in the history of the Crusades, and compare the state of the public mind at the different periods when Godfrey of Bouillon, Louis VII., and Richard I., were chiefs and leaders of the movement. The Crusades themselves were the means of operating a great change in national ideas, and advancing the civilisation of Europe. In the time of Godfrey, the nobles were all-powerful and all-oppressive, and equally obnoxious to kings and people. During their absence along with that portion of the community the deepest sunk in ignorance and superstition, both kings and people fortified themselves against the renewal of aristocratic tyranny, and in proportion as they became free became civilised. It was during this period that in France, the grand centre of the crusading madness, the *communes* began to acquire strength, and the monarch to possess a practical and not a merely theoretic authority. Order and comfort began to take root, and, when the second Crusade was preached, men were in consequence much less willing to abandon their homes than they had been during the first. Such pilgrims as had returned from the Holy Land came back with minds more liberal and expanded than when they set out. They had come in contact with a people more civilised than themselves ; they had seen something more of the world, and had lost some portion, however small, of the prejudice and bigotry of ignorance. The institution of chivalry had also exercised its humanising influence, and coming bright and fresh through the ordeal of the Crusades, had softened the character and improved the hearts of the aristocratic order. The *trouvères* and *troubadours*, singing of love and war in strains pleasing to every class of society, helped to root out the gloomy superstitions which, at the first Crusade, filled the minds of all those who were able to think. Men became in consequence less exclusively under the mental thraldom of the priesthood, and lost much of the credulity which formerly distinguished them.

The Crusades appear never to have excited so much attention in England as on the continent of Europe ; not because the people were less fanatical than their neighbours, but because they were occupied in matters of graver interest. The English were suffering too severely from the recent successful invasion of their soil, to have much sympathy to bestow upon the distresses of people so far away as the Christians of Palestine ; and we find that they took no part in the first Crusade, and very little in the second. Even then those who engaged in it were chiefly Norman knights and their vassals, and not the Saxon franklins and population, who no doubt thought, in their sorrow, as many wise men have thought since, that charity should begin at home.

Germany was productive of more zeal in the cause, and her raw uncivilised hordes continued to issue forth under the banners of the cross in numbers apparently undiminished, when the enthusiasm had long been on the wane in other countries. They were sunk at that time in a deeper slough of barbarism than the livelier nations around them, and took, in consequence, a longer period to free themselves from their prejudices. In fact, the second Crusade drew its chief supplies of men from that quarter, where alone the expedition can be said to have retained any portion of popularity.

Such was the state of mind of Europe when Pope Eugenius, moved by the reiterated entreaties of the Christians of Syria, commissioned St. Bernard to preach a new Crusade. St. Bernard was a man eminently qualified for the mission. He was endowed with an eloquence of the highest order, could move an auditory to tears, or laughter, or fury, as it pleased him, and had led a life of such rigid and self-denying virtue, that not even calumny could lift her finger and point it at him. He had renounced high prospects in the Church, and contented himself with the simple abbacy of Clairvaux, in order that he might have the leisure he desired, to raise his powerful voice against abuses wherever he found them. Vice met in him an austere and uncompromising reprover ; no man was too high for his reproach, and none too low for his sympathy. He was just as well suited for his age as Peter the Hermit had been for the age preceding. He appealed more to the reason, his predecessor to the passions ; Peter the Hermit collected a mob, while St. Bernard collected an army. Both were endowed with equal zeal and perseverance, springing in the one from impulse, and in the other from conviction, and a desire to increase the influence of the Church, that great body of which he was a pillar and an ornament.

One of the first converts he made was in himself a host. Louis VII. was both superstitious and tyrannical, and, in a fit of remorse for the infamous slaughter he had authorised at the sacking of Vitry, he made a vow to undertake the journey to the Holy Land.* He was in this disposition when St. Bernard began to preach, and wanted but little persuasion to embark in the cause. His example had great influence upon the nobility, who, impoverished as many of them were

---

* The sacking of Vitry reflects indelible disgrace upon Louis VII. His predecessors had been long engaged in resistance to the outrageous powers assumed by the Popes, and Louis continued the same policy. The ecclesiastical chapter of Bourges, having elected an archbishop without his consent, he proclaimed the election to be invalid, and took severe and prompt measures against the refractory clergy. Thibault count de Champagne took up arms in defence of the Papal authority, and entrenched himself in the town of Vitry. Louis immediately took the field to chastise the rebel, and he besieged the town with so much vigour that the count was forced to surrender. Upwards of thirteen hundred of the inhabitants, fully one-half of whom were women and children, took refuge in the church; and when the gates of the city were opened, and all resistance had ceased, Louis inhumanly gave orders to set fire to the sacred edifice, and a thousand persons perished in the flames.

by the sacrifices made by their fathers in the holy wars, were anxious to repair their ruined fortunes by conquests on a foreign shore. These took the field with such vassals as they could command, and in a very short time an army was raised amounting to two hundred

CATHEDRAL OF VEZELAI.

thousand men. At Vezelai the monarch received the cross from the hands of St. Bernard, on a platform elevated in sight of all the people. Several nobles, three bishops, and his queen Eleanor of Aquitaine were present at this ceremony, and enrolled themselves under the banner of the cross, St. Bernard cutting up his red sacerdotal vestments and making crosses of them, to be sewn on the shoulders of the people. An exhortation from the Pope was read to the multitude, granting remission of their sins to all who should join the Crusade, and directing that no man on that holy pilgrimage should encumber himself with heavy baggage and vain superfluities; and that the nobles should not travel with dogs or falcons, to lead them from the direct road, as had happened to so many during the first Crusade.

The command of the army was offered to St. Bernard; but he wisely refused to accept a station for which his habits had unqualified him. After consecrating Louis with great solemnity, at St. Denis, as chief of the expedition, he continued his course through the country, stirring up the people wherever he went. So high an opinion was entertained of his sanctity, that he was thought to be animated by the spirit of prophecy, and to be gifted with the power of working miracles. Many women, excited by his eloquence, and encouraged by his predictions, forsook their husbands and children, and, clothing themselves in male attire, hastened to the war. St. Bernard himself wrote a letter to the Pope detailing his success, and stating, that in several towns there did not remain a single male inhabitant capable of bearing arms, and that every where castles and towns were to be seen filled with women weeping for their absent husbands. But in spite of this apparent enthusiasm, the numbers who really took up arms were inconsiderable, and not to be compared to the swarms of the first Crusade. A levy of no more than two hundred thousand men, which was the utmost the number amounted to, could hardly have depopulated a country like France, to the extent mentioned by St. Bernard. His description of the state of the country appears, therefore, to have been much more poetical than true.

Suger, the able minister of Louis, endeavoured to dissuade him from undertaking so long a journey at a time when his own dominions so much needed his presence. But the king was pricked in his conscience by the cruelties of Vitry, and was anxious to make the only reparation which the religion of that day considered sufficient. He was desirous, moreover, of testifying to the world, that though he could brave the temporal power of the Church when it encroached upon his prerogatives, he could render all due obedience to its spiritual decrees whenever it suited his interest or tallied with his prejudices to do so. Suger, therefore, implored in vain, and Louis received the pilgrim's staff at St. Denis, and made all preparations for his pilgrimage.

In the mean time St. Bernard passed into Germany, where similar success attended his preaching. The renown of his sanctity had gone before him, and he found every where an admiring audience. Thousands of people, who could not understand a word he said, flocked around him to catch a glimpse of so holy a man; and the knights enrolled themselves in great numbers in the service of the cross, each receiving from his hands the symbol of the cause. But the people were not led away as in the days of Gottschalk. We do not find that they rose in such tremendous masses of two and three hundred thousand men, swarming over the country like a plague of locusts. Still the enthusiasm was very great. The extraordinary tales that were told and believed of the miracles worked by the preacher brought the country people from far and near. Devils were said to vanish at his sight, and diseases of the most malignant nature to be cured by his touch.* The Emperor Conrad caught at last the contagion from his subjects, and declared his intention to follow the cross.

The preparations were carried on so vigorously under the orders of Conrad, that in less than three months he found himself at the head of an army containing at least one hundred and fifty thousand effective men, besides a great number of women who followed their husbands and lovers to the war. One troop of them rode in the attitude and armour of men : their chief wore gilt spurs and buskins, and thence acquired the epithet of the golden-footed lady. Conrad was ready to set out long before the French monarch, and in the month of June 1147 he arrived before Constantinople, having passed through Hungary and Bulgaria without offence to the inhabitants.

PILGRIM'S
STAFF.

Manuel Comnenus, the Greek emperor, successor not only to the throne but to the policy of Alexius, looked with alarm upon the new levies who had come to eat up his capital and imperil its tranquillity. Too weak to refuse them a passage through his dominions, too distrustful of them to make them welcome when they came, and too little assured of the advantages likely to result to himself from the war, to feign a friendship which he did not feel, the Greek emperor gave offence at the very outset. His subjects, in the pride of superior civilisation, called the Germans barbarians ; while the latter, who, if

* Philip, Archdeacon of the cathedral of Liege, wrote a detailed account of all the miracles performed by St. Bernard during thirty-four days of his mission. They averaged about ten per day. The disciples of St. Bernard complained bitterly that the people flocked around their master in such numbers, that they could not see half the miracles he performed. But they willingly trusted the eyes of others, as far as faith in the miracles went, and seemed to vie with each other whose credulity should be greatest.

semi-barbarous, were at least honest and straightforward, retorted upon the Greeks by calling them double-faced knaves and traitors. Disputes continually arose between them, and Conrad, who had preserved so much good order among his followers during their passage, was unable to restrain their indignation when they arrived at Constantinople. For some offence or other which the Greeks had given them, but which is rather hinted at than stated by the scanty historians of the day, the Germans broke into the magnificent pleasure-garden of the emperor, where he had a valuable collection of tame animals, for which the grounds had been laid out in woods, caverns, groves, and streams, that each might follow in captivity his natural habits. The enraged Germans, meriting the name of barbarians that had been bestowed upon them, laid waste this pleasant retreat, and killed or let loose the valuable animals it contained. Manuel, who is said to have beheld the devastation from his palace-windows without power or courage to prevent it, was completely disgusted with his guests, and resolved, like his predecessor Alexius, to get rid of them on the first opportunity. He sent a message to Conrad respectfully desiring an interview, but the German refused to trust himself within the walls of Constantinople. The Greek emperor, on his part, thought it compatible neither with his dignity nor his safety to seek the German, and several days were spent in insincere negotiations. Manuel at length agreed to furnish the crusading army with guides to conduct it through Asia Minor ; and Conrad passed over the Hellespont with his forces, the advanced guard being commanded by himself, and the rear by the warlike Bishop of Freysinghen.

Historians are almost unanimous in their belief that the wily Greek gave instructions to his guides to lead the army of the German emperor into dangers and difficulties. It is certain that, instead of guiding them through such districts of Asia Minor as afforded water and provisions, they led them into the wilds of Cappadocia, where neither was to be procured, and where they were suddenly attacked by the sultan of the Seljukian Turks, at the head of an immense force. The guides, whose treachery is apparent from this fact alone, fled at the first sight of the Turkish army, and the Christians were left to wage unequal warfare with their enemy, entangled and bewildered in desert wilds. Toiling in their heavy mail, the Germans could make but little effective resistance to the attacks of the Turkish light horse, who were down upon them one instant, and out of sight the next. Now in the front and now in the rear, the agile foe showered his arrows upon them, enticing them into swamps and hollows, from which they could only extricate themselves after long struggles and great losses. The Germans, confounded by this mode of warfare, lost all conception of the direction they were pursuing, and went back instead of forward. Suffering at the same time for want of provisions, they fell an easy prey to their pursuers. Count Bernhard, one of the bravest leaders of the German expedition, was surrounded, with his whole division, not one of whom escaped the Turkish arrows. The emperor himself had nearly fallen a victim, and was twice severely wounded. So persevering was the enemy, and so little able were the Germans to make even a show of resistance, that when Conrad at last reached the city of Nice, he found that, instead of being at the head of an imposing force of one hundred thousand foot and seventy thousand horse, he had but fifty or sixty thousand men, and these in the most worn and wearied condition.

Totally ignorant of the treachery of the Greek emperor, although he had been warned to beware of it, Louis VII. proceeded at the head of his army, through Worms and Ratisbon, towards Constantinople. At Ratisbon, he was met by a deputation from Manuel, bearing letters so full of hyperbole and flattery, that Louis is reported to have blushed when they were read to him by the Bishop of Langres. The object of the deputation was to obtain from the French king a promise to pass through the Grecian territories in a peaceable and friendly manner, and to yield to the Greek emperor any conquest he might make in Asia Minor. The first part of the proposition was immediately acceded to, but no notice was taken of the second and more unreasonable. Louis marched on, and, passing through Hungary, pitched his tents in the outskirts of Constantinople.

On his arrival, Manuel sent him a friendly invitation to enter the city at the head of a small train. Louis at once accepted it, and was met by the emperor at the porch of his palace. The fairest promises were made; every art that flattery could suggest was resorted to, and every argument employed, to induce him to yield his future conquests to the Greek. Louis obstinately refused to pledge himself, and returned to his army convinced that the emperor was a man not to be trusted. Negotiations were, however, continued for several days, to the great dissatisfaction of the French army. The news that arrived of a treaty entered into between Manuel and the Turkish sultan changed their dissatisfaction into fury, and the leaders demanded to be led against Constantinople, swearing that they would raze the treacherous city to the ground. Louis did not feel inclined to accede to this proposal, and, breaking up his camp, he crossed over into Asia.

Here he heard, for the first time, of the mishaps of the German emperor, whom he found in a woful plight under the walls of Nice. The two monarchs united their forces, and marched together along the sea-coast to Ephesus; but Conrad, jealous, it would appear, of the superior numbers of the French, and not liking to sink into a vassal, for the time being, of his rival, withdrew abruptly with the remnant of his legions, and returned to Constantinople. Manuel was all smiles and courtesy. He condoled with the German so feelingly upon his losses, and cursed the stupidity or treachery of the guides with such apparent heartiness, that Conrad was half inclined to believe in his sincerity.

Louis, marching onward in the direction of Jerusalem, came up with the enemy on the banks of the Meander. The Turks contested the passage of the river, but the French bribed a peasant to point out a ford lower down : crossing the river without difficulty, they attacked the Turks with much vigour, and put them to flight. Whether the Turks were really defeated, or merely pretended to be so, is doubtful ; but the latter supposition seems to be the true one. It is probable that it was part of a concerted plan to draw the invaders onwards to more unfavourable ground, where their destruction might be more certain. If such were the scheme, it succeeded to the heart's wish of its projectors. The Crusaders, on the third day after their victory, arrived at a steep mountain-pass, on the summit of which the Turkish host lay concealed so artfully, that not the slightest vestige of their presence could be perceived. "With labouring steps and slow," they toiled up the steep ascent, when suddenly a tremendous fragment of rock came bounding down the precipices with an awful crash, bearing dismay and death before it. At the same instant the Turkish archers started from their hiding-places, and discharged a shower of arrows upon the foot-soldiers, who fell by hundreds at a time. The arrows rebounded harmlessly against the iron mail of the knights, which the Turks observing, took aim at their steeds, and horse and rider fell down the steep into the rapid torrent which rushed below. Louis, who commanded the rear-guard, received the first intimation of the onslaught from the sight of the wounded and flying soldiers, and, not knowing the numbers of the enemy, he pushed vigorously forward to stay, by his presence, the panic which had taken possession of his army. All his efforts were in vain. Immense stones continued to be hurled upon them as they advanced, bearing men and horse before them ; and those who succeeded in forcing their way to the top were met hand-to-hand by the Turks, and cast down headlong upon their companions. Louis himself fought with the energy of desperation, but had great difficulty to avoid falling into the enemy's hands. He escaped at last under cover of the night, with the remnant of his forces, and took up his position before Attalia. Here he restored the discipline and the courage of his disorganised and disheartened followers, and debated with his

captains the plan that was to be pursued. After suffering severely
both from disease and famine, it was resolved that they should
march to Antioch, which still remained an independent principality
under the successors of Bohemund of Tarentum. At this time the
sovereignty was vested in the person of Raymond, the uncle of Eleanor
of Aquitaine. This prince, presuming upon his relationship to the
French queen, endeavoured to withdraw Louis from the grand object
of the Crusade—the defence of the kingdom of Jerusalem, and secure
his co-operation in extending the limits and the power of his principality of Antioch. The Prince of Tripoli formed a similar design;
but Louis rejected the offers of both, and marched, after a short
delay, to Jerusalem. The Emperor Conrad was there before him,
having left Constantinople with promises of assistance from Manuel
Comnenus—assistance which never arrived, and was never intended.

A great council of the Christian princes of Palestine, and the
leaders of the Crusade, was then summoned, to discuss the future
operations of the war. It was ultimately determined that it would
further the cause of the cross in a greater degree if the united armies,
instead of proceeding to Edessa, laid siege to the city of Damascus,

DAMASCUS.

and drove the Saracens from that strong position. This was a bold
scheme, and, had it been boldly followed out, would have insured,
in all probability, the success of the war. But the Christian leaders

never learned from experience the necessity of union, that very soul of great enterprises. Though they all agreed upon the policy of the plan, yet every one had his own notions as to the means of executing it. The princes of Antioch and Tripoli were jealous of each other, and of the king of Jerusalem. The Emperor Conrad was jealous of the king of France, and the king of France was disgusted with them all. But he had come out to Palestine in accordance with a solemn vow; his religion, though it may be called bigotry, was sincere; and he determined to remain to the very last moment that a chance was left of effecting any good for the cause he had set his heart on.

The siege of Damascus was accordingly commenced, and with so much ability and vigour that the Christians gained a considerable advantage at the very outset. For weeks the siege was pressed, till the shattered fortifications and diminishing resistance of the besieged gave evidence that the city could not hold out much longer. At that moment the insane jealousy of the leaders led to dissensions that soon caused the utter failure, not only of the siege but of the Crusade. A modern cookery-book, in giving a recipe for cooking a hare, says, "first catch your hare, and then kill it"—a maxim of indisputable wisdom. The Christian chiefs, on this occasion, had not so much sagacity, for they began a violent dispute among themselves for the possession of a city which was still unconquered. There being already a prince of Antioch and a prince of Tripoli, twenty claimants started for the principality of Damascus; and a grand council of the leaders was held to determine the individual on whom the honour should devolve. Many valuable days were wasted in this discussion, the enemy in the meanwhile gaining strength from their inactivity. It was at length, after a stormy deliberation, agreed that Count Robert of Flanders, who had twice visited the Holy Land, should be invested with the dignity. The other claimants refused to recognise him or to co-operate in the siege until a more equitable arrangement had been made. Suspicion filled the camp; the most sinister rumours of intrigues and treachery were set afloat; and the discontented candidates withdrew at last to the other side of the city, and commenced operations on their own account without a probability of success. They were soon joined by the rest of the army. The consequence was that the weakest side of the city, and that on which they had already made considerable progress in the work of demolition, was left uncovered. The enemy was prompt to profit by the mistake, and received an abundant supply of provisions, and refortified the walls, before the Crusaders came to their senses again. When this desirable event happened, it was too late. Saph Eddin, the powerful emir of Mousoul, was in the neighbourhood, at the head of a large army, advancing by forced marches to the relief of the city. The siege was abruptly abandoned, and the foolish Crusaders returned to Jerusalem, having done nothing to weaken the enemy, but every thing to weaken themselves.

The freshness of enthusiasm had now completely subsided; even the meanest soldiers were sick at heart. Conrad, from whose fierce zeal at the outset so much might have been expected, was wearied with reverses, and returned to Europe with the poor remnant of his host. Louis lingered a short time longer, for very shame, but the pressing solicitations of his minister Suger induced him to return to France. Thus ended the second Crusade. Its history is but a chronicle of defeats. It left the kingdom of Jerusalem in a worse state than when it quitted Europe, and gained nothing but disgrace for its leaders, and discouragement for all concerned.

St. Bernard, who had prophesied a result so different, fell after this into some disrepute, and experienced, like many other prophets, the fate of being without honour in his own country. What made the matter worse, he could not obtain it in any other. Still, however, there were not wanting zealous advocates to stand forward in his behalf, and stem the tide of incredulity, which, unopposed, would have carried away his reputation. The Bishop of Freysinghen declared that prophets were not always able to prophesy, and that the vices of the Crusaders drew down the wrath of heaven upon them. But the most ingenious excuse ever made for St. Bernard is to be found in his life by Geoffroi de Clairvaux, where he pertinaciously insists that the Crusade was not unfortunate. St. Bernard, he says, had prophesied a happy result, and that result could not be considered other than happy which had peopled heaven with so glorious an army of martyrs. Geoffroi was a cunning pleader, and, no doubt, convinced a few of the zealous; but plain people, who were not wanting even in those days, retained their own opinion, or, what amounts to the same thing, "were convinced against their will."

We now come to the consideration of the third Crusade, and of the causes which rendered it necessary. The epidemic frenzy, which had been cooling ever since the issue of the first expedition, was now extinct, or very nearly so, and the nations of Europe looked with cold indifference upon the armaments of their princes. But chivalry had flourished in its natural element of war, and was now in all its glory. It continued to supply armies for the Holy Land when the popular ranks refused to deliver up their able-bodied swarms. Poetry, which, more than religion, inspired the third Crusade, was then but " *caviare* to the million," who had other matters, of sterner import, to claim all their attention. But the knights and their retainers listened with delight to the martial and amatory strains of the minstrels, minnesängers, trouvères, and troubadours, and burned to win favour in ladies' eyes by shewing prowess in the Holy Land. The third was truly the romantic era of the Crusades. Men fought then, not so much for the sepulchre of Jesus and the maintenance of a Christian kingdom in the East, as to gain glory for themselves in the best and almost only field where glory could be obtained. They fought, not as zealots, but as soldiers; not for religion, but for honour; not for the crown of martyrdom, but for the favour of the lovely.

It is not necessary to enter into a detail of the events by which Saladin attained the sovereignty of the East, or how, after a succession of engagements, he planted the Moslem banner once more upon the battlements of Jerusalem. The Christian knights and population, including the grand orders of St. John, the Hospitallers, and the Templars, were sunk in an abyss of vice, and, torn by unworthy jealousies and dissensions, were unable to resist the well-trained armies which the wise and mighty Saladin brought forward to crush them. But the news of their fall created a painful sensation among the chivalry of Europe, whose noblest members were linked to the dwellers in Palestine by many ties, both of blood and friendship. The news of the great battle of Tiberias, in which Saladin defeated the Christian host with terrible slaughter, arrived first in Europe, and was followed in quick succession by that of the capture of Jerusalem, Antioch, Tripoli, and other cities. Dismay seized upon the clergy. The Pope (Urban III.) was so affected by the news that he pined away for grief, and was scarcely seen to smile again, until he sank into the sleep of death.* His successor, Gregory VIII., felt the loss as acutely, but had better strength to bear it, and instructed all the clergy of the Christian world to stir up the people to arms for the recovery of the Holy Sepulchre. William Archbishop of Tyre, a humble follower in the path of Peter the Hermit, left Palestine to preach to the kings of Europe the miseries he had wit-

SEAL OF BARBAROSSA.

nessed, and to incite them to the rescue. The renowned Frederick Barbarossa, the emperor of Germany, speedily collected an army, and

* James of Vitry; William de Nangis.

passing over into Syria with less delay than had ever before awaited a crusading force, defeated the Saracens, and took possession of the city of Iconium.   He was unfortunately cut off in the middle of his successful career, by imprudently bathing in the Cydnus* while he was overheated, and the Duke of Suabia took the command of the expedition.   The latter did not prove so able a general, and met with nothing but reverses, although he was enabled to maintain a footing at Antioch until assistance arrived from Europe.

HENRY II. OF ENGLAND.

Henry II. of England and Philip Augustus of France, at the head of their chivalry, supported the Crusade with all their influence, until wars and dissensions nearer home estranged them from it for a time. The two kings met at Gisors in Normandy in the month of January,

* The desire of comparing two great men has tempted many writers to drown Frederick in the river Cydnus, in which Alexander so imprudently bathed (Q. Curt. lib. iii. c. 4, 5); but, from the march of the emperor, I rather judge that his Saleph is the Cacadnus, a stream of less fame, but of a longer course.—*Gibbon.*

1188, accompanied by a brilliant train of knights and warriors. William of Tyre was present, and expounded the cause of the cross with considerable eloquence, and the whole assembly bound themselves by oath to proceed to Jerusalem. It was agreed at the same time that

CHATEAU OF GISORS.

a tax, called Saladin's tithe, and consisting of the tenth part of all possessions, whether landed or personal, should be enforced over Christendom, upon every one who was either unable or unwilling to assume the cross. The lord of every feof, whether lay or ecclesiastical, was charged to raise the tithe within his own jurisdiction; and any one who refused to pay his quota became by that act the bondsman and absolute property of his lord. At the same time the greatest indulgence was shewn to those who assumed the cross; no man was at liberty to stay them by process of any kind, whether for debt, or robbery, or murder. The king of France, at the breaking up of the conference, summoned a parliament at Paris, where these resolutions were solemnly confirmed, while Henry II. did the same for his Norman possessions at Rouen, and for England at Geddington, in Northamptonshire. To use the words of an ancient chronicler,* " he

* Stowe.

held a parliament about the voyage into the Holy Land, and troubled the whole land with the paying of tithes towards it."

PHILIP AUGUSTUS.

But it was not England alone that was "*troubled*" by the tax. The people of France also looked upon it with no pleasant feelings, and appear from that time forth to have changed their indifference for the Crusade into aversion. Even the clergy, who were exceedingly willing that other people should contribute half, or even all their goods in furtherance of their favourite scheme, were not at all anxious to contribute a single sous themselves. Millot* relates that several of them cried out against the impost. Among the rest, the clergy of Rheims were called upon to pay their quota, but sent a deputation to the king, begging him to be contented with the aid of their prayers, as they were too poor to contribute in any other shape. Philip Augustus knew better, and by way of giving them a lesson, employed three nobles of the vicinity to lay waste the Church lands. The clergy, informed of the outrage, applied to the king for redress. "I will aid you with my prayers," said the monarch condescendingly, "and will entreat those gentlemen to let the Church alone." He did as he had promised, but in such a manner that the nobles, who appreciated the joke, continued their devastations as before. Again the clergy applied to the king. "What would you have of me?" he replied, in answer to their remonstrances : "you gave me your prayers in my necessity, and I have given you mine in yours." The clergy understood the argument, and thought it the wiser course to pay their quota of Saladin's tithe without further parley.

This anecdote shews the unpopularity of the Crusade. If the clergy disliked to contribute, it is no wonder that the people felt still greater antipathy. But the chivalry of Europe was eager for the affray : the tithe was rigorously collected, and armies from England, France, Burgundy, Italy, Flanders, and Germany were soon in the

Elémens de l'Histoire de France.

field. The two kings who were to have led it were, however, drawn into broils by an aggression of Richard duke of Guienne, better known as Richard Cœur de Lion, upon the territory of the Count of Toulouse, and the proposed journey to Palestine was delayed. War continued to rage between France and England, and with so little probability of a speedy termination, that many of the nobles, bound to the Crusade, left the two monarchs to settle the differences at their leisure, and proceeded to Palestine without them.

Death at last stepped in and removed Henry II. from the hostility of his foes, and the treachery and ingratitude of his children. His son Richard immediately concluded an alliance with Philip Augustus ; and the two young, valiant, and impetuous monarchs united all their energies to forward the Crusade. They met with a numerous and brilliant retinue at Nonancourt in Normandy, where, in sight of their assembled chivalry, they embraced as brothers, and swore to live as friends and true allies, until a period of forty days after their return from the Holy Land. With a view of purging their camp from the follies and vices which had proved so ruinous to preceding expeditions, they drew up a code of laws for the government of the army. Gambling had been carried to a great extent, and proved the fruitful source of quarrels and bloodshed ; and one of their laws prohibited any person in the army, beneath the degree of a knight, from playing at any game for money.* Knights and clergymen might play for money, but no one was permitted to lose or gain more than twenty shillings in a day, under a penalty of one hundred shillings. The personal attendants of the monarchs were also allowed to play to the same extent. The penalty in their case for infraction was that they should be whipped naked through the army for the space of three days. Any Crusader who struck another and drew blood was ordered to have his hand cut off ; and whoever slew a brother Crusader was condemned to be tied alive to the corpse of his victim, and buried with him. No young women were allowed to follow the army, to the great sorrow of many vicious and of many virtuous dames, who had not courage to elude the decree by dressing in male attire. But many high-minded and affectionate maidens and matrons, bearing the sword or the spear, followed their husbands and lovers to the war in spite of King Richard, and in defiance of danger. The only women allowed to accompany the army in their own habiliments were washerwomen of fifty years complete, and any others of the fair sex who had reached the same age.

These rules having been promulgated, the two monarchs marched together to Lyons, where they separated, agreeing to meet again at

---

* Strutt's *Sports and Pastimes.*

Messina. Philip proceeded across the Alps to Genoa, where he took ship, and was conveyed in safety to the place of rendezvous. Richard turned in the direction of Marseilles, where he also took ship for Messina. His impetuous disposition hurried him into many squabbles by the way, and his knights and followers, for the most part as brave and as foolish as himself, imitated him very zealously in this particular. At Messina the Sicilians charged the most exorbitant prices for every necessary of life. Richard's army in vain remonstrated. From words they came to blows, and, as a last resource, plundered the Sicilians, since they could not trade with them. Continual

THE ISLAND OF RHODES.

battles were the consequence, in one of which Lebrun, the favourite attendant of Richard, lost his life. The peasantry from far and near came flocking to the aid of the townspeople, and the battle soon became general. Richard, irritated at the loss of his favourite, and incited by a report that Tancred, the king of Sicily, was fighting at the head of his own people, joined the *mêlée* with his boldest knights, and, beating back the Sicilians, attacked the city sword in hand, stormed the battlements, tore down the flag of Sicily, and planted his own in its stead. This collision gave great offence to the king of France, who became from that time jealous of Richard, and apprehensive that his design was not so much to re-establish the Christian kingdom of Jerusalem as to make conquests for himself. He, however, exerted his influence to restore peace between the English and Sicilians, and shortly afterwards set sail for Acre, with distrust of his ally germinating in his heart.

Richard remained behind for some weeks in a state of inactivity quite unaccountable in one of his temperament. He appears to have had no more squabbles with the Sicilians, but to have lived an easy, luxurious life, forgetting, in the lap of pleasure, the objects for which he had quitted his own dominions and the dangerous laxity he was introducing into his army. The superstition of his soldiers recalled him at length to a sense of his duty : a comet was seen for several successive nights, which was thought to menace them with the vengeance of Heaven for their delay. Shooting stars gave them similar warning; and a fanatic, of the name of Joachim, with his drawn sword in his hand, and his long hair streaming wildly over his shoulders, went through the camp, howling all night long, and predicting plague, famine, and every other calamity, if they did not set out immediately. Richard did not deem it prudent to neglect the intimations; and, after doing humble penance for his remissness, he set sail for Acre.

A violent storm dispersed his fleet, but he arrived safely at Rhodes with the principal part of the armament. Here he learned that three of his ships had been stranded on the rocky coasts of Cyprus, and that the ruler of the island, Isaac Comnenus, had permitted his people to pillage the unfortunate crews, and had refused shelter to his betrothed bride, the Princess Berengaria, and his sister, who, in one of the vessels, had been driven by stress of weather into the port of Limisso. The fiery monarch swore to be revenged, and, collecting all his vessels, sailed back to Limisso. Isaac Comnenus refused to apologise or explain, and Richard, in no mood to be trifled with, landed on the island, routed with great loss the forces sent to oppose him, and laid the whole country under contribution.

On his arrival at Acre he found the whole of the chivalry of Europe there before him. Guy of Lusignan, the king of Jerusalem, had long before collected the bold Knights of the Temple, the Hospital, and St. John, and had laid siege to Acre, which was resolutely defended by the Sultan Saladin, with an army magnificent both for its numbers and its discipline. For nearly two years the Crusaders had pushed the siege, and made efforts almost superhuman to dis-

RICHARD I. AND BERENGARIA.

lodge the enemy. Various battles had taken place in the open fields with no decisive advantage to either party, and Guy of Lusignan had begun to despair of taking that strong position without aid from

Europe. His joy was extreme on the arrival of Philip with all his chivalry, and he only waited the coming of Cœur de Lion to make one last decisive attack upon the town. When the fleet of England was first seen approaching the shores of Syria, a universal shout arose from the Christian camp; and when Richard landed with his train, one louder still pierced to the very mountains of the south, where Saladin lay with all his army.

It may be remarked as characteristic of this Crusade, that the Christians and the Moslems no longer looked upon each other as barbarians, to whom mercy was a crime. Each host entertained the highest admiration for the bravery and magnanimity of the other, and, in their occasional truces, met upon the most friendly terms. The Moslem warriors were full of courtesy to the Christian knights, and had no other regret than to think that such fine fellows were not Mahomedans. The Christians, with a feeling precisely similar, extolled to the skies the nobleness of the Saracens, and sighed to think that such generosity and valour should be sullied by disbelief in the Gospel of Jesus. But when the strife began, all these feelings disappeared, and the struggle became mortal.

The jealousy excited in the mind of Philip by the events of Messina still rankled, and the two monarchs refused to act in concert. Instead of making a joint attack upon the town, the French monarch assailed it alone, and was repulsed. Richard did the same, and with the same result. Philip tried to seduce the soldiers of Richard from their allegiance by the offer of three gold pieces per month to every knight who would forsake the banners of England for those of France. Richard endeavoured to neutralise the offer by a larger one, and promised four pieces to every French knight who should join the Lion of England. In this unworthy rivalry their time was wasted, to the great detriment of the discipline and efficiency of their followers. Some good was nevertheless effected; for the mere presence of two such armies prevented the besieged city from receiving supplies, and the inhabitants were reduced by famine to the most woful straits. Saladin did not deem it prudent to risk a general engagement by coming to their relief, but preferred to wait till dissension had weakened his enemy, and made him an easy prey. Perhaps if he had been aware of the real extent of the extremity in Acre, he would have changed his plan; but, cut off from the town, he did not know its misery till it was too late. After a short truce the city capitulated upon terms so severe that Saladin afterwards refused to ratify them. The chief conditions were, that the precious wood of the true cross, captured by the Moslems in Jerusalem, should be restored; that a sum of two hundred thousand gold pieces should be paid; and that all the Christian prisoners in Acre should be released, together with two hundred knights and a thousand soldiers detained in captivity by Saladin. The eastern monarch, as may be well conceived, did not set much store on the wood of the cross, but was nevertheless anxious to keep it, as he knew its possession by the Christians would do more than a victory to restore their courage. He refused, therefore, to deliver it up, or to accede to any of the conditions ; and Richard, as he had previously threatened, barbarously ordered all the Saracen prisoners in his power to be put to death.

The possession of the city only caused new and unhappy dissensions between the Christian leaders. The Archduke of Austria unjustifiably hoisted his flag on one of the towers of Acre, which Richard no sooner saw than he tore it down with his own hands, and trampled it under his feet. Philip, though he did not sympathise with the archduke, was piqued at the assumption of Richard, and the breach between the two monarchs became wider than ever. A foolish dispute arose at the same time between Guy of Lusignan and Conrad of Montferrat for the crown of Jerusalem. The inferior knights were not slow to imitate the pernicious example, and jealousy, distrust, and ill-will reigned in the Christian camp. In the midst of this confusion the king of France suddenly announced his intention to return to his own country. Richard was filled with indignation, and exclaimed, " Eternal shame light on him, and on all France, if, for any cause, he leave this work unfinished !" But Philip was not to be stayed. His health had suffered by his residence in the East ; and, ambitious of playing a first part, he preferred to play none at all than to play second to King Richard. Leaving a small detachment of Burgundians behind, he returned to France with the remainder of his army ; and Cœur de Lion, without feeling, in the multitude of his rivals, that he had lost the greatest, became painfully convinced that the right arm of the enterprise was lopped off.

After his departure, Richard refortified Acre, restored the Christian worship in the churches, and leaving a Christian garrison to protect it, marched along the sea-coast towards Ascalon. Saladin was on the alert, and sent his light horse to attack the rear of the Christian army, while he himself, miscalculating their weakness since the defection of Philip, endeavoured to force them to a general engagement. The rival armies met near Azotus. A fierce battle ensued, in which Saladin was defeated and put to flight, and the road to Jerusalem left free for the Crusaders.

Again discord exerted its baleful influence, and prevented Richard from following up his victory. His opinion was constantly opposed by the other leaders, all jealous of his bravery and influence ; and the army, instead of marching to Jerusalem, or even to Ascalon, as was first intended, proceeded to Jaffa, and remained in idleness until Saladin was again in a condition to wage war against them.

Many months were spent in fruitless hostilities and as fruitless negotiations. Richard's wish was to recapture Jerusalem ; but there were difficulties in the way, which even his bold spirit could not conquer. His own intolerable pride was not the least cause of the evil ; for it estranged many a generous spirit, who would have been willing to co-operate with him in all cordiality. At length it was agreed to march to the Holy City ; but the progress made was so slow and painful, that the soldiers murmured, and the leaders meditated retreat. The weather was hot and dry, and there was little water to be pro-

BETHLEHEM.

cured. Saladin had choked up the wells and cisterns on the route, and the army had not zeal enough to push forward amid such privation. At Bethlehem a council was held, to debate whether they should retreat or advance. Retreat was decided upon, and immediately commenced. It is said, that Richard was first led to a hill, whence he could obtain a sight of the towers of Jerusalem, and that he was so affected at being so near it, and so unable to relieve it, that he hid his face behind his shield, and sobbed aloud. The army separated into two divisions, the smaller falling back upon Jaffa, and the larger, commanded by Richard and the Duke of Burgundy, returning to Acre. Before the English monarch had made all his preparations for his return to Europe, a messenger reached Acre with the intelligence that Jaffa was besieged by Saladin, and that unless relieved immediately, the city would be taken. The French, under the Duke of Burgundy, were so wearied with the war, that they refused to aid their brethren in Jaffa. Richard, blushing with shame at their pusillanimity, called his English to the rescue, and arrived just in time to save the city. His very name put the Saracens to flight, so great was their dread of his prowess. Saladin regarded him with the warmest admiration, and when Richard, after his victory, demanded peace, willingly acceded. A truce was concluded for three years and eight months, during which Christian pilgrims were to enjoy the liberty of visiting Jerusalem without hindrance or payment of any tax. The Crusaders were allowed to retain the cities of Tyre and Jaffa, with the country intervening. Saladin, with a princely generosity, invited many of the Christians to visit Jerusalem; and several of the leaders took advantage of his offer to feast their eyes upon a spot which all considered so sacred. Many of them were entertained for days in the sultan's own palace, from which they returned with their tongues laden with the praises of the noble infidel. Richard and Saladin never met, though the impression that they did will remain on many minds, who have been dazzled by the glorious fiction of Sir Walter Scott. But each admired the prowess and nobleness of soul of his rival, and agreed to terms far less onerous than either would have accepted, had this mutual admiration not existed.*

The king of England no longer delayed his departure, for messengers from his own country brought imperative news that his presence was required to defeat the intrigues that were fomenting against his crown. His long imprisonment in the Austrian dominions and final ransom are too well known to be dwelt upon. And thus ended the third Crusade, less destructive of human life than the two first, but quite as useless.

---

* Richard left a high reputation in Palestine. So much terror did his name occasion, that the women of Syria used it to frighten their children for ages afterwards. Every disobedient child became still when told that King Richard was coming. Even men shared the panic that his name created; and a hundred years afterwards, whenever a horse shied at any object in the way, his rider would exclaim, "What! dost thou think King Richard is in the bush?"

The flame of popular enthusiasm now burned pale indeed, and all the efforts of popes and potentates were insufficient to rekindle it. At last, after flickering unsteadily, like a lamp expiring in the socket, it burned up brightly for one final instant, and was extinguished for ever.

The fourth Crusade, as connected with popular feeling, requires little or no notice. At the death of Saladin, which happened a year after the conclusion of his truce with Richard of England, his vast empire fell to pieces. His brother Saif Eddin, or Saphaddin, seized upon Syria, in the possession of which he was troubled by the sons of Saladin. When this intelligence reached Europe, the pope, Celestine III., judged the moment favourable for preaching a new Crusade. But every nation in Europe was unwilling and cold towards it. The people had no ardour, and kings were occupied with more weighty matters at home. The only monarch of Europe who encouraged it was the Emperor Henry of Germany, under whose auspices the Dukes of Saxony and Bavaria took the field at the head of a considerable force. They landed in Palestine, and found any thing but a welcome from the Christian inhabitants. Under the mild sway of Saladin, they had enjoyed repose and toleration, and both were endangered by the arrival of the Germans. They looked upon them in consequence as over-officious intruders, and gave them no encouragement in the warfare against Saphaddin. The result of this Crusade was even more disastrous than the last; for the Germans contrived not only to embitter the Saracens against the Christians of Judea, but to lose the strong city of Jaffa, and cause the destruction of nine-tenths of the army with which they had quitted Europe. And so ended the fourth Crusade.

The fifth was more important, and had a result which its projectors never dreamed of—no less than the sacking of Constantinople, and the placing of a French dynasty upon the imperial throne of the eastern Cæsars. Each succeeding pope, however much he may have differed from his predecessors on other points, zealously agreed in one, that of maintaining by every possible means the papal ascendency. No scheme was so likely to aid in this endeavour as the Crusades. As long as they could persuade the kings and nobles of Europe to fight and die in Syria, their own sway was secured over the minds of men at home. Such being their object, they never inquired whether a Crusade was or was not likely to be successful, whether the time were well or ill chosen, or whether men and money could be procured in sufficient abundance. Pope Innocent III would have been proud if he could have bent the refractory monarchs of England and France into so much submission. But John and Philip Augustus

were both engaged. Both had deeply offended the Church, and had
been laid under her ban, and both were occupied in important reforms
at home; Philip in bestowing immunities upon his subjects, and
John in having them forced from him. The emissaries of the pope
therefore plied them in vain; but as in the first and second Crusades,
the eloquence of a powerful preacher incited the nobility, and through
them a certain portion of the people: Foulque bishop of Neuilly, an
ambitious and enterprising prelate, entered fully into the views of
the court of Rome, and preached the Crusade wherever he could find
an audience. Chance favoured him to a degree he did not himself
expect, for he had in general found but few proselytes, and those few
but cold in the cause. Theobald count of Champagne had instituted a grand tournament, to which he had invited all the nobles
from far and near. Upwards of two thousand knights were present
with their retainers, besides a vast concourse of people to witness the
sports. In the midst of the festivities Foulque arrived upon the spot,
and conceiving the opportunity to be a favourable one, he addressed
the multitude in eloquent language, and passionately called upon
them to enrol themselves for the new Crusade. The Count de Champagne, young, ardent, and easily excited, received the cross at his
hands. The enthusiasm spread rapidly. Charles count of Blois followed the example, and of the two thousand knights present, scarcely
one hundred and fifty refused. The popular phrensy seemed on the
point of breaking out as in the days of yore. The Count of Flanders,
the Count of Bar, the Duke of Burgundy, and the Marquis of Montferrat brought all their vassals to swell the train, and in a very short
space of time an effective army was on foot and ready to march to
Palestine.

The dangers of an overland journey were too well understood,
and the Crusaders endeavoured to make a contract with some of the
Italian states to convey them over in their vessels. Dandolo, the
aged doge of Venice, offered them the galleys of the Republic; but
the Crusaders, on their arrival in that city, found themselves too poor
to pay even half the sum demanded. Every means was tried to raise
money; the Crusaders melted down their plate, and ladies gave up
their trinkets. Contributions were solicited from the faithful, but
came in so slowly as to make it evident to all concerned, that the
faithful of Europe were outnumbered by the prudent. As a last resource, Dandolo offered to convey them to Palestine at the expense
of the Republic, if they would previously aid in the recapture of
the city of Zara, which had been seized from the Venetians a short
time previously by the king of Hungary. The Crusaders consented,
much to the displeasure of the pope, who threatened excommunica-

tion upon all who should be turned aside from the voyage to Jerusalem. But notwithstanding the fulminations of the Church, the expedition never reached Palestine. The siege of Zara was speedily undertaken. After a long and brave defence, the city surrendered at discretion, and the Crusaders were free, if they had so chosen it, to use their swords against the Saracens. But the ambition of the chiefs had been directed, by unforeseen circumstances, elsewhere.

After the death of Manuel Comnenus, the Greek empire had fallen a prey to intestine divisions. His son Alexius II. had succeeded him, but was murdered after a short reign by his uncle Andronicus, who seized upon the throne. His reign also was but of short duration. Isaac Angelus, a member of the same family, took up arms against the usurper, and having defeated and captured him in a pitched battle, had him put to death. He also mounted the throne only to be cast down from it. His brother Alexius deposed him, and to incapacitate him from reigning, put out his eyes, and shut him up in a dungeon. Neither was Alexius III. allowed to remain in peaceable possession of the throne; the son of the unhappy Isaac, whose name also was Alexius, fled from Constantinople, and hearing that the Crusaders had undertaken the siege of Zara, made them the most magnificent offers if they would afterwards aid him in deposing his uncle. His offers were, that if by their means he was re-established in his father's dominions, he would place the Greek Church under the authority of the Pope of Rome, lend the whole force of the Greek empire to the conquest of Palestine, and distribute two hundred thousand marks of silver among the crusading army. The offer was accepted, with a proviso on the part of some of the leaders, that they should be free to abandon the design, if it met with the disapproval of the pope. But this was not to be feared. The submission of the schismatic Greeks to the See of Rome was a greater bribe to the pontiff than the utter annihilation of the Saracen power in Palestine would have been.

The Crusaders were soon in movement for the imperial city. Their operations were skilfully and courageously directed, and spread such dismay as to paralyse the efforts of the usurper to retain possession of his throne. After a vain resistance, he abandoned the city to its fate, and fled no one knew whither. The aged and blind Isaac was taken from his dungeon by his subjects, and placed upon the throne ere the Crusaders were apprised of the flight of his rival. His son Alexius IV. was afterwards associated with him in the sovereignty.

But the conditions of the treaty gave offence to the Grecian people, whose prelates refused to place themselves under the dominion of the See of Rome. Alexius at first endeavoured to persuade his subjects to submission, and prayed the Crusaders to remain in Constantinople until they had fortified him in the possession of a throne which was yet far from secure. He soon became unpopular with his subjects; and breaking faith with regard to the subsidies, he offended the Crusaders. War was at length declared upon him by both parties; by his people for his tyranny, and by his former friends for his treachery. He was seized in his palace by his own guards, and thrown into prison, while the Crusaders were making ready to besiege his capital. The Greeks immediately proceeded to the election of a new monarch; and looking about for a man of courage, energy, and perseverance, they fixed upon Alexius Ducas, who, with almost every bad quality, was possessed of the virtues they needed. He ascended

CONSTANTINOPLE.

the throne under the name of Murzuphlis. One of his first acts was to rid himself of his youngest predecessor—a broken heart had already removed the blind old Isaac, no longer a stumbling-block in his way—and the young Alexius was soon after put to death in his prison.

War to the knife was now declared between the Greeks and the Franks; and early in the spring of the year 1204, preparations were commenced for an assault upon Constantinople. The French and Venetians entered into a treaty for the division of the spoils among their soldiery; for so confident were they of success, that failure never once entered into their calculations. This confidence led them on to victory; while the Greeks, cowardly as treacherous people always are, were paralysed by a foreboding of evil. It has been a matter of astonishment to all historians, that Murzuphlis, with the reputation for courage which he had acquired, and the immense resources at his disposal, took no better measures to repel the onset of the Crusaders. Their numbers were as a mere handful in comparison with those which he could have brought against them; and if they had the hopes of plunder to lead them on, the Greeks had their homes to fight for, and their very existence as a nation to protect. After an impetuous assault, repulsed for one day, but renewed with double impetuosity on another, the Crusaders lashed their vessels against the walls, slew every man who opposed them, and, with little loss to themselves, entered the city. Murzuphlis fled, and Constantinople was given over to be pillaged by the victors. The wealth they found was enormous. In money alone there was sufficient to distribute twenty marks of silver to each knight, ten to each squire or servant at arms, and five to each archer. Jewels, velvets, silks, and every luxury of attire, with rare wines and fruits, and valuable merchandise of every description, also fell into their hands, and were bought by the trading Venetians, and the proceeds distributed among the army. Two thousand persons were put to the sword; but had there been less plunder to take up the attention of the victors, the slaughter would in all probability have been much greater.

In many of the bloody wars which defile the page of history, we find that soldiers, utterly reckless of the works of God, will destroy his masterpiece, man, with unsparing brutality, but linger with respect round the beautiful works of art. They will slaughter women and children, but spare a picture; will hew down the sick, the helpless, and the hoary-headed, but refrain from injuring a fine piece of sculpture. The Latins, on their entrance into Constantinople, respected neither the works of God nor man, but vented their brutal ferocity upon the one, and satisfied their avarice upon the other. Many beautiful bronze statues, above all price as works of art, were broken into pieces to be sold as old metal. The finely-chiselled marble, which could be put to no such vile uses, was also destroyed with a recklessness, if possible, still more atrocious.*

---

* The following is a list of some of the works of art thus destroyed, from Nicetas, a contemporary Greek author: 1st. A colossal Juno, from the forum of Constantine, the head of which was so large that four horses could scarcely draw it from the place where it stood to the palace. 2d. The statue of Paris, presenting the apple to Venus. 3d. An immense bronze pyramid, crowned by a female figure, which turned with the wind. 4th. The colossal statue of Bellerophon, in bronze, which was broken down and cast into the furnace. Under the inner nail of the horse's hind foot on the left side, was found a seal wrapped in a woollen cloth. 5th. A figure of Hercules, by Lysimachus, of such vast

The carnage being over, and the spoil distributed, six persons were chosen from among the Franks and six from among the Venetians, who were to meet and elect an emperor, previously binding themselves by oath to select the individual best qualified among the candidates. The choice wavered between Baldwin count of Flanders and Boniface marquis of Montferrat, but fell eventually upon the former. He was straightway robed in the imperial purple, and became the founder of a new dynasty. He did not live long to enjoy his power, or to consolidate it for his successors, who, in their turn, were soon swept away. In less than sixty years the rule of the Franks at Constantinople was brought to as sudden and disastrous a termination as the reign of Murzuphlis : and this was the grand result of the fifth Crusade.

Pope Innocent III., although he had looked with no very unfavourable eye upon these proceedings, regretted that nothing had been done for the relief of the Holy Land; still, upon every convenient occasion, he enforced the necessity of a new Crusade. Until the year 1213, his exhortations had no other effect than to keep the subject in the mind of Europe. Every spring and summer detachments of pilgrims continued to set out for Palestine to the aid of their brethren, but not in sufficient numbers to be of much service. These periodical passages were called the *passagium Martii*, or the passage of March, and the *passagium Johannis*, or the passage of the festival of St. John. These did not consist entirely of soldiers, armed against the Saracen, but of pilgrims led by devotion, and in performance of their vows, bearing nothing with them but their staff and their wallet. Early in the spring of 1213 a more extraordinary body of Crusaders was raised in France and Germany. An immense number of boys and girls, amounting, according to some accounts, to thirty thousand, were incited by the persuasion of two monks to undertake the journey to Palestine. They were no doubt composed of the idle and deserted children who generally swarm in great cities, nurtured in vice and daring, and ready for any thing. The object of the monks seems to have been the atrocious one of inveigling them into slave-ships, on pretence of sending them to Syria, and selling them for slaves on the coast of Africa.* Great numbers of these poor victims were shipped

dimensions that the thumb was equal in circumference to the waist of a man. 6th. The Ass and his Driver, cast by order of Augustus after the battle of Actium, in commemoration of his having discovered the position of Anthony through the means of an ass-driver. 7th. The Wolf suckling the Twins of Rome. 8th. The Gladiator in combat with a Lion. 9th. The Hippopotamus. 10th. The Sphinxes. 11th. An Eagle fighting with a Serpent. 12th. A beautiful statue of Helen. 13th. A group, with a monster somewhat resembling a bull engaged in deadly conflict with a serpent; and many other works of art, too numerous to mention.

* See Jacob de Voragine and Albericus.

at Marseilles; but the vessels, with the exception of two or three, were wrecked on the shores of Italy, and every soul perished. The remainder arrived safely in Africa, and were bought up as slaves, and sent off into the interior of the country. Another detachment arrived at Genoa; but the accomplices in this horrid plot having taken no measures at that port, expecting them all at Marseilles, they were induced to return to their homes by the Genoese.

Fuller, in his quaint history of the *Holy Warre*, says that this Crusade was done by the instinct of the devil; and he adds a reason, which may provoke mirth now, but which was put forth by the worthy historian in all soberness and sincerity He says, "the devil, being cloyed with the murdering of men, desired a cordial of children's blood to comfort his weak stomach;" as epicures, when tired of mutton, resort to lamb for a change.

It appears from other authors that the preaching of the vile monks had such an effect upon these deluded children that they ran about the country, exclaiming, "O Lord Jesus, restore thy cross to us!" and that neither bolts nor bars, the fear of fathers, nor the love of mothers, was sufficient to restrain them from journeying to Jerusalem.

The details of these strange proceedings are exceedingly meagre and confused, and none of the contemporary writers who mention the subject have thought it worth while to state the names of the monks who originated the scheme, or the fate they met for their wickedness. Two merchants of Marseilles, who were to have shared in the profits, were, it is said, brought to justice for some other crime, and suffered death; but we are not informed whether they divulged any circumstances relating to this matter.

Pope Innocent III. does not seem to have been aware that the causes of this juvenile Crusade were such as have been stated, for, upon being informed that numbers of them had taken the cross, and were marching to the Holy Land, he exclaimed, "These children are awake while we sleep!" He imagined, apparently, that the mind of Europe was still bent on the recovery of Palestine, and that the zeal of these children implied a sort of reproach upon his own lukewarmness. Very soon afterwards, he bestirred himself with more activity, and sent an encyclical letter to the clergy of Christendom, urging them to preach a new Crusade. As usual, a number of adventurous nobles, who had nothing else to do, enrolled themselves with their retainers. At a Council of Lateran, which was held while these bands were collecting, Innocent announced that he himself would take the Cross, and lead the armies of Christ to the defence of his sepulchre· In all probability he would have done so, for he was zealous enough; but death stepped in, and destroyed his project ere it was ripe. His successor encouraged the Crusade, though he refused to accompany it ; and the armament continued in France, England, and Germany. No leaders of any importance joined it from the former countries. Andrew king of Hungary was the only monarch who had leisure or inclination to leave his dominions. The Dukes of Austria and Bavaria joined him with a considerable army of Germans, and marching to Spalatro, took ship for Cyprus, and from thence to Acre. The whole conduct of the king of Hungary was marked by pusillanimity and irresolution. He found himself in the Holy Land at the head of a very efficient army ; the Saracens were taken by surprise, and were for some weeks unprepared to offer any resistance to his arms. He defeated the first body sent to oppose him, and marched towards Mount Tabor with the intention of seizing upon an important fortress which the Saracens had recently constructed. He arrived without impediment at the mount, and might have easily taken it ; but a sudden fit of cowardice came over him, and he returned to Acre without striking a blow. He very soon afterwards abandoned the enterprise altogether, and returned to his own country.

Tardy reinforcements arrived at intervals from Europe ; and the Duke of Austria, now the chief leader of the expedition, had still sufficient forces at his command to trouble the Saracens very seriously. It was resolved by him, in council with the other chiefs, that the whole energy of the Crusade should be directed upon Egypt, the seat of the Saracen power in its relationship to Palestine, and from whence were drawn the continual levies that were brought against them by the sultan. Damietta, which commanded the river Nile, and was one of the most important cities of Egypt, was chosen as the first point of attack. The siege was forthwith commenced, and carried on with considerable energy, until the Crusaders gained possession of a tower, which projected into the middle of the stream, and was looked upon as the very key of the city.

While congratulating themselves upon this success, and wasting in revelry the time which should have been employed in turning it to further advantage, they received the news of the death of the wise Sultan Saphaddin. His two sons, Camhel and Cohreddin, divided his empire between them. Syria and Palestine fell to the share of Cohreddin, while Egypt was consigned to the other brother, who had for some time exercised the functions of lieutenant of that country. Being unpopular among the Egyptians, they revolted against him, giving the Crusaders a finer opportunity for making a conquest than they had ever enjoyed before. But, quarrelsome and licentious as they had been from time immemorial, they did not see that the favourable moment had come ; or seeing, could not profit by it. While they were revelling or fighting among themselves under the walls of Damietta, the revolt was suppressed, and Camhel firmly established on the throne of Egypt. In conjunction with his brother Cohreddin, his next care was to drive the Christians from Damietta, and for upwards of three months they bent all their efforts to throw in supplies to the besieged, or draw on the besiegers to a general engagement. In neither were they successful ; and the famine in Damietta became so dreadful that vermin of every description were thought luxuries, and sold for exorbitant prices. A dead dog became more valuable than a live ox in time of prosperity. Unwholesome food brought on disease, and the city could hold out no longer for absolute want of men to defend the walls.

Cohreddin and Camhel were alike interested in the preservation of so important a position, and, convinced of the certain fate of the city, they opened a conference with the crusading chiefs, offering to yield the whole of Palestine to the Christians upon the sole condition of the evacuation of Egypt. With a blindness and wrong-headedness almost incredible, these advantageous terms were refused, chiefly through the persuasion of Cardinal Pelagius, an ignorant and obstinate fanatic, who urged upon the Duke of Austria and the French and English leaders, that infidels never kept their word ; that their offers were deceptive, and merely intended to betray. The conferences were brought to an abrupt termination by the Crusaders, and a last attack made upon the walls of Damietta. The besieged made but slight resistance, for they had no hope, and the Christians entered the city, and found, out of seventy thousand people, but three thousand remaining : so fearful had been the ravages of the twin fiends plague and famine.

Several months were spent in Damietta. The climate either weakened the frames or obscured the understandings of the Christians ; for, after their conquest, they lost all energy, and abandoned themselves more unscrupulously than ever to riot and debauchery. John of Brienne, who by right of his wife was the nominal sovereign of Jerusalem, was so disgusted with the pusillanimity, arrogance, and dissensions of the chiefs, that he withdrew entirely from them and retired to Acre. Large bodies also returned to Europe, and Cardinal Pelagius was left at liberty to blast the whole enterprise whenever it pleased him. He managed to conciliate John of Brienne, and marched forward with these combined forces to attack Cairo. It was only when he had approached within a few hours' march of that city that he discovered the inadequacy of his army. He turned back immediately ; but the Nile had risen since his departure ; the sluices were opened, and there was no means of reaching Damietta. In this strait, he sued for the peace he had formerly spurned, and, happily for himself, found the generous brothers Camhel and Cohreddin still willing to grant it. Damietta was soon afterwards given up, and the cardinal returned to Europe. John of Brienne retired to Acre, to mourn the loss of his kingdom, embittered against the folly of his pretended friends, who had ruined where they should have aided him. And thus ended the sixth Crusade.

The seventh was more successful. Frederic II., emperor of Germany, had often vowed to lead his armies to the defence of Palestine, but was as often deterred from the journey by matters of more pressing importance. Cohreddin was a mild and enlightened monarch, and the Christians of Syria enjoyed repose and toleration under his rule : but John of Brienne was not willing to lose his kingdom without an effort ; and the popes in Europe were ever willing to embroil the nations for the sake of extending their own power. No monarch of that age was capable of rendering more effective assistance than Frederic of Germany. To inspire him with more zeal, it was proposed that he should wed the young Princess Violante, daughter of John of Brienne, and heiress of the kingdom of Jerusalem. Frederic consented with joy and eagerness. The princess was brought from Acre to Rome without delay, and her marriage celebrated on a scale of great magnificence. Her father, John of Brienne, abdicated all his rights in favour of his son-in-law, and Jerusalem had once more a king, who had not only the will, but the power, to enforce his claims. Preparations for the new Crusade were immediately commenced, and in the course of six months the emperor was at the head of a well-disciplined army of sixty thousand men. Matthew Paris informs us, that an army of the same amount was gathered in England ; and most of the writers upon the Crusades adopt his statement. When John of Brienne was in England, before his daughter's marriage with the emperor was thought of, praying for the aid of Henry III. and his nobles to recover his lost kingdom, he did not meet with much encouragement. Grafton, in his *Chronicle*, says, "he departed again without any great comfort." But when a man of more influence in European politics appeared upon the scene, the English nobles were as ready to sacrifice themselves in the cause as they had been in the time of Cœur de Lion.

The army of Frederic encamped at Brundusium ; but a pestilential disease having made its appearance among them, their departure was delayed for several months. In the mean time the Empress Violante died in childbed. John of Brienne, who had already repented of his abdication, and was besides incensed against Frederic for many acts of neglect and insult, no sooner saw the only tie which bound them severed by the death of his daughter, than he began to bestir himself, and make interest with the pope to undo what he had done, and regain the honorary crown he had renounced. Pope Gregory IX., a man of a proud, unconciliating, and revengeful character, owed the emperor a grudge for many an act of disobedience to his authority, and encouraged the overtures of John of Brienne more than he should have done. Frederic, however, despised them both, and, as soon as his army was convalescent, set sail for Acre. He had not been many days at sea when he was himself attacked with the malady, and obliged to return to Otranto, the nearest port. Gregory, who had by this time decided in the interest of John of Brienne, excommunicated the emperor for returning from so holy an expedition on any pretext whatever. Frederic at first treated the excommunication with supreme contempt; but when he got well, he gave his holiness to understand that he was not to be outraged with impunity, and sent some of his troops to ravage the papal territories. This, however, only made the matter worse, and Gregory despatched messengers to Palestine forbidding the faithful, under severe pains and penalties, to hold any intercourse with the excommunicated emperor. Thus, between them both, the scheme which they had so much at heart bade fair to be as effectually ruined as even the Saracens could have wished. Frederic still continued his zeal in the Crusade, for he was now king of Jerusalem, and fought for himself, and not for Christendom, or its representative, Pope Gregory. Hearing that John of Brienne was preparing to leave Europe, he lost no time in taking his own departure, and arrived safely at Acre. It was here that he first experienced the evil effects of excommunication. The Christians of Palestine refused to aid him in any way, and looked with distrust, if not with abhorrence, upon him. The Templars, Hospitallers, and other knights, shared at first the general feeling; but they were not men to yield a blind obedience to a distant potentate, especially when it compromised their own interests. When, therefore, Frederic prepared to march upon Jerusalem without them, they joined his banners to a man.

It is said that, previous to quitting Europe, the German emperor had commenced a negotiation with the Sultan Camhel for the restoration of the Holy Land, and that Camhel, who was jealous of the ambition of his brother Cohreddin, was willing to stipulate to that effect, on condition of being secured by Frederic in the possession of the more important territory of Egypt. But before the Crusaders reached Palestine, Camhel was relieved from all fears by the death of his brother. He nevertheless did not think it worth while to contest with the Crusaders the barren corner of the earth which had already been dyed with so much Christian and Saracen blood, and proposed a truce of three years, only stipulating, in addition, that the Moslems should be allowed to worship freely in the temple of Jerusalem. This happy termination did not satisfy the bigoted Christians of Palestine. The tolerance they sought for themselves, they were not willing to extend to others, and they complained bitterly of the privilege of free worship allowed to their opponents. Unmerited good fortune had made them insolent, and they contested the right of the emperor to become a party to any treaty, as long as he remained under the ecclesiastical ban. Frederic was disgusted with his new subjects; but, as the Templars and Hospitallers remained true to him, he marched to Jeru-

TEMPLAR AND HOSPITALLER.

salem to be crowned. All the churches were shut against him, and he could not even find a priest to officiate at his coronation. He had despised the papal authority too long to quail at it now, when it was so unjustifiably exerted, and, as there was nobody to crown him, he very wisely crowned himself. He took the royal diadem from the altar with his own hands, and boldly and proudly placed it on his brow. No shouts of an applauding populace made the welkin ring;

no hymns of praise and triumph resounded from the ministers of religion; but a thousand swords started from their scabbards to testify that their owners would defend the new monarch to the death.

It was hardly to be expected that he would renounce for any long period the dominion of his native land for the uneasy crown and barren soil of Palestine. He had seen quite enough of his new subjects before he was six months among them, and more important interests called him home. John of Brienne, openly leagued with Pope Gregory against him, was actually employed in ravaging his territories at the head of a papal army. This intelligence decided his return. As a preliminary step, he made those who had contemned his authority feel, to their sorrow, that he was their master. He then set sail, loaded with the curses of Palestine. And thus ended the seventh Crusade, which, in spite of every obstacle and disadvantage, had been productive of more real service to the Holy Land than any that had gone before; a result solely attributable to the bravery of Frederic and the generosity of the Sultan Camhel.

Soon after the emperor's departure a new claimant started for the throne of Jerusalem, in the person of Alice queen of Cyprus, and half-sister of the Mary who, by her marriage, had transferred her right to John of Brienne. The grand military orders, however, clung to Frederic, and Alice was obliged to withdraw.

So peaceful a termination to the Crusade did not give unmixed pleasure in Europe. The chivalry of France and England were unable to rest, and long before the conclusion of the truce, were collecting their armies for an eighth expedition. In Palestine also the contentment was far from universal. Many petty Mahomedan states in the immediate vicinity were not parties to the truce, and harassed the frontier towns incessantly. The Templars, ever turbulent, waged bitter war with the sultan of Aleppo, and in the end were almost exterminated. So great was the slaughter among them that Europe resounded with the sad story of their fate, and many a noble knight took arms to prevent the total destruction of an order associated with so many high and inspiring remembrances. Camhel, seeing the preparations that were making, thought that his generosity had been sufficiently shewn, and the very day the truce was at an end assumed the offensive, and marching forward to Jerusalem, took possession of it, after routing the scanty forces of the Christians. Before this intelligence reached Europe a large body of Crusaders was on the march, headed by the King of Navarre, the Duke of Burgundy, the Count de Bretagne, and other leaders. On their arrival, they learned that Jerusalem had been taken, but that the sultan was dead, and his kingdom torn by rival claimants to the supreme power. The dissensions of their foes ought to have made them united; but, as in all previous Crusades, each feudal chief was master of his own host, and acted upon his own responsibility, and without reference to any general plan. The consequence was that nothing could be done. A temporary advantage was gained by one leader, who had no means of improving it; while another was defeated, without means of retrieving himself. Thus the war lingered till the battle of Gaza, when the king of Navarre was defeated with great loss, and compelled to save himself from total destruction by entering into a hard and oppressive treaty with the emir of Karac.

At this crisis aid arrived from England, commanded by Richard earl of Cornwall, the namesake of Cœur de Lion, and inheritor of his valour. His army was strong and full of hope. They had confidence in themselves and in their leader, and looked like men accustomed to victory. Their coming changed the aspect of affairs. The new sultan of Egypt was at war with the sultan of Damascus, and had not forces to oppose two enemies so powerful. He therefore sent messengers to meet the English earl, offering an exchange of prisoners and the complete cession of the Holy Land. Richard, who had not come to fight for the mere sake of fighting, agreed at once to terms so advantageous, and became the deliverer of Palestine without striking a blow. The sultan of Egypt then turned his whole force against his Moslem enemies, and the Earl of Cornwall returned to Europe. Thus ended the eighth Crusade, the most beneficial of all. Christendom had no further pretence for sending her fierce levies to the East. To all appearance the holy wars were at an end: the Christians had entire possession of Jerusalem, Tripoli, Antioch, Edessa, Acre, Jaffa, and, in fact, of nearly all Judea; and, could they have been at peace among themselves, they might have overcome, without great difficulty, the jealousy and hostility of their neighbours. A circumstance, as unforeseen as it was disastrous, blasted this fair prospect, and reillumed, for the last time, the fervour and fury of the Crusades.

Gengis Khan and his successors had swept over Asia like a tropical storm, overturning in their progress the landmarks of ages. Kingdom after kingdom was cast down as they issued, innumerable, from the far recesses of the North and East, and, among others, the empire of Korasmin was overrun by these all-conquering hordes. The Korasmins, a fierce, uncivilised race, thus driven from their homes, spread themselves, in their turn, over the south of Asia with fire and sword, in search of a resting-place. In their impetuous course they directed themselves towards Egypt, whose sultan, unable to withstand the swarm that had cast their longing eyes on the fertile valleys of the Nile, endeavoured to turn them from their course. For this purpose, he sent emissaries to Barbaquan, their leader, inviting them to settle in Palestine; and the offer being accepted by the wild horde, they entered the country before the Christians received the slightest intimation of their coming. It was as sudden as it was overwhelming. Onwards, like the simoom, they came, burning and slaying, and were at the walls of Jerusalem before the inhabitants had time to look round them. They spared neither life nor property; they slew women and children, and priests at the altar, and profaned even the graves of those who had slept for ages. They tore down every vestige of the Christian faith, and committed horrors unparalleled in the history of warfare. About seven thousand of the inhabitants of Jerusalem sought safety in retreat; but before they were out of sight, the banner of the cross was hoisted upon the walls by the savage foe to decoy them back. The artifice

JAFFA.

was but too successful. The poor fugitives imagined that help had arrived from another direction, and turned back to regain their homes. Nearly the whole of them were massacred, and the streets of Jerusalem ran with blood.

The Templars, Hospitallers, and Teutonic knights forgot their long and bitter animosities, and joined hand in hand to rout out this desolating foe. They entrenched themselves in Jaffa, with all the chivalry of Palestine that yet remained, and endeavoured to engage the sultans of Emissa and Damascus to assist them against the common enemy. The aid obtained from the Moslems amounted at first to only four thousand men, but with these reinforcements Walter of Brienne, the lord of Jaffa, resolved to give battle to the Korasmins. The conflict was as deadly as despair on the one side, and unmitigated ferocity on the other, could make it. It lasted with varying fortune for two days, when the sultan of Emissa fled to his fortifications, and Walter of Brienne fell into the enemy's hands. The brave knight was suspended by the arms to a cross in sight of the walls of Jaffa, and the Korasminian leader declared that he should remain in that position until the city surrendered. Walter raised his feeble voice, not to advise surrender, but to command his soldiers to hold out to the last. But his gallantry was unavailing. So great had been the slaughter, that out of the grand array of knights, there now remained but sixteen Hospitallers, thirty-three Templars, and three Teutonic cavaliers. These, with the sad remnant of the army, fled to Acre, and the Korasmins were masters of Palestine.

The sultans of Syria preferred the Christians to this fierce horde for their neighbours. Even the sultan of Egypt began to regret the aid he had given to such barbarous foes, and united with those of Emissa and Damascus to root them from the land. The Korasmins amounted to but twenty thousand men, and were unable to resist the determined hostility which encompassed them on every side. The sultans defeated them in several engagements, and the peasantry rose up in masses to take vengeance upon them. Gradually their numbers were diminished. No mercy was shewn them in defeat. Barbaquan their leader was slain; and after five years of desperate struggles, they were finally extirpated, and Palestine became once more the territory of the Mussulmans.

A short time previous to this devastating eruption, Louis IX. fell sick in Paris, and dreamed in the delirium of his fever that he saw the Christian and Moslem host fighting before Jerusalem, and the Christians defeated with great slaughter. The dream made a great impression on his superstitious mind, and he made a solemn vow, that if ever he recovered his health, he would take a pilgrimage to the Holy Land. When the news of the misfortunes of Palestine, and the awful massacres at Jerusalem and Jaffa, arrived in Europe, St. Louis remembered him of his dream. More persuaded than ever that it was an intimation direct from heaven, he prepared to take the cross at the head of his armies, and march to the deliverance of the Holy Sepulchre. From that moment he doffed the royal mantle of purple and ermine, and dressed in the sober serge becoming a pilgrim. All his thoughts were directed to the fulfilment of his design, and although his kingdom could but ill spare him, he made every preparation to leave it. Pope Innocent IV applauded his zeal and afforded him every assistance. He wrote to Henry III. of England to forward the cause in his dominions, and called upon the clergy and laity all over Europe to contribute towards it. William Longsword,

WILLIAM LONGSWORD.

the celebrated Earl of Salisbury, took the cross at the head of a great number of valiant knights and soldiers. But the fanaticism of the people was not to be awakened either in France or England. Great armies were raised, but the masses no longer sympathised. Taxation had been the great cooler of zeal. It was no longer a disgrace even to a knight if he refused to take the cross. Rutebeuf, a French minstrel, who flourished about this time (1250), composed a dialogue between a Crusader and a non-Crusader, which the reader will find translated in Way's *Fabliaux*. The Crusader uses every argument to persuade the non-Crusader to take up arms, and forsake every thing in the holy cause; but it is evident from the greater force of the arguments used by the non-Crusader, that he was the favourite of the minstrel. To a most urgent solicitation of his friend the Crusader, he replies:

> " I read thee right, thou holdest good
>   To this same land I straight should hie,
> And win it back with mickle blood,
>   Nor gaine one foot of soil thereby ;
> While here dejected and forlorn
> My wife and babes are left to mourn ;
> My goodly mansion rudely marred,
> All trusted to my dogs to guard.
> But I, fair comrade, well I wot
>   An ancient saw of pregnant wit
> Doth bid us keep what we have got ;
>   And troth I mean to follow it."

This being the general feeling, it is not to be wondered at that Louis IX. was occupied fully three years in organising his forces, and in making the necessary preparations for his departure. When all was ready he set sail for Cyprus, accompanied by his queen, his two brothers, the Counts d'Anjou and d'Artois, and a long train of the noblest chivalry of France. His third brother, the Count de Poitiers, remained behind to collect another corps of Crusaders, and followed him in a few months afterwards. The army united at Cyprus, and amounted to fifty thousand men, exclusive of the English Crusaders under William Longsword. Again, a pestilential disease made its appearance, to which many hundreds fell victims. It was in consequence found necessary to remain in Cyprus until the spring. Louis then embarked for Egypt with his whole host ; but a violent tempest separated his fleet, and he arrived before Damietta with only a few thousand men. They were, however, impetuous and full of hope ; and although the Sultan Melick Shah was drawn up on the shore with a force infinitely superior, it was resolved to attempt a landing without waiting the arrival of the rest of the army. Louis himself, in wild impatience, sprang from his boat, and waded on shore ; while his army, inspired by his enthusiastic bravery, followed, shouting the old war-cry of the first Crusaders, *Dieu le veut! Dieu le veut!* A panic seized the Turks. A body of their cavalry attempted to bear down upon the Crusaders, but the knights fixed their large shields deep in the sands of the shore, and rested their lances upon them, so that they projected above, and formed a barrier so imposing, that the Turks, afraid to breast it, turned round and fairly took to flight. At the moment of this panic, a false report was spread in the Saracen host, that the sultan had been slain. The confusion immediately became general—the *deroute* was complete: Damietta itself was abandoned, and the same night the victorious Crusaders fixed their head-quarters in that city. The soldiers who had been separated from their chief by the tempest arrived shortly afterwards; and Louis was in a position to justify the hope, not only of the conquest of Palestine, but of Egypt itself.

But too much confidence proved the bane of his army. They thought, as they had accomplished so much, that nothing more remained to be done, and gave themselves up to ease and luxury. When, by the command of Louis, they marched towards Cairo, they were no longer the same men; success, instead of inspiring, had unnerved them; debauchery had brought on disease, and disease was aggravated by the heat of a climate to which none of them were accustomed. Their progress towards Massoura, on the road to Cairo, was checked by the Thanisian canal, on the banks of which the Saracens were drawn up to dispute the passage. Louis gave orders that a bridge should be thrown across: and the operations commenced under cover of two cat-castles, or high movable towers. The Saracens soon destroyed them by throwing quantities of Greek fire, the artillery of that day, upon them, and Louis was forced to think of some other means of effecting his design. A peasant agreed, for a considerable bribe, to point out a ford where the army might wade across, and the Count d'Artois was despatched with fourteen hundred men to attempt it, while Louis remained to face the Saracens with the main body of the army. The Count d'Artois got safely over, and defeated the detachment that had been sent to oppose his landing. Flushed with the victory, the brave count forgot the inferiority of his numbers, and pursued the panic-stricken enemy into Massoura. He was now completely cut off from the aid of his brother Crusaders, which the Moslems perceiving, took courage and returned upon him, with a force swollen by the garrison of Massoura, and by reinforcements from the surrounding districts. The battle now became hand to hand. The Christians fought with the energy of desperate men, but the continually increasing numbers of the foe surrounded them completely, and cut off all hope, either of victory or escape. The Count d'Artois was among the foremost of the slain; and when Louis arrived to the rescue, the brave advanced-guard was nearly cut to pieces. Of the fourteen hundred, but three hundred remained. The fury of the battle was now increased threefold. The French king and his troops performed prodigies of valour, and the Saracens, under the command of the Emir Ceccidun, fought as if they were determined to exterminate, in one last decisive effort, the new European swarm that had settled upon their coast. At the fall of the evening dews the Christians were masters of the field of Massoura, and flattered themselves that they were the victors. Self-love would not suffer them to confess that the Saracens had withdrawn, and not retreated; but their leaders were too wofully convinced that that fatal field had completed the disorganisation of the Christian army, and that all hopes of future conquest were at an end.

Impressed with this truth, the Crusaders sued for peace. The sultan insisted upon the immediate evacuation of Damietta, and that Louis himself should be delivered as hostage for the fulfilment of the condition. His army at once refused, and the negotiations were broken off. It was now resolved to attempt a retreat; but the agile Saracens, now in the front and now in the rear, rendered it a matter of extreme difficulty, and cut off the stragglers in great numbers. Hundreds of them were drowned in the Nile; and sickness and famine worked sad ravages upon those who escaped all other casualties. Louis himself was so weakened by disease, fatigue, and discouragement, that he was hardly able to sit upon his horse. In the confusion of the flight he was separated from his attendants, and left a total stranger upon the sands of Egypt, sick, weary, and almost friendless. One knight, Geffry de Sergines, alone attended him, and led him to a miserable hut in a small village, where for several days he lay in the hourly expectation of death. He was at last discovered and taken prisoner by the Saracens, who treated him with all the honour due to his rank and all the pity due to his misfortunes. Under their care his health rapidly improved, and the next consideration was that of his ransom.

The Saracens demanded, besides money, the cession of Acre, Tripoli, and other cities of Palestine. Louis unhesitatingly refused, and conducted himself with so much pride and courage that the sultan declared he was the proudest infidel he had ever beheld. After a good deal of haggling, the sultan agreed to waive these conditions, and a treaty was finally concluded. The city of Damietta was restored, a truce of ten years agreed upon, and ten thousand golden bezants paid for the release of Louis and the liberation of all the captives. Louis then withdrew to Jaffa, and spent two years in putting that city, and Cesarea, with the other possessions of the Christians in Palestine, into a proper state of defence. He then returned to his own country, with great reputation as a saint, but very little as a soldier.

Matthew Paris informs us that, in the year 1250, while Louis was in Egypt, " thousands of the English were resolved to go to the holy war, had not the king strictly guarded his ports and kept his people from running out of doors." When the news arrived of the reverses and captivity of the French king, their ardour cooled ; and the Crusade was sung of only, but not spoken of.

In France, a very different feeling was the result. The news of the king's capture spread consternation through the country. A fanatic monk of Citeaux suddenly appeared in the villages, preaching to the people, and announcing that the Holy Virgin, accompanied by a whole army of saints and martyrs, had appeared to him, and commanded him to stir up the shepherds and farm-labourers, to the defence of the cross. To them only was his discourse addressed ; and his eloquence was such, that thousands flocked around him, ready to follow wherever he should lead. The pastures and the corn-fields were deserted, and the shepherds, or *pastoureaux*, as they were termed, became at last so numerous as to amount to upwards of fifty thousand,—Millot says one hundred thousand men.* The Queen Blanche, who governed as regent during the absence of the king, encouraged at first the armies of the *pastoureaux ;* but they soon gave way to such vile excesses that the peaceably disposed were driven to resistance. Robbery, murder, and violation marked their path ; and all good men, assisted by the government, united in putting them down. They were finally dispersed, but not before three thousand of them had been massacred. Many authors say that the slaughter was still greater.

The ten years' truce concluded in 1264, and St. Louis was urged by two powerful motives to undertake a second expedition for the relief of Palestine. These were, fanaticism on the one hand, and a desire of retrieving his military fame on the other, which had suffered more than his parasites liked to remind him of. The pope, of course, encouraged his design, and once more the chivalry of Europe began to bestir themselves. In 1268, Edward, the heir of the English monarchy, announced his determination to join the Crusade ; and the pope (Clement IV.) wrote to the prelates and clergy to aid the cause by their persuasions and their revenues. In England, they agreed to contribute a tenth of their possessions ; and by a parliamentary order, a twentieth was taken from the corn and movables of all the laity at Michaelmas.

In spite of the remonstrances of the few clear-headed statesmen who surrounded him, urging the ruin that might in consequence fall upon his then prosperous kingdom, Louis made every preparation for

* *Elémens de l'Histoire de France.*

his departure.   The warlike nobility were nothing loath ; and in the spring of 1270, the king set sail with an army of sixty thousand men. He was driven by stress of weather into Sardinia, and while there, a change in his plans took place.   Instead of proceeding to Acre, as he originally intended, he shaped his course for Tunis, on the African coast.   The king of Tunis had some time previously expressed himself favourably disposed towards the Christians and their religion, and Louis, it appears, had hopes of converting him, and securing his aid against the sultan of Egypt.   " What honour would be mine," he used to say, " if I could become godfather to this Mussulman king !" Filled with this idea he landed in Africa, near the site of the city of Carthage, but found that he had reckoned without his host.   The king of Tunis had no thoughts of renouncing his religion, nor intention of aiding the Crusaders in any way.   On the contrary, he opposed their landing with all the forces that could be collected on so sudden an emergency.   The French, however, made good their first position, and defeated the Moslems with considerable loss.   They also gained some advantage over the reinforcements that were sent to oppose them ; but an infectious flux appeared in the army, and put a stop to all future victories.   The soldiers died at the rate of a hundred in a day.   The enemy, at the same time, made as great havoc as the plague.   St. Louis himself was one of the first attacked by the disease. His constitution had been weakened by fatigues, and even before he left France he was unable to bear the full weight of his armour.   It was soon evident to his sorrowing soldiers that their beloved monarch could not long survive.   He lingered for some days, and died in Carthage in the fifty-sixth year of his age, deeply regretted by his army and his subjects, and leaving behind him one of the most singular reputations in history.   He is the model king of ecclesiastical writers, in whose eyes his very defects became virtues, because they were manifested in furtherance of their cause.   More unprejudiced historians, while they condemn his fanaticism, admit that he was endowed with many high and rare qualities ; that he was in no one point behind his age, and in many in advance of it.

His brother, Charles of Anjou, in consequence of a revolution in Sicily, had become king of that country.   Before he heard of the death of Louis, he had sailed from Messina with large reinforcements. On his landing near Carthage, he advanced at the head of his army, amid the martial music of drums and trumpets.   He was soon informed how inopportune was his rejoicing, and shed tears before his whole army, such as no warrior would have been ashamed to shed. A peace was speedily agreed upon with the king of Tunis, and the armies of France and Sicily returned to their homes.

So little favour had the Crusade found in England, that even the exertions of the heir to the throne had only collected a small force of fifteen hundred men. With these few Prince Edward sailed from Dover to Bourdeaux, in the expectation that he would find the French king in that city. St. Louis, however, had left a few weeks previously; upon which Edward followed him to Sardinia, and afterwards to Tunis. Before his arrival in Africa, St. Louis was no more, and peace had been concluded between France and Tunis. He determined, however, not to relinquish the Crusade. Returning to Sicily, he passed the winter in that country, and endeavoured to augment his little army. In the spring he set sail for Palestine, and arrived in safety at Acre. The Christians were torn, as usual, by mutual jealousies and animosities. The two great military orders were as virulent and as intractable as ever; opposed to each other, and to all the world. The arrival of Edward had the effect of causing them to lay aside their unworthy contention, and of uniting heart

SEAL OF EDWARD I.

to heart in one last effort for the deliverance of their adopted country. A force of six thousand effective warriors was soon formed to join those of the English prince, and preparations were made for the renewal of hostilities. The Sultan Bibars or Bendocdar,* a fierce Mamluke, who had been placed on the throne by a bloody revolution, was

* Mills, in his history, gives the name of this chief as "Al Malek al Dhaker Rok neddin Abulfeth Bibars al Ali al Bundokdari al Salehi."

at war with all his neighbours, and unable, for that reason, to concentrate his whole strength against them. Edward took advantage of this, and marching boldly forward to Nazareth, defeated the Turks and gained possession of that city. This was the whole amount of his successes. The hot weather engendered disease among his troops, and he himself, the life and soul of the expedition, fell sick among the first. He had been ill for some time, and was slowly recovering, when a messenger desired to speak with him on important matters, and to deliver some despatches into his own hand. While the prince was occupied in examining them, the traitorous messenger drew a dagger from his belt and stabbed him in the breast. The wound fortunately was not deep, and Edward had regained a portion of his strength. He struggled with the assassin, and put him to death with his own dagger, at the same time calling loudly for assistance.* His attendants came at his call, and found him bleeding profusely, and ascertained on inspection that the dagger was poisoned. Means were instantly taken to purify the wound, and an antidote was sent by the Grand Master of the Templars which removed all danger from the effects of the poison. Camden, in his history, has adopted the more popular, and certainly more beautiful version of this story, which says that the Princess Eleonora, in her love for her gallant husband, sucked the poison from his wound at the risk of her own life : to use the words of old Fuller, " it is a pity so pretty a story should not be true ; and that so sovereign a remedy as a woman's tongue, anointed with the virtue of loving affection," should not have performed the good deed.

Edward suspected, and doubtless not without reason, that the assassin was employed by the sultan of Egypt. But it amounted to suspicion only ; and by the sudden death of the assassin the principal clue to the discovery of the truth was lost for ever. Edward, on his recovery, prepared to resume the offensive ; but the sultan, embarrassed by the defence of interests which, for the time being, he considered of more importance, made offers of peace to the Crusaders. This proof of weakness on the part of the enemy was calculated to render a man of Edward's temperament more anxious to prosecute the war ; but he had also other interests to defend. News arrived in Palestine of the death of his father, King Henry III. ; and his presence being necessary in England, he agreed to the terms of the sultan. These were, that the Christians should be allowed to retain their possessions in the Holy Land, and that a truce of ten years

---

* The reader will recognise the incident which Sir Walter Scott has introduced into his beautiful romance, *The Talisman*, and which, with the license claimed by poets and romancers, he represents as having befallen King Richard I.

should be proclaimed. Edward then set sail for England; and thus ended the last Crusade.

The after-fate of the Holy Land may be told in a few words. The Christians, unmindful of their past sufferings and of the jealous neighbours they had to deal with, first broke the truce by plundering some

TOMB OF QUEEN ELEANOR.

Egyptian traders near Margat. The sultan immediately revenged the outrage by taking possession of Margat, and war once more raged between the nations. Margat made a gallant defence, but no reinforcements arrived from Europe to prevent its fall. Tripoli was the next, and other cities in succession, until at last Acre was the only city of Palestine that remained in possession of the Christians.

The Grand Master of the Templars collected together his small and devoted band, and with the trifling aid afforded by the king of Cyprus, prepared to defend to the death the last possession of his order. Europe was deaf to his cry for aid, the numbers of the foe were overwhelming, and devoted bravery was of no avail. In that disastrous siege the Christians were all but exterminated. The king of Cyprus fled when he saw that resistance was vain, and the Grand Master fell at the head of his knights, pierced with a hundred wounds. Seven Templars, and as many Hospitallers, alone escaped from the dreadful carnage. The victorious Moslems then set fire to the city, and the rule of the Christians in Palestine was brought to a close for ever.

This intelligence spread alarm and sorrow among the clergy of Europe, who endeavoured to rouse once more the energy and enthusiasm of the nations in the cause of the Holy Land. But the popular mania had run its career; the spark of zeal had burned its appointed time, and was never again to be re-illumined. Here and there a solitary knight announced his determination to take up arms, and now and then a king gave cold encouragement to the scheme; but it dropped almost as soon as spoken of, to be renewed again, still more feebly, at some longer interval.

Now what was the grand result of all these struggles? Europe expended millions of her treasures, and the blood of two millions of her children; and a handful of quarrelsome knights retained possession of Palestine for about one hundred years! Even had Christendom retained it to this day, the advantage, if confined to that, would have been too dearly purchased. But notwithstanding the fanaticism that originated, and the folly that conducted them, the Crusades were not productive of unmitigated evil. The feudal chiefs became better members of society by coming in contact, in Asia, with a civilisation superior to their own; the people secured some small instalments of their rights; kings, no longer at war with their nobility, had time to pass some good laws; the human mind learned some little wisdom from hard experience, and, casting off the slough of superstition in which the Roman clergy had so long enveloped it, became prepared to receive the seeds of the approaching Reformation. Thus did the all-wise Disposer of events bring good out of evil, and advance the civilisation and ultimate happiness of the nations of the West by means of the very fanaticism that had led them against the East. But the whole subject is one of absorbing interest, and if carried fully out in all its bearings, would consume more space than the plan of this work will allow. The philosophic student will draw his own conclusions; and he can have no better field for the exercise of his powers than this European madness—its advantages and disadvantages, its causes and results.

ARRAS.

THE WITCH MANIA.

> What wrath of gods, or wicked influence
> Of tears, conspiring wretched men t' afflict,
> Hath pour'd on earth this noyous pestilence
> That mortal minds doth inwardly infect
> With love of blindness and of ignorance?
>
> *Spencer's Tears of the Muses.*

Countrymen. Hang her! beat her! kill her!

Justice. How now? Forbear this violence!

Mother Sawyer. A crew of villains—a knot of bloody hangmen! set to torment me! I know not why.

Justice. Alas, neighbour Banks! are you a ringleader in mischief? Fie! to abuse an aged woman!

Banks. Woman! a she hell-cat, a witch! To prove her one, we no sooner set fire on the thatch of her house, but in she came running, as if the devil had sent her in a barrel of gunpowder.

> *Ford's Witch of Edmonton.*

THE belief that disembodied spirits may be permitted to revisit this world has its foundation upon that sublime hope of immortality which is at once the chief solace and greatest triumph of our reason. Even if revelation did not teach us, we feel that we have that within us which shall never die; and all our experience of this life but makes us cling the more fondly to that one repaying hope. But in the early days of "little knowledge" this grand belief became the source of a whole train of superstitions, which, in their turn, became the fount from whence flowed a deluge of blood and horror. Europe, for a period of two centuries and a half, brooded upon the idea, not only that parted spirits walked the earth to meddle in the affairs of men, but that men had power to summon evil spirits to their aid to work woe upon their fellows. An epidemic terror seized upon the nations; no man thought himself secure, either in his person or possessions, from the machinations of the devil and his agents. Every calamity that befell him he attributed to a witch. If a storm arose and blew down his barn, it was witchcraft; if his cattle died of a murrain—if disease fastened upon his limbs, or death entered suddenly and snatched a beloved face from his hearth—they were not visitations of Providence, but the works of some neighbouring hag, whose wretchedness or insanity caused the ignorant to raise their finger and point at her as a witch. The word was upon every body's tongue. France, Italy, Germany, England, Scotland, and the far north successively ran mad upon this subject, and for a long series of years furnished their tribunals with so many trials for witchcraft, that other crimes were seldom or never spoken of. Thousands upon thousands of unhappy persons fell victims to this cruel and absurd delusion. In many cities of Germany, as will be shewn more fully in its due place hereafter, the average number of executions for this pretended crime was six hundred annually, or two every day, if we leave out the Sundays, when it is to be supposed that even this madness refrained from its work.

A misunderstanding of the famous text of the Mosaic law, "Thou shalt not suffer a witch to live," no doubt led many conscientious men astray, whose superstition, warm enough before, wanted but a little corroboration to blaze out with desolating fury. In all ages of the world men have tried to hold converse with superior beings, and to pierce by their means the secrets of futurity. In the time of Moses, it is evident that there were impostors who trafficked upon the credulity of mankind, and insulted the supreme majesty of the true God by pretending to the power of divination. Hence the law which Moses, by divine command, promulgated against these criminals; but it did not follow, as the superstitious monomaniacs of the middle ages imagined, that the Bible established the existence of the power of divination by its edicts against those who pretended to it. From the best authorities, it appears that the Hebrew word, which has been rendered *venefica* and *witch*, means a poisoner and divineress, a dabbler in spells, or fortune-teller. The modern witch was a very different character, and joined to her pretended power of foretelling future events that of working evil upon the life, limbs, and possessions of mankind. This power was only to be acquired by an express compact, signed in blood, with the devil himself, by which the wizard or witch renounced baptism, and sold his or her immortal soul to the evil one, without any saving clause of redemption.

There are so many wondrous appearances in nature for which science and philosophy cannot even now account, that it is not surprising that, when natural law's were still less understood, men should have attributed to supernatural agency every appearance which they could not otherwise explain. The merest tyro now understands various phenomena which the wisest of old could not fathom. The schoolboy knows why, upon high mountains, there should on certain occasions appear three or four suns in the firmament at once, and why the figure of a traveller upon one eminence should be reproduced, inverted and of a gigantic stature, upon another. We all know the strange pranks which imagination can play in certain diseases; that the hypochondriac can see visions and spectres; and that there have been cases in which men were perfectly persuaded that they were teapots. Science has lifted up the veil, and rolled away all the fantastic horrors in which our forefathers shrouded these and similar cases. The man who now imagines himself a wolf is sent to the hospital instead of to the stake, as in the days of the witch mania; and earth, air, and sea are unpeopled of the grotesque spirits that were once believed to haunt them.

Before entering further into the history of Witchcraft, it may be as well if we consider the absurd impersonation of the evil principle formed by the monks in their legends. We must make acquaintance with the *primum mobile*, and understand what sort of a personage it was who gave the witches, in exchange for their souls, the power to torment their fellow-creatures. The popular notion of the devil was, that he was a large, ill-formed, hairy sprite, with horns, a long tail, cloven feet, and dragon's wings. In this shape he was constantly brought on the stage by the monks in their early "miracles" and "mysteries." In these representations he was an important personage, and answered the purpose of the clown in the modern pantomime. The great fun for the people was to see him well belaboured by the saints with clubs or cudgels, and to hear him howl with pain as he limped off, maimed by the blow of some vigorous anchorite. St. Dunstan generally served him the glorious trick for which he is renowned, catching hold of his nose with a pair of red-hot pincers, till

"Rocks and distant dells resounded with his cries."

Some of the saints spat in his face, to his very great annoyance; and others chopped pieces off of his tail, which, however, always grew on again. This was paying him in his own coin, and amused the populace mightily, for they all remembered the scurvy tricks he had played them and their forefathers. It was believed that he endeavoured to trip people up by laying his long invisible tail in their way, and giving it a sudden whisk when their legs were over it:—that he used to get drunk, and swear like a trooper, and be so mischievous in his cups as to raise tempests and earthquakes, to destroy the fruits of the earth, and the barns and homesteads of true believers;—that he used to run invisible spits into people by way of amusing himself in the long winter evenings, and to proceed to taverns and regale himself with the best, offering in payment pieces of gold which, on the dawn of the following morning, invariably turned into slates. Sometimes, disguised as a large drake, he used to lurk among the bulrushes, and frighten the weary traveller out of his wits by his awful quack. The reader will remember the lines of Burns in his address to the "De'il," which so well express the popular notion on this point :

> " Ae dreary, windy, winter night,
>   The stars shot down wi' sklentin light,
>   Wi' you mysel' I got a fright
>   Ayont the lough;
>   Ye, like a rash-bush, stood in sight
>   Wi' waving sough.
>
>   The cudgel in my nieve did shake,
>   Each bristled hair stood like a stake,
>   When wi' an eldritch stour, 'quaick! quaick!'
>   Among the springs
>   Awa' ye squattered, like a drake,
>   On whistling wings."

In all the stories circulated and believed about him, he was represented as an ugly, petty, mischievous spirit, who rejoiced in playing off all manner of fantastic tricks upon poor humanity. Milton seems to have been the first who succeeded in giving any but a ludicrous description of him. The sublime pride, which is the quintessence of evil, was unconceived before his time. All other limners made him merely grotesque, but Milton made him awful. In this the monks shewed themselves but miserable romancers; for their object undoubtedly was to represent the fiend as terrible as possible. But there was nothing grand about their Satan; on the contrary, he was a low, mean devil, whom it was easy to circumvent, and fine fun to play tricks with. But, as is well and eloquently remarked by a modern writer,*

---

* See article on "Demonology" in the sixth volume of the *Foreign Quarterly Review.*

the subject has also its serious side. An Indian deity, with its wild distorted shape and grotesque attitude, appears merely ridiculous when separated from its accessories and viewed by daylight in a museum ; but restore it to the darkness of its own hideous temple, bring back to our recollection the victims that have bled upon its altar or been crushed beneath its car, and our sense of the ridiculous subsides into aversion and horror. So, while the superstitious dreams of former times are regarded as mere speculative insanities, we may be for a moment amused with the wild incoherencies of the patients; but when we reflect that out of these hideous misconceptions of the principle of evil arose the belief in witchcraft—that this was no dead faith, but one operating on the whole being of society, urging on the wisest and the mildest to deeds of murder, or cruelties scarcely less than murder—that the learned and the beautiful, young and old, male and female, were devoted by its influence to the stake and the scaffold—every feeling disappears, except that of astonishment that such things could be, and humiliation at the thought that the delusion was as lasting as it was universal.

Besides this chief personage, there was an infinite number of inferior demons, who played conspicuous parts in the creed of witchcraft. The pages of Bekker, Leloyer, Bodin, Delrio, and De Lancre, abound with descriptions of the qualities of these imps, and the functions which were assigned them. From these authors, — three of whom were commissioners for the trial of witches, and who wrote from the confessions made by the supposed criminals and the evidence delivered against them,—and from the more recent work of M. Jules Garinet, the following summary of the creed has been, with great pains, extracted. The student who is desirous of knowing more is referred to the works in question ; he will find enough in every leaf to make his blood curdle with shame and horror : but the purity of these pages shall not be soiled by any thing so ineffably humiliating and disgusting as a complete exposition of them ; what is here culled will be a sufficient sample of the popular belief, and the reader would but lose time who should seek in the writings of the demonologists for more ample details. He will gain nothing by lifting the veil which covers their unutterable obscenities, unless, like Sterne, he wishes to gather fresh evidence of "what a beast man is." In that case, he will find plenty there to convince him that the beast would be libelled by the comparison.

It was thought that the earth swarmed with millions of demons of both sexes, many of whom, like the human race, traced their lineage up to Adam, who after the fall was led astray by devils, assuming the forms of beautiful women to deceive him. These demons "increased and multiplied" among themselves with the most extraordinary rapidity. Their bodies were of the thin air, and they could pass through the hardest substances with the greatest ease. They had no fixed residence or abiding-place, but were tossed to and fro in the immensity of space. When thrown together in great multitudes, they excited whirlwinds in the air and tempests in the waters, and took delight in destroying the beauty of nature and the monuments of the industry of man. Although they increased among themselves like ordinary creatures, their numbers were daily augmented by the souls of wicked men, of children still-born, of women who died in childbed, and of persons killed in duels. The whole air was supposed to be full of them, and many unfortunate men and women drew them by thousands into their mouths and nostrils at every inspiration; and the demons, lodging in their bowels or other parts of their bodies, tormented them with pains and diseases of every kind, and sent them frightful dreams. St. Gregory of Nice relates a story of a nun who forgot to say her *benedicite* and make the sign of the cross before she sat down to supper, and who in consequence swallowed a demon concealed among the leaves of a lettuce. Most persons said the number of these demons was so great that they could not be counted, but Wierus asserted that they amounted to no more than seven millions four hundred and five thousand nine hundred and twenty-six; and that they were divided into seventy-two companies or battalions, to each of which there was a prince or captain. They could assume any shape they pleased. When they were male, they were called incubi; and when female, succubi. They sometimes made themselves hideous; and at other times they assumed shapes of such transcendent loveliness, that mortal eyes never saw beauty to compete with theirs.

Although the devil and his legions could appear to mankind at any time, it was generally understood that he preferred the night between Friday and Saturday. If Satan himself appeared in human shape, he was never perfectly and in all respects like a man. He was either too black or too white, too large or too small, or some of his limbs were out of proportion to the rest of his body. Most commonly his feet were deformed, and he was obliged to curl up and conceal his tail in some part of his habiliments; for, take what shape he would, he could not get rid of that encumbrance. He sometimes changed himself into a tree or a river; and upon one occasion he transformed himself into a barrister, as we learn from Wierus, book iv. chapter 9. In the reign of Philippe le Bel, he appeared to a monk in the shape of a dark man riding a tall black horse, then as a friar, afterwards as an ass, and finally as a coach-wheel. Instances are not rare in which both he and his inferior demons have taken the form of handsome young men, and, successfully concealing their tails, have married beautiful young women, who have had children by them. Such children were easily recognisable by their continual shrieking, by their requiring five nurses to suckle them, and by their never growing fat.

All these demons were at the command of any individual who would give up his immortal soul to the prince of evil for the privilege of enjoying their services for a stated period. The wizard or witch could send them to execute the most difficult missions : whatever the witch commanded was performed, except it was a good action, in which case the order was disobeyed, and evil worked upon herself instead.

At intervals, according to the pleasure of Satan, there was a general meeting of the demons and all the witches. This meeting was called the Sabbath, from its taking place on the Saturday, or immediately after midnight on Fridays. These sabbaths were sometimes held for one district, sometimes for another, and once at least every year it was held on the Brocken, or among other high mountains, as a general sabbath of the fiends for the whole of Christendom.

The devil generally chose a place where four roads met as the scene of this assembly, or if that was not convenient, the neighbourhood of a lake. Upon this spot nothing would ever afterwards grow, as the hot feet of the demons and witches burnt the principle of fecundity from the earth, and rendered it barren for ever. When orders had been once issued for the meeting of the sabbath, all the wizards and witches who failed to attend it were lashed by demons with a rod made of serpents or scorpions, as a punishment for their inattention or want of punctuality.

In France and England the witches were supposed to ride uniformly upon broomsticks; but in Italy and Spain, the devil himself, in the shape of a goat, used to transport them on his back, which lengthened or shortened according to the number of witches he was desirous of accommodating. No witch, when proceeding to the sabbath, could get out by a door or window, were she to try ever so much. Their general mode of ingress was by the keyhole, and of egress by the chimney, up which they flew, broom and all, with the greatest ease. To prevent the absence of the witches from being noticed by their neighbours, some inferior demon was commanded to assume their shapes and lie in their beds, feigning illness, until the sabbath was over.

When all the wizards and witches had arrived at the place of rendezvous, the infernal ceremonies of the sabbath began. Satan,

having assumed his favourite shape of a large he-goat, with a face in
front and another in his haunches, took his seat upon a throne ; and
all present, in succession, paid their respects to him, and kissed him in
his face behind. This done, he appointed a master of the ceremonies,
in company with whom he made a personal examination of all the
wizards and witches, to see whether they had the secret mark about
them by which they were stamped as the devil's own. This mark
was always insensible to pain. Those who had not yet been marked,
received the mark from the master of the ceremonies, the devil at
the same time bestowing nicknames upon them. This done, they all
began to sing and dance in the most furious manner, until some one
arrived who was anxious to be admitted into their society. They
were then silent for a while, until the new-comer had denied his salvation, kissed the devil, spat upon the Bible, and sworn obedience to
him in all things. They then began dancing again with all their
might, and singing these words,

> " Alegremos, Alegremos !
> Que gente va tenemos !"

In the course of an hour or two they generally became wearied
of this violent exercise, and then they all sat down and recounted the
evil deeds they had done since their last meeting. Those who had
not been malicious and mischievous enough towards their fellow-
creatures, received personal chastisement from Satan himself, who
flogged them with thorns or scorpions till they were covered with
blood, and unable to sit or stand.

When this ceremony was concluded, they were all amused by a
dance of toads. Thousands of these creatures sprang out of the earth,
and standing on their hind legs, danced, while the devil played the
bagpipes or the trumpet. These toads were all endowed with the
faculty of speech, and entreated the witches to reward them with the
flesh of unbaptised babes for their exertions to give them pleasure.
The witches promised compliance. The devil bade them remember
to keep their word ; and then stamping his foot, caused all the
toads to sink into the earth in an instant. The place being thus
cleared, preparation was made for the banquet, where all manner
of disgusting things were served up and greedily devoured by the
demons and witches ; although the latter were sometimes regaled
with choice meats and expensive wines from golden plates and
crystal goblets ; but they were never thus favoured unless they had
done an extraordinary number of evil deeds since the last period of
meeting.

After the feast, they began dancing again ; but such as had no
relish for any more exercise in that way, amused themselves by mock-

ing the holy sacrament of baptism. For this purpose, the toads were again called up, and sprinkled with filthy water; the devil making the sign of the cross, and all the witches calling out, "*In nomine Patricâ, Aragueaco Petrica, agora! agora! Valentia, jouando goure gaits goustia!*" which meant, "In the name of Patrick, Petrick of Aragon, now, now, all our ills are over!"

When the devil wished to be particularly amused, he made the witches strip off their clothes and dance before him, each with a cat tied round her neck, and another dangling from her body in form of a tale. When the cock crew, they all disappeared, and the sabbath was ended.

This is a summary of the belief which prevailed for many centuries nearly all over Europe, and which is far from eradicated even at this day. It was varied in some respects in several countries, but the main points were the same in France, Germany, Great Britain, Italy, Spain, and the far North of Europe.

The early annals of France abound with stories of supposed sorcery, but it was not until the time of Charlemagne that the crime acquired any great importance. "This monarch," says M. Jules Garinet,* "had several times given order, that all necromancers, astrologers, and witches should be driven from his states; but as the number of criminals augmented daily, he found it necessary at last to resort to severer measures. In consequence, he published several edicts, which may be found at length in the *Capitulaire de Baluse*. By these, every sort of magic, enchantment, and witchcraft was forbidden; and the punishment of death decreed against those who in any way evoked the devil, compounded love-philters, afflicted either man or woman with barrenness, troubled the atmosphere, excited tempests, destroyed the fruits of the earth, dried up the milk of cows, or tormented their fellow-creatures with sores and diseases. All persons found guilty of exercising these execrable arts were to be executed immediately upon conviction, that the earth might be rid of the burden and curse of their presence; and those even who consulted them might also be punished with death."†

After this time, prosecutions for witchcraft are continually mentioned, especially by the French historians. It was a crime imputed with so much ease, and repelled with so much difficulty, that the

---

* *Histoire de la Magie en France.* Rois de la seconde race, p. 29.

† M. Michaud, in his *History of the Crusades*, M. Guinguené, in his *Literary History of Italy*, and some other critics, have objected to Tasso's poem, that he has attributed to the Crusaders a belief in magic, which did not exist at that time. If these critics had referred to the edicts of Charlemagne, they would have seen that Tasso was right, and that a disposition too eager to spy out imperfections in a great work was leading themselves into error.

powerful, whenever they wanted to ruin the weak, and could fix no other imputation upon them, had only to accuse them of witchcraft to ensure their destruction. Instances in which this crime was made the pretext for the most violent persecution, both of individuals and of communities, whose real offences were purely political or religious, must be familiar to every reader. The extermination of the Stedinger in 1234, of the Templars from 1307 to 1313, the execution of Joan of Arc in 1429, and the unhappy scenes of Arras in 1459, are the most prominent. The first of these is perhaps the least known, but is not among the least remarkable. The following account, from Dr. Kortüm's interesting history* of the republican confederacies of the middle ages, will shew the horrible convenience of imputations of witchcraft when royal or priestly wolves wanted a pretext for a quarrel with the sheep.

The Frieslanders, inhabiting the district from the Weser to the Zuydersee, had long been celebrated for their attachment to freedom, and their successful struggles in its defence. As early as the eleventh century they had formed a general confederacy against the encroachments of the Normans and the Saxons, which was divided into seven *seelands*, holding annually a diet under a large oak-tree at Aurich, near the Upstalboom. Here they managed their own affairs, without the control of the clergy and ambitious nobles who surrounded them, to the great scandal of the latter. They already had true notions of a representative government. The deputies of the people levied the necessary taxes, deliberated on the affairs of the community, and performed, in their simple and patriarchal manner, nearly all the functions of the representative assemblies of the present day. Finally, the Archbishop of Bremen, together with the Count of Oldenburgh and other neighbouring potentates, formed a league against that section of the Frieslanders known by the name of the Stedinger, and succeeded, after harassing them and sowing dissensions among them for many years, in bringing them under the yoke. But the Stedinger, devotedly attached to their ancient laws, by which they had attained a degree of civil and religious liberty very uncommon in that age, did not submit without a violent struggle. They arose in insurrection in the year 1204, in defence of the ancient customs of their country, refused to pay taxes to the feudal chiefs or tithes to the clergy—who had forced themselves into their peaceful retreats—and drove out many of their oppressors. For a period of eight-and-twenty years the brave Stedinger continued the struggle single-handed against the forces of the Archbishops of Bremen and the Counts of Oldenburg, and destroyed, in the year 1232, the strong castle of Slutterberg, near

* *Entstehungsgeschichte der freistädtischen Bünde im Mittelalter*, von Dr. F. Kortüm. 1827.

Delmenhorst, built by the latter nobleman as a position from which he could send out his marauders to plunder and destroy the possessions of the peasantry.

The invincible courage of these poor people proving too strong for their oppressors to cope with by the ordinary means of warfare, the Archbishop of Bremen applied to Pope Gregory IX. for his spiritual aid against them. That prelate entered cordially into the cause, and launching forth his anathema against the Stedinger as heretics and witches, encouraged all true believers to assist in their extermination. A large body of thieves and fanatics broke into their country in the year 1233, killing and burning wherever they went, and not sparing either women or children, the sick or the aged, in their rage. The Stedinger, however, rallied in great force, routed their invaders, and killed in battle their leader, Count Burckhardt of Oldenburg, with many inferior chieftains.

Again the pope was applied to, and a crusade against the Stedinger was preached in all that part of Germany. The pope wrote to all the bishops and leaders of the faithful an exhortation to arm, to root out from the land those abominable witches and wizards. " The Stedinger," said his holiness, " seduced by the devil, have abjured all the laws of God and man, slandered the Church, insulted the holy sacraments, consulted witches to raise evil spirits, shed blood like water, taken the lives of priests, and concocted an infernal scheme to propagate the worship of the devil, whom they adore under the name of Asmodi. The devil appears to them in different shapes,—sometimes as a goose or a duck, and at others in the figure of a pale black-eyed youth, with a melancholy aspect, whose embrace fills their hearts with eternal hatred against the holy Church of Christ. This devil presides at their sabbaths, when they all kiss him and dance around him. He then envelopes them in total darkness, and they all, male and female, give themselves up to the grossest and most disgusting debauchery."

In consequence of these letters of the pope, the emperor of Germany, Frederic II., also pronounced his ban against them. The Bishops of Ratzebourg, Lubeck, Osnabrück, Munster, and Minden took up arms to exterminate them, aided by the Duke of Brabant, the Counts of Holland, of Clêves, of the Mark, of Oldenburg, of Egmond, of Diest, and many other powerful nobles. An army of forty thousand men was soon collected, which marched, under the command of the Duke of Brabant, into the country of the Stedinger. The latter mustered vigorously in defence of their lives and liberties, but could raise no greater force, including every man capable of bearing arms, than eleven thousand men, to cope against the overwhelming numbers of their foe. They fought with the energy of despair, but all in vain. Eight thousand of them were slain on the field of battle; the whole race was exterminated; and the enraged conquerors scoured the country in all directions, slew the women and children and old men, drove away the cattle, fired the woods and cottages, and made a total waste of the land.

Just as absurd and effectual was the charge brought against the Templars in 1307, when they had rendered themselves obnoxious to the potentates and prelacy of Christendom. Their wealth, their power, their pride, and their insolence had raised up enemies on every side; and every sort of accusation was made against them, but failed to work their overthrow, until the terrible cry of witchcraft was let loose upon them. This effected its object, and the Templars were extirpated. They were accused of having sold their souls to the devil, and of celebrating all the infernal mysteries of the witches' sabbath. It was pretended that, when they admitted a novice into their order, they forced him to renounce his salvation and curse Jesus Christ; that they then made him submit to many unholy and disgusting ceremonies, and forced him to kiss the superior on the cheek, the navel, and the breech, and spit three times upon a crucifix; that all the members were forbidden to have connexion with women, but might give themselves up without restraint to every species of unmentionable debauchery; that when by any mischance a Templar infringed this order, and a child was born, the whole order met, and tossed it about like a shuttlecock from one to the other until it expired; that they then roasted it by a slow fire, and with the fat which trickled from it anointed the hair and beard of a large image of the devil. It was also said that when one of the knights died, his body

PHILIP IV

was burnt into a powder, and then mixed with wine and drunk by every member of the order. Philip IV., who, to exercise his own implacable hatred, invented, in all probability, the greater part of these charges, issued orders for the immediate arrest of all the Templars in his dominions. The pope afterwards took up the cause with almost as much fervour as the king of France ; and in every part of Europe the Templars were thrown into prison, and their goods and estates confiscated. Hundreds of them, when put to the rack, confessed even the most preposterous of the charges against them, and by so doing increased the popular clamour and the hopes of their enemies. It is true that, when removed from the rack, they denied all they had previously confessed ; but this circumstance only increased the outcry, and was numbered as an additional crime against them. They were considered in a worse light than before, and condemned forthwith to the flames as relapsed heretics. Fifty-nine of these unfortunate victims were all burned together by a slow fire in a field in the suburbs of Paris, protesting to the very last moment of their lives their innocence of the crimes imputed to them, and refusing to accept of pardon upon condition of acknowledging themselves guilty. Similar scenes were enacted in the provinces ; and for four years hardly a month passed without witnessing the execution of one or more of these unhappy men. Finally, in 1313, the last scene of this tragedy closed by the burning of the Grand-Master, Jacques de Molay, and his companion Guy, the commander of Normandy. Any thing more atrocious it is impossible to conceive,—disgraceful alike to the monarch who originated, the pope who supported, and the age which tolerated the monstrous iniquity. That the malice of a few could invent such a charge is a humiliating thought for the lover of his species ; but that millions of mankind should credit it is still more so.

The execution of Joan of Arc is the next most notorious example which history affords us of the imputation of witchcraft against a political enemy. Instances of similar persecution, in which this crime was made the pretext for the gratification of political or religious hatred, might be multiplied to a great extent. But it is better to proceed at once to the consideration of the bull of Pope Innocent, the torch that set fire to the long laid train, and caused so fearful an explosion over the Christian world. It will be necessary, however, to go back for some years anterior to that event, the better to understand the motives that influenced the Church in the promulgation of that fearful document.

Towards the close of the fourteenth and beginning of the fifteenth century, many witches were burned in different parts of Europe. As a natural consequence of the severe persecution, the crime, or the pretenders to it, increased. Those who found themselves accused and threatened with the penalties, if they happened to be persons of a bad and malicious disposition, wished they had the power imputed to them, that they might be revenged upon their persecutors. Numer-

JOAN OF ARC.

ous instances are upon record of half-crazed persons being found muttering the spells which were supposed to raise the evil one. When religion and law alike recognised the crime, it is no wonder that the weak in reason and the strong in imagination, especially when they were of a nervous temperament, fancied themselves endued with the terrible powers of which all the world was speaking. The belief of their neighbours did not lag behind their own, and execution was the speedy consequence.

As the fear of witchcraft increased, the Catholic clergy strove to fix the imputation of it upon those religious sects, the pioneers of the Reformation, who began about this time to be formidable to the Church of Rome. If a charge of heresy could not ensure their destruction, that of sorcery and witchcraft never failed. In the year 1459, a devoted congregation of the Waldenses at Arras, who used to repair at night to worship God in their own manner in solitary places, fell victims to an accusation of sorcery. It was rumoured in Arras that in the desert places to which they retired the devil appeared before them in human form, and read from a large book his laws and ordinances, to which they all promised obedience; that he then distributed money and food among them, to bind them to his service, which done, they gave themselves up to every species of lewdness and debauchery. Upon these rumours several creditable persons in Arras were seized and imprisoned, together with a number of decrepit and idiotic old women. The rack, that convenient instrument for making the accused confess any thing, was of course put in requisition. Monstrelet, in his chronicle, says that they were tortured until some of them admitted the truth of the whole accusations, and said, besides, that they had seen and recognised in their nocturnal assemblies many persons of rank; many prelates, seigneurs, governors of bailliages, and mayors of cities, being such names as the examiners had themselves suggested to the victims. Several who had been thus informed against were thrown into prison, and so horribly tortured, that reason fled, and in their ravings of pain they also confessed their midnight meetings with the devil, and the oaths they had taken to serve him. Upon these confessions judgment was pronounced. The poor old women, as usual in such cases, were hanged and burned in the market-place; the more wealthy delinquents were allowed to escape upon payment of large sums. It was soon after universally recognised that these trials had been conducted in the most odious manner, and that the judges had motives of private vengeance against many of the more influential persons who had been implicated. The parliament of Paris afterwards declared the sentence illegal, and the judges iniquitous; but its *arrêt* was too late to be of service even to those who had paid the fine, or to punish the authorities who had misconducted themselves, for it was not delivered until thirty-two years after the executions had taken place.

In the mean time, accusations of witchcraft spread rapidly in France, Italy, and Germany. Strange to say, that although in the first instance chiefly directed against heretics, the latter were as firm believers in the crime as even the Catholics themselves. In after times we also find that the Lutherans and Calvinists became greater witch-burners than ever the Romanists had been, so deeply was the prejudice rooted. Every other point of belief was in dispute, but that was considered by every sect to be as well established as the authenticity of the Scriptures or the existence of a God.

But at this early period of the epidemic the persecutions were directed by the heads of the Catholic Church. The spread of heresy betokened, it was thought, the coming of Antichrist. Florimond, in his work concerning Antichrist, exposed the secret of these prosecutions. He says: " All who have afforded us some signs of the approach of Antichrist agree that the increase of sorcery and witchcraft is to distinguish the melancholy period of his advent; and was ever age so afflicted as ours? The seats destined for criminals in our courts of justice are blackened with persons accused of this guilt.

There are not judges enough to try them. Our dungeons are gorged with them. No day passes that we do not render our tribunals bloody by the dooms which we pronounce, or in which we do not return to our homes discountenanced and terrified at the horrible confessions which we have heard. And the devil is accounted so good a master, that we cannot commit so great a number of his slaves to the flames but what there shall arise from their ashes a sufficient number to supply their place."

Florimond here spoke the general opinion of the Church of Rome; but it never suggested itself to the mind of any person engaged in these trials, that if it were indeed a devil who raised up so many new witches to fill the places of those consumed, it was no other than one in their own employ—the devil of persecution. But so it was. The more they burned, the more they found to burn, until it became a

GATE OF CONSTANCE.

common prayer with women in the humbler walks of life, that they might never live to grow old. It was sufficient to be aged, poor, and half-crazed, to ensure death at the stake or the scaffold.

In the year 1487 there was a severe storm in Switzerland, which laid waste the country for four miles around Constance. Two wretched old women, whom the popular voice had long accused of witchcraft, were arrested on the preposterous charge of having raised the tempest. The rack was displayed, and the two poor creatures were extended upon it. In reply to various questions from their tormentors, they owned in their agony that they were in the constant habit of meeting the devil; that they had sold their souls to him; and that at their command he had raised the tempest. Upon this insane and blasphemous charge they were condemned to die. In the criminal registers of Constance there stands against the name of each the simple but significant phrase, "*convicta et combusta.*"

This case and hundreds of others were duly reported to the ecclesiastical powers. There happened at that time to be a pontiff at the head of the Church who had given much of his attention to the subject of witchcraft, and who, with the intention of rooting out the supposed crime, did more to increase it than any other man that ever lived. John Baptist Cibo, elected to the papacy in 1485, under the designation of Innocent VIII., was sincerely alarmed at the number of witches, and launched forth his terrible manifesto against them. In his celebrated bull of 1488, he called the nations of Europe to the rescue of the Church of Christ upon earth, imperilled by the arts of Satan, and set forth the horrors that had reached his ears; how that numbers of both sexes had intercourse with the infernal fiends; how by their sorceries they afflicted both man and beast; how they blighted the marriage-bed, destroyed the births of women and the increase of cattle; and how they blasted the corn on the ground, the grapes of the vineyard, the fruits of the trees, and the herbs of the field. In order that criminals so atrocious might no longer pollute the earth, he appointed inquisitors in every country, armed with the apostolic power to convict and punish.

It was now that the *Witch Mania,* properly so called, may be said to have fairly commenced. Immediately a class of men sprang up in Europe, who made it the sole business of their lives to discover and burn the witches. Sprenger, in Germany, was the most celebrated of these national scourges. In his notorious work, the *Malleus Maleficarum,* he laid down a regular form of trial, and appointed a course of examination by which the inquisitors in other countries might best discover the guilty. The questions, which were always enforced by torture, were of the most absurd and disgusting nature. The inquisitors were required to ask the suspected whether they had midnight meetings with the devil? whether they attended the witches' sabbath on the Brocken? whether they had their familiar spirits? whether they could raise whirlwinds and call down the lightning? and whether they had had sexual intercourse with Satan?

Straightway the inquisitors set to work : Cumanus, in Italy, burned forty-one poor women in one province alone ; and Sprenger, in Germany, burned a number which can never be ascertained correctly, but which, it is agreed on all hands, amounted to more than five hundred in a year. The great resemblance between the confessions of the unhappy victims was regarded as a new proof of the existence of the crime. But this is not astonishing. The same questions from the *Malleus Maleficarum* were put to them all, and torture never failed to educe the answer required by the inquisitor. Numbers of people, whose imaginations were filled with these horrors, went further in the way of confession than even their tormentors anticipated, in the hope that they would thereby be saved from the rack, and put out of their misery at once. Some confessed that they had had children by the devil ; but no one who had ever been a mother gave utterance to such a frantic imagining, even in the extremity of her anguish. The childless only confessed it, and were burned instanter as unworthy to live.

For fear the zeal of the enemies of Satan should cool, successive popes appointed new commissions. One was appointed by Alexander VI. in 1494, another by Leo X. in 1521, and a third by Adrian VI. in 1522. They were all armed with the same powers to hunt out and destroy, and executed their fearful functions but too rigidly. In Geneva alone five hundred persons were burned in the years 1515 and 1516, under the title of Protestant witches. It would appear that their chief crime was heresy, and their witchcraft merely an aggravation. Bartolomeo de Spina has a list still more fearful. He informs us that in the year 1524 no less than a thousand persons suffered death for witchcraft in the district of Como, and that for several years afterwards the average number of victims exceeded a hundred annually. One inquisitor, Remigius, took great credit to himself for having, during fifteen years, convicted and burned nine hundred.

In France, about the year 1520, fires for the execution of witches blazed in almost every town. Danæus, in his *Dialogues of Witches*, says they were so numerous that it would be next to impossible to tell the number of them. So deep was the thraldom of the human mind, that the friends and relatives of the accused parties looked on and approved. The wife or sister of a murderer might sympathise in his fate, but the wives and husbands of sorcerers and witches had no pity. The truth is, that pity was dangerous, for it was thought no one could have compassion on the sufferings of a witch who was not a dabbler in sorcery : to have wept for a witch would have insured the stake. In some districts, however, the exasperation of the people broke out, in spite of superstition. The inquisitor of a rural township in Piedmont burned the victims so plentifully and so fast, that there was not a family in the place which did not lose a member. The people at last arose, and the inquisitor was but too happy to escape from the country with whole limbs. The archbishop of the diocese proceeded afterwards to the trial of such as the inquisitor had left in prison.

Some of the charges were so utterly preposterous that the poor wretches were at once liberated; others met a harder, but the usual fate. Some of them were accused of having joined the witches' dance at midnight under a blasted oak, where they had been seen by creditable people. The husbands of several of these women (two of whom were young and beautiful) swore positively that at the time stated their wives were comfortably asleep in their arms; but it was all in vain. Their word was taken, but the archbishop told them they had been deceived by the devil and their own senses. It was true they might have had the semblance of their wives in their beds, but the originals were far away at the devil's dance under the oak. The honest fellows were confounded, and their wives burned forthwith.

CHARLES IX.

In the year 1561, five poor women of Verneuil were accused of transforming themselves into cats, and in that shape attending the sabbath of the fiends—prowling around Satan, who presided over them in the form of a goat, and dancing, to amuse him, upon his back. They were found guilty, and burned.*

In 1564, three wizards and a witch appeared before the Presidents Salvert and D'Avanton : they confessed, when extended on the rack, that they anointed the sheep-pens with infernal unguents to kill the sheep; that they attended the sabbath, where they saw a great black goat,

* Bodin, p. 95; Garinet, p. 125; *Anti-demon de Serclier*, p. 346.

which spoke to them, and made them kiss him, each holding a lighted candle in his hand while he performed the ceremony. They were all executed at Poitiers.

In 1571 the celebrated sorcerer Trois Echelles was burned in the Place de Grêve in Paris. He confessed, in the presence of Charles IX., and of the Marshals de Montmorency, De Retz, and the Sieur du Mazille, physician to the king, that he could perform the most wonderful things by the aid of a devil to whom he had sold himself. He described at great length the saturnalia of the fiends, the sacrifices which they offered up, the debaucheries they committed with the young and handsome witches, and the various modes of preparing the infernal unguent for blighting cattle. He said he had upwards of twelve hundred accomplices in the crime of witchcraft in various parts of France, whom he named to the king, and many of whom were afterwards arrested and suffered execution.

At Dôle, two years afterwards, Gilles Garnier, a native of Lyons, was indicted for being a *loup-garou*, or man-wolf, and for prowling in that shape about the country at night to devour little children. The indictment against him, as read by Henri Camus, doctor of laws and counsellor of the king, was to the effect that he, Gilles Garnier, had seized upon a little girl, twelve years of age, whom he drew into a vineyard and there killed, partly with his teeth and partly with his hands, seeming like wolf's paws; that from thence he trailed her bleeding body along the ground with his teeth into the wood of La Serre, where he ate the greatest portion of her at one meal, and carried the remainder home to his wife; that upon another occasion, eight days before the festival of All Saints, he was seen to seize another child in his teeth, and would have devoured her had she not been rescued by the country people, and that the said child died a few days afterwards of the injuries he had inflicted; that fifteen days after the same festival of All Saints, being again in the shape of a wolf, he devoured a boy thirteen years of age, having previously torn off his leg and thigh with his teeth, and hid them away for his breakfast on the morrow. He was furthermore indicted for giving way to the same diabolical and unnatural propensities even in his shape of a man; and that he had strangled a boy in a wood with the intention of eating him, which crime he would have effected if he had not been seen by the neighbours and prevented.

Gilles Garnier was put to the rack after fifty witnesses had deposed against him. He confessed every thing that was laid to his charge. He was thereupon brought back into the presence of his judges, when Dr. Camus, in the name of the parliament of Dôle, pronounced the following sentence:

" Seeing that Gilles Garnier has, by the testimony of credible witnesses, and by his own spontaneous confession, been proved guilty of the abominable crimes of lycanthropy and witchcraft, this court condemns him, the said Gilles, to be this day taken in a cart from this spot to the place of execution, accompanied by the executioner (*maître exécuteur de la haute justice*), where he, by the said executioner, shall be tied to a stake and burned alive, and that his ashes be then scattered to the winds. The court further condemns him, the said Gilles, to the costs of this prosecution.

" Given at Dôle, this 18th day of January, 1573."

In 1578, the parliament of Paris was occupied for several days with the trial of a man named Jacques Rollet. He also was found guilty of being a *loup-garou*, and in that shape devouring a little boy. He was burnt alive in the Place de Grève.

In 1579, so much alarm was excited in the neighbourhood of Melun by the increase of witches and *loup-garous*, that a council was held to devise some measures to stay the evil. A decree was passed that all witches and consulters with witches should be punished with death ; and not only those, but fortune-tellers and conjurors of every kind. The parliament of Rouen took up the same question in the following year, and decreed that the possession of a *grimoire*, or book of spells, was sufficient evidence of witchcraft, and that all persons on whom such books were found should be burned alive. Three councils were held in different parts of France in the year 1583, all in relation to the same subject. The parliament of Bordeaux issued strict injunctions to all curates and clergy whatever to use redoubled efforts to root out the crime of witchcraft. The parliament of Tours was equally peremptory, and feared the judgments of an offended God, if all these dealers with the devil were not swept from the face of the land. The parliament of Rheims was particularly severe against the *noueurs d'aiguillette*, or "tyers of the knot"—people of both sexes who took pleasure in preventing the consummation of marriage, that they might counteract the command of God to our first parents to increase and multiply. This parliament held it to be sinful to wear amulets to preserve from witchcraft ; and that this practice might not be continued within its jurisdiction, drew up a form of exorcism, which would more effectually defeat the agents of the devil, and put them to flight.

A case of witchcraft, which created a great sensation in its day, occurred in 1588, at a village in the mountains of Auvergne, about two leagues from Apchon. A gentleman of that place being at his window, there passed a friend of his who had been out hunting, and who was then returning to his own house. The gentleman asked his friend what sport he had had ; upon which the latter informed him that he had been attacked in the plain by a large and savage wolf, which he had shot at without wounding, and that he had then drawn out his hunting-knife and cut off the animal's fore-paw as it sprang upon his neck to devour him. The huntsman upon this put his hand into his bag to pull out the paw, but was shocked to find that it was a woman's hand, with a wedding-ring on the finger. The gentleman immediately recognised his wife's ring, "which," says the indictment against her, "made him begin to suspect some evil of her." He immediately went in search of her, and found her sitting by the fire in the kitchen, with her arm hidden underneath her apron. He tore off her apron with great vehemence, and found that she had no hand, and that the stump was even then bleeding. She was given into custody, and burnt at Riom, in presence of some thousands of spectators.*

In the midst of these executions, rare were the gleams of mercy. Few instances are upon record of any acquittal taking place when the crime was witchcraft. The discharge of fourteen persons by the parliament of Paris, in the year 1589, is almost a solitary example of a return to reason. Fourteen persons condemned to death for witchcraft appealed against the judgment to the parliament of Paris, which for political reasons had been exiled to Tours. The parliament named four commissioners—Pierre Pigray, the king's surgeon, and Messieurs Leroi, Renard, and Falaiseau, the king's physicians—to visit and examine these witches, and see whether they had the mark of the devil upon them. Pigray, who relates the circumstance in his work on Surgery (book vii. chap. 10), says the visit was made in presence of two counsellors of the court. The witches were all stripped naked, and the physicians examined their bodies very diligently, pricking them in all the marks they could find to see whether they were insensible to pain, which was always considered a certain proof of guilt. They were, however, very sensible of the pricking, and some of them called out very lustily when the pins were driven into them. "We found them," continues Pierre Pigray, "to be very poor, stupid people, and some of them insane. Many of them were quite indifferent about life, and one or two of them desired death as a relief from their sufferings. Our opinion was, that they stood more in need of medicine than of punishment ; and so we reported to the parliament. Their case was thereupon taken into further consideration ; and the parliament, after mature counsel amongst all the mem-

* Tablier. See also Boguet, *Discours sur les Sorciers ;* and M. Jules Garinet, *Histoire de la Magie,* p. 150.

bers, ordered the poor creatures to be sent to their homes, without inflicting any punishment upon them."

Such was the dreadful state of Italy, Germany, and France during the sixteenth century, which was far from being the worst crisis of the popular madness with regard to witchcraft. Let us see what was the state of England during the same period. The Reformation, which in its progress had rooted out so many errors, stopped short at this, the greatest error of all. Luther and Calvin were as firm believers in witchcraft as Pope Innocent himself; and their followers shewed themselves more zealous persecutors than the Romanists. Dr. Hutchinson, in his work on Witchcraft, asserts that the mania manifested itself later in England, and raged with less virulence than on the continent. The first assertion only is true; for though the persecution began later both in England and Scotland, its progress was as fearful as elsewhere.

It was not until more than fifty years after the issuing of the bull of Innocent VIII. that the legislature of England thought fit to make any more severe enactments against sorcery than those already in operation. The statute of 1541 was the first that specified the particular crime of witchcraft. At a much earlier period many persons had suffered death for sorcery, in addition to other offences; but no executions took place for attending the witches' sabbath, raising tempests, afflicting cattle with barrenness, and all the fantastic trumpery of the continent. Two statutes were passed in 1551 : the first relating to false prophecies, caused mainly, no doubt, by the impositions of Elizabeth Barton, the holy maid of Kent, in 1534; and the second against conjuration, witchcraft, and sorcery. But even this enactment did not consider witchcraft as penal in itself, and only condemned to death those who, by means of spells, incantations, or contracts with the devil, attempted the lives of their neighbours. The statute of Elizabeth, in 1562, at last recognised witchcraft as a crime of the highest magnitude, whether exerted or not to the injury of the lives, limbs, and possessions of the community. From that date the persecution may be fairly said to have commenced in England. It reached its climax in the early part of the seventeenth century, which was the hottest period of the mania all over Europe.

A few cases of witch persecution in the sixteenth century will enable the reader to form a more accurate idea of the progress of this great error than if he plunged at once into that busy period of its history when Matthew Hopkins and his coadjutors exercised their infernal calling. Several instances occur in England during the latter years of the reign of Elizabeth. At this time the public mind had become pretty familiar with the details of the crime. Bishop

Jewell, in his sermons before her majesty, used constantly to conclude them by a fervent prayer that she might be preserved from witches. Upon one occasion, in 1598, his words were, "It may

JEWELL.

please your grace to understand that witches and sorcerers within these last four years are marvellously increased within this your grace's realm. Your grace's subjects pine away even unto the death; their colour fadeth—their flesh rotteth—their speech is benumbed—their senses are bereft! I pray God they may never practise further than upon the *subject !*"

By degrees, an epidemic terror of witchcraft spread into the villages. In proportion as the doctrine of the Puritans took root, this dread increased, and, of course, brought persecution in its train. The Church of England has claimed, and is entitled to the merit, of having been less influenced in these matters than any other sect of Christians; but still they were tainted with the superstition of the age. One of the most flagrant instances of cruelty and delusion upon record was consummated under the authority of the Church, and commemorated till a very late period by an annual lecture at the University of Cambridge.

This is the celebrated case of the witches of Warbois, who were executed about thirty-two years after the passing of the statute of Elizabeth. Although in the interval but few trials are recorded, there is, unfortunately, but too much evidence to shew the extreme length to which the popular prejudice was carried. Many women lost their lives in every part of England without being brought to trial at all, from the injuries received at the hands of the people. The number of these can never be ascertained.

The case of the witches of Warbois merits to be detailed at length, not only from the importance attached to it for so many years by the learned of the University, but from the singular absurdity of the evidence upon which men, sensible in all other respects, could condemn their fellow-creatures to the scaffold.

The principal actors in this strange drama were the families of Sir Samuel Cromwell and a Mr. Throgmorton, both gentlemen of landed property near Warbois in the county of Huntingdon. Mr. Throgmorton had several daughters, the eldest of whom, Mistress Joan, was an imaginative and melancholy girl, whose head was filled with stories of ghosts and witches. Upon one occasion she chanced to pass the cottage of one Mrs., or, as she was called, Mother Samuel, a very aged, a very poor, and a very ugly woman. Mother Samuel was sitting at her door knitting, with a black cap upon her head, when this silly young lady passed, and taking her eyes from her work she looked stedfastly at her. Mistress Joan immediately fancied that she felt sudden pains in all her limbs, and from that day forth never ceased to tell her sisters, and every body about her, that Mother Samuel had bewitched her. The other children took up the cry, and actually frightened themselves into fits whenever they passed within sight of this terrible old woman.

Mr. and Mrs. Throgmorton, not a whit wiser than their children, believed all the absurd tales they had been told; and Lady Cromwell, a gossip of Mrs. Throgmorton, made herself very active in the business, and determined to bring the witch to the ordeal. The sapient Sir Samuel joined in the scheme; and the children, thus encouraged, gave loose reins to their imaginations, which seem to have been of the liveliest. They soon invented a whole host of evil spirits, and names for them besides, which they said were sent by Mother Samuel to torment them continually. Seven spirits especially, they said, were raised from hell by this wicked woman to throw them into fits; and as the children were actually subject to fits, their mother and her commeres gave the more credit to the story. The names of these spirits were, " First Smack," " Second Smack," " Third Smack," " Blue," " Catch," " Harduame," and " Pluck."

Throgmorton, the father, was so pestered by these idle fancies, and yet so well inclined to believe them, that he marched valiantly forth to the hut where Mother Samuel resided with her husband and daughter, and dragged her forcibly into his own grounds. Lady Cromwell, Mrs. Throgmorton, and the girls were in waiting, armed with long pins to prick the witch, and see if they could draw blood from her. Lady Cromwell, who seems to have been the most violent of the party, tore the old woman's cap off her head, and plucking out a handful of her grey hair, gave it to Mrs. Throgmorton to burn, as a charm which would preserve them all from her future machinations. It was no wonder that the poor creature, subjected to this rough usage, should give vent to an involuntary curse upon her tormentors. She did so, and her curse was never forgotten. Her hair, however, was supposed to be a grand specific, and she was allowed to depart, half dead with terror and ill-usage. For more than a year the families of Cromwell and Throgmorton continued to persecute her, and to assert that her imps afflicted them with pains and fits, turned the milk sour in their pans, and prevented their cows and ewes from bearing. In the midst of these fooleries, Lady Cromwell was taken ill and died. It was then remembered that her death had taken place exactly a year and a quarter since she was cursed by Mother Samuel, and that on several occasions she had dreamed of the witch and a black cat, the latter being of course the arch-enemy of mankind himself.

Sir Samuel Cromwell now conceived himself bound to take more energetic measures against the sorceress, since he had lost his wife by her means. The year and a quarter and the black cat were proofs positive. All the neighbours had taken up the cry of witchcraft against Mother Samuel; and her personal appearance, unfortunately for her the very ideal of what a witch ought to be, increased the popular suspicion. It would appear that at last the poor woman believed, even to her own disadvantage, that she was what every body represented her to be. Being forcibly brought into Mr. Throgmorton's house, when his daughter Joan was in one of her customary fits, she was commanded by him and Sir Samuel Cromwell to expel the devil from the young lady. She was told to repeat her exorcism, and to add, "As I am a witch, and the causer of Lady Cromwell's death, I charge thee, fiend, to come out of her!" She did as was required of her; and moreover confessed that her husband and daughter were leagued with her in witchcraft, and had, like her, sold their souls to the devil. The whole family were immediately arrested, and sent to Huntingdon to prison.

The trial was instituted shortly afterwards before Mr. Justice Fenner, when all the crazy girls of Mr. Throgmorton's family gave evidence against Mother Samuel and her family. They were all three put to the torture. The old woman confessed in her anguish that she was a witch; that she had cast her spells upon the young ladies; and that she had caused the death of Lady Cromwell. The father and daughter, stronger in mind than their unfortunate wife and parent, refused to confess any thing, and asserted their innocence to the last. They were all three condemned to be hanged, and their bodies burned. The daughter, who was young and good-looking, excited the pity of many persons, and she was advised to plead pregnancy, that she might gain at least a respite from death. The poor girl refused proudly, on the ground that she would not be accounted both a witch and a strumpet. Her half-witted old mother caught at the idea of a few weeks' longer life, and asserted that she was pregnant. The court was convulsed with laughter, in which the wretched victim herself joined; and this was accounted an additional proof that she was a witch. The whole family were executed on the 7th of April, 1593.

Sir Samuel Cromwell, as lord of the manor, received the sum of 40l. out of the confiscated property of the Samuels, which he turned into a rent-charge of 40s. yearly, for the endowment of an annual sermon or lecture upon the enormity of witchcraft, and this case in particular, to be preached by a doctor or bachelor of divinity of Queen's College, Cambridge. I have not been able to ascertain the exact date at which this annual lecture was discontinued; but it appears to have been preached so late as 1718, when Dr. Hutchinson published his work upon witchcraft.

To carry on in proper chronological order the history of the witch delusion in the British isles, it will be necessary to examine into what was taking place in Scotland during all that part of the sixteenth century anterior to the accession of James VI. to the crown of England. We naturally expect that the Scotch—a people renowned from the earliest times for their powers of imagination—should be more deeply imbued with this gloomy superstition than their neighbours of the south. The nature of their soil and climate tended to encourage the dreams of early ignorance. Ghosts, goblins, wraiths, kelpies, and a whole host of spiritual beings, were familiar to the dwellers by the misty glens of the Highlands and the romantic streams of the Lowlands. Their deeds, whether of good or ill, were enshrined in song, and took a greater hold upon the imagination because "verse had sanctified them." But it was not till the religious reformers began the practice of straining Scripture to the severest extremes that the arm of the law was called upon to punish witchcraft as a crime *per se*. What Pope Innocent VIII. had done for Germany and France, the preachers of the Reformation did for the Scottish people. Witchcraft, instead of being a mere article of faith, became enrolled in the statute-book, and all good subjects and true Christians were called upon to take arms against it. The ninth parliament of Queen Mary passed an act in 1563, which decreed the punishment of death against witches and consulters with witches; and immediately the whole bulk of the people were smitten with an epidemic fear of the devil and his mortal agents. Persons in the highest ranks of life shared and encouraged the delusion of the vulgar. Many were themselves accused of witchcraft; and noble ladies were shewn to have dabbled in mystic arts, and proved to the world that if they were not witches, it was not for want of the will.

Among the dames who became notorious for endeavouring to effect their wicked ends by the devil's aid may be mentioned the celebrated Lady Buccleugh of Branxholme (familiar to all the readers of Sir Walter Scott), the Countess of Lothian, the Countess of Angus, the Countess of Atholl, Lady Kerr, the Countess of Huntley, Euphemia Macalzean (the daughter of Lord Cliftonhall), and Lady Fowlis. Among the celebrated of the other sex who were accused of wizardism was Sir Lewis Ballantyne, the Lord Justice-Clerk for Scotland, who, if we may believe Scot of Scotstarvet, "dealt by curiosity with a warlock called Richard Grahame," and prayed him to raise the devil. The warlock consented, and raised him *in propriâ personâ* in the yard of his house in the Canongate, "at sight of him the Lord Justice-Clerk was so terrified, that he took sickness and thereof died." By such idle reports as these did the envious ruin the reputation of those they hated; though it would appear in this case that Sir Lewis had been fool enough to make the attempt of which he was accused, and that the success of the experiment was the only apocryphal part of the story.

JOHN KNOX.

The enemies of John Knox invented a similar tale, which found ready credence among the Roman Catholics, glad to attach any stigma to that grand scourge of the vices of their Church. It was reported that he and his secretary went into the churchyard of St. Andrew's with the intent to raise "some sanctes ;" but that, by a mistake in their conjurations, they raised the great fiend himself instead of the saints they wished to consult. The popular rumour added, that Knox's secretary was so frightened at the great horns, goggle eyes, and long tail of Satan, that he went mad, and shortly afterwards died. Knox himself was built of sterner stuff, and was not to be frightened.

The first name that occurs in the records of the High Court of Justiciary of persons tried or executed for witchcraft, is that of Janet Bowman in 1572, nine years after the passing of the act of Mary. No particulars of her crimes are given, and against her name there only stands the words, "convict and brynt." It is not, however, to be inferred, that in this interval no trials or executions took place ; for it appears, on the authority of documents of unquestioned authenticity in the Advocates' Library at Edinburgh,* that the Privy Council made a practice of granting commissions to resident gentlemen and ministers in every part of Scotland to examine, try, and execute witches within their own parishes. No records of those who suffered from the sentence of these tribunals have been preserved ; but if popular tradition may be believed even to the amount of one-fourth of its assertions, their number was fearful. After the year 1572, the entries of executions for witchcraft in the records of the High Court become more frequent, but do not average more than one per annum,—another proof that trials for this offence were in general entrusted to the local magistracy. The latter appear to have ordered witches to the stake with as little compunction, and after as summary a mode, as modern justices of the peace order a poacher to the stocks.

As James VI. advanced in manhood, he took great interest in the witch trials. One of them especially—that of Gellie Duncan, Dr. Fian, and their accomplices, in the year 1591—engrossed his whole attention, and no doubt suggested in some degree the famous work on Demonology, which he wrote shortly afterwards. As these witches had made an attempt upon his own life, it is not surprising, with his habits, that he should have watched the case closely, or become strengthened in his prejudice and superstition by its singular details. No other trial that could be selected would give so fair an idea of the delusions of the Scottish people as this. Whether we consider the number of victims, the absurdity of the evidence, and the real villany of some of the persons implicated, it is equally extraordinary.

Gellie Duncan, the prime witch in these proceedings, was servant to the deputy bailiff of Tranent, a small town in Haddingtonshire,

* *Foreign Quarterly Review*, vol. vi. p. 41.

about ten miles from Edinburgh. Though neither old nor ugly (as witches usually were), but young and good-looking, her neighbours, from some suspicious parts of her behaviour, had long considered her a witch. She had, it appears, some pretensions to the healing art. Some cures which she effected were so sudden, that the worthy bailiff, her master, who, like his neighbours, mistrusted her, considered them no less than miraculous. In order to discover the truth, he put her to the torture; but she obstinately refused to confess that she had dealings with the devil. It was the popular belief that no witch would confess as long as the mark which Satan had put upon her remained undiscovered upon her body. Somebody present reminded the torturing bailie of this fact, and on examination, the devil's mark was found upon the throat of poor Gellie. She was put to the torture again, and her fortitude giving way under the extremity of her anguish, she confessed that she was indeed a witch— that she had sold her soul to the devil, and effected all her cures by his aid. This was something new in the witch creed, according to which, the devil delighted more in laying diseases on than in taking them off; but Gellie Duncan fared no better on that account. The torture was still applied, until she had named all her accomplices, among whom were one Cunningham, a reputed wizard, known by the name of Dr. Fian; a grave and matron-like witch, named Agnes Sampson; Euphemia Macalzean, the daughter of Lord Cliftonhall, already mentioned, and nearly forty other persons, some of whom were the wives of respectable individuals in the city of Edinburgh. Every one of these persons was arrested, and the whole realm of Scotland thrown into commotion by the extraordinary nature of the disclosures which were anticipated.

About two years previous to this time, James had suddenly left his kingdom, and proceeded gallantly to Denmark, to fetch over his bride, the Princess of Denmark, who had been detained by contrary weather in the harbour of Upslo. After remaining for some months in Copenhagen, he set sail with his young bride, and arrived safely in Leith on the 1st of May 1590, having experienced a most boisterous passage, and been nearly wrecked. As soon as the arrest of Gellie Duncan and Fian became known in Scotland, it was reported by every body who pretended to be well-informed, that these witches and their associates had, by the devil's means, raised the storms which had endangered the lives of the king and queen. Gellie, in her torture, had confessed that such was the fact, and the whole kingdom waited aghast and open-mouthed for the corroboration about to be furnished by the trial.

Agnes Sampson, the "grave and matron-like" witch implicated

by Gellie Duncan, was put to the horrible torture of the *pilliewinkis*. She laid bare all the secrets of the sisterhood before she had suffered an hour, and confessed that Gellie Duncan, Dr. Fian, Marian Lincup, Euphemia Macalzean, herself, and upwards of two hundred witches and warlocks, used to assemble at midnight in the kirk of North Berwick, where they met the devil; that they had plotted there to attempt the king's life ; that they were incited to this by the old fiend himself, who had asserted with a thundering oath that James was the greatest enemy he ever had, and that there would be no peace for the devil's children upon earth until he were got rid of ; that the devil upon these occasions always liked to have a little music, and that Gellie Duncan used to play a reel before him on a trump or Jew's harp, to which all the witches danced.

James was highly flattered at the idea that the devil should have said that he was the greatest enemy he ever had. He sent for Gellie Duncan to the palace, and made her play before him the same reel which she had played at the witches' dance in the kirk.

TORTURE OF THE BOOTS.

Dr. Fian, or rather Cunningham, a petty schoolmaster of Tranent, was put to the torture among the rest. He was a man who had led an infamous life, was a compounder of and dealer in poisons, and a pretender to magic. Though not guilty of the preposterous crimes laid to his charge, there is no doubt that he was a sorcerer in will, though not in deed, and that he deserved all the misery he endured. When put on the rack, he would confess nothing, and held out so long unmoved, that the severe torture of the *boots* was resolved upon. He endured this till exhausted nature could bear no longer, when insensibility kindly stepped in to his aid. When it was seen that he was utterly powerless, and that his tongue cleaved to the roof of his mouth, he was released. Restoratives were administered; and during the first faint gleam of returning consciousness, he was prevailed upon to sign, ere he well knew what he was about, a full confession, in strict accordance with those of Gellie Duncan and Agnes Sampson. He was then remanded to his prison, from which, after two days, he managed, some how or other, to escape. He was soon recaptured, and brought before the Court of Justiciary, James himself being present. Fian now denied all the circumstances of the written confession which he had signed ; whereupon the king, enraged at his " stubborn wilfulness," ordered him once more to the torture. His finger-nails were riven out with pincers, and long needles thrust up to the eye into the quick ; but he did not wince. He was then consigned again to the *boots*, in which, to quote a pamphlet published at the time,* he continued " so long, and abode so many blows in them, that his legs were crushed and beaten together as small as might be, and the bones and flesh so bruised, that the blood and marrow spouted forth in great abundance, whereby they were made unserviceable for ever."

The astonishing similarity of the confessions of all the persons implicated in these proceedings has often been remarked. It would appear that they actually endeavoured to cause the king's death by their spells and sorceries. Fian, who was acquainted with all the usual tricks of his profession, deceived them with pretended apparitions, so that many of them were really convinced that they had seen the devil. The sum of their confessions was to the following effect :

Satan, who was, of course, a great foe of the reformed religion, was alarmed that King James should marry a Protestant princess. To avert the consequences to the realms of evil, he had determined to put an end to the king and his bride by raising a storm on their voyage home. Satan, first of all, sent a thick mist over the waters, in the hope that the king's vessel might be stranded on the coast amid the darkness. This failing, Dr. Fian, who, from his superior scholarship, was advanced to the dignity of the devil's secretary, was commanded to summon all the witches to meet their master, each one sailing on a sieve on the high seas.

* *News from Scotland, declaring the Damnable Life of Dr. Fian.*

On All Hallowmas Eve, they assembled to the number of upwards of two hundred, including Gellie Duncan, Agnes Sampson, Euphemia Macalzean, one Barbara Napier, and several warlocks ; and each embarking in a riddle or sieve, they sailed " over the ocean very substantially." After cruising about for some time, they met with the fiend, bearing in his claws a cat, which had been previously drawn nine times through the fire. This he delivered to one of the warlocks, telling him to cast it into the sea and cry " Hola !" This was done with all solemnity, and immediately the ocean became convulsed, the waters hissed loudly, and the waves rose mountains high,

" Twisting their arms to the dun-coloured heaven."

The witches sailed gallantly through the tempest they had raised, and landing on the coast of Scotland, took their sieves in their hands and marched on in procession to the haunted kirk of North Berwick, where the devil had resolved to hold a preaching. Gellie Duncan, the musician of the party, tripped on before, playing on her Jew's harp and singing,

" Cummer, go ye before, cummer, go ye ;
Gif ye will not go before, cummer, let me !"

Arrived at the kirk, they paced around it *withershins*, that is, in reverse of the apparent motion of the sun. Dr. Fian then blew into the keyhole of the door, which opened immediately, and all the witches entered. As it was pitch-dark, Fian blew with his mouth upon the candles, which immediately lighted, and the devil was seen occupying the pulpit. He was attired in a black gown and hat, and the witches saluted him by crying " All hail, master !" His body was hard, like iron ; his face terrible ; his nose like the beak of an eagle ; he had great burning eyes ; his hands and legs were hairy ; and he had long claws upon his hands and feet, and spake with an exceedingly gruff voice. Before commencing his sermon he called over the names of his congregation, demanding whether they had been good servants, and what success had attended their operations against the life of the king and his bride.

Gray Meill, a crazy old warlock, who acted as beadle or doorkeeper, was silly enough to answer " that nothing ailed the king yet, God be thanked ;" upon which the devil, in a rage, stepped down from the pulpit and boxed his ears for him. He then remounted and commenced the preaching, commanding them to be dutiful servants to him and do all the evil they could. Euphemia Macalzean and Agnes Sampson, bolder than the rest, asked him whether he had brought the image or picture of King James, that they might, by pricking it, cause pains and diseases to fall upon him. " The father of lies" spoke truth for once, and confessed that he had forgotten it ; upon which Euphemia Macalzean upbraided him loudly for his carelessness. The devil, however, took it all in good part, although Agnes Sampson and several other women let loose their tongues at him immediately. When they had done scolding, he invited them all to a grand entertainment. A newly-buried corpse was dug up and divided among them, which was all they had in the way of edibles. He was more liberal in the matter of drink, and gave them so much excellent wine that they soon became jolly. Gellie Duncan then played the old tune upon her trump, and the devil himself led off the dance with Euphemia Macalzean. Thus they kept up the sport till the cock crew.

Agnes Sampson, the wise woman of Keith, as she was called, added some other particulars in her confession. She stated that, on a previous occasion, she had raised an awful tempest in the sea by throwing a cat into it, with four joints of men tied to its feet. She said also, that on their grand attempt to drown King James, they did not meet with the devil after cruising about, but that he had accompanied them from the first, and that she had seen him dimly in the distance, rolling himself before them over the great waves, in shape and size not unlike a huge haystack. They met with a foreign ship richly laden with wines and other good things, which they boarded, and sunk after they had drunk all the wine and made themselves quite merry.

JAMES THE DEMONOLOGIST.

Some of these disclosures were too much even for the abundant faith of King James, and he more than once exclaimed, that the witches were like their master, " extreme lyars." But they confessed many other things of a less preposterous nature, and of which they were no doubt really guilty. Agnes Sampson said she was to have taken the king's life by anointing his linen with a strong poison. Gellie Duncan used to threaten her neighbours by saying she would send the devil after them ; and many persons of weaker minds than usual were frightened into fits by her, and rendered subject to them for the remainder of their lives. Dr. Fian also made no scruple in aiding and abetting murder, and would rid any person of an enemy by means of poison, who could pay him his fee for it. Euphemia Macalzean also was far from being pure. There is no doubt that she meditated the king's death, and used such means to compass it as the superstition of the age directed. She was a devoted partisan of Bothwell, who was accused by many of the witches as having consulted them on the period of the king's death. They were all found guilty, and sentenced to be hanged and burned. Barbara Napier, though found guilty upon other counts, was acquitted upon the charge of having been present at the great witch meeting in Berwick kirk. The king was highly displeased, and threatened to have the jury indicted for a wilful error upon an assize. They accordingly reconsidered their verdict, and threw themselves upon the king's mercy for the fault they had committed. James was satisfied, and Barbara Napier was hanged along with Gellie Duncan, Agnes Sampson, Dr. Fian, and five-and-twenty others. Euphemia Macalzean met a harder fate. Her connexion with the bold and obnoxious Bothwell, and her share in poisoning one or two individuals who had stood in her way, were thought deserving of the severest punishment the law could inflict. Instead of the ordinary sentence, directing the criminal to be first strangled and then burned, the wretched woman was doomed "to be bound to a stake, and burned in ashes, *quick* to the death." This cruel sentence was executed on the 25th of June, 1591.

These trials had the most pernicious consequences all over Scotland. The lairds and ministers in their districts, armed with due power from the privy council, tried and condemned old women after the most summary fashion. Those who still clung to the ancient faith of Rome were the severest sufferers, as it was thought, after the disclosures of the fierce enmity borne by the devil towards a Protestant king and his Protestant wife, that all the Catholics were leagued with the powers of evil to work woe on the realm of Scotland. Upon a very moderate calculation, it is presumed that from the passing of the act of Queen Mary till the accession of James to the throne of England, a period of thirty-nine years, the average number of executions for witchcraft in Scotland was two hundred annually, or upwards of seventeen thousand altogether For the first nine years the number was not one quarter so great; but towards the years 1590 to 1593, the number must have been more than four hundred. The case last cited was one of an extraordinary character. The general aspect of the trials will be better seen from that of Isabel Gowdie, which, as it would be both wearisome and disgusting to go through them all, is given as a

fair specimen, although it took place at a date somewhat later than
the reign of James. This woman, wearied of her life by the persecutions of her neighbours, voluntarily gave herself up to justice, and
made a confession, embodying the whole witch-creed of the period.
She was undoubtedly a monomaniac of the most extraordinary kind.
She said that she deserved to be stretched upon an iron rack, and
that her crimes could never be atoned for, even if she were to be
drawn asunder by wild horses. She named a long list of her associates, including nearly fifty women and a few warlocks. They dug
up the graves of unchristened infants, whose limbs were serviceable
in their enchantments. When they wanted to destroy the crops
of an enemy, they yoked toads to his plough, and on the following
night Satan himself ploughed the land with his team, and blasted it
for the season. The witches had power to assume almost any shape ;
but they generally chose either that of a cat or a hare, oftenest the
latter. Isabel said, that on one occasion, when she was in this disguise, she was sore pressed by a pack of hounds, and had a very narrow escape with her life. She reached her own door at last, feeling
the hot breath of the pursuing dogs at her haunches. She managed,
however, to hide herself behind a chest, and got time to pronounce
the magic words that could alone restore her to her proper shape.
They were :

> " Hare ! hare !
> God send thee care !
> I am in a hare's likeness now ;
> But I shall be a woman e en now !
> Hare ! hare !
> God send thee care !"

If witches, when in this shape, were bitten by the dogs, they always
retained the marks in their human form ; but she had never heard
that any witch had been bitten to death. When the devil appointed
any general meeting of the witches, the custom was that they should
proceed through the air mounted on broomsticks, or on corn or bean-
straws, pronouncing as they went :

> " Horse and pattock, horse and go,
> Horse and pellats, ho ! ho ! ho !"

They generally left behind them a broom or a three-legged stool,
which, when placed in their beds and duly charmed, assumed the
human shape till their return. This was done that the neighbours
might not know when they were absent.

She added that the devil furnished his favourite witches with servant imps to attend upon them. These imps were called " The

Roaring Lion," "Thief of Hell," "Wait-upon-Herself," "Ranting Roarer," "Care-for-Naught," &c., and were known by their liveries, which were generally yellow, sad-dun, sea-green, pea-green, or grass-green. Satan never called the witches by the names they had received at baptism ; neither were they allowed, in his presence, so to designate each other. Such a breach of the infernal etiquette assuredly drew down his most severe displeasure. But as some designation was necessary, he re-baptised them in their own blood by the names of "Able-and-Stout," "Over-the-dike-with-it," "Raise-the-wind," "Pickle-nearest-the-wind," "Batter-them-down-Maggy," "Blow-Kale," and such like. The devil himself was not very particular what name they called him, so that it was not "Black John." If any witch was unthinking enough to utter these words, he would rush out upon her and beat and buffet her unmercifully, or tear her flesh with a wool-card. Other names he did not care about ; and once gave instructions to a noted warlock that whenever he wanted his aid, he was to strike the ground three times and exclaim, "Rise up, foul thief !"

Upon this confession many persons were executed. So strong was the popular feeling, that no one once accused of witchcraft was acquitted ; at least, acquittals did not average one in a hundred trials. Witch-finding, or witch-pricking, became a trade, and a set of mercenary vagabonds roamed about the country provided with long pins to run into the flesh of supposed criminals. It was no unusual thing then, nor is it now, that in aged persons there should be some spot on the body totally devoid of feeling. It was the object of the witch-pricker to discover this spot, and the unhappy wight who did not bleed when pricked upon it was doomed to the death. If not immediately cast into prison, her life was rendered miserable by the persecution of her neighbours. It is recorded of many poor women, that the annoyances they endured in this way were so excessive, that they preferred death. Sir George Mackenzie, the Lord Advocate, at the time when witch trials were so frequent, and himself a devout believer in the crime, relates, in his *Criminal Law*, first published in 1678, some remarkable instances of it. He says, "I went, when I was a justice-depute, to examine some women who had confessed judicially ; and one of them, who was a silly creature, told me, under secrecy, that she had not confessed because she was guilty, but being a poor creature, who wrought for her meat, and being defamed for a witch, she knew she should starve, for no person thereafter would either give her meat or lodging, and that all men would beat her and set dogs at her, and that, therefore, she desired to be out of the world ; whereupon she wept most bitterly, and upon her knees called God to witness to

what she said." Sir George, though not wholly elevated above the
prejudices of his age upon this subject, was clear-sighted enough to
see the danger to society of the undue encouragement given to the

SIR G. MACKENZIE.

witch prosecutions. He was
convinced that three-fourths of
them were unjust and unfound-
ed. He says in the work already quoted, that the persons
who were in general accused of
this crime were poor ignorant
men and women who did not
understand the nature of the
accusation, and who mistook
their own superstitious fears for
witchcraft. One poor wretch,
a weaver, confessed that he was
a warlock, and, being asked
why, he replied, because "he
had seen the devil dancing,
like a fly, about the candle!"
A simple woman, who, because

she was called a witch, believed that she was, asked the judge upon
the bench whether a person might be a witch and not know it?
Sir George adds, that all the supposed criminals were subjected to
severe torture in prison from their gaolers, who thought they did God
good service by vexing and tormenting them; "and I know," says
this humane and enlightened magistrate, "that this usage was the
ground of all their confession; and albeit, the poor miscreants cannot prove this usage, the actors in it being the only witnesses; yet
the judge should be jealous of it, as that which did at first elicit the
confession, and for fear of which they dare not retract it." Another
author,* also a firm believer in witchcraft, gives a still more lamentable instance of a woman who preferred execution as a witch to live
on under the imputation. This woman, who knew that three others
were to be strangled and burned on an early day, sent for the minister
of the parish, and confessed that she had sold her soul to Satan.
"Whereupon being called before the judges, she was condemned to
die with the rest. Being carried forth to the place of execution, she
remained silent during the first, second, and third prayer, and then,
perceiving that there remained no more but to rise and go to the stake,
she lifted up her body, and, with a loud voice, cried out, 'Now all
you that see me this day, know that I am now to die as a witch, by

* *Satan's Invisible World Discovered*, by the Rev. G. Sinclair.

my own confession; and I free all men, especially the ministers and magistrates, of the guilt of my blood. I take it wholly upon myself. My blood be upon my own head. And, as I must make answer to the God of heaven presently, I declare 1 am as free of witchcraft as any child. But, being delated by a malicious woman, and put in prison under the name of a witch, disowned by my husband and friends, and seeing no ground of hope of ever coming out again, I made up that confession to destroy my own life, being weary of it, and choosing rather to die than to live.'" As a proof of the singular obstinacy and blindness of the believers in witches, it may be stated that the minister who relates this story only saw in the dying speech of the unhappy woman an additional proof that she was a witch. True, indeed, is it, that "none are so blind as those who will not see."

It is time, however, to return to James VI., who is fairly entitled to share with Pope Innocent, Sprenger, Bodinus, and Matthew Hopkins the glory or the odium of being at the same time a chief enemy and chief encourager of witchcraft. Towards the close of the sixteenth century, many learned men, both on the continent and in the isles of Britain, had endeavoured to disabuse the public mind on this subject. The most celebrated were Wierus, in Germany; Pietro d'Apone, in Italy; and Reginald Scot, in England. Their works excited the attention of the zealous James, who, mindful of the involuntary compliment which his merits had extorted from the devil, was ambitious to deserve it by still continuing "his greatest enemie." In the year 1597, he published in Edinburgh his famous treatise on Demonology. Its design may be gathered from the following passage in the introduction : "The fearful abounding," says the king, "at this time and in this country of these detestable slaves of the devil, the witches or enchanters, hath moved me, beloved reader, to despatch in post this following treatise of mine, not in any wise, as I protest, to serve for a show of mine own learning and in-gene [ingenuity], but only (moved of conscience) to press thereby, so far as I can, to resolve the doubting hearts of many, both that such assaults of Satan are most certainly practised, and that the instrument thereof merits most severely to be punished, against the damnable opinions of two, principally in our age; whereof the one called Scot, an Englishman, is not ashamed in public print to deny that there can be such thing as witchcraft, and so maintains the old error of the Sadducees in denying of spirits. The other, called Wierus, a German physician, sets out a public apology for all these crafts-folks, whereby procuring for them impunity, he plainly betrays himself to have been one of that profession." In other parts of this treatise, which the author had put into the form of a dialogue, to " make it more pleasant and facile," he says: " Witches ought to be put to death, according to the law of God, the civil and imperial law, and the municipal law of all Christian nations: yea, to spare the life, and not strike whom God bids strike, and so severely punish in so odious a treason against God, is not only unlawful, but doubtless as great a sin in the magistrate as was Saul's sparing Agag." He says also that the crime is so abominable, that it may be proved by evidence which would not be received against any other offenders,—young children, who knew not the nature of an oath, and persons of an infamous character, being sufficient witnesses against them; but lest the innocent should be accused of a crime so difficult to be acquitted of, he recommends that in all cases the

PIETRO D'APONE.

ordeal should be resorted to. He says, " Two good helps may be used: the one is the finding of their mark, and the trying the insensibleness thereof; the other is their floating on the water, — for, as in a secret murther, if the dead carcass be at any time thereafter handled by the murtherer, it will gush out of blood, as if the blood were crying to Heaven for revenge of the murtherer (God having appointed that secret supernatural sign for trial of that secret unnatural crime), so that it appears that God hath appointed (for a supernatural sign of the monstrous impiety of witches) that the water shall refuse to receive them in her bosom that have shaken off them the sacred water of baptism, and wilfully refused the benefit thereof;—no, not so much as their eyes are able to shed tears (threaten and torture them as you please), while first they repent (God not permitting them to dissemble their obstinacy in so horrible a crime); albeit, the womenkind especially, be able otherwise to shed tears at every light occasion when they will, yea, although it were dissembling like the crocodiles."

When such doctrines as these were openly promulgated by the highest authority in the realm, and who, in promulgating them, flattered, but did not force the public opinion, it is not surprising that the sad delusion should have increased and multiplied until the race of wizards and witches replenished the earth. The reputation which he lost by being afraid of a naked sword, he more than regained by his courage in combating the devil. The Kirk shewed itself a most zealous coadjutor, especially during those halcyon days when it was not at issue with the king upon other matters of doctrine and prerogative.

On his accession to the throne of England in 1603, James came amongst a people who had heard with admiration of his glorious deeds against the witches. He himself left no part of his ancient prejudices behind him ; and his advent was the signal for the persecution to burst forth in England with a fury equal to that in Scotland. It had languished a little during the latter years of the reign of Elizabeth ; but the very first parliament of King James brought forward the subject. James was flattered by their promptitude, and the act passed in 1604. On the second reading in the House of Lords, the bill passed into a committee, in which were twelve bishops. By it was enacted, " That if any person shall use, practise, or exercise any conjuration of any wicked or evil spirit, or shall consult, covenant with, or feed any such spirit, the first offence to be imprisonment for a year, and standing in the pillory once a quarter ; the second offence to be death."

The minor punishment seems but rarely to have been inflicted. Every record that has been preserved mentions that the witches were hanged and burned, or burned, without the previous strangling, "alive and quick." During the whole of James's reign, amid the civil wars of his successor, the sway of the Long Parliament, the usurpation of Cromwell, and the reign of Charles II., there was no abatement of the persecution. If at any time it raged with less virulence, it was when Cromwell and the Independents were masters. Dr. Zachary Grey, the editor of an edition of " Hudibras," informs us, in a note to that work, that he himself perused a list of three thousand witches who were executed in the time of the Long Parliament alone. During the first eighty years of the seventeenth century, the number executed has been estimated at five hundred annually, making the frightful total of forty thousand. Some of these cases deserve to be cited. The great majority resemble closely those already mentioned ; but two or three of them let in a new light upon the popular superstition.

Every one has heard of the " Lancashire witches," a phrase now used to compliment the ladies of that county for their bewitching beauty; but it is not every one who has heard the story in which it originated. A villanous boy, named Robinson, was the chief actor in the tragedy. He confessed many years afterwards that he had been suborned by his father and other persons to give false evidence against the unhappy witches whom he brought to the stake. The time of this famous trial was about the year 1634. This boy Robinson, whose father was a wood-cutter, residing on the borders of Pendle Forest, in Lancashire, spread abroad many rumours against one Mother Dickenson, whom he accused of being a witch. These rumours coming to the ears of the local magistracy, the boy was sent for and strictly examined. He told the following extraordinary story without hesitation or prevarication, and apparently in so open and honest a manner, that no one who heard him doubted the truth of it. He said, that as he was roaming about in one of the glades of the forest, amusing himself by gathering blackberries, he saw two greyhounds before him, which he thought at the time belonged to some gentleman of the neighbourhood. Being fond of sport, he proposed to have a course; and a hare being started, he incited the hounds to run. Neither of them would stir. Angry at the beasts, he seized hold of a switch, with which he was about to punish them, when one of them suddenly started up in the form of a woman, and the other of a little boy. He at once recognised the woman to be the witch Mother Dickenson. She offered him some money to induce him to sell his soul to the devil; but he refused. Upon this she took a bridle out of her pocket, and shaking it over the head of the other little boy, he was instantly turned into a horse. Mother Dickenson then seized him in her arms, sprang upon the horse, and placing him before her, rode with the swiftness of the wind over forests, fields, bogs, and rivers, until they came to a large barn. The witch alighted at the door, and, taking him by the hand, led him inside. There he saw seven old women pulling at seven halters which hung from the roof. As they pulled, large pieces of meat, lumps of butter, loaves of bread, basins of milk, hot puddings, black-puddings, and other rural dainties, fell from the halters on to the floor. While engaged in this charm, they made such ugly faces, and looked so fiendish, that he was quite frightened. After they had pulled in this manner enough for an ample feast, they set-to, and shewed, whatever might be said of the way in which their supper was procured, that their epicurism was a little more refined than that of the Scottish witches, who, according to Gellie Duncan's confession, feasted upon dead men's flesh in the old kirk of Berwick. The boy added, that as soon as supper was ready, many other witches came to partake of it, several of whom he named.

In consequence of this story, many persons were arrested, and the boy Robinson was led about from church to church, in order that he might point out to the officers by whom he was accompanied the hags he had seen in the barn. Altogether, about twenty persons were thrown into prison ; eight of them were condemned to die; including Mother Dickenson, upon this evidence alone, and executed accordingly. Among the wretches who concocted this notable story, not one was ever brought to justice for his perjury ; and Robinson, the father, gained considerable sums by threatening persons who were rich enough to buy off exposure.

Among the ill-weeds which flourished amid the long dissensions of the civil war, Matthew Hopkins, the witch-finder, stands eminent in his sphere. This vulgar fellow resided, in the year 1644, at the town of Manningtree, in Essex, and made himself very conspicuous in discovering the devil's marks upon several unhappy witches. The credit he gained by his skill in this instance seems to have inspired him to renewed exertions. In the course of a very short time, whenever a witch was spoken of in Essex, Matthew Hopkins was sure to be present, aiding the judges with his knowledge of "such cattle," as he called them. As his reputation increased, he assumed the title of " Witch-finder General," and travelled through the counties of Norfolk, Essex, Huntingdon, and Sussex, for the sole purpose of finding out witches. In one year he brought sixty poor creatures to the stake. The test he commonly adopted was that of swimming, so highly recommended by King James in his *Demonologie*. The hands and feet of the suspected persons were tied together crosswise, the thumb of the right hand to the toe of the left foot, and *vice versa*. They were then wrapped up in a large sheet or blanket, and laid upon their backs in a pond or river. If they sank, their friends and relatives had the poor consolation of knowing they were innocent ; but there was an end of them : if they floated, which, when laid carefully on the water, was generally the case, there was also an end of them ; for they were deemed guilty of witchcraft, and burned accordingly.

Another test was to make them repeat the Lord's prayer and creed. It was affirmed that no witch could do so correctly. If she missed a word, or even pronounced one incoherently, which in her trepidation it was most probable she would, she was accounted guilty. It was thought that witches could not weep more than three tears, and those only from the left eye. Thus the conscious innocence of many persons, which gave them fortitude to bear unmerited torture without flinching, was construed by their unmerciful tormentors into proofs of guilt. In some districts the test resorted to was to weigh the culprit against the church Bible. If the suspected witch proved heavier than the Bible, she was set at liberty. This mode was far too humane for the witch-finders by profession. Hopkins always maintained that the most legitimate modes were pricking and swimming.

Hopkins used to travel through his counties like a man of consideration, attended by his two assistants, always putting up at the chief inn of the place, and always at the cost of the authorities. His charges were twenty shillings a town, his expenses of living while there, and his carriage thither and back. This he claimed whether he found witches or not. If he found any, he claimed twenty shillings a head in addition when they were brought to execution. For about three years he carried on this infamous trade, success making him so insolent and rapacious that high and low became his enemies. The Rev. Mr. Gaul, a clergyman of Houghton, in Huntingdonshire, wrote a pamphlet impugning his pretensions, and accusing him of being a common nuisance. Hopkins replied in an angry letter to the functionaries of Houghton, stating his intention to visit their town; but desiring to know whether it afforded many such sticklers for witchcraft as Mr. Gaul, and whether they were willing to receive and entertain him with the customary hospitality, if he so far honoured them. He added, by way of threat, that in case he did not receive a satisfactory reply, "he would waive their shire altogether, and betake himself to such places where he might do and punish, not only without control, but with thanks and recompense." The authorities of Houghton were not much alarmed at this awful threat of letting them alone. They very wisely took no notice either of him or his letter.

Mr. Gaul describes in his pamphlet one of the modes employed by Hopkins, which was sure to swell his revenues very considerably. It was a proof even more atrocious than the swimming. He says, that the " Witch-finder General" used to take the suspected witch and place her in the middle of a room, upon a stool or table, cross-legged, or in some other uneasy posture. If she refused to sit in this manner, she was bound with strong cords. Hopkins then placed persons to watch her for four-and-twenty hours, during which time she was to be kept without meat or drink. It was supposed that one of her imps would come during that interval and suck her blood. As the imp might come in the shape of a wasp, a moth, a fly, or other insect, a hole was made in the door or window to let it enter. The watchers were ordered to keep a sharp look out, and endeavour to kill any insect that appeared in the room. If any fly escaped, and they could not kill it, the woman was guilty; the fly was her imp, and she was sentenced to be burned, and twenty shillings went into the pockets of Master Hopkins. In this manner he made one old

MATTHEW HOPKINS.*

woman confess, because four flies had appeared in the room, that she was attended by four imps, named "Ilemazar," "Pye-wackett," "Peck-in-the-crown," and "Grizel-Greedigut."

* This illustration, representing Matthew Hopkins examining two witches who are confessing to him the names of their imps and familiars, is copied from Caulfield's *Memoirs of Remarkable Persons*, 1794, where it is taken from an extremely rare print.

It is consoling to think that this impostor perished in his own snare. Mr. Gaul's exposure and his own rapacity weakened his influence among the magistrates; and the populace, who began to find that not even the most virtuous and innocent were secure from his persecution, looked upon him with undisguised aversion. He was beset by a mob at a village in Suffolk, and accused of being himself a wizard. An old reproach was brought against him, that he had, by means of sorcery, cheated the devil out of a certain memorandum-book, in which he, Satan, had entered the names of all the witches in England. "Thus," said the populace, "you find out witches, not by God's aid, but by the devil's." In vain he denied his guilt. The populace longed to put him to his own test. He was speedily stripped, and his thumbs and toes tied together. He was then placed in a blanket, and cast into a pond. Some say that he floated, and that he was taken out, tried, and executed upon no other proof of his guilt. Others assert that he was drowned. This much is positive, that there was an end of him. As no judicial entry of his trial and execution is to be found in any register, it appears most probable that he expired by the hands of the mob. Butler has immortalised this scamp in the following lines of his *Hudibras:*

> " Hath not this present Parliament
> A lieger to the devil sent,
> Fully empower'd to treat about
> Finding revolted witches out ?
> And has he not within a year
> Hang'd threescore of them in one shire ?
> Some only for not being drown'd,
> And some for sitting above ground
> Whole days and nights upon their breeches,
> And feeling pain, were hang'd for witches ;
> And some for putting knavish tricks
> Upon green geese or turkey chicks ;
> Or pigs that suddenly deceased
> Of griefs unnatural, as he guess'd ;
> Who proved himself at length a witch,
> And made a rod for his own breech."

In Scotland also witch-finding became a trade. They were known under the designation of "common prickers," and, like Hopkins, received a fee for each witch they discovered. At the trial of Janet Peaston, in 1646, the magistrates of Dalkeith "caused John Kincaid of Tranent, the common pricker, to exercise his craft upon her. He found two marks of the devil's making; for she could not feel the pin when it was put into either of the said marks, nor did the marks bleed when the pin was taken out again. When she was asked where she thought the pins were put in her, she pointed to a part of her body distant from the real place. They were pins of three inches in length."*

These common prickers became at last so numerous that they were considered nuisances. The judges refused to take their evidence; and in 1678 the privy council of Scotland condescended to hear the complaint of an honest woman who had been indecently exposed by one of them, and expressed their opinion that common prickers were common cheats.

But such an opinion was not formed in high places before hundreds of innocent persons had fallen victims. The parliaments had encouraged the delusion both in England and Scotland; and by arming these fellows with a sort of authority, had in a manner forced the magistrates and ministers to receive their evidence. The fate of one poor old gentleman, who fell a victim to the arts of Hopkins in 1646, deserves to be recorded. Mr. Louis, a venerable clergyman, upwards of seventy years of age, and who had been rector of Framlingham, in Suffolk, for fifty years, excited suspicion that he was a wizard. Being a violent royalist, he was likely to meet with no sympathy at that time; and even his own parishioners, whom he had served so long and so faithfully, turned their backs upon him as soon as he was accused. Placed under the hands of Hopkins, who knew so well how to bring the refractory to confession, the old man, the light of whose intellect had become somewhat dimmed from age, confessed that he was a wizard. He said he had two imps that continually excited him to do evil; and that one day, when he was walking on the sea-coast, one of them prompted him to express a wish that a ship, whose sails were just visible in the distance, might sink. He consented, and saw the vessel sink before his eyes. He was, upon this confession, tried and condemned. On his trial, the flame of reason burned up as brightly as ever. He denied all that had been alleged against him, and cross-examined Hopkins with great tact and severity. After his condemnation, he begged that the funeral service of the Church might be read for him. The request was refused, and he repeated it for himself from memory as he was led to the scaffold.

A poor woman in Scotland was executed upon evidence even less strong than this. John Bain, a common pricker, swore that, as he passed her door, he heard her talking to the devil. She said, in defence, that it was a foolish practice she had of talking to herself, and several of her neighbours corroborated her statement; but the evidence of the pricker was received. He swore that none ever talked

* Pitcairn's *Records of Justiciary*.

to themselves who were not witches. The devil's mark being found upon her, the additional testimony of her guilt was deemed conclusive, and she was "convict and brynt."

From the year 1652 to 1682, these trials diminished annually in number, and acquittals were by no means so rare as they had been. To doubt in witchcraft was no longer dangerous. Before country justices, condemnations on the most absurd evidence still continued; but when the judges of the land had to charge the jury, they took a more humane and philosophical view. By degrees, the educated classes (comprised in those days within very narrow limits) openly expressed their unbelief of modern witchcraft, although they were not bold enough to deny its existence altogether. Between them and the believers in the old doctrine fierce arguments ensued, and the sceptics were designated Sadducees. To convince them, the learned and Reverend Joseph Glanvil wrote his well-known work, *Sadducismus Triumphatus*, and *The Collection of Relations;* the first part intended as a philosophical inquiry into witchcraft, and the power of the devil "to assume a mortal shape:" the latter containing what he considered a multitude of well-authenticated modern instances.

SIR MATTHEW HALE.

But though progress was made, it was slow In 1664, the venerable Sir Matthew Hale condemned two women, named Amy Duny and Rose Cullender, to the stake at St. Edmondsbury, upon evidence the most ridiculous. These two old women, whose ugliness gave their neighbours the first idea that they were witches, went to a shop to purchase herrings, and were refused. Indignant at the prejudice against them, they were not sparing of their abuse. Shortly afterward, the daughter of the herring-dealer fell sick, and a cry was raised that she was bewitched by the old women who had been refused the herrings. This girl was subject to epileptic fits. To discover the guilt of Amy Duny and Rose Cullender, the girl's eyes were blinded closely with a shawl, and the witches were commanded to touch her. They did so, and she was immediately seized with a fit. Upon this evidence they were sent to prison. The girl was afterwards touched by an indifferent person, and the force of her imagination was so great, that, thinking it was again the witches, she fell down in a violent fit as before. This, however, was not received in favour of the accused.

The following extract, from the published reports of the trial, will shew the sort of evidence which was received :

"Samuel Pacey, of Leystoff (a good, sober man), being sworn, said that, on Thursday the 10th of October last, his younger daughter, Deborah, about nine years old, was suddenly taken so lame that she could not stand on her legs, and so continued till the 17th of the same month, when the child desired to be carried to a bank on the east side of the house, looking towards the sea ; and, while she was sitting there, Amy Duny came to this examinant's house to buy some herrings, but was denied. Then she came twice more, but, being as often denied, she went away discontented and grumbling. At this instant of time, the child was taken with terrible fits, complaining of a pain in her stomach, as if she was pricked with pins, shrieking out with a voice like a whelp, and thus continued till the 30th of the same month. This examinant further saith, that Amy Duny, having long had the reputation of a witch, and his child having, in the intervals of her fits, constantly cried out on her as the cause of her disorder, saying, that the said Amy did appear to her and fright her ; he himself did suspect the said Amy to be a witch, and charged her with being the cause of his child's illness, and set her in the stocks. Two days after, his daughter Elizabeth was taken with such strange fits, that they could not force open her mouth without a tap ; and the younger child being in the same condition, they used to her the same remedy. Both children grievously complained that Amy Duny and another woman, whose habit and looks they described, did appear to them and torment them, and would cry out, 'There stands Amy Duny ! There stands Rose Cullender !' the other person who afflicted them. Their fits were not alike. Sometimes they were lame on the right side ; sometimes on the left ; and sometimes so sore, that they could not bear to be touched. Sometimes they were perfectly well in other respects, but they could not *hear ;* at other times they could not *see.* Sometimes they lost their speech for one, two, and once for eight days together. At times they had swooning fits, and, when they could speak, were taken with a fit of coughing, and vomited phlegm and crooked pins; and once a great twopenny nail, with above forty pins; which nail he, the examinant, saw vomited up, with many of the pins. The nail and pins were produced in the court. Thus the children continued for two months, during which time the examinant often made them read in the New Testament, and observed, when they came to the words *Lord Jesus*, or *Christ*, they could not pronounce them, but fell into a fit. When they came to the word *Satan*, or *devil*, they would point, and say, ' This bites, but makes me speak right well.' Finding his children thus tormented without hopes of recovery, he sent them to his sister, Margaret Arnold, at Yarmouth, being willing to try whether change of air would help them.

" Margaret Arnold was the next witness. Being sworn, she said, that about the 30th of November, Elizabeth and Deborah Pacey came to her house with her brother, who told her what had happened, and that he thought his children bewitched. She, this examinant, did not much regard it, supposing the children had played tricks, and put the pins into their mouths themselves. She therefore took all the pins from their clothes, sewing them with thread instead of pinning them. But, notwithstanding, they raised, at times, at least thirty pins in her presence, and had terrible fits; in which fits they would cry out upon Amy Duny and Rose Cullender, saying, that they saw them and heard them threatening, as before; that they saw things like mice running about the house; and one of them catched one, and threw it into the fire, which made a noise like a rat. Another time the younger child, being out of doors, a thing like a bee would have forced itself into her mouth, at which the child ran screaming into the house, and before this examinant could come at her, fell into a fit, and vomited a twopenny nail, with a broad head. After that, this examinant asked the child how she came by this nail, when she answered, ' The bee brought the nail, and forced it into my mouth.' At other times the eldest child told this examinant that she saw flies bring her crooked pins. She would then fall into a fit, and vomit such pins. One time the said child said she saw a mouse, and crept under the table to look for it; and afterwards, the child seemed to put something into her apron, saying, ' She had caught it.' She then ran to the fire, and threw it in, on which there did appear to this examinant something like a flash of gunpowder, although she does own she saw nothing in the child's hand. Once the child, being speechless, but otherwise very sensible, ran up and down the house crying, ' Hush! hush!' as if she had seen poultry; but this examinant saw nothing. At last the child catched at something, and threw it into the fire. Afterwards, when the child could speak, this examinant asked her what she saw at the time? She answered that she saw a duck. Another time the youngest child said, after a fit, that Amy Duny had been with her, and tempted her to drown herself, or cut her throat, or otherwise destroy herself. Another time they both cried out upon Amy Duny and Rose Cullender, saying, 'Why don't you come yourselves? Why do you send your imps to torment us?'"

The celebrated Sir Thomas Brown, the author of *Vulgar Errors*, was also examined as a witness upon the trial. Being desired to give his opinion of the three persons in court, he said he was clearly of opinion that they were bewitched. He said there had lately been a discovery of witches in Denmark, who used the same way of tormenting persons, by conveying crooked pins, needles, and nails into their bodies. That he thought, in such cases, the devil acted upon human bodies by natural means, namely, by exciting and stirring up the superabundant humours; he did afflict them in a more surprising manner by the same diseases their bodies were usually subject to; that these fits might be natural, only raised to a great degree by the subtlety of the devil, co-operating with the malice of these witches.

SIR THOMAS BROWN

The evidence being concluded, Sir Matthew Hale addressed the jury. He said, he would waive repeating the evidence, to prevent any mistake, and told the jury there were two things they had to inquire into. First, Whether or not these children were bewitched; secondly, Whether these women did bewitch them. He said, he did not in the least doubt there were witches; first, Because the Scriptures affirmed it; secondly, Because the wisdom of all nations, particularly our own, had provided laws against witchcraft, which implied their belief of such a crime. He desired them strictly to observe the evidence, and begged of God to direct their hearts in the weighty concern they had in hand, since, to condemn the innocent and let the guilty go free are both an abomination to the Lord.

The jury then retired, and in about half an hour returned a verdict of guilty upon all the indictments, being thirteen in number. The next morning the children came with their father to the lodgings of Sir Matthew Hale, very well, and quite restored to their usual health. Mr. Pacey, being asked at what time their health began to improve, replied, that they were quite well in half an hour after the conviction of the prisoners.

Many attempts were made to induce the unfortunate women to confess their guilt; but in vain, and they were both hanged.

Eleven trials were instituted before Chief Justice Holt for witch-craft, between the years 1694 and 1701. The evidence was of the usual character; but Holt appealed so successfully in each case to the common sense of the jury, that they were every one acquitted. A general feeling seemed to pervade the country that blood enough had been shed upon these absurd charges. Now and then the flame of persecution burnt up in a remote district; but these instances were no longer looked upon as mere matters of course. They appear, on the contrary, to have excited much attention; a sure proof, if no other were to be obtained, that they were becoming unfrequent.

A case of witchcraft was tried in 1711, before Lord Chief Justice Powell; in which, however, the jury persisted in a verdict of guilty, though the evidence was of the usual absurd and contradictory cha-racter, and the enlightened judge did all in his power to bring them to a right conclusion. The accused person was one Jane Wenham, better known as the Witch of Walkerne; and the persons who were alleged to have suffered from her witchcraft were two young women, named Thorne and Street. A witness, named Mr. Arthur Chauncy, deposed that he had seen Ann Thorne in several of her fits, and that she always recovered upon prayers being said, or if Jane Wenham came to her. He related, that he had pricked the prisoner several times in the arms, but could never fetch any blood from her; that he had seen her vomit pins, when there were none in her clothes or within her reach; and that he had preserved several of them, whic he was ready to produce. The judge, however, told him that was needless, *as he supposed they were crooked pins.*

Mr. Francis Bragge, another witness, deposed, that strange " cakes" of bewitched feathers having been taken from Ann Thorne's pillow, he was anxious to see them. He went into a room where some of these feathers were, and took two of the cakes, and compared them together. They were both of a circular figure, something larger than a crown piece; and he observed that the small feathers were placed in a nice and curious order, at equal distances from each other, making so many radii of the circle, in the centre of which the quill-ends of the feathers met. He counted the number of these feathers, and found them to be exactly thirty-two in each cake. He afterwards endeavoured to pull off two or three of them, and observed that they were all fastened together by a sort of viscous matter, which would stretch seven or eight times in a thread before it broke. Having taken off several of these feathers, he removed the viscous matter with his fingers, and found under it, in the centre, some short hairs, black and grey, matted together, which he verily believed to be cat's hair. He also said, that Jane Wenham confessed to him that she had bewitched the pillow, and had practised witchcraft for sixteen years.

The judge interrupted the witness at this stage, and said, he should very much like to see an enchanted feather, and seemed to wonder when he was told that none of these strange cakes had been preserved. His lordship asked the witness why he did not keep one or two of them, and was informed that they had all been burnt, in order to relieve the bewitched person of the pains she suffered, which could not be so well effected by any other means.

A man, named Thomas Ireland, deposed, that hearing several times a great noise of cats crying and screaming about his house, he went out and frightened them away, and they all ran towards the cottage of Jane Wenham. One of them he swore positively had a face very like Jane Wenham's. Another man, named Burville, gave similar evidence, and swore that he had often seen a cat with Jane Wenham's face. Upon one occasion he was in Ann Thorne's chamber, when several cats came in, and among them the cat above stated. This witness would have favoured the court with a much longer statement, but was stopped by the judge, who said he had heard quite enough.

The prisoner, in her defence, said nothing, but that " she was a clear woman." The learned judge then summed up, leaving it to the jury to determine whether such evidence as they had heard was sufficient to take away the prisoner's life upon the indictment. After a long deliberation they brought in their verdict, that she was guilty upon the evidence. The judge then asked them whether they found her guilty upon the indictment of conversing with the devil in the shape of a cat? The sapient foreman very gravely answered, " We find her guilty of *that*." The learned judge then very reluctantly proceeded to pass sentence of death; but, by his persevering exertions, a pardon was at last obtained, and the wretched old woman was set at liberty.

In the year 1716, a woman and her daughter—the latter only nine years of age—were hanged at Huntingdon for selling their souls to the devil, and raising a storm by pulling off their stockings and making a lather of soap. This appears to have been the last judicial execution in England. From that time to the year 1736, the populace raised at intervals the old cry, and more than once endangered the lives of poor women by dragging them through ponds on suspicion; but the philosophy of those who, from their position, sooner or later give the tone to the opinions and morals of the poor, was silently working a cure for the evil. The fear of witches ceased to be epidemic, and became individual, lingering only in minds fettered by inveterate prejudice or brutalising superstition. In the year 1736, the penal statute of James I. was finally blotted from the statute-book, and suffered no longer to disgrace the advancing intelligence of the country. Pretenders to witchcraft, fortune-tellers, conjurors, and all their train, were liable only to the common punishment of rogues and impostors—imprisonment and the pillory.

In Scotland, the delusion also assumed the same phases, and was gradually extinguished in the light of civilisation. As in England, the progress of improvement was slow. Up to the year 1665, little or no diminution of the mania was perceptible. In 1643, the General Assembly recommended that the privy council should institute a standing commission, composed of any " understanding gentlemen or magistrates," to try the witches, who were stated to have increased enormously of late years. In 1649, an act was passed, confirmatory of the original statute of Queen Mary, explaining some points of the latter which were doubtful, and enacting severe penalties, not only against witches themselves, but against all who covenanted with them, or sought by their means to pry into the secrets of futurity, or cause any evil to the life, lands, or limbs of their neighbours. For the next ten years, the popular madness upon this subject was perhaps more furious than ever; upwards of four thousand persons suffered for the crime during that interval. This was the consequence of the act of parliament and the unparalleled severity of the magistrates; the latter frequently complained that for two witches they burned one day, there were ten to burn the next : they never thought that they themselves were the cause of the increase. In a single circuit, held at Glasgow, Ayr, and Stirling, in 1659, seventeen unhappy creatures were burned by judicial sentence for trafficking with Satan. In one day (November 7, 1661), the privy council issued no less than fourteen commissions for trials in the provinces. Next year, the violence of the persecution seems to have abated. From 1662 to 1668, although "the understanding gentlemen and magistrates" already mentioned continued to try and condemn, the High Court of Justiciary had but one offender of this class to deal with, and she was acquitted. James Welsh, a common pricker, was ordered to be publicly whipped through the streets of Edinburgh for falsely accusing a woman of witchcraft; a fact which alone proves that the superior court sifted the evidence in these cases with much more care and severity than it had done a few years previously. The enlightened Sir George Mackenzie, styled by Dryden "the noble wit of Scotland," laboured hard to introduce this rule into court, that the confessions of the witches should be held of little worth, and that the evidence of the prickers and other interested persons should be received with distrust and jealousy. This was reversing the old practice, and saved many innocent lives. Though a firm believer both in ancient and modern witchcraft, he could not shut his eyes to the atrocities daily committed under the name of justice. In his work on the Criminal Law of Scotland, published in 1678, he says, "From the horridness of this crime, I do conclude that, of all others, it requires the clearest relevancy and most convincing probature; and I condemn, next to the witches themselves, those cruel and too forward judges who burn persons by thousands as guilty of this crime." In the same year, Sir John Clerk plumply refused to serve as a commissioner on trials for witchcraft, alleging, by way of excuse, "that he was not himself good conjuror enough to be duly qualified." The views entertained by Sir George Mackenzie were so favourably received by the Lords of Session, that he was deputed, in 1680, to report to them on the cases of a number of poor women who were then in prison awaiting their trial. Sir George stated that there was no evidence against them whatever but their own confessions, which were absurd and contradictory, and drawn from them by severe torture. They were immediately discharged.

For the next sixteen years the Lords of Session were unoccupied with trials for witchcraft. Not one is entered upon the record. But in 1697 a case occurred which equalled in absurdity any of those that signalised the dark reign of King James. A girl named Christiana Shaw, eleven years of age, the daughter of John Shaw of Bargarran, was subject to fits; and being of a spiteful temper, she accused her maid-servant, with whom she had frequent quarrels, of bewitching her. Her story unfortunately was believed. Encouraged to tell all the persecutions of the devil which the maid had sent to torment her, she in the end concocted a romance that involved twenty-one persons. There was no other evidence against them but the fancies of this lying child, and the confessions which pain had extorted from them; but upon this no less than five women were condemned before Lord Blantyre and the rest of the commissioners, appointed specially by the privy council to try this case. They were burned on the Green at Paisley. The warlock of the party, one John Reed, who was also condemned, hanged himself in prison. It was the general belief in Paisley that the devil had strangled him lest he should have revealed in his last moments too many of the unholy secrets of witchcraft. This trial excited considerable disgust in Scotland. The Rev. Mr. Bell, a contemporary writer, observed that, in this business, "persons of more goodness and esteem than most of their calumniators were defamed for witches." He adds, that the persons chiefly to blame were "certain ministers of too much forwardness and absurd credulity, and some topping professors in and about Glasgow."*

After this trial, there again occurs a lapse of seven years, when the subject was painfully forced upon public attention by the brutal cruelty of the mob at Pittenween. Two women were accused of having bewitched a strolling beggar who was subject to fits, or who pretended to be so, for the purpose of exciting commiseration. They were cast into prison, and tortured until they confessed. One of them, named Janet Cornfoot, contrived to escape, but was brought back to Pittenween next day by a party of soldiers. On her approach to the town she was unfortunately met by a furious mob, composed principally of fishermen and their wives, who seized upon her with the intention of swimming her. They forced her away to the sea-shore, and tying a rope around her body, secured the end of it to the mast of a fishing-boat lying alongside. In this manner they ducked her several times. When she was half dead, a sailor in the boat cut away the rope, and the mob dragged her through the sea to the beach. Here, as she lay quite insensible, a brawny ruffian took down the door of his hut, close by, and placed it on her back. The mob gathered large stones from the beach and piled them upon her till the wretched woman was pressed to death. No magistrate made the slightest attempt to interfere; and the soldiers looked on, delighted spectators. A great outcry was raised against this culpable remissness, but no judicial inquiry was set on foot. This happened in 1704.

The next case we hear of is that of Elspeth Rule, found guilty of witchcraft before Lord Anstruther, at the Dumfries circuit, in 1708. She was sentenced to be marked in the cheek with a red-hot iron, and banished the realm of Scotland for life.

Again there is a long interval. In 1718, the remote county of Caithness, where the delusion remained in all its pristine vigour for years after it had ceased elsewhere, was startled from its propriety by the cry of witchcraft. A silly fellow, named William Montgomery, a carpenter, had a mortal antipathy to cats; and somehow or other these animals generally chose his back-yard as the scene of their cat-

---

* Preface to *Law's Memorials*, edited by Sharpe.

terwaulings. He puzzled his brains for a long time to know why he, above all his neighbours, should be so pestered. At last he came to the sage conclusion that his tormentors were no cats, but witches. In this opinion he was supported by his maid-servant, who swore a round oath that she had often heard the aforesaid cats talking together in human voices. The next time the unlucky tabbies assembled in his back-yard, the valiant carpenter was on the alert. Arming himself with an axe, a dirk, and a broadsword, he rushed out among them. One of them he wounded in the back, a second in the hip, and the leg of a third he maimed with his axe; but he could not capture any of them. A few days afterwards, two old women of the parish died; and it was said, that when their bodies were laid out, there appeared upon the back of one the mark as of a recent wound, and a similar scar upon the hip of the other. The carpenter and his maid were convinced that they were the very cats, and the whole county repeated the same story. Every one was upon the look-out for proofs corroborative; a very remarkable one was soon discovered. Nanny Gilbert, a wretched old creature of upwards of seventy years of age, was found in bed with her leg broken. As she was ugly enough for a witch, it was asserted that she also was one of the cats that had fared so ill at the hands of the carpenter. The latter, when informed of the popular suspicion, asserted that he distinctly remembered to have struck one of the cats a blow with the back of his broadsword, which ought to have broken her leg. Nanny was immediately dragged from her bed and thrown into prison. Before she was put to the torture, she explained in a very natural and intelligible manner how she had broken her limb; but this account did not give satisfaction. The professional persuasions of the torturer made her tell a different tale, and she confessed that she was indeed a witch, and had been wounded by Montgomery on the night stated; that the two old women recently deceased were witches also, besides about a score of others whom she named. The poor creature suffered so much by the removal from her own home, and the tortures inflicted upon her, that she died the next day in prison. Happily for the persons she had named in her confession, Dundas of Arniston, at that time the king's advocate-general, wrote to the sheriff-depute, one Captain Ross of Littledean, cautioning him not to proceed to trial, the "thing being of too great difficulty, and beyond the jurisdiction of an inferior court." Dundas himself examined the precognition with great care, and was so convinced of the utter folly of the whole case, that he quashed all further proceedings.

We find this same sheriff-depute of Caithness very active four years afterwards in another trial for witchcraft. In spite of the warning he had received that all such cases were to be tried in future by the superior courts, he condemned to death an old woman at Dornoch, upon the charge of bewitching the cows and pigs of her neighbours. This poor creature was insane, and actually laughed and clapped her hands at sight of "the bonnie fire" that was to consume her. She had a daughter who was lame both of her hands and feet, and one of the charges brought against her was, that she had used this daughter as a pony in her excursions to join the devil's sabbath, and that the devil himself had shod her, and produced lameness.

This was the last execution that took place in Scotland for witchcraft. The penal statutes were repealed in 1736; and, as in England, whipping, the pillory, or imprisonment, were declared the future punishments of all pretenders to magic or witchcraft.

Still for many years after this the superstition lingered both in England and Scotland, and in some districts is far from being extinct even at this day. But before we proceed to trace it any further than to its legal extinction, we have yet to see the frightful havoc it made in continental Europe from the commencement of the seventeenth to the middle of the eighteenth century. France, Germany, and Switzerland were the countries which suffered most from the epidemic. The number of victims in these countries during the sixteenth century has already been mentioned; but at the early part of the seventeenth, the numbers are so great, especially in Germany, that were they not to be found in the official records of the tribunals, it would be almost impossible to believe that mankind could ever have been so maddened and deluded. To use the words of the learned and indefatigable Horst,* "the world seemed to be like a large madhouse for witches and devils to play their antics in." Satan was believed to be at every body's call to raise the whirlwind, draw down the lightning, blight the productions of the earth, or destroy the health and paralyse the limbs of man. This belief, so insulting to the majesty and beneficence of the Creator, was shared by the most pious ministers of religion. Those who in their morning and evening prayers acknowledged the one true God, and praised him for the blessings of the seed-time and the harvest, were convinced that frail humanity could enter into a compact with the spirits of hell to subvert his laws and thwart all his merciful intentions. Successive popes, from Innocent VIII. downwards, promulgated this degrading doctrine, which spread so rapidly, that society seemed to be divided into two great factions, the bewitching and the bewitched.

The commissioners named by Innocent VIII. to prosecute the witch-trials in Germany were, Jacob Sprenger, so notorious for his

* *Zauberbibliothek*, Thiel 5.

work on demonology, entitled the *Malleus Malleficarum, or Hammer to knock down Witches;* Henry Institor, a learned jurisconsult; and the Bishop of Strasburgh. Bamberg, Trèves, Cologne, Paderborn, and Würzburg, were the chief seats of the commissioners, who, during their lives alone, condemned to the stake, on a very moderate calculation, upwards of three thousand victims. The number of witches so increased, that new commissioners were continually appointed in Germany, France, and Switzerland. In Spain and Portugal the Inquisition alone took cognisance of the crime. It is impossible to search the records of those dark, but now happily non-existing tribunals; but the mind recoils with affright even to form a guess of the multitudes who perished.

The mode of trial in the other countries is more easily ascertained. Sprenger in Germany, and Bodinus and Delrio in France, have left but too ample a record of the atrocities committed in the much-abused names of justice and religion. Bodinus, of great repute and authority in the seventeenth century, says, "The trial of this offence must not be conducted like other crimes. Whoever adheres to the ordinary course of justice perverts the spirit of the law, both divine and human. He who is accused of sorcery should never be acquitted, unless the malice of the prosecutor be clearer than the sun; for it is so difficult to bring full proof of this secret crime, that out of a million of witches not one would be convicted if the usual course were followed!" Henri Boguet, a witch-finder, who styled himself "The Grand Judge of Witches for the Territory of St. Claude," drew up a code for the guidance of all persons engaged in the witch trials, consisting of seventy articles, quite as cruel as the code of Bodinus. In this document he affirms, that a mere suspicion of witchcraft justifies the immediate arrest and torture of the suspected person. If the prisoner muttered, looked on the ground, and did not shed any tears, all these were proofs positive of guilt! In all cases of witchcraft, the evidence of the child ought to be taken against its parent; and persons of notoriously bad character, although not to be believed upon their oaths on the ordinary occasions of dispute that might arise between man and man, were to be believed, if they swore that any person had bewitched them! Who, when he hears that this diabolical doctrine was the universally received opinion of the ecclesiastical and civil authorities, can wonder that thousands upon thousands of unhappy persons should be brought to the stake? that Cologne should for many years burn its three hundred witches annually? the district of Bamberg its four hundred? Nuremberg, Geneva, Paris, Toulouse, Lyons, and other cities, their two hundred?

A few of these trials may be cited, taking them in the order of priority, as they occurred in different parts of the Continent. In 1595 an old woman residing in a village near Constance, angry at not being invited to share the sports of the country people on a day of public

CITY OF LYONS.

rejoicing, was heard to mutter something to herself, and was afterwards seen to proceed through the fields towards a hill, where she was lost sight of. A violent thunder-storm arose about two hours afterwards, which wet the dancers to the skin, and did considerable damage to the plantations. This woman, suspected before of witchcraft, was seized and imprisoned, and accused of having raised the storm, by filling a hole with wine, and stirring it about with a stick. She was tortured till she confessed, and was burned alive the next evening.

About the same time two sorcerers in Toulouse were accused of having dragged a crucifix about the streets at midnight, stopping at times to spit upon and kick it, and uttering at intervals an exorcism to raise the devil. The next day a hail-storm did considerable damage to the crops ; and a girl, the daughter of a shoemaker in the town, remembered to have heard in the night the execrations of the wizards. Her story led to their arrest. The usual means to produce confession were resorted to. The wizards owned that they could raise tempests whenever they pleased, and named several persons who possessed similar powers. They were hanged, and then burned in the market-place, and seven of the persons they had mentioned shared the same fate.

Hoppo and Stadlin, two noted wizards of Germany, were executed in 1599. They implicated twenty or thirty witches, who went about causing women to miscarry, bringing down the lightning of heaven, and making maidens bring forth toads. To this latter fact several girls were found to swear most positively! Stadlin confessed that he had killed seven infants in the womb of one woman.

Bodinus highly praises the exertions of a witch-finder named Nider, in France, who prosecuted so many that he could not calculate them. Some of these witches could, by a single word, cause people to fall down dead ; others made women go with child three years instead of nine months ; while others, by certain invocations and ceremonies, could turn the faces of their enemies upside down, or twist them round to their backs. Although no witness was ever procured who saw persons in this horrible state, the witches confessed that they had the power and exercised it. Nothing more was wanting to ensure the stake.

At Amsterdam a crazy girl confessed that she could cause sterility in cattle, and bewitch pigs and poultry, by merely repeating the magic words *Turius und Shurius Inturius!* She was hanged and burned. Another woman in the same city, named Kornelis van Purmerund, was arrested in consequence of some disclosures the former had made. A witness came forward and swore that she one day looked through the window of her hut, and saw Kornelis sitting before a fire muttering something to the devil. She was sure it was to the devil, because she heard him answer her. Shortly afterwards twelve black cats ascended out of the floor, and danced on their hind legs around the witch for the space of about half an hour. They then vanished with a horrid noise, and leaving a disagreeable smell behind them. She also was hanged and burned.

At Bamberg, in Bavaria, the executions from the year 1610 to 1640 were at the rate of about a hundred annually. One woman, suspected of witchcraft, was seized because, having immoderately praised the beauty of a child, it had shortly afterwards fallen ill and died. She confessed upon the rack that the devil had given her the power to work evil upon those she hated, by speaking words in their praise. If she said with unwonted fervour, " What a strong man !" " What a lovely woman !" " What a sweet child !" the devil understood her, and afflicted them with diseases immediately. It is quite unnecessary to state the end of this poor creature. Many women were executed for causing strange substances to lodge in the bodies of those who offended them. Bits of wood, nails, hair, egg-shells, bits of glass, shreds of linen and woollen cloth, pebbles, and even hot

cinders and knives, were the articles generally chosen. These were
believed to remain in the body till the witches confessed or were
executed, when they were voided from the bowels, or by the mouth,

BAMBERG.

nostrils, or ears. Modern physicians have often had cases of a similar
description under their care, where girls have swallowed needles,
which have been voided on the arms, legs, and other parts of the
body. But the science of that day could not account for these phenomena otherwise than by the power of the devil ; and every needle
swallowed by a servant-maid cost an old woman her life. Nay, if no
more than one suffered in consequence, the district might think itself
fortunate. The commissioners seldom stopped short at one victim.
The revelations of the rack in most cases implicated half a score.
     Of all the records of the witch-trials preserved for the wonder
of succeeding ages, that of Würzburg, from 1627 to 1629, is the

most frightful. Hauber, who has preserved this list in his *Acta et Scripta Magica*, says, in a note at the end, that it is far from complete, and that there were a great many other burnings too numerous to specify. This record, which relates to the city only, and not to the province of Würzburg, contains the names of one hundred and fifty-seven persons who were burned in two years in twenty-nine burnings, averaging from five to six at a time. The list comprises three play-actors, four innkeepers, three common councilmen of Würzburg, fourteen vicars of the cathedral, the burgomaster's lady, an apothecary's wife and daughter, two choristers of the cathedral, Göbel Babelin, the prettiest girl in the town, and the wife, the two little sons, and the daughter of the councillor Stolzenberg. Rich and poor, young and old, suffered alike. At the seventh of these recorded burnings, the victims are described as a wandering boy, twelve years of age, and four strange men and women found sleeping in the market-place. Thirty-two of the whole number appear to have been vagrants, of both sexes, who, failing to give a satisfactory account of themselves, were accused and found guilty of witchcraft. The number of children on the list is horrible to think upon. The thirteenth and fourteenth burnings comprised four persons, who are stated to have been a little maiden nine years of age, a maiden still less, her sister, their mother, and their aunt, a pretty young woman of twenty-four. At the eighteenth burning, the victims were two boys of twelve, and a girl of fifteen ; at the nineteenth, the young heir of the noble house of Rotenhahn, aged nine, and two other boys, one aged ten, and the other twelve. Among other entries appear the names of Baunach, the fattest, and Steinacher, the richest burgher in Würzburg. What tended to keep up the delusion in this unhappy city, and, indeed, all over Europe, was the number of hypochondriac and diseased persons who came voluntarily forward and made confession of witchcraft. Several of the victims in the foregoing list had only themselves to blame for their fate. Many, again, including the apothecary's wife and daughter already mentioned, pretended to sorcery, and sold poisons, or attempted, by means of charms and incantations, to raise the devil. But throughout all this fearful period the delusion of the criminals was as great as that of the judges. Depraved persons, who in ordinary times would have been thieves or murderers, added the desire of sorcery to their depravity, sometimes with the hope of acquiring power over their fellows, and sometimes with the hope of securing impunity in this world by the protection of Satan. One of the persons executed at the first burning, a prostitute, was heard repeating the exorcism which was supposed to have the power of raising the arch enemy in the form of a goat.

This precious specimen of human folly has been preserved by Horst in his *Zauberbibliothek*. It ran as follows, and was to be repeated slowly, with many ceremonies and wavings of the hand:

> " Lalle, Bachera, Magotte, Baphia, Dajam,
> Vagoth Heneche Ammi Nagaz, Adomator
> Raphael Immanuel Christus, Tetragrammaton
> Agra Jod Loi. König! König!"

The last two words were uttered quickly, and with a sort of scream, and were supposed to be highly agreeable to Satan, who loved to be called a king. If he did not appear immediately, it was necessary to repeat a further exorcism. The one in greatest repute was as follows, and was to be read backwards, with the exception of the last two words:

> " Anion, Lalle, Sabolos, Sado, Pater, Aziel
> Adonai Sado Vagoth Agra, Jod,
> Baphra! Komm! Komm!"

When the witch wanted to get rid of the devil, who was sometimes in the habit of prolonging his visits to an unconscionable length, she had only to repeat the following, also backwards, when he generally disappeared, leaving behind him a suffocating smell:

> "Zellianelle Heotti Bonus Vagotha
> Plisos sother osech unicus Beelzebub
> Dax! Komm! Komm!"

This nonsensical jargon soon became known to all the idle and foolish boys of Germany. Many an unhappy urchin, who in a youthful frolic had repeated it, paid for his folly the penalty of his life. Three, whose ages varied from ten to fifteen, were burned alive at Würzburg for no other offence. Of course every other boy in the city became still more convinced of the power of the charm. One boy confessed that he would willingly have sold himself to the devil, if he could have raised him, for a good dinner and cakes every day of his life, and a pony to ride upon. This luxurious youngster, instead of being horsewhipped for his folly, was hanged and burned.

The small district of Lindheim was, if possible, even more notorious than Würzburg for the number of its witch-burnings. In the year 1633 a famous witch, named Pomp Anna, who could cause her foes to fall sick by merely looking at them, was discovered and burned, along with three of her companions. Every year in this parish, consisting at most of a thousand persons, the average number of executions was five. Between the years 1660 and 1664, the number consumed was thirty. If the executions all over Germany had been in this frightful proportion, hardly a family could have escaped losing one of its members.

In 1627, a ballad entitled the *Druten Zeitung*, or the *Witches' Gazette*, was very popular in Germany. It detailed, according to the title-page of a copy printed at Smalcald in 1627, "An account of the remarkable events which took place in Franconia, Bamberg, and Würzburg, with those wretches who, from avarice or ambition, have sold themselves to the devil, and how they had their reward at last: set to music, and to be sung to the tune of Dorothea." The sufferings of the witches at the stake are explained in it with great minuteness, the poet waxing extremely witty when he describes the horrible contortions of pain upon their countenances, and the shrieks that rent the air when any one of more than common guilt was burned alive. A trick resorted to in order to force one witch to confess, is told in this doggrel as an excellent joke. As she obstinately refused to own that she was in league with the powers of evil, the commissioners suggested that the hangman should dress himself in a bear's skin, with the horns, tail, and all the et-ceteras, and in this form penetrate into her dungeon. The woman, in the darkness of her cell, could not detect the imposture, aided as it was by her own superstitious fears. She thought she was actually in the presence of the prince of hell; and when she was told to keep up her courage, and that she should be relieved from the power of her enemies, she fell on her knees before the supposed devil, and swore to dedicate herself hereafter, body and soul, to his service. Germany is perhaps the only country in Europe where the delusion was so great as to have made such detestable verses as these the favourites of the people:

> " Man shickt ein Henkersknecht
> Zu ihr in Gefängniss n'unter,
>   Den man hat kleidet recht,
>   Mit einer Bärnhaute,
>   Als wenns der Teufel wär ;
>   Als ihm die Drut anschaute
>   Meints ihr Buhl kam daher.
>
> Sie sprach zu ihm behende,
> Wie lässt du mich so lang
> In der Obrigkeit Hände?
>   Hilf mir aus ihren Zwang,
>   Wie du mir hast verheissen,
>   Ich bin ja eben dein,
> Thu mich aus der Angst entreissen
>   O liebster Buhle mein !"*

* They sent a hangman's assistant down to her in her prison; they clothed him properly in a bear's skin, as if he were the devil. Him, when the witch saw, she thought he was her familiar. She said to him quickly, "Why hast thou left me so long in the magistrates' hands? Help me out of their power, as thou hast promised, and I will be thine alone. Help me from this anguish, O thou dearest devil [or lover] mine!"

This rare poet adds, that in making such an appeal to the hangman, the witch never imagined the roast that was to be made of her, and puts in, by way of parenthesis, " was not that fine fun !—*was das war für ein Spiel!*" As feathers thrown into the air shew how the wind blows, so this trumpery ballad serves to shew the current of popular feeling at the time of its composition.

All readers of history are familiar with the celebrated trial of the Maréchale d'Ancre, who was executed in Paris in the year 1617. Although witchcraft was one of the accusations brought against her, the real crime for which she suffered was her ascendency over the mind of Mary of Medicis, and the consequent influence she exercised indirectly over the unworthy king, Louis XIII. Her coachman gave evidence that she had sacrificed a cock at midnight in one of the churches, and others swore they had seen her go secretly into the house of a noted witch named Isabella. When asked by what means she had acquired so extraordinary an influence over the mind of the Queen Mother, she replied boldly that she exercised no other power over her than that which a strong mind can always exercise over the weak. She died with great firmness.

In two years afterwards, scenes far more horrible than any that had yet taken place in France were enacted at Labourt, at the foot of the Pyrenees. The parliament of Bourdeaux, scandalised at the number of witches who were said to infest Labourt and its neighbourhood, deputed one of its own members, the noted Pierre de l'Ancre, and its president, Espaignel, to inquire into the matter, with full powers to punish the offenders. They arrived at Labourt in May 1619. De l'Ancre wrote a book setting forth all his great deeds in this battle against the powers of evil. It is full of obscenity and absurdity, but the facts may be relied on as far as they relate to the number of trials and executions, and the strange confessions which torture forced from the unhappy criminals.

De l'Ancre states as a reason why so many witches were to be found at Labourt, that the country was mountainous and sterile ! He discovered many of them from their partiality to smoking tobacco. It may be inferred from this that he was of the opinion of King James, that tobacco was the " devil's weed." When the commission first sat, the number of persons brought to trial was about forty a day. The acquittals did not average so many as five per cent. All the witches confessed that they had been present at the great Domdaniel, or Sabbath. At these saturnalia the devil sat upon a large gilded throne, sometimes in the form of a goat ; sometimes as a gentleman, dressed all in black, with boots, spurs, and sword ; and very often as a shapeless mass, resembling the trunk of a blasted tree, seen indistinctly amid the darkness. They generally proceeded to the Domdaniel, riding on spits, pitchforks, or broomsticks, and on their arrival indulged with the fiends in every species of debauchery. Upon one occasion they had had the audacity to celebrate this festival in the very heart of the city of Bourdeaux. The throne of the arch fiend was placed in the middle of the Place de Gallienne, and the whole space was covered with the multitude of witches and wizards who flocked to it from far and near, some arriving even from distant Scotland.

After two hundred poor wretches had been hanged and burned, there seemed no diminution in the number of criminals to be tried. Many of the latter were asked upon the rack what Satan had said when he found that the commissioners were proceeding with such severity? The general reply was, that he did not seem to care much about it. Some of them asserted that they had boldly reproached him for suffering the execution of their friends, saying, " *Out upon thee, false fiend! thy promise was that they should not die! Look, how thou hast kept thy word! They have been burned, and are a heap of ashes!*" Upon these occasions he was never offended : he would give orders that the sports of the Domdaniel should cease, and producing illusory fires that did not burn, he encouraged them to walk through, assuring them that the fires lighted by the executioner gave no more pain than those. They would then ask him, where their friends were, since they had not suffered ; to which the " Father of Lies" invariably replied, that they were happy in a far country, and could see and hear all that was then passing ; and that, if they called by name those they wished to converse with, they might hear their voices in reply. Satan then imitated the voices of the defunct witches so successfully that they were all deceived. Having answered all objections, the orgies recommenced and lasted till the cock crew.

De l'Ancre was also very zealous in the trial of unhappy monomaniacs for the crime of lycanthropy. Several who were arrested confessed, without being tortured, that they were *weir-wolves,* and that at night they rushed out among the flocks and herds killing and devouring. One young man at Besançon, with the full consciousness of the awful fate that awaited him, voluntarily gave himself up to the Commissioner Espaignel, and confessed that he was the servant of a strong fiend, who was known by the name of "Lord of the Forests :" by his power he was transformed into the likeness of a wolf. The "Lord of the Forests" assumed the same shape ; but was much larger, fiercer, and stronger. They prowled about the pastures together at midnight, strangling the watch-dogs that defended the folds, and killing more sheep than they could devour. He felt, he said, a fierce pleasure in these excursions, and howled in excess of joy as he tore with his fangs the warm flesh of the sheep asunder. This youth was not alone in this horrid confession ; many others voluntarily owned that they were *weir-wolves*, and many more were forced by torture to make the same avowal. Such criminals were thought to be too atrocious to be hanged first and then burned: they were generally sentenced to be burned alive, and their ashes to be scattered to the winds. Grave and learned doctors of divinity openly sustained the possibility of these transformations, relying mainly upon the history of Nebuchadnezzar. They could not imagine why, if he had been an ox, modern men could not become wolves by Divine permission and the power of the devil. They also contended that, if men should confess, it was evidence enough, if there had been no other. Delrio mentions that one gentleman accused of lycanthropy was put to the torture no less than twenty times; but still he would not confess. An intoxicating draught was then given him, and under its influence he confessed that he was a *weir-wolf*. Delrio cites this to shew the extreme equity of the commissioners. They never burned any body till he confessed ; and if one course of torture would not suffice, their patience was not exhausted, and they tried him again and again, even to the twentieth time ! Well may we exclaim, when such atrocities have been committed in the name of religion,

> " Quel lion, quel tigre égale en cruauté,
> Une injuste fureur qu'arme la piété ?"

The trial of the unhappy Urbain Grandier, the curate of Loudun, for bewitching a number of girls in the convent of the Ursulines in that town, was, like that of the Maréchale d'Ancre, an accusation resorted to by his enemies to ruin one against whom no other charge could be brought so readily. This noted affair, which kept France in commotion for months, and the true character of which was known even at that time, merits no more than a passing notice in this place. It did not spring from the epidemic dread of sorcery then so prevalent, but was carried on by wretched intriguers, who had sworn to have the life of their foe. Such a charge could not be refuted in 1634 ; the accused could not, as Bodinus expresses it, " make the malice of the prosecutors more clear than the sun ;" and his own denial, however intelligible, honest, and straightforward, was held as nothing in refutation of the testimony of the crazy women who imagined themselves bewitched. The more absurd and contradictory their assertions, the stronger the argument employed by his enemies that the devil was in them. He was burned alive, under circumstances of great cruelty.*

A singular instance of the epidemic fear of witchcraft occurred at Lille, in 1639. A pious but not very sane lady, named Antoinette Bourignon, founded a school, or *hospice*, in that city. One day, on entering the schoolroom, she imagined that she saw a great number of little black angels flying about the heads of the children. In great alarm she told her pupils of what she had seen, warning them to beware of the devil, whose imps were hovering about them. The foolish woman continued daily to repeat the same story, and Satan and his power became the only subject of conversation, not only between the girls themselves, but between them and their instructors. One of them at this time ran away from the school. On being brought back and interrogated, she said she had not run away, but had been carried away by the devil ; she was a witch, and had been one since the age of seven. Some other little girls in the school went into fits at this announcement, and, on their recovery, confessed that they also were witches. At last the whole of them, to the number of fifty, worked upon each other's imaginations to such a degree that they also confessed that they wére witches—that they attended the Domdaniel, or meeting of the fiends—that they could ride through the air on broomsticks, feast on infants' flesh, or creep through a keyhole.

The citizens of Lille were astounded at these disclosures. The clergy hastened to investigate the matter ; many of them, to their credit, openly expressed their opinion that the whole affair was an imposture—not so the majority ; they strenuously insisted that the confessions of the children were valid, and that it was necessary to make an example by burning them all for witches. The poor parents, alarmed for their offspring, implored the examining Capuchins with tears in their eyes to save their young lives, insisting that they were bewitched, and not bewitching. This opinion also gained ground in the town. Antoinette Bourignon, who had put these absurd notions into the heads of the children, was accused of witchcraft, and examined before the council. The circumstances of the case seemed so unfavourable towards her that she would not stay for a second examination. Disguising herself as she best could, she hastened out of Lille and escaped pursuit. If she had remained four hours longer, she

* A very graphic account of the execution of this unfortunate gentleman is to be found in the excellent romance of M. Alfred de Vigny, entitled *Cinq Mars;* but if the eader wishes for a full and accurate detail of all the circumstances of one of the most extraordinary trials upon record, he is referred to a work published anonymously, at Amsterdam, in 1693, entitled *Histoire des Diables de Loudun, ou de la Possession des Religieuses Ursulines, et de la Condemnation et du Supplice d'Urbain Grandier.*

would have been burned by judicial sentence as a witch and a heretic. It is to be hoped that, wherever she went, she learned the danger of tampering with youthful minds, and was never again entrusted with the management of children.

The Duke of Brunswick and the Elector of Menz were struck with the great cruelty exercised in the torture of suspected persons, and convinced, at the same time, that no righteous judge would consider a confession extorted by pain, and contradictory in itself, as sufficient evidence to justify the execution of any accused person. It is related of the Duke of Brunswick that he invited two learned Jesuits to his house, who were known to entertain strong opinions upon the subject of witchcraft, with a view of shewing them the cruelty and absurdity of such practices. A woman lay in the dungeon of the city accused of witchcraft, and the duke, having given previous instructions to the officiating torturers, went with the two Jesuits to hear her confession. By a series of artful leading questions the poor creature, in the extremity of her anguish, was induced to confess that she had often attended the sabbath of the fiends upon the Brocken; that she had seen two Jesuits there, who had made themselves notorious, even among witches, for their abominations; that she had seen them assume the form of goats, wolves, and other animals; and that many noted witches had born them five, six, and seven children at a birth, who had heads like toads, and legs like spiders. Being asked if the Jesuits were far from her, she replied that they were in the room beside her. The Duke of Brunswick led his astounded friends away, and explained the stratagem. This was convincing proof to both of them that thousands of persons had suffered unjustly; they knew their own innocence, and shuddered to think what their fate might have been if an enemy instead of a friend had put such a confession into the mouth of a criminal. One of these Jesuits was Frederick Spee, the author of the *Cautio Criminalis*, published in 1631. This work, exposing the horrors of the witch-trials, had a most salutary effect in Germany: Schonbrunn, Archbishop and Elector of Menz, abolished the torture entirely within his dominions, and his example was imitated by the Duke of Brunswick and other potentates. The number of supposed witches immediately diminished, and the violence of the mania began to subside. The Elector of Brandenburg issued a rescript, in 1654, with respect to the case of Anna of Ellerbrock, a supposed witch, forbidding the use of torture, and stigmatising the swimming of witches as an unjust, cruel, and deceitful test,

This was the beginning of the dawn after the long-protracted darkness. The tribunals no longer condemned witches to execution by hundreds in a year. Würzburg, the grand theatre of the burnings, burned but one where, forty years previously, it had burned three score. From 1660 to 1670 the electoral chambers, in all parts of Germany, constantly commuted the sentence of death passed by the provincial tribunals into imprisonment for life, or burning on the cheek.

ROUEN.

A truer philosophy had gradually disabused the public mind. Learned men freed themselves from the trammels of a debasing superstition, and governments, both civil and ecclesiastical, repressed the popular delusion they had so long encouraged. The parliament of Normandy condemned a number of women to death, in the year 1670, on the old charge of riding on broomsticks to the Domdaniel; but Louis XIV. commuted the sentence into banishment for life. The parliament remonstrated, and sent the king the following remarkable request. The reader will perhaps be glad to see this document at length. It is of importance, as the last effort of a legislative assembly to uphold this great error; and the arguments they used and the instances they quoted are in the highest degree curious. It reflects honour upon the memory of Louis XIV. that he was not swayed by it.

"REQUEST OF THE PARLIAMENT OF ROUEN TO THE KING, IN 1670.

"SIRE,—Emboldened by the authority which your majesty has
committed into our hands in the province of Normandy, to try and
punish offences, and more particularly those offences of the nature of
witchcraft, which tend to the destruction of religion and the ruin of
nations, we, your parliament, remonstrate humbly with your majesty
upon certain cases of this kind which have been lately brought before
us. We cannot permit the letter addressed by your majesty's command to the attorney-general of this district, for the reprieve of certain persons condemned to death for witchcraft, and for the staying
of proceedings in several other cases, to remain unnoticed, and without remarking upon the consequences which may ensue. There is
also a letter from your secretary of state, declaring your majesty's
intention to commute the punishment of these criminals into one of
perpetual banishment, and to submit to the opinion of the procureur-
general, and of the most learned members of the parliament of Paris,
whether, in the matter of witchcraft, the jurisprudence of the parliament of Rouen is to be followed in preference to that of the parliament of Paris, and of the other parliaments of the kingdom which
judge differently.

" Although by the ordinances of the kings your predecessors, parliaments have been forbidden to pay any attention to *lettres de cachet ;*
we, nevertheless, from the knowledge which we have, in common
with the whole kingdom, of the care bestowed by your majesty for
the good of your subjects, and from the submission and obedience to
your commandments which we have always manifested, have stayed
all proceedings, in conformity to your orders ; hoping that your majesty, considering the importance of the crime of witchcraft, and the
consequences likely to ensue from its impunity, will be graciously
pleased to grant us once more your permission to continue the trials,
and execute judgment upon those found guilty. And as, since we
received the letter of your secretary of state, we have also been made
acquainted with the determination of your majesty, not only to commute the sentence of death passed upon these witches into one of
perpetual banishment from the province, but to re-establish them in
the possession of their goods and chattels, and of their good fame and
character, your parliament have thought it their duty, on occasion of
these crimes, the greatest which men can commit, to make you
acquainted with the general and uniform feelings of the people of
this province with regard to them ; it being, moreover, a question in
which are concerned the glory of God and the relief of your suffering
subjects, who groan under their fears from the threats and menaces of

this sort of persons, and who feel the effects of them every day in the mortal and extraordinary maladies which attack them, and the surprising damage and loss of their possessions.

'Your majesty knows well that there is no crime so opposed to the commands of God as witchcraft, which destroys the very foundation of religion, and draws strange abominations after it. It is for this reason, sire, that the Scriptures pronounce the punishment of death against offenders, and that the Church and the holy fathers have fulminated their anathemas, and that canonical decisions have one and all decreed the most severe punishments, to deter from this crime; and that the Church of France, animated by the piety of the kings your predecessors, has expressed so great a horror at it, that, not judging the punishment of perpetual imprisonment, the highest it has the power to inflict, sufficiently severe, it has left such criminals to be dealt with by the secular power.

" It has been the general feeling of all nations that such criminals ought to be condemned to death, and all the ancients were of the same opinion. The law of the 'Twelve Tables,' which was the principal of the Roman laws, ordains the same punishment. All jurisconsults agreed in it, as well as the constitutions of the emperors, and more especially those of Constantine and Theodosius, who, enlightened by the Gospel, not only renewed the same punishment, but also deprived, expressly, all persons found guilty of witchcraft of the right of appeal, and declared them to be unworthy of a prince's mercy. And Charles VIII., sire, inspired by the same sentiments, passed that beautiful and severe ordinance (*cette belle et sévère ordonnance*), which enjoined the judges to punish witches according to the exigencies of the case, under a penalty of being themselves fined or imprisoned, or dismissed from their office; and decreed, at the same time, that all persons who refused to denounce a witch, should be punished as accomplices; and that all, on the contrary, who gave evidence against one should be rewarded.

" From these considerations, sire, and in the execution of so holy an ordinance, your parliaments, by their decrees, proportion their punishments to the guilt of the offenders; and your parliament of Normandy has never, until the present time, found that its practice was different from that of other courts; for all the books which treat upon this matter cite an infinite number of decrees condemning witches to be burnt, or broken on the wheel, or to other punishments. The following are examples :—In the time of Chilperic, as may be seen in Gregory of Tours, b. vi. c. 35 of his *History of France*, all the decrees of the parliament of Paris passed according to, and in conformity with, this ancient jurisprudence of the kingdom, cited by

Imbert, in his *Judicial Practice;* all those cited by Monstrelet, in
1459, against the witches of Artois; the decrees of the same parliament, of the 13th of October 1573, against Mary le Fief, native of
Saumur; of the 21st of October 1596, against the Sieur de Beaumont,
who pleaded, in his defence, that he had only sought the aid of the
devil for the purpose of unbewitching the afflicted and of curing
diseases; of the 4th of July 1606, against Francis du Bose; of the
20th of July 1582, against Abel de la Rue, native of Coulommiers; of
the 2d of October 1593, against Rousseau and his daughter; of 1608,
against another Rousseau and one Peley, for witchcraft and adoration
of the devil at the Sabbath, under the figure of a he-goat, as confessed
by them; the decree of 4th of February 1615, against Leclerc, who appealed from the sentence of the parliament of Orleans, and who was
condemned for having attended the Sabbath, and confessed, as well
as two of his accomplices, who died in prison, that he had adored the
devil, renounced his baptism and his faith in God, danced the witches'
dance, and offered up unholy sacrifices; the decrees of the 6th of May
1616, against a man named Leger, on a similar accusation; the pardon granted by Charles IX. to Trois Echelles, upon condition of revealing his accomplices, but afterwards revoked for renewed sorcery
on his part; the decree of the parliament of Paris, cited by Mornac
in 1595; the judgments passed in consequence of the commission
given by Henry IV. to the Sieur de l'Ancre, councillor of the parliament of Bourdeaux; of the 20th of March 1619, against Etienne
Audibert; those passed by the chamber of Nerac, on the 26th of June
1620, against several witches; those passed by the parliament of Toulouse in 1577, as cited by Gregory Tolosanus, against four hundred
persons accused of this crime, and who were all marked with the sign
of the devil.   Besides all these, we might recal to your majesty's recollection the various decrees of the parliament of Provence, especially
in the case of Gaufrédy in 1611; the decrees of the parliament of
Dijon, and those of the parliament of Rennes, following the example
of the condemnation of the Marshal de Rays, who was burned in
1441, for the crime of witchcraft, in presence of the Duke of Brittany;—all these examples, sire, prove that the accusation of witchcraft has always been punished with death by the parliaments of your
kingdom, and justify the uniformity of their practice.

" These, sire, are the motives upon which your parliament of Normandy has acted in decreeing the punishment of death against the
persons lately brought before it for this crime.   If it has happened
that, on any occasion, these parliaments, and the parliament of Normandy among the rest, have condemned the guilty to a less punishment than that of death, it was for the reason that their guilt was

not of the deepest dye ; your majesty, and the kings your predecessors, having left full liberty to the various tribunals to whom they delegated the administration of justice, to decree such punishment as was warranted by the evidence brought before them.

" After so many authorities, and punishments ordained by human and divine laws, we humbly supplicate your majesty to reflect once more upon the extraordinary results which proceed from the malevolence of this sort of people ; on the deaths from unknown diseases, which are often the consequences of their menaces, on the loss of the goods and chattels of your subjects, on the proofs of guilt continually afforded by the insensibility of the marks upon the accused, on the sudden transportation of bodies from one place to another, on the sacrifices and nocturnal assemblies, and other facts, corroborated by the testimony of ancient and modern authors, and verified by so many eye-witnesses, composed partly of accomplices, and partly of people who had no interest in the trials beyond the love of truth, and confirmed, moreover, by the confessions of the accused parties themselves ; and that, sire, with so much agreement and conformity between the different cases, that the most ignorant persons convicted of this crime have spoken to the same circumstances, and in nearly the same words, as the most celebrated authors who have written about it, all of which may be easily proved to your majesty's satisfaction by the records of various trials before your parliaments.

" These, sire, are truths so intimately bound up with the principles of our religion, that, extraordinary although they be, no person has been able to this time to call them in question. If some have cited, in opposition to these truths, the pretended canon of the Council of Ancyre, and a passage from St. Augustin, in a treatise upon the *Spirit and the Soul*, it has been without foundation ; and it would be easy to convince your majesty that neither the one nor the other ought to be accounted of any authority ; and besides that the canon, in this sense, would be contrary to the opinion of all succeeding councils of the Church, Cardinal Baronius and all learned commentators agree that it is not to be found in any old edition. In effect, in those editions wherein it is found, it is in another language, and is in direct contradiction to the twenty-third canon of the same council, which condemns sorcery, according to all preceding constitutions. Even supposing that this canon was really promulgated by the Council of Ancyre, we must observe that it was issued in the second century, when the principal attention of the Church was directed to the destruction of paganism. For this reason, it condemns that class of women who said they could pass through the air, and over immense regions, with Diana and Herodias, and enjoins all

reachers to teach the falsehood of such an opinion, in order to deter
people from the worship of these false divinities; but it does not
question the power of the devil over the human body, which is, in
fact, proved by the holy Gospel of Jesus Christ himself. And with
regard, sire, to the pretended passage of St. Augustin, every body
knows that it was not written by him, because the writer, whoever
he was, cites Bœtius, who died more than eighty years after the time
of St. Augustin. Besides, there is still more convincing proof in the
act, that the same father establishes the truth of witchcraft in all
his writings, and more particularly in his *City of God;* and in his
first volume, question the 25th, wherein he states that sorcery is a
communion between man and the devil, which all good Christians
ought to look upon with horror.

" Taking all these things into consideration, sire, the officers of
your parliament hope, from the justice of your majesty, that you will
be graciously pleased to receive the humble remonstrances they have
taken the liberty to make. They are compelled, for the acquittal of
their own consciences and in discharge of their duty, to make known
to your majesty, that the decrees they passed against the sorcerers
and witches brought before them were passed after a mature deliberation on the part of all the judges present, and that nothing has been
done therein which is not conformable to the universal jurisprudence
of the kingdom, and for the general welfare of your majesty's subjects, of whom there is not one who can say that he is secure from
the malevolence of such criminals. We therefore supplicate your
majesty to suffer us to carry into effect the sentences we passed, and
to proceed with the trial of the other persons accused of the same
crime ; and that the piety of your majesty will not suffer to be introduced during your reign an opinion contrary to the principles of that
holy religion for which you have always employed so gloriously both
your cares and your arms."

Louis, as we have already mentioned, paid no attention to this
appeal. The lives of the old women were spared, and prosecutions
for mere witchcraft, unconnected with other offences, were discontinued throughout France. In 1680 an act was passed for the punishment, not of witches, but of pretenders to witchcraft, fortune-tellers,
divineresses, and poisoners.

Thus the light broke in upon Germany, France, England, and
Scotland about the same time, gradually growing clearer and clearer
till the middle of the eighteenth century, when witchcraft was finally
reckoned amongst exploded doctrines, and the belief in it confined to
the uttermost vulgar. Twice, however, did the madness burst forth

again as furious, while it lasted, as ever it had been. The first time in Sweden, in 1669, and the second in Germany so late as 1749. Both these instances merit particular mention. The first is one of the most extraordinary upon record, and for atrocity and absurdity is unsurpassed in the annals of any nation.

It having been reported to the king of Sweden that the little village of Mohra, in the province of Dalecarlia, was troubled exceedingly with witches, he appointed a commission of clergy and laymen to trace the rumour to its source, with full powers to punish the guilty. On the 12th of August 1669, the commissioners arrived in the bewitched village, to the great joy of the credulous inhabitants. On the following day the whole population, amounting to three

LOUIS XIV

thousand persons, assembled in the church. A sermon was preached, " declaring the miserable case of those people that suffered themselves to be deluded by the devil," and fervent prayer was offered up that God would remove the scourge from among them.

The whole assembly then adjourned to the rector's house, filling all the street before it, when the king's commission was read, charging every person who knew any thing of the witchery to come forward and declare the truth. A passion of tears seized upon the multitude ; men, women, and children began to weep and sob, and all promised to divulge what they had heard or knew. In this frame of mind they were dismissed to their homes. On the following day they were again called together, when the depositions of several persons were taken publicly before them all. The result was that seventy persons, including fifteen children, were taken into custody. Numbers also were arrested in the neighbouring district of Elfdale. Being put to the torture, they all confessed their guilt. They said they used to go to a gravel-pit, that lay hard by the cross-way, where they put a vest upon their heads, and danced " round and round and round about." They then went to the cross-way, and called three times upon the devil ; the first time in a low still voice ; the second, somewhat louder ; and the third, very loudly, with these words, "Antecessor, come, and carry us to Blockula !" This invocation never failed to bring him to their view. He generally appeared as a little old man, in a grey coat, with red and blue stockings, with exceedingly long garters. He had besides a very high-crowned hat, with bands of many-coloured linen enfolded about it, and a long red beard that hung down to his middle.

The first question he put to them was, whether they would serve him soul and body ? On their answering in the affirmative, he told them to make ready for the journey to Blockula. It was necessary to procure, in the first place, "some scrapings of altars and filings of church clocks." Antecessor then gave them a horn with some salve in it, wherewith they anointed themselves. These preparations ended, he brought beasts for them to ride upon,—horses, asses, goats, and monkeys ; and giving them a saddle, a hammer, and a nail, uttered the word of command, and away they went. Nothing stopped them. They flew over churches, high walls, rocks, and mountains, until they came to the green meadow where Blockula was situated. Upon these occasions they carried as many children with them as they could ; for the devil, they said, "did plague and whip them if they did not procure him children, insomuch that they had no peace or quiet for him."

Many parents corroborated a part of this evidence, stating that their children had repeatedly told them that they had been carried away in the night to Blockula, where the devil had beaten them black and blue. They had seen the marks in the morning, but they soon disappeared. One little girl was examined, who swore positively that she was carried through the air by the witches, and when at a great height she uttered the holy name of Jesus. She immediately fell to the ground, and made a great hole in her side. "The devil, however, picked her up, healed her side, and carried her away to Blockula." She added (and her mother confirmed her statement), that she had till that day "an exceeding great pain in her side." This was a clencher, and the nail of conviction was driven home to the hearts of the judges.

The place called Blockula, whither they were carried, was a large house, with a gate to it, "in a delicate meadow, whereof they could see no end." There was a very long table in it, at which the witches sat down ; and in other rooms "there were very lovely and delicate beds for them to sleep upon."

After a number of ceremonies had been performed, by which they bound themselves body and soul to the service of Antecessor, they sat down to a feast composed of broth, made of colworts and bacon, oatmeal, bread and butter, milk and cheese. The devil always took the chair, and sometimes played to them on the harp or the fiddle while they were eating. After dinner they danced in a ring, sometimes naked and sometimes in their clothes, cursing and swearing all the time. Some of the women added particulars too horrible and too obscene for repetition.

Once the devil pretended to be dead, that he might see whether his people regretted him. They instantly set up a loud wail, and wept three tears each for him; at which he was so pleased, that he jumped up among them, and hugged in his arms those who had been most obstreperous in their sorrow.

Such were the principal details given by the children, and corroborated by the confessions of the full-grown witches. Any thing more absurd was never before stated in a court of justice. Many of the accused contradicted themselves most palpably; but the commissioners gave no heed to discrepancies. One of them, the parson of the district, stated in the course of the inquiry, that on a particular night, which he mentioned, he had been afflicted with a headache so agonising, that he could not account for it otherwise than by supposing he was bewitched. In fact, he thought a score of witches must have been dancing on the crown of his head. This announcement excited great horror among the pious dames of the auditory, who loudly expressed their wonder that the devil should have power to hurt so good a man. One poor witch, who lay in the very jaws of death, confessed that she knew too well the cause of the minister's headache. The devil had sent her with a sledge-hammer and a large nail to drive into the good man's skull. She had hammered at it for some time, but the skull was so enormously *thick*, that she made no impression upon it. Every hand was held up in astonishment. The pious minister blessed God that his skull was so solid, and he became renowned for his thick head all the days of his life. Whether the witch intended a joke does not appear, but she was looked upon as a criminal more than usually atrocious. Seventy persons were condemned to death on these so awful, yet so ridiculous confessions. Twenty-three of them were burned together in one fire in the village of Mohra, in the presence of thousands of delighted spectators. On the following day fifteen children were murdered in the same manner, offered up in sacrifice to the bloody Moloch of superstition. The remaining thirty-two were executed at the neighbouring town of Fahluna. Besides these, fifty-six children were found guilty of witchcraft in a minor degree, and sentenced to various punishments, such as running the gauntlet, imprisonment, and public whipping once a week for a twelvemonth.

Long after the occurrence of this case, it was cited as one of the most convincing proofs upon record of the prevalence of witchcraft. When men wish to construct or support a theory, how they torture facts into their service ! The lying whimsies of a few sick children, encouraged by foolish parents, and drawn out by superstitious neighbours, were sufficient to set a country in a flame. If, instead of commissioners as deeply sunk in the slough of ignorance as the people they were sent amongst, there had been deputed a few men firm in courage and clear in understanding, how different would have been the result ! Some of the poor children who were burned would have been sent to an infirmary ; others would have been well flogged ; the credulity of the parents would have been laughed at ; and the lives of seventy persons spared. The belief in witchcraft remains in Sweden to this day ; but happily the annals of that country present no more such instances of lamentable aberration of intellect as the one just cited.

In New England, about the same time, the colonists were scared by similar stories of the antics of the devil. All at once a fear seized upon the multitude, and supposed criminals were arrested day after day in such numbers, that the prisons were found too small to contain them. A girl named Goodwin, the daughter of a mason, who was hypochondriac and subject to fits, imagined that an old Irish woman, named Glover, had bewitched her. Her two brothers, in whose constitutions there was apparently a predisposition to similar fits, went off in the same way, crying out that the devil and dame Glover were tormenting them. At times their joints were so stiff that they could not be moved; while at others, said the neighbours, they were so flexible, that the bones appeared softened into sinews. The supposed witch was seized, and as she could not repeat the Lord's Prayer without making a mistake in it, she was condemned and executed.

But the popular excitement was not allayed. One victim was not enough ; the people waited agape for new disclosures. Suddenly two hysteric girls in another family fell into fits daily, and the cry of witchcraft resounded from one end of the colony to the other. The feeling of suffocation in the throat, so common in cases of hysteria, was said by the patients to be caused by the devil himself, who had stuck balls in the windpipe to choke them. They felt the pricking of thorns in every part of the body, and one of them vomited needles. The case of these girls, who were the daughter and niece of a Mr. Parvis, the minister of a Calvinist chapel, excited so much attention, that all the weak women in the colony began to fancy themselves similarly afflicted. The more they brooded on it, the more convinced they became. The contagion of this mental disease was as great as if it had been a pestilence. One after the other the women fainted away, asserting on their recovery that they had seen the spectres of witches. Where there were three or four girls in a family, they so worked each upon the diseased imagination of the other, that they fell into fits five or six times in a day. Some related that the devil himself appeared to them, bearing in his hand a parchment-roll, and promising that if they would sign an agreement, transferring to him their immortal souls, they should be immediately relieved from fits and all the ills of the flesh. Others asserted that they saw witches only, who made them similar promises, threatening that they should never be free from aches and pains till they had agreed to become the devil's. When they refused, the witches pinched, or bit, or pricked them with long pins and needles. More than two hundred persons named by these mischievous visionaries were thrown into prison. They were of all ages and conditions of life, and many of them of exemplary character. No less than nineteen were condemned and executed before reason returned to the minds of the colonists. The most horrible part of this lamentable history is, that among the victims there was a little child only five years old. Some women swore that they had seen it repeatedly in company with the devil, and that it had bitten them often with its little teeth for refusing to sign a compact with the evil one. It can hardly increase our feelings of disgust and abhorrence when we learn that this insane community actually tried and executed a dog for the same offence!

One man, named Cory, stoutly refused to plead to the preposterous indictment against him. As was the practice in such cases, he was pressed to death. It is told of the Sheriff of New England, who superintended the execution, that when this unhappy man thrust out his tongue in his mortal agony, he seized hold of a cane, and crammed it back again into the mouth. If ever there were a fiend in human form, it was this sheriff : a man who, if the truth were known, perhaps plumed himself upon his piety—thought he was doing God good service, and

> "Hoped to merit heaven by making earth a hell."

Arguing still in the firm belief of witchcraft, the bereaved people began to inquire, when they saw their dearest friends snatched away from them by these wide-spreading accusations, whether the whole proceedings were not carried on by the agency of the devil. Might not the great enemy have put false testimony into the mouths of the witnesses, or might not the witnesses be witches themselves? Every man who was in danger of losing his wife, his child, or his sister, embraced this doctrine with avidity. The revulsion was as sudden as the first frenzy. All at once, the colonists were convinced of their error.   The judges put a stop to the prosecutions, even of those who had confessed their guilt.   The latter were no sooner at liberty than they retracted all they had said, and the greater number hardly remembered the avowals which agony had extorted from them.   Eight persons, who had been tried and condemned, were set free; and gradually girls ceased to have fits and to talk of the persecutions of the devil.   The judge who had condemned the first criminal executed on this charge, was so smitten with sorrow and humiliation at his folly, that he set apart the anniversary of that day as one of solemn penitence and fasting.   He still clung to the belief in witchcraft; no new light had broken in upon him on that subject, but, happily for the community, the delusion had taken a merciful turn.   The whole colony shared the feeling; the jurors on the different trials openly expressed their penitence in the churches; and those who had suffered were regarded as the victims, and not as the accomplices of Satan.

It is related that the Indian tribes in New England were sorely puzzled at the infatuation of the settlers, and thought them either a race inferior to, or more sinful than the French colonists in the vicinity, amongst whom, as they remarked, " the Great Spirit sent no witches."

Returning again to the continent of Europe, we find that, after the year 1680, men became still wiser upon this subject.   For twenty years the populace were left to their belief, but governments in general gave it no aliment in the shape of executions.   The edict of Louis XIV. gave a blow to the superstition, from which it never recovered. The last execution in the Protestant cantons of Switzerland was at Geneva, in 1652.   The various potentates of Germany, although they could not stay the trials, invariably commuted the sentence into imprisonment, in all cases where the pretended witch was accused of pure witchcraft, unconnected with any other crime.   In the year 1701, Thomasius, the learned professor at the University of Halle, delivered his inaugural thesis *De Crimine Magiæ*, which struck another blow at the falling monster of popular error.   But a faith so strong as that in witchcraft was not to be eradicated at once; the arguments of learned men did not penetrate to the villages and hamlets: but still they achieved great things; they rendered the belief an unworking faith, and prevented the supply of victims, on which for so many ages it had battened and grown strong.

Once more the delusion broke out; like a wild beast wounded to the death, it collected all its remaining energies for the final convulsion, which was to shew how mighty it had once been.   Germany, which had nursed the frightful error in its cradle, tended it on its death-ded, and Würzburg, the scene of so many murders on the same pretext, was destined to be the scene of the last. That it might lose no portion of its bad renown, the last murder was as atrocious as the first. This case offers a great resemblance to that of the witches of Mohra and New England, except in the number of its victims. It happened so late as the year 1749, to the astonishment and disgust of the rest of Europe.

VIEW IN WURZBURG.

A number of young women in a convent at Würzburg fancied themselves bewitched; they felt, like all hysteric subjects, a sense of suffocation in the throat. They went into fits repeatedly; and one of them, who had swallowed needles, evacuated them at abscesses, which formed in different parts of the body. The cry of sorcery was raised, and a young woman, named Maria Renata Sänger, was arrested on the charge of having leagued with the devil to bewitch five of the young ladies. It was sworn on the trial that Maria had been frequently seen to clamber over the convent-walls in the shape of a pig—that, proceeding to the cellar, she used to drink the best wine till she was intoxicated, and then start suddenly up in her own form. Other girls asserted that she used to prowl about the roof like a cat, and often penetrate into their chamber, and frighten them by her dreadful howlings. It was also said that she had been seen in the shape of a hare, milking the cows dry in the meadows belonging to the convent; that she used to perform as an actress on the boards of Drury Lane Theatre in London, and, on the very same night, return upon a broomstick to Würzburg, and afflict the young ladies with pains in all their limbs. Upon this evidence she was condemned, and burned alive in the market-place of Würzburg.

Here ends this frightful catalogue of murder and superstition. Since that day, the belief in witchcraft has fled from the populous abodes of men, and taken refuge in remote villages and districts too wild, rugged, and inhospitable to afford a resting-place for the foot of civilisation. Rude fishers and uneducated labourers still attribute every phenomenon of nature which they cannot account for, to the devil and witches. Catalepsy, that wondrous disease, is still thought by ignorant gossips to be the work of Satan; and hypochondriacs, uninformed by science of the nature of their malady, devoutly believe in the reality of their visions. The reader would hardly credit the extent of the delusion upon this subject in the very heart of England at this day. Many an old woman leads a life of misery from the unfeeling insults of her neighbours, who raise the scornful finger and hooting voice at her, because in her decrepitude she is ugly, spiteful, perhaps insane, and realises in her personal appearance the description preserved by tradition of the witches of yore. Even in the neighbourhood of great towns the taint remains of this once widely-spread contagion. If no victims fall beneath it, the enlightenment of the law is all that prevents a recurrence of scenes as horrid as those of the seventeenth century. Hundreds upon hundreds of witnesses could be found to swear to absurdities as great as those asserted by the infamous Matthew Hopkins.

In the *Annual Register* for 1760, an instance of the belief in witchcraft is related, which shews how superstition lingers. A dispute arose in the little village of Glen, in Leicestershire, between two old women, each of whom vehemently accused the other of witchcraft. The quarrel at last ran so high that a challenge ensued, and they both agreed to be tried by the ordeal of swimming. They accordingly stripped to their shifts—procured some men, who tied their thumbs and great toes together, cross-wise, and then, with a cart-rope about their middle, suffered themselves to be thrown into a pool of water. One of them sank immediately, but the other continued struggling a short time upon the surface of the water, which the mob deeming an infallible sign of her guilt, pulled her out, and insisted that she should immediately impeach all her accomplices in the craft. She accordingly told them that, in the neighbouring village of Burton, there were several old women as "much witches as she was." Happily for her, this negative information was deemed sufficient, and a student in astrology, or "white-witch," coming up at the time, the mob, by his direction, proceeded forthwith to Burton in search of all the delinquents. After a little consultation on their arrival, they went to the old woman's house on whom they had fixed the strongest suspicion. The poor old creature on their approach locked the outer door, and from the window of an upstairs room asked what they wanted. They informed her that she was charged with being guilty of witchcraft, and that they were come to duck her ; remonstrating with her at the same time upon the necessity of submission to the ordeal, that, if she were innocent, all the world might know it. Upon her persisting in a positive refusal to come down, they broke open the door and carried her out by force, to a deep gravel-pit full of water. They tied her thumbs and toes together and threw her into the water, where they kept her for several minutes, drawing her out and in two or three times by the rope round her middle. Not being able to satisfy themselves whether she were a witch or no, they at last let her go, or, more properly speaking, they left her on the bank to walk home by herself, if she ever recovered. Next day they tried the same experiment upon another woman, and afterwards upon a third ; but fortunately, neither of the victims lost her life from this brutality. Many of the ringleaders in the outrage were apprehended during the week, and tried before the justices at quarter-sessions. Two of them were sentenced to stand in the pillory and to be imprisoned for a month ; and as many as twenty more were fined in small sums for the assault, and bound over to keep the peace for a twelvemonth.

"So late as the year 1785," says Arnot, in his collection and abridgment of *Criminal Trials in Scotland*, "it was the custom among the sect of Seceders to read from the pulpit an annual confession of sins, national and personal ; amongst the former of which was particularly mentioned the 'Repeal by parliament of the penal statute against witches, contrary to the express laws of God.' "

Many houses are still to be found in England with the horse-shoe (the grand preservative against witchcraft) nailed against the threshold. If any over-wise philosopher should attempt to remove them, the chances are that he would have more broken bones than thanks

LADY HATTON'S HOUSE, CROSS STREET, HATTON GARDEN.

for his interference. Let any man walk into Cross Street, Hatton Garden, and from thence into Bleeding-heart Yard, and learn the tales still told and believed of one house in that neighbourhood, and he will ask himself in astonishment if such things can be in the nineteenth century. The witchcraft of Lady Hatton, the wife of the famous Sir Christopher, so renowned for his elegant dancing in the days of Elizabeth, is as devoutly believed as the Gospels. The room is to be seen where the devil seized her after the expiration of the contract he had made with her, and bore her away bodily to the pit of Tophet : the pump against which he dashed her is still pointed out, and the spot where her heart was found, after he had torn it out of her bosom with his iron claws, has received the name of Bleeding-heart Yard, in confirmation of the story. Whether the horse-shoe still remains upon the door of the haunted house, to keep away other witches, is uncertain. A former inmate relates that, " about twenty years ago, more than one old woman begged for admittance repeatedly, to satisfy themselves that it was in its proper place. One poor creature, apparently insane, and clothed in rags, came to the door with a tremendous double-knock, as loud as that of a fashionable footman, and walked straight along the passage to the horse-shoe. Great was the wonderment of the inmates, especially when the woman spat upon the horse-shoe, and expressed her sorrow that she could do no harm while it remained there. After spitting upon, and kicking it again and again, she coolly turned round and left the house, without saying a word to any body. This poor creature perhaps intended a joke, but the probability is that she imagined herself a witch. In Saffron Hill, where she resided, her ignorant neighbours gave her that character, and looked upon her with no little fear and aversion."

More than one example of the popular belief in witchcraft occurred in the neighbourhood of Hastings so lately as the year 1830. An aged woman, who resided in the Rope-walk of that town, was so repulsive in her appearance, that she was invariably accused of being a witch by all the ignorant people who knew her. She was bent completely double; and though very old, her eye was unusually bright and malignant. She wore a red cloak, and supported herself on a crutch; she was, to all outward appearance, the very *beau ideal* of a witch. So dear is power to the human heart, that this old woman actually encouraged the popular superstition; she took no pains to remove the ill impression, but seemed to delight that she, old and miserable as she was, could keep in awe so many happier and stronger fellow-creatures. Timid girls crouched with fear when they met her, and many would go a mile out of their way to avoid her. Like the witches of the olden time, she was not sparing of her curses against those who offended her. The child of a woman who resided within two doors of her was afflicted with lameness, and the mother constantly asserted that the old woman had bewitched her. All the neighbours credited the tale. It was believed, too, that she could assume the form of a cat. Many a harmless puss has been hunted almost to the death by mobs of men and boys, upon the supposition that the animal would start up before them in the true shape of Mother ——

In the same town there resided a fisherman, who was the object of unceasing persecution, because it was said that he had sold himself to the devil. It was currently reported that he could creep through a keyhole, and that he had made a witch of his daughter, in order that he might have the more power over his fellows. It was also believed that he could sit on the points of pins and needles and feel no pain. His brother fishermen put him to this test whenever they had an opportunity. In the alehouses which he frequented, they often placed long needles in the cushions of the chairs in such a manner that he could not fail to pierce himself when he sat down. The result of these experiments tended to confirm their faith in his supernatural powers. It was asserted that he never flinched. Such was the popular feeling in the fashionable town of Hastings a few years ago; very probably it is the same now.

In the north of England, the superstition lingers to an almost inconceivable extent. Lancashire abounds with witch-doctors, a set of quacks who pretend to cure diseases inflicted by the devil. The practices of these worthies may be judged of by the following case, reported in the *Hertford Reformer* of the 23d of June 1838. The witch-doctor alluded to is better known by the name of the *cunning man*, and has a large practice in the counties of Lincoln and Nottingham. According to the writer in the *Reformer*, the dupe, whose name is not mentioned, had been for about two years afflicted with a painful abscess, and had been prescribed for without relief by more than one medical gentleman. He was urged by some of his friends, not only in his own village but in neighbouring ones, to consult the witch-doctor, as they were convinced he was under some evil influence. He agreed, and sent his wife to the *cunning man*, who lived in New St. Swithin's, in Lincoln. She was informed by this ignorant impostor that her husband's disorder was an infliction of the devil, occasioned by his next-door neighbours, who had made use of certain charms for that purpose. From the description he gave of the process, it appears to be the same as that employed by Dr. Fian and Gellie Duncan to work woe upon King James. He stated that the neighbours, instigated by a witch, whom he pointed out, took some wax and moulded it before the fire into the form of her husband, as near as they could represent him; they then pierced the image with pins on all sides, repeated the Lord's Prayer backwards, and offered prayers to the devil that he would fix his stings into the person whom that figure represented, in like manner as they pierced *it* with pins. To counteract the effects of this diabolical process, the witch-doctor prescribed a certain medicine, and a charm to be worn next the body, on that part where the disease principally lay. The patient was to repeat the 109th and 119th Psalms every day, or the cure would not be effectual. The fee which he claimed for this advice was a guinea.

So efficacious is faith in the cure of any malady, that the patient actually felt much better after a three weeks' course of this prescription. The notable charm which the quack had given was afterwards opened, and found to be a piece of parchment covered with some cabalistic characters and signs of the planets.

The next-door neighbours were in great alarm that the witch-doctor would, on the solicitation of the recovering patient, employ some means to punish them for their pretended witchcraft. To escape the infliction, they feed another cunning man, in Nottinghamshire, who told them of a similar charm, which would preserve them from all the malice of their enemies. The writer concludes by saying, that " the doctor, not long after he had been thus consulted, wrote to say, that he had discovered that his patient was not afflicted by Satan, as he had imagined, but by God, and would continue more or less in the same state till his life's end."

An impostor carried on a similar trade in the neighbourhood of Tunbridge Wells about the year 1830. He had been in practice for several years, and charged enormous fees for his advice. This fellow pretended to be the seventh son of a seventh son, and to be endowed in consequence with miraculous powers for the cure of all diseases, but especially of those resulting from witchcraft. It was not only the poor who employed him, but ladies who rode in their carriages. He was often sent for from a distance of sixty or seventy miles by these people, who paid all his expenses to and fro, besides rewarding him handsomely. He was about eighty years of age, and his extremely venerable appearance aided his imposition in no slight degree. His name was Okey or Oakley.

In France the superstition at this day is even more prevalent than it is in England. Garinet, in his history of Magic and Sorcery in that country, cites upwards of twenty instances which occurred between the years 1805 and 1818. In the latter year no less than three tribunals were occupied with trials originating in this humiliating belief : we shall cite only one of them. Julian Desbourdes, aged fifty-three, a mason, and inhabitant of the village of Thilouze, near Bourdeaux, was taken suddenly ill, in the month of January 1818. As he did not know how to account for his malady, he suspected at last that he was bewitched. He communicated this suspicion to his son-in-law Bridier, and they both went to consult a sort of idiot, named Baudouin, who passed for a conjuror or *white-witch*. This man told them that Desbourdes was certainly bewitched, and offered to accompany them to the house of an old man named Renard, who, he said, was undoubtedly the criminal. On the night of the 23d of January all three proceeded stealthily to the dwelling of Renard, and accused him of afflicting persons with diseases by the aid of the devil. Desbourdes fell on his knees and earnestly entreated to be restored to his former health, promising that he would take no measures against him for the evil he had done. The old man denied in the strongest terms that he was a wizard ; and when Desbourdes still pressed him to remove the spell from him, he said he knew nothing about the spell, and refused to remove it. The idiot Boudouin, the *white-witch*, now interfered, and told his companions that no relief for the malady could ever be procured until the old man confessed his guilt. To force him to confession they lighted some sticks of sulphur which they had brought with them for the purpose, and placed them under the old man's nose. In a few moments he fell down suffocated and apparently lifeless. They were all greatly alarmed ; and thinking that they had killed the man, they carried him out and threw him into a neighbouring pond, hoping to make it appear that he had fallen in accidentally. The pond, however, was not very deep, and the coolness of the water reviving the old man, he opened his eyes and sat up. Desbourdes and Bridier, who were still waiting on the bank, were now more alarmed than before, lest he should recover and inform against them. They therefore waded into the pond, seized their victim by the hair of the head, beat him severely, and then held him under water till he was drowned.

They were all three apprehended on the charge of murder a few days afterwards. Desbourdes and Bridier were found guilty of aggravated manslaughter only, and sentenced to be burnt on the back, and to work in the galleys for life. The *white-witch* Boudouin was acquitted on the ground of insanity.

M. Garinet further informs us that France, at the time he wrote (1818), was overrun by a race of fellows who made a trade of casting out devils and finding out witches. He adds also, that many of the priests in the rural districts encouraged the superstition of their parishioners by resorting frequently to exorcisms whenever any foolish persons took it into their heads that a spell had been thrown over them. He recommended, as a remedy for the evil, that all these exorcists, whether lay or clerical, should be sent to the galleys, and felt assured that the number of witches would then very sensibly diminish.

Many other instances of this lingering belief might be cited both in France and Great Britain, and indeed in every other country in Europe. So deeply rooted are some errors, that ages cannot remove them. The poisonous tree that once overshadowed the land may be cut down by the sturdy efforts of sages and philosophers ; the sun may shine clearly upon spots where venomous things once nestled in security and shade ; but still the entangled roots are stretched beneath the surface, and may be found by those who dig. Another king like James I. might make them vegetate again ; and more mis-

chievous still, another Pope like Innocent VIII. might raise the de-
caying roots to strength and verdure. Still it is consoling to think
that the delirium has passed away; that the raging madness has given
place to a milder folly; and that we may now count by units the
votaries of a superstition which in former ages numbered its victims
by tens of thousands, and its votaries by millions.

FLOATING A WITCH.

THE SLOW POISONERS.

Pescara. The like was never read of.
Stephano. In my judgment,
To all that shall but hear it, 'twill appear
A most impossible fable.
Pescara. Troth, I'll tell you,
And briefly as I can, by what degrees
They fell into this madness.—*Duke of Milan.*

THE atrocious system of poisoning by poisons so slow in their operation as to make the victim appear, to ordinary observers, as if dying from a gradual decay of nature, has been practised in all ages. Those who are curious in the matter may refer to Beckmann on secret poisons, in his *History of Inventions*, in which he has collected several instances of it from the Greek and Roman writers. Early in the sixteenth century, the crime seems to have gradually increased, till in the seventeenth it spread over Europe like a pestilence. It was often exercised by pretended witches and sorcerers, and finally became a branch of education amongst all who laid any claim to magical and supernatural arts. In the twenty-first year of Henry VIII. an act was passed rendering it high treason. Those found guilty of it were to be boiled to death.

One of the first in point of date, and hardly second to any in point of atrocity, is the murder by this means of Sir Thomas Overbury, which disgraced the court of James I. in the year 1613. A slight sketch of it will be a fitting introduction to the history of the poisoning mania, which was so prevalent in France and Italy fifty years later.

Robert Kerr, a Scottish youth, was early taken notice of by James I., and loaded with honours, for no other reason that the world could ever discover than the beauty of his person. James, even in his own day, was suspected of being addicted to the most abominable of all offences; and the more we examine his history now, the stronger the suspicion becomes. However that may be, the handsome Kerr, lending his smooth cheek even in public to the disgusting kisses of his royal master, rose rapidly in favour. In the year 1613, he was made Lord High Treasurer of Scotland, and created an English peer by the style and title of Viscount Rochester. Still further honours were in store for him.

In this rapid promotion he had not been without a friend. Sir Thomas Overbury, the king's secretary—who appears, from some threats in his own letters, to have been no better than a pander to the vices of the king, and privy to his dangerous secrets—exerted all his backstair influence to forward the promotion of Kerr, by whom he was doubtless repaid in some way or other. Overbury did not confine his friendship to this—if friendship ever could exist between two such men—but acted the part of an *entremetteur*, and assisted Rochester to carry on an adulterous intrigue with the Lady Frances Howard, the wife of the Earl of Essex. This woman was a person of violent passions, and lost to all sense of shame. Her husband was in her way, and to be freed from him she instituted proceedings for a divorce, on grounds which a woman of any modesty or delicacy of feeling would die rather than avow. Her scandalous suit was successful, and was no sooner decided than preparations on a scale of the greatest magnificence were made for her marriage with Lord Rochester.

Sir Thomas Overbury, who had willingly assisted his patron to intrigue with the Countess of Essex, seems to have imagined that his marriage with so vile a woman might retard his advancement. He accordingly employed all his influence to dissuade him from it; but Rochester was bent on the match, and his passions were as violent as those of the countess. On one occasion, when Overbury and the viscount were walking in the gallery of Whitehall, Overbury was overheard to say, "Well, my lord, if you do marry that base woman, you will utterly ruin your honour and yourself. You shall never do it with my advice or consent; and if you do, you had best look to stand

fast." Rochester flung from him in a rage, exclaiming with an oath,
" I will be even with you for this." These words were the death-
warrant of the unfortunate Overbury. He had mortally wounded the
pride of Rochester in insinuating that by his (Overbury's) means he
might be lowered in the king's favour ; and he had endeavoured to
curb the burning passions of a heartless, dissolute, and reckless man.

Overbury's imprudent remonstrances were reported to the countess ; and from that moment she also vowed the most deadly vengeance
against him. With a fiendish hypocrisy, however, they both concealed their intentions ; and Overbury, at the solicitation of Rochester, was appointed ambassador to the court of Russia. This apparent
favour was but the first step in a deep and deadly plot. Rochester,
pretending to be warmly attached to the interests of Overbury,
advised him to refuse the embassy, which he said was but a trick to
get him out of the way. He promised at the same time to stand
between him and any evil consequences which might result from
his refusal. Overbury fell into the snare, and declined the embassy.
James, offended, immediately ordered his committal to the Tower.

He was now in safe custody, and his enemies had opportunity to
commence the work of vengeance. The first thing Rochester did was
to procure, by his influence at court, the dismissal of the Lieutenant
of the Tower, and the appointment of Sir Jervis Elwes, one of his
creatures, to the vacant post. This man was but one instrument ;
and another being necessary, was found in Richard Weston, a fellow
who had formerly been shopman to a druggist. He was installed in
the office of under-keeper, and as such had the direct custody of
Overbury. So far all was favourable to the designs of the conspirators.

In the mean time the insidious Rochester wrote the most friendly
letters to Overbury, requesting him to bear his ill-fortune patiently,
and promising that his imprisonment should not be of long duration ;
for that his friends were exerting themselves to soften the king's displeasure. Still pretending the extreme of sympathy for him, he followed up the letters by presents of pastry and other delicacies, which
could not be procured in the Tower. These articles were all poisoned. Occasionally, presents of a similar description were sent to
Sir Jervis Elwes, with the understanding that these articles were not
poisoned when they were unaccompanied by letters : of these the
unfortunate prisoner never tasted. A woman named Turner, who
had formerly kept a house of ill-fame, and who had more than once
lent it to further the guilty intercourse of Rochester and Lady Essex,
was the agent employed to procure the poisons. They were prepared
by Dr. Forman, a pretended fortune-teller of Lambeth, assisted by

an apothecary named Franklin. Both these persons knew for what purposes the poisons were needed, and employed their skill in mixing them in the pastry and other edibles, in such small quantities as gradually to wear out the constitution of their victim. Mrs. Turner regularly furnished the poisoned articles to the under-keeper, who placed them before Overbury. Not only his food but his drink was

SIR THOMAS OVERBURY.

poisoned. Arsenic was mixed with the salt he ate, and cantharides with the pepper. All this time his health declined sensibly. Daily he grew weaker and weaker ; and with a sickly appetite craved for sweets and jellies. Rochester continued to condole with him, and anticipated all his wants in this respect, sending him abundance of pastry, and occasionally partridges and other game, and young pigs. With the sauce for the game, Mrs. Turner mixed a quantity of cantharides, and poisoned the pork with lunar-caustic. As stated on the trial

Overbury took in this manner poison enough to have poisoned twenty men; but his constitution was strong, and he still lingered. Franklin, the apothecary, confessed that he prepared with Dr. Forman seven different sorts of poisons, viz. aquafortis, arsenic, mercury, powder of diamonds, lunar-caustic, great spiders, and cantharides. Overbury held out so long that Rochester became impatient, and in a letter to Lady Essex, expressed his wonder that things were not sooner despatched. Orders were immediately sent by Lady Essex to the keeper to finish with the victim at once. Overbury had not been all this time without suspicion of treachery, although he appears to have had no idea of poison. He merely suspected that it was intended to confine him for life, and to set the king still more bitterly against him. In one of his letters he threatened Rochester that, unless he were speedily liberated, he would expose his villany to the world. He says, "You and I, ere it be long, will come to a public trial of another nature." * * * "Drive me not to extremities, lest I should say something that both you and I should repent." * * * "Whether I live or die, your shame shall never die, but ever remain to the world, to make you the most odious man living." * * * "I wonder much you should neglect him to whom such secrets of all kinds have passed." * * * "Be these the fruits of common secrets, common dangers?"

All these remonstrances, and hints as to the dangerous secrets in his keeping, were ill calculated to serve him with a man so reckless as Lord Rochester: they were more likely to cause him to be sacrificed than to be saved. Rochester appears to have acted as if he thought so. He doubtless employed the murderer's reasoning, that "dead men tell no tales," when, after receiving letters of this description, he complained to his paramour of the delay. Weston was spurred on to consummate the atrocity; and the patience of all parties being exhausted, a dose of corrosive sublimate was administered to him in October 1613, which put an end to his sufferings, after he had been for six months in their hands. On the very day of his death, and before his body was cold, he was wrapped up carelessly in a sheet, and buried without any funeral ceremony in a pit within the precincts of the Tower.

Sir Anthony Weldon, in his *Court and Character of James I.*, gives a somewhat different account of the closing scene of this tragedy. He says, "Franklin and Weston came into Overbury's chamber, and found him in infinite torment, with contention between the strength of nature and the working of the poison; and it being very like that nature had gotten the better in this contention, by the thrusting out of boils, blotches, and blains, they, fearing it might come to light by the judgment of physicians, the foul play that had been offered him, consented to stifle him with the bedclothes, which accordingly was performed ; and so ended his miserable life, with the assurance of the conspirators that he died by the poison ; none thinking otherwise than these two murderers."

The sudden death, the indecent haste of the funeral, and the non-holding of an inquest upon the body, strengthened the suspicions that were afloat. Rumour, instead of whispering, began to speak out ; and the relatives of the deceased openly expressed their belief that their kinsman had been murdered. But Rochester was still all powerful at court, and no one dared to utter a word to his discredit. Shortly afterwards, his marriage with the Countess of Essex was celebrated with the utmost splendour, the king himself being present at the ceremony.

It would seem that Overbury's knowledge of James's character was deeper than Rochester had given him credit for, and that he had been a true prophet when he predicted that his marriage would eventually estrange James from his minion. At this time, however, Rochester stood higher than ever in the royal favour ; but it did not last long—conscience, that busy monitor, was at work. The tongue of rumour was never still ; and Rochester, who had long been a guilty, became at last a wretched man. His cheeks lost their colour —his eyes grew dim ; and he became moody, careless, and melancholy. The king, seeing him thus, took at length no pleasure in his society, and began to look about for another favourite. George Villiers, Duke of Buckingham, was the man to his mind : quick-witted, handsome, and unscrupulous. The two latter qualities alone were sufficient to recommend him to James I. In proportion as the influence of Rochester declined, that of Buckingham increased. A falling favourite has no friends ; and rumour wagged her tongue against Rochester louder and more pertinaciously than ever. A new favourite, too, generally endeavours to hasten by a kick the fall of the old one; and Buckingham, anxious to work the complete ruin of his forerunner in the king's good graces, encouraged the relatives of Sir Thomas Overbury to prosecute their inquiries into the strange death of their kinsman.

James was rigorous enough in the punishment of offences when he was not himself involved. He piqued himself, moreover, on his dexterity in unravelling mysteries. The affair of Sir Thomas Overbury found him congenial occupation. He set to work by ordering the arrest of Sir Jervis Elwes. James, at this early stage of the proceedings, does not seem to have been aware that Rochester was so deeply implicated. Struck with horror at the atrocious system of slow poisoning, the king sent for all the judges. According to Sir Anthony Weldon, he knelt down in the midst of them, and said, "My lords the judges, it is lately come to my hearing that you have now in examination a business of poisoning. Lord! in what a miserable

DUKE OF BUCKINGHAM.

condition shall this kingdom be (the only famous nation for hospitality in the world), if our tables should become such a snare, as that none could eat without danger of life, and that Italian custom should be introduced among us! Therefore, my lords, I charge you, as you will answer it at that great and dreadful day of judgment, that you examine it strictly, without favour, affection, or partiality. And if you shall spare any guilty of this crime, God's curse light on you and your posterity! and if I spare any that are guilty, God's curse light on me and my posterity for ever!"

The imprecation fell but too surely upon the devoted house of Stuart. The solemn oath was broken, and God's curse *did* light upon him and his posterity!

The next person arrested after Sir Jervis Elwes, was Weston, the under-keeper; then Franklin and Mrs. Turner; and lastly, the Earl and Countess of Somerset, to which dignity Rochester had been advanced since the death of Overbury.

Weston was first brought to trial. Public curiosity was on the stretch. Nothing else was talked of, and the court on the day of trial was crowded to suffocation. The *State Trials* report, that Lord Chief Justice Coke "laid open to the jury the baseness and cowardliness of poisoners, who attempt that secretly against which there is no means of preservation or defence for a man's life; and how rare it was to hear of any poisoning in England, so detestable it was to our nation. But the devil had taught divers to be cunning in it, so that they can poison in what distance of space they please, by consuming the *nativum calidum*, or *humidum radicale*, in one month, two or three, or more, as they list, which they four manner of ways do execute, viz. *haustu, gustu, odore,* and *contactu.*"

LORD COKE.

When the indictment was read over, Weston made no other reply than "Lord have mercy upon me! Lord have mercy upon me!" On being asked how he would be tried, he refused to throw himself upon a jury of his country, and declared that he would be tried by God alone. In this he persisted for some time. The fear of the dreadful punishment for contumacy* induced him at length to plead "Not guilty," and take his trial in due course of law.

All the circumstances against him were fully proved, and he was found guilty and executed at Tyburn. Mrs. Turner, Franklin, and Sir Jervis Elwes were also brought to trial, found guilty, and executed between the 19th of October and the 4th of December 1615; but the grand trial of the Earl and Countess of Somerset did not take place till the month of May following.

On the trial of Sir Jervis Elwes, circumstances had transpired, shewing a guilty knowledge of the poisoning on the part of the Earl of Northampton, the uncle of Lady Somerset, and the chief falconer Sir Thomas Monson. The former was dead; but Sir Thomas Monson was arrested and brought to trial. It appeared, however, that he was too dangerous a man to be brought to the scaffold. He knew too many of the odious secrets of James I., and his dying speech might contain disclosures which would compromise the king. To conceal old guilt it was necessary to incur new: the trial of Sir Thomas Monson was brought to an abrupt conclusion, and himself set at liberty.

---

* The punishment for the contumacious was expressed by the words *onere, frigore, et fame.* By the first was meant, that the culprit should be extended on his back on the ground, and weights placed over his body, gradually increased, until he expired. Sometimes the punishment was not extended to this length, and the victim being allowed to recover, underwent the second portion, the *frigore,* which consisted in his standing naked in the open air, for a certain space, in the sight of all the people. The third, or *fame,* was more dreadful, the statute saying, "That he was to be preserved with the coarsest bread that could be got, and water out of the next sink, or puddle, to the place of execution; and that day he had water he should have no bread, and that day he had bread he should have no water;" and in this torment he was to linger as long as nature would hold out.

Already James had broken his oath. He now began to fear that he had been rash in engaging so zealously to bring the poisoners to

THE EARL OF SOMERSET.

punishment. That Somerset would be declared guilty there was no doubt, and that he looked for pardon and impunity was equally evident to the king. Somerset, while in the Tower, asserted confidently that James would not *dare* to bring him to trial. In this he was mistaken; but James was in an agony. What the secret was between them will now never be known with certainty; but it may be surmised. Some have imagined it to be the vice to which the king was addicted; while others have asserted that it related to the death of Prince Henry, a virtuous young man, who had held Somerset in especial abhorrence. This prince died early, unlamented by his father, and, as public opinion whispered at the time, poisoned by Somerset. Probably some crime or other lay heavy upon the soul of the king; and Somerset, his accomplice, could not be brought to public execution with safety. Hence the dreadful tortures of James when he discovered that his favourite was so deeply implicated in the murder of Overbury. Every means was taken by the agonised king to bring the prisoner into what was called a safe frame of mind. He was secretly advised to plead guilty, and trust to the clemency of the king. The same advice was conveyed to the countess. Bacon was instructed by the king to draw up a paper of all the points of "mercy and favour" to Somerset which might result from the evidence; and Somerset was again recommended to plead guilty, and promised that no evil should ensue to him.

The countess was first tried. She trembled and shed tears during the reading of the indictment, and, in a low voice, pleaded guilty. On being asked why sentence of death should not be passed against her, she replied meekly, "I can much aggravate, but nothing extenuate my fault. I desire mercy, and that the lords will intercede for me with the king." Sentence of death was passed upon her.

Next day the earl was brought to trial. He appears to have mistrusted the promises of James, and he pleaded not guilty. With a self-possession and confidence which he felt, probably, from his knowledge of the king's character, he rigorously cross-examined the witnesses, and made a stubborn defence. After a trial which lasted eleven hours, he was found guilty, and condemned to the felon's death.

Whatever may have been the secrets between the criminal and the king, the latter, notwithstanding his terrific oath, was afraid to sign the death-warrant. It might, perchance, have been his own. The earl and countess were committed to the Tower, where they remained for nearly five years. At the end of this period, to the surprise and scandal of the community, and the disgrace of its chief magistrate, they both received the royal pardon, but were ordered to reside at a distance from the court. Having been found guilty of felony, the estates of the earl had become forfeited; but James granted

THE COUNTESS OF SOMERSET.

him out of their revenues an income of 4000*l.* per annum ! Shamelessness could go no further.

Of the after-life of these criminals nothing is known, except that the love they had formerly borne each other was changed into aversion, and that they lived under the same roof for months together without the interchange of a word.

The exposure of their atrocities did not put a stop to the practice of poisoning. On the contrary, as we shall see hereafter, it engendered that insane imitation which is so strange a feature of the human character. James himself is supposed, with great probability, to have fallen a victim to it. In the notes to Harris's *Life and Writings of James I.*, there is a good deal of information on the subject. The guilt of Buckingham, although not fully established, rests upon circumstances of suspicion stronger than have been sufficient to lead hundreds to the scaffold. His motives for committing the crime are stated to have been a desire of revenge for the coldness with which the king, in the latter years of his reign, began to regard him ; his fear that James intended to degrade him ; and his hope that the great influence he possessed over the mind of the heir apparent would last through a new reign, if the old one were brought to a close.

In the second volume of the *Harleian Miscellany*, there is a tract, entitled the *Forerunner of Revenge*, written by George Eglisham, doctor of medicine, and one of the physicians to King James. Harris, in quoting it, says that it is full of rancour and prejudice. It is evidently exaggerated, but forms nevertheless a link in the chain of

evidence.   Eglisham says, "The king being sick of an ague, the
duke took this opportunity, when all the king's doctors of physic
were at dinner, and offered to him a white powder to take, the which
he a long time refused ; but, overcome with his flattering importunity, he took it in wine, and immediately became worse and worse,
falling into many swoonings and pains, and violent fluxes of the belly,
so tormented, that his majesty cried out aloud of this white powder,
' Would to God I had never taken it !'" He then tells us "of the Countess of Buckingham (the duke's mother) applying the plaister to the
king's heart and breast, whereupon he grew faint and short-breathed,
and in agony ; that the physicians exclaimed that the king was poisoned ; that Buckingham commanded them out of the room, and committed one of them close prisoner to his own chamber, and another to
be removed from court; and that, after his majesty's death, his body
and head swelled above measure ; his hair, with the skin of his head,
stuck to his pillow, and his nails became loose on his fingers and
toes." Clarendon, who, by the way, was a partisan of the duke's,
gives a totally different account of James's death.   He says, "It was
occasioned by an ague (after a short indisposition by the gout), which
meeting many humours in a fat unwieldy body of fifty-eight years
old, in four or five fits carried him out of the world,—after whose
death many scandalous and libellous discourses were raised, without
the least colour or ground, as appeared upon the strictest and most
malicious examination that could be made, long after, in a time of
license, when nobody was afraid of offending majesty, and when pro-
secuting the highest reproaches and contumelies against the royal
family was held very meritorious."   Notwithstanding this confident
declaration, the world will hardly be persuaded that there was not
some truth in the rumours that were abroad.   The inquiries which
were instituted were not strict, as he asserts, and all the unconstitu-
tional influence of the powerful favourite was exerted to defeat them.
In the celebrated accusations brought against Buckingham by the
Earl of Bristol, the poisoning of King James was placed last on the
list ; and the pages of history bear evidence of the summary mode in
which they were, for the time, got rid of.

The man from whom Buckingham is said to have procured his
poisons was one Dr. Lamb, a conjuror and empiric, who, besides dealing in poisons, pretended to be a fortune-teller.   The popular fury,
which broke with comparative harmlessness against his patron, was
directed against this man, until he could not appear with safety in
the streets of London.   His fate was melancholy.   Walking one day
in Cheapside, disguised, as he thought, from all observers, he was
recognised by some idle boys, who began to hoot and pelt him with

stones, calling out, "The poisoner! the poisoner! Down with the wizard! down with him!" A mob very soon collected, and the doctor took to his heels and ran for his life. He was pursued and seized in Wood Street, and from thence dragged by the hair through the mire to St. Paul's Cross; the mob beating him with sticks and stones, and calling out, "Kill the wizard! kill the poisoner!"

Charles I., on hearing of the riot, rode from Whitehall to quell it; but he arrived too late to save the victim. Every bone in his body was broken, and he was quite dead. Charles was excessively indignant, and fined the city six hundred pounds for its inability to deliver up the ring-leaders to justice.

PAUL'S CROSS; SEVENTEENTH CENTURY.

But it was in Italy that poisoning was most prevalent. From a very early period, it seems to have been looked upon in that country as a perfectly justifiable means of getting rid of an enemy. The Italians of the sixteenth and seventeenth centuries poisoned their opponents with as little compunction as an Englishman of the present day brings an action at law against any one who has done him an injury. The writings of contemporary authors informs us that, when La Spara and La Tophania carried on their infernal trade, ladies put poison-bottles on their dressing-tables as openly, and used them with as little scruple upon others, as modern dames use *eau de Cologne* or lavender-water upon themselves. So powerful is the influence of fashion, it can even cause murder to be regarded as a venial peccadillo.

In the memoirs of the last Duke of Guise, who made a Quixotic attempt, in 1648, to seize upon the government of Naples, we find some curious particulars relative to the popular feeling with regard to poisoning. A man named Gennaro Annese, who, after the short and extraordinary career of Masaniello the fisherman, had established himself as a sort of captain-general of the populace, rendered himself so obnoxious to the Duke of Guise, that the adherents of the latter determined to murder him. The captain of the guard, as the duke himself very coolly informs us, was requested to undertake this office. It was suggested to him that the *poniard* would be the most effectual instrument, but the man turned up his eyes with pious horror at the proposition. He was ready to *poison* Gennaro Annese whenever he might be called upon to do so; but to poniard him, he said, would be disgraceful, and unbecoming an officer of the guards! At last, poison was agreed upon, and Augustino Molla, an attorney in the duke's confidence, brought the bottle containing the liquid to shew it to his master. The following is the duke's own account :

"Augustino came to me at night, and told me : ' I have brought you something which will free you from Gennaro. He deserves death, and it is no great matter after what fashion justice is done upon him. Look at this vial, full of clear and beautiful water : in four days' time, it will punish all his treasons. The captain of the guard has undertaken to give it him ; and as it has no taste at all, Gennaro will suspect nothing.' "

The duke further informs us that the dose was duly administered ; but that Gennaro, fortunately for himself, ate nothing for dinner that day but cabbage dressed with oil, which acting as an antidote, caused him to vomit profusely, and saved his life. He was exceedingly ill for five days, but never suspected that he had been poisoned.

In process of time, poison-vending became a profitable trade. Eleven years after this period, it was carried on at Rome to such an extent, that the sluggish government was roused to interference. Beckmann, in his *History of Inventions,* and Lebret, in his *Magazin zum Gebrauche der Staaten Kirche Geschichte,* or *Magazine of Materials for a History of a State Church,* relates that, in the year 1659, it was made known to Pope Alexander VII. that great numbers of young women had avowed in the confessional that they had poisoned their husbands with slow poison. The Catholic clergy, who in general hold the secrets of the confessional so sacred, were shocked and alarmed at the extraordinary prevalence of the crime. Although they refrained from revealing the names of the penitents, they conceived themselves bound to apprise the head of the Church of the enormities that were practised. It was also the subject of general conversation in Rome that young widows were unusually abundant. It was remarked too, that if any couple lived unhappily together, the husband soon took ill and died. The papal authorities, when once they began to inquire, soon learned that a society of young wives had been formed, and met nightly, for some mysterious purpose, at the house of an old woman named Hieronyma Spara. This hag was a reputed witch and fortune-teller, and acted as president of the young viragos, several of whom, it was afterwards ascertained, belonged to the first families of Rome.

In order to have positive evidence of the practices of this female conclave, a lady was employed by the government to seek an interview with them. She dressed herself out in the most magnificent style ; and having been amply provided with money, she found but little difficulty, when she had stated her object, of procuring an audience of La Spara and her sisterhood. She pretended to be in extreme distress of mind on account of the infidelities and ill-treatment of her husband, and implored La Spara to furnish her with a few drops of the wonderful elixir, the efficacy of which in sending cruel husbands to "their last long sleep" was so much vaunted by the ladies of Rome. La Spara fell into the snare, and sold her some of her "drops" at a price commensurate with the supposed wealth of the purchaser.

The liquor thus obtained was subjected to an analysis, and found to be, as was suspected, a slow poison ; clear, tasteless, and limpid, like that spoken of by the Duke of Guise. Upon this evidence, the house was surrounded by the police, and La Spara and her companions taken into custody. La Spara, who is described as having been a little ugly old woman, was put to the torture, but obstinately refused to confess her guilt. Another of the women, named La Gratiosa, had less firmness, and laid bare all the secrets of the infernal sisterhood. Taking a confession extorted by anguish on the rack at its true value (nothing at all), there is still sufficient evidence to warrant posterity in a belief of their guilt. They were found guilty, and condemned, according to their degrees of culpability, to various punishments. La Spara, Gratiosa, and three young women, who had poisoned their husbands, were hanged together at Rome. Upwards of thirty women were whipped publicly through the streets ; and several, whose high rank screened them from more degrading punishment, were banished from the country, and mulcted in heavy fines. In a few months afterwards, nine women more were hanged for poisoning ; and another bevy, including many young and beautiful girls, were whipped half naked through the streets of Rome.

This severity did not put a stop to the practice, and jealous women and avaricious men, anxious to step into the inheritance of fathers, uncles, or brothers, resorted to poison. As it was quite free from taste, colour, and smell, it was administered without exciting suspicion. The skilful vendors compounded it of different degrees of strength, so that the poisoners had only to say whether they wanted their victims to die in a week, a month, or six months, and they were suited with corresponding doses. The vendors were chiefly women, of whom the most celebrated was a hag named Tophania, who was in this way accessory to the death of upwards of six hundred persons. This woman appears to have been a dealer in poisons from her girlhood, and resided first at Palermo and then at Naples. That entertaining traveller, Father Lebat, has given, in his letters from Italy, many curious particulars relating to her. When he was at Civita Vecchia, in 1719, the Viceroy of Naples discovered that poison was extensively sold in the latter city, and that it went by the name of *aqueta*, or little-water. On making further inquiry, he ascertained that Tophania (who was by this time near seventy years of age, and who seems to have begun her evil courses very soon after the execution of La Spara,) sent large quantities of it to all parts of Italy in small vials, with the inscription, "Manna of St. Nicholas of Barri."

The tomb of St. Nicholas of Barri was celebrated throughout Italy. A miraculous oil was said to ooze from it, which cured nearly all the maladies that flesh is heir to, provided the recipient made use of it with the due degree of *faith*. La Tophania artfully gave this name to her poison, to elude the vigilance of the custom-house officers, who, in common with every body else, had a pious respect for St. Nicholas de Barri and his wonderful oil.

The poison was similar to that manufactured by La Spara. Hahnemann the physician, and father of the homœopathic doctrine, writing upon this subject, says it was compounded of arsenical neutral salts, occasioning in the victim a gradual loss of appetite, faintness, gnawing pains in the stomach, loss of strength, and wasting of the lungs. The Abbé Gagliardi says, that a few drops of it were generally poured into tea, chocolate, or soup, and its effects were slow, and almost imperceptible. Garelli, physician to the Emperor of Austria, in a letter to Hoffmann, says it was crystallised arsenic, dissolved in a large quantity of water by decoction, with the addition (for some unexplained purpose) of the herb *cymbalaria*. The Neapolitans called it *Aqua Toffnina*; and it became notorious all over Europe under the name of *Aqua Tophania*.

Although this woman carried on her infamous traffic so extensively, it was extremely difficult to meet with her. She lived in continual dread of discovery. She constantly changed her name and residence; and pretending to be a person of great godliness, resided in monasteries for months together. Whenever she was more than usually apprehensive of detection she sought ecclesiastical protection. She was soon apprised of the search made for her by the Viceroy of Naples, and, according to her practice, took refuge in a monastery. Either the search after her was not very rigid, or her measures were exceedingly well taken ; for she contrived to elude the vigilance of the authorities for several years. What is still more extraordinary, as shewing the ramifications of her system, her trade was still carried on to as great an extent as before. Lebat informs us that she had so great a sympathy for poor wives who hated their husbands and wanted to get rid of them, but could not afford to buy her wonderful *aqua*, that she made them presents of it.

She was not allowed, however, to play at this game for ever; she was at length discovered in a nunnery, and her retreat cut off. The viceroy made several representations to the superior to deliver her up, but without effect. The abbess, supported by the archbishop of the diocese, constantly refused. The public curiosity was in consequence so much excited at the additional importance thus thrust upon the criminal, that thousands of persons visited the nunnery in order to catch a glimpse of her.

The patience of the viceroy appears to have been exhausted by these delays. Being a man of sense, and not a very zealous Catholic, he determined that even the Church should not shield a criminal so atrocious. Setting the privileges of the nunnery at defiance, he sent a troop of soldiers, who broke over the walls, and carried her away, *vi et armis*. The archbishop, Cardinal Pignatelli, was highly indignant, and threatened to excommunicate and lay the whole city under interdict. All the inferior clergy, animated by the *esprit du corps*, took up the question, and so worked upon the superstitious and bigoted people, that they were ready to rise in a mass to storm the palace of the viceroy and rescue the prisoner.

These were serious difficulties; but the viceroy was not a man to be daunted. Indeed he seems to have acted throughout with a rare union of astuteness, coolness, and energy. To avoid the evil consequences of the threatened excommunication, he placed a guard round the palace of the archbishop, judging that the latter would not be so foolish as to launch out an anathema which would cause the city to be starved, and himself in it. The market-people would not have dared to come to the city with provisions so long as it remained under the ban. There would have been too much inconvenience to himself and his ghostly brethren in such a measure ; and, as the viceroy anticipated, the good cardinal reserved his thunders for some other occasion.

Still there was the populace. To quiet their clamour and avert the impending insurrection, the agents of the government adroitly mingled with the people, and spread abroad a report that Tophania had poisoned all the wells and fountains of the city. This was enough. The popular feeling was turned against her immediately. Those who, but a moment before, had looked upon her as a saint, now reviled her as a devil, and were as eager for her punishment as they had before been for her escape. Tophania was then put to the torture. She confessed the long catalogue of her crimes, and named all the persons who had employed her. She was shortly afterwards strangled, and her corpse thrown over the wall into the garden of the convent from whence she had been taken. This appears to have been done to conciliate the clergy, by allowing them, at least, the burial of one who had taken refuge within their precincts.

After her death the mania for poisoning seems to have abated; but we have yet to see what hold it took upon the French people at a somewhat earlier period. So rooted had it become in France between the years 1670 and 1680, that Madame de Sevigné, in one of her letters, expresses her fear that Frenchman and poisoner would become synonymous terms.

As in Italy, the first notice the government received of the prevalence of this crime was given by the clergy, to whom females of high rank, and some among the middle and lower classes, had avowed in the confessional that they had poisoned their husbands. In consequence of these disclosures, two Italians, named Exili and Glaser, were arrested, and thrown into the Bastille, on the charge of compounding and selling the drugs used for these murders. Glaser died in prison, but Exili remained without trial for several months; and there, shortly afterwards, he made the acquaintance of another prisoner, named Sainte Croix, by whose example the crime was still further disseminated among the French people.

The most notorious of the poisoners that derived their pernicious knowledge from this man was Madame de Brinvilliers, a young woman connected both by birth and marriage with some of the noblest families of France. She seems, from her very earliest years, to have been heartless and depraved; and, if we may believe her own confession, was steeped in wickedness ere she had well entered her teens. She was, however, beautiful and accomplished; and in the eye of the world, seemed exemplary and kind. Guyot de Pitaval, in the *Causes Célèbres*, and Madame de Sevigné, in her letters, represent her as mild and agreeable in her manners, and offering no traces on her countenance of the evil soul within. She was married in 1651 to the Marquis de Brinvilliers, with whom she lived unhappily for some years. He was a loose, dissipated character, and was the means of introducing Sainte Croix to his wife, a man who cast a blight upon her life, and dragged her on from crime to crime, till her offences became so great that the mind shudders to dwell upon them. For this man she conceived a guilty passion, to gratify which she plunged at once into the gulf of sin. She was drawn to its most loathsome depths ere retribution overtook her.

She had as yet shewn a fair outside to the world, and found but little difficulty in effecting a legal separation from her husband, who had not the art to conceal his vices. The proceeding gave great offence to her family. She appears, after this, to have thrown off the mask completely, and carried on her intrigues so openly with her lover, Sainte Croix, that her father, M. D'Aubray, scandalised at her conduct, procured a *lettre de cachet*, and had him imprisoned in the Bastille for a twelvemonth.

THE BASTILLE.

Sainte Croix, who had been in Italy, was a dabbler in poisons. He knew something of the secrets of the detestable La Spara, and improved himself in them from the instructions of Exili, with whom he speedily contracted a sort of friendship. By him he was shewn how to prepare, not only the liquid poisons employed in Italy, but that known as *succession-powder*, which afterwards became so celebrated in France. Like his mistress, he appeared amiable, witty, and intelligent, and shewed no signs to the world of the two fierce passions, revenge and avarice, which were gnawing at his heart. Both these passions were to be sated on the unfortunate family of D'Aubray; his revenge, because they had imprisoned him; and his avarice, because they were rich. Reckless and extravagant, he was always in want of money, and he had no one to supply him but Madame de Brinvilliers, whose own portion was far from sufficient to satisfy his need. Groaning to think that any impediment should stand between him and wealth, he conceived the horrid idea of poisoning M. D'Aubray her father, and her two brothers, that she might inherit the property. Three murders were nothing to such a villain. He communicated his plan to Madame de Brinvilliers; and she, without the slightest scruple, agreed to aid him: he undertook to compound the poisons, and she to administer them. The zeal and alacrity with which she set to work seem hardly credible. Sainte Croix found her an apt scholar; and she soon became as expert as himself in the manufacture of poisons. To try the strength of the first doses, she used to administer them to dogs, rabbits, and pigeons. Afterwards, wishing to be more certain of their effects, she went round to the hospitals, and administered them to the sick poor in the soups which she brought in apparent charity.* None of the poisons were intended to kill at the first dose; so that she could try them once upon an individual without fear of murder. She tried the same atrocious experiment upon the guests at her father's table, by poisoning a pigeon-pie! To be more certain still, she next poisoned herself! When convinced by this desperate essay of the potency of the draught, she procured an antidote from Sainte Croix, and all doubts being removed, commenced operations upon her grey-headed father. She administered the first dose with her own hands, in his chocolate. The poison worked well. The old man was taken ill, and his daughter, apparently full of tenderness and anxiety, watched by his bedside. The next day she gave him some broth, which she recommended as highly nourishing. This also was poisoned. In this manner she gradually wore out his frame, and in less than ten days he was a corpse! His death seemed so much the result of disease, that no suspicions were excited.

When the two brothers arrived from the provinces to render the last sad duties to their sire, they found their sister as grieved, to all outward appearance, as even filial affection could desire: but the young men only came to perish. They stood between Sainte Croix and the already half-clutched gold, and their doom was sealed. A man, named La Chaussée, was hired by Sainte Croix to aid in admi-

* This is denied by Voltaire in his *Age of Louis XIV.;* but he does not state for what reason. His words are, "Il est faux qu'elle eut essaye ses poisons dans les hôpitaux, comme le disait le peuple, et comme il est écrit dans les *Causes Célèbres,* ouvrage d'un avocat sans cause, et fait pour le peuple."

nistering the poisons; and in less than six weeks time they had both gone to their long home.

Suspicion was now excited ; but so cautiously had all been done, that it found no one upon whom to attach itself. The marquise had a sister, and she was entitled, by the death of her relatives, to half the property. Less than the whole would not satisfy Sainte Croix, and he determined that she should die the same death as her father and brothers. She was too distrustful, however; and, by quitting Paris, she escaped the destruction that was lurking for her.

The marquise had undertaken these murders to please her lover. She was now anxious to perpetrate another on her own account. She wished to marry Sainte Croix; but, though separated from her husband, she was not divorced. She thought it would be easier to poison him than to apply to the tribunals for a divorce, which might, perhaps, be refused. But Sainte Croix had no longer any love for his guilty instrument. Bad men do not admire others who are as bad as themselves. Though a villain himself, he had no desire to marry one, and was not at all anxious for the death of the marquis. He seemed, however, to enter into the plot, and supplied her with poison for her husband ; but he took care to provide a remedy. La Brinvilliers poisoned him one day, and Sainte Croix gave him an antidote the next. In this manner he was buffeted about between them for some time, and finally escaped, with a ruined constitution and a broken heart.

But the day of retribution was at hand, and a terrible mischance brought the murders to light. The nature of the poisons compounded by Sainte Croix was so deadly, that, when working in his laboratory, he was obliged to wear a mask, to preserve himself from suffocation. One day, the mask slipped off, and the miserable wretch perished in his crimes. His corpse was found, on the following morning, in the obscure lodging where he had fitted up his laboratory. As he appeared to be without friends or relatives, the police took possession of his effects. Among other things, was found a small box, to which was affixed the following singular document :

" I humbly beg, that those into whose hands this box may fall, will do me the favour to deliver it into the hands only of the Marchioness de Brinvilliers, who resides in the Rue Neuve St. Paul, as every thing it contains concerns her, and belongs to her alone ; and as, besides, there is nothing in it that can be of use to any person but her. In case she shall be dead before me, it is my wish that it be burned, with every thing it contains, without opening or altering any thing. In order that no one may plead ignorance, I swear by the God that I adore, and by all that is held most sacred, that I assert nothing but the truth : and if my intentions, just and reasonable as they are, be thwarted in this point by any persons, I charge their consciences with it, both in this world and that which is to come, in order that I may unload mine. I protest that this is my last will. Done at Paris, May 25, 1672. (Signed) SAINTE CROIX."

This earnest solicitation, instead of insuring respect, as was intended, excited curiosity. The box was opened, and found to contain some papers, and several vials and powders. The latter were handed to a chemist for analysis, and the documents were retained by the police, and opened. Among them was found a promissory note of the Marchioness de Brinvilliers, for thirty thousand francs, to the order of Sainte Croix. The other papers were of greater importance, as they implicated both her and her servant, La Chaussée, in the recent murders. As soon as she was informed of the death of Sainte Croix, she made an attempt to gain possession of his papers and the box; but, being refused, she saw that there was no time to be lost, and immediately quitted. Next morning the police were on her trail; but she succeeded in escaping to England. La Chaussée was not so fortunate. Altogether ignorant of the fatal mischance which had brought his villanies to light, he did not dream of danger. He was arrested and brought to trial: being put to the torture, he confessed that he had administered poison to the Messieurs d'Aubray, and that he had received a hundred pistoles, and the promise of an annuity for life, from Sainte Croix and Madame de Brinvilliers, for the job. He was condemned to be broken alive on the wheel, and the marchioness was, by default, sentenced to be beheaded. He was executed accordingly, in March 1673, on the Place de Grève, in Paris.

La Brinvilliers appears to have resided for nearly three years in England. Early in 1676, thinking that the rigour of pursuit was over, and that she might venture to return to the Continent, she proceeded secretly to Liège. Notwithstanding her care, the French authorities were soon apprised of her return; and arrangements were promptly made with the municipality of that city to permit the agents of the French police to arrest her within the limits of their jurisdiction. Desgrais, an officer of the maréchaussée, accordingly left Paris for that purpose. On his arrival in Liège, he found that she had sought shelter within the walls of a convent. Here the arm of the law, long as it is said to be, could not reach her; but Desgrais was not a man to be baffled, and he resorted to stratagem to accomplish what force could not. Having disguised himself as a priest, he sought admission to the convent, and obtained an interview with La Brinvilliers. He said, that being a Frenchman, and passing through Liège, he could not leave that city without paying a visit to a lady whose beauty and misfortunes were so celebrated. Her vanity was flattered by the compliment. Desgrais saw, to use a vulgar but forcible expression, "that he had got on the blind side of her;" and he adroitly continued to pour out the language of love and admiration till the deluded marchioness was completely thrown off her guard. She agreed, without much solicitation, to meet him outside the walls of the convent, where their amorous intrigue might be carried on more conveniently than within. Faithful to her appointment with her supposed new lover, she came, and found herself, not in the embrace of a gallant, but in the custody of a policeman.

Her trial was not long delayed. The proofs against her were abundant. The dying declaration of La Chaussée would have been alone enough to convict her; but besides that, there were the mysterious document attached to the box of Sainte Croix, her flight from France, and, stronger and more damning proof than all, a paper, in her own handwriting, found among the effects of Sainte Croix, in which she detailed to him the misdeeds of her life, and spoke of the murder of her father and brothers in terms that left no doubt of her guilt. During the trial, all Paris was in commotion. La Brinvilliers was the only subject of conversation. All the details of her crimes were published, and greedily devoured; and the idea of secret poisoning first put into the heads of hundreds, who afterwards became guilty of it.

On the 16th of July, 1676, the Superior Criminal Court of Paris pronounced a verdict of guilty against her, for the murder of her father and brothers, and the attempt upon the life of her sister. She was condemned to be drawn on a hurdle, with her feet bare, a rope about her neck, and a burning torch in her hand, to the great entrance of the cathedral of Notre Dame, where she was to make the *amende honorable* in sight of all the people; to be taken from thence to the Place de Grève, and there to be beheaded. Her body was afterwards to be burned, and her ashes scattered to the winds.

After her sentence, she made a full confession of her guilt. She seems to have looked upon death without fear; but it was recklessness, not courage, that supported her. Madame de Sevigné says, that when on the hurdle, on her way to the scaffold, she entreated her confessor to exert his influence with the executioner to place himself next to her, that his body might hide from her view "that scoundrel Desgrais, who had entrapped her." She also asked the ladies, who had been drawn to their windows to witness the procession, what they were looking at? adding, "A pretty sight you have come to see, truly!" She laughed when on the scaffold, dying as she had lived, impenitent and heartless. On the morrow, the populace came in crowds to collect her ashes, to preserve them as relics. She was regarded as a martyred saint, and her ashes were supposed to be endowed, by divine grace, with the power of curing all diseases. Popular folly has often canonised persons whose pretensions to sanctity were extremely equivocal ; but the disgusting folly of the multitude in this instance has never been surpassed.

Before her death, proceedings were instituted against M. de Penautier, treasurer of the province of Languedoc, and receiver-general for the clergy, who was accused by a lady, named St. Laurent, of having poisoned her husband, the late receiver-general, in order to obtain his appointment. The circumstances of this case were never divulged, and the greatest influence was exerted to prevent it from going to trial. He was known to have been intimate with Sainte Croix and Madame de Brinvilliers, and was thought to have procured his poisons from them. The latter, however, refused to say any thing which might implicate him. The inquiry was eventually stifled, after Penautier had been several months in the Bastille.

The Cardinal de Bonzy was accused by the gossips of the day of being an accomplice of Penautier. The cardinal's estates were burdened with the payment of several heavy annuities ; but, about the time that poisoning became so fashionable, all the annuitants died off, one after the other. The cardinal, in talking of these annuitants, afterwards used to say, "Thanks to my star, I have outlived them all !" A wit, seeing him and Penautier riding in the same carriage, cried out, in allusion to this expression, "There go the Cardinal de Bonzy and his *star !*"

It was now that the mania for poisoning began to take hold of the popular mind. From this time until the year 1682, the prisons of France teemed with persons accused of this crime ; and it is very singular that other offences decreased in a similar proportion. We have already seen the extent to which it was carried in Italy. It was, if possible, surpassed in France. The diabolical ease with which these murders could be effected, by means of these scentless and tasteless poisons, enticed the evil-minded. Jealousy, revenge, avarice, even petty spite, alike resorted to them. Those who would have been deterred, by fear of detection, from using the pistol or the dagger, or even strong doses of poison, which kill at once, employed slow poisons without dread. The corrupt government of the day, although it could wink at the atrocities of a wealthy and influential courtier like Penautier, was scandalised to see the crime spreading among the people. Disgrace was, in fact, entailed, in the eyes of Europe, upon the name of Frenchman. Louis XIV., to put a stop to the evil, instituted what was called the Chambre Ardente, or Burning Chamber, with extensive powers for the trial and punishment of the prisoners.

Two women, especially, made themselves notorious at this time, and were instrumental to the deaths of hundreds of individuals. They both resided in Paris, and were named Lavoisin and Lavigoreux. Like Spara and Tophania, of whom they were imitators, they chiefly sold their poisons to women who wanted to get rid of their husbands; and, in some few instances, to husbands who wanted to get rid of their wives. Their ostensible occupation was that of midwives. They also pretended to be fortune-tellers, and were visited by persons of every class of society. The rich and poor thronged alike to their *mansardes* to learn the secrets of the future. Their prophecies were principally of death. They foretold to women the approaching dissolution of husbands, and to needy heirs the end of rich relatives, who had made them, as Byron expresses it, "wait too, too long already." They generally took care to be instrumental in fulfilling their own predictions. They used to tell their wretched employers that some sign of the approaching death would take place in the house, such as the breaking of glass or china; and they paid servants considerable fees to cause a breakage, as if by accident, exactly at the appointed time. Their occupation as midwives made them acquainted with the secrets of many families, which they afterwards turned to dreadful account.

It is not known how long they had carried on this awful trade before they were discovered. Detection finally overtook them at the close of the year 1679. They were both tried, found guilty, and burned alive on the Place de Grève, on the 22d of February, 1680, after their hands had been bored through with a red-hot iron, and then cut off. Their numerous accomplices in Paris and in the provinces were also discovered and brought to trial. According to some authors, thirty, and to others, fifty of them, chiefly women, were hanged in the principal cities.

Lavoisin kept a list of the visitors who came to her house to purchase poisons. This paper was seized by the police on her arrest, and examined by the tribunals. Among the names were found those of the Marshal de Luxembourg, the Countess de Soissons, and the Duchess de Bouillon. The marshal seems only to have been guilty of a piece of discreditable folly in visiting a woman of this description, but the popular voice at the time imputed to him something more than folly. The author of the *Memoirs of the Affairs of Europe since the Peace of Utrecht*, says, "The miserable gang who dealt in poison and prophecy alleged that he had sold himself to the devil, and that a young girl of the name of Dupin had been poisoned by his means. Among other stories, they said he had made a contract with the devil, in order to marry his son to the daughter of the Marquis of Louvois. To this atrocious and absurd accusation the marshal, who had surrendered himself at the Bastille on the first accusation against him, replied with the mingled sentiment of pride and inno-cence, 'When Mathieu de Montmorenci, my ancestor, married the widow of Louis le Gros, he did not have recourse to the devil, but to the states-general, in order to obtain for the minor king the support of the house of Montmorenci.' This brave man was imprisoned in a cell six feet and a half long, and his trial, which was interrupted for several weeks, lasted altogether fourteen months. No judgment was pronounced upon him."

The Countess of Soissons fled to Brussels, rather than undergo the risk of a trial; and was never able to clear herself from the stigma that attached to her, of having made an attempt to poison the Queen of Spain by doses of succession-powder. The Duchess of Bouillon was arrested, and tried by the Chambre Ardente. It would appear, however, that she had nothing to do with the slow poisons, but had merely endeavoured to pry into the secrets of futurity, and gratify her curiosity with a sight of the devil. One of the presidents of the Chambre, La Reynie, an ugly little old man, very seriously asked her whether she had really seen the devil; to which the lady replied, looking him full in the face, "Oh, yes! I see him now. He is in the form of a little ugly old man, exceedingly ill-natured, and is dressed in the robes of a Counsellor of State." M. la Reynie prudently re-frained from asking any more questions of a lady with so sharp and ready a tongue. The duchess was imprisoned for several months in the Bastille; and nothing being proved against her, she was released at the intercession of her powerful friends. The severe punishment of criminals of this note might have helped to abate the fever of imi-tation among the vulgar;—their comparative impunity had a con-trary tendency. The escape of Penautier, and the wealthy Cardinal de Bonzy his employer, had the most pernicious effect. For two years longer the crime continued to rage, and was not finally suppressed till the stake had blazed, or the noose dangled, for upwards of a hun-dred individuals.*

---

* Slow poisoning is a crime which has unhappily been revived in England within the last few years, and which has been carried to an extent sufficient to cast a stain upon the national character. The poisoners have been principally women of the lowest class, and their victims have been their husbands or their children. The motive for the crime has in most instances been the basest that can be imagined,—the desire to obtain from burial-clubs to which they subscribed, the premium, or burial-money. A recent enactment, re-stricting the sale of arsenic and other poisons, will, it is to be hoped, check, if it do not extirpate this abominable crime.—1851.

PALACE OF WOODSTOCK.

HAUNTED HOUSES.

Here's a knocking indeed! . . . . Knock! knock! knock! . . . ,
Who's there, i' the name o' Beelzebub? . . . . Who's there, i' the devil's
name? Knock! knock! knock!—Never at quiet?—*Macbeth.*

WHO has not either seen or heard of some house, shut up and un-
inhabitable, fallen into decay, and looking dusty and dreary, from
which, at midnight, strange sounds have been heard to issue—aerial
knockings—the rattling of chains, and the groaning of perturbed spirits?—a house that people have thought it unsafe to pass after dark,
and which has remained for years without a tenant, and which no
tenant would occupy, even were he paid to do so? There are hundreds of such houses in England in the present day; hundreds in
France, Germany, and almost every country of Europe, which are
marked with the mark of fear—places for the timid to avoid, and the
pious to bless themselves at, and ask protection from, as they pass—
the abodes of ghosts and evil spirits. There are many such houses in
London; and if any vain boaster of the march of intellect would but
take the trouble to find them out and count them, he would be convinced that intellect must yet make some enormous strides before
such old superstitions can be eradicated.

The idea that such houses exist is a remnant of the witch creed,
which merits separate notice from its comparative harmlessness, and

from its being not so much a madness as a folly of the people. Unlike other notions that sprang from the belief in witchcraft, and which we have already dwelt upon at sufficient length, it has sent no wretches to the stake or the gibbet, and but a few to the pillory only.

Many houses have been condemned as haunted, and avoided by the weak and credulous, from circumstances the most trifling in themselves, and which only wanted a vigorous mind to clear up at once, and dissipate all alarm. A house in Aix-la-Chapelle, a large desolate-looking building, remained uninhabited for five years, on account of the mysterious knockings that there were heard within it at all hours of the day and night. Nobody could account for the noises; and the fear became at last so excessive, that the persons who inhabited the houses on either side relinquished their tenancy, and went to reside in other quarters of the town, where there was less chance of interruption from evil spirits. From being so long without an inhabitant, the house at last grew so ruinous, so dingy, and so miserable in its outward appearance, and so like the place that ghosts might be supposed to haunt, that few persons cared to go past it after sunset. The knocking that was heard in one of the upper rooms was not very loud, but it was very regular. The gossips of the neighbourhood asserted that they often heard groans from the cellars, and saw lights moved about from one window to another immediately after the midnight bell had tolled. Spectres in white habiliments were reported to have gibed and chattered from the windows; but all these stories could bear no investigation. The knocking, however, was a fact which no one could dispute, and several ineffectual attempts were made by the proprietor to discover the cause. The rooms were sprinkled with holy water; the evil spirits were commanded in due form, by a priest, to depart thence to the Red Sea; but the knockings still continued, in spite of all that could be done in that way. Accident at last discovered the cause, and restored tranquillity to the neighbourhood. The proprietor, who suffered not only in his mind but in his pocket, had sold the building at a ruinously small price, to get rid of all future annoyance. The new proprietor was standing in a room on the first floor when he heard the door driven to at the bottom with a considerable noise, and then fly open immediately, about two inches and no more. He stood still a minute and watched, and the same thing occurred a second and a third time. He examined the door attentively, and all the mystery was unravelled. The latch of the door was broken, so that it could not be fastened, and it swung chiefly upon the bottom hinge. Immediately opposite was a window, in which one pane of glass was broken; and when the wind was in a certain quarter, the draught of air was so strong that it blew the door to with some violence. There being no latch, it swung open again; and when there was a fresh gust, was again blown to. The new proprietor lost no time in sending for a glazier, and the mysterious noises ceased for ever. The house was replastered and repainted, and once more regained its lost good name. It was not before two or three years, however, that it was thoroughly established in popular favour; and many persons, even then, would always avoid passing it, if they could reach their destination by any other street.

A similar story is narrated by Sir Walter Scott, in his *Letters on Demonology and Witchcraft*, the hero of which was a gentleman of birth and distinction, well known in the political world. Shortly after he succeeded to his title and estates, there was a rumour among the servants concerning a strange noise that used to be heard at night in the family mansion, and the cause of which no one could ascertain. The gentleman resolved to discover it himself, and to watch for that purpose with a domestic who had grown old in the family, and who, like the rest, had whispered strange things about the knocking having begun immediately upon the death of his old master. These two watched until the noise was heard, and at last traced it to a small store-room, used as a place for keeping provisions of various kinds for the family, and of which the old butler had the key. They entered this place, and remained for some time without hearing the noises which they had traced thither. At length the sound was heard, but much lower than it seemed to be while they were farther off, and their imaginations were more excited. They then discovered the cause without difficulty. A rat, caught in an old-fashioned trap, had occasioned the noise by its efforts to escape, in which it was able to raise the trap-door of its prison to a certain height, but was then obliged to drop it. The noise of the fall resounding through the house had occasioned the mysterious rumours, which but for the investigation of the proprietor, would in all probability have acquired so bad a name for the dwelling that no servants would have inhabited it. The circumstance was told to Sir Walter Scott by the gentleman to whom it happened.

But in general, houses that have acquired this character have been more indebted for it to the roguery of living men than to accidents like these. Six monks played off a clever trick of the kind upon that worthy king, Louis, whose piety has procured him in the annals of his own country the designation of "the Saint." Having heard his confessor speak in terms of warm eulogy of the goodness and learning of the monks of the order of St. Bruno, he expressed his wish to establish a community of them near Paris. Bernard de

la Tour, the superior, sent six of the brethren, and the king gave
them a handsome house to live in in the village of Chantilly. It so
happened that from their windows they had a very fine view of the
ancient palace of Vauvert, which had been built for a royal residence
by King Robert, but deserted for many years.

SAINT LOUIS.

The worthy monks thought the palace would
just suit them ; but their modesty was so
excessive that they were ashamed to ask the
king for a grant of it in due form. This
difficulty was not to be overcome, and the
monks set their ingenuity to work to discover another plan. The palace of Vauvert
had never laboured under any imputation
upon its character until they became its
neighbours; but, somehow or other, it almost immediately afterwards began to acquire a bad name. Frightful shrieks were
heard to proceed from it at night; blue,
red, and green lights were suddenly seen to
glimmer from the windows, and as suddenly
to disappear; the clanking of chains was
heard, and the howling as of persons in
great pain. These disturbances continued for
several months, to the great terror of all the
country round, and even of the pious King
Louis, to whom, at Paris, all the rumours
were regularly carried with whole heaps of
additions that accumulated on the way. At
last a great spectre, clothed all in pea-green,
with a long white beard and a serpent's tail,
took his station regularly at midnight in
the principal window of the palace, and
howled fearfully, and shook his fists at the passengers. The six
monks at Chantilly, to whom all these things were duly narrated,
were exceedingly wrath that the devil should play such antics right
opposite their dwelling, and hinted to the commissioners sent down
by Saint Louis to investigate the matter, that if they were allowed
to inhabit the palace, they would very soon make a clearance of
the evil spirits. The king was quite charmed with their piety, and
expressed to them how grateful he felt for their disinterestedness.
A deed was forthwith drawn up, the royal sign-manual was affixed
to it, and the palace of Vauvert became the property of the monks
of St. Bruno. The deed is dated 1259. The disturbances ceased im-

mediately, the lights disappeared, and the green ghost (so said the monks) was laid at rest for ever under the waves of the Red Sea.*

In the year 1580, one Gilles Blacre had taken the lease of a house in the suburbs of Tours, but repenting him of his bargain with the landlord, Peter Piquet, he endeavoured to prevail upon him to cancel the agreement. Peter, however, was satisfied with his tenant and his terms, and would listen to no compromise. Very shortly afterwards, the rumour was spread all over Tours that the house of Gilles Blacre was haunted. Gilles himself asserted that he verily believed his house to be the general rendezvous of all the witches and evil spirits of France. The noise they made was awful, and quite prevented him from sleeping. They knocked against the wall, howled in the chimneys, broke his window-glass, scattered his pots and pans all over his kitchen, and set his chairs and tables a-dancing the whole night through. Crowds of persons assembled round the house to hear the mysterious noises; and the bricks were observed to detach themselves from the wall, and fall into the streets upon the heads of those who had not said their paternoster before coming out in the morning. These things having continued for some time, Gilles Blacre made his complaint to the Civil Court of Tours, and Peter Piquet was summoned to shew cause why the lease should not be annulled. Poor Peter could make no defence, and the court unanimously agreed that no lease could hold good under such circumstances, and annulled it accordingly, condemning the unlucky owner to all the expenses of the suit. Peter appealed to the parliament of Paris; and after a long examination, the parliament confirmed the lease. "Not," said the judge, "because it has not been fully and satisfactorily proved that the house is troubled by evil spirits, but that there was an informality in the proceedings before the Civil Court of Tours, that rendered its decision null and of no effect."

A similar cause was tried before the parliament of Bourdeaux, in the year 1595, relative to a house in that city which was sorely troubled by evil spirits. The parliament appointed certain ecclesiastics to examine and report to them, and on their report in the affirmative that the house was haunted, the lease was annulled, and the tenant absolved from all payment of rent and taxes.†

One of the best stories of a haunted house is that of the royal palace of Woodstock, in the year 1649, when the commissioners sent from London by the Long Parliament to take possession of it, and efface all the emblems of royalty about it, were fairly driven out by their fear of the devil, and the annoyances they suffered from a roguish cavalier, who played the imp to admiration. The commis-

---

* Garinet, *Histoire de la Magie en France*, p. 75. † Ibid. p. 156.

sioners, dreading at that time no devil, arrived at Woodstock on the 13th of October, 1649. They took up their lodgings in the late king's apartments—turned the beautiful bedrooms and withdrawing-rooms into kitchens and sculleries — the council-hall into a brew-house, and made the dining-room a place to keep firewood in. They pulled down all the insignia of royal state, and treated with the ut-most indignity every thing that recalled to their memory the name or the majesty of Charles Stuart. One Giles Sharp accompanied them in the capacity of clerk, and seconded their efforts, apparently with the greatest zeal. He aided them to uproot a noble old tree, merely because it was called the *King's* Oak, and tossed the fragments into the dining-room to make cheerful fires for the commissioners. During the first two days, they heard some strange noises about the house, but they paid no great attention to them. On the third, however, they began to suspect they had got into bad company; for they heard, as they thought, a supernatural dog under their bed, which gnawed their bed-clothes. On the next day, the chairs and tables began to dance, apparently of their own accord. On the fifth day, something came into the bedchamber and walked up and down ; and fetching the warming-pan out of the withdrawing-room, made so much noise with it that they thought five church-bells were ringing in their ears. On the sixth day, the plates and dishes were thrown up and down the dining-room. On the seventh, they penetrated into the bedroom in company with several logs of wood, and usurped the soft pillows intended for the commissioners. On the eighth and ninth nights, there was a cessation of hostilities ; but on the tenth, the bricks in the chimneys became locomotive, and rattled and danced about the floors, and round the heads of the commissioners, all the night long. On the eleventh, the demon ran away with their breeches ; and on the twelfth filled their beds so full of pewter platters that they could not get into them. On the thirteenth night, the glass became unaccount-ably seized with a fit of cracking, and fell into shivers in all parts of the house. On the fourteenth, there was a noise as if forty pieces of artillery had been fired off, and a shower of pebble-stones, which so alarmed the commissioners that, " struck with great horror, they cried out to one another for help."

They first of all tried the efficacy of prayers to drive away the evil spirits; but these proving unavailing, they began seriously to reflect whether it would not be much better to leave the place altogether to the devils that inhabited it. They ultimately resolved, however, to try it a little longer ; and having craved forgiveness of all their sins, betook themselves to bed. That night they slept in tolerable com-fort, but it was merely a trick of their tormentor to lull them into false security. When, on the succeeding night, they heard no noises, they began to flatter themselves that the devil was driven out, and prepared accordingly to take up their quarters for the whole winter in the palace. These symptoms on their part became the signal for renewed uproar among the fiends. On the 1st of November, they heard something walking with a slow and solemn pace up and down the withdrawing-room, and immediately afterwards a shower of stones, bricks, mortar, and broken glass pelted about their ears. On the 2d the steps were again heard in the withdrawing-room, sounding to their fancy very much like the treading of an enormous bear, which continued for about a quarter of an hour. This noise having ceased, a large warming-pan was thrown violently upon the table, followed by a number of stones and the jawbone of a horse. Some of the boldest walked valiantly into the withdrawing-room, armed with swords and pistols; but could discover nothing. They were afraid that night to go to sleep, and sat up, making fires in every room, and burning candles and lamps in great abundance; thinking that, as the fiends loved darkness, they would not disturb a company surrounded with so much light. They were deceived, however: buckets of water came down the chimneys and extinguished the fires; and the candles were blown out, they knew not how. Some of the servants who had betaken themselves to bed were drenched with putrid ditchwater as they lay, and arose in great fright, muttering incoherent prayers, and exposing to the wondering eyes of the commissioners their linen all dripping with green moisture, and their knuckles red with the blows they had at the same time received from some invisible tormentors. While they were still speaking, there was a noise like the loudest thunder, or the firing of a whole park of artillery, upon which they all fell down upon their knees and implored the protection of the Almighty. One of the commissioners then arose, the others still kneeling, and asked in a courageous voice, and in the name of God, who was there, and what they had done that they should be troubled in that manner. No answer was returned, and the noises ceased for a while. At length, however, as the commissioners said, "the devil came again, and brought with it seven devils worse than itself." Being again in darkness, they lighted a candle and placed it in the doorway, that it might throw a light upon the two chambers at once; but it was suddenly blown out, and one commissioner said that he had "seen the similitude of a horse's hoof striking the candle and candlestick into the middle of the chamber, and afterwards making three scrapes on the snuff to put it out." Upon this, the same person was so bold as to draw his sword; but he asserted positively that he had hardly withdrawn it from the scabbard before an invisible hand seized hold of it and tugged with him for it, and prevailing, struck him so violent a blow with the pommel that he was quite stunned. Then the noises began again; upon which, with one accord, they all retired into the presence-chamber, where they passed the night, praying and singing psalms.

They were by this time convinced that it was useless to struggle any longer with the powers of evil that seemed determined to make Woodstock their own. These things happened on the Saturday night and being repeated on the Sunday, they determined to leave the place immediately, and return to London. By Tuesday morning early, all their preparations were completed; and shaking the dust off their feet, and devoting Woodstock and all its inhabitants to the infernal gods, they finally took their departure.*

Many years elapsed before the true cause of these disturbances was discovered. It was ascertained at the Restoration that the whole was the work of Giles Sharp, the trusty clerk of the commissioners. This man, whose real name was Joseph Collins, was a concealed royalist, and had passed his early life within the bowers of Woodstock; so that he knew every hole and corner of the place, and the numerous trap-doors and secret passages that abounded in the building. The commissioners, never suspecting the true state of his opinions, but believing him to be revolutionary to the back-bone, placed the utmost reliance upon him; a confidence which he abused in the manner above detailed, to his own great amusement and that of the few cavaliers whom he let into the secret.

Quite as extraordinary and as cleverly managed was the trick played off at Tedworth, in 1661, at the house of Mr. Mompesson, and which is so circumstantially narrated by the Rev. Joseph Glanvil, under the title of *The Demon of Tedworth*, and appended, among other proofs of witchcraft, to his noted work called *Sadducismus Triumphatus*. About the middle of April, in the year above mentioned, Mr. Mompesson, having returned to his house at Tedworth, from a journey he had taken to London, was informed by his wife, that during his absence they had been troubled with the most extraordinary noises. Three nights afterwards he heard the noise himself; and it appeared to him to be that of "a great knocking at his doors, and on the outside of his walls." He immediately arose, dressed himself, took down a pair of pistols, and walked valiantly forth to discover the disturber, under the impression that it must be a robber; but, as he went, the noise seemed to travel before or behind him; and when he arrived at the door from which he thought it proceeded, he saw nothing, but still heard "a strange hollow sound. He puzzled his

* Dr. H. More's *Continuation of Glanvil's Collection of Relations in proof of Witchcraft.*

brains for a long time, and searched every corner of the house; but discovering nothing, he went to bed again. He was no sooner snug under the clothes than the noise began again more furiously than ever, sounding very much like a "thumping and drumming on the top of his house, and then by degrees going off into the air."

These things continued for several nights, when it came to the recollection of Mr. Mompesson that some time before he had given orders for the arrest and imprisonment of a wandering drummer, who went about the country with a large drum, disturbing quiet people and soliciting alms, and that he had detained the man's drum, and that probably the drummer was a wizard, and had sent evil spirits to haunt his house to be revenged of him. He became strengthened in his opinion every day, especially when the noises assumed, to his fancy, a resemblance to the beating of a drum, "like that at the breaking up of a guard." Mrs. Mompesson being brought to bed, the devil, or the drummer, very kindly and considerately refrained from making the usual riot; but, as soon as she recovered strength, began again "in a ruder manner than before, following and vexing the young children, and beating their bedsteads with so much violence that every one expected they would fall in pieces." For an hour together, as the worthy Mr. Mompesson repeated to his wondering neighbours, this infernal drummer "would beat ' Roundheads and Cuckolds,' the 'Tat-too,' and several other points of war, as cleverly as any soldier." When this had lasted long enough, he changed his tactics, and scratched with his iron talons under the children's bed. "On the 5th of November," says the Rev. Joseph Glanvil, "it made a mighty noise; and a servant observing two boards in the children's room seeming to move, he bid it give him one of them. Upon which the board came (nothing moving it that he saw) within a yard of him. The man added, 'Nay, let me have it in my hand;' upon which the spirit, devil, or drummer pushed it towards him so close that he might touch it." "This," continues Glanvil, "was in the day-time, and was seen by a whole roomful of people. That morning it left a sulphureous smell behind it, which was very offensive. At night the minister, one Mr. Cragg, and several of the neighbours came to the house on a visit. Mr. Cragg went to prayers with them, kneeling at the children's bedside, where it then became very troublesome and loud. During prayer-time, the spirit withdrew into the cock-loft, but returned as soon as prayers were done; and then, in sight of the company, the chairs walked about the room of themselves, the children's shoes were hurled over their heads, and every loose thing moved about the chamber. At the same time, a bed-staff was thrown at the minister, which hit him on the leg, but so favourably, that a lock of

wool could not have fallen more softly." On another occasion, the
blacksmith of the village, a fellow who cared neither for ghost nor
devil, slept with John the footman, that he also might hear the disturbances and be cured of his incredulity, when there "came a noise
in the room as if one had been shoeing a horse, and somewhat came,
as it were, with a pair of pincers," snipping and snapping at the poor
blacksmith's nose the greater part of the night. Next day it came
panting like a dog out of breath; upon which some woman present
took a bed-staff to knock at it, "which was caught suddenly out of
her hand and thrown away; and company coming up, the room was
presently filled with a *bloomy noisome smell*, and was very hot, though
without fire, in a very sharp and severe winter. It continued in the
bed, panting and scratching for an hour and a half, and then went
into the next room, where it knocked a little, and seemed to rattle a
chain."

The rumour of these wonderful occurrences soon spread all over
the country, and people from far and near flocked to the haunted
house of Tedworth, to believe or doubt as their natures led them, but
all filled with intense curiosity. It appears, too, that the fame of
these events reached the royal ear, and that some gentlemen were
sent by the king to investigate the circumstances, and draw up a
report of what they saw or heard. Whether the royal commissioners
were more sensible men than the neighbours of Mr. Mompesson, and
required more clear and positive evidence than they, or whether the
powers with which they were armed to punish any body who might be
found carrying on this deception frightened the evil-doers, is not certain; but Glanvil himself reluctantly confesses that all the time they
were in the house the noises ceased, and nothing was heard or seen.
"However," says he, "as to the quiet of the house when the courtiers
were there, the intermission may have been accidental, or perhaps
the demon was not willing to give so public a testimony of those
transactions which might possibly convince those who he had rather
should continue in unbelief of his existence."

As soon as the royal commissioners took their departure, the infernal drummer recommenced his antics, and hundreds of persons
were daily present to hear and wonder. Mr. Mompesson's servant
was so fortunate as not only to hear, but to see this pertinacious demon, for it came and stood at the foot of his bed. "The exact shape
and proportion of it he could not discover; but he saw a great body,
with two red and glaring eyes, which, for some time, were fixed
steadily on him; and at length disappeared." Innumerable were the
antics it played. Once it purred like a cat; beat the children's legs
black and blue; put a long spike into Mr. Mompesson's bed, and a

knife into his mother's; filled the porringers with ashes; hid a Bible under the grate; and turned the money black in people's pockets. "One night," said Mr. Mompesson in a letter to Mr. Glanvil, "there were seven or eight of these devils in the shape of men, who, as soon as a gun was fired, would shuffle away into an arbour;" a circumstance which might have convinced Mr. Mompesson of the mortal nature of his persecutors, if he had not been of the number of those worse than blind, who shut their eyes and refuse to see.

In the mean time the drummer, the supposed cause of all the mischief, passed his time in Gloucester gaol, whither he had been committed as a rogue and a vagabond. Being visited one day by some person from the neighbourhood of Tedworth, he asked what was the news in Wiltshire, and whether people did not talk a great deal about a drumming in a gentleman's house there? The visitor replied that he heard of nothing else; upon which the drummer observed, "I have done it; I have thus plagued him; and he shall never be quiet until he hath made me satisfaction for taking away my drum." No doubt the fellow, who seems to have been a gipsy, spoke the truth, and that the gang of which he was a member knew more about the noises at Mr. Mompesson's house than any body else. Upon these words, however, he was brought to trial at Salisbury for witchcraft; and, being found guilty, was sentenced to transportation; a sentence which, for its leniency, excited no little wonder in that age, when such an accusation, whether proved or not, generally insured the stake or the gibbet. Glanvil says that the noises ceased immediately the drummer was sent beyond the seas; but that, somehow or other, he managed to return from transportation—"by raising storms and affrighting the seamen, it was said,"—when the disturbances were forthwith renewed, and continued at intervals for several years. Certainly, if the confederates of this roving gipsy were so pertinacious in tormenting poor weak Mr. Mompesson, their pertinacity is a most extraordinary instance of what revenge is capable of. It was believed by many, at the time, that Mr. Mompesson himself was privy to the whole matter, and permitted and encouraged these tricks in his house for the sake of notoriety; but it seems more probable that the gipsies were the real delinquents, and that Mr. Mompesson was as much alarmed and bewildered as his credulous neighbours, whose excited imaginations conjured up no small portion of these stories,

"Which roll'd, and as they roll'd grew larger visibly."

Many instances of a similar kind, during the seventeenth century, might be gleaned from Glanvil and other writers of that period; but they do not differ sufficiently from these to justify a detail of them. The most famous of all haunted houses acquired its notoriety much nearer our own time; and the circumstances connected with it are so curious, and afford so fair a specimen of the easy credulity even of well-informed and sensible people, as to merit a little notice in this chapter. The Cock-Lane Ghost, as it was called, kept London in commotion for a considerable time, and was the theme of conversation among the learned and the illiterate, and in every circle, from that of the prince to that of the peasant.

At the commencement of the year 1760, there resided in Cock Lane, near West Smithfield, in the house of one Parsons, the parish-clerk of St. Sepulchre's, a stockbroker, named Kent. The wife of

THE HAUNTED HOUSE IN COCK LANE.

this gentleman had died in child-bed during the previous year, and his sister-in-law, Miss Fanny, had arrived from Norfolk to keep his house for him. They soon conceived a mutual affection, and each of them made a will in the other's favour. They lived some months in the house of Parsons, who, being a needy man, borrowed money of his lodger. Some difference arose betwixt them, and Mr. Kent left the house and instituted legal proceedings against the parish-clerk for the recovery of his money.

While this matter was yet pending, Miss Fanny was suddenly taken ill of the small-pox; and, notwithstanding every care and attention, she died in a few days, and was buried in a vault under Clerkenwell church. Parsons now began to hint that the poor lady had come unfairly by her death, and that Mr. Kent was accessory to it, from his too great eagerness to enter into possession of the property she had bequeathed him. Nothing further was said for nearly two years; but it would appear that Parsons was of so revengeful a character, that he had never forgotten or forgiven his differences with Mr. Kent, and the indignity of having been sued for the borrowed money. The strong passions of pride and avarice were silently at work during all that interval, hatching schemes of revenge, but dismissing them one after the other as impracticable, until, at last, a notable one suggested itself. About the beginning of the year 1762, the alarm was spread over all the neighbourhood of Cock Lane, that the house of Parsons was haunted by the ghost of poor Fanny, and that the daughter of Parsons, a girl about twelve years of age, had several times seen and conversed with the spirit, who had, moreover, informed her, that she had not died of the small-pox, as was currently reported, but of poison, administered by Mr. Kent. Parsons, who originated, took good care to countenance these reports; and in answer to numerous inquiries, said his house was every night, and had been for two years, in fact, ever since the death of Fanny, troubled by a loud knocking at the doors and in the walls. Having thus prepared the ignorant and credulous neighbours to believe or exaggerate for themselves what he had told them, he sent for a gentleman of a higher class in life, to come and witness these extraordinary occurrences. The gentleman came accordingly, and found the daughter of Parsons, to whom the spirit alone appeared, and whom alone it answered, in bed, trembling violently, having just seen the ghost, and been again informed that she had died from poison. A loud knocking was also heard from every part of the chamber, which so mystified the not very clear understanding of the visitor, that he departed, afraid to doubt and ashamed to believe, but with a promise to bring the clergyman of the parish and several other gentlemen on the following day to report upon the mystery.

On the following night he returned, bringing with him three clergymen, and about twenty other persons, including two negroes, when, upon a consultation with Parsons, they resolved to sit up the whole night, and await the ghost's arrival. It was then explained by Parsons, that although the ghost would never render itself visible to any body but his daughter, it had no objection to answer the questions that might be put to it by any person present, and that it expressed an affirmation by one knock, a negative by two, and its displeasure by a kind of scratching. The child was then put into bed along with her sister, and the clergymen examined the bed and bedclothes to satisfy themselves that no trick was played, by knocking upon any substance concealed among the clothes. As on the previous night, the bed was observed to shake violently.

After some hours, during which they all waited with exemplary patience, the mysterious knocking was heard in the wall, and the child declared that she saw the ghost of poor Fanny. The following

questions were then gravely put by the clergyman, through the medium of one Mary Frazer, the servant of Parsons, and to whom it was said the deceased lady had been much attached. The answers were in the usual fashion, by a knock or knocks :

" Do you make this disturbance on account of the ill-usage you received from Mr. Kent?"—" Yes."

ROOM IN THE HAUNTED HOUSE IN COCK LANE.*

" Were you brought to an untimely end by poison ?"—" Yes."

"How was the poison administered, in beer or purl?"—"In purl."

* The woman whose ghost was said to manifest itself in Cock Lane was buried in the crypt or cloister of St. John, Clerkenwell. The vault is composed of two aisles, that on the south being much narrower than the other,—it was here she was deposited.

About seven years since, I was sketching a picturesque trefoil-headed door leading into this part of the vault; and the place being at that time in great confusion with coffins, remains of bodies, some of which were dried like mummies, &c., I could find no better seat than one of the coffins. The sexton's boy, who held my light, informed me this was the coffin of *Scratching Fanny*, which recalled the Cock-Lane story to my mind. I got off the lid of the coffin, and saw the face of a handsome woman, with an aquiline nose ; this feature remaining perfect, an uncommon case, for the cartilage mostly gives way. The remains had become adipocere, and were perfectly preserved. She was said to have been poisoned by deleterious punch, but this was legally disproved ; and, if I remember rightly, she was otherwise declared to have died of small-pox ; of this disease there was not the least sign, but as some mineral poisons tend to render bodies adipocere, here was some evidence in support of the former allegation. I made particular inquiries at the time of Mr. Bird, churchwarden, a respectable and judicious man; and he gave me good assurance that this coffin had always been looked upon as the one containing the Cock-Lane woman. Since that time the vault has been set in order, and the above-mentioned coffin, with others, put away.

The niche near the window in the drawing of the Ghost Room is the place where the bed-head was, and where the scratching, knocks, &c. were heard. This is the tradition of the house. Mrs. King, who holds the premises, informs me that her family has had the house about eighty years.—J. W. ARCHER.

"How long was that before your death?"—"About three hours."

"Can your former servant, Carrots, give any information about the poison?"—"Yes."

"Are you Kent's wife's sister?"—"Yes."

"Were you married to Kent after your sister's death?"—"No."

"Was any body else, besides Kent, concerned in your murder?"—"No."

"Can you, if you like, appear visibly to any one?"—"Yes."

"Will you do so?"—"Yes."

"Can you go out of this house?"—"Yes."

"Is it your intention to follow this child about every where?"—"Yes."

"Are you pleased in being asked these questions?"—"Yes."

"Does it ease your troubled soul?"—"Yes."

[Here there was heard a mysterious noise, which some wiseacre present compared to the fluttering of wings.]

"How long before your death did you tell your servant, Carrots, that you were poisoned? An hour?"—"Yes."

[Carrots, who was present, was appealed to; but she stated positively that such was not the fact, as the deceased was quite speechless an hour before her death. This shook the faith of some of the spectators, but the examination was allowed to continue.]

"How long did Carrots live with you?"—"Three or four days."

[Carrots was again appealed to, and said that this was true.]

"If Mr. Kent is arrested for this murder, will he confess?"—"Yes."

"Would your soul be at rest if he were hanged for it?"—"Yes."

"Will he be hanged for it?"—"Yes."

"How long a time first?"—"Three years."

"How many clergymen are there in this room?"—"Three."

"How many negroes?"—"Two."

"Is this watch (held up by one of the clergymen) white?"—"No."

"Is it yellow?"—"No."

"Is it blue?"—"No."

"Is it black?"—"Yes."

[The watch was in a black shagreen case.]

"At what time this morning will you take your departure?"

The answer to this question was four knocks, very distinctly heard by every person present; and accordingly, at four o'clock precisely the ghost took its departure to the Wheatsheaf public-house close by, where it frightened mine host and his lady almost out of their wits, by knocking in the ceiling right above their bed.

The rumour of these occurrences very soon spread over London, and every day Cock Lane was rendered impassable by the crowds of people who assembled round the house of the parish-clerk, in expectation of either seeing the ghost or of hearing the mysterious knocks. It was at last found necessary, so clamorous were they for admission within the haunted precincts, to admit those only who would pay a certain fee, an arrangement which was very convenient to the needy and money-loving Mr. Parsons. Indeed, things had taken a turn greatly to his satisfaction ; he not only had his revenge, but he made a profit out of it. The ghost, in consequence, played its antics every night, to the great amusement of many hundreds of people and the great perplexity of a still greater number.

Unhappily, however, for the parish-clerk, the ghost was induced to make some promises which were the means of utterly destroying its reputation. It promised, in answer to the questions of the Rev. Mr. Aldritch of Clerkenwell, that it would not only follow the little Miss Parsons wherever she went, but would also attend him, or any other gentleman, into the vault under St. John's Church, where the body of the murdered woman was deposited, and would there give notice of its presence by a distinct knock upon the coffin. As a preliminary, the girl was conveyed to the house of Mr. Aldritch near the church, where a large party of ladies and gentlemen, eminent for their acquirements, their rank, or their wealth, had assembled. About ten o'clock on the night of the first of February, the girl having been brought from Cock Lane in a coach, was put to bed by several ladies in the house of Mr. Aldritch ; a strict examination having been previously made that nothing was hidden in the bed-clothes. While the gentlemen in an adjoining chamber were deliberating whether they should proceed in a body to the vault, they were summoned into the bedroom by the ladies, who affirmed, in great alarm, that the ghost was come, and that they heard the knocks and scratches. The gentlemen entered accordingly, with a determination to suffer no deception. The little girl, on being asked whether she saw the ghost, replied, " No ; but she felt it on her back like a mouse." She was then required to put her hands out of bed, and they being held by some of the ladies, the spirit was summoned in the usual manner to answer, if it were in the room. The question was several times put with great solemnity ; but the customary knock was not heard in reply in the walls, neither was there any scratching. The ghost was then asked to render itself visible, but it did not choose to grant the request. It was next solicited to give some token of its presence by a sound of any sort, or by touching the hand or cheek of any lady or gentleman in the room ; but even with this request the ghost would not comply.

There was now a considerable pause, and one of the clergymen went downstairs to interrogate the father of the girl, who was waiting the result of the experiment. He positively denied that there was any deception, and even went so far as to say that he himself, upon one occasion, had seen and conversed with the awful ghost. This having been communicated to the company, it was unanimously resolved to give the ghost another trial; and the clergyman called out in a loud voice to the supposed spirit, that the gentleman to whom it had promised to appear in the vault was about to repair to that place, where he claimed the fulfilment of its promise. At one hour after midnight they all proceeded to the church, and the gentleman in question, with another, entered the vault alone, and took up their position alongside of the coffin of poor Fanny. The ghost was then summoned to appear, but it appeared not; it was summoned to knock, but it knocked not; it was summoned to scratch, but it scratched not; and the two retired from the vault, with a firm belief that the whole business was a deception practised by Parsons and his daughter. There were others, however, who did not wish to jump so hastily to a conclusion, and who suggested that they were perhaps trifling with this awful and supernatural being, which, being offended with them for their presumption, would not condescend to answer them. Again, after serious consultation, it was agreed on all hands that if the ghost answered any body at all, it would answer Mr. Kent, the supposed murderer; and he was accordingly requested to go down into the vault. He went with several others, and summoned the ghost to answer whether he had indeed poisoned her. There being no answer, the question was put by Mr. Aldritch, who conjured it, if it were indeed a spirit, to end their doubts, make a sign of its presence, and point out the guilty person. There being still no answer for the space of half an hour, during which time all these boobies waited with the most praiseworthy perseverance, they returned to the house of Mr. Aldritch, and ordered the girl to get up and dress herself. She was strictly examined, but persisted in her statement that she used no deception, and that the ghost had really appeared to her.

So many persons had, by their openly expressed belief of the reality of the visitation, identified themselves with it, that Parsons and his family were far from being the only persons interested in the continuance of the delusion. The result of the experiment convinced most people; but these were not to be convinced by any evidence, however positive, and they therefore spread abroad the rumour, that the ghost had not appeared in the vault because Mr. Kent had taken care beforehand to have the coffin removed. That gentleman, whose position was a very painful one, immediately procured competent witnesses, in whose presence the vault was entered, and the coffin of poor Fanny opened. Their depositions were then published; and Mr. Kent indicted Parsons and his wife, his daughter, Mary Frazer the servant, the Rev. Mr. Moor, and a tradesman, two of the most prominent patrons of the deception, for a conspiracy. The trial came on in the Court of King's Bench, on the 10th of July, before Lord Chief-Justice Mansfield, when, after an investigation which lasted twelve hours, the whole of the conspirators were found guilty. The Rev. Mr. Moor and his friend were severely reprimanded in open court, and recommended to make some pecuniary compensation to the prosecutor for the aspersions they had been instrumental in throwing upon his character. Parsons was sentenced to stand three times in the pillory, and to be imprisoned for two years; his wife to one year's, and his servant to six months' imprisonment in the Bridewell. A printer, who had been employed by them to publish an account of the proceedings for their profit, was also fined fifty pounds, and discharged.

The precise manner in which the deception was carried on has never been explained. The knocking in the wall appears to have been the work of Parsons' wife, while the scratching part of the business was left to the little girl. That any contrivance so clumsy could have deceived any body cannot fail to excite our wonder. But thus it always is. If two or three persons can only be found to take the lead in any absurdity, however great, there is sure to be plenty of imitators. Like sheep in a field, if one clears the stile, the rest will follow.

About ten years afterwards, London was again alarmed by the story of a haunted house. Stockwell, near Vauxhall, the scene of the antics of this new ghost, became almost as celebrated in the annals of superstition as Cock Lane. Mrs. Golding, an elderly lady, who resided alone with her servant, Anne Robinson, was sorely surprised on the evening of Twelfth-Day, 1772, to observe a most extraordinary commotion among her crockery. Cups and saucers rattled down the chimney—pots and pans were whirled downstairs, or through the windows; and hams, cheeses, and loaves of bread disported themselves upon the floor as if the devil were in them. This, at least, was the conclusion that Mrs. Golding came to; and being greatly alarmed, she invited some of her neighbours to stay with her, and protect her from the evil one. Their presence, however, did not put a stop to the insurrection of china, and every room in the house was in a short time strewed with the fragments. The chairs and tables joined, at last, in the tumult, and things looked altogether so serious and inexplicable, that the neighbours, dreading that the house itself would next be seized with a fit of motion, and tumble about their ears, left poor Mrs. Golding to bear the brunt of it by herself. The ghost in this case was solemnly remonstrated with, and urged to take its departure; but the demolition continuing as great as before, Mrs. Golding finally made up her mind to quit the house altogether. She took refuge with Anne Robinson in the house of a neighbour; but his glass and crockery being immediately subjected to the same persecution, he was reluctantly compelled to give her notice to quit. The old lady thus forced back to her own house, endured the disturbance for some days longer, when suspecting that Anne Robinson was the cause of all the mischief, she dismissed her from her service. The extraordinary appearances immediately ceased, and were never afterwards renewed; a fact which is of itself sufficient to point out the real disturber. A long time afterwards, Anne Robinson confessed the whole matter to the Reverend Mr. Brayfield. This gentleman confided the story to Mr. Hone, who has published an explanation of the mystery. Anne, it appears, was anxious to have a clear house, to carry on an intrigue with her lover, and resorted to this trick to effect her purpose. She placed the china on the shelves in such a manner that it fell on the slightest motion, and attached horse-hairs to other articles, so that she could jerk them down from an adjoining room without being perceived by any one. She was exceedingly dexterous at this sort of work, and would have proved a formidable rival to many a juggler by profession. A full explanation of the whole affair may be found in the *Every-day Book*.

The latest instance of the popular panic occasioned by a house supposed to be haunted, occurred in Scotland, in the winter of the year 1838. On the 5th of December, the inmates of the farm-house of Baldarroch, in the district of Banchory, Aberdeenshire, were alarmed by observing a great number of sticks, pebble-stones, and clods of earth flying about their yard and premises. They endeavoured, but in vain, to discover who was the delinquent; and the shower of stones continuing for five days in succession, they came at last to the conclusion that the devil and his imps were alone the cause of it. The rumour soon spread over all that part of the country, and hundreds of persons came from far and near to witness the antics of the devils of Baldarroch. After the fifth day, the shower of clods and stones ceased on the outside of the premises, and the scene shifted to the interior. Spoons, knives, plates, mustard-pots, rolling-pins, and flat-irons appeared suddenly endued with the power of self-motion, and were whirled from room to room, and rattled down the chimneys in a manner which nobody could account for. The lid of a mustard-pot was put into a cupboard by the servant-girl in the presence of scores of people, and in a few minutes afterwards came bouncing down the chimney, to the consternation of every body. There was also a tremendous knocking at the doors and on the roof, and pieces of stick and pebble-stones rattled against the windows and broke them. The whole neighbourhood was a scene of alarm; and not only the vulgar, but persons of education, respectable farmers, within a circle of twenty miles, expressed their belief in the supernatural character of these events, and offered up devout prayers to be preserved from the machinations of the Evil One. The note of fear being once sounded, the visitors, as is generally the case in all tales of wonder, strove with each other who should witness the most extraordinary occurrences; and within a week, it was generally believed in the parishes of Banchory-Ternan, Drumoak, Durris, Kincardine-O'Neil, and all the circumjacent districts of Mearns and Aberdeenshire, that the devil had been seen in the act of hammering upon the house-top of Baldarroch. One old man asserted positively that, one night, after having been to see the strange gambols of the knives and mustard-pots, he met the phantom of a great black man, " who wheeled round his head with a whizzing noise, making a wind about his ears that almost blew his bonnet off," and that he was haunted by him in this manner for three miles. It was also affirmed and believed, that all horses and dogs that approached this enchanted ground were immediately affected; that a gentleman, slow of faith, had been cured of his incredulity by meeting the butter-churn jumping in at the door as he himself was going out; that the roofs of houses had been torn off, and that several ricks in the corn-yard had danced a quadrille together, to the sound of the devil's bagpipes re-echoing from the mountain-tops. The women in the family of the persecuted farmer of Baldarroch also kept their tongues in perpetual motion; swelling with their strange stories the tide of popular wonder. The goodwife herself, and all her servants, said that, whenever they went to bed, they were attacked with stones and other missiles, some of which came below the blankets and gently tapped their toes. One evening, a shoe suddenly darted across a garret where some labourers were sitting, and one of the men, who attempted to catch it, swore positively that it was so hot and heavy he was unable to hold it. It was also said that the bearbeater (a sort of mortar used to bruise barley in)—an object of such weight that it requires several men to move it —spontaneously left the barn and flew over the house-top, alighting at the feet of one of the servant-maids, and hitting her, but without hurting her in the least, or even causing her any alarm; it being a fact well known to her, that all objects thus thrown about by the devil lost their specific gravity, and could harm nobody, even though they fell upon a person's head.

Among the persons drawn to Baldarroch by these occurrences were the heritor, the minister, and all the elders of the Kirk, under whose superintendence an investigation was immediately commenced. Their proceedings were not promulgated for some days; and, in the mean time, rumour continued to travel through all the Highlands, magnifying each mysterious incident the farther it got from home. It was said, that when the goodwife put her potato-pot on the fire, each potato, as the water boiled, changed into a demon, and grinned horribly at her as she lifted the lid; that not only chairs and tables, but carrots and turnips, skipped along the floor in the merriest manner imaginable; that shoes and boots went through all the evolutions of the Highland fling without any visible wearers directing their motions; and that a piece of meat detached itself from the hook on which it hung in the pantry, and placed itself before the fire, whence all the efforts of the people of the house were unable to remove it until it was thoroughly roasted; and that it then flew up the chimney with a tremendous bang. At Baldarroch itself the belief was not quite so extravagant; but the farmer was so convinced that the devil and his imps were alone the cause of all the disturbance, that he travelled a distance of forty miles to an old conjuror, named Willie Foreman, to induce him, for a handsome fee, to remove the enchantment from his property. There were, of course, some sensible and educated people, who, after stripping the stories circulated of their exaggeration, attributed all the rest to one or other of two causes : first, that some gipsies, or strolling mendicants, hidden in the neighbouring plantation, were amusing themselves by working on the credulity of the country people; or, secondly, that the inmates of Baldarroch carried on this deception themselves, for some reason or other, which was not very clear to any body. The last opinion gained but few believers, as the farmer and his family were much respected; and so many persons had, in the most open manner, expressed their belief in the supernatural agency, that they did not like to stultify themselves by confessing that they had been deceived.

At last, after a fortnight's continuance of the noises, the whole trick was discovered. The two servant lasses were strictly examined, and then committed to prison. It appeared that they were alone at the bottom of the whole affair, and that the extraordinary alarm and credulity of their master and mistress, in the first instance, and of the neighbours and country people afterwards, made their task comparatively easy. A little common dexterity was all they had used ; and, being themselves unsuspected, they swelled the alarm by the wonderful stories they invented. It was they who loosened the bricks in the chimneys, and placed the dishes in such a manner on the shelves, that they fell on the slightest motion. In short, they played the same tricks as those used by the servant girl at Stockwell, with the same results, and for the same purpose—the gratification of a love of mischief. They were no sooner secured in the county gaol than the noises ceased, and most people were convinced that human agency alone had worked all the wonder. Some few of the most devoutly superstitious still held out in their first belief, and refused to listen to any explanation.

These tales of haunted houses, especially those of the last and present century, however they may make us blush for popular folly, are yet gratifying in their results; for they shew that society has made a vast improvement. Had Parsons and his wife, and the other contrivers of the Cock-Lane deception, lived two hundred years earlier, they would not perhaps have found a greater number of dupes, but they would have been hanged as witches, instead of being imprisoned as vagabonds. The ingenious Anne Robinson and the sly lasses of Baldarroch would doubtless have met a similar fate. Thus it is pleasant to reflect, that though there may be as much folly and credulity in the world as ever in one class of society, there is more wisdom and mercy in another than ever were known before. Lawgivers, by blotting from the statute-book the absurd or sanguinary enactments of their predecessors, have made one step towards teaching the people. It is to be hoped that the day is not far distant when lawgivers will teach the people by some more direct means, and prevent the recurrence of delusions like these, and many worse, which might be cited, by securing to every child born within their dominions an education in accordance with the advancing state of civilisation. If ghosts and witches are not yet altogether exploded, it is the fault, not so much of the ignorant people, as of the law and the government that have neglected to enlighten them.

POPULAR FOLLIES OF GREAT CITIES.

La faridondaine—la faridondon,
Vive la faridondaine !—*Beranger*.

 HE popular humours of a great city are a never-failing source of amusement to the man whose sympathies are hospitable enough to embrace all his kind, and who, refined though he may be himself, will not sneer at the humble wit or grotesque peculiarities of the boozing mechanic, the squalid beggar, the vicious urchin, and all the motley group of the idle, the reckless, and the imitative that swarm in the alleys and broadways of a metropolis. He who walks through a great city to find subjects for weeping, may find plenty at every corner to wring his heart; but let such a man walk on his course, and enjoy his grief alone—we are not of those who would accompany him. The miseries of us poor earth-dwellers gain no alleviation from the sympathy of those who merely hunt them out to be pathetic over them. The weeping philosopher too often impairs his eyesight by his woe, and becomes unable from his tears to see the remedies for the evils which he deplores. Thus it will often be found that the man of no tears is the truest philanthropist, as he is the best physician who wears a cheerful face, even in the worst of cases.

So many pens have been employed to point out the miseries, and so many to condemn the crimes and vices, and more serious follies of the multitude, that ours shall not increase the number, at least in this chapter. Our present task shall be less ungracious, and wandering through the busy haunts of great cities, we shall seek only for amusement, and note as we pass a few of the harmless follies and whimsies of the poor.

And, first of all, walk where we will, we cannot help hearing from every side a phrase repeated with delight, and received with laughter, by men with hard hands and dirty faces, by saucy butcher-lads and errand-boys, by loose women, by hackney-coachmen, cabriolet drivers, and idle fellows who loiter at the corners of streets. Not one utters this phrase without producing a laugh from all within hearing. It seems applicable to every circumstance, and is the universal answer to every question; in short, it is the favourite slang phrase of the day, a phrase that, while its brief season of popularity lasts, throws a dash of fun and frolicsomeness over the existence of squalid poverty and ill-requited labour, and gives them reason to laugh as well as their more fortunate fellows in a higher stage of society.

London is peculiarly fertile in this sort of phrases, which spring up suddenly, no one knows exactly in what spot, and pervade the whole population in a few hours, no one knows how. Many years ago the favourite phrase (for, though but a monosyllable, it was a phrase in itself) was Quoz. This odd word took the fancy of the multitude in an extraordinary degree, and very soon acquired an almost boundless meaning. When vulgar wit wished to mark its incredulity, and raise a laugh at the same time, there was no resource so sure as this popular piece of slang. When a man was asked a favour which he did not choose to grant, he marked his sense of the suitor's unparalleled presumption by exclaiming *Quoz!* When a mischievous urchin wished to annoy a passenger, and create mirth for his comrades, he looked him in the face, and cried out *Quoz!* and the exclamation never failed in its object. When a disputant was desirous of throwing a doubt upon the veracity of his opponent, and getting summarily rid of an argument which he could not overturn, he uttered the word *Quoz,* with a contemptuous curl of his lip and an impatient shrug of his shoulders. The universal monosyllable conveyed all his meaning, and not only told his opponent that he lied, but that he erred egregiously if he thought that any one was such a nincompoop as to believe him. Every alehouse resounded with *Quoz;* every street-corner was noisy with it, and every wall for miles around was chalked with it.

But, like all other earthly things, *Quoz* had its season, and passed away as suddenly as it arose, never again to be the pet and the idol of the populace. A new claimant drove it from its place, and held undisputed sway, till, in its turn, it was hurled from its pre-eminence, and a successor appointed in its stead.

" *What a shocking bad hat !*" was the phrase that was next in vogue. No sooner had it become universal, than thousands of idle but sharp eyes were on the watch for the passenger whose hat shewed any signs, however slight, of ancient service. Immediately the cry arose, and, like the war-whoop of the Indians, was repeated by a hundred discordant throats. He was a wise man who, finding himself under these circumstances "the observed of all observers," bore his honours meekly. He who shewed symptoms of ill-feeling at the imputations cast upon his hat, only brought upon himself redoubled notice. The mob soon perceive whether a man is irritable, and, if of their own class, they love to make sport of him. When such a man, and with such a hat, passed in those days through a crowded neighbourhood, he might think himself fortunate if his annoyances were confined to the shouts and cries of the populace. The obnoxious hat was often snatched from his head and thrown into the gutter by some practical joker, and then raised, covered with mud, upon the end of a stick, for the admiration of the spectators, who held their sides with laughter, and exclaimed in the pauses of their mirth, " *Oh, what a shocking bad hat !*" " *What a shocking bad hat !*" Many a nervous poor man, whose purse could but ill spare the outlay, doubtless purchased a new hat before the time, in order to avoid exposure in this manner.

The origin of this singular saying, which made fun for the metropolis for months, is not involved in the same obscurity as that which shrouds the origin of *Quoz* and some others. There had been a hotly contested election for the borough of Southwark, and one of the candidates was an eminent hatter. This gentleman, in canvassing the electors, adopted a somewhat professional mode of conciliating their good-will, and of bribing them without letting them perceive that they were bribed. Whenever he called upon or met a voter whose hat was not of the best material, or, being so, had seen its best days, he invariably said, " *What a shocking bad hat you have got; call at my warehouse, and you shall have a new one !*" Upon the day of election this circumstance was remembered, and his opponents made the most of it, by inciting the crowd to keep up an incessant cry of " *What a shocking bad hat !*" all the time the honourable candidate was addressing them. From Southwark the phrase spread over all London, and reigned for a time the supreme slang of the season.

Hookey Walker, derived from the chorus of a popular ballad, was also high in favour at one time, and served, like its predecessor *Quoz,* to answer all questions. In the course of time the latter word alone became the favourite, and was uttered with a peculiar drawl upon the first syllable, and a sharp turn upon the last. If a lively servant girl was importuned for a kiss by a fellow she did not care about, she cocked her little nose, and cried " *Walker !*" If a dustman asked his friend for the loan of a shilling, and his friend was either unable or unwilling to accommodate him, the probable answer he would receive was, " *Walker !* "   If a drunken man was reeling about the streets, and a boy pulled his coat-tails, or a man knocked his hat over his eyes to make fun of him, the joke was always accompanied by the same exclamation. This lasted for two or three months, and "*Walker !*" walked off the stage, never more to be revived for the entertainment of that or any future generation.

The next phrase was a most preposterous one. Who invented it, how it arose, or where it was first heard, are alike unknown. Nothing about it is certain, but that for months it was *the* slang *par excellence* of the Londoners, and afforded them a vast gratification. " *There he goes with his eye out !* " or " *There she goes with her eye out !*" as the sex of the party alluded to might be, was in the mouth of every body who knew the town. The sober part of the community were as much puzzled by this unaccountable saying as the vulgar were delighted with it.   The wise thought it very foolish, but the many thought it very funny, and the idle amused themselves by chalking it upon walls, or scribbling it upon monuments. But "all that's bright must fade," even in slang.   The people grew tired of their hobby, and " *There he goes with his eye out !* " was heard no more in its accustomed haunts.

Another very odd phrase came into repute in a brief space afterwards, in the form of the impertinent and not universally apposite query, "*Has your mother sold her mangle ?*" But its popularity was not of that boisterous and cordial kind which ensures a long continuance of favour. What tended to impede its progress was, that it could not be well applied to the older portions of society.   It consequently ran but a brief career, and then sank into oblivion. Its successor enjoyed a more extended fame, and laid its foundations so deep, that years and changing fashions have not sufficed to eradicate it.   This phrase was "*Flare up !*" and it is, even now, a colloquialism in common use. It took its rise in the time of the Reform riots, when Bristol was nearly half burned by the infuriated populace. The flames were said to have *flared up* in the devoted city. Whether there was any thing peculiarly captivating in the sound, or in the idea of these words, is hard to say ; but whatever was the reason, it tickled the mob-fancy mightily, and drove all other slang out of the field before it. Nothing was to be heard all over London but "*flare up !*" It answered all questions, settled all disputes, was applied to all persons, all things, and all circumstances, and became suddenly the most comprehensive phrase in the English language.   The man who had overstepped the bounds of decorum in his speech was said to have *flared up ;* he who had paid visits too repeated to the gin-shop, and got damaged in consequence, had *flared up*. To put one's self into a passion; to stroll out on a nocturnal frolic, and alarm a neighbourhood, or to create a disturbance in any shape, was to *flare up*. A lover's quarrel was a *flare up;* so was a boxing-match between two blackguards in the streets; and the preachers of sedition and revolution recommended the English nation to *flare up*, like the French. So great a favourite was the word, that people loved to repeat it for its very sound. They delighted apparently in hearing their own organs articulate it; and labouring men, when none who could respond to the call were within hearing, would often startle the aristocratic echoes of the West by the well-known slang phrase of the East. Even in the dead hours of the night, the ears of those who watched late, or who could not sleep, were saluted with the same sound. The drunkard reeling home shewed that he was still a man and a citizen by calling *"flare up!"* in the pauses of his hiccough. Drink had deprived him of the power of arranging all other ideas; his intellect was sunk to the level of the brute's; but he clung to humanity by the one last link of the popular cry. While he could vociferate that sound, he had rights as an Englishman, and would not sleep in a gutter, like a dog! Onwards he went, disturbing quiet streets and comfortable people by his whoop, till exhausted nature could support him no more, and he rolled powerless into the road. When, in due time afterwards, the policeman stumbled upon him as he lay, that guardian of the peace turned the full light of his lantern on his face, and exclaimed, " Here's a poor devil who has been *flaring up!*" Then came the stretcher, on which the victim of deep potations was carried to the watch-house, and pitched into a dirty cell, among a score of wretches about as far gone as himself, who saluted their new comrade by a loud, long shout of *"flare up!"*

So universal was this phrase, and so enduring seemed its popularity, that a speculator, who knew not the evanescence of slang, established a weekly newspaper under its name. But he was like the man who built his house upon the sand; his foundation gave way under him, and the phrase and the newspaper were washed into the mighty sea of the things that were. The people grew at last weary of the monotony, and *" flare up"* became vulgar even among them. Gradually it was left to little boys who did not know the world, and in process of time sank altogether into neglect. It is now heard no more as a piece of popular slang; but the words are still used to signify any sudden outburst either of fire, disturbance, or ill-nature.

The next phrase that enjoyed the favour of the million was less concise, and seems to have been originally aimed against precocious youths who gave themselves the airs of manhood before their time. " *Does your mother know you're out?*" was the provoking query addressed to young men of more than reasonable swagger, who smoked cigars in the streets, and wore false whiskers to look irresistible. We have seen many a conceited fellow who could not suffer a woman to pass him without staring her out of countenance, reduced at once into his natural insignificance by the mere utterance of this phrase. Apprentice lads and shopmen in their Sunday clothes held the words in abhorrence, and looked fierce when they were applied to them. Altogether the phrase had a very salutary effect, and in a thousand instances shewed young Vanity that it was not half so pretty and engaging as it thought itself. What rendered it so provoking was the doubt it implied as to the capability of self-guidance possessed by the individual to whom it was addressed. " *Does your mother know you're out?*" was a query of mock concern and solicitude, implying regret and concern that one so young and inexperienced in the ways of a great city should be allowed to wander abroad without the guidance of a parent. Hence the great wrath of those who verged on manhood, but had not reached it, whenever they were made the subject of it. Even older heads did not like it; and the heir of a ducal house, and inheritor of a warrior's name, to whom they were applied by a cabriolet-driver who was ignorant of his rank, was so indignant at the affront, that he summoned the offender before the magisterial bench. The fellow had wished to impose upon his lordship by asking double the fare he was entitled to; and when his lordship resisted the demand, he was insultingly asked, " if his mother knew he was out?" All the drivers on the stand joined in the query, and his lordship was fain to escape their laughter by walking away with as much haste as his dignity would allow. The man pleaded ignorance that his customer was a lord, but offended justice fined him for his mistake.

When this phrase had numbered its appointed days, it died away like its predecessors, and " *Who are you?*" reigned in its stead. This new favourite, like a mushroom, seems to have sprung up in a night, or, like a frog in Cheapside, to have come down in a sudden shower. One day it was unheard, unknown, uninvented; the next it pervaded London. Every alley resounded with it; every highway was musical with it,

> " And street to street, and lane to lane flung back
> The one unvarying cry."

The phrase was uttered quickly, and with a sharp sound upon the first and last words, leaving the middle one little more than an aspiration. Like all its compeers which had been extensively popular, it was applicable to almost every variety of circumstance. The lovers of a plain answer to a plain question did not like it at all. Insolence made use of it to give offence; ignorance to avoid exposing itself; and waggery to create laughter. Every new comer into an alehouse tap-room was asked unceremoniously, " *Who are you?*" and if he looked foolish, scratched his head, and did not know what to reply, shouts of boisterous merriment resounded on every side. An authoritative disputant was not unfrequently put down, and presumption of every kind checked by the same query. When its popularity was at its height, a gentleman, feeling the hand of a thief in his pocket, turned suddenly round and caught him in the act, exclaiming, " *Who are you?*" The mob which gathered round applauded to the very echo, and thought it the most capital joke they had ever heard, the very acmé of wit, the very essence of humour. Another circumstance of a similar kind gave an additional fillip to the phrase, and infused new life and vigour into it just as it was dying away. The scene occurred in the chief criminal court in the kingdom. A prisoner stood at the bar; the offence with which he had been charged was clearly proved against him; his counsel had been heard, not in his defence, but in extenuation, insisting upon his previous good life and character as reasons for the lenity of the court. " And where are your witnesses?" inquired the learned judge who presided. " Please you, my lord, I knows the prisoner at the bar, and a more honester feller never breathed," said a rough voice in the gallery. The officers of the court looked aghast, and the strangers tittered with ill-suppressed laughter. " *Who are you?*" said the judge, looking suddenly up, but with imperturbable gravity. The court was convulsed; the titter broke out into a laugh; and it was several minutes before silence and decorum could be restored. When the ushers recovered their self-possession, they made diligent search for the profane transgressor; but he was not to be found. Nobody knew him; nobody had seen him. After a while the business of the court again proceeded. The next prisoner brought up for trial augured favourably of his prospects when he learned that the solemn lips of the representative of justice had uttered the popular phrase, as if he felt and appreciated it. There was no fear that such a judge would use undue severity. His heart was with the people; he understood their language and their manners, and would make allowances for the temptations which drove them into crime. So thought many of the prisoners, if we may infer it from the fact that the learned judge suddenly acquired an immense increase of popularity. The praise of his wit was in every mouth, and " *Who are you?*" renewed its lease, and remained in possession of public favour for another term in consequence.

But it must not be supposed that there were no interregna between the dominion of one slang phrase and another. They did not arise in one long line of unbroken succession, but shared with song the possession of popular favour. Thus, when the people were in the mood for music, slang advanced its claims to no purpose ; and when they were inclined for slang, the sweet voice of music wooed them in vain. About thirty years ago London resounded with one chorus, with the love of which every body seemed to be smitten. Girls and boys, young men and old, maidens and wives and widows, were all alike musical. There was an absolute mania for singing ; and the worst of it was, that, like good Father Philip in the romance of *The Monastery*, they seemed utterly unable to change their tune. " Cherry ripe !" " Cherry ripe !" was the universal cry of all the idle in the town. Every unmelodious voice gave utterance to it ; every crazy fiddle, every cracked flute, every wheezy pipe, every street-organ was heard in the same strain, until studious and quiet men stopped their ears in desperation, or fled miles away into the fields or woodlands to be at peace. This plague lasted for a twelvemonth, until the very name of cherries became an abomination in the land. At last the excitement wore itself away, and the tide of favour set in a new direction. Whether it was another song or a slang phrase is difficult to determine at this distance of time ; but certain it is, that very shortly afterwards people went mad upon a dramatic subject, and nothing was to be heard of but " *Tommy and Jerry.*" Verbal wit had amused the multitude long enough, and they became more practical in their recreation. Every youth on the town was seized with the fierce desire of distinguishing himself by knocking down the " *charlies,*" being locked up all night in a watch-house, or kicking up a row among loose women and blackguard men in the low dens of St. Giles's. Imitative boys vied with their elders in similar exploits, until this unworthy passion (for such it was) had lasted, like other follies, its appointed time, and the town became merry after another fashion. It was next thought the height of vulgar wit to answer all questions by placing the point of the thumb upon the tip of the nose, and twirling the fingers in the air. If one man wished to insult or annoy another, he had only to make use of this cabalistic sign in his face, and his object was accomplished. At every street-corner where a group was assembled, the spectator who was curious enough to observe their movements would be sure to see the fingers of some of them at their noses, either as a mark of incredulity, surprise, refusal, or mockery, before he had watched two minutes. There is some remnant of this absurd custom to be seen to this day ; but it is thought low even among the vulgar.

About sixteen years ago, London became again most preposterously musical. The *vox populi* wore itself hoarse by singing the praises of "The Sea, the Sea!" If a stranger (and a philosopher) had walked through London, and listened to the universal chorus, he might have constructed a very pretty theory upon the love of the English for the sea-service, and our acknowledged superiority over all other nations upon that element. "No wonder," he might have said, "that this people is invincible upon the ocean. The love of it mixes with their daily thoughts; they celebrate it even in the market-place; their street-minstrels excite charity by it; and high and low, young and old, male and female, chant *Io pæans* in its praise. Love is not honoured in the national songs of this warlike race—Bacchus is no god to them; they are men of sterner mould, and think only of ' the Sea, the Sea!' and the means of conquering upon it."

Such would, doubtless, have been his impression if he had taken the evidence only of his ears. Alas, in those days for the refined ears that *were* musical! great was their torture when discord, with its thousand diversities of tone, struck up this appalling anthem—there was no escape from it. The migratory minstrels of Savoy caught the strain, and pealed it down the long vistas of quiet streets, till their innermost and snuggest apartments re-echoed with the sound. Men were obliged to endure this crying evil for full six months, wearied to desperation, and made *sea-*sick on the dry land.

Several other songs sprang up in due succession afterwards, but none of them, with the exception of one, entitled "All round my hat," enjoyed any extraordinary share of favour, until an American actor introduced a vile song called "Jim Crow." The singer sang his verses in appropriate costume, with grotesque gesticulations, and a sudden whirl of his body at the close of each verse. It took the taste of the town immediately, and for months the ears of orderly people were stunned by the senseless chorus—

> " Turn about and wheel about,
> And do just so—
> Turn about and wheel about,
> And jump, Jim Crow !"

Street-minstrels blackened their faces in order to give proper effect to the verses; and fatherless urchins, who had to choose between thieving and singing for their livelihood, took the latter course, as likely to be the more profitable, as long as the public taste remained in that direction. The uncouth dance, its accompaniment, might be seen in its full perfection on market nights in any great thoroughfare; and the words of the song might be heard, piercing above all the din and buzz of the ever-moving multitude. He, the calm observer, who during the hey-day popularity of this doggrel,

> " Sate beside the public way,
> Thick strewn with summer dust, and saw the stream
> Of people there was hurrying to and fro,
> Numerous as gnats upon the evening gleam,"

might have exclaimed with Shelley, that

> " The million, with fierce song and maniac dance,
> Did rage around."

The philosophic theorist we have already supposed soliloquising upon the English character, and forming his opinion of it from their exceeding love for a sea-song, might, if he had again dropped suddenly into London, have formed another very plausible theory to account for our unremitting efforts for the abolition of the slave-trade. " Benevolent people ! " he might have said, " how unbounded are your sympathies ! Your unhappy brethren of Africa, differing from you only in the colour of their skins, are so dear to you, and you be-grudge so little the twenty millions you have paid on their behalf, that you love to have a memento of them continually in your sight. Jim Crow is the representative of that injured race, and as such is the idol of your populace ! See how they all sing his praises ! how they imitate his peculiarities ! how they repeat his name in their moments of leisure and relaxation ! They even carve images of him to adorn their hearths, that his cause and his sufferings may never be forgotten ! Oh, philanthropic England ! oh, vanguard of civili-sation !"

Such are a few of the peculiarities of the London multitude, when no riot, no execution, no murder, no balloon, disturbs the even cur-rent of their thoughts. These are the whimsies of the mass—the harmless follies by which they unconsciously endeavour to lighten the load of care which presses upon their existence. The wise man, even though he smile at them, will not altogether withhold his sym-pathy, and will say, " Let them enjoy their slang phrases and their choruses if they will ; and if they cannot be happy, at least let them be merry." To the Englishman, as well as to the Frenchman of whom Beranger sings, there may be some comfort in so small a thing as a song, and we may own with him that

> " Au peuple attristé
> Ce qui rendra la gaîté,
> C'est la GAUDRIOLE !
> O gué !
> C'est la GAUDRIOLE !"

SHERWOOD FOREST.

POPULAR ADMIRATION OF GREAT THIEVES.

Jack. Where shall we find such another set of practical philosophers, who,
to a man, are above the fear of death!
Wat. Sound men and true!
Robin. Of tried courage and indefatigable industry!
Ned. Who is there here that would not die for his friend?
Harry. Who is there here that would betray him for his interest?
Mat. Shew me a gang of courtiers that could say as much!

Dialogue of Thieves in the Beggar's Opera.

WHETHER it be that the multitude, feeling the pangs of poverty,
sympathise with the daring and ingenious depredators who take away
the rich man's superfluity, or whether it be the interest that mankind
in general feel for the records of perilous adventure, it is certain that
the populace of all countries look with admiration upon great and
successful thieves. Perhaps both these causes combine to invest
their career with charms in the popular eye. Almost every country

in Europe has its traditional thief, whose exploits are recorded with
all the graces of poetry, and whose trespasses

> " Are cited up in rhymes,
> And sung by children in succeeding times."*

Those travellers who have made national manners and character-
istics their peculiar study, have often observed and remarked upon
this feeling. The learned Abbé le Blanc, who resided for some time
in England at the commencement of the eighteenth century, says, in
his amusing letters on the English and French nations, that he continually met with Englishmen who were not less vain in boasting of
the success of their highwaymen than of the bravery of their troops.
Tales of their address, their cunning, or their generosity, were in the
mouths of every body, and a noted thief was a kind of hero in high
repute. He adds that the mob, in all countries, being easily moved,
look in general with concern upon criminals going to the gallows;
but an English mob looked upon such scenes with extraordinary interest: they delighted to see them go through their last trials with
resolution, and applauded those who were insensible enough to die
as they had lived, braving the justice both of God and men : such, he
might have added, as the noted robber Macpherson, of whom the old
ballad says :

> " Sae rantingly, sae wantonly,
> Sae dauntingly gaed he :
> He played a spring, and danced it round
> Beneath the gallows tree."

Among these traditional thieves the most noted in England, or
perhaps in any country, is Robin Hood, a name which popular affection has encircled with a peculiar halo. " He robbed the rich to give
to the poor;" and his reward has been an immortality of fame, a
tithe of which would be thought more than sufficient to recompense
a benefactor of his species. Romance and poetry have been emulous
to make him all their own; and the forest of Sherwood, in which he
roamed with his merry men, armed with their long bows, and clad
in Lincoln green, has become the resort of pilgrims, and a classic spot
sacred to his memory. The few virtues he had, which would have en-
sured him no praise if he had been an honest man, have been blazoned
forth by popular renown during seven successive centuries, and will
never be forgotten while the English tongue endures. His charity to
the poor, and his gallantry and respect for women, have made him the
pre-eminent thief of all the world.

Among English thieves of a later date, who has not heard of

* Shakspeare's *Rape of Lucretia.*

Claude Duval, Dick Turpin, Jonathan Wild, and Jack Sheppard, those knights of the road and of the town, whose peculiar chivalry formed at once the dread and the delight of England during the eighteenth century? Turpin's fame is unknown to no portion of the male population of England after they have attained the age of ten. His wondrous ride from London to York has endeared him to the imagination of millions; his cruelty in placing an old woman upon a fire, to force her to tell him where she had hidden her money, is regarded as a good joke; and his proud bearing upon the scaffold is looked upon as a virtuous action. The Abbé le Blanc, writing in 1737, says he was continually entertained with stories of Turpin—how, when he robbed gentlemen, he would generously leave them enough to continue their journey, and exact a pledge from them never to inform against him, and how scrupulous such gentlemen were in keeping their word. He was one day told a story with which the relator was in the highest degree delighted. Turpin, or some other noted robber, stopped a man whom he knew to be very rich, with the usual salutation—"Your money or your life!" but not finding more than five or six guineas about him, he took the liberty of entreating him, in the most affable manner, never to come out so ill-provided; adding that, if he fell in with him, and he had no more than such a paltry sum, he would give him a good licking. Another story, told by one of Turpin's admirers, was of a robbery he had committed upon a Mr. C. near Cambridge. He took from this gentleman his watch, his snuff-box, and all his money but two shillings, and, before he left him, required his word of honour that he would not cause him to be pursued or brought before a justice. The promise being given, they both parted very courteously. They afterwards met at Newmarket, and renewed their acquaintance. Mr. C. kept his word religiously; he not only refrained from giving Turpin into custody, but made a boast that he had fairly won some of his money back again in an honest way. Turpin offered to bet with him on some favourite horse, and Mr. C. accepted the wager with as good a grace as he could have done from the best gentleman in England. Turpin lost his bet and paid it immediately, and was so smitten with the generous behaviour of Mr. C., that he told him how deeply he regretted that the trifling affair which had happened between them did not permit them to drink together. The narrator of this anecdote was quite proud that England was the birthplace of such a highwayman.*

---

* The Abbé, in the second volume, in the letter No. 79, addressed to Monsieur de Buffon, gives the following curious particulars of the robbers of 1737, which are not without interest at this day, if it were only to shew the vast improvement which has taken place since that period. "It is usual in travelling to put ten or a dozen guineas in a separate pocket, as a tribute to the first that comes to demand them; the right of

Not less familiar to the people of England is the career of Jack Sheppard, as brutal a ruffian as ever disgraced his country, but who has claims upon the popular admiration which are very generally acknowledged. He did not, like Robin Hood, plunder the rich to relieve the poor, nor rob with an uncouth sort of courtesy, like Turpin; but he escaped from Newgate with the fetters on his limbs. This achievement, more than once repeated, has encircled his felon brow with the wreath of immortality, and made him quite a pattern thief among the populace. He was no more than twenty-three years of age at the time of his execution, and he died much pitied by the crowd. His adventures were the sole topics of conversation for months; the print-shops were filled with his effigies, and a fine painting of him was made by Sir Richard Thornhill. The following complimentary verses to the artist appeared in the *British Journal* of November 28th, 1724:

> " Thornhill! 'tis thine to gild with fame
> Th' obscure, and raise the humble name;
> To make the form elude the grave,
> And Sheppard from oblivion save!
>
> Apelles Alexander drew—
> Cæsar is to Aurelius due;
> Cromwell in Lilly's works doth shine,
> And Sheppard, Thornhill, lives in thine !"

This was a very equivocal sort of compliment, and might have meant, that if Apelles were worthy to paint a monarch, Thornhill was worthy to paint a thief. But the artist did not view it in that light, nor did the public; for they considered the verses to be very neat, pointed, and flattering. So high was Jack's fame, that he was thought a very fit subject for the stage; and a pantomime entertainment, called *Harlequin Jack Sheppard*, was devised by one Thurmond, and brought out with considerable success at Drury Lane

passport, which custom has established here in favour of the robbers, who are almost the only highway surveyors in England, has made this necessary; and accordingly the English call these fellows the 'Gentlemen of the Road,' the government letting them exercise their jurisdiction upon travellers without giving them any great molestation. To say the truth, they content themselves with only taking the money of those who obey without disputing; but notwithstanding their boasted humanity, the lives of those who endeavour to get away are not always safe. They are very strict and severe in levying their impost; and if a man has not wherewithal to pay them, he may run the chance of getting himself knocked on the head for his poverty.

" About fifteen years ago, these robbers, with the view of maintaining their rights, fixed up papers at the doors of rich people about London, expressly forbidding all persons, of whatsoever quality or condition, from going out of town without ten guineas and a watch about them, on pain of death. In bad times, when there is little or nothing to be got on the roads, these fellows assemble in gangs, to raise contributions even in London itself, and the watchmen seldom trouble themselves to interfere with them in their vocation."

Theatre. All the scenes were painted from nature, including the public-house that the robber frequented in Clare Market, and the condemned cell from which he had made his escape in Newgate.* The Rev. Mr. Villette, the editor of the *Annals of Newgate*, published in 1754, relates a curious sermon, which he says a friend of his heard delivered by a street-preacher about the time of Jack's execution. The orator, after animadverting on the great care men took of their bodies, and the little care they bestowed upon their souls, continued as follows, by way of exemplifying the position : — " We have a remarkable instance of this in a notorious malefactor, well

* Since the publication of the first edition of this volume, Jack Sheppard's adventures have been revived. A novel upon the real or fabulous history of the burglar has afforded, by its extraordinary popularity, a further exemplification of the allegations in the text. The *Sixth Report of the Inspector of Prisons for the Northern Districts of England* contains a mass of information upon the pernicious effect of such romances, and of the dramas founded upon them. The Inspector examined several boys attending the prison school in the New Bailey at Manchester, from whose evidence the following passages bearing upon the subject are extracted :

" J. L. (aged 14). The first time I was ever at the theatre was to see *Jack Sheppard*. There were two or three boys near to the house who were going, and they asked me. I took sixpence from the money I used to lay up weekly for clothes. The next time I went, which was the week after, I borrowed the money from a boy ; I returned it to him the Saturday after. I then went many times. I took the money from my mother out of her pocket as she was sitting down, and I beside her. There was more than sixpence in her pocket. I got a great love for the theatre, and stole from people often to get there. *I thought this Jack Sheppard was a clever fellow* for making his escape and robbing his master. *If I could get out of gaol, I think I should be as clever as him:* but, after all his exploits, he got done at last. I have had the book out of a library at Dole Field. I had paid two-pence a book for three volumes. I also got *Richard Turpin*, in two volumes, and paid the same. I have seen *Oliver Twist*, and think the Artful Dodger is very like some of the boys here. I am here for picking a pocket of 25*l.*

" H. C. (aged 15). When we came to Manchester, I went to the play, and saw *Jack Sheppard* the first night it came out. There were pictures of him about the streets on boards and on the walls ; one of them was his picking a pocket in the church. I liked *Jack Sheppard* much. I had not been in prison there. I was employed in a warehouse at 6*s.* 6*d.* a week, and was allowed 6*d.* out of it for myself, and with that I went regularly to the play. I saw *Jack Sheppard* afterwards four times in one week. I got the money out of my money-bag by stealth, and without my master's knowledge. I once borrowed 10*s.* in my mother's name from Mrs. ———, a shopkeeper, with whom she used to deal ; I went to the play with it.

" J. M'D. (aged 15). I have heard of *Jack Sheppard:* a lad whom I know told me of it, who had seen it, and said it was *rare fun* to see him break out of prison.

" J. L. (aged 11). Has been to the play twice, and seen *Jack Sheppard*. Went with his brother the first time, and by himself the second. I took the money to go a second time out of mother's house, off the chimney-piece, where she had left a sixpence. It was the first night *Jack Sheppard* was played. There was great talk about it, and there were nice pictures about it all over the walls. I thought him a very clever fellow ; but Blueskin made the most fun. I first went to the markets, and begun by stealing apples. I also knew a lad, ———, who has been transported, and went with him two or three times. The most I ever got was 10*s.* out of a till."

The Inspector's *Report on Juvenile Delinquency at Liverpool* contains much matter of the same kind ; but sufficient has been already quoted to shew the injurious effects of the deification of great thieves by thoughtless novelists.

known by the name of Jack Sheppard. What amazing difficulties has he overcome! what astonishing things has he performed! and all for the sake of a stinking, miserable carcase, hardly worth the hanging! How dexterously did he pick the chain of his padlock with a crooked nail! how manfully he burst his fetters asunder, climb up the chimney, wrench out an iron bar, break his way through a stone wall, make the strong door of a dark entry fly before him, till he got upon the leads of the prison, then, fixing a blanket to the wall with a spike, he stole out of the chapel! How intrepidly did he descend to the top of the turner's house! how cautiously pass down the stair, and make his escape to the street-door!

"Oh, that ye were all like Jack Sheppard! Mistake me not, my brethren—I don't mean in a carnal, but in a spiritual sense; for I propose to spiritualise these things. What a shame it would be if we should not think it worth our while to take as much pains, and employ as many deep thoughts to save our souls as he has done to preserve his body!

"Let me exhort ye, then, to open the locks of your hearts with the nail of repentance! Burst asunder the fetters of your beloved lusts, mount the chimney of hope, take from thence the bar of good resolution, break through the stone wall of despair, and all the strongholds in the dark entry of the valley of the shadow of death! Raise yourselves to the leads of divine meditation, fix the blanket of faith with the spike of the Church, let yourselves down to the turner's house of resignation, and descend the stairs of humility! So shall you come to the door of deliverance from the prison of iniquity, and escape the clutches of that old executioner the devil!"

Jonathan Wild, whose name has been immortalised by Fielding, was no favourite with the people. He had none of the virtues which, combined with crimes, make up the character of the great thief. He was a pitiful fellow, who informed against his comrades, and was afraid of death. This meanness was not to be forgiven by the crowd; and they pelted him with dirt and stones on his way to Tyburn, and expressed their contempt by every possible means. How different was their conduct to Turpin and Jack Sheppard, who died in their neatest attire, with nosegays in their button-holes, and with the courage that a crowd expects! It was anticipated that the body of Turpin would have been delivered up to the surgeons for dissection; and the people seeing some men very busily employed in removing it, suddenly set upon them, rescued the body, bore it about the town in triumph, and then buried it in a very deep grave, filled with quick lime, to hasten the progress of decomposition. They would not suffer the corpse of their hero—of the man who had ridden from London to

York in four-and-twenty hours—to be mangled by the rude hands of unmannerly surgeons.

The death of Claude Duval would appear to have been no less triumphant. Claude was a gentlemanly thief. According to Butler, in the famous ode to his memory, he

> " Taught the wild Arabs of the road
> To rob in a more gentle mode;
> Take prizes more obligingly than those
> Who never had been bred *filous;*
> And how to hang in a more graceful fashion
> Than e'er was known before to the dull English nation."

In fact, he was the pink of politeness, and his gallantry to the fair sex was proverbial. When he was caught at last, pent in " stone walls and chains and iron grates," their grief was in proportion to his rare merits and his great fame. Butler says, that to his dungeon

> " Came ladies from all parts,
> To offer up close prisoners their hearts,
> Which he received as tribute due—
> *   *   *   *
> Never did bold knight to relieve
> Distress'd dames, such dreadful feats achieve,
> As feeble damsels for his sake
> Would have been proud to undertake,
> And, bravely ambitious to redeem
> The world's loss and their own,
> Strove who should have the honour to lay down,
> And change a life with him."

Among the noted thieves of France, there is none to compare with the famous Aimerigot Tétenoire, who flourished in the reign of Charles VI. This fellow was at the head of four or five hundred men, and possessed two very strong castles in Limousin and Auvergne. There was a good deal of the feudal baron about him, although he possessed no revenues but such as the road afforded him. At his death he left a singular will. " I give and bequeath," said the robber, " one thousand five hundred francs to St. George's Chapel, for such repairs as it may need; to my sweet girl, who so loyally loved me, I give two thousand five hundred; and the surplus I give to my companions. I hope they will all live as brothers, and divide it amicably among them. If they cannot agree, and the devil of contention gets among them, it is no fault of mine; and I advise them to get a good strong sharp axe, and break open my strong-box. Let them scramble for what it contains, and the devil seize the hindmost." The people of Auvergne still recount with admiration the daring feats of this brigand.

Of later years, the French thieves have been such unmitigated scoundrels as to have left but little room for popular admiration. The famous Cartouche, whose name has become synonymous with ruffian in their language, had none of the generosity, courtesy, and devoted bravery which are so requisite to make a robber-hero. He was born at Paris, towards the end of the seventeenth century, and broken alive on the wheel in November 1727. He was, however, sufficiently popular to have been pitied at his death, and afterwards to have formed the subject of a much-admired drama, which bore his name, and was played with great success in all the theatres of France during the years 1734, 5, and 6. In our own day the French have been more fortunate in a robber; Vidocq bids fair to rival the fame of Turpin and Jack Sheppard. Already he has become the hero of many an apocryphal tale—already his compatriots boast of his manifold achievements, and express their doubts whether any other country in Europe could produce a thief so clever, so accomplished, so gentlemanly, as Vidocq.

Germany has its Schinderhannes, Hungary its Schubry, and Italy and Spain a whole host of brigands, whose names and exploits are familiar as household words in the mouths of the children and populace of those countries.

The Italian banditti are renowned over the world;. and many of them are not only very religious (after a fashion) but very charitable. Charity from such a source is so unexpected, that the people doat upon them for it. One of them, when he fell into the hands of the police, exclaimed, as they led him away, " Ho fatto più carità !"— " I have given away more in charity than any three convents in these provinces." And the fellow spoke truth.

In Lombardy, the people cherish the memory of two notorious robbers, who flourished about two centuries ago under the Spanish government. Their story, according to Macfarlane, is contained in a little book well known to all the children of the province, and read by them with much more gusto than their Bibles.

Schinderhannes, the robber of the Rhine, is a great favourite on the banks of the river which he so long kept in awe. Many amusing stories are related by the peasantry* of the scurvy tricks he played off upon rich Jews, or too-presuming officers of justice—of his princely generosity, and undaunted courage. In short, they are proud of him, and would no more consent to have the memory of his achievements dissociated from their river than they would have the rock of Ehrenbreitstein blown to atoms by gunpowder.

* For a full account of this noted robber, and indeed of European thieves and banditti in general, see the very amusing work upon the subject by Mr. Charles Macfarlane.

There is another robber-hero, of whose character and exploits the people of Germany speak admiringly. Mausch Nadel was captain of a considerable band that infested the Rhine, Switzerland, Alsatia, and Lorraine, during the years 1824, 5, and 6. Like Jack Sheppard, he endeared himself to the populace by his most hazardous escape from prison. Being confined at Bremen, in a dungeon on the third story of the prison of that town, he contrived to let himself down without exciting the vigilance of the sentinels, and to swim across the Weser, though heavily laden with irons. When about half-way over, he was espied by a sentinel, who fired at him, and shot him in the calf of the leg; but the undaunted robber struck out manfully, reached the shore, and was out of sight before the officers of justice could get ready their boats to follow him. He was captured again in 1826, tried at Mayence, and sentenced to death. He was a tall, strong, handsome man, and his fate, villain as he was, excited much sympathy all over Germany. The ladies especially were loud in their regret that nothing could be done to save a hero so good-looking, and of adventures so romantic, from the knife of the headsman.

Mr. Charles Macfarlane, in speaking of Italian banditti, remarks, that the abuses of the Catholic religion, with its confessions and absolutions, have tended to promote crime of this description. But he adds more truly, that priests and monks have not done half the mischief which has been perpetrated by ballad-mongers and story-tellers. If he had said playwrights also, the list would have been complete. In fact, the theatre, which can only expect to prosper, in a pecuniary sense, by pandering to the tastes of the people, continually recurs to the annals of thieves and banditti for its most favourite heroes. These theatrical robbers, with their picturesque attire, wild haunts, jolly, reckless, devil-may-care manners, take a wonderful hold upon the imagination, and whatever their advocates may say to the contrary, exercise a very pernicious influence upon public morals. In the Memoirs of the Duke of Guise upon the Revolution of Naples in 1647 and 1648, it is stated, that the manners, dress, and mode of life of the Neapolitan banditti were rendered so captivating upon the stage, that the authorities found it absolutely necessary to forbid the representation of dramas in which they figured, and even to prohibit their costume at the masquerades. So numerous were the banditti at this time, that the duke found no difficulty in raising an army of them, to aid him in his endeavours to seize on the throne of Naples. He thus describes them :* "They were three thousand five hundred men, of whom the oldest came short of five-and-forty years, and the youngest was above twenty. They were all tall and well made, with long black

* See also *Foreign Quarterly Review*, vol. iv. p. 398.

hair, for the most part curled; coats of black Spanish leather, with
sleeves of velvet, or cloth of gold; cloth breeches with gold lace, most
of them scarlet; girdles of velvet, laced with gold, with two pistols
on each side; a cutlass hanging at a belt, suitably trimmed, three
fingers broad and two feet long; a hawking-bag at their girdle, and
a powder-flask hung about their neck with a great silk riband. Some
of them carried firelocks, and others blunderbusses; they had all
good shoes, with silk stockings, and every one a cap of cloth of gold,
or cloth of silver, of different colours, on his head, which was very
delightful to the eye."

The *Beggar's Opera,* in our own country, is another instance of
the admiration that thieves excite upon the stage. Of the extraordinary success of this piece, when first produced, the following account
is given in the notes to *The Dunciad,* and quoted by Johnson in his
Lives of the Poets: " This piece was received with greater applause
than was ever known. Besides being acted in London sixty-three
days without interruption, and renewed the next season with equal
applause, it spread into all the great towns of England; was played
in many places to the thirtieth and fortieth time; at Bath and
Bristol, &c. fifty. It made its progress into Wales, Scotland, and
Ireland, where it was performed twenty-four days successively. The
ladies carried about with them the favourite songs of it in fans, and
houses were furnished with it in screens. The fame of it was not confined to the author only. The person who acted Polly, till then
obscure, became all at once the favourite of the town;* her pictures
were engraved and sold in great numbers; her life written, books of
letters and verses to her published, and pamphlets made even of her
sayings and jests. Furthermore, it drove out of England, for that
season, the Italian Opera, which had carried all before it for ten years."
Dr. Johnson, in his life of the author, says, that Herring, afterwards
Archbishop of Canterbury, censured the opera, as giving encouragement, not only to vice, but to crimes, by making the highwayman
the hero, and dismissing him at last unpunished; and adds, that it
was even said, that after the exhibition the gangs of robbers were
evidently multiplied. The Doctor doubts the assertion, giving as his
reason, that highwaymen and housebreakers seldom frequent the play-
house, and that it was not possible for any one to imagine that he
might rob with safety, because he saw Macheath reprieved upon the
stage. But if Johnson had wished to be convinced, he might very
easily have discovered that highwaymen and housebreakers did frequent the theatre, and that nothing was more probable than that a
laughable representation of successful villany should induce the young

* Lavinia Fenton, afterwards Duchess of Bolton.

and the already vicious to imitate it. Besides, there is the weighty authority of Sir John Fielding, the chief magistrate of Bow Street, who asserted positively, and proved his assertion by the records of his office, that the number of thieves was greatly increased at the time when that opera was so popular.

We have another instance of the same result much nearer our own times. Schiller's *Räuber*, that wonderful play, written by a green youth, perverted the taste and imagination of all the young men in Germany. An accomplished critic of our own country (Hazlitt), speaking of this play, says it was the first he ever read, and such was the effect it produced on him, that it " stunned him, like a blow." After the lapse of five-and-twenty years, he could not forget it ; it was still, to use his own words, " an old dweller in the chambers of his brain," and he had not even then recovered enough from it to describe how it was. The high-minded, metaphysical thief, its hero, was so warmly admired, that several raw students, longing to imitate a character they thought so noble, actually abandoned their homes and their colleges, and betook themselves to the forests and the wilds to levy contributions upon travellers. They thought they would, like Moor, plunder the rich, and deliver eloquent soliloquies to the setting sun or the rising moon ; relieve the poor when they met them, and drink flasks of Rhenish with their free companions in rugged mountain-passes, or in tents in the thicknesses of the forests. But a little experience wonderfully cooled their courage ; they found that real, every-day robbers were very unlike the conventional banditti of the stage, and that three months in prison, with bread and water for their fare, and damp straw to lie upon, was very well to read about by their own firesides, but not very agreeable to undergo in their own proper persons.

Lord Byron, with his soliloquising, high-souled thieves, has, in a slight degree, perverted the taste of the juvenile rhymers of his country. As yet, however, they have shewn more good sense than their fellows of Germany, and have not taken to the woods or the highways. Much as they admire Conrad the Corsair, they will not go to sea, and hoist the black flag for him. By words only, and not by deeds, they testify their admiration, and deluge the periodicals and music-shops of the land with verses describing pirates' and bandits' brides, and robber adventures of every kind.

But it is the playwright who does most harm ; and Byron has fewer sins of this nature to answer for than Gay or Schiller. With the aid of scenery, fine dresses, and music, and the very false notions they convey, they vitiate the public taste, not knowing,

" Vulgaires rimeurs !
Quelle force ont les arts pour demolir les mœurs."

In the penny theatres that abound in the poor and populous districts of London, and which are chiefly frequented by striplings of idle and dissolute habits, tales of thieves and murderers are more admired, and draw more crowded audiences, than any other species of representation. There the footpad, the burglar, and the highwayman are portrayed in their natural colours, and give pleasant lessons in crime to their delighted listeners. There the deepest tragedy and the broadest farce are represented in the career of the murderer and the thief, and are applauded in proportion to their depth and their breadth. There, whenever a crime of unusual atrocity is committed, it is brought out afresh, with all its disgusting incidents copied from the life, for the amusement of those who will one day become its imitators.

With the mere reader the case is widely different; and most people have a partiality for knowing the adventures of noted rogues. Even in fiction they are delightful: witness the eventful story of Gil Blas de Santillane, and of that great rascal Don Guzman d'Alfarache. Here there is no fear of imitation. Poets, too, without doing mischief, may sing of such heroes when they please, wakening our sympathies for the sad fate of Jemmy Dawson, or Gilderoy, or Macpherson the Dauntless; or celebrating in undying verse the wrongs and the revenge of the great thief of Scotland, Rob Roy. If, by the music of their sweet rhymes, they can convince the world that such heroes are but mistaken philosophers, born a few ages too late, and having both a theoretical and practical love for

> " The good old rule, the simple plan,
> That they should take who have the power,
> That they should keep who can ;"

the world may perhaps become wiser, and consent to some better distribution of its good things, by means of which thieves may become reconciled to the age, and the age to them. The probability, however, seems to be, that the charmers will charm in vain, charm they ever so wisely.

DUELS AND ORDEALS.

There was an ancient sage philosopher,
Who swore the world, as he could prove,
Was mad of fighting.—*Hudibras.*

MOST writers, in accounting for the origin of duelling, derive it from
the warlike habits of those barbarous nations who overran Europe in
the early centuries of the Christian era, and who knew no mode so
effectual for settling their differences as the point of the sword. In
fact, duelling, taken in its primitive and broadest sense, means nothing more than combating, and is the universal resort of all wild
animals, including man, to gain or defend their possessions, or avenge
their insults. Two dogs who tear each other for a bone, or two ban-
tams fighting on a dunghill for the love of some beautiful hen, or two
fools on Wimbledon Common, shooting at each other to satisfy the
laws of offended honour, stand on the same footing in this respect,
and are each and all mere duellists. As civilisation advanced, the
best-informed men naturally grew ashamed of such a mode of adjust-
ing disputes, and the promulgation of some sort of laws for obtaining
redress for injuries was the consequence. Still there were many cases

in which the allegations of an accuser could not be rebutted by any positive proof on the part of the accused; and in all these, which must have been exceedingly numerous in the early stages of European society, the combat was resorted to. From its decision there was no appeal. God was supposed to nerve the arm of the combatant whose cause was just, and to grant him the victory over his opponent. As Montesquieu well remarks,* this belief was not unnatural among a people just emerging from barbarism. Their manners being wholly warlike, the man deficient in courage, the prime virtue of his fellows, was not unreasonably suspected of other vices besides cowardice, which is generally found to be co-existent with treachery. He, therefore, who shewed himself most valiant in the encounter was absolved by public opinion from any crime with which he might be charged. As a necessary consequence, society would have been reduced to its original elements, if the men of thought, as distinguished from the men of action, had not devised some means for taming the unruly passions of their fellows. With this view, governments commenced by restricting within the narrowest possible limits the cases in which it was lawful to prove or deny guilt by the single combat. By the law of Gondebaldus king of the Burgundians, passed in the year 501, the proof by combat was allowed in all legal proceedings in lieu of swearing. In the time of Charlemagne, the Burgundian practice had spread over the empire of the Francs, and not only the suitors for justice, but the witnesses, and even the judges, were obliged to defend their cause, their evidence, or their decision at the point of the sword. Louis the Debonnaire, his successor, endeavoured to remedy the growing evil by permitting the duel only in appeals of felony, in civil cases, or issue joined in a writ of right, and in cases of the court of chivalry, or attacks upon a man's knighthood. None were exempt from these trials but women, the sick and the maimed, and persons under fifteen or above sixty years of age. Ecclesiastics were allowed to produce champions in their stead. This practice, in the course of time, extended to all trials of civil and criminal cases, which had to be decided by battle.

The clergy, whose dominion was an intellectual one, never approved of a system of jurisprudence which tended so much to bring all things under the rule of the strongest arm. From the first they set their faces against duelling, and endeavoured, as far as the prejudices of their age would allow them, to curb the warlike spirit, so alien from the principles of religion. In the Council of Valentia, and afterwards in the Council of Trent, they excommunicated all persons engaged in duelling; and not only them, but even the assistants

* *Esprit des Loix*, liv. xxviii. chap. xvii.

and spectators, declaring the custom to be hellish and detestable, and introduced by the devil for the destruction both of body and soul. They added also, that princes who connived at duels should be deprived of all temporal power, jurisdiction, and dominion over the places where they had permitted them to be fought. It will be seen hereafter that this clause only encouraged the practice which it was intended to prevent.

But it was the blasphemous error of these early ages to expect that the Almighty, whenever he was called upon, would work a miracle in favour of a person unjustly accused. The priesthood, in condemning the duel, did not condemn the principle on which it was founded. They still encouraged the popular belief of divine interference in all the disputes or differences that might arise among nations or individuals. It was the very same principle that regulated the ordeals, which with all their influence they supported against the duel. By the former, the power of deciding the guilt or innocence was vested wholly in their hands; while by the latter they enjoyed no power or privilege at all. It is not to be wondered at that, for this reason, if for no other, they should have endeavoured to settle all differences by the peaceful mode. While that prevailed, they were, as they wished to be, the first party in the state; but while the strong arm of individual prowess was allowed to be the judge in all doubtful cases, their power and influence became secondary to those of the nobility.

Thus it was not the mere hatred of bloodshed which induced them to launch the thunderbolts of excommunication against the combatants: it was a desire to retain the power, which, to do them justice, they were in those times the persons best qualified to wield. The germs of knowledge and civilisation lay within the bounds of their order; for they were the representatives of the intellectual, as the nobility were of the physical power of man. To centralise this power in the Church, and make it the judge of the last resort in all appeals, both in civil and criminal cases, they instituted five modes of trial, the management of which lay wholly in their hands. These were, the oath upon the evangelists; the ordeal of the cross and the fire-ordeal, for persons in the higher ranks; the water-ordeal, for the humbler classes; and, lastly, the *corsned*, or bread and cheese ordeal, for members of their own body.

The oath upon the evangelists was taken in the following manner. The accused who was received to this proof, says Paul Hay, Count du Chastelet, in his *Memoirs of Bertrand du Guesclin*, swore upon a copy of the New Testament, and on the relics of the holy martyrs, or on their tombs, that he was innocent of the crime imputed to him. He was also obliged to find twelve persons of acknowledged probity who should take oath at the same time that they believed him innocent. This mode of trial led to very great abuses, especially in cases of disputed inheritance, where the hardest swearer was certain of the victory. This abuse was one of the principal causes which led to the preference given to the trial by battle. It is not at all surprising that a feudal baron, or captain of the early ages, should have preferred the chances of a fair fight with his opponent to a mode by which firm perjury would always be successful.

The trial by, or judgment of, the cross, which Charlemagne begged his sons to have recourse to, in case of disputes arising between them, was performed thus :—When a person accused of any crime had declared his innocence upon oath, and appealed to the cross for its judgment in his favour, he was brought into the church, before the altar. The priest previously prepared two sticks exactly like one another, upon one of which was carved a figure of the cross. They were both wrapped up, with great care and many ceremonies, in a quantity of fine wool, and laid upon the altar, or on the relics of the saints. A solemn prayer was then offered up to God, that he would be pleased to discover, by the judgment of his holy cross, whether the accused person were innocent or guilty. A priest then approached the altar, and took up one of the sticks, and the assistants unswathed it reverently. If it was marked with the cross, the accused person was innocent ; if unmarked, he was guilty. It would be unjust to assert, that the judgments thus delivered were in all cases erroneous; and it would be absurd to believe that they were left altogether to chance. Many true judgments were doubtless given, and, in all probability, most conscientiously; for we cannot but believe that the priests endeavoured beforehand to convince themselves by strict inquiry and a strict examination of the circumstances, whether the appellant were innocent or guilty, and that they took up the crossed or uncrossed stick accordingly. Although, to all other observers, the sticks, as enfolded in the wool, might appear exactly similar, those who enwrapped them could, without any difficulty, distinguish the one from the other.

By the fire-ordeal the power of deciding was just as unequivocally left in their hands. It was generally believed that fire would not burn the innocent, and the clergy, of course, took care that the innocent, or such as it was their pleasure or interest to declare so, should be so warned before undergoing the ordeal, as to preserve themselves without any difficulty from the fire. One mode of ordeal was to place red-hot ploughshares on the ground at certain distances, and then, blindfolding the accused person, make him walk barefooted over them. If he stepped regularly in the vacant spaces, avoiding the fire, he was adjudged innocent; if he burned himself, he was declared guilty. As none but the clergy interfered with the arrangement of the ploughshares, they could always calculate beforehand the result of the ordeal. To find a person guilty, they had only to place them at irregular distances, and the accused was sure to tread upon one of them. When Emma, the wife of King Ethelred, and mother of Edward the Confessor, was accused of a guilty familiarity with Alwyn Bishop of Winchester, she cleared her character in this manner. The reputation, not only of their order, but of a queen, being at stake, a verdict of guilty was not to be apprehended from any ploughshares which priests had the heating of. This ordeal was called the *Judicium Dei*, and sometimes the *Vulgaris Purgatio*, and might also be tried by several other methods. One was to hold in the hand, unhurt, a piece of red-hot iron, of the weight of one, two, or three pounds. When we read not only that men with hard hands, but women of softer and more delicate skin, could do this with impunity, we must be convinced that the hands were previously rubbed with some preservative, or that the apparently hot iron was merely cold iron painted red. Another mode was to plunge the naked arm into a caldron of boiling water. The priests then enveloped it in several folds of linen and flannel, and kept the patient confined within the church, and under their exclusive care, for three days. If, at the end of that time, the arm appeared without a scar, the innocence of the accused person was firmly established.*

As regards the water-ordeal, the same trouble was not taken. It was a trial only for the poor and humble, and, whether they sank or

---

* Very similar to this is the fire-ordeal of the modern Hindoos, which is thus described in Forbes's *Oriental Memoirs*, vol. i. ch. xi.:—"When a man, accused of a capital crime, chooses to undergo the ordeal trial, he is closely confined for several days, his right hand and arm are covered with thick wax-cloth, tied up and sealed, in the presence of proper officers, to prevent deceit. In the English districts the covering was always sealed with the Company's arms, and the prisoner placed under a European guard. At the time fixed for the ordeal, a caldron of oil is placed over a fire; when it boils, a piece of money is dropped into the vessel; the prisoner's arm is unsealed and washed in the presence of his judges and accusers. During this part of the ceremony the attendant Brahmins supplicate the Deity. On receiving their benediction, the accused plunges his hand into the boiling fluid, and takes out the coin. The arm is afterwards again sealed up until the time appointed for a re-examination. The seal is then broken: if no blemish appears, the prisoner is declared innocent; if the contrary, he suffers the punishment due to his crime." . . . . . On this trial the accused thus addresses the element before plunging his hand into the boiling oil:—"Thou, O fire! pervadest all things. O cause of purity! who givest evidence of virtue and of sin, declare the truth in this my hand!" If no juggling were practised, the decisions by this ordeal would be all the same way; but as some are by this means declared guilty, and others innocent, it is clear that the Brahmins, like the Christian priests of the middle ages, practise some deception in saving those whom they wish to be thought guiltless.

swam, was thought of very little consequence. Like the witches of more modern times, the accused were thrown into a pond or river; if they sank, and were drowned, their surviving friends had the consolation of knowing that they were innocent; if they swam, they were guilty. In either case society was rid of them.

But of all the ordeals, that which the clergy reserved for themselves was the one least likely to cause any member of their corps to be declared guilty. The most culpable monster in existence came off clear when tried by this method. It was called the *Corsned*, and was thus performed. A piece of barley bread and a piece of cheese were laid upon the altar, and the accused priest, in his full canonicals, and surrounded by all the pompous adjuncts of Roman ceremony, pronounced certain conjurations, and prayed with great fervency for several minutes. The burden of the prayer was, that if he were guilty of the crime laid to his charge, God would send his angel Gabriel to stop his throat, that he might not be able to swallow the bread and cheese. There is no instance upon record of a priest having been choked in this manner.*

When, under Pope Gregory VII., it was debated whether the Gregorian chant should be introduced into Castile, instead of the Musarabic, given by St. Isidore of Seville to the churches of that kingdom, very much ill-feeling was excited. The churches refused to receive the novelty, and it was proposed that the affair should be decided by a battle between two champions, one chosen from each side. The clergy would not consent to a mode of settlement which they considered impious, but had no objection to try the merits of each chant by the fire-ordeal. A great fire was accordingly made, and a book of the Gregorian and one of the Musarabic chant were thrown into it, that the flames might decide which was most agreeable to God by refusing to burn it. Cardinal Baronius, who says he was an eye-witness of the miracle, relates, that the book of the Gregorian chant was no sooner laid upon the fire, than it leaped out uninjured, visibly, and with a great noise. Every one present thought that the saints had decided in favour of Pope Gregory. After a slight interval, the fire was extinguished; but, wonderful to relate! the other book of St. Isidore was found covered with ashes, but not injured

* An ordeal very like this is still practised in India. Consecrated rice is the article chosen, instead of bread and cheese. Instances are not rare in which, through the force of imagination, guilty persons are not able to swallow a single grain. Conscious of their crime, and fearful of the punishment of Heaven, they feel a suffocating sensation in their throat when they attempt it, and they fall on their knees, and confess all that is laid to their charge. The same thing, no doubt, would have happened with the bread and cheese of the Roman Church, if it had been applied to any others but ecclesiastics. The latter had too much wisdom to be caught in a trap of their own setting.

in the slightest degree.   The flames had not even warmed it.   Upon
this it was resolved, that both were alike agreeable to God, and that
they should be used by turns in all the churches of Seville.*

If the ordeals had been confined to questions like this, the laity
would have had little or no objection to them; but when they
were introduced as decisive in all the disputes that might arise between man and man, the opposition of all those whose prime virtue
was personal bravery, was necessarily excited.   In fact, the nobility,
from a very early period, began to look with jealous eyes upon them.
They were not slow to perceive their true purport, which was no
other than to make the Church the last court of appeal in all cases,
both civil and criminal; and not only did the nobility prefer the
ancient mode of single combat from this cause, in itself a sufficient
one, but they clung to it because an acquittal gained by those dis-
plays of courage and address which the battle afforded, was more
creditable in the eyes of their compeers than one which it required
but little or none of either to accomplish.   To these causes may be
added another, which was perhaps more potent than either in raising the credit of the judicial combat at the expense of the ordeal.
The noble institution of chivalry was beginning to take root, and,
notwithstanding the clamours of the clergy, war was made the sole
business of life, and the only elegant pursuit of the aristocracy.   The
fine spirit of honour was introduced, any attack upon which was only
to be avenged in the lists, within sight of applauding crowds, whose
verdict of approbation was far more gratifying than the cold and
formal acquittal of the ordeal.   Lothaire, the son of Louis I., abolished that by fire and the trial of the cross within his dominions;
but in England they were allowed so late as the time of Henry III.,
in the early part of whose reign they were prohibited by an order of
council.   In the mean time, the Crusades had brought the institution of chivalry to the full height of perfection.   The chivalric spirit
soon achieved the downfall of the ordeal system, and established the
judicial combat on a basis too firm to be shaken.   It is true that with
the fall of chivalry, as an institution, fell the tournament and the
encounter in the lists; but the duel, their offspring, has survived to
this day, defying the efforts of sages and philosophers to eradicate it.
Among all the errors bequeathed to us by a barbarous age, it has proved
the most pertinacious.   It has put variance between men's reason
and their honour; put the man of sense on a level with the fool, and
made thousands who condemn it submit to it or practise it.

Those who are curious to see the manner in which these combats
were regulated, may consult the learned Montesquieu, where they

* *Histoire de Messire Bertrand du Guesclin*, par Paul Hay du Chastelet, liv. i. ch. xix.

will find a copious summary of the code of ancient duelling.* Truly does he remark, in speaking of the clearness and excellence of the arrangements, that, as there were many wise matters which were conducted in a very foolish manner, so there were many foolish matters conducted very wisely. No greater exemplification of it could be given than the wise and religious rules of the absurd and blasphemous trial by battle.

In the ages that intervened between the Crusades and the new era that was opened out by the invention of gunpowder and printing, a more rational system of legislation took root. The inhabitants of cities, engaged in the pursuits of trade and industry, were content to acquiesce in the decisions of their judges and magistrates whenever any differences arose among them. Unlike the class above them, their habits and manners did not lead them to seek the battle-field on every slight occasion. A dispute as to the price of a sack of corn, a bale of broad-cloth, or a cow, could be more satisfactorily adjusted before the mayor or bailiff of their district. Even the martial knights and nobles, quarrelsome as they were, began to see that the trial by battle would lose its dignity and splendour if too frequently resorted to. Governments also shared this opinion, and on several occasions restricted the cases in which it was legal to proceed to this extremity. In France, before the time of Louis IX., duels were permitted only in cases of *lèse majestè, rape, incendiarism, assassination,* and *burglary.* Louis IX., by taking off all restriction, made them legal in civil cases. This was not found to work well, and, in 1303, Philip the Fair judged it necessary to confine them, in criminal matters, to state offences, rape, and incendiarism ; and in civil cases, to questions of disputed inheritance. Knighthood was allowed to be the best judge of its own honour, and might defend or avenge it as often as occasion arose.

Among the earliest duels upon record, is a very singular one that took place in the reign of Louis II. (A. D. 878). Ingelgerius count of Gastinois was one morning discovered by his countess dead in bed at her side. Gontran, a relation of the count, accused the countess of having murdered her husband, to whom, he asserted, she had long been unfaithful, and challenged her to produce a champion to do battle in her behalf, that he might establish her guilt by killing him.† All the friends and relatives of the countess believed in her innocence; but Gontran was so stout and bold and renowned a warrior that no one dared to meet him, for which, as Brantôme quaintly says, "mauvais et poltrons parens estaient." The unhappy countess began to

---

* *Esprit des Loix,* liv. xxviii. ch. xxv.
† *Mémoires de Brantôme touchant les Duels.*

despair, when a champion suddenly appeared in the person of Ingelgerius count of Anjou, a boy of sixteen years of age, who had been
held by the countess on the baptismal font, and received her husband's
name.   He tenderly loved his godmother, and offered to do battle in
her cause against any and every opponent.   The king endeavoured
to persuade the generous boy from his enterprise, urging the great
strength, tried skill, and invincible courage of the challenger ; but

DUEL BETWEEN INGELGERIUS AND GONTRAN.

he persisted in his resolution, to the great sorrow of all the court,
who said it was a cruel thing to permit so brave and beautiful a child
to rush to such butchery and death.

When the lists were prepared, the countess duly acknowledged her champion, and the combatants commenced the onset. Gontran rode so fiercely at his antagonist, and hit him on the shield with such impetuosity, that he lost his own balance and rolled to the ground. The young count, as Gontran fell, passed his lance through his body, and then dismounting, cut off his head, which, Brantôme says, "he presented to the king, who received it most graciously, and was very joyful, as much so as if any one had made him a present of a city." The innocence of the countess was then proclaimed with great rejoicings; and she kissed her godson, and wept over his neck with joy, in the presence of all the assembly.

When the Earl of Essex was accused by Robert de Montfort, before King Henry II., in 1162, of having traitorously suffered the royal standard of England to fall from his hands in a skirmish with the Welsh at Coleshill, five years previously, the latter offered to prove the truth of the charge by single combat. The Earl of Essex accepted the challenge, and the lists were prepared near Reading. An immense concourse of persons assembled to witness the battle. Essex at first fought stoutly, but, losing his temper and self-command, he gave an advantage to his opponent which soon decided the struggle. He was unhorsed, and so severely wounded, that all present thought he was dead. At the solicitation of his relatives, the monks of the Abbey of Reading were allowed to remove the body for interment, and Montfort was declared the victor. Essex, however, was not dead, but stunned only, and, under the care of the monks, recovered in a few weeks from his bodily injuries. The wounds of his mind were not so easily healed. Though a loyal and brave subject, the whole realm believed him a traitor and a coward because he had been vanquished. He could not brook to return to the world deprived of the good opinion of his fellows; he therefore made himself a monk, and passed the remainder of his days within the walls of the abbey.

Du Chastelet relates a singular duel that was proposed in Spain.* A Christian gentleman of Seville sent a challenge to a Moorish cavalier, offering to prove against him, with whatever weapons he might choose, that the religion of Jesus Christ was holy and divine, and that of Mahomet impious and damnable. The Spanish prelates did not choose that Christianity should be compromised within their jurisdiction by the result of any such combat; the Moorish cavalier might, perchance, have proved to be the stronger, and they commanded the knight, under pain of excommunication, to withdraw the challenge.

The same author relates that, under Otho I., a question arose among jurisconsults, viz. whether grandchildren, who had lost their

* *Histoire de Messire Bertrand du Guesclin*, liv. i. ch. xix.

father, should share equally with their uncles in the property of their grandfather, at the death of the latter. The difficulty of this question was found so insurmountable, that none of the lawyers of that day could resolve it. It was at last decreed that it should be decided by single combat. Two champions were accordingly chosen; one for, and the other against, the claims of the little ones. After a long struggle, the champion of the uncles was unhorsed and slain; and it was therefore decided that the right of the grandchildren was established, and that they should enjoy the same portion of their grandfather's possessions that their father would have done had he been alive.

Upon pretexts just as strange, and often more frivolous than these, duels continued to be fought in most of the countries of Europe, during the whole of the fourteenth and fifteenth centuries. A memorable instance of the slightness of the pretext on which a man could be forced to fight a duel to the death, occurs in the memoirs of the brave Constable, Du Guesclin. The advantage he had obtained, in a skirmish before Rennes, against William Brembre, an English captain, so preyed on the spirits of William Troussel, the chosen friend and companion of the latter, that nothing would satisfy him but a mortal combat with the Constable. The Duke of Lancaster, to whom Troussel applied for permission to fight the great Frenchman, forbade the battle, as not warranted by the circumstances. Troussel nevertheless burned with a fierce desire to cross his weapon with Du Guesclin, and sought every occasion to pick a quarrel with him. Having so good a will for it, of course he found a way. A relative of his had been taken prisoner by the Constable, in whose hands he remained till he was able to pay his ransom. Troussel resolved to make a quarrel out of this, and despatched a messenger to Du Guesclin, demanding the release of his prisoner, and offering a bond, at a distant date, for the payment of the ransom. Du Guesclin, who had received intimation of the hostile purposes of the Englishman, sent back word that he would not accept his bond, neither would he release his prisoner until the full amount of his ransom was paid. As soon as this answer was received, Troussel sent a challenge to the Constable, demanding reparation for the injury he had done his honour, by refusing his bond, and offering a mortal combat, to be fought three strokes with the lance, three with the sword, and three with the dagger. Du Guesclin, although ill in bed with the ague, accepted the challenge, and gave notice to the Marshal d'Andreghem, the king's lieutenant-general in Lower Normandy, that he might fix the day and the place of combat. The marshal made all necessary arrangements, upon condition that he who was beaten should pay a hundred florins of gold to feast the nobles and gentlemen who were witnesses of the encounter.

The Duke of Lancaster was very angry with his captain, and told him that it would be a shame to his knighthood and his nation if he forced on a combat with the brave Du Guesclin at a time when he was enfeebled by disease and stretched on the couch of suffering. Upon these representations, Troussel, ashamed of himself, sent notice to Du Guesclin that he was willing to postpone the duel until such time as he should be perfectly recovered. Du Guesclin replied, that he could not think of postponing the combat after all the nobility had received notice of it; that he had sufficient strength left not only to meet, but to conquer such an opponent as he was; and that if he did not make his appearance in the lists at the time appointed, he would publish him every where as a man unworthy to be called a knight, or to wear an honourable sword by his side. Troussel carried this haughty message to the Duke of Lancaster, who immediately gave permission for the battle.

On the day appointed, the two combatants appeared in the lists, in the presence of several thousand spectators. Du Guesclin was attended by the flower of the French nobility, including the Marshal de Beaumanoir, Olivier de Mauny, Bertrand de Saint Pern, and the Viscount de la Bellière; while the Englishman appeared with no more than the customary retinue of two seconds, two squires, two coutilliers or daggermen, and two trumpeters. The first onset was unfavourable to the Constable. He received so heavy a blow on his shield-arm, that he fell forward to the left upon his horse's neck; and being weakened by his fever, was nearly thrown to the ground. All his friends thought he could never recover himself, and began to deplore his ill-fortune; but Du Guesclin collected his energies for a decisive effort, and at the second charge aimed a blow at the shoulder of his enemy, which felled him to the earth, mortally wounded. He then sprang from his horse, sword in hand, with the intention of cutting off the head of his fallen foe, when the Marshal d'Andreghem threw a golden wand into the arena as a signal that hostilities should cease. Du Guesclin was proclaimed the victor amid the joyous acclamations of the crowd, and retiring, left the field to the meaner combatants, who were afterwards to make sport for the people. Four English and as many French squires fought for some time with pointless lances, when the French gaining the advantage, the sports were declared at an end.

In the time of Charles VI., about the beginning of the fifteenth century, a famous duel was ordered by the parliament of Paris. The Sieur de Carrouges being absent in the Holy Land, his lady was violated by the Sieur Legris. Carrouges, on his return, challenged Legris to mortal combat for the twofold crime of violation and slander, inasmuch as he had denied his guilt by asserting that the lady was a willing party. The lady's asseverations of innocence were held to be no evidence by the parliament, and the duel was commanded, with all the ceremonies. "On the day appointed," says Brantôme,* "the lady came to witness the spectacle in her chariot; but the king made her descend, judging her unworthy, because she was criminal in his eyes till her innocence was proved, and caused her to stand upon a scaffold to await the mercy of God and this judgment by the battle. After a short struggle, the Sieur de Carrouges overthrew his enemy, and made him confess both the rape and the slander. He was then taken to the gallows and hanged in the presence of the multitude; while the innocence of the lady was proclaimed by the heralds, and recognised by her husband, the king, and all the spectators."

Numerous battles of a similar description constantly took place, until the unfortunate issue of one encounter of the kind led the French king, Henry II., to declare solemnly that he would never again permit any such encounter, whether it related to a civil or criminal case, or the honour of a gentleman.

This memorable combat was fought in the year 1547. François de Vivonne, lord of La Chataigneraie, and Guy de Chabot, lord of Jarnac, had been friends from their early youth, and were noted at the court of Francis I. for the gallantry of their bearing and the magnificence of their retinue. Chataigneraie, who knew that his friend's means were not very ample, asked him one day in confidence how it was that he contrived to be so well provided? Jarnac replied, that his father had married a young and beautiful woman, who, loving the son far better than the sire, supplied him with as much money as he desired. La Chataigneraie betrayed the base secret to the dauphin, the dauphin to the king, the king to his courtiers, and the courtiers to all their acquaintance. In a short time it reached the ears of the old Lord de Jarnac, who immediately sent for his son, and demanded to know in what manner the report had originated, and whether he had been vile enough not only to carry on such a connexion but to boast of it? De Jarnac indignantly denied that he had ever said so, or given reason to the world to say so, and requested his father to accompany him to court and confront him with his accuser, that he might see the manner in which he would confound him. They went accordingly; and the younger de Jarnac, entering a room where the dauphin, La Chataigneraie, and several courtiers were present, exclaimed aloud, "That whoever had asserted that he maintained a criminal connexion with his mother-in-law was a liar and a coward!" Every eye was turned to the dauphin and La Chataigneraie, when the

* *Mémoires de Brantôme touchant les Duels.*

latter stood forward and asserted, that De Jarnac had himself avowed that such was the fact, and he would extort from his lips another confession of it. A case like this could not be met or rebutted by any legal proof, and the royal council ordered that it should be decided by single combat. The king, however, set his face against the duel,* and forbade them both, under pain of his high displeasure, to proceed any further in the matter. But Francis died in the following year, and the dauphin, now Henry II., who was himself compromised, resolved that the combat should take place.

The lists were prepared in the court-yard of the chateau of St. Germain-en-Laye, and the 10th of July, 1547, was appointed for the encounter. The cartels of the combatants, which are preserved in the *Mémoires de Castelnau*, were as follow :

> "*Cartel of François de Vivonne, lord of La Chataigneraie.*
>
> "SIRE,
>   "Having learned that Guy Chabot de Jarnac, being lately at Compiegne, asserted that whoever had said that he boasted of having criminal intercourse with his mother-in-law was wicked and a wretch, I, sire, with your good will and pleasure, do answer that he has wickedly lied, and will lie as many times as he denies having said that which I affirm he did say ; for I repeat, that he told me several times, and boasted of it, that he had slept with his mother-in-law.
> "FRANÇOIS DE VIVONNE."

To this cartel De Jarnac replied :

> "SIRE,
>   "With your good will and permission, I say, that François de Vivonne has lied in the imputation which he has cast upon me, and of which I spoke to you at Compiegne. I therefore entreat you, sire, most humbly, that you be pleased to grant us a fair field, that we may fight this battle to the death."
> "GUY CHABOT."

The preparations were conducted on a scale of the greatest magnificence, the king having intimated his intention of being present. La Chataigneraie made sure of the victory, and invited the king and a hundred and fifty of the principal personages of the court to sup with him in the evening, after the battle, in a splendid tent which

---

* Although Francis shewed himself in this case an enemy to duelling, yet in his own case he had not the same objection. Every reader of history must remember his answer to the challenge of the Emperor Charles V. The emperor wrote that he had failed i n his word, and that he would sustain their quarrel single-handed against him. Francis replied, that he lied—*qu'il en avait menti par la gorge*, and that he was ready to meet him in single combat whenever and wherever he pleased.

he had prepared at the extremity of the lists. De Jarnac was not so confident, though perhaps more desperate. At noon, on the day appointed, the combatants met, and each took the customary oath that he bore no charms or amulets about him, or made use of any magic, to aid him against his antagonist. They then attacked each other, sword in hand. La Chataigneraie was a strong robust man, and over confident; De Jarnac was nimble, supple, and prepared for the worst. The combat lasted for some time doubtful, until De Jarnac, overpowered by the heavy blows of his opponent, covered his head with his shield, and stooping down, endeavoured to make amends by his agility for his deficiency of strength. In this crouching posture he aimed two blows at the left thigh of La Chataigneraie, who had left it uncovered, that the motion of his leg might not be impeded. Each blow was successful, and, amid the astonishment of all the spectators, and to the great regret of the king, La Chataigneraie rolled over upon the sand. He seized his dagger, and made a last effort to strike De Jarnac: but he was unable to support himself, and fell powerless into the arms of the assistants. The officers now interfered, and De Jarnac being declared the victor, fell down upon his knees, uncovered his head, and, clasping his hands together, exclaimed: " *O Domine, non sum dignus!*" La Chataigneraie was so mortified by the result of the encounter, that he resolutely refused to have his wounds dressed. He tore off the bandages which the surgeons applied, and expired two days afterwards. Ever since that time, any sly and unforeseen attack has been called by the French a *coup de Jarnac*. Henry was so grieved at the loss of his favourite, that he made the solemn oath already alluded to, that he would never again, so long as he lived, permit a duel. Some writers have asserted, and among others, Mezerai, that he issued a royal edict forbidding them. This has been doubted by others, and as there appears no registry of the edict in any of the courts, it seems most probable that it was never issued. This opinion is strengthened by the fact, that, two years afterwards, the council ordered another duel to be fought with similar forms, but with less magnificence, on account of the inferior rank of the combatants. It is not any where stated that Henry interfered to prevent it, notwithstanding his solemn oath; but that, on the contrary, he encouraged it, and appointed the Marshal de la Marque to see that it was conducted according to the rules of chivalry. The disputants were Fendille and D'Aguerre, two gentlemen of the household, who, quarrelling in the king's chamber, had proceeded from words to blows. The council, being informed of the matter, decreed that it could only be decided in the lists. Marshal de la Marque, with the king's permission, appointed the city of Sedan as the place of combat. Fendille, who was a bad swordsman, was anxious to avoid an encounter with D'Aguerre, who was one of the most expert men of the age; but the council authoritatively commanded that he should fight, or be degraded from all his honours. D'Aguerre appeared in the field attended by François de Vendôme, Count de Chartres, while Fendille was accompanied by the Duke of Nevers. Fendille appears to have been not only an inexpert swordsman, but a thorough coward; one who, like Cowley, might have heaped curses on the man,

> " (Death's factor sure), who brought
> Dire swords into this peaceful world."

On the very first encounter he was thrown from his horse, and, confessing on the ground all that his victor required of him, slunk away ignominiously from the arena.

One is tempted to look upon the death of Henry II. as a judgment upon him for his perjury in the matter of duelling. In a grand tournament instituted on the occasion of the marriage of his daughter, he broke several lances in encounters with some of the bravest knights of the time. Ambitious of still further renown, he would not rest satisfied until he had also engaged the young Count de Montgommeri. He received a wound in the eye from the lance of his antagonist, and died from its effects shortly afterwards, in the forty-first year of his age.

In the succeeding reigns of Francis II., Charles IX., and Henry III., the practice of duelling increased to an alarming extent. Duels were not rare in the other countries of Europe at the same period; but in France they were so frequent, that historians, in speaking of that age, designate it as "l'époque de la fureur des duels." The parliament of Paris endeavoured, as far as in its power lay, to discourage the practice. By a decree dated the 26th of June 1559, it declared all persons who should be present at duels, or aiding and abetting in them, to be rebels to the king, transgressors of the law, and disturbers of the public peace.

When Henry III. was assassinated at St. Cloud in 1589, a young gentleman, named L'Isle-Marivaut, who had been much beloved by him, took his death so much to heart, that he resolved not to survive him. Not thinking suicide an honourable death, and wishing, as he said, to die gloriously in revenging his king and master, he publicly expressed his readiness to fight any body to the death, who should assert that Henry's assassination was not a great misfortune to the community. Another youth, of a fiery temper and tried courage, named Marolles, took him at his word, and the day and place of the combat were forthwith appointed. When the hour had come, and all were ready, Marolles turned to his second, and asked whether his opponent had a casque or helmet only, or whether he wore a *sallade*, or headpiece. Being answered a helmet only, he said gaily, " So much the better; for, sir my second, you shall repute me the wickedest man in all the world, if I do not thrust my lance right through the middle of his head and kill him." Truth to say, he did so at the very first onset, and the unhappy L'Isle-Marivaut expired without a groan. Brantôme, who relates this story, adds, that the victor might have done as he pleased with the body, cut off the head, dragged it out of the camp, or exposed it upon an ass; but that being a wise and very courteous gentleman, he left it to the relatives of the deceased to be honourably buried, contenting himself with the glory of his triumph, by which he gained no little renown and honour among the ladies of Paris.

On the accession of Henry IV., that monarch determined to set his face against duelling; but such was the influence of early education and the prejudices of society upon him, that he never could find it in his heart to punish a man for this offence. He thought it tended to foster a warlike spirit among his people. When the chivalrous Créqui demanded his permission to fight Don Philippe de Savoire, he is reported to have said, " Go, and if I were not a king, I would be your second." It is no wonder that when such was known to be the king's disposition, his edicts attracted but small attention. A calculation was made by M. de Lomenie, in the year 1607, that since the accession of Henry, in 1589, no less than four thousand French gentlemen had lost

HENRY IV.

their lives in these conflicts; which, for the eighteen years, would have been at the rate of four or five in a week, or eighteen per month! Sully, who reports this fact in his Memoirs, does not throw the slightest doubt upon its exactness; and adds, that it was chiefly owing to the facility and ill-advised good-nature of his royal master that the bad example had so empoisoned the court, the city, and the whole country. This wise minister devoted much of his time and attention to the subject; for the rage, he says, was such as to cause him a thousand pangs, and the king also. There was hardly a man moving in what was called good society, who had not been engaged in a duel either as principal or second; and if there were such a man, his chief desire was to free himself from the imputation of non-duelling, by picking a quarrel with somebody. Sully constantly wrote letters to the king, in which he prayed him to renew the edicts against this barbarous custom, to aggravate the punishment against offenders, and never, in any instance, to grant a pardon, even to a person who had wounded another in a duel, much less to any one who had taken away life. He also advised, that some sort of tribunal, or court of honour, should be established, to take cognisance of injurious and slanderous language, and of all such matters as usually led to duels; and that the justice to be administered by this court should be sufficiently prompt and severe to appease the complainant, and make the offender repent of his aggression.

Henry, being so warmly pressed by his friend and minister, called together an extraordinary council in the gallery of the palace of Fontainebleau, to take the matter into consideration. When all the

GALLERY AT FONTAINEBLEAU.

members were assembled, his majesty requested that some person conversant with the subject would make a report to him on the origin, progress, and different forms of the duel. Sully complacently remarks that none of the councillors gave the king any great reason to felicitate them on their erudition. In fact, they all remained silent. Sully held his peace with the rest; but he looked so knowing, that the king turned towards him, and said—" Great master! by your face I conjecture that you know more of this matter than you would have us believe. I pray you, and indeed I command, that you tell us what you think, and what you know." The coy minister refused, as he says, out of mere politeness to his more ignorant colleagues ; but, being again pressed by the king, he entered into a history of duelling both in ancient and modern times. He has not preserved this history in his Memoirs ; and, as none of the ministers or councillors present thought proper to do so, the world is deprived of a discourse which was, no doubt, a learned and remarkable one. The result was, that a royal edict was issued, which Sully lost no time in transmitting to the most distant provinces, with a distinct notification to all parties concerned that the king was in earnest, and would exert the full rigour of the law in punishment of the offenders. Sully himself does not inform us what were the provisions of the new law ; but Father Matthias has been more explicit, and from him we learn, that the marshals of France were created judges of a court of chivalry, for the hearing of all causes wherein the honour of a noble or gentleman was concerned, and that such as resorted to duelling should be punished by death and confiscation of property, and that the seconds and assistants should lose their rank, dignity, or offices, and be banished from the court of their sovereign.*

But so strong a hold had the education and prejudice of his age upon the mind of the king, that though his reason condemned, his sympathies approved the duel. Notwithstanding this threatened severity, the number of duels did not diminish, and the wise Sully had still to lament the prevalence of an evil which menaced society with utter disorganisation. In the succeeding reign the practice prevailed, if possible, to a still greater extent, until the Cardinal de Richelieu, better able to grapple with it than Sully had been, made some severe examples in the very highest classes. Lord Herbert, the English ambassador at the court of Louis XIII., repeats, in his letters, an observation that had been previously made in the reign of Henry IV., that it was rare to find a Frenchman moving in good society who had not killed his man in a duel. The Abbé Millot says of this period, that the duel madness made the most terrible ravages. Men had actually a frenzy for combating. Caprice and vanity, as well as the excitement of passion, imposed the necessity of fighting. Friends were obliged to enter into the quarrels of their friends, or be themselves called out for their refusal, and revenge became hereditary in many families. It was reckoned that in twenty years eight thou-

* *Le Père Matthias*, tome ii. livre iv.

sand letters of pardon had been issued to persons who had killed
others in single combat.*

Other writers confirm this statement. Amelot de Houssaye, in
his Memoirs, says, upon this subject, that duels were so common
in the first years of the reign of Louis XIII., that the ordinary conversation of persons when they met in the morning was, "*Do you
know who fought yesterday?*" and after dinner, "*Do you know who
fought this morning?*" The most infamous duellist at that period
was De Bouteville. It was not at all necessary to quarrel with this
assassin, to be forced to fight a duel with him. When he heard that
any one was very brave, he would go to him, and say, "*People tell me
that you are brave; you and I must fight together!*" Every morning the
most notorious bravos and duellists used to assemble at his house, to
take a breakfast of bread and wine, and practice fencing. M. de Valençay, who was afterwards elevated to the rank of a cardinal, stood
very high in the estimation of De Bouteville and his gang. Hardly
a day passed but what he was engaged in some duel or other, either
as principal or second; and he once challenged De Bouteville himself, his best friend, because De Bouteville had fought a duel without
inviting him to become his second. This quarrel was only appeased
on the promise of De Bouteville that, in his next encounter, he would
not fail to avail himself of his services. For that purpose he went
out the same day and picked a quarrel with the Marquis des Portes.
M. de Valençay, according to agreement, had the pleasure of serving
as his second, and of running through the body M. de Cavois, the
second of the Marquis des Portes, a man who had never done him any
injury, and whom he afterwards acknowledged he had never seen before.

Cardinal Richelieu devoted much attention to this lamentable state
of public morals, and seems to have concurred with his great predecessor Sully, that nothing but the most rigorous severity could put a
stop to the evil. The subject indeed was painfully forced upon him
by his enemies. The Marquis de Themines, to whom Richelieu, then
Bishop of Luçon, had given offence by some representations he had
made to Mary of Medicis, determined, since he could not challenge an
ecclesiastic, to challenge his brother. An opportunity was soon found.
Themines, accosting the Marquis de Richelieu, complained, in an insulting tone, that the Bishop of Luçon had broken his faith. The
marquis resented both the manner and matter of his speech, and
readily accepted a challenge. They met in the Rue d'Angoulême,
and the unfortunate Richelieu was stabbed to the heart, and instantly
expired. From that moment the bishop became the steady foe of the
practice of duelling. Reason and the impulse of brotherly love alike

* *Elémens de l'Histoire de France,* vol. iii. p. 219.

combined to make him detest it, and when his power in France was firmly established, he set vigorously about repressing it. In his *Testament Politique*, he has collected his thoughts upon the subject, in the chapter entitled "Des moyens d'arrêter les Duels." In spite of the edicts that he published, the members of the nobility persisted in fighting upon the most trivial and absurd pretences. At last Richelieu made a terrible example. The infamous De Bouteville challenged and fought the Marquis de Beuvron; and although the duel itself was not fatal to either, its consequences were fatal to both. High as they were, Richelieu resolved that the law should reach them both, and they were both tried, found guilty, and beheaded. Thus did society get rid of one of the most bloodthirsty scoundrels that ever polluted it.

In 1632 two noblemen fought a duel in which they were both killed. The officers of justice had notice of the breach of the law, and arrived at the scene of combat before the friends of the parties had time to remove the bodies. In conformity with the cardinal's severe code upon the subject, the bodies were ignominiously stripped and hanged upon a gallows with their heads downwards, for several hours, within sight of all the people.* This severity sobered the frenzy of the nation for a time; but it was soon forgotten. Men's minds were too deeply imbued with a false notion of honour to be brought to a right way of thinking : by such examples, however striking, Richelieu was unable to persuade them to walk in the right path, though he could punish them for choosing the wrong one. He

SULLY.

had, with all his acuteness, miscalculated the spirit of duelling. It was not death that a duellist feared; it was shame, and the contempt of his fellows. As Addison remarked more than eighty years afterwards, "Death was not sufficient to deter men who made it their glory to despise it; but if every one who fought a duel were to stand in the pillory, it would quickly diminish the number of those imaginary men of honour, and put an end to so absurd a practice." Richelieu never thought of this.

Sully says, that in his time the Germans were also much addicted to duelling. There were three places where it was legal to fight;

* *Mercure de France*, vol. xiii.

Witzburg in Franconia, and Uspach and Halle in Swabia. Thither, of course, vast numbers repaired, and murdered each other under sanction of the law. At an earlier period in Germany, it was held highly disgraceful to refuse to fight. Any one who surrendered to his adversary for a simple wound that did not disable him, was reputed infamous, and could neither cut his beard, bear arms, mount on horseback, or hold any office in the state. He who fell in a duel was buried with great pomp and splendour.

In the year 1652, just after Louis XIV. had attained his majority, a desperate duel was fought between the Dukes de Beaufort and de Nemours, each attended by four gentlemen. Although brothers-in-law, they had long been enemies, and their constant dissensions had introduced much disorganisation among the troops which they severally commanded. Each had long sought an opportunity for combat, which at last arose on a misunderstanding relative to the places they were to occupy at the council-board. They fought with pistols, and, at the first discharge, the Duke de Nemours was shot through the body, and almost instantly expired. Upon this the Marquis de Villars, who seconded Nemours, challenged Héricourt, the second of the Duke de Beaufort, a man whom he had never before seen ; and the challenge being accepted, they fought even more desperately than their principals. This combat, being with swords, lasted longer than the first, and was more exciting to the six remaining gentlemen who stayed to witness it. The result was fatal to Héricourt, who fell pierced to the heart by the sword of De Villars. Any thing more savage than this can hardly be imagined. Voltaire says such duels were frequent, and the compiler of the *Dictionnaire d'Anecdotes* informs us that the number of seconds was not fixed. As many as ten, or twelve, or twenty, were not unfrequent, and they often fought together after their principals were disabled. The highest mark of friendship one man could manifest towards another, was to choose him for his second ; and many gentlemen were so desirous of serving in this capacity, that they endeavoured to raise every slight misunderstanding into a quarrel, that they might have the pleasure of being engaged in it. The Count de Bussy-Rabutin relates an instance of this in his Memoirs. He says, that as he was one evening coming out of the theatre, a gentleman named Bruc, whom he had not before known, stopped him very politely; and, drawing him aside, asked him if it was true that the Count de Thianges had called him (Bruc) a drunkard ? Bussy replied that he really did not know, for he saw the count very seldom. "Oh, he is your uncle !" replied Bruc ; "and, as I cannot have satisfaction from him, because he lives so far off in the country, I apply to you." "I see what you are at," replied Bussy, "and, since you wish to put me in my uncle's place, I answer, that whoever asserted that he called you a drunkard, told a lie !" "My brother said so," replied Bruc, "and he is a child." "Horsewhip him, then, for his falsehood," returned De Bussy. "I will not have my brother called a liar," returned Bruc, determined to quarrel with him ; "so draw, and defend yourself !" They both drew their swords in the public street, but were separated by the spectators. They agreed, however, to fight on a future occasion, and with all the regular forms of the duello. A few days afterwards, a gentleman, whom De Bussy had never before seen, and whom he did not know even by name, called upon him and asked if he might have the privilege of serving as his second. He added, that he neither knew him nor Bruc, except by reputation, but having made up his mind to be second of one of them, he had decided upon accompanying De Bussy as the braver man of the two. De Bussy thanked him very sincerely for his politeness, but begged to be excused, as he had already engaged four seconds to accompany him, and he was afraid that if he took any more the affair would become a battle instead of a duel.

When such quarrels as these were looked upon as mere matters of course, the state of society must have been indeed awful. Louis XIV. very early saw the evil, and as early determined to remedy it. It was not, however, till the year 1679, when he instituted the "Chambre Ardente," for the trial of the slow poisoners and pretenders to sorcery, that he published any edict against duelling. In that year his famous edict was promulgated, in which he reiterated and confirmed the severe enactments of his predecessors Henry IV. and Louis XIII., and expressed his determination never to pardon any offender. By this celebrated ordinance, a supreme court of honour was established, composed of the marshals of France. They were bound, on taking the office, to give to every one who brought a well-founded complaint before them, such reparation as would satisfy the justice of the case. Should any gentleman against whom complaint was made refuse to obey the mandate of the court of honour, he might be punished by fine and imprisonment ; and when that was not possible, by reason of his absenting himself from the kingdom, his estates might be confiscated till his return.

Every man who sent a challenge, be the cause of offence what it might, was deprived of all redress from the court of honour—suspended three years from the exercise of any office in the state—was further imprisoned for two years, and sentenced to pay a fine of half his yearly income.

He who accepted a challenge was subject to the same punishment.

Any servant or other person, who knowingly became the bearer of a challenge, was, if found guilty, sentenced to stand in the pillory and be publicly whipped for the first offence; and for the second, sent for three years to the galleys.

Any person who actually fought was to be held guilty of murder, even though death did not ensue, and was to be punished accordingly. Persons in the higher ranks of life were to be beheaded, and those of the middle class hanged upon a gallows, and their bodies refused Christian burial.

At the same time that Louis published this severe edict, he exacted a promise from his principal nobility that they would never engage in a duel on any pretence whatever. He never swerved from his resolution to pursue all duellists with the utmost rigour, and many were executed in various parts of the country. A slight abatement of the evil was the consequence, and in the course of a few years one duel was not fought where twelve had been fought previously. A medal was struck to commemorate the circumstance, by the express command of the king. So much had he this object at heart, that, in his will, he particularly recommended to his successor the care of his edict against duelling, and warned him against any ill judged lenity to those who disobeyed it.

A singular law formerly existed in Malta with regard to duelling. By this law it was permitted, but only upon condition that the parties should fight in one particular street. If they presumed to settle their quarrel elsewhere, they were held guilty of murder, and punished accordingly. What was also very singular, they were bound, under heavy penalties, to put up their swords when requested to do so by a priest, a knight, or a woman. It does not appear, however, that the ladies or the knights exercised this mild and beneficent privilege to any great extent ; the former were too often themselves the cause of duels, and the latter sympathised too much in the wounded honour of the combatants to attempt to separate them. The priests alone were the great peacemakers. Brydone says, that a cross was always painted on the wall opposite to the spot where a knight had been killed, and that in the " street of duels " he counted about twenty of them.*

In England the private duel was also practised to a scandalous extent towards the end of the sixteenth and beginning of the seventeenth centuries. The judicial combat now began to be more rare, but several instances of it are mentioned in history. One was instituted in the reign of Elizabeth, and another so late as the time of Charles I. Sir Henry Spelman gives an account of that which took

* Brydone's *Tour in Malta*, 1772.

place in Elizabeth's reign, which is curious, perhaps the more so when we consider that it was perfectly legal, and that similar combats remained so till the year 1819. A proceeding having been instituted in the Court of Common Pleas for the recovery of certain manorial rights in the county of Kent, the defendant offered to prove by single combat his right to retain possession. The plaintiff accepted the challenge, and the Court having no power to stay the proceedings, agreed to the champions who were to fight in lieu of the principals. The queen commanded the parties to compromise; but it being represented to her majesty that they were justified by law in the course they were pursuing, she allowed them to proceed. On the day appointed, the justices of the Common Pleas, and all the counsel engaged in the cause, appeared as umpires of the combat, at a place in Tothill-fields, where the lists had been prepared. The champions were ready for the encounter, and the plaintiff and defendant were publicly called to come forward and acknowledge them. The defendant answered to his name, and recognised his champion with the due formalities, but the plaintiff did not appear. Without his presence and authority the combat could not take place; and his absence being considered an abandonment of his claim, he was declared to be nonsuited, and barred for ever from renewing his suit before any other tribunal whatever.

The queen appears to have disapproved personally of this mode of settling a disputed claim, but her judges and legal advisers made no attempt to alter the barbarous law. The practice of private duelling excited more indignation, from its being of every-day occurrence. In the time of James I. the English were so infected with the French madness, that Bacon, when he was attorney-general, lent the aid of his powerful eloquence to effect a reformation of the evil. Informations were exhibited in the Star Chamber against two persons, named Priest and Wright, for being engaged, as principal and second, in a duel, on which occasion he delivered a charge that was so highly approved of by the Lords of the Council, that they ordered it to be printed and circulated over the country, as a thing " very meet and worthy to be remembered and made known unto the world." He began by considering the nature and greatness of the mischief of duelling. " It troubleth peace—it disfurnisheth war—it bringeth calamity upon private men, peril upon the state, and contempt upon the law. Touching the cause of it," he observed, "that the first motive of it, no doubt, is a false and erroneous imagination of honour and credit; but then, the seed of this mischief being such, it is nourished by vain discourses and green and unripe conceits. Hereunto may be added, that men have almost lost the true notion and understanding of fortitude and valour. For fortitude distinguisheth of the grounds of quarrel whether they be just; and not only so, but whether they be worthy, and setteth a better price upon men's lives than to bestow them idly. Nay, it is weakness and disesteem of a man's self to put a man's life upon such liedger performances. A man's life is not to be trifled with; it is to be offered up and sacrificed to honourable services, public merits, good causes, and noble adventures. It is in expense of blood as it is in expense of money. It is no liberality to make a profusion of money upon every vain occasion, neither is it fortitude to make effusion of blood, except the cause of it be worth."*

LORD BACON.

The most remarkable event connected with duelling in this reign was that between Lord Sanquir, a Scotch nobleman, and one Turner, a fencing-master. In a trial of skill between them, his lordship's eye was accidentally thrust out by the point of Turner's sword. Turner expressed great regret at the circumstance, and Lord Sanquir bore his loss with as much philosophy as he was master of, and forgave his antagonist. Three years afterwards, Lord Sanquir was at Paris, where he was a constant visitor at the court of Henry IV. One day, in the course of conversation, the affable monarch inquired how he had lost his eye. Sanquir, who prided himself on being the most expert swordsman of the age, blushed as he replied that it was inflicted by the sword of a fencing-master. Henry, forgetting his assumed character of an anti-duellist, carelessly, and as a mere matter of course, inquired whether the man lived? Nothing more was said; but the query sank deep into the proud heart of the Scotch baron, who returned shortly afterwards to England, burning for revenge. His first intent was to challenge the fencing-master to single combat; but, on further consideration, he deemed it inconsistent with his dignity to meet him as an equal in fair and open fight. He therefore hired two bravos, who set upon the fencing-master, and murdered him in his own house at Whitefriars. The assassins were taken and executed, and a reward of one thousand pounds offered for the apprehension of their employer. Lord Sanquir concealed himself for seve-

* See *Life and Character of Lord Bacon*, by Thomas Martin, Barrister-at-Law.

ral days, and then surrendered to take his trial, in the hope (happily false) that Justice would belie her name, and be lenient to a murderer because he was a nobleman, who on a false point of honour had thought fit to take revenge into his own hands. The most powerful intercessions were employed in his favour, but James, to his credit, was deaf to them all. Bacon, in his character of attorney-general, prosecuted the prisoner to conviction; and he died the felon's death on the 29th of June, 1612, on a gibbet erected in front of the gate of Westminster Hall.

With regard to the public duel, or trial by battle, demanded under the sanction of the law, to terminate a quarrel which the ordinary course of justice could with difficulty decide, Bacon was equally opposed to it, and thought that in no case should it be granted. He suggested that there should be declared a constant and settled resolution in the state to abolish it altogether; that care should be taken that the evil be no more cockered, nor the humour of it fed, but that all persons found guilty should be rigorously punished by the Star Chamber, and those of eminent quality banished from the court.

In the succeeding reign, when Donald Mackay, the first Lord Reay, accused David Ramsay of treason, in being concerned with the Marquis of Hamilton in a design upon the crown of Scotland, he was challenged by the latter to make good his assertion by single combat.* It had been at first the intention of the government to try the case by the common law, but Ramsay thought he would stand a better chance of escape by recurring to the old and almost exploded custom, but which was still the right of every man in appeals of treason. Lord Reay readily accepted the challenge, and both were confined in the Tower until they found security that they would appear on a certain day appointed by the court to determine the question. The management of the affair was delegated to the Marischal Court of Westminster, and the Earl of Lindsay was created Lord Constable of England for the purpose. Shortly before the day appointed, Ramsay confessed in substance all that Lord Reay had laid to his charge, upon which Charles I. put a stop to the proceedings.

But in England, about this period, sterner disputes arose among men than those mere individual matters which generate duels. The men of the Commonwealth encouraged no practice of the kind, and the subdued aristocracy carried their habits and prejudices elsewhere, and fought their duels at foreign courts. Cromwell's parliament, however—although the evil at that time was not so crying—published an order in 1654 for the prevention of duels, and the punishment of all concerned in them. Charles II., on his restoration, also

* See *History of the House and Clan of Mackay.*

issued a proclamation upon the subject. In his reign an infamous duel was fought—infamous not only from its own circumstances, but from the lenity that was shewn to the principal offenders.

The worthless duke of Buckingham, having debauched the Countess of Shrewsbury, was challenged by her husband to mortal combat in January 1668. Charles II. endeavoured to prevent the duel, not from any regard to public morality, but from fear for the life of his favourite. He gave commands to the Duke of Albemarle to confine Buckingham to his house, or take some other measures to prevent him from fighting. Albemarle neglected the order, thinking that the king himself might prevent the combat by some surer means. The meeting took place at Barn Elms; the injured Shrewsbury being attended by Sir John Talbot, his relative, and Lord Bernard Howard, son of the Earl of Arundel. Buckingham was accompanied by two of his dependants, Captain Holmes and Sir John Jenkins. According to the barbarous custom of the age, not only the principals, but the seconds engaged each other. Jenkins was pierced to the heart, and left dead upon the field, and Sir John Talbot severely wounded in both arms. Buckingham himself escaping with slight wounds, ran his unfortunate antagonist through the body, and then left the field with the wretched woman, the cause of all the mischief, who, in the dress of a page, awaited the issue of the conflict in a neighbouring wood, holding her paramour's horse to avoid suspicion. Great influence was exerted to save the guilty parties from punishment, and the master, as base as the favourite, made little difficulty in granting a free pardon to all concerned. In a royal proclamation issued shortly afterwards, Charles II. formally pardoned the murderers, but declared his intention never to extend in future any mercy to such offenders. It would be hard, after this, to say who was the most infamous, the king, the favourite, or the courtesan.

In the reign of Queen Anne, repeated complaints were made of the prevalence of duelling. Addison, Swift, Steele, and other writers employed their powerful pens in reprobation of it. Steele especially, in the *Tatler* and *Guardian*, exposed its impiety and absurdity, and endeavoured both by argument and by ridicule to bring his countrymen to a right way of thinking.* His comedy of *The Conscious Lovers* contains an admirable exposure of the abuse of the word *honour*, which led men into an error so lamentable. Swift, writing upon the subject, remarked that he could see no harm in rogues and fools shooting each other. Addison and Steele took higher ground; and the latter, in the *Guardian*, summed up nearly all that could be

---

* See *Spectator*, Nos. 84, 97, and 99; and *Tatler*, Nos. 25, 26, 29, 31, 38, and 39; and *Guardian*, No 20.

said upon the subject in the following impressive words :—" A Christian and a gentleman are made inconsistent appellations of the same person. You are not to expect eternal life if you do not forgive injuries, and your mortal life is rendered uncomfortable if you are not ready to commit a murder in resentment of an affront ; for good sense, as well as religion, is so utterly banished the world, that men glory in their very passions, and pursue trifles with the utmost vengeance, so little do they know that to forgive is the most arduous pitch human nature can arrive at. A coward has often fought, a coward has often conquered ; but a coward never forgave." Steele also published a pamphlet, in which he gave a detailed account of the edict of Louis XIV., and the measures taken by that monarch to cure his subjects of their murderous folly.

On the 8th of May, 1711, Sir Cholmely Decring, M.P. for the county of Kent, was slain in a duel by Mr. Richard Thornhill, also a member of the House of Commons. Three days afterwards Sir Peter King brought the subject under the notice of the legislature ; and after dwelling at considerable length on the alarming increase of the practice, obtained leave to bring in a bill for the prevention and punishment of duelling. It was read a first time that day, and ordered for a second reading in the ensuing week.

About the same time, the attention of the Upper House of Parliament was also drawn to the subject in the most painful manner. Two of its most noted members would have fought had it not been that Queen Anne received notice of their intention, and exacted a pledge that they would desist ; while a few months afterwards two other of its members lost their lives in one of the most remarkable duels upon record. The first affair, which happily terminated without a meeting, was between the Duke of Marlborough and the Earl Pawlet ; the latter and fatal encounter was between the Duke of Hamilton and Lord Mohun.

The first arose out of a debate in the Lords upon the conduct of the Duke of Ormond in refusing to hazard a general engagement with the enemy, in which Earl Pawlet remarked that nobody could doubt the courage of the Duke of Ormond. " He was not like a certain general, who led troops to the slaughter, to cause great numbers of officers to be knocked on the head in a battle, or against stone walls, in order to fill his pockets by disposing of their commissions." Every one felt that the remark was aimed at the Duke of Marlborough, but he remained silent, though evidently suffering in mind. Soon after the House broke up, the Earl Pawlet received a visit from Lord Mohun, who told him that the Duke of Marlborough was anxious to come to an explanation with him relative to some expressions he had made use of in that day's debate, and therefore prayed him to "go and take a little air in the country." Earl Pawlet did not affect to misunderstand the hint, but asked him in plain terms whether he brought a challenge from the duke. Lord Mohun said his message needed no explanation, and that he (Lord Mohun) would accompany the Duke of Marlborough. He then took his leave, and Earl Pawlet returned home and told his lady that he was going out to fight a duel with the Duke of Marlborough. His lady, alarmed for her lord's safety, gave notice of his intention to the Earl of Dartmouth, who immediately, in the queen's name, sent to the Duke of Marlborough, and commanded him not to stir abroad. He also caused Earl Pawlet's house to be guarded by two sentinels; and having taken these precautions, informed the queen of the whole affair. Her Majesty sent at once for the duke, expressed her abhorrence of the custom of duelling, and required his word of honour that he would proceed no further. The duke pledged his word accordingly, and the affair terminated.

The lamentable duel between the Duke of Hamilton and Lord Mohun took place in November 1712, and sprang from the following circumstances. A lawsuit had been pending for eleven years between these two noblemen, and they looked upon each other in consequence with a certain degree of coldness. They met together on the 13th of November in the chambers of Mr. Orlebar, a master in Chancery, when, in the course of conversation, the Duke of Hamilton reflected upon the conduct of one of the witnesses in the cause, saying that he was a person who had neither truth nor justice in him. Lord Mohun, somewhat nettled at this remark applied to a witness favourable to his side, made answer hastily, that Mr. Whiteworth, the person alluded to, had quite as much truth and justice in him as the Duke of Hamilton. The duke made no reply, and no one present imagined that he took offence at what was said; and when he went out of the room he made a low and courteous salute to the Lord Mohun. In the evening, General Macartney called twice upon the duke with a challenge from Lord Mohun, and failing in seeing him, sought him a third time at a tavern, where he found him, and delivered his message. The duke accepted the challenge, and the day after the morrow, which was Sunday, the 15th of November, at seven in the morning, was appointed for the meeting.

At that hour they assembled in Hyde Park, the duke being attended by his relative Colonel Hamilton, and the Lord Mohun by General Macartney. They jumped over a ditch into a place called the Nursery, and prepared for the combat. The Duke of Hamilton, turning to General Macartney, said, "*Sir, you are the cause of this, let the event be what it will."* Lord Mohun did not wish that the seconds should engage, but the duke insisted that " *Macartney should have a share in the dance.*" All being ready, the two principals took up their positions, and fought with swords so desperately, that after a short time they both fell down mortally wounded. The Lord Mohun expired upon the spot, and the Duke of Hamilton in the arms of his servants as they were carrying him to his coach.

This unhappy termination caused the greatest excitement not only in the metropolis, but all over the country. The Tories, grieved at the loss of the Duke of Hamilton, charged the fatal combat on the Whig party, whose leader, the Duke of Marlborough, had so recently set the example of political duels. They called Lord Mohun the bully of the Whig faction (he had already killed three men in duels, and been twice tried for murder), and asserted openly that the quarrel was concocted between him and General Macartney to rob the country of the services of the Duke of Hamilton by murdering him. It was also asserted that the wound of which the duke died was not inflicted by Lord Mohun, but by Macartney ; and every means was used to propagate this belief. Colonel Hamilton, against whom and Macartney the coroner's jury had returned a verdict of wilful murder, surrendered a few days afterwards, and was examined before a privy council sitting at the house of Lord Dartmouth. He then deposed, that seeing Lord Mohun fall, and the duke upon him, he ran to the duke's assistance ; and that he might with the more ease help him, he flung down both their swords, and as he was raising the duke up, *he saw Macartney make a push at him.* Upon this deposition, a royal proclamation was immediately issued, offering a reward of 500*l.* for the apprehension of Macartney, to which the Duchess of Hamilton afterwards added a reward of 300*l.*

Upon the further examination of Colonel Hamilton, it was found that reliance could not be placed on all his statements, and that he contradicted himself in several important particulars. He was arraigned at the Old Bailey for the murder of Lord Mohun, the whole political circles of London being in a fever of excitement for the result. All the Tory party prayed for his acquittal, and a Tory mob surrounded the doors and all the avenues leading to the court of justice for many. hours before the trial began. The examination of witnesses lasted seven hours. The criminal still persisted in accusing General Macartney of the murder of the Duke of Hamilton, but in other respects, say the newspapers of the day, prevaricated foully. He was found guilty of manslaughter. This favourable verdict was received with universal applause, "not only from the court and all the gentlemen present, but the common people shewed a mighty satisfaction, which they testified by loud and repeated huzzas."*

As the popular delirium subsided, and men began to reason coolly upon the subject, they disbelieved the assertions of Colonel Hamilton, that Macartney had stabbed the duke, although it was universally admitted that he had been much too busy and presuming. Hamilton was shunned by all his former companions, and his life rendered so irksome to him, that he sold out of the Guards and retired to private life, in which he died heart-broken four years afterwards.

General Macartney surrendered about the same time, and was tried for murder in the Court of King's Bench. He was, however, found guilty of manslaughter only.

At the opening of the session of Parliament of 1713, the queen made pointed allusion in her speech to the frequency of duelling, and recommended to the legislature to devise some speedy and effectual remedy for it. A bill to that effect was brought forward, but thrown out on the second reading, to the very great regret of all the sensible portion of the community.

A famous duel was fought in 1765 between Lord Byron and Mr. Chaworth. The dispute arose at a club-dinner, and was relative to which of the two had the largest quantity of game on his estates. Infuriated by wine and passion, they retired instantly into an adjoining room, and fought with swords across a table, by the feeble glimmer of a tallow candle. Mr. Chaworth, who was the more expert swordsman of the two, received a mortal wound, and shortly afterwards expired. Lord Byron was brought to trial for the murder before the House of Lords ; and it appearing clearly that the duel was not premeditated, but fought at once, and in the heat of passion, he was found guilty of manslaughter only, and ordered to be discharged upon payment of his fees. This was a very bad example for the country, and duelling of course fell into no disrepute after such a verdict.

In France more severity was exercised. In the year 1769, the parliament of Grenoble took cognisance of the delinquency of the Sieur Duchelas, one of its members, who challenged and killed in a duel a captain of the Flemish legion. The servant of Duchelas officiated as second, and was arraigned with his master for the murder of the captain. They were both found guilty. Duchelas was broken alive on the wheel, and the servant condemned to the galleys for life.

A barbarous and fiercely-contested duel was fought in November 1778, between two foreign adventurers, at Bath, named Count Rice and the Vicomte du Barri. Some dispute arose relative to a gambling

* *Post-Boy,* December 13th, 1712.

transaction, in the course of which Du Barri contradicted an assertion of the other, by saying "That is not true!" Count Rice immediately asked him if he knew the very disagreeable meaning of the words he had employed. Du Barri said he was perfectly well aware of their meaning, and that Rice might interpret them just as he pleased. A challenge was immediately given and accepted. Seconds were sent for, who, arriving with but little delay, the whole party, though it was not long after midnight, proceeded to a place called Claverton Down, where they remained with a surgeon until daylight. They then prepared for the encounter, each being armed with two pistols and a sword. The ground having been marked out by the seconds, Du Barri fired first, and wounded his opponent in the thigh. Count Rice then levelled his pistol, and shot Du Barri mortally in the breast. So angry were the combatants, that they refused to desist; both stepped back a few paces, and then rushing forward, discharged their second pistols at each other. Neither shot took effect, and both throwing away their pistols, prepared to finish the sanguinary struggle by the sword. They took their places, and were advancing towards each other, when the Vicomte du Barri suddenly staggered, grew pale, and, falling on the ground, exclaimed, "*Je vous demande ma vie.*" His opponent had but just time to answer that he granted it, when the unfortunate Du Barri turned upon the grass, and expired with a heavy groan. The survivor of this savage conflict was then removed to his lodgings, where he lay for some weeks in a dangerous state. The coroner's jury, in the mean while, sat upon the body of Du Barri, and disgraced themselves by returning a verdict of manslaughter only. Count Rice, upon his recovery, was indicted for the murder notwithstanding this verdict. On his trial he entered into a long defence of his conduct, pleading the fairness of the duel, and its unpremeditated nature ; and, at the same time, expressing his deep regret for the unfortunate death of Du Barri, with whom for many years he had been bound in ties of the strictest friendship. These considerations appear to have weighed with the jury, and this fierce duellist was again found guilty of manslaughter only, and escaped with a merely nominal punishment.

A duel, less remarkable from its circumstances, but more so from the rank of the parties, took place in 1789. The combatants on this occasion were the Duke of York and Colonel Lenox, the nephew and heir of the Duke of Richmond. The cause of offence was given by the Duke of York, who had said in presence of several officers of the Guards, that words had been used to Colonel Lenox at Daubigny's to which no gentleman ought to have submitted. Colonel Lenox went up to the duke on parade, and asked him publicly whether he had made such an assertion. The Duke of York, without answering his question, coldly ordered him to his post. When parade was over, he took an opportunity of saying publicly in the orderly-room before Colonel Lenox, that he desired no protection from his rank as a prince and his station as commanding-officer; adding that, when he was off duty, he wore a plain brown coat like a private gentleman, and was ready as such to give satisfaction. Colonel Lenox desired nothing better than satisfaction; that is to say, to run the chance of shooting the duke through the body, or being himself shot. He accordingly challenged his Royal Highness, and they met on Wimbledon Common. Colonel Lenox fired first, and the ball whizzed past the head of his opponent, so near to it as to graze his projecting curl. The duke refused to return the fire, and the seconds interfering, the affair terminated.

Colonel Lenox was very shortly afterwards engaged in another duel arising out of this. A Mr. Swift wrote a pamphlet in reference to the dispute between him and the Duke of York, at some expressions in which he took so much offence, as to imagine that nothing but a shot at the writer could atone for them. They met on the Uxbridge Road, but no damage was done to either party.

The Irish were for a long time renowned for their love of duelling. The slightest offence which it is possible to imagine that one man could offer to another was sufficient to provoke a challenge. Sir Jonah Barrington relates, in his *Memoirs*, that, previous to the Union, during the time of a disputed election in Dublin, it was no unusual thing for three-and-twenty duels to be fought in a day. Even in times of less excitement they were so common as to be deemed unworthy of note by the regular chroniclers of events, except in cases where one or both of the combatants were killed.

In those days, in Ireland, it was not only the man of the military, but of every profession, who had to work his way to eminence with the sword or the pistol. Each political party had its regular corps of bullies, or fire-eaters, as they were called, who qualified themselves for being the pests of society by spending all their spare time in firing at targets. They boasted that they could hit an opponent in any part of his body they pleased, and made up their minds before the encounter began whether they should kill him, disable, or disfigure him for life—lay him on a bed of suffering for a twelvemonth, or merely graze a limb.

The evil had reached an alarming height, when, in the year 1808, an opportunity was offered to King George III. of shewing in a striking manner his detestation of the practice, and of setting an example to the Irish that such murders were not to be committed with impunity. A dispute arose, in the month of June 1807, between Major Campbell and Captain Boyd, officers of the 21st regiment, stationed in Ireland, about the proper manner of giving the word of command on parade. Hot words ensued on this slight occasion, and the result was a challenge from Campbell to Boyd. They retired into the mess-room shortly afterwards, and each stationed himself at a corner, the distance obliquely being but seven paces. Here, without friends or seconds being present, they fired at each other, and Captain Boyd fell mortally wounded between the fourth and fifth ribs. A surgeon, who came in shortly, found him sitting in a chair, vomiting and suffering great agony. He was led into another room, Major Campbell following, in great distress and perturbation of mind. Boyd survived but eighteen hours, and just before his death, said, in reply to a question from his opponent, that the duel was not fair, and added, "You hurried me, Campbell—you're a bad man."— "Good God!" replied Campbell, "will you mention before these gentlemen, was not every thing fair? Did you not say that you were ready?" Boyd answered faintly, "Oh, no! you know I wanted you to wait and have friends." On being again asked whether all was fair, the dying man faintly murmured, "Yes:" but in a minute after, he said, "You're a bad man!" Campbell was now in great agitation, and wringing his hands convulsively, he exclaimed, "Oh, Boyd! you are the happiest man of the two! Do you forgive me?" Boyd replied, "I forgive you—I feel for you, as I know you do for me." He shortly afterwards expired, and Major Campbell made his escape from Ireland, and lived for some months with his family under an assumed name, in the neighbourhood of Chelsea. He was, however, apprehended, and brought to trial at Armagh, in August 1808. He said we in prison, that, if found guilty of murder, he should suffer as an example to duellists in Ireland; but he endeavoured to buoy himself up with the hope that the jury would only convict him of manslaughter. It was proved in evidence upon the trial, that the duel was not fought immediately after the offence was given, but that Major Campbell went home and drank tea with his family before he sought Boyd for the fatal encounter. The jury returned a verdict of wilful murder against him, but recommended him to mercy on the ground that the duel had been a fair one. He was condemned to die on the Monday following, but was afterwards respited for a few days longer. In the mean time the greatest exertions were made in his behalf. His unfortunate wife went upon her knees before the Prince of Wales, to move him to use his influence with the king in favour of her unhappy husband. Every thing a fond wife and a courageous woman could do she tried, to gain the royal clemency; but George III. was inflexible, in consequence of the representations of the Irish viceroy that an example was necessary. The law was therefore allowed to take its course, and the victim of a false spirit of honour died the death of a felon.

The most inveterate duellists of the present day are the students in the Universities of Germany. They fight on the most frivolous pretences, and settle with swords and pistols the schoolboy disputes which in other countries are arranged by the more harmless medium of the fisticuffs. It was at one time the custom among these savage youths to prefer the sword-combat, for the facility it gave them of cutting off the noses of their opponents. To disfigure them in this manner was an object of ambition, and the German duellists reckoned the number of these disgusting trophies which they had borne away, with as much satisfaction as a successful general the provinces he had reduced or the cities he had taken.

But it would be wearisome to enter into the minute detail of all the duels of modern times. If an examination were made into the general causes which produced them, it would be found that in every case they had been either of the most trivial or the most unworthy nature. Parliamentary duels were at one time very common, and amongst the names of those who have soiled a great reputation by conforming to the practice, may be mentioned those of Warren Hastings, Sir Philip Francis, Wilkes, Pitt, Fox, Grattan, Curran, Tierney, and Canning. So difficult is it even for the superior mind to free itself from the trammels with which foolish opinion has enswathed it— not one of these celebrated persons who did not in his secret soul condemn the folly to which he lent himself. The bonds of reason, though iron-strong, are easily burst through; but those of folly, though lithe and frail as the rushes by a stream, defy the stoutest heart to snap them asunder. Colonel Thomas, an officer in the Guards, who was killed in a duel, added the following clause to his will the night before he died:—" In the first place, I commit my soul to Almighty God, in hope of his mercy and pardon for the irreligious step I now (in compliance with the unwarrantable customs of this wicked world) put myself under the necessity of taking." How many have been in the same state of mind as this wise, foolish man ! He knew his error, and abhorred it, but could not resist it for fear of the opinion of the prejudiced and unthinking. No other could have blamed him for refusing to fight a duel.

The list of duels that have sprung from the most degrading causes might be stretched out to an almost indefinite extent. Sterne's father fought a duel about a goose, and the great Raleigh about a tavern-bill.* Scores of duels (many of them fatal) have been fought from disputes at cards, or a place at a theatre; while hundreds of challenges, given and accepted over-night in a fit of drunkenness, have been fought out the next morning to the death of one or both of the antagonists.

Two of the most notorious duels of modern times had their origin in causes no more worthy than the quarrel of a dog and the favour of a prostitute: that between Macnamara and Montgomery arising from the former; and that between Best and Lord Camelford from the latter. The dog of Montgomery attacked a dog belonging to Macnamara, and each master interfering in behalf of his own animal, high words ensued. The result was the giving and accepting a challenge to mortal combat. The parties met on the following day, when Montgomery was shot dead, and his antagonist severely wounded. The affair created a great sensation at the time, and Heaviside, the surgeon who attended at the fatal field to render his assistance if necessary, was arrested as an accessory to the murder, and committed to Newgate.

In the duel between Best and Lord Camelford, two pistols were used which were considered to be the best in England. One of them was thought slightly superior to the other, and it was agreed that the belligerents should toss up a piece of money to decide the choice of weapons. Best gained it, and at the first discharge, Lord Camelford fell mortally wounded. But little sympathy was expressed for his fate; he was a confirmed duellist, had been engaged in many meetings of the kind, and the blood of more than one fellow-creature lay at his door. As he had sowed, so did he reap; and the violent man met an appropriate death.

It now only remains to notice the means that have been taken to stay the prevalence of this madness of false honour in the various countries of the civilised world. The efforts of the governments of France and England have already been mentioned, and their want of

---

* Raleigh at one period of his life appeared to be an inveterate duellist, and it was said of him that he had been engaged in more encounters of the kind than any man of note among his contemporaries. More than one fellow-creature he had deprived of life; but he lived long enough to be convinced of the sinfulness of his conduct, and made a solemn vow never to fight another duel. The following anecdote of his forbearance is well known, but it will bear repetition:

A dispute arose in a coffee-house between him and a young man on some trivial point, and the latter, losing his temper, impertinently spat in the face of the veteran. Sir Walter, instead of running him through the body, as many would have done, or challenging him to mortal combat, coolly took out his handkerchief, wiped his face, and said, "Young man, if I could as easily wipe from my conscience the stain of killing you, as I can this spittle from my face, you should not live another minute." The young man immediately begged his pardon.

success is but too well known. The same efforts have been attended
with the same results elsewhere. In despotic countries, where the
will of the monarch has been strongly expressed and vigorously supported, a diminution of the evil has for a time resulted, but only to
be increased again, when death relaxed the iron grasp, and a successor appeared of less decided opinions on the subject. This was
the case in Prussia, under the great Frederick, of whose aversion to
duelling a popular anecdote is recorded. It is stated of him that he
permitted duelling in his army, but only upon the condition that the
combatants should fight in presence of a whole battalion of infantry,
drawn up on purpose to see fair play. The latter received strict
orders, when one of the belligerents fell, to shoot the other immediately. It is added, that the known determination of the king
effectually put a stop to the practice.

The Emperor Joseph II. of Austria was as firm as Frederick,
although the measures he adopted were not so singular. The following letter explains his views on the subject :

" To GENERAL   *   *   *   *.

" MY GENERAL,
        " You will immediately arrest the Count of K. and Captain W.
The count is young, passionate, and influenced by wrong notions of
birth and a false spirit of honour. Captain W. is an old soldier, who
will adjust every dispute with the sword and pistol, and who has received the challenge of the young count with unbecoming warmth.

        " I will suffer no duelling in my army. I despise the principles
of those who attempt to justify the practice, and who would run each
other through the body in cold blood.

        " When I have officers who bravely expose themselves to every
danger in facing the enemy—who at all times exhibit courage,
valour, and resolution in attack and defence, I esteem them highly.
The coolness with which they meet death on such occasions is serviceable to their country, and at the same time redounds to their
own honour ; but should there be men amongst them who are ready
to sacrifice every thing to their vengeance and hatred, I despise them.
I consider such a man as no better than a Roman gladiator.

        " Order a court-martial to try the two officers. Investigate the
subject of their dispute with that impartiality which I demand from
every judge ; and he that is guilty, let him be a sacrifice to his fate
and the laws.

        " Such a barbarous custom, which suits the age of the Tamerlanes
and Bajazets, and which has often had such melancholy effects on
single families, I will have suppressed and punished, even if it should

deprive me of one-half of my officers. There are still men who know how to unite the character of a hero with that of a good subject; and he only can be so who respects the laws.

" *August*, 1771. JOSEPH."*

In the United States of America the code varies considerably. In one or two of the still wild and simple states of the far west, where no duel has yet been fought, there is no specific law upon the subject beyond that in the Decalogue, which says, " Thou shalt do no murder:" but duelling every where follows the steps of modern civilisation; and by the time the backwoodsman is transformed into the citizen, he has imbibed the false notions of honour which are prevalent in Europe and around him, and is ready, like his progenitors, to settle his differences with the pistol. In the majority of the States the punishment for challenging, fighting, or acting as second, is solitary imprisonment and hard labour for any period less than a year, and disqualification for serving any public office for twenty years. In Vermont the punishment is total disqualification for office, deprivation of the rights of citizenship, and a fine ; in fatal cases the same punishment as that of murderers. In Rhode Island, the combatant, though death does not ensue, is liable to be carted to the gallows, with a rope about his neck, and to sit in this trim for an hour exposed to the peltings of the mob. He may be further imprisoned for a year, at the option of the magistrate. In Connecticut the punishment is total disqualification for office or employ, and a fine varying from one hundred to a thousand dollars. The laws of Illinois require certain officers of the state to make oath, previous to their instalment, that they have never been, nor ever will be, concerned in a duel.†

Amongst the edicts against duelling promulgated at various times in Europe, may be mentioned that of Augustus king of Poland, in 1712, which decreed the punishment of death against principals and seconds, and minor punishments against the bearers of a challenge. An edict was also published at Munich in 1773, according to which both principals and seconds, even in duels where no one was either killed or wounded, should be hanged, and their bodies buried at the foot of the gallows.

The king of Naples issued an ordinance against duelling in 1738, in which the punishment of death is decreed against all concerned in

---

* Vide the Letters of Joseph II. to distinguished Princes and Statesmen, published for the first time in England in *The Pamphleteer* for 1821. They were originally published in Germany a few years previously, and throw a great light upon the character of that monarch and the events of his reign.

† *Encyclopedia Americana*, art. Duelling.

a fatal duel. The bodies of those killed, and of those who may be executed in consequence, are to be buried in unconsecrated ground, and without any religious ceremony; nor is any monument to be erected on the spot. The punishment for duels in which either or both are wounded, and for those in which no damage whatever is done, varies according to the case, and consists of fine, imprisonment, loss of rank and honours, and incapacity for filling any public situation. Bearers of challenges may also be punished with fine and imprisonment.

It might be imagined that enactments so severe all over the civilised world would finally eradicate a custom, the prevalence of which every wise and good man must deplore. But the frowns of the law never yet have taught, and never will teach, men to desist from this practice, as long as it is felt that the lawgiver sympathises with it in his heart. The stern judge upon the bench may say to the unfortunate wight who has been called a liar by some unmannerly opponent, " If you challenge him, you meditate murder, and are guilty of murder!" but the same judge divested of his robes of state, and mixing in the world with other men, would say, " If you do not challenge him, if you do not run the risk of making yourself a murderer, you will be looked upon as a mean-spirited wretch, unfit to associate with your fellows, and deserving nothing but their scorn and their contempt!" It is society, and not the duellist, who is to blame. Female influence too, which is so powerful in leading men either to good or to evil, takes in this case the evil part. Mere animal bravery has, unfortunately, such charms in the female eye, that a successful duellist is but too often regarded as a sort of hero; and the man who refuses to fight, though of truer courage, is thought a poltroon, who may be trampled on. Mr. Graves, a member of the American legislature, who, early in 1838, killed a Mr. Cilley in a duel, truly and eloquently said, on the floor of the House of Representatives, when lamenting the unfortunate issue of that encounter, that society was more to blame than he was. " Public opinion," said the repentant orator, " is practically the paramount law of the land. Every other law, both human and divine, ceases to be observed; yea, withers and perishes in contact with it. It was this paramount law of this nation and of this House that forced me, under the penalty of dishonour, to subject myself to the code, which impelled me unwillingly into this tragical affair. Upon the heads of this nation, and at the doors of this House, rests the blood with which my unfortunate hands have been stained!"

As long as society is in this mood; as long as it thinks that the man who refuses to resent an insult, deserved that insult, and should be scouted accordingly; so long, it is to be feared, will duelling exist, however severe the laws may be. Men must have redress for injuries inflicted ; and when those injuries are of such a nature that no tribunal will take cognisance of them, the injured will take the law into their own hands, and right themselves in the opinion of their fellows, at the hazard of their lives. Much as the sage may affect to despise the opinion of the world, there are few who would not rather expose their lives a hundred times than be condemned to live on in society, but not of it—a by-word of reproach to all who know their history, and a mark for scorn to point his finger at.

The only practicable means for diminishing the force of a custom which is the disgrace of civilisation, seems to be the establishment of a court of honour, which should take cognisance of all those delicate and almost intangible offences which yet wound so deeply. The court established by Louis XIV. might be taken as a model. No man now fights a duel when a fit apology has been offered ; and it should be the duty of this court to weigh dispassionately the complaint of every man injured in his honour, either by word or deed, and to force the offender to make a public apology. If he refused the apology, he would be the breaker of a second law ; an offender against a high court, as well as against the man he had injured, and might be punished with fine and imprisonment, the latter to last until he saw the error of his conduct, and made the concession which the court demanded.

If, after the establishment of this tribunal, men should be found of a nature so bloodthirsty as not to be satisfied with its peaceful decisions, and should resort to the old and barbarous mode of an appeal to the pistol, some means might be found of dealing with them. To hang them as murderers would be of no avail ; for to such men death would have few terrors. Shame alone would bring them to reason. Transportation, the tread-wheel, or a public whipping, would perhaps be sufficient.

RELICS.

A fouth o' auld knick-knackets,
Rusty airn caps and jinglin' jackets,
Wad haud the Lothians three, in tackets,
A towmond guid;
An' parritch pats, and auld saut backets,
Afore the flood.

BURNS.

HE love for relics is one which will never be eradicated as long as feeling and affection are denizens of the heart. It is a love which is most easily excited in the best and kindliest natures, and which few are callous enough to scoff at. Who would not treasure the lock of hair that once adorned the brow of the faithful wife now cold in death, or that hung down the neck of a beloved infant now sleeping under the sward ? Not one ! They are home-relics, whose sacred worth is intelligible to all : spoils rescued from the devouring grave, which to the affectionate are beyond all price. How dear to a forlorn survivor the book over whose pages he has pored with one departed ! How much greater its value, if that hand, now cold, had written a thought, an opinion, or a name, upon the leaf ! Besides these sweet domestic relics, there are others which no one can condemn : relics sanctified by that admiration of greatness and goodness which is akin to love ; such as the copy of Montaigne's *Florio*, with the name of Shakspeare upon the leaf, written by the poet of all time himself ; the chair preserved at Antwerp, in which Rubens sat when he painted the immortal Descent from the Cross ; or the telescope, preserved in the Museum of Florence, which aided Galileo in his sublime discoveries. Who would not look with veneration upon the undoubted arrow of William Tell—the swords of Wallace or of Hampden—or the Bible whose leaves were turned by some stern old father of the faith?

Thus the principle of reliquism is hallowed and enshrined by love. But from this germ of purity how numerous the progeny of errors and superstitions! Men, in their admiration of the great, and of all that appertained to them, have forgotten that goodness is a component part of true greatness, and have made fools of themselves for the jawbone of a saint, the toe-nail of an apostle, the handkerchief a king blew his nose in, or the rope that hanged a criminal. Desiring to rescue some slight token from the graves of their predecessors, they have confounded the famous and the infamous, the renowned and the notorious. Great saints, great sinners; great philosophers, great quacks; great conquerors, great murderers; great ministers, great thieves; each and all have had their admirers, ready to ransack earth, from the equator to either pole, to find a relic of them.

The reliquism of modern times dates its origin from the centuries immediately preceding the Crusades. The first pilgrims to the Holy Land brought back to Europe thousands of apocryphal relics, in the purchase of which they had expended all their store. The greatest favourite was the wood of the true cross, which, like the oil of the widow, never was diminished. It is generally asserted, in the traditions of the Romish Church, that the Empress Helen, the mother of Constantine the Great, first discovered the veritable "*true cross*" in her pilgrimage to Jerusalem. The Emperor Theodosius made a present of the greater part of it to St. Ambrose, Bishop of Milan, by whom it was studded with precious stones, and deposited in the principal church of that city. It was carried away by the Huns, by whom it was burnt, after they had extracted the valuable jewels it contained. Fragments, purporting to have been cut from it, were, in the eleventh and twelfth centuries, to be found in almost every church in Europe, and would, if collected together in one place, have been almost sufficient to have built a cathedral. Happy was the sinner who could get a sight of one of them; happier he who possessed one! To obtain them the greatest dangers were cheerfully braved. They were thought to preserve from all evils, and to cure the most inveterate diseases. Annual pilgrimages were made to the shrines that contained them, and considerable revenues collected from the devotees.

Next in renown were those precious relics, the tears of the Saviour. By whom and in what manner they were preserved, the pilgrims did not inquire. Their genuineness was vouched by the Christians of the Holy Land, and that was sufficient. Tears of the Virgin Mary, and tears of St. Peter, were also to be had, carefully enclosed in little caskets, which the pious might wear in their bosoms. After the tears, the next most precious relics were drops of the blood of Jesus and the martyrs, and the milk of the Virgin Mary. Hair and toe-nails were also in great repute, and were sold at extravagant prices. Thousands of pilgrims annually visited Palestine in the eleventh and twelfth centuries, to purchase pretended relics for the home market. The majority of them had no other means of subsistence than the profits thus obtained. Many a nail, cut from the filthy foot of some unscrupulous ecclesiastic, was sold at a diamond's price, within six months after its severance from its parent toe, upon the supposition that it had once belonged to a saint or an apostle. Peter's toes were uncommonly prolific, for there were nails enough in Europe, at the time of the Council of Clermont, to have filled a sack, all of which were devoutly believed to have grown on the sacred feet of that great apostle. Some of them are still shewn in the cathedral of Aix-la-Chapelle. The pious come from a distance of a hundred German miles to feast their eyes upon them.

At Port Royal, in Paris, is kept with great care a thorn, which the priests of that seminary assert to be one of the identical thorns that bound the holy head of the Son of God. How it came there, and by whom it was preserved, has never been explained. This is the famous thorn, celebrated in the long dissensions of the Jansenists and the Molenists, and which worked the miraculous cure upon Mademoiselle Perrier : by merely kissing it she was cured of a disease of the eyes of long standing.*

What traveller is unacquainted with the Santa Scala, or Holy Stairs, at Rome ? They were brought from Jerusalem along with the true cross, by the Empress Helen, and were taken from the house which, according to popular tradition, was inhabited by Pontius Pilate. They are said to be the steps which Jesus ascended and descended when brought into the presence of the Roman governor. They are held in the greatest veneration at Rome : it is sacrilegious to walk upon them. The knees of the faithful must alone touch them in ascending or descending, and that only after the pilgrims have reverentially kissed them.

Europe still swarms with these religious relics. There is hardly a Roman Catholic church in Spain, Portugal, Italy, France, or Belgium, without one or more of them. Even the poorly endowed churches of the villages boast the possession of miraculous thigh-bones of the innumerable saints of the Romish calendar. Aix-la-Chapelle is proud of the veritable *châsse*, or thigh-bone of Charlemagne, which cures lameness. Halle has a thigh-bone of the Virgin

* Voltaire, *Siècle de Louis XIV.*

Mary; Spain has seven or eight, all said to be undoubted relics. Brussels at one time preserved, and perhaps does now, the teeth of St. Gudule. The faithful, who suffered from the toothache, had only to pray, look at them, and be cured. Some of these holy bones have been buried in different parts of the Continent. After a certain lapse of time, water is said to ooze from them, which soon forms a spring, and cures all the diseases of the faithful.

It is curious to remark the avidity manifested in all ages, and in all countries, to obtain possession of some relic of any persons who have been much spoken of, even for their crimes. When William Longbeard, leader of the populace of London in the reign of Richard I., was hanged at Smithfield, the utmost eagerness was shewn to obtain a hair from his head, or a shred from his garments. Women came from Essex, Kent, Suffolk, Sussex, and all the surrounding counties, to collect the mould at the foot of his gallows. A hair of his beard was believed to preserve from evil spirits, and a piece of his clothes from aches and pains.

In more modern days, a similar avidity was shewn to obtain a relic of the luckless Masaniello, the fisherman of Naples. After he had been raised by mob favour to a height of power more despotic than monarch ever wielded, he was shot by the same populace in the streets, as if he had been a mad dog. His headless trunk was dragged through the mire for several hours, and cast at night-fall into the city ditch. On the morrow the tide of popular feeling turned once more in his favour. His corpse was sought, arrayed in royal robes, and buried magnificently by torch-light in the cathedral, ten thousand armed men, and as many mourners, attending at the ceremony. The fisherman's dress which he had worn was rent into shreds by the crowd, to be preserved as relics; the door of his hut was pulled off its hinges by a mob of women, and eagerly cut up into small pieces, to be made into images, caskets, and other mementos. The scanty furniture of his poor abode became of more value than the adornments of a palace; the ground he had walked upon was considered sacred, and, being collected in small phials, was sold at its weight in gold, and worn in the bosom as an amulet.

Almost as extraordinary was the frenzy manifested by the populace of Paris on the execution of the atrocious Marchioness de Brinvilliers. There were grounds for the popular wonder in the case of Masaniello, who was unstained with personal crimes. But the career of Madame de Brinvilliers was of a nature to excite no other feelings than disgust and abhorrence. She was convicted of poisoning several persons, and sentenced to be burned in the Place de Grève, and to have her ashes scattered to the winds. On the day of her execution, the populace, struck by her gracefulness and beauty, inveighed against the severity of her sentence. Their pity soon increased to admiration, and, ere evening, she was considered a saint. Her ashes were industriously collected ; even the charred wood, which had aided to consume her, was eagerly purchased by the populace. Her ashes were thought to preserve from witchcraft.

In England many persons have a singular love for the relics of thieves and murderers, or other great criminals. The ropes with which they have been hanged are very often bought by collectors at a guinea per foot. Great sums were paid for the rope which hanged Dr. Dodd, and for those more recently which did justice upon Mr. Fauntleroy for forgery, and on Thurtell for the murder of Mr. Weare. The murder of Maria Marten, by Corder, in the year 1828, excited the greatest interest all over the country. People came from Wales and Scotland, and even from Ireland, to visit the barn where the body of the murdered woman was buried. Every one of them was anxious to carry away some memorial of his visit. Pieces of the barndoor, tiles from the roof, and, above all, the clothes of the poor victim, were eagerly sought after. A lock of her hair was sold for two guineas, and the purchaser thought himself fortunate in getting it so cheaply.

So great was the concourse of people to visit the house in Camberwell Lane, where Greenacre murdered Hannah Brown, in 1837, that it was found necessary to station a strong detachment of police on the spot. The crowd was so eager to obtain a relic of the house of this atrocious criminal, that the police were obliged to employ force to prevent the tables and chairs, and even the doors, from being carried away.

In earlier times, a singular superstition was attached to the hand of a criminal who had suffered execution. It was thought that by merely rubbing the dead hand on the body, the patient afflicted with the king's evil would be instantly cured. The executioner at Newgate formerly derived no inconsiderable revenue from this foolish practice. The possession of the hand was thought to be of still greater efficacy in the cure of diseases and the prevention of misfortunes. In the time of Charles II., as much as ten guineas was thought a small price for one of these disgusting relics.

When the maniac Thom, or Courtenay, was shot, in the spring of 1838, the relic-hunters were immediately in motion to obtain a memento of so extraordinary an individual. His long black beard and hair, which were cut off by the surgeons, fell into the hands of his disciples, by whom they were treasured with the utmost reverence. A lock of his hair commanded a great price, not only amongst his followers, but among the more wealthy inhabitants of Canterbury and its neighbourhood. The tree against which he fell when he was shot, was stripped of all its bark by the curious; while a letter, with his signature to it, was paid for in gold coins; and his favourite horse became as celebrated as its master. Parties of ladies and gentlemen went to Boughton from a distance of a hundred and fifty miles, to visit the scene of that fatal affray, and stroke on the back the horse of the "mad knight of Malta." If a strict watch had not been kept over his grave for months, the body would have been disinterred, and the bones carried away as memorials.

Among the Chinese no relics are more valued than the *boots* which have been worn by an upright magistrate. In Davis's interesting description of the empire of China, we are informed, that whenever a judge of unusual integrity resigns his situation, the people all congregate to do him honour. If he leaves the city where he has presided, the crowd accompany him from his residence to the gates, where his boots are drawn off with great ceremony, to be preserved in the hall of justice. Their place is immediately supplied by a new pair, which, in their turn, are drawn off to make room for others before he has worn them five minutes, it being considered sufficient to consecrate them that he should have merely drawn them on.

Among the most favourite relics of modern times, in Europe, are Shakspeare's mulberry-tree, Napoleon's willow, and the table at Waterloo on which the emperor wrote his despatches. Snuff-boxes of Shakspeare's mulberry-tree are comparatively rare, though there are doubtless more of them in the market than were ever made of the wood planted by the great bard. Many a piece of alien wood passes under this name. The same may be said of Napoleon's table at Waterloo. The original has long since been destroyed, and a round dozen of counterfeits along with it. Many preserve the simple stick of wood; others have them cut into brooches and every variety of ornament; but by far the greater number prefer them as snuff-boxes. In France they are made into *bonbonnières*, and are much esteemed by the many thousands whose cheeks still glow and whose eyes still sparkle at the name of Napoleon.

Bullets from the field of Waterloo, and buttons from the coats of the soldiers who fell in the fight, are still favourite relics in Europe. But the same ingenuity which found new tables after the old one was destroyed, has cast new bullets for the curious. Many a one who thinks himself the possessor of a bullet which aided in giving peace to the world on that memorable day, is the owner of a dump, first extracted from the ore a dozen years afterwards. Let all lovers of genuine relics look well to their money before they part with it to the ciceroni that swarm in the village of Waterloo !

Few travellers stopped at the lonely isle of St. Helena without cutting a twig from the willow that drooped over the grave of Napoleon, prior to the removal of the body by the government of Louis Philippe, Many of them have since been planted in different parts of Europe, and have grown into trees as large as their parent. Relic-hunters, who are unable to procure a twig of the original, are content with one from these. Several of them are growing in the neighbourhood of London.

But in relics, as in every thing else, there is the use and the abuse. The undoubted relics of great men, or great events, will always possess attractions for the thinking and refined. There are few who would not join with Cowley in the extravagant wish introduced in his lines " written while sitting in a chair made of the remains of the ship in which Sir Francis Drake sailed round the world :"

> " And I myself, who now love quiet too,
> Almost as much as any chair can do,
> Would yet a journey take
> An old wheel of that chariot to see,
> Which Phaeton so rashly brake."

INDEX.

Hatton, Lady, her reputation for witchcraft; her house in Hatton Garden, (*engraving*), ii. 186.

"HAUNTED HOUSES," popular belief in, ii. 217-238; a house at Aix la Chapelle, cause of the noises discovered, ii. 218; alarm caused by a rat, 219; the monks of St. Bruno, their trick to obtain the haunted palace of Vauvert, 220; houses at Tours and Bordeaux, 221; the story of Woodstock Palace, 222; Mr. Mompesson's house at Tedworth, 224; the "Cock Lane Ghost," history of the deception; believed in by the learned (*engravings*), 228; the Stockwell ghost, 234; Baldarroch farm-house, 235; effect of education and civilisation, 238.

Hawkins, Mr., *engravings* from his Collection of Caricatures, i. 29, 44.

Haygarth, Dr., his exposure of Perkins's "Metallic Tractors," i. 289.

Hell, Father, his magnetic cures; his connexion with Mesmer, i. 283.

Henry I., his hair cut short by Serlo, his chaplain (*engraving*), i. 262, 264.

Henry II. joins the third crusade (*engraving*), ii. 64.

Henry VI. issues patents to encourage alchymy, i. 118, 135.

Henry VIII., his invitation to Cornelius Agrippa, i. 140.

Henry, Prince, son of James I. suspected to have been poisoned, ii. 200.

Henry II. of France, his patronage of Nostradamus, i. 246; said to have prohibited duelling, ii. 273, 275; his death in the lists, 276.

Henry IV. of France, *portrait* of, ii. 277; his opposition to duelling, 277, 279.

Hermes Trismegistus, the founder of alchymy, i. 95.

Hermetic Philosophy. (*See* the Alchymists.)

Heydon, John, an English Rosicrucian, i. 175.

Heywood, his life and prophecies of Merlin, i. 233.

Highwaymen. (*See* Thieves.)

Hogarth's caricature of the South - Sea Bubble (*engraving*), i. 82.

Holland, the tulip mania. (*See* Tulip Mania.)

Holloway's lectures on animal magnetism, i. 287.

Holt, Chief Justice, his opposition to the belief in witchcraft, ii. 152.

"Holy Lance," the, its pretended discovery (*engraving*), ii. 37.

Hopkins, Matthew, the "witch-finder general," his cruelty and retributive fate, (*engraving*), ii. 143-146.

Horoscope of Louis XIV., i. 249.

Hugh count of Vermandois imprisoned at Constantinople, ii. 21, 23; at the siege of Nice, 26; quits the Crusaders, 42.

Human remains ingredients in charms and nostrums, i. 272.

Hungary plundered by the Crusaders, ii. 15, 16, 20, 21.

Hutchinson, Dr., his work on witchcraft, ii. 123.

Imps in the service of witches. (*See* Demons and Witchcraft.)

Ingelgerius count of Anjou, his duel with Gontran (*engraving*), ii. 269.

Innocent III. and IV., promoters of the Crusades, ii. 75, 80, 81.

Innocent VIII., his bull against witchcraft, ii. 117.

Innspruck, view of (*engraving*), i. 181.

Invisibility pretended by the Rosicrucians, i. 169, 178.

Isaac Comnenus attacked by Richard I., ii. 69.

Isaac of Holland, an alchymist, i. 136.

Isnik, the Crusaders defeated at (with *view* of Isnik), ii. 19.

Italy, slow poisoning in (*see* Poisoning); the banditti of, ii. 256.

Jaques Cœur the alchymist, memoir of, i. 132.

Jaffa besieged by Saladin, and saved by Richard I., ii. 74; *view* of, ii. 89; defended by the Templars against the Korasmins, ii. 90.

James I., his belief in the virtue of "weapon salve," i. 266; *portrait* of, ii. 134; charges Gellie Duncan and others with witchcraft,129; their trial, confessions and execution, 129-135; his work on "Demonology," 139; his supposed secret vices; his favoritism to the Earl of Somerset, the poisoner of Sir Thomas Overbury; himself thought to have died by poison, 193-202; his severity against duelling,287.

Jean De Meung. (*See* De Meung.)

Jerusalem (and *see* Crusades), *engravings*, ii. 44, 47, 49; first pilgrims to, ii. 2; besieged and taken by the Crusaders, 45; its state under the Christian kings, 48, 49; council of the second Crusade there, 60; captured by Saladin, 63.

Jewell, Bishop, his exclamations against witchcraft, ii. 124.

Jews plundered and murdered by the Crusaders, ii. 20.

Joan of Arc, her execution (*engraving*), ii. 114.

John XXII. (Pope), his study of Alchymy, i. 111.

Johnson, Dr., on the "Beggar's Opera," ii. 258.

Joseph II. of Austria, his opposition to duelling, ii. 298.

Judicial astrology. (*See* Astrology.)

Judicial combats. (*See* Duels.)

Karloman, King of Hungary, his contest with the Crusaders, ii. 20.

Kelly, Edward, the Alchymist, memoir of, i. 152.

Kendal, Duchess of, her participation in the South-Sea fraud, i. 76, 77.

Kent, Mr., accused of murder by the "Cock Lane Ghost," ii. 122.

Kepler, his excuse for astrology, i. 250.

Kerbogha, made of the Turks defeated at Antioch, ii. 34, 38, 39.

Kerr, Robert, afterwards Earl of Somerset. (*See* Somerset.)

Kircher abandons his belief in alchymy,

i. 185, 186; his belief in magnetism as a remedy for disease, 264.

Knight, —, Treasurer of the South-Sea Company, his apprehension and escape, i. 76.

Knox, John, *portrait* of; accused of witch-craft, ii. 128.

Koffstky, a Polish alchymist, i. 136.

Labourt, France, 200 witches executed, ii. 166.

La Chataigneraie and De Jarnac, their famous duel, ii. 273.

La Chaussée, the accomplice of Madame de Brinvilliers, his execution, ii. 212.

Lady-day, superstitions on, i. 258.

Lamb, Dr., the poisoner, attacked and killed in the streets (*engraving*), ii. 202.

" Lancashire witches" executed, ii. 141.

Laski, Count Albert, his reception by Queen Elizabeth, his studies in alchymy, i. 155; is victimised by Dee and Kelly, 157.

Lavigoreux and Lavoisin, the French poisoners executed, ii. 215.

Law, J., projector of the Mississippi scheme, his romantic history, i. 1; his house in the Rue de Quincampoix, Paris (*engraving*), i. 13.

Law, Wm., his participation in the Mississippi scheme, i. 9, 42.

Le Blanc, the Abbé, on the popularity of Great Thieves, ii. 251.

Lennox, Col., his duel with the Duke of York, ii. 293.

Liège, Madame de Brinvilliers arrested there, ii. 213.

Lille, singular charges of witchcraft at, ii. 169.

Lilly, the astrologer, account of, i. 243.

Lipsius, his passion for tulips, i. 86.

London, the plague of 1665, i 228; inundation prophesied in 1524, i 228; the Great Fire, 230. (*See* also Cagliostro, Change Alley, Cornhill, Merchant Taylors' Hall, Tower, Westminster.

Longbeard, William, cause of his name, 300.

Longsword, William (*engraving*), joins the ninth Crusade, ii. 91.

Loudun, the curate of, executed for witchcraft, ii. 168.

Louis VII. cuts short his hair, and loses his queen, i. 299; joins the Crusaders, ii. 53; is consecrated at St. Denis, 55; reaches Constantinople and Nice, 58; his conflicts with the Saracens, 59; arrival at Jerusalem, 60; his sincerity as a Crusader, 61; returns to France, 62.

Louis IX. undertakes the ninth Crusade, ii. 90; his valour at the battle of Massoura, 94; taken prisoner, 94; his ransom and return, 94; his second Crusade, 95; effigy of (*engravin g*). 220.

Louis XI., his encouragement of astrologers, i. 246.

Louis XIII., prevalence of duelling in his reign, ii. 280.

Louis XIV., his bigotry and extravagance, i. 5, 6; remonstrated with by his Parliament on his leniency to supposed witches, ii. 171; *portrait* of, 177; establishes the " chambre ardente" for the trial of poi-

soners, 214, 283; his horoscope, 249; his severe edict against duelling, 283.

Louis XV., his patronage of the Court St. Germain, i. 201, 204.

" Loup-garou" executed in France, ii. 120.

Loutherbourg, the painter, his alleged cures by animal magnetism, i. 288.

Lulli, Raymond, a famous alchymist, his romantic history, with *portrait*, i. 105; his treatment by Edward II., 135.

Lyons, *view* of, ii. 160.

Macartney, General, second to Lord Mohun, his trial for murder, ii. 292.

Mackenzie, Sir George, *portrait* of, ii. 138; his enlightened views on witchcraft, 137.

Macnamara and Montgomery, frivolous cause of their fatal duel, ii. 297.

MAGNETISERS, the, i. 262-295; effect of imagination in the cure of diseases, i. 262, 272. *Mineral Magnetism:* Paracelsus its first professor, 263; diseases transplanted to the earth; Kircher; " weapon-salve," 264; controversy on its merits, 265; Sir Kenelm Digby's " powder of sympathy," 266; other delusions, 268. *Animal Magnetism:* wonderful cures by Valentine Greatraks, i. 269-272; Francisco Bagnoni, Van Helmont, Gracian, Baptista Porta, &c., 272; Wirdig, Maxwell, 273; the convulsionaires of St. Medard, i. 273; Father Hell, 274; Anthony Mesmer, his history and theory, 275; Mesmer, 276-283; D'Eslon adopts his views, 278, 280, 281; encouragement to depravity afforded by his experiments, 282, 293; exposures by MM. Dupotet and Bailly, 279, 281; Marquis de Puysegur, 283; Chevalier de Barbarin, 286; Mainauduc, Holloway, Loutherbourg, 287, 288; Perkins's " Metallic Tractors" exposed by Dr. Haygarth, 289; absurd theories of Deleuze, 291; the Abbé Faria, fallacies of the theory of, 294.

Mainauduc, Dr., his experiments in animal magnetism, i. 287.

Malta, its singular laws on duelling, ii 284.

Mansfield, Lord, trial of the " Cock-lane Ghost" conspirators before him, ii. 234.

Manuel Comnenus, his treatment of the Crusaders, ii. 56, 58, 59.

Marie Antoinette, history of the diamond necklace, i. 216-220.

Marlborough, Duke of, his duel with Earl Pawlet, ii. 289.

Massaniello, relics of his fate treasured by the populace, ii. 305.

Massoura, battle of, the Saracens defeated, ii. 94.

Mayer, Michael his report on the Rosicrucian doctrines, i. 168.

Maxwell, William, the magnetiser, i. 273.

Medicis, Catherine di, her encouragement of astrologers, i. 246.

Medici family, predictions respecting them, i. 247.

Merchant Taylors' Hall, *view* of gateway, i. 62.

Merlin, his pretended prophecies, i. 232; his miraculous birth, 236; Spenser's description of his cave, 237.

THE END.

LONDON :

PRINTED BY LEVEY, ROBSON, AND FRANKLYN,
Great New Street, Fetter Lane.

Breinigsville, PA USA
15 March 2011
257712BV00001B/26/P